HarperCollins POCKET
WORLDATLAS

☰ HarperCollins **POCKET**

WORLD**ATLAS**

HarperResource
An Imprint of HarperCollins*Publishers*

world

states and territories		8-23
countries		24-25
physical features		26-27
climate		28-29
land cover		30-31
population and cities		32-33
timezones		34-35

europe

physical features	1:35 000 000	36-37
countries	1:35 000 000	38-39
western russian federation	1:20 000 000	40-41
baltic states and moscow region	1:8 000 000	42-43
ukraine and moldova	1:8 000 000	44-45
scandinavia and iceland	1:10 000 000	46-47
british isles	1:8 000 000	48-49
scotland	1:4 000 000	50
ireland	1:4 000 000	51
england and wales	1:4 000 000	52-53
northwest europe	1:4 000 000	54-55
central europe	1:8 000 000	56-57
france and switzerland	1:8 000 000	58-59
spain and portugal	1:8 000 000	60-61
italy and the balkans	1:8 000 000	62-63
southeast europe	1:8 000 000	64-65

asia

physical features	1:78 000 000	66-67
countries	1:78 000 000	68-69
southeast asia	1:30 000 000	70-71
malaysia and western indonesia	1:15 000 000	72-73
myanmar, thailand and indo-china	1:15 000 000	74-75
philippines	1:15 000 000	76
north korea and south korea	1:9 000 000	77
japan	1:10 000 000	78-79
china and mongolia	1:30 000 000	80-81
central china	1:15 000 000	82-83
southern asia	1:20 000 000	84-85
pakistan, northern india, nepal and bangladesh	1:15 000 000	86-87
central asia	1:20 000 000	88-89
arabian peninsula	1:15 000 000	90-91
eastern mediterranean	1:15 000 000	92-93
russian federation	1:42 000 000	94-95

africa

physical features	1:60 000 000	96-97
countries	1:60 000 000	98-99
northwest africa	1:26 000 000	100-101
northeast africa	1:26 000 000	102-103
central africa	1:20 000 000	104-105
southern africa	1:20 000 000	106-107
republic of south africa	1:10 000 000	108-109

oceania

physical features	1:65 000 000	110-111
countries	1:65 000 000	112-113
australia	1:25 000 000	114-115
southeast australia	1:10 000 000	116-117
new zealand	1:10 000 000	118
antarctica	1:60 000 000	119

north america

physical features	1:65 000 000	120-121
countries	1:65 000 000	122-123
canada	1:30 000 000	124-125
western canada	1:15 000 000	126-127
eastern canada	1:15 000 000	128-129
united states of america	1:25 000 000	130-131
western united states	1:11 000 000	132-133
north central united states	1:11 000 000	134-135
northeast united states	1:11 000 000	136-137
southeast united states	1:11 000 000	138-139
south central united states	1:11 000 000	140-141
mexico	1:15 000 000	142-143
the caribbean	1:20 000 000	144-145

south america

physical features	1:50 000 000	146-147
countries	1:50 000 000	148-149
northern south america	1:25 000 000	150-151
southern south america	1:25 000 000	152-153
southeast brazil	1:10 000 000	154-155

oceans

features		156-157
pacific ocean	1:100 000 000	158-159
atlantic ocean and indian ocean	1:100 000 000	160-161
arctic ocean	1:60 000 000	162

index

	163-256

INTRODUCTION

The atlas is introduced by details of the world's states and territories and by maps and information on major geographical themes. The reference maps which follow this world section have been compiled to provide the best coverage for each part of the world through careful selection of scales and map projections. Maps are arranged on a continental basis, with each continent being introduced by maps and statistics on the continent's physical features and countries. Maps of Antarctica and the world's oceans complete the worldwide coverage.

Map symbolization

Maps show information by using symbols which are designed to reflect the features on the earth that they represent. Map symbols can be in the form of points – such as those used to show towns and airports; lines – used to represent roads and rivers; or areas – such as lakes. Variation in size, shape and colour of these types of symbol allow a great range of information to be shown. The symbols used in this atlas are explained here. Not all details can be shown at the small map scales used in this atlas, so information is generalized to allow easy interpretation. This generalization takes the form of selection – the inclusion of some features and the omission of others of less importance; and simplification – where lines are smoothed, areas combined, or symbols displaced slightly to add clarity. This is done in such a way that the overall character of the area mapped is retained. The degree of generalization varies, and is determined largely by the scale at which the map is drawn.

Scale

Scale is the relationship between the size of an area shown on the map and the actual size of the area on the ground. It determines the amount of detail shown on a map – larger scales show more, smaller scales show less – and can be used to measure the distance between two points, although the projection of the map must also be taken into account when measuring distances.

Geographical names

The spelling of place names on maps is a complex problem for the cartographer. There is no single standard way of converting them from one alphabet, or symbol set, to another. Changes in official languages also have to be taken into account when creating maps and policies need to be established for the spelling of names on individual atlases and maps. Such policies must take account of the local official position, international conventions or traditions, as well as the purpose of the atlas or map. The policy in this atlas is to use local name forms which are officially recognized by the governments of the countries concerned, but with English conventional name forms being used for the most well-known places. In these cases, the local form is often included in brackets on the map and also appears as a cross-reference in the index. All country names and those for international features appear in their English forms.

Boundaries

The status of nations and their boundaries are shown in this atlas as they are in reality at the time of going to press, as far as can be ascertained. Where international boundaries are the subject of disputes the aim is to take a strictly neutral viewpoint, based on advice from expert consultants.

MAP SYMBOLS

Settlements

Population	National Capital	Administrative Capital	City or Town
over 5 million	⊡ **BEIJING**	⊙ **Tianjin**	⊙ **New York**
1 million – 5 million	☐ **MADRID**	○ **Sydney**	○ **Madurai**
500 000 – 1 million	☐ **BANGUI**	○ **Douala**	○ **Barranquilla**
100 000 – 500 000	☐ WELLINGTON	○ Mansa	○ Yong'an
50 000 – 100 000	☐ PORT OF SPAIN	○ Lubango	○ Puruliya
under 50 000	▫ MALABO	○ Chinhoyi	○ El Tigre

Styles of lettering

Country name	**FRANCE**	Island	*Gran Canaria*
Overseas territory / Dependency	**Guadaloupe**	Lake	*Lake Erie*
Administrative name	**SCOTLAND**	Mountain	*Mt Blanc*
Area name	PATAGONIA	River	*Thames*

Physical features

		Communications	
	Freshwater lake		Motorway
	Seasonal freshwater lake		Main road
	Salt lake		Track
	Seasonal salt lake		Railway
	Dry salt lake	✈	Main airport
	Ice cap		Canal
———	River		
≊ 2188	Mountain pass		
△ 6960	Summit		

Other features

		Boundaries	
∴	Site of special interest	———	International
ᴡᴡᴡ	Wall	- - - - -	International disputed
		———	Administrative (selected countries only)
		··········	Ceasefire line

introduction and map symbols

EUROPE COUNTRIES		area sq km	area sq miles	population	capital
ALBANIA		28 748	11 100	3 166 000	Tirana
ANDORRA		465	180	71 000	Andorra la Vella
AUSTRIA		83 855	32 377	8 116 000	Vienna
BELARUS		207 600	80 155	9 895 000	Minsk
BELGIUM		30 520	11 784	10 318 000	Brussels
BOSNIA-HERZEGOVINA		51 130	19 741	4 161 000	Sarajevo
BULGARIA		110 994	42 855	7 897 000	Sofia
CROATIA		56 538	21 829	4 428 000	Zagreb
CZECH REPUBLIC		78 864	30 450	10 236 000	Prague
DENMARK		43 075	16 631	5 364 000	Copenhagen
ESTONIA		45 200	17 452	1 323 000	Tallinn
FINLAND		338 145	130 559	5 207 000	Helsinki
FRANCE		543 965	210 026	60 144 000	Paris
GERMANY		357 022	137 849	82 476 000	Berlin
GREECE		131 957	50 949	10 976 000	Athens
HUNGARY		93 030	35 919	9 877 000	Budapest
ICELAND		102 820	39 699	290 000	Reykjavik
IRELAND, REPUBLIC OF		70 282	27 136	3 956 000	Dublin
ITALY		301 245	116 311	57 423 000	Rome
LATVIA		63 700	24 595	2 307 000	Riga
LIECHTENSTEIN		160	62	34 000	Vaduz
LITHUANIA		65 200	25 174	3 444 000	Vilnius
LUXEMBOURG		2 586	998	453 000	Luxembourg
MACEDONIA (F.Y.R.O.M.)		25 713	9 928	2 056 000	Skopje
MALTA		316	122	394 000	Valletta
MOLDOVA		33 700	13 012	4 267 000	Chişinău
MONACO		2	1	34 000	Monaco-Ville
NETHERLANDS		41 526	16 033	16 149 000	Amsterdam/The Hague
NORWAY		323 878	125 050	4 533 000	Oslo
POLAND		312 683	120 728	38 587 000	Warsaw
PORTUGAL		88 940	34 340	10 062 000	Lisbon
ROMANIA		237 500	91 699	22 334 000	Bucharest
RUSSIAN FEDERATION		17 075 400	6 592 849	143 246 000	Moscow

languages	religions	currency
Albanian, Greek	Sunni Muslim, Albanian Orthodox, Roman Catholic	Lek
Spanish, Catalan, French	Roman Catholic	Euro
German, Croatian, Turkish	Roman Catholic, Protestant	Euro
Belorussian, Russian	Belorussian Orthodox, Roman Catholic	Belarus rouble
Dutch (Flemish), French (Walloon), German	Roman Catholic, Protestant	Euro
Bosnian, Serbian, Croatian	Sunni Muslim, Serbian Orthodox, Roman Catholic, Protestant	Marka
Bulgarian, Turkish, Romany, Macedonian	Bulgarian Orthodox, Sunni Muslim	Lev
Croatian, Serbian	Roman Catholic, Serbian Orthodox, Sunni Muslim	Kuna
Czech, Moravian, Slovak	Roman Catholic, Protestant	Czech koruna
Danish	Protestant	Danish krone
Estonian, Russian	Protestant, Estonian and Russian Orthodox	Kroon
Finnish, Swedish	Protestant, Greek Orthodox	Euro
French, Arabic	Roman Catholic, Protestant, Sunni Muslim	Euro
German, Turkish	Protestant, Roman Catholic	Euro
Greek	Greek Orthodox, Sunni Muslim	Euro
Hungarian	Roman Catholic, Protestant	Forint
Icelandic	Protestant	Icelandic króna
English, Irish	Roman Catholic, Protestant	Euro
Italian	Roman Catholic	Euro
Latvian, Russian	Protestant, Roman Catholic, Russian Orthodox	Lats
German	Roman Catholic, Protestant	Swiss franc
Lithuanian, Russian, Polish	Roman Catholic, Protestant, Russian Orthodox	Litas
Letzeburgish, German, French	Roman Catholic	Euro
Macedonian, Albanian, Turkish	Macedonian Orthodox, Sunni Muslim	Macedonian denar
Maltese, English	Roman Catholic	Maltese lira
Romanian, Ukrainian, Gagauz, Russian	Romanian Orthodox, Russian Orthodox	Moldovan leu
French, Monegasque, Italian	Roman Catholic	Euro
Dutch, Frisian	Roman Catholic, Protestant, Sunni Muslim	Euro
Norwegian	Protestant, Roman Catholic	Norwegian krone
Polish, German	Roman Catholic, Polish Orthodox	Zloty
Portuguese	Roman Catholic, Protestant	Euro
Romanian, Hungarian	Romanian Orthodox, Protestant, Roman Catholic	Romanian leu
Russian, Tatar, Ukrainian, local languages	Russian Orthodox, Sunni Muslim, Protestant	Russian rouble

EUROPE COUNTRIES (continued)		area sq km	area sq miles	population	capital
SAN MARINO		61	24	28 000	San Marino
SERBIA AND MONTENEGRO		102 173	39 449	10 527 000	Belgrade
SLOVAKIA		49 035	18 933	5 402 000	Bratislava
SLOVENIA		20 251	7 819	1 984 000	Ljubljana
SPAIN		504 782	194 897	41 060 000	Madrid
SWEDEN		449 964	173 732	8 876 000	Stockholm
SWITZERLAND		41 293	15 943	7 169 000	Bern
UKRAINE		603 700	233 090	48 523 000	Kiev
UNITED KINGDOM		243 609	94 058	58 789 194	London
VATICAN CITY		0.5	0.2	472	Vatican City

EUROPE DEPENDENT TERRITORIES			area sq km	area sq miles	populati
Azores		Autonomous Region of Portugal	2 300	888	242 0
Faroe Islands		Self-governing Danish Territory	1 399	540	47 0
Gibraltar		United Kingdom Overseas Territory	7	3	27 0
Guernsey		United Kingdom Crown Dependency	78	30	62 7
Isle of Man		United Kingdom Crown Dependency	572	221	75 0
Jersey		United Kingdom Crown Dependency	116	45	87 1

ASIA COUNTRIES		area sq km	area sq miles	population	capital
AFGHANISTAN		652 225	251 825	23 897 000	Kābul
ARMENIA		29 800	11 506	3 061 000	Yerevan
AZERBAIJAN		86 600	33 436	8 370 000	Baku
BAHRAIN		691	267	724 000	Manama
BANGLADESH		143 998	55 598	146 736 000	Dhaka
BHUTAN		46 620	18 000	2 257 000	Thimphu
BRUNEI		5 765	2 226	358 000	Bandar Seri Begawan
CAMBODIA		181 000	69 884	14 144 000	Phnom Penh
CHINA		9 584 492	3 700 593	1 289 161 000	Beijing
CYPRUS		9 251	3 572	802 000	Nicosia
EAST TIMOR		14 874	5 743	778 000	Dili
GEORGIA		69 700	26 911	5 126 000	T'bilisi

languages	religions	currency
Italian	Roman Catholic	Euro
Serbian, Albanian, Hungarian	Serbian Orthodox, Montenegrin Orthodox, Sunni Muslim	Serbian dinar, Euro
Slovak, Hungarian, Czech	Roman Catholic, Protestant, Orthodox	Slovakian koruna
Slovene, Croatian, Serbian	Roman Catholic, Protestant	Tólar
Castilian, Catalan, Galician, Basque	Roman Catholic	Euro
Swedish	Protestant, Roman Catholic	Swedish krona
German, French, Italian, Romansch	Roman Catholic, Protestant	Swiss franc
Ukrainian, Russian	Ukrainian Orthodox, Ukrainian Catholic, Roman Catholic	Hryvnia
English, Welsh, Gaelic	Protestant, Roman Catholic, Muslim	Pound sterling
Italian	Roman Catholic	Euro

capital	languages	religions	currency
Ponta Delgada	Portuguese	Roman Catholic, Protestant	Euro
Tórshavn	Faroese, Danish	Protestant	Danish krone
Gibraltar	English, Spanish	Roman Catholic, Protestant, Sunni Muslim	Gibraltar pound
St Peter Port	English, French	Protestant, Roman Catholic	Pound sterling
Douglas	English	Protestant, Roman Catholic	Pound sterling
St Helier	English, French	Protestant, Roman Catholic	Pound sterling

languages	religions	currency
Dari, Pushtu, Uzbek, Turkmen	Sunni Muslim, Shi'a Muslim	Afghani
Armenian, Azeri	Armenian Orthodox	Dram
Azeri, Armenian, Russian, Lezgian	Shi'a Muslim, Sunni Muslim, Russian and Armenian Orthodox	Azerbaijani manat
Arabic, English	Shi'a Muslim, Sunni Muslim Christian	Bahrain dinar
Bengali, English	Sunni Muslim, Hindu	Taka
Dzongkha, Nepali, Assamese	Buddhist, Hindu	Ngultrum, Indian rupee
Malay, English, Chinese	Sunni Muslim, Buddhist, Christian	Brunei dollar
Khmer, Vietnamese	Buddhist, Roman Catholic, Sunni Muslim	Riel
Mandarin, Wu, Cantonese, Hsiang, regional languages	Confucian, Taoist, Buddhist, Christian, Sunni Muslim	Yuan, Hong Kong dollar, Macau pataca
Greek, Turkish, English	Greek Orthodox, Sunni Muslim	Cyprus pound
Portuguese, Tetun, English	Roman Catholic	US dollar
Georgian, Russian, Armenian, Azeri, Ossetian, Abkhaz	Georgian Orthodox, Russian Orthodox, Sunni Muslim	Lari

ASIA
COUNTRIES (continued)

		area sq km	area sq miles	population	capital
INDIA		3 064 898	1 183 364	1 065 462 000	New Delhi
INDONESIA		1 919 445	741 102	219 883 000	Jakarta
IRAN		1 648 000	636 296	68 920 000	Tehrān
IRAQ		438 317	169 235	25 175 000	Baghdād
ISRAEL		20 770	8 019	6 433 000	Jerusalem (De facto capital Disputed)
JAPAN		377 727	145 841	127 654 000	Tōkyō
JORDAN		89 206	34 443	5 473 000	'Ammān
KAZAKHSTAN		2 717 300	1 049 155	15 433 000	Astana
KUWAIT		17 818	6 880	2 521 000	Kuwait
KYRGYZSTAN		198 500	76 641	5 138 000	Bishkek
LAOS		236 800	91 429	5 657 000	Vientiane
LEBANON		10 452	4 036	3 653 000	Beirut
MALAYSIA		332 965	128 559	24 425 000	Kuala Lumpur/Putrajaya
MALDIVES		298	115	318 000	Male
MONGOLIA		1 565 000	604 250	2 594 000	Ulan Bator
MYANMAR		676 577	261 228	49 485 000	Rangoon
NEPAL		147 181	56 827	25 164 000	Kathmandu
NORTH KOREA		120 538	46 540	22 664 000	P'yŏngyang
OMAN		309 500	119 499	2 851 000	Muscat
PAKISTAN		803 940	310 403	153 578 000	Islamabad
PALAU		497	192	20 000	Koror
PHILIPPINES		300 000	115 831	79 999 000	Manila
QATAR		11 437	4 416	610 000	Doha
RUSSIAN FEDERATION		17 075 400	6 592 849	143 246 000	Moscow
SAUDI ARABIA		2 200 000	849 425	24 217 000	Riyadh
SINGAPORE		639	247	4 253 000	Singapore
SOUTH KOREA		99 274	38 330	47 700 000	Seoul
SRI LANKA		65 610	25 332	19 065 000	Sri Jayewardenepura Kott
SYRIA		185 180	71 498	17 800 000	Damascus
TAIWAN		36 179	13 969	22 548 000	T'aipei
TAJIKISTAN		143 100	55 251	6 245 000	Dushanbe
THAILAND		513 115	198 115	62 833 000	Bangkok
TURKEY		779 452	300 948	71 325 000	Ankara

languages	religions	currency
Hindi, English, many regional languages	Hindu, Sunni Muslim, Shi'a Muslim, Sikh, Christian	Indian rupee
Indonesian, local languages	Sunni Muslim, Protestant, Roman Catholic, Hindu, Buddhist	Rupiah
Farsi, Azeri, Kurdish, regional languages	Shi'a Muslim, Sunni Muslim	Iranian rial
Arabic, Kurdish, Turkmen	Shi'a Muslim, Sunni Muslim, Christian	Iraqi dinar
Hebrew, Arabic	Jewish, Sunni Muslim, Christian, Druze	Shekel
Japanese	Shintoist, Buddhist, Christian	Yen
Arabic	Sunni Muslim, Christian	Jordanian dinar
Kazakh, Russian, Ukrainian, German, Uzbek, Tatar	Sunni Muslim, Russian Orthodox, Protestant	Tenge
Arabic	Sunni Muslim, Shi'a Muslim, Christian, Hindu	Kuwaiti dinar
Kyrgyz, Russian, Uzbek	Sunni Muslim, Russian Orthodox	Kyrgyz som
Lao, local languages	Buddhist, traditional beliefs	Kip
Arabic, Armenian, French	Shi'a Muslim, Sunni Muslim, Christian	Lebanese pound
Malay, English, Chinese, Tamil, local languages	Sunni Muslim, Buddhist, Hindu, Christian, traditional beliefs	Ringgit
Divehi (Maldivian)	Sunni Muslim	Rufiyaa
Khalka (Mongolian), Kazakh, local languages	Buddhist, Sunni Muslim	Tugrik (tögrög)
Burmese, Shan, Karen, local languages	Buddhist, Christian, Sunni Muslim	Kyat
Nepali, Maithili, Bhojpuri, English, local languages	Hindu, Buddhist, Sunni Muslim	Nepalese rupee
Korean	Traditional beliefs, Chondoist, Buddhist	North Korean won
Arabic, Baluchi, Indian languages	Ibadhi Muslim, Sunni Muslim	Omani riyal
Urdu, Punjabi, Sindhi, Pushtu, English	Sunni Muslim, Shi'a Muslim, Christian, Hindu	Pakistani rupee
Palauan, English	Roman Catholic, Protestant, traditional beliefs	US dollar
English, Pilipino, Cebuano, local languages	Roman Catholic, Protestant, Sunni Muslim, Aglipayan	Philippine peso
Arabic	Sunni Muslim	Qatari riyal
Russian, Tatar, Ukrainian, local languages	Russian Orthodox, Sunni Muslim, Protestant	Russian rouble
Arabic	Sunni Muslim, Shi'a Muslim	Saudi Arabian riyal
Chinese, English, Malay, Tamil	Buddhist, Taoist, Sunni Muslim, Christian, Hindu	Singapore dollar
Korean	Buddhist, Protestant, Roman Catholic	South Korean won
Sinhalese, Tamil, English	Buddhist, Hindu, Sunni Muslim, Roman Catholic	Sri Lankan rupee
Arabic, Kurdish, Armenian	Sunni Muslim, Shi'a Muslim, Christian	Syrian pound
Mandarin, Min, Hakka, local languages	Buddhist, Taoist, Confucian, Christian	Taiwan dollar
Tajik, Uzbek, Russian	Sunni Muslim	Somoni
Thai, Lao, Chinese, Malay, Mon-Khmer languages	Buddhist, Sunni Muslim	Baht
Turkish, Kurdish	Sunni Muslim, Shi'a Muslim	Turkish lira

world states and territories
asia

ASIA
COUNTRIES (continued)

		area sq km	area sq miles	population	capital
TURKMENISTAN		488 100	188 456	4 867 000	Ashgabat
UNITED ARAB EMIRATES		77 700	30 000	2 995 000	Abu Dhabi
UZBEKISTAN		447 400	172 742	26 093 000	Tashkent
VIETNAM		329 565	127 246	81 377 000	Ha Nôi
YEMEN		527 968	203 850	20 010 000	Şan'ā'

ASIA
DEPENDENT AND DISPUTED TERRITORIES

		area sq km	area sq miles	population
Christmas Island	Australian External Territory	135	52	1 560
Cocos Islands	Australian External Territory	14	5	632
Gaza	Semi-autonomous region	363	140	1 203 591
Jammu and Kashmir	Disputed territory (India/Pakistan)	222 236	85 806	13 000 000
West Bank	Disputed territory	5 860	2 263	2 303 660

AFRICA
COUNTRIES

		area sq km	area sq miles	population	capital
ALGERIA		2 381 741	919 595	31 800 000	Algiers
ANGOLA		1 246 700	481 354	13 625 000	Luanda
BENIN		112 620	43 483	6 736 000	Porto-Novo
BOTSWANA		581 370	224 468	1 785 000	Gaborone
BURKINA		274 200	105 869	13 002 000	Ouagadougou
BURUNDI		27 835	10 747	6 825 000	Bujumbura
CAMEROON		475 442	183 569	16 018 000	Yaoundé
CAPE VERDE		4 033	1 557	463 000	Praia
CENTRAL AFRICAN REPUBLIC		622 436	240 324	3 865 000	Bangui
CHAD		1 284 000	495 755	8 598 000	Ndjamena
COMOROS		1 862	719	768 000	Moroni
CONGO		342 000	132 047	3 724 000	Brazzaville
CONGO, DEMOCRATIC REP. OF		2 345 410	905 568	52 771 000	Kinshasa
CÔTE D'IVOIRE		322 463	124 504	16 631 000	Yamoussoukro
DJIBOUTI		23 200	8 958	703 000	Djibouti
EGYPT		1 000 250	386 199	71 931 000	Cairo
EQUATORIAL GUINEA		28 051	10 831	494 000	Malabo
ERITREA		117 400	45 328	4 141 000	Asmara

guages	religions	currency
kmen, Uzbek, Russian	Sunni Muslim, Russian Orthodox	Turkmen manat
bic, English	Sunni Muslim, Shi'a Muslim	United Arab Emirates dirham
ek, Russian, Tajik, Kazakh	Sunni Muslim, Russian Orthodox	Uzbek som
namese, Thai, Khmer, Chinese, local languages	Buddhist, Taoist, Roman Catholic, Cao Dai, Hoa Hao	Dong
bic	Sunni Muslim, Shi'a Muslim	Yemeni rial

ital	languages	religions	currency
Settlement	English	Buddhist, Sunni Muslim, Protestant, Roman Catholic	Australian dollar
st Island	English	Sunni Muslim, Christian	Australian dollar
a	Arabic	Sunni Muslim, Shi'a Muslim	Israeli shekel
nagar			
	Arabic, Hebrew	Sunni Muslim, Jewish, Shi'a Muslim, Christian	Jordanian dinar, Israeli shekel

guages	religions	currency
bic, French, Berber	Sunni Muslim	Algerian dinar
tuguese, Bantu, local languages	Roman Catholic, Protestant, traditional beliefs	Kwanza
nch, Fon, Yoruba, Adja, local languages	Traditional beliefs, Roman Catholic, Sunni Muslim	CFA franc*
lish, Setswana, Shona, local languages	Traditional beliefs, Protestant, Roman Catholic	Pula
nch, Moore (Mossi), Fulani, local languages	Sunni Muslim, traditional beliefs, Roman Catholic	CFA franc*
ndi (Hutu, Tutsi), French	Roman Catholic, traditional beliefs, Protestant	Burundian franc
nch, English, Fang, Bamileke, local languages	Roman Catholic, traditional beliefs, Sunni Muslim, Protestant	CFA franc*
tuguese, creole	Roman Catholic, Protestant	Cape Verde escudo
nch, Sango, Banda, Baya, local languages	Protestant, Roman Catholic, traditional beliefs, Sunni Muslim	CFA franc*
bic, French, Sara, local languages	Sunni Muslim, Roman Catholic, Protestant, traditional beliefs	CFA franc*
orian, French, Arabic	Sunni Muslim, Roman Catholic	Comoros franc
nch, Kongo, Monokutuba, local languages	Roman Catholic, Protestant, traditional beliefs, Sunni Muslim	CFA franc*
nch, Lingala, Swahili, Kongo, local languages	Christian, Sunni Muslim	Congolese franc
nch, creole, Akan, local languages	Sunni Muslim, Roman Catholic, traditional beliefs, Protestant	CFA franc*
nali, Afar, French, Arabic	Sunni Muslim, Christian	Djibouti franc
bic	Sunni Muslim, Coptic Christian	Egyptian pound
nish, French, Fang	Roman Catholic, traditional beliefs	CFA franc*
nya, Tigre	Sunni Muslim, Coptic Christian	Nakfa

world states and territories
asia, africa

		area sq km	area sq miles	population	capital
ETHIOPIA		1 133 880	437 794	70 678 000	Addis Ababa
GABON		267 667	103 347	1 329 000	Libreville
THE GAMBIA		11 295	4 361	1 426 000	Banjul
GHANA		238 537	92 100	20 922 000	Accra
GUINEA		245 857	94 926	8 480 000	Conakry
GUINEA-BISSAU		36 125	13 948	1 493 000	Bissau
KENYA		582 646	224 961	31 987 000	Nairobi
LESOTHO		30 355	11 720	1 802 000	Maseru
LIBERIA		111 369	43 000	3 367 000	Monrovia
LIBYA		1 759 540	679 362	5 551 000	Tripoli
MADAGASCAR		587 041	226 658	17 404 000	Antananarivo
MALAWI		118 484	45 747	12 105 000	Lilongwe
MALI		1 240 140	478 821	13 007 000	Bamako
MAURITANIA		1 030 700	397 955	2 893 000	Nouakchott
MAURITIUS		2 040	788	1 221 000	Port Louis
MOROCCO		446 550	172 414	30 566 000	Rabat
MOZAMBIQUE		799 380	308 642	18 863 000	Maputo
NAMIBIA		824 292	318 261	1 987 000	Windhoek
NIGER		1 267 000	489 191	11 972 000	Niamey
NIGERIA		923 768	356 669	124 009 000	Abuja
RWANDA		26 338	10 169	8 387 000	Kigali
SÃO TOMÉ AND PRÍNCIPE		964	372	161 000	São Tomé
SENEGAL		196 720	75 954	10 095 000	Dakar
SEYCHELLES		455	176	81 000	Victoria
SIERRA LEONE		71 740	27 699	4 971 000	Freetown
SOMALIA		637 657	246 201	9 890 000	Mogadishu
SOUTH AFRICA, REPUBLIC OF		1 219 090	470 693	45 026 000	Pretoria/Cape Town
SUDAN		2 505 813	967 500	33 610 000	Khartoum
SWAZILAND		17 364	6 704	1 077 000	Mbabane
TANZANIA		945 087	364 900	36 977 000	Dodoma
TOGO		56 785	21 925	4 909 000	Lomé
TUNISIA		164 150	63 379	9 832 000	Tunis
UGANDA		241 038	93 065	25 827 000	Kampala

nguages	religions	currency
omo, Amharic, Tigrinya, local languages	Ethiopian Orthodox, Sunni Muslim, traditional beliefs	Birr
ench, Fang, local languages	Roman Catholic, Protestant, traditional beliefs	CFA franc*
glish, Malinke, Fulani, Wolof	Sunni Muslim, Protestant	Dalasi
glish, Hausa, Akan, local languages	Christian, Sunni Muslim, traditional beliefs	Cedi
ench, Fulani, Malinke, local languages	Sunni Muslim, traditional beliefs, Christian	Guinea franc
rtuguese, crioulo, local languages	Traditional beliefs, Sunni Muslim, Christian	CFA franc*
vahili, English, local languages	Christian, traditional beliefs	Kenyan shilling
sotho, English, Zulu	Christian, traditional beliefs	Loti, S. African rand
glish, creole, local languages	Traditional beliefs, Christian, Sunni Muslim	Liberian dollar
abic, Berber	Sunni Muslim	Libyan dinar
alagasy, French	Traditional beliefs, Christian, Sunni Muslim	Malagasy franc
ichewa, English, local languages	Christian, traditional beliefs, Sunni Muslim	Malawian kwacha
ench, Bambara, local languages	Sunni Muslim, traditional beliefs, Christian	CFA franc*
abic, French, local languages	Sunni Muslim	Ouguiya
glish, creole, Hindi, Bhojpuri, French	Hindu, Roman Catholic, Sunni Muslim	Mauritius rupee
abic, Berber, French	Sunni Muslim	Moroccan dirham
rtuguese, Makua, Tsonga, local languages	Traditional beliefs, Roman Catholic, Sunni Muslim	Metical
glish, Afrikaans, German, Ovambo, local languages	Protestant, Roman Catholic	Namibian dollar
ench, Hausa, Fulani, local languages	Sunni Muslim, traditional beliefs	CFA franc*
glish, Hausa, Yoruba, Ibo, Fulani, local languages	Sunni Muslim, Christian, traditional beliefs	Naira
nyarwanda, French, English	Roman Catholic, traditional beliefs, Protestant	Rwandan franc
rtuguese, creole	Roman Catholic, Protestant	Dobra
ench, Wolof, Fulani, local languages	Sunni Muslim, Roman Catholic, traditional beliefs	CFA franc*
glish, French, creole	Roman Catholic, Protestant	Seychelles rupee
glish, creole, Mende, Temne, local languages	Sunni Muslim, traditional beliefs	Leone
mali, Arabic	Sunni Muslim	Somali shilling
rikaans, English, nine official local languages	Protestant, Roman Catholic, Sunni Muslim, Hindu	Rand
abic, Dinka, Nubian, Beja, Nuer, local languages	Sunni Muslim, traditional beliefs, Christian	Sudanese dinar
vazi, English	Christian, traditional beliefs	Emalangeni, S. African rand
vahili, English, Nyamwezi, local languages	Shi'a Muslim, Sunni Muslim, traditional beliefs, Christian	Tanzanian shilling
ench, Ewe, Kabre, local languages	Traditional beliefs, Christian, Sunni Muslim	CFA franc*
abic, French	Sunni Muslim	Tunisian dinar
glish, Swahili, Luganda, local languages	Roman Catholic, Protestant, Sunni Muslim, traditional beliefs	Ugandan shilling

AFRICA
COUNTRIES (continued)

		area sq km	area sq miles	population	capital
ZAMBIA		752 614	290 586	10 812 000	Lusaka
ZIMBABWE		390 759	150 873	12 891 000	Harare

AFRICA
DEPENDENT AND DISPUTED TERRITORIES

		area sq km	area sq miles	populati
Canary Islands	Autonomous Community of Spain	7 447	2 875	1 694 4
Madeira	Autonomous Region of Portugal	779	301	242 6
Mayotte	French Territorial Collectivity	373	144	171 0
Réunion	French Overseas Department	2 551	985	756 0
St Helena and Dependencies	United Kingdom Overseas Territory	121	47	5 6
Western Sahara	Disputed territory (Morocco)	266 000	102 703	308 0

OCEANIA
COUNTRIES

		area sq km	area sq miles	population	capital
AUSTRALIA		7 692 024	2 969 907	19 731 000	Canberra
FIJI		18 330	7 077	839 000	Suva
KIRIBATI		717	277	88 000	Bairiki
MARSHALL ISLANDS		181	70	53 000	Delap-Uliga-Djarrit
MICRONESIA, FED. STATES OF		701	271	109 000	Palikir
NAURU		21	8	13 000	Yaren
NEW ZEALAND		270 534	104 454	3 875 000	Wellington
PAPUA NEW GUINEA		462 840	178 704	5 711 000	Port Moresby
SAMOA		2 831	1 093	178 000	Apia
SOLOMON ISLANDS		28 370	10 954	477 000	Honiara
TONGA		748	289	104 000	Nuku'alofa
TUVALU		25	10	11 000	Vaiaku
VANUATU		12 190	4 707	212 000	Port Vila

OCEANIA
DEPENDENT TERRITORIES

		area sq km	area sq miles	populati
American Samoa	United States Unincorporated Territory	197	76	67 0
Cook Islands	Self-governing New Zealand Territory	293	113	18 0
French Polynesia	French Overseas Territory	3 265	1 261	244 0
Guam	United States Unincorporated Territory	541	209	163 0
New Caledonia	French Overseas Territory	19 058	7 358	228 0

languages	religions	currency
English, Bemba, Nyanja, Tonga, local languages	Christian, traditional beliefs	Zambian kwacha
English, Shona, Ndebele	Christian, traditional beliefs	Zimbabwean dollar

capital	languages	religions	currency
Santa Cruz de Tenerife, Las Palmas	Spanish	Roman Catholic	Euro
Funchal	Portuguese	Roman Catholic, Protestant	Euro
Mamoudzou	French, Mahorian	Sunni Muslim, Christian	Euro
St-Denis	French, creole	Roman Catholic	Euro
Jamestown	English	Protestant, Roman Catholic	St Helena pound
Laâyoune	Arabic	Sunni Muslim	Moroccan dirham

*Communauté Financière Africaine franc

languages	religions	currency
English, Italian, Greek	Protestant, Roman Catholic, Orthodox	Australian dollar
English, Fijian, Hindi	Christian, Hindu, Sunni Muslim	Fiji dollar
Gilbertese, English	Roman Catholic, Protestant	Australian dollar
English, Marshallese	Protestant, Roman Catholic	US dollar
English, Chuukese, Pohnpeian, local languages	Roman Catholic, Protestant	US dollar
Nauruan, English	Protestant, Roman Catholic	Australian dollar
English, Maori	Protestant, Roman Catholic	New Zealand dollar
English, Tok Pisin (creole), local languages	Protestant, Roman Catholic, traditional beliefs	Kina
Samoan, English	Protestant, Roman Catholic	Tala
English, creole, local languages	Protestant, Roman Catholic	Solomon Islands dollar
Tongan, English	Protestant, Roman Catholic	Pa'anga
Tuvaluan, English	Protestant	Australian dollar
English, Bislama (creole), French	Protestant, Roman Catholic, traditional beliefs	Vatu

capital	languages	religions	currency
Pago Pago	Samoan, English	Protestant, Roman Catholic	US dollar
Alofi	English, Maori	Protestant, Roman Catholic	New Zealand dollar
Papeete	French, Tahitian, Polynesian languages	Protestant, Roman Catholic	CFP franc*
Agaña	Chamorro, English, Tapalog	Roman Catholic	US dollar
Nouméa	French, local languages	Roman Catholic, Protestant, Sunni Muslim	CFP franc*

OCEANIA DEPENDENT TERRITORIES (continued)			area sq km	area sq miles	population
Niue		Self-governing New Zealand Territory	258	100	2 00
Norfolk Island		Australian External Territory	35	14	2 03
Northern Mariana Islands		United States Commonwealth	477	184	79 00
Pitcairn Islands		United Kingdom Overseas Territory	45	17	5
Tokelau		New Zealand Overseas Territory	10	4	2 00
Wallis and Futuna Islands		French Overseas Territory	274	106	15 00

NORTH AMERICA COUNTRIES		area sq km	area sq miles	population	capital
ANTIGUA AND BARBUDA		442	171	73 000	St John's
THE BAHAMAS		13 939	5 382	314 000	Nassau
BARBADOS		430	166	270 000	Bridgetown
BELIZE		22 965	8 867	256 000	Belmopan
CANADA		9 984 670	3 855 103	31 510 000	Ottawa
COSTA RICA		51 100	19 730	4 173 000	San José
CUBA		110 860	42 803	11 300 000	Havana
DOMINICA		750	290	79 000	Roseau
DOMINICAN REPUBLIC		48 442	18 704	8 745 000	Santo Domingo
EL SALVADOR		21 041	8 124	6 515 000	San Salvador
GRENADA		378	146	80 000	St George's
GUATEMALA		108 890	42 043	12 347 000	Guatemala City
HAITI		27 750	10 714	8 326 000	Port-au-Prince
HONDURAS		112 088	43 277	6 941 000	Tegucigalpa
JAMAICA		10 991	4 244	2 651 000	Kingston
MEXICO		1 972 545	761 604	103 457 000	Mexico City
NICARAGUA		130 000	50 193	5 466 000	Managua
PANAMA		77 082	29 762	3 120 000	Panama City
ST KITTS AND NEVIS		261	101	42 000	Basseterre
ST LUCIA		616	238	149 000	Castries
ST VINCENT AND THE GRENADINES		389	150	120 000	Kingstown
TRINIDAD AND TOBAGO		5 130	1 981	1 303 000	Port of Spain
UNITED STATES OF AMERICA		9 826 635	3 794 085	294 043 000	Washington DC

apital	languages	religions	currency
ilofi	English, Polynesian	Christian	New Zealand dollar
ingston	English	Protestant, Roman Catholic	Australian dollar
apitol Hill	English, Chamorro, local languages	Roman Catholic	US dollar
damstown	English	Protestant	New Zealand dollar
	English, Tokelauan	Christian	New Zealand dollar
latã'utu	French, Wallisian, Futunian	Roman Catholic	CFP franc*

*Franc des Comptoirs Français du Pacifique

anguages	religions	currency
nglish, creole	Protestant, Roman Catholic	East Caribbean dollar
nglish, creole	Protestant, Roman Catholic	Bahamian dollar
nglish, creole	Protestant, Roman Catholic	Barbados dollar
nglish, Spanish, Mayan, creole	Roman Catholic, Protestant	Belize dollar
nglish, French	Roman Catholic, Protestant, Eastern Orthodox, Jewish	Canadian dollar
panish	Roman Catholic, Protestant	Costa Rican colón
panish	Roman Catholic, Protestant	Cuban peso
nglish, creole	Roman Catholic, Protestant	East Caribbean dollar
panish, creole	Roman Catholic, Protestant	Dominican peso
panish	Roman Catholic, Protestant	El Salvador colón, US dollar
nglish, creole	Roman Catholic, Protestant	East Caribbean dollar
panish, Mayan languages	Roman Catholic, Protestant	Quetzal, US dollar
rench, creole	Roman Catholic, Protestant, Voodoo	Gourde
panish, Amerindian languages	Roman Catholic, Protestant	Lempira
nglish, creole	Protestant, Roman Catholic	Jamaican dollar
panish, Amerindian languages	Roman Catholic, Protestant	Mexican peso
panish, Amerindian languages	Roman Catholic, Protestant	Córdoba
panish, English, Amerindian languages	Roman Catholic, Protestant, Sunni Muslim	Balboa
nglish, creole	Protestant, Roman Catholic	East Caribbean dollar
nglish, creole	Roman Catholic, Protestant	East Caribbean dollar
nglish, creole	Protestant, Roman Catholic	East Caribbean dollar
nglish, creole, Hindi	Roman Catholic, Hindu, Protestant, Sunni Muslim	Trinidad and Tobago dollar
nglish, Spanish	Protestant, Roman Catholic, Sunni Muslim, Jewish	US dollar

world states and territories
oceania, north america

NORTH AMERICA DEPENDENT TERRITORIES			area sq km	area sq miles	population
Anguilla		United Kingdom Overseas Territory	155	60	12 000
Aruba		Self-governing Netherlands Territory	193	75	100 000
Bermuda		United Kingdom Overseas Territory	54	21	82 000
Cayman Islands		United Kingdom Overseas Territory	259	100	40 000
Greenland		Self-governing Danish Territory	2 175 600	840 004	57 000
Guadeloupe		French Overseas Department	1 780	687	440 000
Martinique		French Overseas Department	1 079	417	393 000
Montserrat		United Kingdom Overseas Territory	100	39	4 000
Netherlands Antilles		Self-governing Netherlands Territory	800	309	221 000
Puerto Rico		United States Commonwealth	9 104	3 515	3 879 000
St Pierre and Miquelon		French Territorial Collectivity	242	93	6 000
Turks and Caicos Islands		United Kingdom Overseas Territory	430	166	21 000
Virgin Islands (U.K.)		United Kingdom Overseas Territory	153	59	21 000
Virgin Islands (U.S.A.)		United States Unincorporated Territory	352	136	111 000

SOUTH AMERICA COUNTRIES		area sq km	area sq miles	population	capital
ARGENTINA		2 766 889	1 068 302	38 428 000	Buenos Aires
BOLIVIA		1 098 581	424 164	8 808 000	La Paz/Sucre
BRAZIL		8 514 879	3 287 613	178 470 000	Brasília
CHILE		756 945	292 258	15 805 000	Santiago
COLOMBIA		1 141 748	440 831	44 222 000	Bogotá
ECUADOR		272 045	105 037	13 003 000	Quito
GUYANA		214 969	83 000	765 000	Georgetown
PARAGUAY		406 752	157 048	5 878 000	Asunción
PERU		1 285 216	496 225	27 167 000	Lima
SURINAME		163 820	63 251	436 000	Paramaribo
URUGUAY		176 215	68 037	3 415 000	Montevideo
VENEZUELA		912 050	352 144	25 699 000	Caracas

SOUTH AMERICA DEPENDENT TERRITORIES			area sq km	area sq miles	population
Falkland Islands		United Kingdom Overseas Territory	12 170	4 699	3 000
French Guiana		French Overseas Department	90 000	34 749	178 000

apital	languages	religions	currency
ne Valley	English	Protestant, Roman Catholic	East Caribbean dollar
ranjestad	Papiamento, Dutch, English	Roman Catholic, Protestant	Arubian florin
amilton	English	Protestant, Roman Catholic	Bermuda dollar
eorge Town	English	Protestant, Roman Catholic	Cayman Islands dollar
luuk	Greenlandic, Danish	Protestant	Danish krone
asse-Terre	French, creole	Roman Catholic	Euro
ort-de-France	French, creole	Roman Catholic, traditional beliefs	Euro
lymouth	English	Protestant, Roman Catholic	East Caribbean dollar
illemstad	Dutch, Papiamento, English	Roman Catholic, Protestant	Netherlands guilder
an Juan	Spanish, English	Roman Catholic, Protestant	US dollar
t-Pierre	French	Roman Catholic	Euro
rand Turk	English	Protestant	US dollar
oad Town	English	Protestant, Roman Catholic	US dollar
harlotte Amalie	English, Spanish	Protestant, Roman Catholic	

anguages	religions	currency
panish, Italian, Amerindian languages	Roman Catholic, Protestant	Argentinian peso
panish, Quechua, Aymara	Roman Catholic, Protestant, Baha'í	Boliviano
ortuguese	Roman Catholic, Protestant	Real
panish, Amerindian languages	Roman Catholic, Protestant	Chilean peso
panish, Amerindian languages	Roman Catholic, Protestant	Colombian peso
panish, Quechua, other Amerindian languages	Roman Catholic	US dollar
nglish, creole, Amerindian languages	Protestant, Hindu, Roman Catholic, Sunni Muslim	Guyana dollar
panish, Guaraní	Roman Catholic, Protestant	Guarani
panish, Quechua, Aymara	Roman Catholic, Protestant	Sol
utch, Surinamese, English, Hindi	Hindu, Roman Catholic, Protestant, Sunni Muslim	Suriname guilder
panish	Roman Catholic, Protestant, Jewish	Uruguayan peso
panish, Amerindian languages	Roman Catholic, Protestant	Bolivar

apital	languages	religions	currency
tanley	English	Protestant, Roman Catholic	Falkland Islands pound
ayenne	French, creole	Roman Catholic	Euro

World extremes – capitals

Largest national capital (population)	**Tōkyō**, Japan	26 849 000
Smallest national capital (population)	**Vatican City**	472
Most northerly national capital	**Reykjavík**, Iceland	64° 08'N
Most southerly national capital	**Wellington**, New Zealand	41° 18'S
Highest capital	**La Paz**, Bolivia	3 630 m 11 909 ft

AL.	ALBANIA
A.	ANDORRA
ARM.	ARMENIA
AUS.	AUSTRIA
AZ.	AZERBAIJAN
B.	BURUNDI
BE.	BENIN
BEL.	BELGIUM
B.H.	BOSNIA-HERZEGOVINA
BN.	BAHRAIN
BUR.	BURKINA
CAM.	CAMEROON
C.A.R.	CENTRAL AFRICAN REPUBLIC
C.D'I.	CÔTE D'IVOIRE
CR.	CROATIA
CYP.	CYPRUS
CZ.R.	CZECH REPUBLIC
DEN.	DENMARK
EQ.G.	EQUATORIAL GUINEA
FR.G.	FRENCH GUIANA
GEOR.	GEORGIA
GER.	GERMANY
GH.	GHANA
GUY.	GUYANA
HUN.	HUNGARY
ISR.	ISRAEL

JOR.	JORDAN
K.	KUWAIT
KYR.	KYRGYZSTAN
LEB.	LEBANON
LITH.	LITHUANIA
LUX.	LUXEMBOURG
M.	MACEDONIA
MO.	MOLDOVA
NETH.	NETHERLANDS
NI.	NIGERIA
POL.	POLAND
Q.	QATAR
R.	RWANDA
SLA.	SLOVAKIA
SL.	SLOVENIA
S.M.	SERBIA AND MONTENEGRO
SUR.	SURINAME
SW.	SWITZERLAND
T.	TOGO
TAJIK.	TAJIKISTAN
TURKM.	TURKMENISTAN
U.A.E.	UNITED ARAB EMIRATES
UZBEK.	UZBEKISTAN

1:180 000 000

0 — 1000 — 2000 — 3000 miles
0 — 2000 — 4000 km

FACTS

The longest single continuous land border stretches for 6 416 kilometres between Canada and the USA

Both China and the Russian Federation have borders with 14 different countries

All countries of the world are members of the United Nations except Taiwan and Vatican City

Map labels:

Svalbard (Norway)

Arctic Circle

NAY

FINLAND
Archangel
RUSSIAN FEDERATION
Magadan

ESTONIA
Yekaterinburg
LATVIA
Moscow
Novosibirsk
LITH.
BELARUS
POL.
Kiev
R.SLA. UKRAINE
Astana
HUN. MO.
Ulan Bator
ROMANIA
KAZAKHSTAN
MONGOLIA
BULGARIA GEOR.
Istanbul ARM.
UZBEK.
KYR.
GREECE TURKEY AZ.
TURKM.
TAJIK.
Ürümqi
Beijing
N.KOREA
ISM.
SYRIA
Tehran
AFGHAN.
Tianjin
Seoul
JAPAN
tipoli
LEB.
IRAQ
ISTAN
Xi'an
S.KOREA
Tōkyō
Cairo
ISR. JOR.
IRAN
CHINA
Osaka
EGYPT
Riyadh
PAKISTAN
New Delhi
Chengdu
Wuhan
Shanghai
SAUDI
U.A.E.
NEPAL
BHUTAN
Chongqing
ARABIA
INDIA
BANGLA-
T'aipei
Khartoum
YEMEN
OMAN
DESH
Ha Nôi
TAIWAN
ERITREA
Mumbai
MYANMAR
Hong Kong
Tropic of Cancer
SUDAN
DJIBOUTI
Rangoon
THAILAND
Northern
Addis
Chennai
Mariana
Ababa
ETHIOPIA
SRI
Bangkok
CAM-
Manila
Islands
(U.S.A.)
C.A.R.
LANKA
BODIA
PHILIPPINES
PACIFIC
DEM. UGANDA
SOMALIA
KENYA
BRUNEI
REP.
Mogadishu
MALDIVES
MALAYSIA
PALAU
FEDERATED STATES
MARSHALL
ISLANDS
CONGO
Nairobi
SINGAPORE
OF MICRONESIA
anda
R.
Dodoma
SEYCHELLES
OCEAN
TANZANIA
INDONESIA
Equator
ZAMBIA
COMOROS
Jakarta
PAPUA
NAURU
KIRIBATI
GOLA
ZIM-
MOZAMBIQUE
Dili
NEW
SOLOMON
TUVALU
IBIA
BABWE
MADAGASCAR
EAST
GUINEA
ISLANDS
WANA
MAURITIUS
TIMOR
Port
SAMOA
BOTS-
Réunion
Moresby
American
Pretoria
(France)
VANUATU
Samoa
SWAZILAND
New
FIJI
TONGA
LESOTHO
Caledonia
REP. OF
(France)
Tropic of Capricorn
OUTH AFRICA
OCEAN
AUSTRALIA
lhoek
INDIAN
Perth

French Southern
and Antarctic Lands
Îles Kerguélen

Sydney
Canberra

Wellington

NEW
ZEALAND

Antarctic Circle

A

World extremes – countries

Largest country	Russian Federation	17 075 400 sq km	6 592 849 sq miles
Smallest country	Vatican City	0.5 sq km	0.2 sq miles
Largest population	China	1 289 161 000	
Smallest population	Vatican City	472	
Most densely populated country	Monaco	17 000 per sq km	34 000 per sq mile
Least densely populated country	Mongolia	2 per sq km	4 per sq mile

FACTS

The Pacific Ocean is larger than all the continents' land areas combined

52% of the earth's land surface is below 500 metres

Lake Baikal, in the Russian Federation, is the world's deepest lake with a maximum depth of 1 637 metres

Earth's dimensions

Total area	509 450 000 sq km	196 699 746 sq miles
Land area	148 721 936 sq km	57 421 861 sq miles
Water area	360 728 064 sq km	139 277 885 sq miles
Equatorial diameter	12 756 km	7 927 miles
Polar diameter	12 714 km	7 901 miles
Equatorial circumference	40 075 km	24 903 miles
Meridional circumference	40 008 km	24 861 miles

1:180 000 000

0	1000	2000	3000 miles
0	2000		4000 km

World extremes

Highest mountain	**Mt Everest**, China/Nepal	8 848 metres	29 028 feet
Longest river	**Nile**, Africa	6 695 km	4 160 miles
Largest lake	**Caspian Sea**, Asia/Europe	371 000 sq km	143 244 sq miles
Largest island	**Greenland**, North America	2 175 600 sq km	840 004 sq miles
Largest drainage basin	**Amazon**, South America	7 050 000 sq km	2 722 005 sq miles
Lowest point	**Dead Sea**, Asia	-398 miles	-1 306 feet
Deepest water	**Challenger Deep**, Pacific Ocean	10 920 metres	35 826 feet

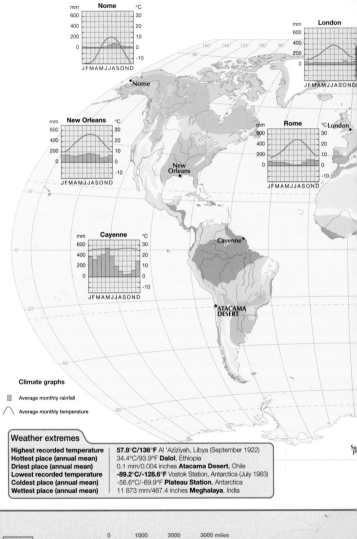

Nome
mm / °C

600 / 30
400 / 20
200 / 10
0 / 0
/ -10

J F M A M J J A S O N D

London
mm / °C

600
400 / 30
200 / 20
0 / 10
/ 0

J F M A M J J A S O N D

New Orleans
mm / °C

600 / 30
400 / 20
200 / 10
0 / 0
/ -10

J F M A M J J A S O N D

Rome
mm / °C

600
400 / 30
200 / 20
0 / 10
/ 0
/ -10

J F M A M J J A S O N D

Cayenne
mm / °C

600 / 30
400 / 20
200 / 10
0 / 0
/ -10

J F M A M J J A S O N D

Nome
London
New Orleans
Rome
Cayenne
ATACAMA DESERT

Climate graphs

Average monthly rainfall

Average monthly temperature

Weather extremes

Highest recorded temperature	**57.8°C/136°F** Al 'Aziziyah, Libya (September 1922)
Hottest place (annual mean)	34.4°C/93.9°F **Dalol**, Ethiopia
Driest place (annual mean)	0.1 mm/0.004 inches **Atacama Desert**, Chile
Lowest recorded temperature	**-89.2°C/-128.6°F** Vostok Station, Antarctica (July 1983)
Coldest place (annual mean)	-56.6°C/-69.9°F **Plateau Station**, Antarctica
Wettest place (annual mean)	11 873 mm/467.4 inches **Meghalaya**, India

1:180 000 000

0   1000   2000   3000 miles
0   2000   4000 km

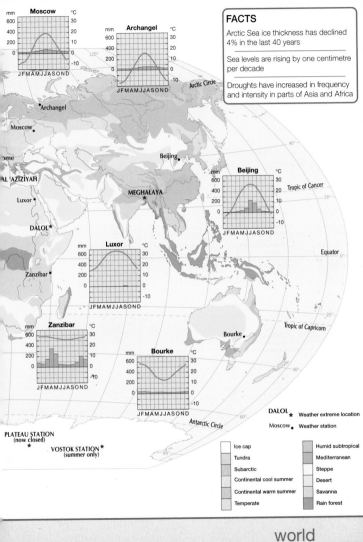

FACTS

Arctic Sea ice thickness has declined 4% in the last 40 years

Sea levels are rising by one centimetre per decade

Droughts have increased in frequency and intensity in parts of Asia and Africa

Ice cap
Tundra
Subarctic
Continental cool summer
Continental warm summer
Temperate

Humid subtropical
Mediterranean
Steppe
Desert
Savanna
Rain forest

DALOL ★ Weather extreme location

Moscow ● Weather station

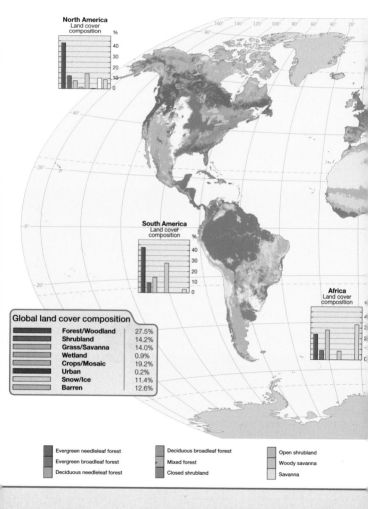

North America
Land cover composition
%

South America
Land cover composition
%

Africa
Land cover composition

Global land cover composition

Forest/Woodland	27.5%
Shrubland	14.2%
Grass/Savanna	14.0%
Wetland	0.9%
Crops/Mosaic	19.2%
Urban	0.2%
Snow/Ice	11.4%
Barren	12.6%

Evergreen needleleaf forest

Evergreen broadleaf forest

Deciduous needleleaf forest

Deciduous broadleaf forest

Mixed forest

Closed shrubland

Open shrubland

Woody savanna

Savanna

1:180 000 000

0   1000   2000   3000 miles
0   2000   4000 km

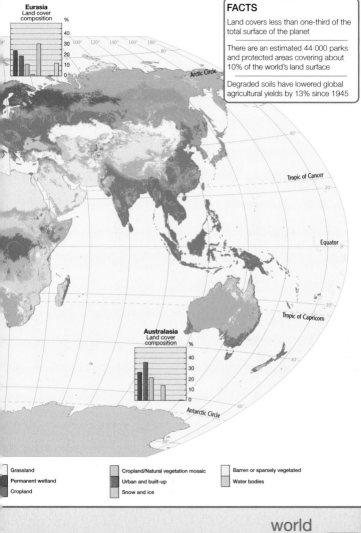

Eurasia
Land cover composition

%
40
30
20
10
0

100°   120°   140°   160°   180°

Arctic Circle

FACTS

Land covers less than one-third of the total surface of the planet

There are an estimated 44 000 parks and protected areas covering about 10% of the world's land surface

Degraded soils have lowered global agricultural yields by 13% since 1945

40°

Tropic of Cancer

20°

Equator   0°

Australasia
Land cover composition

%
40
30
20
10
0

20°

Tropic of Capricorn

40°

60°

Antarctic Circle

80°

Grassland

Permanent wetland

Cropland

Cropland/Natural vegetation mosaic

Urban and built-up

Snow and ice

Barren or sparsely vegetated

Water bodies

world
land cover   31

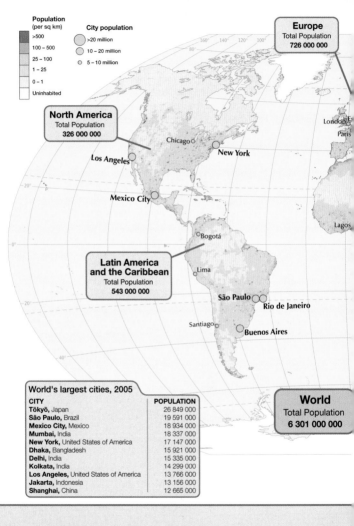

Population (per sq km)
- >500
- 100 – 500
- 25 – 100
- 1 – 25
- 0 – 1
- Uninhabited

City population
- >20 million
- 10 – 20 million
- 5 – 10 million

Europe
Total Population
726 000 000

North America
Total Population
326 000 000

Chicago

New York

Los Angeles

London

Paris

Mexico City

Lagos

Bogotá

Latin America and the Caribbean
Total Population
543 000 000

Lima

São Paulo

Rio de Janeiro

Santiago

Buenos Aires

World's largest cities, 2005	
CITY	**POPULATION**
Tōkyō, Japan	26 849 000
São Paulo, Brazil	19 591 000
Mexico City, Mexico	18 934 000
Mumbai, India	18 337 000
New York, United States of America	17 147 000
Dhaka, Bangladesh	15 921 000
Delhi, India	15 335 000
Kolkata, India	14 299 000
Los Angeles, United States of America	13 766 000
Jakarta, Indonesia	13 156 000
Shanghai, China	12 665 000

World
Total Population
6 301 000 000

1:180 000 000

0	1000	2000	3000 miles
0	2000	4000 km	

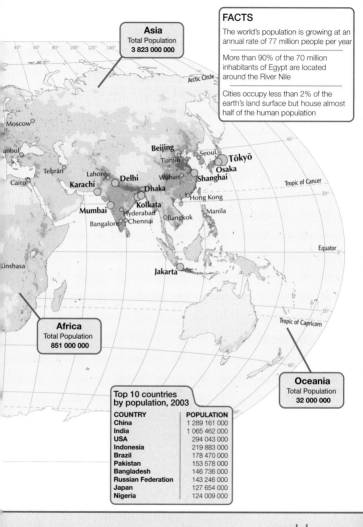

Asia
Total Population
3 823 000 000

FACTS

The world's population is growing at an annual rate of 77 million people per year

More than 90% of the 70 million inhabitants of Egypt are located around the River Nile

Cities occupy less than 2% of the earth's land surface but house almost half of the human population

Arctic Circle

Moscow

anbul

Tehrān

Cairo

Lahore

Karachi

Delhi

Beijing

Tianjin

Seoul

Tōkyō

Osaka

Wuhan

Shanghai

Dhaka

Kolkata

Hong Kong

Mumbai

Hyderabad

Bangalore

Chennai

Bangkok

Manila

Tropic of Cancer

Equator

Kinshasa

Jakarta

Africa
Total Population
851 000 000

Tropic of Capricorn

Oceania
Total Population
32 000 000

Top 10 countries by population, 2003

COUNTRY	POPULATION
China	1 289 161 000
India	1 065 462 000
USA	294 043 000
Indonesia	219 883 000
Brazil	178 470 000
Pakistan	153 578 000
Bangladesh	146 736 000
Russian Federation	143 246 000
Japan	127 654 000
Nigeria	124 009 000

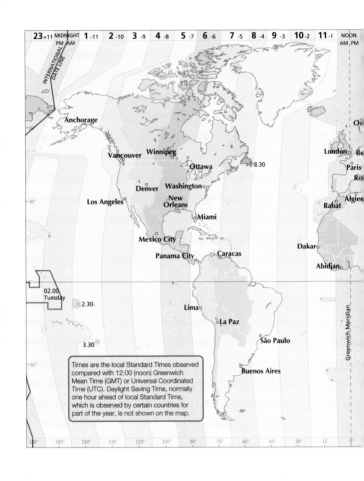

23 +11	MIDNIGHT	1 -11	2 -10	3 -9	4 -8	5 -7	6 -6	7 -5	8 -4	9 -3	10 -2	11 -1	NOON
	PM | AM												AM | PM

INTERNATIONAL DATELINE

Anchorage

Vancouver   Winnipeg

Os

London   B

Paris   R

Ottawa   8.30

Denver   Washington

Algie

Los Angeles   New Orleans

Rabat

Miami

Mexico City

Dakar

Panama City   Caracas

Abidjan

02.00 Tuesday

2.30

Lima

La Paz

São Paulo

3.30

-30°

Buenos Aires

Times are the local Standard Times observed compared with 12:00 (noon) Greenwich Mean Time (GMT) or Universal Coordinated Time (UTC). Daylight Saving Time, normally one hour ahead of local Standard Time, which is observed by certain countries for part of the year, is not shown on the map.

Greenwich Meridian

180°   165°   150°   135°   120°   105°   90°   75°   60°   45°   30°   15°   0°

1:180 000 000

0	1000	2000	3000 miles
0	2000		4000 km

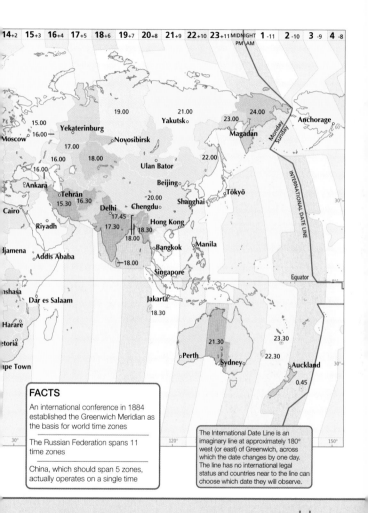

19.00   21.00   24.00

15.00   Yakutsk   23.00   Anchorage

16.00   Yekaterinburg

Moscow   Novosibirsk   Magadan

17.00

Ankara   16.00   18.00   Ulan Bator   22.00

16.00   Tehrān   16.30   Beijing   Tōkyō

15.30   Delhi   Chengdu   Shanghai

Cairo   17.45   20.00

Riyadh   17.30   Hong Kong

Djamena   18.00   18.30   Manila

Addis Ababa   Bangkok

18.00   Singapore   Equator

nshasa   Dar es Salaam   Jakarta

Harare   18.30

etoria   21.30   23.30

Cape Town   Perth   22.30   Auckland
Sydney

0.45

FACTS

An international conference in 1884
established the Greenwich Meridian as
the basis for world time zones

The Russian Federation spans 11
time zones

China, which should span 5 zones,
actually operates on a single time

The International Date Line is an
imaginary line at approximately 180°
west (or east) of Greenwich, across
which the date changes by one day.
The line has no international legal
status and countries near to the line can
choose which date they will observe.

Horn

Fontur

Vesterålen

Lofoten

Faxaflói **Iceland**

Snæfell
1833

Vestfjorden

Vestmannaeyjar

Vatnajökull

N o r w e g i a n

S e a

Faroe
Islands

Galdhøpiggen
2470

Shetland

Scandin

ATLANTIC

OCEAN

Cape
Wrath

Outer
Hebrides

Orkney

Vänern

**British
Isles**

Grampian
Mountains

N o r t h

Skagerrak

Kattegat

Vättern

S e a

Pennines

Jutland

Irish Sea

Zealand

Ireland

Bal

**Great
Britain**

Thames

Rhine

Weser

Elbe

Nor

Böhmer Wald

Sude

English Channel

Channel Islands

Seine

Ardennes

Danube

Bay of
Biscay

Loire

Jura Lake
Geneva

Vosges

A l p s

Dolomites

Po

Din

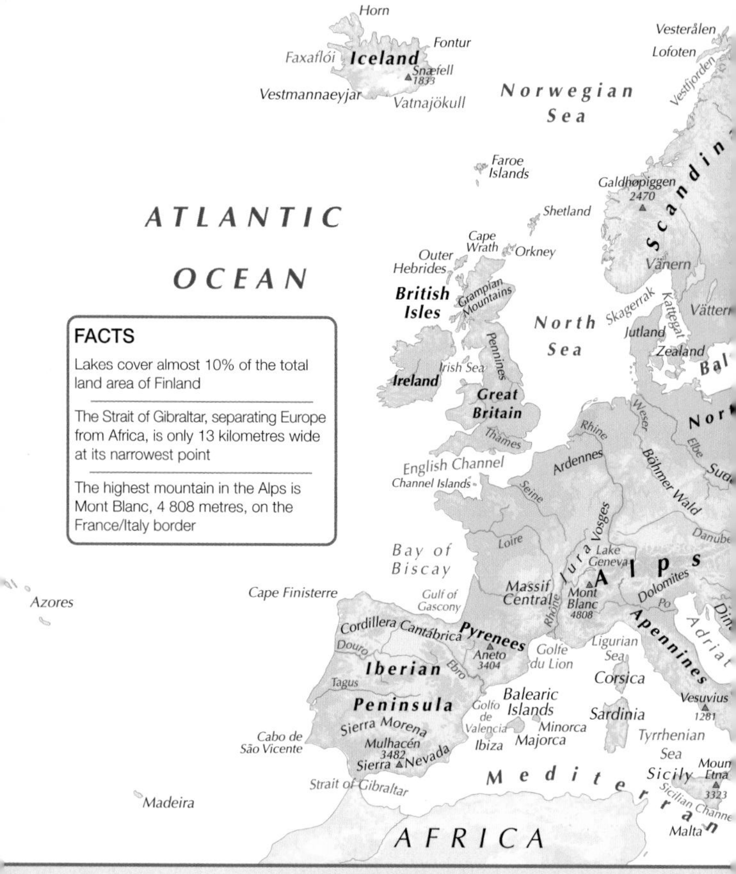

Azores

Cape Finisterre

Gulf of
Gascony

Massif
Central

Mont
Blanc
4808

Rhône

Apennines

Adriat

Cordillera Cantábrica

Pyrenees

Ligurian
Sea

Douro

Aneto
3404

Golfe
du Lion

Corsica

Ebro

Iberian

Golfo
de
Valencia

Balearic
Islands

Sardinia

Vesuvius
1281

Tagus

Peninsula

Sierra Morena

Minorca

Tyrrhenian

Cabo de
São Vicente

Mulhacén
3482
Sierra ▲Nevada

Ibiza

Majorca

Sea

Sicily

Moun
Etna
3323

Madeira

Strait of Gibraltar

M e d i t e r r a

Sicilian Channe

Malta

AFRICA

0   150   300   450 miles
0   300   600 km

Novaya
Zemlya

*Barents
Sea* Ostrov
Kolguyev

orth Cape

appland

**Kola
Peninsula**

White
Sea

Timanskiy Kryazh

Ural Mountains

Usa

Pechora

Bothnia

Severnaya Dvina

Lake
Onega

Kama

Kamskoye
Vodokhranilishche

and
ands

Lake
Ladoga

Rybinskoye
Vodokhranilishche

Gulf of Finland

Lake
Peipus

and

Volga

Kuybyshevskoye
Vodokhranilishche

ropean Plain

Valdayskaya
Vozvyshennost'

**Central
Russian
Upland**

Dnieper

Don

Pripet
Marshes

Tsimlyanskoye
Vodokhranilishche

la

Dniester

Don

Volga

**Carpathian
Mountains**

Stavropol'skaya
Vozvyshennost'

Sea
of Azov

Caspian Sea

Transylvanian Alps

Crimea

Kerchyns'ka
Zatoka

Caucasus
▲ El'brus
5642

Danube

**Balkan
Mountains**

Black Sea

Bosporus

Rhodope
Mountains

a

Pindus Mts

Aegean

nian
ands
i a n

Peloponnese

Krytiko
Pelagos

Dodecanese

Rhodes

e a

n

Crete

Sea

ASIA

Europe's longest rivers

Volga	3 688 km	2 291 miles
Danube	2 850 km	1 770 miles
Dnieper	2 285 km	1 419 miles
Kama	2 028 km	1 260 miles
Don	1 931 km	1 199 miles

Europe's highest mountains

El'brus, Russian Federation	5 642 m	18 510 ft
Gora Dykh-Tau, Russian Federation	5 204 m	17 073 ft
Shkhara, Georgia/Russian Federation	5 201 m	17 063 ft
Kazbek, Georgia/Russian Federation	5 047 m	16 558 ft
Mont Blanc, France/Italy	4 808 m	15 774 ft

europe
physical features

Europe's countries			
Largest country	Russian Federation	17 075 400 sq km	6 592 812 sq miles
Smallest country	Vatican City	0.5 sq km	0.2 sq miles
Largest population	Russian Federation	143 246 000	
Smallest population	Vatican City	472	
Most densely populated country	Monaco	17 000 per sq km	34 000 per sq mile
Least densely populated country	Iceland	3 per sq km	7 per sq mile

Reykjavík · ICELAND

Norwegian Sea

Tórshavn · Faroe Islands (Denmark)

ATLANTIC

OCEAN

Bergen · Oslo

Stockholm

NORWAY

SWEDEN

Glasgow · Edinburgh

North Sea

Belfast · UNITED KINGDOM

REPUBLIC OF IRELAND · Dublin

Manchester

Aalborg

DENMARK Malmö

Copenhagen

Bal

AL. ALBANIA
B.H. BOSNIA-HERZEGOVINA
CR. CROATIA
CZ.R. CZECH REPUBLIC
HUN. HUNGARY
LIE. LIECHTENSTEIN
LUX. LUXEMBOURG
M. MACEDONIA
NETH. NETHERLANDS
S.M. SERBIA AND MONTENEGRO
SW. SWITZERLAND

Birmingham

Cardiff · The Hague · Amsterdam

NETH. · Berlin

London · Brussels · Essen

English Channel · BELGIUM · Rhine · GERMANY

Channel Islands (U.K.) · LUX. · Frankfurt am Main · Prague

Nantes · Paris · Luxembourg · CZ.R.

Seine · Strasbourg · Munich · Vienn

Orléans · Zürich · LIE. · Bratisla

Bay of Biscay · FRANCE · Bern · SW. · Vaduz · AUSTRIA

Loire · Danube · SLOVEN

Bordeaux · Lyon · Geneva · Ljubljana · Zag

Turin · Milan · Po · CR.

Azores (Portugal)

Andorra la Vella · Marseille · MONACO · SAN MARINO · Sp

ANDORRA · ITALY

Oporto · Vatican City · Corsica

Lisbon · Madrid · Barcelona · Rome

Tagus · PORTUGAL · SPAIN · Palma de Mallorca · *Sardinia* · Naples

Seville · Valencia · *Balearic Islands* · *Tyrrhenian Sea*

Cádiz · Cartagena · *Mediterra* · Palermo · *Sicily*

Madeira (Portugal)

Gibraltar (U.K.)

AFRICA

Valletta · MALTA

38   1:35 000 000

0 150 300 450 miles
0 300 600 km

Novaya Zemlya

Barents Sea

Ostrov Kolguyev

Vorkuta

Lappland

Kola Peninsula

White Sea

Archangel

R U S S I A N

Severnaya Dvina

FINLAND *Lake Ladoga*

F E D E R A T I O N

Perm'

Helsinki

St Petersburg

Izhevsk

Gulf of Finland Tallinn

Yaroslavl'

Nizhniy

Kazan'

Ufa

ESTONIA

Volga

Novgorod

LATVIA

Moscow

Ul'yanovsk

Samara

Riga

Tula

Orenburg

A S I A

LITHUANIA Vilnius

S. FED.

Kaliningrad

Saratov

BELARUS Homyel'

Voronezh

Minsk

Warsaw

Brest

Volgograd

Volga

LAND Rivne **Kiev**

Kharkiv

Astrakhan'

Katowice

U K R A I N E Donets'k

Don

L'viv *Dniester* Dnipropetrovs'k

Rostov-

na-Donu

Caspian Sea

VAKIA

MOLDOVA

Budapest Chişinău

Odesa

Krasnodar

Groznyy

N.

Caucasus

ROMANIA

Belgrade **Bucharest** Constanta

Black Sea

Sarajevo Niš *Danube*

dgorica Sofia

İstanbul

irana M **BULGARIA**

AL. Skopje

T U R K E Y

Thessaloniki

Aegean Sea

GREECE

Athens

nian Sea

Crete

Europe's capitals

Largest capital (population)	**Paris**, France	9 753 000
Smallest capital (population)	**Vatican City**	472
Most northerly capital	**Reykjavík**, Iceland	64° 39'N
Most southerly capital	**Valletta**, Malta	35° 54'N
Highest capital	**Andorra la Vella**, Andorra	1 029 metres 3 376 feet

europe
countries

europe
baltic states and moscow region

43

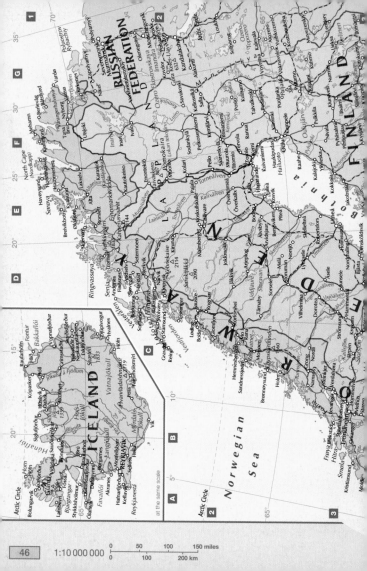

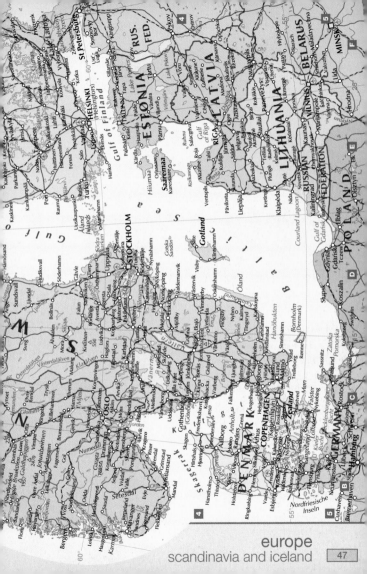

europe
scandinavia and iceland

47

ATLANTIC
OCEAN

North
Ronaldsay
Westray
Rousay
Sanday
Birsay
Stronsay
Orkney
Islands
Mainland
Kirkwall
Scapa
Stromness
Flow
Loth
Ward Hills
Scapa
Hoy
Flow
South
Ronaldsay
Pentland Firth
Dunnet Head
John
o'Groats
Duncansby
Head

Herma Ness
Unst
Yell
Isbister
Uyea
Toft
Fetlar
Ronas Hill
450?
Walls
Mainland
Whalsay
Foula
Lerwick
Bressay
Shetland
Islands
Sumburgh
Sumburgh
Head
Fair Isle

Cape
Wrath
Durness
Tongue
Ben
Hope
927
Thurso
Wick

Butt of Lewis
Port Ness
West
Loch Roag
Stornoway
Loch a'
Tuath
Scourie
Point of
Stoer
Ben More
Assynt
998
Loch
Shin
Laird
Helmsdale
Golspie
Dornoch
Dornoch Firth

Isle
of
Lewis
Clisham
799
Tarbert
Harris
Lochinver
Ullapool
Loch
Maree
Gairloch
An Teallach
1062
Ben
Wyvis
1046
Invergordon
Alness
Black
Isle
Dingwall
Lossiemouth
Elgin
Forres
Buckie
Fraserburgh
Banff
Rattray
Head
Peterhead

North
Uist
Lochmaddy
Benbecula
Skye
Portree
Achnasheen
Torridon
Carn
Eighe
1183
Strathspey
Inverness
Nairn
Aberchirder
Huntly
Ellon
Dyce
Inverurie

South Uist
Lochboisdale
Uig
Sgurr Alasdair
993
Kyle of
Lochalsh
Fort
Augustus
Loch Ness
Monadhliath Mountains
Aviemore
Grantown-
on-Spey
Cairngorm
Mountains
1309
Dufftown
Don
Dyce
Aberdeen

Canna
Rum
Eigg
Mallaig
Garry
Loch
Laggan
Loch Shiel
Fort
William
1344
Ben Nevis
Kingussie
Ben
Macdhui
1309
Braemar
Ballater
Lochnagar
1155
Dee
Stonehaven

Barra
Castlebay

Coll
Point of
Ardnamurchan
Salen
Tobermory
Morvern
Arinagour
Mull
Ben More
966
Loch
Linnhe
Glen Coe
Rannoch
Moor
Ben
Lawers
1214
GRAMPIAN MOUNTAINS
Blair
Atholl
Pitlochry
Kirriemuir
Blairgowrie
Forfar
Brechin
Montrose

North
Sea

Tiree
Scarinish
Iona
Fionnphort
Colonsay
Oban
Loch Awe
Dalmally
Crianlarich
Killin
Loch Tay
Crieff
Perth
Dundee
Arbroath
Sidlaw Hills
St Andrews
Fife Ness

Jura
Islay
Port Askaig
Port Ellen
Gigha
Mull of Oa
Inveraray
Ben Lomond
974
Lochgilphead
Tarbert
Loch
Fyne
Helensburgh
Greenock
Rothesay
Dumbarton
Clydebank
Paisley
Glasgow
Largs
Ardrossan
East Kilbride
Kilmarnock
Prestwick
Ayr
Callander
Stirling
Alloa
Falkirk
Cumbernauld
Coatbridge
Motherwell
Hamilton
Lanark
Maybole
Cumnock
Loch
Lomond
Forth
Glenrothes
Kirkcaldy
Cowdenbeath
Dunfermline
Firth of Forth
North Berwick
Dunbar
Haddington
Musselburgh
Edinburgh
Dalkeith
Penicuik
Peebles
Biggar
Galashiels
St Abb's Head
Duns
Berwick-
upon-Tweed
Holy Island
Lindisfarne

Goat Fell
874
Brodick
Arran
Campbeltown
Mull of
Kintyre
Kintyre
Girvan
Merrick
843
Thornhill
Dumfries
Southern Uplands
Broad
Law
840
Moffat
Selkirk
Hawick
Kelso
Jedburgh
The Cheviot
815
Cheviot
Hills
Wooler
Rothbury
Ashington
Morpeth

CamRaphy / NORTHERN IRELAND

Malin Head
Carndonagh
Inishowen
Giant's
Causeway
Portrush
Ballycastle
Rathlin
Island
North
Channel
Newton
Stewart
Castle
Douglas
Dalbeattie
Annan
Carlisle
Cross
Fell
893
Spennymoor

Buncrana
Londonderry
Letterkenny
Lifford
Strabane
Newtownstewart
Castlederg
Cookstown
Limavady
Dungiven
Magherafelt
Cullybackey
Ballymena
Antrim
Ballyclare
Newtownabbey
Larne
Whitehead
Bangor
Donaghadee
Stranraer
Luce
Bay
Kirkcudbright
Whithorn
Mull of Galloway
Solway Firth
Workington
Cockermouth
Skiddaw
931
Penrith
Consett
Durham
Gateshead
Newcastle
upon Tyne
Hexham
ENGLAND

Coleraine
Ballymoney
Ballymena
Ballynahinch
Ballyclare

S C O T L A N D

0   20   40   60 mi
0   50   100 km

europe
ireland

51

1:4 000 000

europe
central europe

europe
italy and the balkans
63

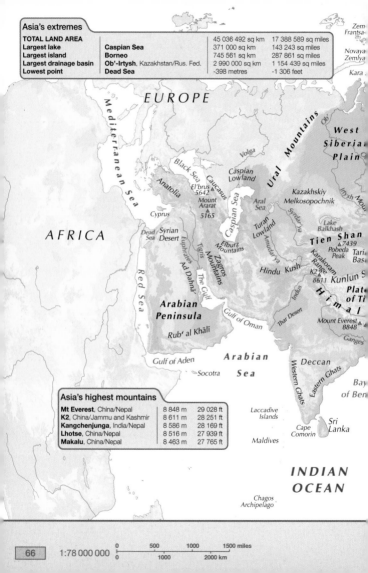

Asia's extremes

TOTAL LAND AREA		45 036 492 sq km	17 388 589 sq miles
Largest lake	Caspian Sea	371 000 sq km	143 243 sq miles
Largest island	Borneo	745 561 sq km	287 861 sq miles
Largest drainage basin	Ob'-Irtysh, Kazakhstan/Rus. Fed.	2 990 000 sq km	1 154 439 sq miles
Lowest point	Dead Sea	-398 metres	-1 306 feet

Zem Frantsa-

Novaya Zemlya

Kara

EUROPE

West Siberia Plain

Ob

M e d i t e r r a n e a n   S e a

Ural Mountains

Volga

Black Sea

Caspian Lowland

Irtysh Mou

Anatolia

Caucasus

El'brus 5642

Mount Ararat 5165

Kazakhskiy Melkosopochnik

Cyprus

Caspian Sea

Aral Sea

Syrdar'ya

Lake Balkhash

AFRICA

Dead Sea

Syrian Desert

Turan Lowland

Amudar'ya

Tien Shan 7439

Tari Bas

Pobeda Peak

Elburz Mountains

Euphrates

Zagros Mountains

Tigris

Karakoram Range

K2 8611

Kunlun S

Hindu Kush

Ad Dahnā

The Gulf

Red Sea

Plat of Ti

Arabian Peninsula

Rub' al Khālī

Gulf of Oman

Indus

Thar Desert

Himal

Mount Everest 8848

Ganges

Gulf of Aden

Socotra

A r a b i a n   S e a

Deccan

Western Ghats

Eastern Ghats

Bay of Ben

Asia's highest mountains

Mt Everest, China/Nepal	8 848 m	29 028 ft
K2, China/Jammu and Kashmir	8 611 m	28 251 ft
Kangchenjunga, India/Nepal	8 586 m	28 169 ft
Lhotse, China/Nepal	8 516 m	27 939 ft
Makalu, China/Nepal	8 463 m	27 765 ft

Laccadive Islands

Sri Lanka

Cape Comorin

Maldives

INDIAN OCEAN

Chagos Archipelago

1:78 000 000

0	500	1000	1500 miles
0	1000	2000 km	

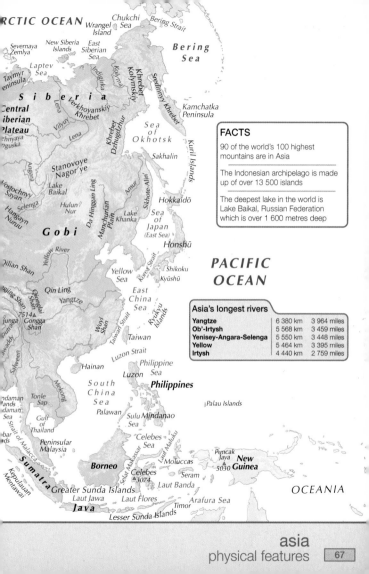

FACTS

90 of the world's 100 highest mountains are in Asia

The Indonesian archipelago is made up of over 13 500 islands

The deepest lake in the world is Lake Baikal, Russian Federation which is over 1 600 metres deep

Asia's longest rivers

Yangtze	6 380 km	3 964 miles
Ob'-Irtysh	5 568 km	3 459 miles
Yenisey-Angara-Selenga	5 550 km	3 448 miles
Yellow	5 464 km	3 395 miles
Irtysh	4 440 km	2 759 miles

asia
physical features

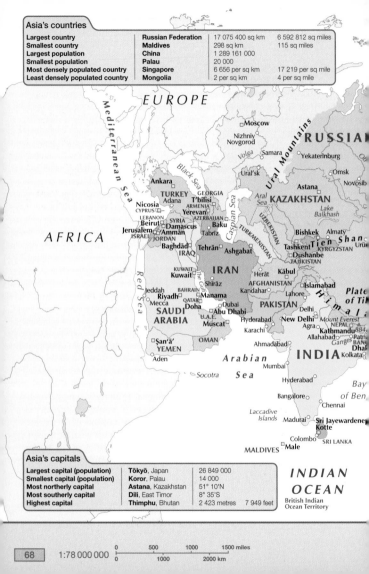

Asia's countries

Largest country	**Russian Federation**	17 075 400 sq km	6 592 812 sq miles
Smallest country	**Maldives**	298 sq km	115 sq miles
Largest population	**China**	1 289 161 000	
Smallest population	**Palau**	20 000	
Most densely populated country	**Singapore**	6 656 per sq km	17 219 per sq mile
Least densely populated country	**Mongolia**	2 per sq km	4 per sq mile

EUROPE

Mediterranean Sea

AFRICA

Moscow

Nizhniy Novgorod

Volga

Samara

Ural Mountains

RUSSIA

Yekaterinburg

Omsk

Novosib

Black Sea

Ankara

TURKEY

Adana

GEORGIA

T'bilisi

ARMENIA

Nicosia

CYPRUS

Yerevan

AZERBAIJAN

Baku

Astana

KAZAKHSTAN

Aral Sea

Lake Balkhash

Ural'sk

Caspian Sea

LEBANON

Beirut

Damascus

SYRIA

Jerusalem

ISRAEL

Amman

JORDAN

Baghdād

IRAQ

Tabrīz

Tehrān

TURKMENISTAN

Ashgabat

UZBEKISTAN

Bishkek

Tashkent

Dushanbe

TAJIKISTAN

KYRGYZSTAN

Almaty

Ürür

Tien Shan

KUWAIT

Kuwait

The Gulf

Shīrāz

IRAN

Herāt

Kābul

AFGHANISTAN

Islamabad

Riyadh

BAHRAIN

Manama

QATAR

Doha

Dubai

Abu Dhabi

U.A.E.

Kandahar

Lahore

Delhi

PAKISTAN

Plateau of Tib

Himalaya

Mount Everest

8848

Jeddah

Mecca

SAUDI ARABIA

Muscat

OMAN

Hyderabad

Karachi

New Delhi

Agra

NEPAL

Kathmandu

Allahabad

BANG

Dha

Ṣan'ā'

YEMEN

Aden

Ahmadabad

Gange

INDIA

Kolkata

Socotra

Arabian Sea

Mumbai

Hyderabad

Bay of Ben

Bangalore

Chennai

Laccadive Islands

Madurai

Sri Jayewardene Kotte

Colombo

SRI LANKA

MALDIVES

Male

INDIAN

OCEAN

British Indian Ocean Territory

Asia's capitals

Largest capital (population)	**Tōkyō**, Japan	26 849 000	
Smallest capital (population)	**Koror**, Palau	14 000	
Most northerly capital	**Astana**, Kazakhstan	51° 10'N	
Most southerly capital	**Dili**, East Timor	8° 35'S	
Highest capital	**Thimphu**, Bhutan	2 423 metres	7 949 feet

1:78 000 000

0	500	1000	1500 miles
0	1000	2000 km	

ARCTIC OCEAN

Bering Sea

Magadan

iril'sk

Lena

Petropavlovak-Kamchatskiy

EDERATION

Sea of Okhotsk

Irkutsk   *Lake Baikal*

Harbin   Sapporo

Ulan Bator   Hakodate

Vladivostock   *Sea of Japan (East Sea)*   JAPAN

MONGOLIA   Shenyang   NORTH KOREA

Beijing   Dalian   P'yŏngyang   Tōkyō

Yellow River   Tianjin   Seoul   SOUTH KOREA   Ōsaka

Lanzhou   *Yellow Sea*   Hiroshima   Fukuoka

HINA   Xi'an   Nanjing   Shanghai   *East China Sea*

Chengdu   Yangtze   Hangzhou

u   Chongqing   Wuhan

PACIFIC OCEAN

Kunming   Liuzhou   Guangzhou   T'aipei

Nanning   Hong Kong   TAIWAN   Kaoshiung

Ha Nôi   *Luzon Strait*

ANMAR   LAOS   Hai Phong

ein   Vientiane   Quezon City   PHILIPPINES

ngoon   THAILAND   *South China Sea*   Manila

Bangkok

CAMBODIA   PALAU

daman   Phnom Penh   Hô Chi Minh   Koror

nds   dia)

icobar   Kota Kinabalu   Davao

lands   Bandar Seri Begawan

ndia)

MALAYSIA   BRUNEI   *Celebes Sea*   Jayapura

Medan   Kuala Lumpur   Putrajaya   Kuching   Borneo

Singapore   Pontianak   New Guinea

INDONESIA   OCEANIA

Palembang   Banjarmasin   *Laut Banda*

Jakarta   *Laut Jawa*   Makassar   EAST TIMOR

Bandung   Semarang   Surabaya   Dili

Java

asia
southeast asia

South China Sea

Natuna Besar (Indonesia)

Panaik

Quang Ngai
Kong Son
Qui Nhon
Tuy Hoa
Kinh Hoa
Nha Trang
Cam Ranh
Phan Rang

Sông Da

Buôn Mê Thuột
Krong
Play Cu
Kon Tum
Da Lat
Đức Trong
Phan Thiết

Salavan
Pakxé
Thapangthong
Bolovens
Attapu
Muang Không
Stung Treng
Sekong
Ratanakiri
Đức Cơ
Tây Ninh
Vung Tau

Ho Chi Minh City (Saigon)

Mouths of the Mekong

Côn Son

A M

C A M B O D I A

Kâmpóng Cham
Kâmpóng Spœu

PHNOM PENH

Takêv
Svay Riĕng
Tân Châu
Long Xuyên
My Tho
Vinh Long
Cân Tho

Rach Gia
Bac Liêu
Soc Trang
Ca Mau

Mui Ca Mau

Battambang
Pouthisat
Kâmpóng Chhnang
Kôngpông Thum
Kâmpông Saôm
Sihanoukville

Krŏng Kaôh Kŏng
Kâmpôt

Tônlé Sap

Siĕmréab
Rôviĕng
Preah Vihéar
Phumi Vihéar

T H A I L A N D

Gulf
of
Thailand

Kota Bharu
Pasir Putih
Kuala Terengganu
Dungun
Kuantan

Peninsular Malaysia

M A L A Y S I A

Kuala Talan
Gunung Tahan 2189
Cukai

Pekan

Kuala Lipis
Kuala Kubu
Teluk Intan
KUALA LUMPUR

Narathiwat
Yala
Pattani
Songkhla
Nakhon Si Thammarat
Khao Chum Thong
Phatthalung
Trang
Thung Song

Pat Yai
Sadao
Kota Tinggi
Alor Setar

Kangar
Sungai Petani
George Town
Butterworth
Taiping
Ipoh

Strait of Malacca

Kampar
Bagan Datuk

Parit
Sitiawan

Kedah Peak
Peak

A

B

Narcondam Island

INDIAN
OCEAN

Banda Aceh
Calang
Sigli
Bireun
Lhokseumawe
Peureula
Takengon
Gunung Abongabong
Blangkejeren
Gunung Leuser 3145

Ujangsa
Langsa
Pangkalansusu
Pangkalanbrandan
Belawan

Medan
Tebingtinggi
Binjai

Sibolga
Tapaktuan
Singkil

I N D O N E S I A

1 **A** 120° Itbayat *Batan* **B** **1**
Islands
20° — *Luzon* *Batan* — 20°
Strait

Babuyan
Calayan Babuyan **Philippine**
Fuga Islands
Camiguin **Sea**

Laoag
Cordillera Central Aparri
Bangued Tuguegarao
Vigan Mount Chico Palanan
Tagudin Sapodoy
Bontoc Ilagan
San Fernando Mount Santiago
La Trinidad Polog
Dagupan 2929 Bayombong
Baguio
Lingayen San Carlos **Luzon**
Tarlac San Jose
Iba Cabanatuan
Angeles San Fernando
Olongapo Valenzuela *Polillo Islands*

2 *Scarborough* Balanga Quezon City **2**
Shoal **MANILA**
Santa Cruz Labo
South Tagaytay City San Pablo Daet *Catanduanes*
Batangas Tucena Lopez
China Calapan Boac Naga Virac
Mount Oas
Halcon Legaspi Sorsogon
Sea 2505 Iriosin
Mindoro San Jose Roxas *Sibuyan* Calbayog
Busuanga Romblon Masbate **Samar**
Calamian *Sibuyan Sea* Catbalogan
Group Culion Roxas *Masbate*
Visayan Tacloban
El Nido *Cuyo* Roxas *Sea* Ormoc Guiuan
Linapacan *Islands* **Panay** **Leyte**
Taytay San Jose de Iloilo **Cebu**
Buenavista Bacolod *Dinagat*
Roxas *Dumaran* **Negros** Talisay *Bohol* *Siargao*
10° — **Palawan** Puerto Princesa Cauayan **Cebu** Tagbilaran Surigo — 10°
Tanjay *Bohol Sea*
Quezon Aborlan Bayawan Tandag
Mount Dumaguete
Mantalingajan Dipolog Cagayan Butuan
2051 Brooke's Point Roxas de Oro
Bugsuk Oroquieta Iligan
Balabac Liloy Ozamiz Malaybalay
Balabac Pagadian **Mindanao**
Balabac Strait *Zamboanga* Mount Tagum
Kudat *Peninsula* Kitanglad **Davao**
Mapin 2815 Digos
Kota Belud *Banggi* Cotabato Mount Mati
3 Kota Zamboanga *Moro* Datu Piang Apo *Davao* **3**
Gunung *Gulf* 2954 *Gulf*
Kinabalu Isabela Banga
Beaufort 4095 *Basilan* General Santos
Labuan Ranau Sandakan Jolo
Crocker Lamag *Sulu* *Sarangani*
Lawas Lahad **MALAYSIA** Jolo *Archipelago* *Islands*
BANDAR SERI Kuamut Datu *Kepulauan*
BEGAWAN Pensiangan **SABAH** Tawitawi **Celebes** Karakelong *Nanusa*
Lumbis *Kepulauan*
INDONESIA **A** Sempoma Tawau *Tumindao* **Sea** **B** **INDONESIA** *Talaud*
120° *Sangir* Kaburuang

1:15 000 000

0 100 200 300 miles
0 150 300 450 km

asia
north korea and south korea

77

asia
central china

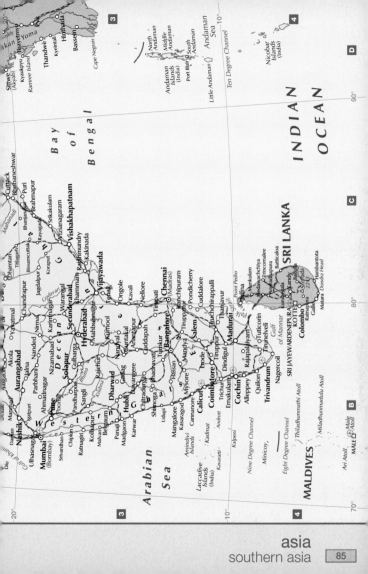

asia
southern asia

asia
arabian peninsula

asia
russian federation

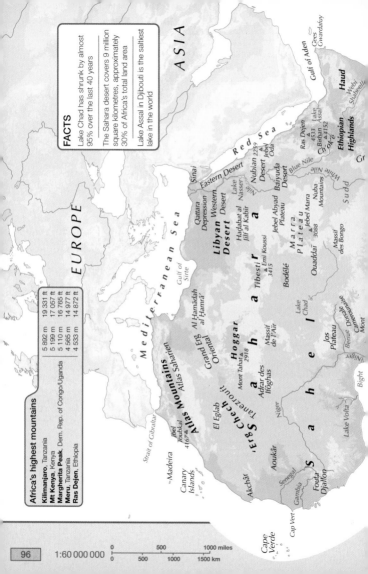

1:60 000 000

ASIA

EUROPE

FACTS

Lake Chad has shrunk by almost 95% over the last 40 years

The Sahara desert covers 9 million square kilometres, approximately 30% of Africa's total land area

Lake Assal in Djibouti is the saltiest lake in the world

Africa's highest mountains

Kilimanjaro, Tanzania	5 892 m	19 331 ft
Mt Kenya, Kenya	5 199 m	17 057 ft
Margherita Peak, Dem. Rep. of Congo/Uganda	5 110 m	16 765 ft
Meru, Tanzania	4 565 m	14 977 ft
Ras Dejen, Ethiopia	4 533 m	14 872 ft

Mediterranean Sea

Red Sea

Gulf of Aden

Gulf of Sirte

Strait of Gibraltar

Madeira

Canary Islands

Cap Vert

Cape Verde

Atlas Mountains

Jbel Toubkal ▲4167

Anti Atlas Saharien

El Eglab

Tanezrouft

'Erg Chech

Akchâr

Aoukâr

Adrar des Ifoghas

Grand Erg Oriental

Al Hamādah al Ḥamrā'

Hoggar

Mont Tahat ▲2918

Massif de l'Air

Tibesti

▲Emi Koussi 3415

Libyan Desert

Western Desert

Qattara Depression

Eastern Desert

Sinai

Hadabat al Jilf al Kabīr

Nile

Lake Nasser

Nubian Desert

Jebel Oda ▲2259

Ras Dejen ▲4533

Lake Assal

Birhan ▲4152

Choke

Ethiopian Highlands

Blue Nile

White Nile

Gr

Haud

Wehi Shebelli

Webi Shabeelle

Gees Gwardafuy

Bajuda Desert

Jebel Abyad Plateau

Nuba Mountains

Jebel Marra ▲3088

Marra Plateau

Ouaddaï

Massif des Bongo

Sudd

Bodélé

Lake Chad

Jos Plateau

Benue

Dorsale Camerounaise

Mont

Niger

Bight

Lake Volta

Senegal

Gambia

Fouta Djallon

Sahara

Sahel

Niger

0   500   1000 miles
0   500   1000   1500 km

Africa's longest rivers

Nile	6 695 km	4 160 miles
Congo	4 667 km	2 900 miles
Niger	4 184 km	2 599 miles
Zambezi	2 736 km	1 700 miles
Webi Shabeelle	2 490 km	1 547 miles

Africa's extremes

TOTAL LAND AREA		30 343 578 sq km	11 715 655 sq miles
Largest lake	Lake Victoria	68 800 sq km	26 564 sq miles
Largest island	Madagascar	587 040 sq km	226 656 sq miles
Largest drainage basin	Congo, Congo/Dem. Rep. Congo	3 700 000 sq km	1 428 570 sq miles
Lowest point	Lake Assal, Djibouti	-152 metres	-499 feet

africa
physical features

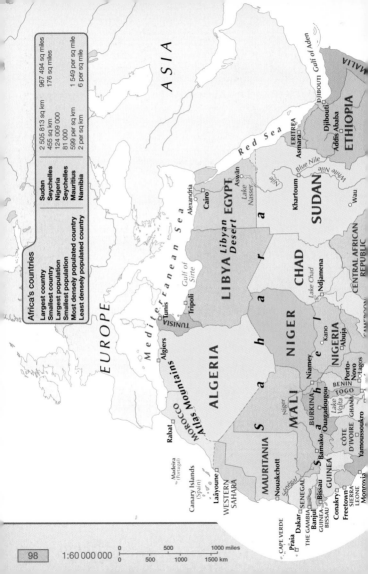

Africa's countries

Largest country	Sudan	2 505 813 sq km	967 494 sq miles
Smallest country	Seychelles	455 sq km	176 sq miles
Largest population	Nigeria	124 009 000	
Smallest population	Seychelles	81 000	
Most densely populated country	Mauritius	599 per sq km	1 549 per sq mile
Least densely populated country	Namibia	2 per sq km	6 per sq mile

ASIA

EUROPE

Mediterranean Sea

Gulf of Sirte

Gulf of Aden

Red Sea

SOMALIA

DJIBOUTI
Djibouti

ERITREA
Asmara

ETHIOPIA
Addis Ababa

Blue Nile
White Nile
Nile

EGYPT
Cairo
Alexandria
Aswân
Lake Nasser

Libyan Desert

LIBYA
Tripoli

TUNISIA
Tunis

Algiers

Atlas Mountains

MOROCCO
Rabat

Madeira (Portugal)

Canary Islands (Spain)

Laâyoune

WESTERN SAHARA

MAURITANIA
Nouakchott

Senegal

SENEGAL
Dakar
THE GAMBIA
Banjul
GUINEA-BISSAU
Bissau
GUINEA
Conakry
SIERRA LEONE
Freetown
Monrovia

CAPE VERDE
Praia

ALGERIA

S a h a r a

MALI
Bamako

Niger

BURKINA
Ouagadougou

CÔTE D'IVOIRE
Yamoussoukro

GHANA
Lake Volta

TOGO
BENIN
Porto-Novo

Lagos

NIGERIA
Abuja
Kano

Niamey
NIGER

S a h e l

CHAD
Ndjamena
Lake Chad

SUDAN
Khartoum
Wau

CENTRAL AFRICAN REPUBLIC

98

1:60 000 000

0	500	1000 miles
0	500	1000 1500 km

Victoria

MAURITIUS
Port Louis
St-Denis
Réunion
(France)

SEYCHELLES

Aldabra Islands

Mount Kenya
5199

KENYA

▲ Kilimanjaro
5892

Nairobi

Zanzibar Island

Moroni
COMOROS
Mayotte
(France)

Dzaoudzi

Dar es Salaam

Dodoma

Nampula

TANZANIA

Lake Nyasa

MADAGASCAR

Antananarivo

INDIAN

OCEAN

MALAWI

Lilongwe

Harare

ZIMBABWE

Maputo

Mbabane
SWAZILAND

Mozambique Channel

Lumbashi

ZAMBIA

Lusaka

Bulawayo

MOZAMBIQUE

Limpopo

Okavango
Delta

BOTSWANA

Gaborone

Pretoria
Johannesburg

Maseru LESOTHO

Durban

DEMOCRATIC
REPUBLIC
OF CONGO

Kinshasa

RWANDA
Kigali
BURUNDI
Bujumbura

Lake Tanganyika

Kampala

Lake Victoria

Brazzaville

CONGO

GABON

Libreville

São Tomé

ANGOLA

Huambo

Luanda

Cubango

Cuango

Zambezi

REPUBLIC OF
SOUTH AFRICA

Windhoek

NAMIBIA

Namib Desert

Orange

Cape Town
Cape of
Good Hope

Cape Agulhas

Port Elizabeth

ATLANTIC

OCEAN

Ascension

St Helena

St Helena and
Dependencies
(U.K.)

Guinea

Africa's capitals

Largest capital (population)	Cairo, Egypt	9 462 000
Smallest capital (population)	Victoria, Seychelles	30 000
Most northerly capital	Tunis, Tunisia	36° 46'N
Most southerly capital	Cape Town, Republic of South Africa	33° 57'S
Highest capital	Addis Ababa, Ethiopia	2 408 metres	7 900 feet

africa
northwest africa

101

1:26 000 000

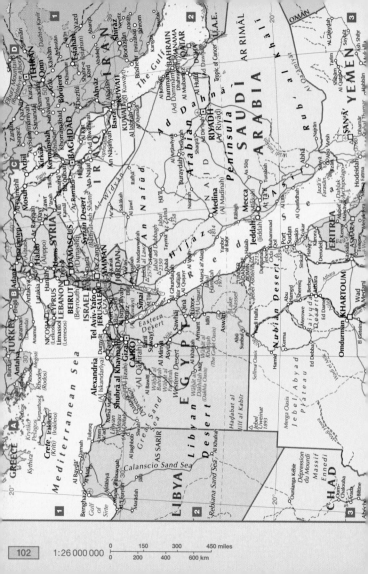

africa
northeast africa

africa
southern africa

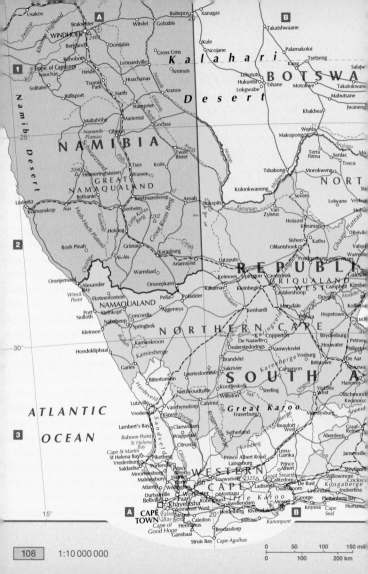

africa
republic of south africa

109

Northern Mariana Islands
Pagan
Saipan
Guam
Wake Island

ASIA

Yap

M i c r o n e s i a

Marshall Islands
Kwajalein
Ralik Chain
Ratak Chain
Majuro

Gaferut
Chuuk
Pohnpei
Kosrae

Caroline Islands

M e l a n e s i a

Gilbert Islands
Tarawa
Nauru
Be
Onotoa
Kingsmill Group
Nanumea

Bismarck Archipelago
New Ireland
Bismarck Sea
New Britain
Bougainville I.
Choiseul
Santa Isabel
Solomon Islands

Puncak Jaya 5030
Mount Wilhelm 4509
New Guinea

Mount Victoria 4073
Solomon Sea
Guadalcanal
Malaita
San Cristobal
Santa Cruz Islands
Banks Islands
Rotuma

Arafura Sea
Torres Strait
Cape York
Louisiade Archipelago
Rennell
Espíritu Santo

C o r a l

Fiji
Viti Levu
Kada

Melville Island
Cape Arnhem
Cape York Peninsula
Gulf of Carpentaria
Great Barrier Reef
Malakula
Éfaté
S e a
Erromango
Tanna
Îles Loyauté
Hur...
Islar...

Timor Sea
Cape Londonderry
Arnhem Land
Barkly Tableland

Cape Lévêque
Kimberley Plateau
Lake Argyle
Great Dividing Range
Nouvelle Calédonie

INDIAN OCEAN

Great Sandy Desert

A u s t r a l i a

Gibson Desert
Macdonnell Ranges
Uluru 867
Musgrave Ranges
Simpson Desert

North West Cape
Great Victoria Desert
Lake Eyre
Darling
Norfolk Island
Lord Howe Island
North Cape

Nullarbor Plain
Lake Torrens
Murray
Mount Kosciuszko 2230

T a s m a n
Nor... Isla...

Cape Leeuwin
Great Australian Bight
Kangaroo Island
Bass Strait
S e a
New Zealand

Aoraki 3754
Southern Alps

South East Cape
Tasmania
South Island

Stewart Island
Antip... Isla...
Auckland Islands
Campbell Island
Macquarie Island

Oceania's longest rivers

Murray-Darling	3 750 km	2 330 miles
Darling	2 739 km	1 702 miles
Murray	2 589 km	1 608 miles
Murrumbidgee	1 690 km	1 050 miles
Lachlan	1 480 km	919 miles

Oceania's highest mountains

Puncak Jaya, Indonesia	5 030 m	16 502 ft
Puncak Trikora, Indonesia	4 730 m	15 518 ft
Puncak Mandala, Indonesia	4 700 m	15 420 ft
Puncak Yamin, Indonesia	4 595 m	15 075 ft
Mt Wilhelm, Papua New Guinea	4 509 m	14 793 ft

1:65 000 000

0	500	1000	1500 miles
0	1000	2000 km	

PACIFIC OCEAN

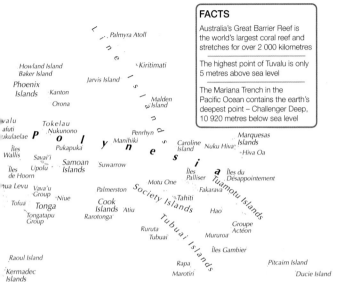

FACTS

Australia's Great Barrier Reef is the world's largest coral reef and stretches for over 2 000 kilometres

The highest point of Tuvalu is only 5 metres above sea level

The Mariana Trench in the Pacific Ocean contains the earth's deepest point – Challenger Deep, 10 920 metres below sea level

Oceania's extremes

TOTAL LAND AREA		8 844 516 sq km	3 414 868 sq miles
Largest lake	Lake Eyre, Australia	0–8 900 sq km	0–3 436 sq miles
Largest island	New Guinea, Indonesia/Papua New Guinea	808 510 sq km	312 166 sq miles
Largest drainage basin	Murray-Darling, Australia	1 058 000 sq km	408 494 sq miles
Lowest point	Lake Eyre, Australia	-16 metres	-53 feet

Wake Island
(U.S.A.)

Pagan
Northern
Mariana Islands
(U.S.A.)

Saipan

MARSHALL
ISLANDS

Guam □Capitol Hill
(U.S.A.) ■Hagåtña

Yap

Gaferut

Chuuk Pohnpei ■Palikir
Caroline Islands

Majuro □Delap-Ulig
Djarrit

Kosrae

FEDERATED STATES
OF MICRONESIA

Gilbert
Islands □Tarawa
■Bairiki

Kingsmill
Group

ASIA

Yaren
■NAURU

TUVA

Mount
Wilhelm
New Rabaul New Ireland
Guinea 4509 PAPUA
NEW
GUINEA

Bougainville I.

SOLOMON ISLANDS

Funa

*Arafura
Sea*

New
Britain Solomon
Sea ■Honiara

Malaita

Santa Cruz
Islands

Rotuma

Torres Strait Port
■Moresby

VANUATU

Banks
Islands

FIJI

Espíritu Santo

Malakula Éfaté

Su
Viti Lev.

Timor Sea

Darwin

Gulf
of
Carpentaria

Cairns

Coral Sea
Islands Territory
(Australia)

*Coral
Sea*

■Port Vila

Cape Lévêque

*Lake
Argyle*

Townsville

New
Caledonia
(France)

Îles
Loyauté

■Nouméa

Broome

INDIAN
OCEAN

AUSTRALIA

Uluru ▲Alice Springs
867

Brisbane

Norfolk
Island
(Australia)

North West
Cape

Lake Eyre

Darling

Lord Howe
Island
(Australia)

North Cape

*Lake
Torrens*

Sydney

Auckland
**North
Island**

Kalgoorlie

Great
Australian Bight

Murray
■Canberra
▲Mount
Kosciuszko
2229

■Wellington

*Tasman
Sea*

Adelaide

Perth

Kangaroo
Island

Melbourne

Christchu

Cape Leeuwin

Bass Strait

Tasmania

■Hobart

Aoraki
3754▲

South Island

**NEW
ZEALA**

Stewart Island

Auckland Islands
(N.Z.)

Oceania's capitals		
Largest capital (population)	**Canberra**, Australia	387 000
Smallest capital (population)	**Vaiaku**, Tuvalu	5 100
Most northerly capital	**Delap-Uliga-Djarrit**, Marshall Islands	7° 7'N
Most southerly capital	**Wellington**, New Zealand	41° 18'S
Highest capital	**Canberra**, Australia	581 metres 1 906 feet

Campbell Island
(N.Z.)

Macquarie Island
(Australia)

1:65 000 000

0	500	1000	1500 miles
0	1000	2000 km	

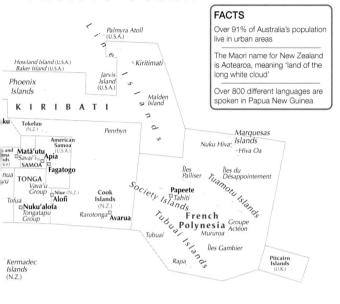

Hawaiian
Islands
(U.S.A.)

PACIFIC OCEAN

Palmyra Atoll
(U.S.A.)

Line Islands

Kiritimati

Howland Island (U.S.A.)
Baker Island (U.S.A.)

Phoenix
Islands

Jarvis
Island
(U.S.A.)

Malden
Island

K I R I B A T I

...ku

Tokelau
(N.Z.)

Penrhyn

Marquesas
Islands

Nuku Hiva   Hiva Oa

American
Samoa
(U.S.A.)

...s and
...ma
...ds
...ce)

Matā'utu   Apia
Savai'i   SAMOA

...nua

TONGA   Fagatogo
Vava'u
Group

...yu

Tofua

Niue (N.Z.)
Alofi

Nuku'alofa
Tongatapu
Group

Cook
Islands
(N.Z.)

Rarotonga   Avarua

Society Islands

Îles
Palliser

Îles du
Désappointement

Papeete
Tahiti

Tuamotu Islands

French
Polynesia   Groupe
Actéon
Mururoa

Tubuai Islands

Tubuai

Îles Gambier

Kermadec
Islands
(N.Z.)

Rapa

Pitcairn
Islands
(U.K.)

Chatham
Islands
(N.Z.)

...odes
...ds

Oceania's countries

Largest country	**Australia**	7 692 024 sq km	2 969 907 sq miles
Smallest country	**Nauru**	21 sq km	8 sq miles
Largest population	**Australia**	19 731 000	
Smallest population	**Tuvalu**	11 000	
Most densely populated country	**Nauru**	619 per sq km	1 625 per sq mile
Least densely populated country	**Australia**	3 per sq km	7 per sq mile

1

A 170° **B** North Cape 175° **C** 1

Te Paki

35° Awanui North 35
Kaitaia Cape Cavalle
Kerikeri Bay of
Russell Islands
Kawakawa
Whangarei

Donnellys Crossing

Dargaville
Great Barrier
Island
Wellsford Port Fitzroy

Hauraki
Gulf
Takapuna East Coast Bays Whitianga
Auckland Manukau **Coromandel**
Papakura **Peninsula**

2

Waiuku Pukekohe Thames 2
Paeroa Mount
North Ngaruawahia Huntly Maunganui
Katikati Hicks Bay
Island Hamilton Tauranga Whakatane
Te Awamutu Cambridge Opotiki
Rotorua Kawerau Te Kaha Matawai
Te Kuiti Tokoroa Lake
Rotorua Murupara
T a s m a n Mokau Mangakino Lake Taupo Kaitawa
Taumarunui Turangi Wairoa Gisborne
North Mahia
S e a Waitara **Taranaki Bight** Peninsula
New Plymouth **Mount** Raurimu **Hawke**
Mount Taranaki Stratford Rapehu **Bay**
2518 Raetihi Napier
Opunake Waiouru Hastings
Hawera Patea Havelock North
South Taihape Cape
Waverley Tikokino Kidnappers
Taranaki Bight Hunterville
Marton Waipawa

40° Feilding Dannevirke 40
Cape Palmerston North
Farewell Woodville
Collingwood Foxton Cape Turnagain
D'Urville Levin
Takaka **Golden Bay** Island Otaki
Tasman Paraparaumu Masterton
Karamea **Mountains** **Bay** Porirua Featherston
Richmond Riwaka Picton Te Wharau
Karamea Wakefield Nelson Blenheim **WELLINGTON** Lower Hutt
Bight Renwick Seddon
Westport Reefton **Inland Kaikoura** Cape
Punakaiki **Spenser** **Range** Campbell

3

Runanga **Mountains** Hanmer Kaikoura 3
Greymouth Springs Clarence
Hokitika Junction Waiau
Kowhitirangi Arthur's Pass Parnassus
Franz Josef **Southern Alps** Oxford Waipara
Glacier 920 Rangiora
Fox Glacier 754 **Pegasus Bay**
Lake Paringa Aoraki Kaiapoi
(Mt Cook) **Canterbury** Christchurch
Jackson Head Haast **Plains** Lake Ellesmere
Mount Lake Tekapo Ashburton **Banks Peninsula**
Aspiring Twizel Pleasant
3030 Lake Point **Canterbury**
Milford Sound **Mount** Wanaka Pukaki Geraldine **Bight**
Christina Hawea Lake Temuka
2502 Wanaka Benmore Timaru
Lake Wakatipu Waimate

45° **Lake** Cromwell Oamaru **South** 45
Anau Queenstown Alexandra **Island**
Te Anau
Doubtful Teviot
Sound Lumsden Beaumont Mosgiel **PACIFIC**
Winton Gore Brighton Port Chalmers
Tuatapere **Otago Peninsula**
Mataura Milton **Dunedin** **OCEAN**

4

Orepuki Balclutha 4
Halfmoon Bay Invercargill
Foveaux Bluff 170°
Stewart Ruapuke
Island Island Chaslands
Mistake

A **B** 175° **C**

oceania
new zealand

1:10 000 000   50   100 mil
100 km

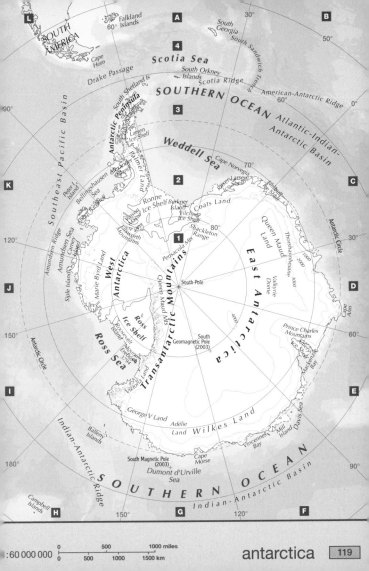

L SOUTH AMERICA · Falkland Islands · 60° · Cape Horn · Drake Passage

A · 30° · South Georgia · South Sandwich Trench · **B** · 50°

4 Scotia Sea · South Orkney Islands · Scotia Ridge · 60° · American-Antarctic Ridge · 0°

SOUTHERN OCEAN · Atlantic-Indian-Antarctic Basin

3 · Antarctic Peninsula · Larsen Ice Shelf · Weddell Sea · Cape Norvegia · 70° · Queen Maud Land · Ekström Ice Shelf

Southeast Pacific Basin · 90° · Palmer Land · Alexander Island · **2** · Coats Land · **C**

Bellingshausen Sea · Peter I Island · George VI Ice Shelf · Ronne Ice Shelf · Berkner Island · Filchner Ice Shelf · Shackleton Range · Queen Maud Land · Thorshavnheiane · Antarctic Circle · 30°

K · 80° · Pensacola Mts · **1** · Valkyrie Dome · 2000

120° · Amundsen Ridge · Amundsen Sea · Carney Island · Ellsworth Mountains · Ellsworth Land · South Pole · 1000 · **D**

Siple Island · West Antarctica · Marie Byrd Land · Queen Maud Mts · East Antarctica · Prince Charles Mountains · Cape Ann · 60°

J · Transantarctic Mountains · Amery Ice Shelf · Mac. Robertson Land · Lambert Glacier

150° · Ross Ice Shelf · Roosevelt Island · Ross Sea · South Geomagnetic Pole (2003) · Prydz Bay

Antarctic Circle · Victoria Land · **E**

I · George V Land · Adélie Land · Wilkes Land · Mill Island · Davis Sea

180° · Balleny Islands · Indian-Antarctic Ridge · Vincennes Bay · 90°

South Magnetic Pole (2003) · Cape Morse · **F**

Dumont d'Urville Sea

Campbell Islands · **H** · SOUTHERN OCEAN · Indian-Antarctic Basin · **G** · 120°

150°

:60 000 000 · 0 · 500 · 1000 miles · 0 · 500 · 1000 · 1500 km

antarctica · 119

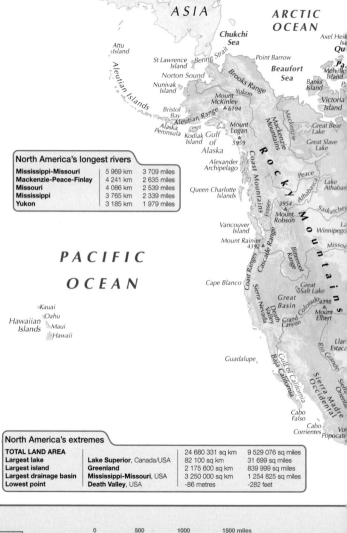

ASIA

ARCTIC OCEAN

Axel Hei
Isl
Qu

Chukchi Sea

Point Barrow

Pa
Melville
Island
P

Attu
Island

St Lawrence
Island

Bering Strait

Beaufort Sea

Banks
Island

Norton Sound

Yukon

Brooks Range

Nunivak
Island

Mount
McKinley
▲6194

Victoria
Island

Bristol
Bay

Mackenzie
Mountains

Great Bear
Lake

Aleutian Range

Mount
Logan
5959

Great Slave
Lake

Alaska
Peninsula

Kodiak
Island

Gulf
of
Alaska

Peace

ROCKY

Aleutian Islands

Alexander
Archipelago

Coast Mountains

Athabasca

Lake
Athaba

North America's longest rivers

Mississippi-Missouri	5 969 km	3 709 miles
Mackenzie-Peace-Finlay	4 241 km	2 635 miles
Missouri	4 086 km	2 539 miles
Mississippi	3 765 km	2 339 miles
Yukon	3 185 km	1 979 miles

Queen Charlotte
Islands

Fraser

3954
Mount
Robson

Saskatche

La
Winnipego

Vancouver
Island

Mount Rainier
4392

Misso

M o u n t a i n s

Cascade Range

Bitterroot
Range

PACIFIC

OCEAN

Cape Blanco

Coast Ranges

Great
Salt Lake

Great
Basin

Colorado

4398
Mount
Elbert

Kauai

Oahu

Hawaiian
Islands

Maui

Hawaii

Sierra Nevada

Death
Valley

Grand
Canyon

Llar
Estaca

Rio Grande

Guadalupe

Gulf of California

Baja California

Sierra Madre Occidental

Sierra
Orienta

Cabo
Falso

Cabo
Corrientes

Vo
Popocate

North America's extremes

TOTAL LAND AREA		24 680 331 sq km	9 529 076 sq miles
Largest lake	**Lake Superior**, Canada/USA	82 100 sq km	31 699 sq miles
Largest island	**Greenland**	2 175 600 sq km	839 999 sq miles
Largest drainage basin	**Mississippi-Missouri**, USA	3 250 000 sq km	1 254 825 sq miles
Lowest point	**Death Valley**, USA	-86 metres	-282 feet

1:65 000 000

0	500	1000	1500 miles
0	1000	2000 km	

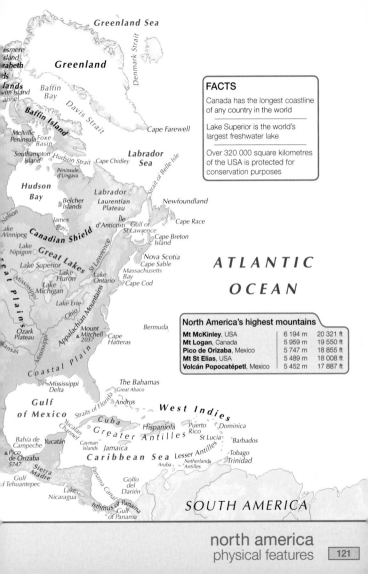

Greenland Sea

Denmark Strait

esmere
sland
zabeth
ds
lands
von Island
annel

Greenland

Baffin
Bay

Davis Strait

Cape Farewell

Melville
Peninsula

Foxe
Basin

Baffin Island

Southampton
Island

Hudson Strait

Cape Chidley

**Labrador
Sea**

Péninsule
d'Ungava

Strait of Belle Isle

**Hudson
Bay**

James
Bay

Belcher
Islands

Nelson

Labrador

Laurentian
Plateau

Newfoundland

Lake
Winnipeg

Canadian Shield

Île
d'Anticosti

Cape Race

Lake
Nipigon

Great Lakes

Gulf of
St Lawrence

Cape Breton
Island

Lake
Superior

St Lawrence

Nova Scotia
Cape Sable

Mississippi

Lake
Huron

Lake
Michigan

Lake
Ontario

Massachusetts
Bay
Cape Cod

eat Plain's

Lake Erie

Ohio

Appalachian Mountains

Ozark
Plateau

Mount
Mitchell
▲2037

Cape
Hatteras

Bermuda

ansas

Mississippi

Coastal Plain

Mississippi
Delta

The Bahamas
Great Abaco

**Gulf
of Mexico**

Straits of Florida

Andros

West Indies

Bahía de
Campeche

Yucatán

Yucatan
Channel

Cuba

Greater Antilles

Hispaniola

Puerto
Rico

Dominica

Pico
de Orizaba
5747

Cayman
Islands

Jamaica

St Lucia

Barbados

Sierra
Madre

Caribbean Sea

Lesser Antilles

Netherlands
Antilles

Tobago
Trinidad

Gulf
f Tehuantepec

Lake
Nicaragua

Panama Canal

Golfo
del
Darién

Aruba

Isthmus of Panama
Gulf
of Panama

SOUTH AMERICA

ATLANTIC

OCEAN

FACTS

Canada has the longest coastline of any country in the world

Lake Superior is the world's largest freshwater lake

Over 320 000 square kilometres of the USA is protected for conservation purposes

---

North America's highest mountains

Mt McKinley, USA	6 194 m	20 321 ft
Mt Logan, Canada	5 959 m	19 550 ft
Pico de Orizaba, Mexico	5 747 m	18 855 ft
Mt St Elias, USA	5 489 m	18 008 ft
Volcán Popocatépetl, Mexico	5 452 m	17 887 ft

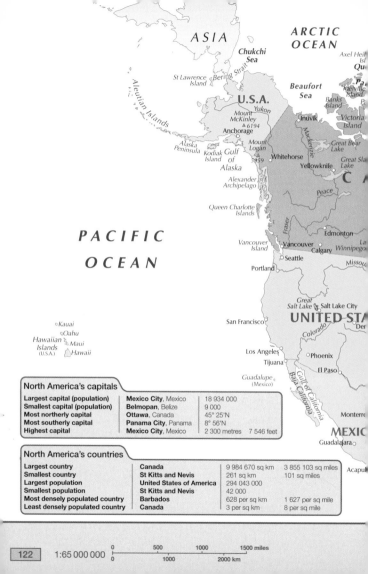

North America's capitals

Largest capital (population)	**Mexico City**, Mexico	18 934 000
Smallest capital (population)	**Belmopan**, Belize	9 000
Most northerly capital	**Ottawa**, Canada	45° 25'N
Most southerly capital	**Panama City**, Panama	8° 56'N
Highest capital	**Mexico City**, Mexico	2 300 metres 7 546 feet

North America's countries

Largest country	Canada	9 984 670 sq km	3 855 103 sq miles
Smallest country	St Kitts and Nevis	261 sq km	101 sq miles
Largest population	United States of America	294 043 000	
Smallest population	St Kitts and Nevis	42 000	
Most densely populated country	Barbados	628 per sq km	1 627 per sq mile
Least densely populated country	Canada	3 per sq km	8 per sq mile

0   500   1000   1500 miles
0   1000   2000 km

Greenland Sea

esmere
sland
abeth
ls
on Island
annel

Greenland

Baffin
Bay

Davis Strait

Denmark Strait

Nuuk

Cape Farewell

Baffin Island

Foxe
Basin

Southampton
Island

Hudson Strait

Labrador
Sea

N A D A

Hudson
Bay

Belcher
Islands

James
Bay

nelson

Newfoundland

St John's

Île
d'Anticosti

Gulf of
St Lawrence

St-Pierre

St Pierre and Miquelon
(France)

ake
innipeg

Lake
Nipigon

Québec

Halifax

Cape Sable

Winnipeg

Thunder
Bay

Great Lakes

Ottawa Montréal

Portland

Boston

Minneapolis

Detroit

Toronto

New York

S OF AMERICA

Chicago

Columbus

Pittsburgh

Philadelphia

Washington

Cleveland

St Louis

Ohio

ansas

Memphis

Cape Hatteras

Bermuda
(U.K.)

Dallas

Atlanta

Houston

Jacksonville

New Orleans

Orlando

*ATLANTIC
OCEAN*

Gulf
of Mexico

THE BAHAMAS

Miami

Nassau

Turks and
Caicos Islands
(U.K.)

Virgin Islands
(U.S.A.)

Virgin Islands
(U.K.)

ST KITTS AND NEVIS

ANTIGUA AND BARBUDA

Guadeloupe (France)

DOMINICA

Martinique (France)

Havana

CUBA

Cayman
Islands
(U.K.)

Kingston

JAMAICA

HAITI

Santo
Domingo

Port-
au-Prince

**San
Juan**

Puerto Rico
(U.S.A)

DOMINICAN
REPUBLIC

ST LUCIA

BARBADOS

ST VINCENT AND THE GRENADINES

Mérida

Yucatán

xico City

Veracruz

7 Pico
de Orizaba

BELIZE

Belmopan

Caribbean Sea

GRENADA

TRINIDAD
AND TOBAGO

GUATEMALA

HONDURAS

Aruba
(Neth.)

Netherlands
Antilles

uatemala City

Tegucigalpa

NICARAGUA

San Salvador

EL SALVADOR

Managua

San José

COSTA RICA

Lake Nicaragua

Panama
Canal

Panama City

PANAMA

SOUTH AMERICA

north america
canada

125

north america
western canada

127

north america
eastern canada

129

north america
north central united states

135

1:11 000 000

100   200 miles

100   200   300 km

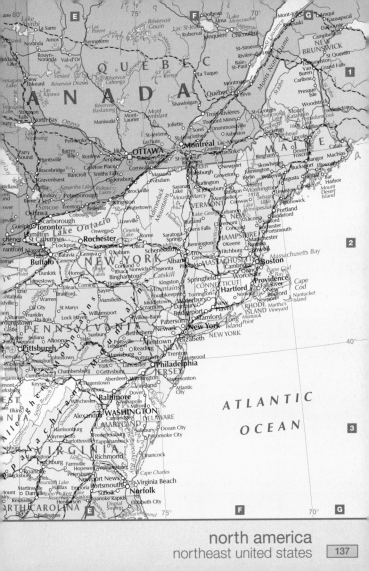

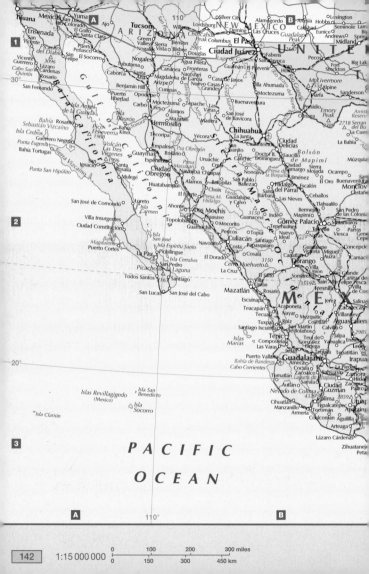

ATLANTIC

OCEAN

C · 70° · D · 60° · E · 30°

2

Tropic of Cancer

THE BAHAMAS

Great Abaco

Eleuthera

ds

NASSAU

Cat Island

Exuma Cays

Long Island

Mayaguana

Acklins Island

Turks and Caicos Islands (U.K.)

□ GRAND TURK (Cockburn Town)

Great Inagua

Caicos Islands

W e s t   I n d i e s

20°

Las Tunas

Holguín

Baracoa

Cruz

Bayamo ● Guantánamo

Cap-Haïtien

H i s p a n i o l a

Windward Passage

Santiago ●

□ Puerto Plata

DOMINICAN

Puerto Rico

(U.S.A.)

Virgin Is

(U.K.)

Anguilla

(U.K.)

L e e w a r d   I s l a n d s

St-Martin

(France)

KINGSTON

Port-au-Prince

de Paix

Gonaïves

Île de la Gonâve

Jérémie ●

Les Cayes

HAITI

PORT-

AU-PRINCE

Jacmel

Isla Beata *Cabo Beata*

Barahona

REPUBLIC

SANTO

DOMINGO

□La Romana

SAN JUAN

Ponce

Virgin Is (U.S.A.)

St Croix

St-Maarten

(Netherlands)

ST KITTS AND NEVIS

Montserrat

(U.K.)

□St John's

□ Antigua

ANTIGUA AND

BARBUDA

BASSETERRE

PLYMOUTH

Guadeloupe

(France)

BASSE-TERRE

Marie-Galante

A n t i l l e s

DOMINICA

□ ROSEAU

3

Martinique

(France)

□ FORT-DE-

FRANCE

CASTRIES

ST LUCIA

L e s s e r

b e a n   S e a

KINGSTOWN

ST VINCENT AND THE

GRENADINES

BRIDGETOWN

□BARBADOS

□ GRENADA

ST GEORGE'S

W i n d w a r d   I s l a n d s

Punta Gallinas

Península de la Guajira

Aruba

(Neth.)

Netherlands

Antilles

Curaçao

Bonaire

Islas Los Roques

La Tortuga

Isla de Margarita

La Asunción

Scarborough Tobago

PORT OF SPAIN

TRINIDAD

AND

TOBAGO

San Trinidad

Fernando

10°

Barranquilla

Cartagena ●

Santa Marta

Ríohacha

Golfo de Venezuela

Punto Fijo

Coro

Maiquetía

Cumaná

Barcelona

Gulf of Paria

Sucre

Orinoco Delta

Maturín

Tucupita

MARACAIBO

Valledupar

El Plato

Machiques

San Carlos del Zulia

MÉRIDA

Trujillo

BARQUISIMETO

Cabimas

Lake Maracaibo

Sierra de Perijá

San Felipe

El Tocuyo

Acarigua

VALENCIA

MARACAY

San Carlos

Valle de la Pascua

CARACAS

Los Teques

Zaraza

Guanipa

Guanare

El Baúl

Calabozo

El Tigre

Maganguéy ●

El Banco

COLOMBIA

Sincelejo

Montería

gulf

el Darién

Turbo

Magdalena

Valera

Barinas

Libertad

Bucaramanga

San Cristóbal

Bolívar

El Piedra

San Fernando de Apure

Arauca

Pamplona

Llanos

VENEZUELA

Ciudad Bolívar

Orinoco

Ciudad

Guayana

Embalse de Guri

El Callao

Mabaruma

GUYANA

4

La Paragua

Cúcuta

70°

60°

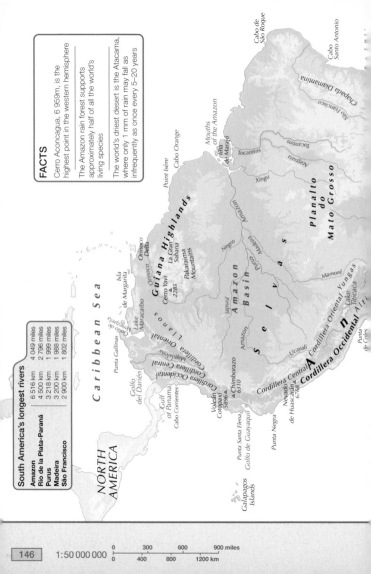

1:50 000 000

| 0 | 300 | 600 | 900 miles |
| 0 | 400 | 800 | 1200 km |

South America's longest rivers

Amazon	6 516 km	4 049 miles
Río de la Plata-Paraná	4 500 km	2 796 miles
Purus	3 218 km	1 999 miles
Madeira	3 200 km	1 988 miles
São Francisco	2 900 km	1 802 miles

FACTS

Cerro Aconcagua, 6 959m, is the highest point in the western hemisphere

The Amazon rain forest supports approximately half of all the world's living species

The world's driest desert is the Atacama, where only 1 mm of rain may fall as infrequently as once every 5–20 years

Caribbean Sea

NORTH AMERICA

Galápagos Islands

Punta Gallinas

Golfo del Darién

Gulf of Panama
Cabo Corrientes

Punta Santa Elena
Golfo de Guayaquil

Punta Negra

Cordillera Occidental
Cordillera Central
Cordillera Oriental

Volcán Cotopaxi 5896▲
▲Chimborazo 6310

Nevado de Huascarán 6768▲

Cordillera Occidental
Cordillera Central
Cordillera Oriental

Punta de Coles

ANDES

Lake Titicaca

Yungas

Cañó de Cérepo
Lake Maracaibo

Isla de Margarita

Orinoco
Orinoco Delta

Cerro Yavi ▲ 2205

Guiana Highlands

La Gran Sabana
Pakaraima Mountains

Llanos

Negro

Amazon

Japurá

Purus

Selvas

Amazon Basin

Ucayali

Mamoré

Madeira

Point Isère

Cabo Orange

Mouths of the Amazon

Ilha de Marajó

Xingu

Tocantins

Amazon

Tocantins

Araguaia

Planalto do Mato Grosso

São Francisco

Chapada Diamantina

Cabo de São Roque

Cabo Santo Antonio

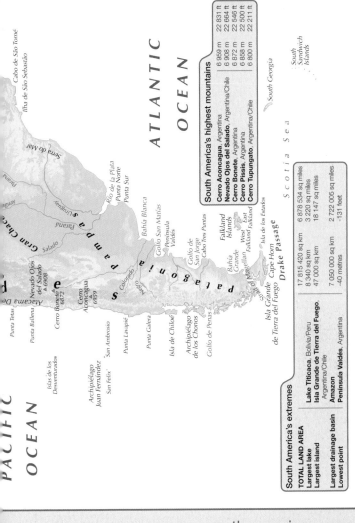

PACIFIC
OCEAN

ATLANTIC
OCEAN

Cabo de São Tomé
Ilha de São Sebastião
Serra do Mar

Paraná
Uruguai
Arroio
Negro
Salado

Río de la Plata
Punta Norte
Punta Sur

Bahía Blanca

Golfo San Matías
Península
Valdés

Gran Chaco
Atacama De
Nevado Ojós
del Salado
▲6908
Cerro
Bonete
6872
Cerro
Aconcagua
▲
6959

Colorado

Golfo de
San Jorge
Punta Tres Puntas

P a t a g o n i a

Punta Tetas
Punta Ballena
San Ambrosio
Islas de los
Desventurados
San Felix

Archipiélago
Juan Fernández

Punta Lavapié
Punta Galera
Isla de Chiloé

Archipiélago
de los Chonos
Golfo de Penas

P a m p a s

Bahía
Grande
Estrecho de Magallanes
Isla Grande
de Tierra del Fuego

Isla de los Estados
Cabo de Hornos Cape Horn
Drake Passage

Falkland
Islands
West   East
Falkland Falkland

Scotia Sea

South Georgia

South
Sandwich
Islands

South America's highest mountains

Cerro Aconcagua, Argentina	6 959 m	22 831 ft
Nevado Ojos del Salado, Argentina/Chile	6 908 m	22 664 ft
Cerro Bonete, Argentina	6 872 m	22 546 ft
Cerro Pissis, Argentina	6 858 m	22 500 ft
Cerro Tupungato, Argentina/Chile	6 800 m	22 211 ft

South America's extremes

TOTAL LAND AREA		17 815 420 sq km	6 878 534 sq miles
Largest lake	Lake Titicaca, Bolivia/Peru	8 340 sq km	3 220 sq miles
Largest island	Isla Grande de Tierra del Fuego, Argentina/Chile	47 000 sq km	18 147 sq miles
Largest drainage basin	Amazon	7 050 000 sq km	2 722 005 sq miles
Lowest point	Península Valdés, Argentina	-40 metres	-131 feet

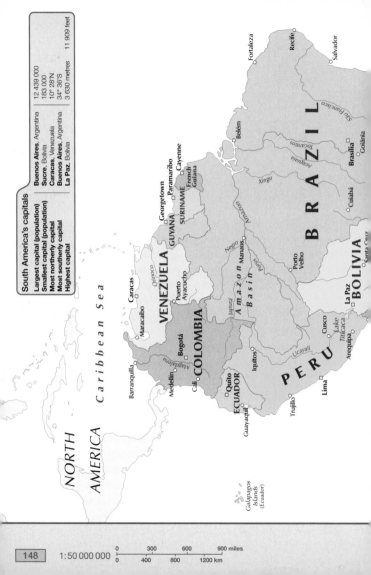

South America's capitals

Largest capital (population)	Buenos Aires, Argentina	12 439 000
Smallest capital (population)	Sucre, Bolivia	183 000
Most northerly capital	Caracas, Venezuela	10° 28'N
Most southerly capital	Buenos Aires, Argentina	34° 36'S
Highest capital	La Paz, Bolivia	3 630 metres	11 909 feet

1:50 000 000

0   300   600   900 miles
0   400   800   1200 km

NORTH AMERICA

Caribbean Sea

Barranquilla

Maracaibo

Caracas

VENEZUELA

Orinoco

GUYANA

Georgetown

Paramaribo

SURINAME

Cayenne

French Guiana

Medellín

COLOMBIA

Bogotá

Cali

Magdalena

Quito

ECUADOR

Guayaquil

Galápagos Islands (Ecuador)

Puerto Ayacucho

Negro

Iquitos

Japurá

Japurá

Amazon Basin

Purus

Manaus

Amazon

Xingu

Belém

Fortaleza

Recife

Salvador

BRAZIL

São Francisco

Tocantins

Araguaia

Brasília

Goiânia

Cuiabá

Porto Velho

BOLIVIA

Santa Cruz

La Paz

Lima

Trujillo

PERU

Cusco

Ucayali

Lake Titicaca

Arequipa

ATLANTIC

OCEAN

Scotia Sea

FACTS

South America is often referred to as 'Latin America', reflecting the historic influences of Spain and Portugal

South America has only 2 landlocked countries – Bolivia and Paraguay

Chile is over 4 000 kilometres long but has an average width of only 177 kilometres

South America's countries

Largest country	Brazil	8 514 879 sq km	3 287 613 sq miles
Smallest country	Uruguay	176 215 sq km	68 037 sq miles
Largest population	Brazil	178 470 000	
Smallest population	Suriname	436 000	
Most densely populated country	Ecuador	48 per sq km	124 per sq mile
Least densely populated country	Suriname	3 per sq km	7 per sq mile

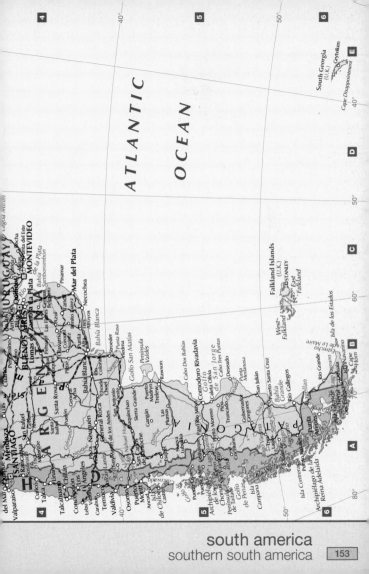

south america
southern south america

ATLANTIC

OCEAN

Tropic of Capricorn

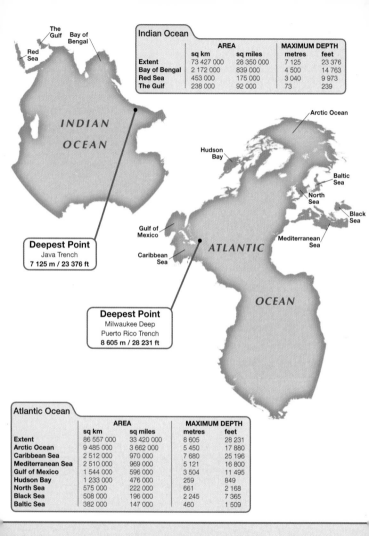

Indian Ocean

	AREA		MAXIMUM DEPTH	
	sq km	sq miles	metres	feet
Extent	73 427 000	28 350 000	7 125	23 376
Bay of Bengal	2 172 000	839 000	4 500	14 763
Red Sea	453 000	175 000	3 040	9 973
The Gulf	238 000	92 000	73	239

The Gulf
Bay of Bengal
Red Sea

INDIAN OCEAN

Arctic Ocean

Hudson Bay

Baltic Sea
North Sea
Black Sea
Mediterranean Sea

Gulf of Mexico

ATLANTIC

Caribbean Sea

OCEAN

Deepest Point
Java Trench
7 125 m / 23 376 ft

Deepest Point
Milwaukee Deep
Puerto Rico Trench
8 605 m / 28 231 ft

Atlantic Ocean

	AREA		MAXIMUM DEPTH	
	sq km	sq miles	metres	feet
Extent	86 557 000	33 420 000	8 605	28 231
Arctic Ocean	9 485 000	3 662 000	5 450	17 880
Caribbean Sea	2 512 000	970 000	7 680	25 196
Mediterranean Sea	2 510 000	969 000	5 121	16 800
Gulf of Mexico	1 544 000	596 000	3 504	11 495
Hudson Bay	1 233 000	476 000	259	849
North Sea	575 000	222 000	661	2 168
Black Sea	508 000	196 000	2 245	7 365
Baltic Sea	382 000	147 000	460	1 509

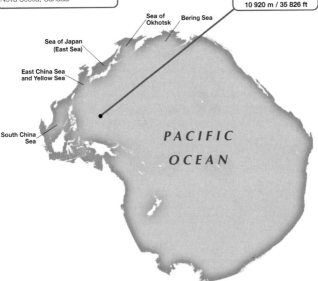

Deepest Point
Challenger Deep
Mariana Trench
10 920 m / 35 826 ft

Sea of Okhotsk

Bering Sea

Sea of Japan (East Sea)

East China Sea and Yellow Sea

South China Sea

PACIFIC OCEAN

Pacific Ocean	AREA		MAXIMUM DEPTH	
	sq km	sq miles	metres	feet
Extent	166 241 000	64 186 000	10 920	35 826
Bering Sea	2 261 000	873 000	4 150	13 615
Sea of Okhotsk	1 392 000	537 000	3 363	11 033
Sea of Japan (East Sea)	1 013 000	391 000	3 743	12 280
East China Sea and Yellow Sea	1 202 000	464 000	2 717	8 913
South China Sea	2 590 000	1 000 000	5 514	18 090

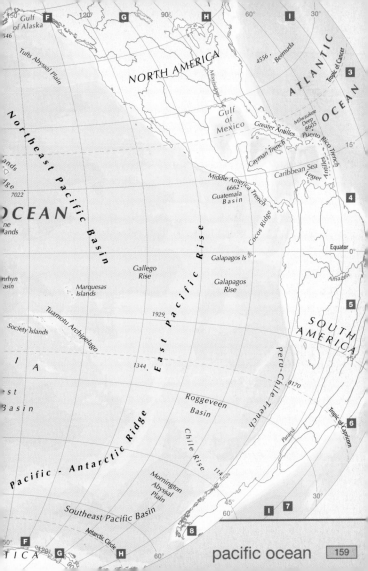

Gulf of Alaska

F 150° **G** 120° **H** 90° **I** 60° 30°

546

Tufts Abyssal Plain

NORTH AMERICA

4556 · Bermuda

3 ATLANTIC

Mississippi

Gulf of Mexico

Greater Antilles

Milwaukee Deep 8605 · Puerto Rico Trench

OCEAN

Tropic of Cancer

15°

N o r t h e a s t   P a c i f i c   B a s i n

...ands

...dge

7022

Cayman Trench

Caribbean Sea

Lesser Antilles

4

OCEAN

Middle America Trench 6662

Guatemala Basin

Cocos Ridge

Galapagos Is

Equator

Amazon

ne Islands

mrhyn asin

Gallego Rise

Galapagos Rise

5 SOUTH AMERICA

Marquesas Islands

Tuamotu Archipelago

1929

E a s t   P a c i f i c   R i s e

Society Islands

I   A

1344

15°

est Basin

Roggeveen Basin

Peru-Chile Trench

8170

P a c i f i c - A n t a r c t i c   R i d g e

Chile Rise

Parang

Tropic of Capricorn

6

Mornington Abyssal Plain

1147

30°

Southeast Pacific Basin

45°

60°

I **7**

Antarctic Circle

8

50°

F **G** **H** 60°

...TICA

...29

90°

pacific ocean   159

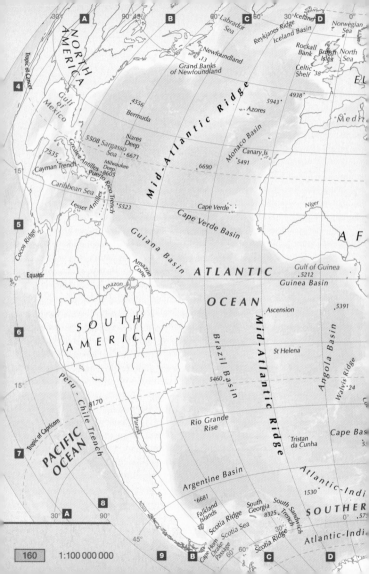

atlantic and
indian oceans

161

arctic ocean

1:60 000 000

INTRODUCTION TO THE INDEX

The index includes all names shown on the reference maps in the atlas. Names are referenced by page number and by a grid reference. The grid reference correlates to the alphanumeric values along the edges of each map which reflect the lines of latitude and longitude. Names are generally referenced to the largest scale map on which they appear. Each entry also includes the country or geographical area in which the feature is located. Where relevant, the index clearly indicates [inset] if a feature appears on an inset map.

Name forms are as they appear on the maps, with additional alternative names or name forms included as cross-references which refer the user to the entry for the map form of the name. Names beginning with Mc or Mac are alphabetized exactly as they appear. The terms Saint, Sainte, etc, are abbreviated to St, Ste, etc, but alphabetized as if in the full form.

Names of physical features beginning with generic geographical terms are permuted – the descriptive term is placed after the main part of the name. For example, Lake Superior is indexed as Superior, Lake; Mount Everest as Everest, Mount. This policy is applied to all languages.

Entries, other than those for towns and cities, include a descriptor indicating the type of geographical feature. Descriptors are not included where the type of feature is implicit in the name itself.

Administrative divisions are included to differentiate entries of the same name and feature type within the one country. In such cases duplicate names are alphabetized in order of administrative division. Additional qualifiers are also included for names within selected geographical areas.

INDEX ABBREVIATIONS

admin. div.	administrative division	**Ger.**	Germany	**Port.**	Portugal
Afgh.	Afghanistan	**Guat.**	Guatemala	**prov.**	province
Alg.	Algeria	**h.**	hill	**pt.**	point
Arg.	Argentina	**hd**	headland	**r.**	river
Austr.	Australia	**Hond.**	Honduras	**reg.**	region
aut. reg.	autonomous region	**i.**	island	**Rep.**	Republic
aut. rep.	autonomous republic	**imp. l.**	impermanent lake	**resr**	reservoir
		Indon.	Indonesia	**rf**	reef
Azer.	Azerbaijan	**is**	islands	**Rus. Fed.**	Russian Federation
b.	bay	**isth.**	isthmus		
Bangl.	Bangladesh	**Kazakh.**	Kazakhstan	**S.**	South
B.I.O.T.	British Indian Ocean Territory	**Kyrg.**	Kyrgyzstan	**Serb. and Mont.**	Serbia and Montenegro
		l.	lake		
Bol.	Bolivia	**lag.**	lagoon	**str.**	strait
Bos.-Herz.	Bosnia Herzegovina	**Lith.**	Lithuania	**Switz.**	Switzerland
Bulg.	Bulgaria	**Lux.**	Luxembourg	**Tajik.**	Tajikistan
c.	cape	**Madag.**	Madagascar	**Tanz.**	Tanzania
Can.	Canada	**Maur.**	Mauritania	**terr.**	territory
C.A.R.	Central African Republic	**Mex.**	Mexico	**Thai.**	Thailand
		Moz.	Mozambique	**Trin. and Tob.**	Trinidad and Tobago
Col.	Colombia	**mt.**	mountain		
Czech Rep.	Czech Republic	**mts**	mountains	**Turkm.**	Turkmenistan
Dem. Rep. Congo	Democratic Republic of Congo	**mun.**	municipality	**U.A.E.**	United Arab Emirates
		N.	North		
depr.	depression	**Neth.**	Netherlands	**U.K.**	United Kingdom
des.	desert	**Nic.**	Nicaragua	**Ukr.**	Ukraine
Dom. Rep.	Dominican Republic	**N.Z.**	New Zealand	**Uru.**	Uruguay
		Pak.	Pakistan	**U.S.A.**	United States of America
esc.	escarpment	**Para.**	Paraguay		
est.	estuary	**pen.**	peninsula	**Uzbek.**	Uzbekistan
Eth.	Ethiopia	**Phil.**	Philippines	**Venez.**	Venezuela
Fin.	Finland	**plat.**	plateau	**vol.**	volcano
for.	forest	**P.N.G.**	Papua New Guinea		
g.	gulf	**Pol.**	Poland		

100 Mile House Can. **126** C2

Aabenraa Denmark **47** B4
Aachen Ger. **54** C2
Aalborg Denmark **47** B4
Aalst Belgium **54** B2
Aarschot Belgium **54** B2
Aba China **80** C2
Aba Nigeria **101** C4
Ābādān Iran **93** C2
Ābādeh Iran **93** D2
Abadla Alg. **100** B1
Abakaliki Nigeria **101** C4
Abakan Rus. Fed. **95** I3
Abakanskiy Khrebet mts Rus. Fed. **89** F1
Abancay Peru **150** B4
Abarqū Iran **93** D2
Abashiri Japan **78** D2
Abaya, Lake Eth. **103** B4
Âbay Wenz r. Eth./Sudan see **Blue Nile**
Abaza Rus. Fed. **89** G1
Abbasanta Italy **62** A2
Abbeville France **58** C1
Abbeville U.S.A. **138** B3
Abbot Ice Shelf Antarctica **119** J2
Abbottabad Pak. **86** B1
Abéché Chad **101** F3
Abengourou Côte d'Ivoire **100** B4
Abeokuta Nigeria **100** C4
Aberaeron U.K. **53** A3
Aberchirder U.K. **50** C2
Aberdare U.K. **53** B4
Aberdaron U.K. **52** A3
Aberdeen S. Africa **108** B3
Aberdeen U.K. **50** C2
Aberdeen MD U.S.A. **137** E3
Aberdeen SD U.S.A. **135** D1
Aberdeen WA U.S.A. **132** B1
Aberdeen Lake Can. **127** F1
Aberystwyth U.K. **53** A3
Abez' Rus. Fed. **40** F2
Abhā Saudi Arabia **90** B3
Abiad, Bahr el r. Sudan/Uganda see **White Nile**
Abidjan Côte d'Ivoire **100** B4
Abilene KS U.S.A. **135** D3
Abilene TX U.S.A. **141** E2
Abingdon U.K. **53** C4
Abinsk Rus. Fed. **45** E3
Abitibi, Lake Can. **128** E2
Abohar India **86** B1
Abomey Benin **100** C4
Abongabong, Gunung mt. Indon. **72** A1
Aborlan Phil. **76** A3
Abou Déia Chad **101** D3
Abrantes Port. **60** B2
Abra Pampa Arg. **152** B3
Absaroka Range mts U.S.A. **134** A2
Abşeron Yarımadası pen. Azer. **93** C1
Abū 'Arīsh Saudi Arabia **90** B3
Abu Deleiq Sudan **90** A3
Abu Dhabi U.A.E. **90** C2
Abu Hamed Sudan **102** B3
Abuja Nigeria **101** C4
Abū Kamāl Syria **93** C2
Abunã r. Bol. **152** B1
Abunã Brazil **150** C2
Abu Road India **86** B2
Abū Sunbul Egypt **102** B2

Abu Zabad Sudan **103** A3
Abū Zabī U.A.E. see **Abu Dhabi**
Abyei Sudan **103** A4
Acambaro Mex. **143** B2
A Cañiza Spain **60** B1
Acaponeta Mex. **142** B2
Acapulco Mex. **143** C3
Acará Brazil **151** E3
Acaray, Represa de resr Para. **154** A3
Acatlan Mex. **143** C3
Acayucan Mex. **143** C3
Accra Ghana **100** B4
Accrington U.K. **52** B3
Achalpur India **86** B2
Achicourt France **54** A2
Achim Ger. **55** D1
Achnasheen U.K. **50** B2
Achuyevo Rus. Fed. **45** E2
Acıpayam Turkey **65** C3
Acireale Italy **62** C3
Acklins Island Bahamas **145** C2
Aconcagua, Cerro mt. Arg. **152** A4
A Coruña Spain **60** B1
Acqui Terme Italy **62** A2
Ács Hungary **57** D3
Actéon, Groupe is Fr. Polynesia **111**
Actopán Mex. **143** C2
Ada r. Italy **62** A1
Adam Oman **91** C2
'Adan Yemen see **Aden**
Adana Turkey **92** B2
Adapazarı Turkey **65** D2
Adda r. Italy **62** A1
Ad Dafinah Saudi Arabia **90** B2
Ad Dahnā' des. Saudi Arabia **91** B2
Ad Dakhla Western Sahara **100** A2
Ad Dammām Saudi Arabia see **Dammam**
Ad Dār al Ḥamrā' Saudi Arabia **90** A2
Ad Darb Saudi Arabia **90** B3
Ad Dawādimī Saudi Arabia **90** B2
Ad Dawḥah Qatar see **Doha**
Aḍ Ḍiffah plat. Egypt see **Libyan Plateau**
Ad Dilam Saudi Arabia **90** B2
Ad Dirʻīyah Saudi Arabia **102** C2
Addis Ababa Eth. **103** B4
Ad Dīwānīyah Iraq **93** C2
Adelaide Austr. **116** B2
Adelaide River Austr. **114** C1
Adelebsen Ger. **55** D2
Adélie Land reg. Antarctica **119** G3
Aden Yemen **90** B3
Aden, Gulf of Somalia/Yemen **91** B3
Adenau Ger. **54** C2
Adh Dhayd U.A.E. **91** C2
Adra Spain **60** C2
Adrar Alg. **100** B2
Adrian MI U.S.A. **136** D2
Adrian TX U.S.A. **141** D1
Adriatic Sea Europe **62** B2
Âdwa Eth. **102** B3
Adycha r. Rus. Fed. **95** L2
Adygeysk Rus. Fed. **45** E3
Adzopé Côte d'Ivoire **100** B4
Aegean Sea Greece/Turkey **65** B3
Aerzen Ger. **55** D1
A Estrada Spain **60** B1

Afabet Eritrea **102** B3
Afghanistan country Asia **86** A1
'Afif Saudi Arabia **90** B2
Africa 66
Afyon Turkey **92** B2
Agadez Niger **101** C3
Agadir Morocco **100** B1
Agadyr' Kazakh. **89** E2
Agar India **86** B2
Agartala India **87** B3
Ağdam Azer. **93** C2
Agde France **59** C3
Agen France **58** C3
Aggeneys S. Africa **108** A2
Agia Vervara Greece **65** C3
Agios Dimitrios Greece **65** B3
Agios Efstratios i. Greece **65** C3
Agios Konstantinos Greece **92** A2
Agios Nikolaos Greece **65** C3
Agirwat Hills Sudan **90** A3
Agra India **87** B2
Ağrı Turkey **93** C2
Agrigento Italy **62** B3
Agrinio Greece **65** B3
Agropoli Italy **62** B2
Agua Clara Brazil **154** B2
Aguadulce Panama **144** B4
Aguanaval r. Mex. **142** B2
Agua Prieta Mex. **142** B1
Aguascalientes Mex. **142** B2
Águas Formosas Brazil **155** D1
Águeda Port. **60** B1
Aguilar de Campóo Spain **60** C1
Águilas Spain **61** C2
Aguililla Mex. **142** B3
Agulhas, Cape S. Africa **108** B3
Agulhas Negras mt. Brazil **155** D2
Ağva Turkey **65** C2
Ahar Iran **93** C2
Ahaus Ger. **54** C1
Ahlat Turkey **93** C2
Ahlen Ger. **54** C2
Ahmadabad India **86** B2
Ahmadnagar India **85** B3
Ahmadpur East Pak. **86** B2
Ahmadpur Sial Pak. **86** B1
Ahome Mex. **142** B2
Ahram Iran **93** D3
Ahrensburg Ger. **55** E1
Ahun France **58** C2
Ahvāz Iran **93** C2
Ai-Ais Namibia **108** A2
Aigialousa Cyprus **92** B2
Aigio Greece **65** B3
Aiken U.S.A. **139** D2
Aimorés Brazil **155** D1
Aimorés, Serra dos hills Brazil **155** D1
Ain r. France **56** B3
Aïn Azel Alg. **61** E2
'Aïn Ben Tili Maur. **100** B2
Aïn Defla Alg. **61** D2
Aïn Oulmene Alg. **61** E2
Aïn Sefra Alg. **100** B1
Ainsworth U.S.A. **134** D2
Aintab Turkey see **Gaziantep**
Aïn Taya Alg. **61** D2
Aïn Tédélès Alg. **61** D2
Aïn Temouchent Alg. **61** C2
Aïr, Massif de l' mts Niger **101** C3
Airbangis Indon. **72** A1
Airdrie Can. **126** D2
Aire-sur-l'Adour France **58** B3
Aisch r. Ger. **55** E3
Aishihik Lake Can. **126** B1
Aisne r. France **54** A3
Aitape P.N.G. **71** D3
Aiud Romania **44** E2
Aix-en-Provence France **59** D3
Aix-les-Bains France **59** D2

Aizawl India **74** A1
Aizkraukle Latvia **42** C2
Aizu-wakamatsu Japan **79** C3
Ajaccio France **59** D3
Ajdābiyā Libya **101** E1
Ajmer India **86** B2
Ajo U.S.A. **140** B2
Akçakale Turkey **92** B2
Akçakoca Turkey **92** B2
Akchâr *reg.* Maur. **96**
Akdağmadeni Turkey **92** B2
Åkersberga Sweden **42** A2
Aketi Dem. Rep. Congo **104** C2
Akhalk'alak'i Georgia **41** D4
Akhḍar, Jabal *mts* Oman **91** C2
Akhisar Turkey **65** C3
Akhtubinsk Rus. Fed. **41** D4
Akita Japan **78** D3
Akjoujt Maur. **100** A3
Akkol' Kazakh. **89** E1
Akmenrags *pt* Latvia **42** B2
Akmola Kazakh. *see* Astana
Akobo Sudan **103** B4
Akola India **86** B2
Akpatok Island Can. **125** G3
Akranes Iceland **46** [inset]
Akrathos, Akra *pt* Greece **65** B2
Akrehamn Norway **48** E2
Akron U.S.A. **136** D2
Aksai Chin *terr.* Asia **87** B1
Aksaray Turkey **92** B2
Aksay Kazakh. **88** C1
Aksay Rus. Fed. **45** E2
Akşehir Turkey **92** B2
Akshiganak Kazakh. **88** D2
Aksu China **89** F2
Aksu Eth. **90** A3
Aktau Kazakh. **88** C2
Aktobe Kazakh. **88** C1
Aktogay Kazakh. **89** E2
Aktsyabrski Belarus **42** C3
Akure Nigeria **101** C4
Akureyri Iceland **46** [inset]
Akyab Myanmar *see* Sittwe
Alabama *r.* U.S.A. **139** C2
Alabama *state* U.S.A. **138** C2
Alaçatı Turkey **65** C3
Alagir Rus. Fed. **93** C1
Alagoinhas Brazil **151** F4
Alagón Spain **61** C1
Al Aḥmadi Kuwait **91** B2
Al 'Alayyah Saudi Arabia **90** B3
Al 'Amādīyah Iraq **93** C2
Al 'Amīrīyah Egypt **92** A2
Alamo U.S.A. **133** C3
Alamogordo U.S.A. **140** C2
Alamos *Sonora* Mex. **142** B2
Alamos *Sonora* Mex. **142** B2
Alamos *r.* Mex. **142** B2
Alamosa U.S.A. **134** B3
Åland Islands Fin. **47** D3
Alanya Turkey **92** B2
Al 'Aqiq Saudi Arabia **90** B2
Alarcón, Embalse de *resr* Spain **61** C2
Al 'Arīsh Egypt **92** B2
Al Arṭāwīyah Saudi Arabia **90** B2
Alas Indon. **73** C2
Alaşehir Turkey **65** C3
Alaska *state* U.S.A. **124** C2
Alaska, Gulf of U.S.A. **124** C3
Alaska Peninsula U.S.A. **120**
Alaska Range *mts* U.S.A. **124** C2
Älät Azer. **93** C2
Alatyr' Rus. Fed. **41** D3

Alausí Ecuador **150** B3
Alavus Fin. **47** E3
Alawoona Austr. **116** C2
Alba Italy **62** A2
Albacete Spain **61** C2
Alba Iulia Romania **44** B2
Albania *country* Europe **64** A2
Albany Austr. **114** A3
Albany *r.* Can. **128** B1
Albany *GA* U.S.A. **139** D2
Albany *NY* U.S.A. **137** F2
Albany *OR* U.S.A. **132** B2
Albatross Bay Austr. **115** D1
Al Bawīṭī Egypt **102** A2
Al Bayḍā' Libya **101** E1
Al Bayḍā' Yemen **90** B3
Albemarle U.S.A. **139** D1
Albemarle Sound *sea chan.* U.S.A. **139** E1
Albenga Italy **62** A2
Alberga *watercourse* Austr. **116** B1
Albert France **54** C3
Albert, Lake Dem. Rep. Congo/Uganda **105** D2
Alberta *prov.* Can. **126** D2
Albert Kanaal *canal* Belgium **54** B2
Albert Lea U.S.A. **135** E2
Albi France **58** C3
Al Bi'r Saudi Arabia **90** A2
Al Birk Saudi Arabia **90** B3
Al Biyāḍḥ *reg.* Saudi Arabia **90** B2
Alborz, Reshteh-ye *mts* Iran *see* Elburz Mountains
Albufeira Port. **60** B2
Albuquerque U.S.A. **140** C1
Al Buraymī Oman **91** C2
Albury Austr. **117** D3
Alcácer do Sal Port. **60** B2
Alcalá de Henares Spain **60** C1
Alcalá la Real Spain **60** C2
Alcamo Italy **62** B3
Alcañiz Spain **61** C1
Alcántara Spain **60** B2
Alcaraz Spain **60** C2
Alcaraz, Sierra de *mts* Spain **60** C2
Alcaudete Spain **60** C2
Alcázar de San Juan Spain **60** C2
Alchevs'k Ukr. **45** E2
Alcobaça Brazil **155** E1
Alcora Spain **61** C1
Alcoy-Alcoi Spain **61** C2
Alcúdia Spain **61** D2
Aldabra Islands Seychelles **103** C5
Aldama Mex. **143** C2
Aldan Rus. Fed. **95** K3
Aldan *r.* Rus. Fed. **95** K2
Alderney *i.* Channel Is **53** B5
Aleg Maur. **100** A3
Alegre Brazil **155** D2
Alegrete Brazil **152** C3
Alekhovshchina Rus. Fed. **43** D1
Aleksandrovsk-Sakhalinskiy Rus. Fed. **95** L3
Aleksandry, Zemlya *i.* Rus. Fed. **94** F1
Alekseyevka *Belgorodskaya Oblast'* Rus. Fed. **45** E1
Alekseyevka *Belgorodskaya Oblast'* Rus. Fed. **45** E1
Aleksin Rus. Fed. **43** E3
Aleksinac Serb. and Mont. **64** B2
Alèm Paraíba Brazil **155** D2
Ålen Norway **46** C3
Alençon France **58** C2
Aleppo Syria **92** B2
Alerta Peru **150** B4
Alert Bay Can. **126** C2
Alès France **59** C3
Aleşd Romania **44** B2
Alessandria Italy **62** A2

Ålesund Norway **46** B3
Aleutian Islands U.S.A. **158** E1
Aleutian Range *mts* U.S.A. **120**
Alevina, Mys *c.* Rus. Fed. **95** M3
Alexander Archipelago *is* U.S.A. **126** B3
Alexander Bay S. Africa **108** A2
Alexander City U.S.A. **139** C2
Alexander Island Antarctica **119** K2
Alexandra Austr. **117** D3
Alexandra N.Z. **118** A4
Alexandreia Greece **65** B2
Alexandria Egypt **102** A1
Alexandria Romania **44** C3
Alexandria S. Africa **109** C3
Alexandria *LA* U.S.A. **138** B2
Alexandria *MN* U.S.A. **135** D1
Alexandria *VA* U.S.A. **137** E3
Alexandrina, Lake Austr. **116** B3
Alexandroupoli Greece **65** C2
Alexis *r.* Can. **129** E1
Alexis Creek Can. **126** C2
Aleysk Rus. Fed. **89** F1
Alfaro Spain **61** C1
Al Fāw Iraq **93** C3
Al Fayyūm Egypt **92** B3
Alfeld (Leine) Ger. **55** D2
Alfenas Brazil **155** C2
Al Fujayrah U.A.E. *see* Fujairah
Algeciras Spain **60** B2
Algemesí Spain **61** C2
Algena Eritrea **90** A3
Alger Alg. *see* Algiers
Algeria *country* Africa **100** C2
Al Ghaydah Yemen **91** C3
Alghero Italy **62** A2
Al Ghurdaqah Egypt **102** A2
Al Ghwaybīyah Saudi Arabia **91** B2
Algiers Alg. **100** C1
Algoa Bay S. Africa **109** C3
Algona U.S.A. **135** E2
Algorta Spain **60** C1
Al Ḥadīthah Iraq **93** C2
Al Hajar al Gharbī *mts* Oman **91** C2
Al Ḥamādah al Ḥamrā' *plat.* Libya **101** D2
Alhama de Murcia Spain **61** C2
Al Ḥammām Egypt **92** A2
Al Ḥanākīyah Saudi Arabia **90** B2
Al Ḥasakah Syria **93** C2
Al Ḥayy Iraq **93** C2
Al Ḥazm al Jawf Yemen **90** B3
Al Hibāk *des.* Saudi Arabia **91** C3
Al Ḥillah Saudi Arabia **90** B2
Al Ḥinnāh Saudi Arabia **91** B2
Al Hoceima Morocco **60** C2
Al Ḥudaydah Yemen *see* Hodeidah
Al Ḥufūf Saudi Arabia **91** B2
Al Ḥulayq al Kabir *hills* Libya **101** D2
'Alīābād Iran **93** D3
Aliağa Turkey **65** C3
Aliakmonas *r.* Greece **65** B2
Alicante Spain **61** C2
Alice U.S.A. **141** E3
Alice, Punta *pt* Italy **63** C3
Alice Springs Austr. **114** C2
Aligarh India **87** B2
Alīgūdarz Iran **93** C2
Alihe China **81** E1
Alima *r.* Congo **104** B3
Aliova *r.* Turkey **65** C3
Ali Sabieh Djibouti **103** C3
Al Iskandarīyah Egypt *see* Alexandria
Al Ismā'īlīyah Egypt **102** B1
Aliwal North S. Africa **109** C3
Al Jaghbūb Libya **101** E2
Al Jahrah Kuwait **91** B2
Al Jamalīyah Qatar **91** C2
Al Jawf Libya **101** E2
Al Jawf Saudi Arabia **90** A2

Al Jawsh Libya **101** D1
Aljezur Port. **60** B2
Al Jubayl Saudi Arabia **91** B2
Al Junaynah Saudi Arabia **90** B2
Aljustrel Port. **60** B2
Al Kahfah Saudi Arabia **90** B2
Al Kāmil Oman **91** C2
Al Karak Jordan **92** B2
Al Khābūrah Oman **91** C2
Al Khamāsin Saudi Arabia **90** B2
Al Khārijah Egypt **102** B2
Al Khaşab Oman **91** C2
Al Khawkhah Yemen **90** B3
Al Khawr Qatar **91** C2
Al Khufrah Libya **102** A2
Al Khums Libya **101** D1
Al Khunn Saudi Arabia **91** B2
Al Kir'ānah Qatar **91** C2
Alkmaar Neth. **54** B1
Al Kūt Iraq **93** C2
Al Kuwayt Kuwait *see* Kuwait
Al Lādhiqīyah Syria *see* Latakia
Allahabad India **87** C2
Allakh-Yun' Rus. Fed. **95** L2
'Allāqī, Wādī al *watercourse* Egypt **90** A2
Allegheny *r.* U.S.A. **137** D2
Allegheny Mountains U.S.A. **137** D3
Allen, Lough *l.* Rep. of Ireland **51** B1
Allende *Coahuila* Mex. **143** B2
Allende *Nuevo León* Mex. **143** B2
Allentown U.S.A. **137** D2
Alleppey India **85** B4
Aller *r.* Ger. **55** D1
Alliance *NE* U.S.A. **134** C2
Alliance *OH* U.S.A. **136** D2
Al Līth Saudi Arabia **90** B2
Alloa U.K. **50** C2
Alma Can. **129** C2
Almada Port. **60** B2
Almadén Spain **60** C2
Al Madīnah Saudi Arabia *see* Medina
Al Mahwīt Yemen **90** B3
Almanor, Lake U.S.A. **132** B2
Almansa Spain **61** C2
Al Manşūrah Egypt **102** B2
Al Mariyyah U.A.E. **91** C2
Al Marj Libya **101** E1
Almaty Kazakh. **89** E1
Almazán Spain **60** C1
Almeirim Brazil **151** D3
Almelo Neth. **54** C1
Almenara Brazil **155** D1
Almendra, Embalse de *resr* Spain **60** B1
Almendralejo Spain **60** B2
Almería Spain **60** C2
Almería, Golfo de *b.* Spain **60** C2
Al'met'yevsk Rus. Fed. **41** E3
Al Mindak Saudi Arabia **90** B2
Al Minyā Egypt **102** B2
Al Mish'āb Saudi Arabia **91** B2
Almodôvar Port. **60** B2
Almonte Spain **60** B2
Almora India **87** B2
Al Mubarrez Saudi Arabia **91** B2
Al Muḍaibī Oman **91** C2
Al Mudawwarah Jordan **92** B3
Al Mukallā Yemen *see* Mukalla
Al Mukhā Yemen *see* Mocha
Almuñécar Spain **60** C2
Al Muwayliḥ Saudi Arabia **90** A2
Almyros Greece **65** B3
Alness U.K. **50** C2
Alnwick U.K. **52** C2
Alofi Niue **113**
Along India **74** A1
Alonnisos *i.* Greece **65** B3
Alor *i.* Indon. **71** C3

Alor, Kepulauan *is* Indon. **71** C3
Alor Setar Malaysia **72** B1
Alozero Rus. Fed. **46** G2
Alpena U.S.A. **136** D1
Alpine U.S.A. **141** D2
Alps *mts* Europe **59** D2
Al Qa'āmīyāt *reg.* Saudi Arabia **91** B3
Al Qaddāḥīyah Libya **101** D1
Al Qāhirah Egypt *see* Cairo
Al Qā'īyah Saudi Arabia **90** B2
Al Qāmishlī Syria **93** C2
Al Qaryatayn Syria **92** B2
Al Qaṭn Yemen **91** B3
Al Qunayṭirah Syria **92** B2
Al Qunfidhah Saudi Arabia **90** B3
Al Quşayr Egypt **102** B2
Al Quwayīyah Saudi Arabia **90** B2
Alsfeld Ger. **55** D2
Alta Norway **46** E2
Altaelva *r.* Norway **46** E2
Altai Mountains Asia **89** F2
Altamaha *r.* U.S.A. **135** D2
Altamira Brazil **151** D3
Altamura Italy **63** C2
Altay China **89** F2
Altay Mongolia **80** C1
Altdorf Switz. **59** D2
Altea Spain **61** C2
Altenburg Ger. **55** F2
Altenkirchen (Westerwald) Ger. **54** C2
Altentreptow Ger. **55** F1
Altınoluk Turkey **65** C3
Altıntaş Turkey **65** D3
Altiplano *plain* Bol. **152** B2
Alto Araguaia Brazil **154** B1
Alto del Moncayo *mt.* Spain **61** C1
Alto Garças Brazil **154** B1
Alto Molócuè Moz. **107** C1
Altona Can. **127** F3
Altoona U.S.A. **137** D2
Alto Sucuriú Brazil **154** B1
Alto Taquari Brazil **154** B1
Altötting Ger. **56** C3
Altun Shan *mts* China **89** F3
Alturas U.S.A. **132** B2
Alus U.S.A. **141** E2
Alūksne Latvia **42** C2
Al 'Ulā Saudi Arabia **90** A2
Al 'Uqaylah Libya **101** D1
Al Uqşur Egypt *see* Luxor
Alushta Ukr. **45** D3
Alva U.S.A. **141** E1
Alvarado Mex. **143** C3
Älvdalen Sweden **47** C3
Ålvik Norway **48** B1
Älvsbyn Sweden **46** E2
Al Wajh Saudi Arabia **90** A2
Alwar India **86** B2
Al Widyān *plat.* Iraq/Saudi Arabia **93** C2
Alxa Youqi China *see* Ehen Hudag
Alyangula Austr. **115** C1
Alytus Lith. **42** B3
Alzada U.S.A. **134** C1
Alzey Ger. **54** D3
Amadeus, Lake *salt flat* Austr. **114** C2
Amadora Port. **60** B2
Amā'ir Saudi Arabia **90** B2
Åmål Sweden **47** C4
Amaliada Greece **65** B3
Amamapare Indon. **71** D3
Amambaí Brazil **154** A2
Amambaí *r.* Brazil **154** B2
Amambaí, Serra de *hills* Brazil/Para. **154** A2
Amami-Ō-shima *i.* Japan **81** E3
Amami-shotō *is* Japan **81** E3
Amangel'dy Kazakh. **89** D1
Amantea Italy **63** C3

Amanzimtoti S. Africa **109** D3
Amapá Brazil **151** D2
Amareleja Port. **60** B2
Amarillo U.S.A. **141** D1
Amaro, Monte *mt.* Italy **62** B2
Amasya Turkey **92** B1
Amazon *r.* S. America **150** D2
Amazon, Mouths of the Brazil **151** E2
Amazonas *r.* S. America *see* Amazon
Ambala India **86** B1
Ambalavao Madag. **107** [inset] D2
Ambanja Madag. **107** [inset] D1
Ambato Ecuador **150** B3
Ambato Boeny Madag. **107** [inset] D1
Ambato Finandrahana Madag. **107** [inset] D2
Ambatolampy Madag. **107** [inset] D1
Ambatondrazaka Madag. **107** [inset] D1
Amberg Ger. **55** E3
Ambergris Cay *i.* Belize **144** B3
Ambikapur India **87** C2
Ambilobe Madag. **107** [inset] D1
Ambleside U.K. **52** B2
Amboasary Madag. **107** [inset] D2
Ambohimahasoa Madag. **107** [inset] D2
Ambon Indon. **71** C3
Ambon *i.* Indon. **71** C3
Ambositra Madag. **107** [inset] D2
Ambovombe Madag. **107** [inset] D2
Amboy U.S.A. **133** C4
Ambriz Angola **104** B3
Amdo China **87** D1
Amealco Mex. **143** B2
Ameca Mex. **142** B2
Ameland *i.* Neth. **54** B1
American Falls U.S.A. **132** D2
American Falls Reservoir U.S.A. **132** D2
American Fork U.S.A. **132** D2
American Samoa *terr.* S. Pacific Ocean **113**
Americus U.S.A. **139** D2
Amersfoort Neth. **54** B1
Amery Ice Shelf Antarctica **119** D2
Ames U.S.A. **135** E2
Amfissa Greece **65** B3
Amga Rus. Fed. **95** K2
Amgu Rus. Fed. **78** C1
Amguid Alg. **101** C2
Amgun' *r.* Rus. Fed. **95** L3
Amherst Can. **129** D2
Amiens France **58** C2
Amindivi Islands India **85** B3
Amirante Islands Seychelles **105** [inset]
Amirabad Iran **88** C2
Amisk Lake Can. **127** E2
Amistad Reservoir Mex./U.S.A. **141** D3
Amlwch U.K. **52** A3
'Ammān Jordan **92** B2
Ammassalik Greenland **125** J2
Am Nābiyah Yemen **90** B3
Amol Iran **93** D2
Amorgos *i.* Greece **65** C3
Amory U.S.A. **138** C2
Amos Can. **128** C2
Amoy China *see* Xiamen
Amparo Brazil **155** C2
Amposta Spain **61** D1
Amqui Can. **137** G2
Amravati India **87** B2
Amritsar India **86** B1
Amstelveen Neth. **54** B1
Amsterdam Neth. **54** B1
Amstetten Austria **56** C2
Am Timan Chad **101** E3
Amudar'ya *r.* Asia **88** C2
Amund Ringnes Island Can. **124** F1

Amundsen Gulf Can. **124** D2
Amuntai Indon. **73** C2
Amur r. China see Heilong Jiang
'Amur, Wadi watercourse Sudan **90** A3
Anabanua Indon. **73** D2
Anabar r. Rus. Fed. **95** J2
Anabarskiy Zaliv b. Rus. Fed. **95** J2
Anaconda U.S.A. **132** D1
Anadarko U.S.A. **141** E1
Anadolu Dağları mts Turkey **92** B1
Anadyr' r. Rus. Fed. **95** N2
'Ānah Iraq **93** C2
Anáhuac Mex. **143** B2
Anambas, Kepulauan is Indon. **72** B1
Anamosa U.S.A. **135** E2
Anamur Turkey **92** B2
Anan Japan **79** B4
Anantapur India **85** B3
Anantnag India **86** B1
Anan'yiv Ukr. **44** C2
Anapa Rus. Fed. **45** E3
Anápolis Brazil **154** C1
Añatuya Arg. **152** B3
Anbyon N. Korea **77** B2
Ancenis France **58** B2
Anchorage U.S.A. **124** C2
Ancona Italy **62** B2
Ancud Chile **153** A5
Åndalsnes Norway **46** E3
Andalucía aut. comm. Spain **60** C2
Andalusia U.S.A. **138** C2
Andaman Islands India **85** D3
Andaman Sea Indian Ocean **75** A2
Andapa Madag. **107** [inset] D1
Andelst Neth. **54** B2
Andenes Norway **46** D2
Andenne Belgium **54** B2
Anderlecht Belgium **54** B2
Anderson r. Can. **124** C2
Anderson AK U.S.A. **124** C2
Anderson IN U.S.A. **136** C2
Anderson SC U.S.A. **139** D2
Andes mts S. America **152** A1
Andijon Uzbek. **89** E2
Andilamena Madag. **107** [inset] D1
Andilanatoby Madag. **107** [inset] D1
Andizhan Uzbek. see Andijon
Andoany Madag. **107** [inset] D1
Andong S. Korea **77** B2
Andorra country Europe **58** C3
Andorra la Vella Andorra **58** C3
Andover U.K. **53** C4
Andradina Brazil **154** B2
Andreapol' Rus. Fed. **43** D2
Andrelândia Brazil **155** D2
Andrews U.S.A. **141** D2
Andria Italy **63** C2
Androka Madag. **107** [inset] D2
Andros i. Bahamas **144** C2
Andros i. Greece **65** B3
Andros Town Bahamas **139** E4
Andrott i. India **85** B3
Andrushivka Ukr. **44** C1
Andselv Norway **46** D2
Andújar Spain **60** C2
Andulo Angola **106** A1
Anéfis Mali **100** C3
Aneto mt. Spain **36**
Aney Niger **101** D3
Angara r. Rus. Fed. **95** I3
Angarsk Rus. Fed. **80** C1
Ånge Sweden **47** D3
Ángel de la Guarda, Isla i. Mex. **142** A2
Angeles Phil. **76** B2
Ängelholm Sweden **47** C4
Ångermanälven r. Sweden **46** D3
Angermünde Ger. **55** C1
Angers France **58** B2

Angikuni Lake Can. **127** F1
Anglesey i. U.K. **52** A3
Angoche Moz. **107** C1
Angohrān Iran **91** C2
Angola country Africa **104** B4
Angola U.S.A. **136** D2
Angoon U.S.A. **126** B2
Angoulême France **58** C2
Angren Uzbek. **89** E2
Anguilla terr. West Indies **145** D3
Angul India **87** C2
Anholt i. Denmark **47** C4
Anhua China **83** B3
Anhui prov. China **82** B2
Anhumas Brazil **154** B1
Anicuns Brazil **154** C1
Aniva, Mys c. Rus. Fed. **78** D1
Aniva, Zaliv b. Rus. Fed. **78** D1
Anjū N. Korea **77** B2
Ankang China **82** A2
Ankara Turkey **41** C5
Anlu China **82** B2
Anna Rus. Fed. **43** F3
Annaba Alg. **101** C1
Annaberg-Buchholtz Ger. **55** F2
An Nafūd des. Saudi Arabia **90** B2
An Najaf Iraq **93** C2
Annan U.K. **50** C3
Annapolis U.S.A. **137** E3
Annapurna I mt. Nepal **87** C2
Ann Arbor U.S.A. **136** D2
Anna Regina Guyana **150** D2
An Nāşirīyah Iraq **93** C2
Annecy France **59** D2
An Nimāş Saudi Arabia **90** B3
Anning China **74** B1
Anniston U.S.A. **139** C2
Annonay France **59** C2
An Nu'ayrīyah Saudi Arabia **91** B2
Anorontany, Tanjona hd Madag. **107** [inset] D1
Ano Viannos Greece **65** C3
Anpu China **83** B3
Anqing China **83** B3
Ansan S. Korea **77** B2
Ansbach Ger. **55** E3
Anshan China **82** C1
Anshun China **83** A3
An Sirhān, Wādī watercourse Saudi Arabia **90** A1
Ansongo Mali **100** C3
Antabamba Peru **150** B4
Antakya Turkey **92** B2
Antalaha Madag. **107** [inset] E1
Antalya Turkey **92** B2
Antalya Körfezi g. Turkey **92** B2
Antananarivo Madag. **107** [inset] D1
Antarctica **119**
Antarctic Peninsula Antarctica **119** K3
An Teallach mt. U.K. **50** B2
Antequera Spain **60** C2
Anthony U.S.A. **140** C2
Anti Atlas mts Morocco **100** B2
Antibes France **59** D3
Anticosti, Île d' i. Can. **129** D2
Antigonish Can. **129** D2
Antigua i. Antigua **145** D3
Antigua and Barbuda country West Indies **145** D3
Antiguo-Morelos Mex. **143** C2
Antikythira i. Greece **65** B3
Antipodes Islands N.Z. **110**
Antofagasta Chile **152** A3
Antonina Brazil **154** C3
Antrim U.K. **51** C1
Antrim Hills U.K. **51** C1
Antsalova Madag. **107** [inset] D1
Antsirabe Madag. **107** [inset] D1
Antsirañana Madag. **107** [inset] D1
Antsohihy Madag. **107** [inset] D1

Antwerp Belgium **54** B2
Anupgarh India **86** B2
Anuradhapura Sri Lanka **85** C4
Anxi China **80** C2
Anxious Bay Austr. **116** A2
Anyang China **82** B2
Anzio Italy **62** B2
Aomori Japan **78** D2
Aosta Italy **62** A1
Aoukâr reg. Mali/Maur. **96**
Apalachee Bay U.S.A. **139** D3
Apaporis r. Col. **150** C3
Aparecida do Tabuado Brazil **154** B2
Aparri Phil. **76** B2
Apatity Rus. Fed. **40** C2
Apatzingán Mex. **142** B3
Apeldoorn Neth. **54** B1
Apen Ger. **54** C1
Apennines mts Italy **62** A2
Apia Samoa **113**
Apiaí Brazil **154** C2
Apo, Mount vol. Phil. **76** B3
Apolda Ger. **55** E2
Apollo Bay Austr. **116** C3
Apopka, Lake U.S.A. **139** D3
Aporé Brazil **154** B1
Aporé r. Brazil **154** B1
Apostolos Andreas, Cape Cyprus **92** B2
Appalachian Mountains U.S.A. **131** E3
Appin Austr. **117** C2
Appleton U.S.A. **136** C2
Aprilia Italy **62** B2
Apsheronsk Rus. Fed. **45** E3
Apucarana Brazil **154** B2
Apucarana, Serra da hills Brazil **154** B2
Aqaba, Gulf of Asia **90** A2
Aqqikkol Hu salt l. China **87** C1
Aquidauana Brazil **154** A1
Aquidauana r. Brazil **154** A1
Ara India **87** C2
Arab, Bahr el watercourse Sudan **103** A4
Arabian Peninsula Asia **102** C5
Arabian Sea Indian Ocean **161** G4
Aracaju Brazil **151** F4
Aracati Brazil **151** F3
Araçatuba Brazil **154** B2
Aracruz Brazil **155** D1
Araçuaí Brazil **155** D1
Arad Romania **44** B2
Arada Chad **101** D3
Arafura Sea Austr./Indon. **71** C3
Aragarças Brazil **154** B1
Aragón r. Spain **61** C1
Araguaia r. Brazil **151** E3
Araguaína Brazil **151** E3
Araguari Brazil **154** C1
Arai Japan **79** C3
Arak Alg. **100** C2
Arāk Iran **93** C2
Arakan Yoma mts Myanmar **74** A1
Arak's r. Armenia **93** C1
Aral Sea salt l. Kazakh./Uzbek. **88** C2
Aral'sk Kazakh. **88** C2
Aranda de Duero Spain **60** C1
Arandelovac Serb. and Mont. **64** B2
Aran Islands Rep. of Ireland **51** B2
Aranjuez Spain **60** C1
Aranos Namibia **108** A1
Aransas Pass U.S.A. **141** E3
Arao Japan **79** B4
Araouane Mali **100** B3
Arapiraca Brazil **151** F3
Arapongas Brazil **154** B2
Araquari Brazil **154** C3
'Ar'ar Saudi Arabia **90** B1
Araraquara Brazil **154** C2
Araras Brazil **151** D3

Araras, Serra das *mts* Brazil **154** B3
Ararat Austr. **116** C3
Ararat, Mount Turkey **93** C2
Araruama, Lago de *lag.* Brazil **155** D2
Arauca Col. **150** B2
Araxá Brazil **154** C1
Arbíl Iraq **93** C2
Arbroath U.K. **50** C2
Arbu Lut, Dasht-e *des.* Afgh. **86** A2
Arcachon France **58** B3
Arcadia U.S.A. **139** D3
Arcata U.S.A. **132** B2
Arcelia Mex. **143** B3
Archangel Rus. Fed. **40** D2
Archer *r.* Austr. **115** D1
Arco U.S.A. **132** D2
Arcos de la Frontera Spain **60** B2
Arctic Bay Can. **125** G2
Arctic Ocean **162**
Arctic Red *r.* Can. **126** B1
Ardabīl Iran **93** C2
Ardahan Turkey **93** C1
Årdalstangen Norway **47** B3
Ardennes *plat.* Belgium **54** B3
Ardestān Iran **93** D2
Ardlethan Austr. **117** D2
Ardmore U.S.A. **141** E2
Ardnamurchan, Point of *pt* U.K. **50** A2
Ardrossan Austr. **116** B2
Ardrossan U.K. **50** B3
Arena, Point *pt* U.S.A. **133** B3
Arendal Norway **47** B4
Arendsee (Altmark) Ger. **55** E1
Arequipa Peru **150** B4
Arere Brazil **151** B3
Arévalo Spain **60** C1
Arezzo Italy **62** D3
Argentan France **58** B2
Argentina *country* S. America **153** B4
Argentino, Lago *l.* Arg. **153** A6
Argenton-sur-Creuse France **58** C2
Argeş *r.* Romania **64** C3
Arghandab *r.* Afgh. **86** A1
Argolikos Kolpos *b.* Greece **65** B3
Argos Greece **65** B3
Argostoli Greece **65** B3
Arguis Spain **61** C1
Argun' *r.* China/Rus. Fed. **81** E1
Argyle, Lake Austr. **114** B1
Ar Horqin Qi China *see* Tianshan
Århus Denmark **47** B4
Ariamsvlei Namibia **108** A2
Ari Atoll Maldives **85** B4
Arica Chile **152** A2
Arinagour U.K. **50** A2
Arinos Brazil **155** C1
Aripuanã Brazil **150** D4
Aripuanã *r.* Brazil **150** C3
Ariquemes Brazil **150** C3
Ariranhá *r.* Brazil **154** B1
Arizona *state* U.S.A. **140** B2
Arizpe Mex. **142** A1
'Arjah Saudi Arabia **90** B2
Arjeplog Sweden **46** D2
Arkadelphia U.S.A. **138** B2
Arkalyk Kazakh. **89** D1
Arkansas *r.* U.S.A. **138** B1
Arkansas *state* U.S.A. **138** B1
Arkansas City U.S.A. **135** D3
Arkhangel'sk Rus. Fed. *see* Archangel
Arklow Rep. of Ireland **51** C2
Arkona, Kap *c.* Ger. **56** C2
Arkticheskogo Instituta, Ostrova *is* Rus. Fed. **94** H1
Arles France **59** C3
Arlit Niger **101** C3
Arlon Belgium **54** B3
Armagh U.K. **51** C1
Armant Egypt **102** B2
Armavir Rus. Fed. **45** F2

Ashdown U.S.A. **138** B2
Asheville U.S.A. **139** D1
Ashford Austr. **117** E1
Ashford U.K. **53** C3
Ashgabat Turkm. **88** C3
Ashington U.K. **52** C2
Ashizuri-misaki *pt* Japan **79** B4
Ashkhabad Turkm. *see* Ashgabat
Ashland *KS* U.S.A. **134** D3
Ashland *KY* U.S.A. **136** D3
Ashland *OH* U.S.A. **136** D2
Ashland *OR* U.S.A. **132** B2
Ashland *WI* U.S.A. **136** B1
Ashmyany Belarus **42** C3
Ash Sharawrah Saudi Arabia **90** B3
Ash Shāriqah U.A.E. *see* Sharjah
Ash Sharqāt Iraq **93** C2
Ash Shaṭrah Iraq **93** C2
Ash Shiḥr Yemen **91** B3
Ash Shināş Oman **91** C2
Ash Shu'bah Saudi Arabia **90** B2
Ash Shumlūl Saudi Arabia **91** B2
Ashtabula U.S.A. **137** D2
Ashuanipi Lake Can. **129** D2
Asilah Morocco **60** B2
Asinara, Golfo dell' *b.* Italy **62** A2
Asino Rus. Fed. **94** H3
Asipovichy Belarus **42** C3
'Asīr *reg.* Saudi Arabia **90** B2
Askim Norway **47** C4
Askiz Rus. Fed. **80** C1
Asmara Eritrea **102** B3
Åsnen *l.* Sweden **47** C4
Asoteriba, Jebel *mt.* Sudan **102** B3
Aspang-Markt Austria **57** D3
Aspen U.S.A. **134** B3
Aspiring, Mount N.Z. **118** A3
Assab Eritrea **102** C3
Assal, Lake Djibouti **96**
As Salamiyah Saudi Arabia **91** B2
As Samāwah Iraq **93** C2
As Şanām *reg.* Saudi Arabia **91** C2
As Sarīr *reg.* Libya **101** E2
Assen Neth. **54** C1
Assesse Belgium **54** B2
As Sidrah Libya **101** D1
Assiniboia Can. **127** E3
Assis Brazil **154** B2
Assisi Italy **59** E3
Aş Şubayḩīyah Kuwait **91** B2
As Sulaymānīyah Iraq **93** C2
As Sulaymī Saudi Arabia **90** B2
As Sulayyil Saudi Arabia **90** B2
As Sūq Saudi Arabia **90** B2
As Suwaydā' Syria **92** B2
As Suwayq Oman **91** C2
As Suways Egypt *see* Suez
Astakos Greece **65** B3
Astana Kazakh. **89** E1
Åstārā Iran **93** C2
Asti Italy **62** A2
Astor Jammu and Kashmir **86** B1
Astorga Spain **60** B1
Astoria U.S.A. **132** B1
Astrakhan' Rus. Fed. **41** D4
Astravyets Belarus **42** C3
Astypalaia *i.* Greece **65** C3
Asunción Para. **152** C3
Aswān Egypt **102** B2
Asyūṭ Egypt **102** B2
Atacama, Desierto de *des.* Chile *see* Atacama Desert
Atacama, Salar de *salt flat* Chile **152** B3
Atacama Desert Chile **152** B3
Atakpamé Togo **100** C4
Atalanti Greece **65** B3
Atalaya Peru **150** B4
Atamyrat Turkm. **89** D3
'Ataq Yemen **90** B3

Armenia *country* Asia **93** C1
Armenia Col. **150** B2
Armentières France **54** A2
Armidale Austr. **117** E2
Armstrong Can. **128** B1
Armyans'k Ukr. **92** B1
Arnaoutis, Cape Cyprus **92** B2
Arnaud *r.* Can. **129** D1
Arnhem Neth. **54** B2
Arnhem, Cape Austr. **115** C1
Arnhem Bay Austr. **115** C1
Arnhem Land *reg.* Austr. **115** C1
Arno *r.* Italy **62** B2
Arno Bay Austr. **116** B2
Arnprior Can. **128** C2
Arnsberg Ger. **54** D2
Arnstadt Ger. **55** E2
Aroab Namibia **108** A2
Arolsen Ger. **55** D2
Arona Italy **62** A1
Aros *r.* Mex. **142** B2
Ar Ramādī Iraq **93** C2
Arran *i.* U.K. **50** B3
Ar Raqqah Syria **92** B2
Arras France **58** C1
Ar Rass Saudi Arabia **90** B2
Arriagá Mex. **143** C3
Ar Rimāl *reg.* Saudi Arabia **91** C2
Ar Riyāḑ Saudi Arabia *see* Riyadh
Arroyo Seco Mex. **143** C2
Ar Rustāq Oman **91** C2
Ar Ruṭbah Iraq **92** C2
Arsenaján Iran **93** D3
Arsen'yev Rus. Fed. **78** B2
Arta Greece **65** B3
Arteaga Mex. **142** B3
Artem Rus. Fed. **78** B2
Artemivs'k Ukr. **45** E2
Artenay France **58** C2
Artesia U.S.A. **140** D2
Arthur Point *pt* Austr. **115** E2
Arthur's Pass N.Z. **118** B3
Arthur's Town Bahamas **139** E4
Artigas Uru. **152** C4
Artillery Lake Can. **127** E1
Artsyz Ukr. **44** C2
Artux China **89** C3
Artvin Turkey **93** C1
Aru, Kepulauan *is* Indon. **71** C3
Arua Uganda **105** D2
Aruba *terr.* West Indies **145** D3
Arusha Tanz. **105** D3
Arvayheer Mongolia **80** C1
Arviat Can. **127** F1
Arvidsjaur Sweden **46** D2
Arvika Sweden **47** C4
Arzamas Rus. Fed. **41** D3
Arzew Alg. **61** C2
Arzfeld Ger. **54** C2
Aš Czech Rep. **55** F2
Asaba Nigeria **101** C4
Asahi-dake *vol.* Japan **78** D2
Asahikawa Japan **78** D2
Āsalē *l.* Eth. **90** B3
Asansol India **87** C2
Asbestos Can. **129** C2
Ascea Italy **62** C2
Ascensión Bol. **152** B2
Ascension *i.* S. Atlantic Ocean **97**
Ascensión, Bahía de la *b.* Mex. **143** D3
Aschaffenburg Ger. **55** D3
Ascheberg Ger. **54** C2
Aschersleben Ger. **55** E2
Ascoli Piceno Italy **62** B2
Åsele Sweden **46** D3
Asenovgrad Bulg. **64** B2
Ashburton *watercourse* Austr. **114** A2
Ashburton N.Z. **118** B3

Atâr Maur. **100** A2
Atascadero U.S.A. **133** B3
Atasu Kazakh. **89** E2
Atbara Sudan **102** B3
Atbara r. Sudan **102** B3
Atbasar Kazakh. **89** D1
Atchison U.S.A. **135** D3
Aterno r. Italy **62** B2
Atessa Italy **62** B2
Ath Belgium **54** A2
Athabasca Can. **126** D2
Athabasca r. Can. **127** D2
Athabasca, Lake Can. **127** E2
Athens Greece **65** B3
Athens GA U.S.A. **139** D2
Athens OH U.S.A. **136** D3
Athens TN U.S.A. **139** D1
Athens TX U.S.A. **141** E2
Athies France **54** A2
Athlone Rep. of Ireland **51** C2
Athos mt. Greece **65** B3
Athy Rep. of Ireland **51** C2
Ati Chad **101** D3
Atikokan Can. **128** A2
Atiu i. Cook Is **111**
Atkarsk Rus. Fed. **41** D3
Atlanta U.S.A. **139** D2
Atlantic U.S.A. **135** D2
Atlantic City U.S.A. **137** F3
Atlantic Ocean **160**
Atlantis S. Africa **108** A3
Atlas Mountains Africa **100** B1
Atlas Saharien mts Alg. **100** C1
Atlin Can. **126** B2
Atlin Lake Can. **126** B2
Atmore U.S.A. **138** C2
Atrai r. India **87** C2
Aţ Ţā'if Saudi Arabia **90** B2
Attapu Laos **75** B2
Attawapiskat r. Greece **65** C3
Attawapiskat Can. **128** B1
Attawapiskat r. Can. **128** B1
Attawapiskat Lake Can. **128** B1
Attendorn Ger. **54** C2
Aţ Turbah Yemen **90** B3
Atyrau Kazakh. **88** C2
Aubagne France **59** D3
Aubange Belgium **54** B3
Aube r. France **59** C2
Aubenas France **59** C3
Aubigny-sur-Nère France **59** C2
Aubusson France **58** C2
Auch France **58** C3
Auckland N.Z. **118** B2
Auckland Islands N.Z. **110**
Audo Range mts Eth. **105** C2
Aue r. Ger. **55** F2
Augsburg Ger. **56** C3
Augusta Italy **62** C3
Augusta GA U.S.A. **139** D2
Augusta KS U.S.A. **135** D3
Augusta ME U.S.A. **137** G2
Augustus, Mount Austr. **114** A2
Aulnoye-Aymeries France
 54 A2
Aunglan Myanmar **74** A2
Auob watercourse Namibia/S. Africa
 108 B2
Aurangabad India **86** B3
Aurich Ger. **54** C1
Aurilândia Brazil **154** B1
Aurillac France **58** C3
Aurora CO U.S.A. **134** C3
Aurora IL U.S.A. **136** C2
Aurora NE U.S.A. **135** D2
Aus Namibia **108** A2

Austin MN U.S.A. **135** E2
Austin NV U.S.A. **133** C3
Austin TX U.S.A. **141** E2
Australes, Îles is Fr. Polynesia see
 Tubuai Islands
Australia country Oceania **114**
Australian Capital Territory
 admin. div. Austr. **117** D3
Austria country Europe **56** C2
Autlán Mex. **142** B3
Autun France **59** C2
Auxerre France **59** C2
Auxonne France **59** D2
Avallon France **59** C2
Avaré Brazil **154** C2
Avarua Cook Is **113**
Avdiyivka Ukr. **45** E2
Aveiro Port. **60** B1
Avellino Italy **62** B2
Avesnes-sur-Helpe France **54** A2
Avesta Sweden **47** D3
Avezzano Italy **62** B2
Aviemore U.K. **50** C2
Avignon France **59** C3
Ávila Spain **60** C1
Avilés Spain **60** B1
Avola Italy **62** C3
Avon r. England U.K. **53** B3
Avon r. England U.K. **53** C4
Avranches France **58** B2
Awanui N.Z. **118** B2
Awash Eth. **103** C4
Awash r. Eth. **103** C3
Awbārī Libya **101** D2
Aw Dheegle Somalia **103** C4
Awe, Loch l. U.K. **50** B2
Aweil Sudan **103** A4
Awka Nigeria **104** A2
Axel Heiberg Island Can. **124** F1
Axim Ghana **100** B4
Ay France **54** B3
Ayacucho Peru **150** B4
Ayagoz Kazakh. **89** F2
Ayakkum Hu salt l. China **80** B2
Ayamonte Spain **60** B2
Ayan Rus. Fed. **95** L3
Ayaviri Peru **150** B4
Äybak Afgh. **86** A1
Aybas Rus. Fed. **88** B2
Aydar r. Ukr. **45** E2
Aydarko'l ko'li l. Uzbek. **89** D2
Aydın Turkey **65** C3
Ayeat, Gora r. Kazakh. **89** D2
Ayers Rock h. Austr. see Uluru
Aylesbury U.K. **53** C4
Ayllón Spain **60** C1
Aylmer Lake Can. **127** E1
Ayod Sudan **103** B4
Ayon, Ostrov i. Rus. Fed. **95** N2
'Ayoûn el 'Atroûs Maur. **100** B3
Ayr Austr. **115** D1
Ayr U.K. **50** B3
Ayre, Point of pt Isle of Man **52** A2
Ayteke Bi Kazakh. **88** D2
Aytos Bulg. **64** C2
Ayutla Mex. **143** C3
Ayutthaya Thai. **75** B2
Ayvacık Turkey **65** C3
Ayvalık Turkey **65** C3
Azaouagh, Vallée de watercourse
 Mali/Niger **100** C3
Azopol'ye Rus. Fed. **40** D2
Azores terr. N. Atlantic Ocean **38**
Azores aut. reg. Port. **38**
Azov Rus. Fed. **45** E2
Azov, Sea of Rus. Fed./Ukr. **45** E2
Azraq, Bahr el r. Eth./Sudan see
 Blue Nile

Azuaga Spain **60** B2
Azuero, Península de pen. Panama
 144 B4
Azul Arg. **153** C4
Az Zaqāzīq Egypt **92** B2
Az Zarqā' Jordan **92** B2
Az Zaydīyah Yemen **90** B3
Azzel Matti, Sebkha salt pan Alg.
 100 C2
Az Zilfī Saudi Arabia **90** B2
Az Zuqur i. Yemen **90** B3

Baardheere Somalia **103** C4
Bābā, Kūh-e mts Afgh. **86** A1
Babadag Romania **44** C3
Babaeski Turkey **65** C2
Bāb al Mandab str. Africa/Asia **90** B3
Babana Indon. **73** C2
Babar i. Indon. **71** C3
Babati Tanz. **105** D3
Babayevo Rus. Fed. **43** E2
Babine r. Can. **126** C2
Babine Lake Can. **126** C2
Babo Indon. **71** C3
Bābol Iran **93** D2
Baboon Point h. S. Africa **108** A3
Babruysk Belarus **42** C3
Babuyan i. Phil. **76** B2
Babuyan Islands Phil. **76** B1
Bacabal Brazil **151** E3
Bacan i. Indon. **71** C3
Bacău Romania **44** C2
Bacchus Marsh Austr. **116** C3
Bachu China **89** E3
Back r. Can. **127** F1
Bačka Palanka Serb. and Mont. **64** A1
Bac Lac Vietnam **74** B1
Bac Liêu Vietnam **75** B3
Bacolod Phil. **76** B2
Bacqueville, Lac l. Can. **128** C1
Badajoz Spain **60** B2
Badarpur India **74** A1
Bad Berka Ger. **55** E2
Bad Berleburg Ger. **55** D2
Bad Bevensen Ger. **55** E1
Bad Ems Ger. **54** C2
Baden Austria **57** D3
Baden-Baden Ger. **56** B3
Bad Freienwalde Ger. **55** G1
Bad Harzburg Ger. **55** E2
Bad Hersfeld Ger. **55** D2
Bad Hofgastein Austria **56** C3
Bad Homburg vor der Höhe Ger.
 55 D2
Badin Pak. **86** A2
Bad Ischl Austria **59** E2
Bādiyat ash Shām des. Asia see
 Syrian Desert
Bad Kissingen Ger. **55** E2
Bad Kreuznach Ger. **54** C3
Bad Lauterberg im Harz Ger. **55** E2
Bad Liebenwerda Ger. **55** F2
Bad Lippspringe Ger. **55** D2
Bad Mergentheim Ger. **55** D3
Bad Nauheim Ger. **55** D2
Bad Neuenahr-Ahrweiler Ger. **54** C2
Bad Neustadt an der Saale Ger.
 55 E2
Bad Oldesloe Ger. **55** E1
Bad Pyrmont Ger. **55** D2
Badr Ḥunayn Saudi Arabia **90** A2
Bad Salzuflen Ger. **55** D1
Bad Salzungen Ger. **55** E2
Bad Schwartau Ger. **56** C2
Bad Segeberg Ger. **56** C2
Badulla Sri Lanka **85** C4

Bad Zwischenahn Ger. **54** D1
Baeza Spain **60** C2
Bafatá Guinea-Bissau **100** A3
Baffin Bay *sea* Can./Greenland **125** H2
Baffin Island Can. **125** H2
Bafia Cameroon **104** B2
Bafing *r.* Guinea/Mali **100** A3
Bafoulabé Mali **100** A3
Bafoussam Cameroon **104** B2
Bāfq Iran **91** C2
Bafra Turkey **92** B1
Bāft Iran **91** C2
Bafwasende Dem. Rep. Congo **105** C2
Bagamoyo Tanz. **105** D3
Bagan Datuk Malaysia **72** B1
Bagani Namibia **106** B1
Bagansiapiapi Indon. **72** B1
Bagdad Iraq **93** C2
Bagé Brazil **152** C4
Bagdād Iraq **93** C2
Baghlān Afgh. **86** A1
Bagnères-de-Luchon France **58** C3
Bagrationovsk Rus. Fed. **42** B3
Bagrax China *see* Bohu
Baguio Phil. **76** B2
Bagzane, Monts *mts* Niger **101** C3
Baharampur India **87** C2
Bahau Malaysia **72** B1
Bahawalnagar Pak. **84** B2
Bahawalpur Pak. **86** B2
Bahia, Islas de la *is* Hond. **144** B3
Bahía Blanca Arg. **153** B4
Bahía Kino Mex. **142** A2
Bahía Negra Para. **152** C3
Bahía Tortugas Mex. **142** A2
Bahir Dar Eth. **103** B3
Bahraich India **87** C2
Bahrain *country* Asia **91** C2
Bahriyah, Wāḩāt al *oasis* Egypt **102** A2
Bānū Kālāt Iran **91** D2
Baia Mare Romania **44** B2
Baicheng China **81** E1
Baie-Comeau Can. **129** D2
Baie-St-Paul Can. **129** C2
Baihe China **77** B1
Baikal, Lake Rus. Fed. **81** D1
Baile Átha Cliath Rep. of Ireland *see* Dublin
Băileşti Romania **44** B3
Baima China **80** C2
Bainbridge U.S.A. **139** D2
Bairiki Kiribati **112**
Bairin Youqi China *see* Daban
Bairnsdale Austr. **117** D3
Baishan China **77** B1
Baishanzhen China **77** B1
Baiyin China **82** A2
Baiyuda Desert Sudan **102** B3
Baja Hungary **57** D3
Baja California *pen.* Mex. **142** A1
Bajawa Indon. **73** C2
Bājil Yemen **90** B3
Bakel Senegal **100** A3
Baker *CA* U.S.A. **133** C3
Baker *MT* U.S.A. **134** C1
Baker *OR* U.S.A. **132** C2
Baker, Mount *vol.* U.S.A. **132** B1
Baker Foreland *hd* Can. **127** F1
Baker Island *terr.*
  N. Pacific Ocean **113**
Baker Lake Can. **127** F1
Baker Lake *l.* Can. **127** F1
Bakersfield U.S.A. **133** C3
Bakhchysaray Ukr. **45** D3
Bakherden Turkm. **88** C3
Bakhmach Ukr. **45** D1
Bakı Azer. *see* Baku
Bakırköy Turkey **65** C3
Bakkaflói *b.* Iceland **46** [inset]

Bakouma C.A.R. **104** C2
Baku Azer. **93** C1
Balabac Phil. **76** A3
Balabac *i.* Phil. **76** A3
Balabac Strait Malaysia/Phil. **73** C1
Balaiberkuak Indon. **73** C2
Balaklava Austr. **116** B2
Balaklava Ukr. **45** D3
Balakliya Ukr. **45** E2
Balakovo Rus. Fed. **41** D3
Bālā Morghāb Afgh. **86** A1
Balancán Mex. **143** C3
Balan Daği *h.* Turkey **65** C3
Balangu Phil. **76** B2
Balashov Rus. Fed. **41** D3
Balaton, Lake Hungary **57** D3
Balatonboglár Hungary **57** D3
Balbina, Represa de *resr* Brazil **150** D3
Balbriggan Rep. of Ireland **51** C2
Balcanoona Austr. **116** B2
Balchik Bulg. **64** C2
Balclutha N.Z. **118** A4
Baldock Lake Can. **127** F2
Baldy Mountain *h.* Can. **127** E2
Baldy Peak U.S.A. **140** C2
Baleares, Islas *is* Spain *see* Balearic Islands
Balearic Islands *is* Spain **61** D2
Baleia, Ponta da *pt* Brazil **155** E1
Baleine, Grande Rivière de la *r.* Can. **128** C1
Baleine, Rivière à la *r.* Can. **129** D1
Baleshwar India **87** C2
Bali *i.* Indon. **73** C2
Bali, Laut *sea* Indon. **73** C2
Balige Indon. **72** A1
Baliguda India **87** C2
Balikesir Turkey **65** C3
Balikpapan Indon. **73** C2
Balimo P.N.G. **71** D3
Balingen Ger. **56** B3
Bali Sea Indon. *see* Bali, Laut
Balkanabat Turkm. **88** C3
Balkan Mountains Bulg./Serb. and Mont. **64** B2
Balkhash Kazakh. **89** E2
Balkhash, Lake Kazakh. **89** E2
Balladonia Austr. **114** B3
Ballaghaderreen Rep. of Ireland **51** B2
Ballangen Norway **46** D2
Ballarat Austr. **116** C3
Ballard, Lake *salt flat* Austr. **114** B2
Ballater U.S.A. **50** C2
Ballé Mali **100** B3
Ballena, Punta *pt* Chile **147**
Ballina Austr. **117** E1
Ballina Rep. of Ireland **51** B1
Ballinasloe Rep. of Ireland **51** B2
Ballinger U.S.A. **141** E2
Ballinrobe Rep. of Ireland **51** B2
Ballycastle Rep. of Ireland **51** B1
Ballycastle U.K. **51** C1
Ballyclare U.K. **51** D1
Ballymena U.K. **51** C1
Ballymoney U.K. **51** C1
Ballynahinch U.K. **51** D1
Ballyshannon Rep. of Ireland **51** B1
Balonne *r.* Austr. **115** D2
Balotra India **86** B2
Balrampur India **87** C2
Balranald Austr. **116** C2
Balş Romania **44** B3
Balsas Brazil **151** E3
Balsas Mex. **143** C3
Balta Ukr. **44** C2
Bălţi Moldova **44** C2
Baltic Sea *g.* Europe **47** D4
Balţim Egypt **92** B2
Baltimore U.S.A. **137** E3

Baltiysk Rus. Fed. **42** A3
Balu India **74** A1
Balvi Latvia **42** C2
Balykchy Kyrg. **89** E2
Balykshi Kazakh. **88** C2
Bam Iran **91** C2
Bamaga Austr. **115** D1
Bamaji Lake Can. **128** A1
Bamako Mali **100** B3
Bambari C.A.R. **104** C2
Bamberg Ger. **55** E3
Bambili Dem. Rep. Congo **105** C2
Bambouti C.A.R. **105** C2
Bambuí Brazil **155** C2
Bamenda Cameroon **104** B2
Bāmiān Afgh. **86** A1
Bam Posht, Kūh-e *mts* Iran **86** A2
Bañados del Izozog *swamp* Bol. **152** B2
Banalia Dem. Rep. Congo **105** C2
Bananal, Ilha do *i.* Brazil **151** D4
Banas *r.* India **86** B2
Banaz Turkey **65** C3
Ban Ban Laos **74** B2
Banbridge U.K. **51** C1
Banbury U.K. **53** C3
Bancroft Can. **128** C2
Banda Dem. Rep. Congo **105** C2
Banda India **87** C2
Banda, Kepulauan *is* Indon. **71** C3
Banda, Laut *sea* Indon. **71** C3
Banda Aceh Indon. **72** A1
Bandar-e ʿAbbās Iran **91** C2
Bandar-e Anzalī Iran **93** C2
Bandar-e Chārak Iran **91** C2
Bandar-e Emām Khomeynī Iran **93** C2
Bandar-e Lengeh Iran **91** C2
Bandar-e Maqām Iran **91** C2
Bandar Lampung Indon. **72** B2
Bandar Seri Begawan Brunei **73** C1
Banda Sea Indon. *see* Banda, Laut
Bandeiras, Pico de *mt.* Brazil **155** D2
Banderas, Bahía de *b.* Mex. **142** B2
Bandiagara Mali **100** B3
Bandırma Turkey **65** C2
Bandon Rep. of Ireland **51** B3
Bandundu Dem. Rep. Congo **104** B3
Bandung Indon. **72** B2
Banff Can. **126** D2
Banff U.K. **50** C2
Banfora Burkina **100** B3
Banga Phil. **76** B3
Bangalore India **85** B3
Bangassou C.A.R. **104** C2
Banggai Indon. **73** C2
Banggai, Kepulauan *is* Indon. **73** D2
Banggi *i.* Malaysia **73** C1
Bangka *i.* Indon. **72** B2
Bangkalan Indon. **73** C2
Bangkinang Indon. **72** B1
Bangko Indon. **72** B2
Bangkok Thai. **75** B2
Bangladesh *country* Asia **87** C2
Bangor *Northern Ireland* U.K. **51** D1
Bangor *Wales* U.K. **52** A3
Bangor U.S.A. **137** G2
Bang Saphan Yai Thai. **75** A2
Bangued Phil. **76** B2
Bangui C.A.R. **104** B2
Bangweulu, Lake Zambia **107** B1
Ban Huai Khon Thai. **74** B2
Banī Mazār Egypt **92** B3
Banī Suwayf Egypt **102** B2
Banī Walīd Libya **101** D1
Bāniyās Syria **92** B2
Banja Luka Bos.-Herz. **62** C2
Banjarmasin Indon. **73** C2
Banjul Gambia **100** A3

Banks Island *B.C.* Can. **126** B2
Banks Island *N.W.T.* Can. **124** D2
Banks Islands Vanuatu **110**
Banks Lake Can. **127** F1
Banks Peninsula N.Z. **118** B3
Bankura India **87** C2
Banmauk Myanmar **74** A1
Ban Mouang Laos **74** B2
Bann *r.* U.K. **51** C1
Ban Napè Laos **74** B2
Ban Na San Thai. **75** A3
Bannerman Town Bahamas **139** E4
Bannu Pak. **86** B1
Banswara India **86** B2
Bantry Rep. of Ireland **51** B3
Bantry Bay Rep. of Ireland **51** B3
Banyo Cameroon **104** B2
Banyoles Spain **61** D1
Banyuwangi Indon. **73** C2
Baochang China **82** B1
Baoding China **82** B2
Baoji China **82** A2
Bao Lôc Vietnam **75** B2
Baoqing China **78** B1
Baoshan China **74** A1
Baotou China **82** B1
Baotou Shan *mt.* China/N. Korea **77** B1
Bapaume France **54** A2
Ba'qūbah Iraq **93** C2
Bar Serb. and Mont. **64** C2
Baracoa Cuba **145** C2
Baradine Austl. **117** D2
Barahona *watercourse* Eritrea/Sudan
    102 B3
Baram *r.* Malaysia **73** C1
Baranavichy Belarus **42** C3
Baranis Egypt **90** A2
Baranivka Ukr. **44** C1
Baranul Kazakh. **88** C2
Baranof Island U.S.A. **126** B2
Barat Daya, Kepulauan *is* Indon.
    72 B2
Barbacena Brazil **155** D2
Barbados *country* West Indies **145** E3
Barbastro Spain **61** D1
Barbezieux-St-Hilaire France **58** B2
Barcaldine Austl. **115** D2
Barcelona Spain **61** D1
Barcelona Venez. **150** C1
Barcelos Brazil **150** C3
Barcs Hungary **57** C3
Barddhaman India **87** C2
Bardejov Slovakia **57** E3
Bardsīr Iran **91** C2
Barentin France **54** C1
Barents Sea Arctic Ocean **40** D1
Barentu Eritrea **90** A3
Barfleur, Pointe de *pt* France **53** C5
Barh India **87** C2
Bar Harbor U.S.A. **137** G2
Barika Alg. **61** E2
Barikot Afgh. **86** B1
Barinas Venez. **150** B2
Baripada India **87** C2
Barisal Bangl. **87** D2
Barisan, Pegunungan *mts* Indon.
    72 B2
Barito *r.* Indon. **73** C2
Barkā Oman **91** C2
Barkava Latvia **42** C2
Barkly Tableland *reg.* Austl. **115** C1
Barkol China **80** C2

Bârlad Romania **44** C2
Bar-le-Duc France **59** D2
Barlee, Lake *salt flat* Austl. **114** A2
Barletta Italy **63** C2
Barmedman Austl. **117** D2
Barmouth U.K. **53** A3
Barmstedt Ger. **55** D1
Barnard Castle U.K. **52** C2
Barnato Austl. **117** C2
Barnaul Rus. Fed. **89** F1
Barneveld Neth. **54** B1
Barneville-Carteret France **53** C5
Barnsley U.K. **52** C3
Barnstaple U.K. **53** A4
Barnwell U.S.A. **139** D2
Barra *r.* U.K. **50** A2
Barraba Austl. **117** E2
Barra do Corda Brazil **151** E3
Barra do Garças Brazil **154** B1
Barra do São Manuel Brazil **150** D3
Barranca *Lima* Peru **150** B4
Barranca *Loreto* Peru **150** B3
Barrancaueras Arg. **152** C3
Barranquilla Col. **150** B1
Barreiras Brazil **151** E4
Barretos Brazil **154** C2
Barrie Can. **128** C2
Barrière Can. **126** C2
Barrier Range *hills* Austl. **116** C2
Barrington, Mount Austl. **117** E2
Barrington Lake Can. **127** E2
Barringun Austl. **117** D1
Barrow *r.* Rep. of Ireland **51** C2
Barrow U.S.A. **124** B2
Barrow, Point *pt* U.S.A. **124** B2
Barrow Creek Austl. **114** C2
Barrow-in-Furness U.K. **52** B2
Barrow Island Austl. **114** A2
Barrow Strait Can. **124** F2
Barry U.K. **53** B4
Barrys Bay Can. **128** C2
Barsalpur India **86** B2
Barstow U.S.A. **133** C4
Bar-sur-Aube France **59** D2
Bartın Turkey **92** B1
Bartle Frere, Mount Austl. **115** D1
Bartlesville U.S.A. **141** E1
Bartoszyce Pol. **57** E2
Barung *i.* Indon. **73** C2
Baruun-Urt Mongolia **81** D1
Barvinkove Ukr. **45** E2
Barwon *r.* Austl. **117** D2
Barysaw Belarus **42** C3
Basarabi Romania **44** C3
Basel Switz. **59** D2
Bashtanka Ukr. **45** D2
Basilan *i.* Phil. **76** B3
Basildon U.K. **53** C4
Basingstoke U.K. **53** C4
Başkale Turkey **93** C2
Baskatong, Réservoir *resr* Can.
    128 C2
Basle Switz. *see* Basel
Basoko Dem. Rep. Congo **104** C2
Basra Iraq **93** C2
Bassano Can. **127** D2
Bassar Togo **100** C4
Bassein Myanmar **74** A2
Basse-Terre Guadeloupe **145** D3
Basseterre St Kitts and Nevis **145** D3
Bassikounou Maur. **100** B3
Bass Strait Austl. **115** D3
Bastak Iran **91** C2
Bastheim Ger. **55** E2
Basti India **87** C2
Bastia France **59** D3
Bastogne Belgium **54** B2
Bastrop U.S.A. **138** B2

Bata Equat. Guinea **104** A2
Batagay Rus. Fed. **95** K2
Bataguassu Brazil **154** B2
Batalha Port. **60** B2
Batan *i.* Phil. **76** B1
Batangafo C.A.R. **104** B2
Batangas Phil. **76** B2
Batanghari *r.* Indon. **72** B2
Batan Islands Phil. **76** B1
Batavia U.S.A. **137** E2
Bataysk Rus. Fed. **45** E2
Batchawana Mountain *h.* Can. **128** B2
Batchelor Austl. **114** C1
Bătdâmbâng Cambodia **75** B2
Batemans Bay Austl. **117** E3
Batesville U.S.A. **138** B1
Batetskiy Rus. Fed. **43** D2
Bath U.K. **53** B4
Bathinda India **86** B1
Bathurst Austl. **117** D2
Bathurst Can. **125** H3
Bathurst Inlet Can. **124** E2
Bathurst Inlet *inlet* Can. **124** E2
Bathurst Island Austl. **114** C1
Bathurst Island Can. **124** F1
Bātin, Wādī al *watercourse* Asia **90** B2
Batman Turkey **93** C2
Batna Alg. **101** C1
Baton Rouge U.S.A. **138** B2
Batopilas Mex. **142** B2
Batouri Cameroon **104** B2
Batovi Brazil **154** B1
Båtsfjord Norway **46** F1
Batticaloa Sri Lanka **85** C4
Battipaglia Italy **62** B2
Battle *r.* Can. **127** E2
Battle Creek U.S.A. **136** C2
Battle Mountain U.S.A. **132** C2
Batu *mt.* Eth. **103** B4
Batu, Pulau-pulau *is* Indon. **72** A2
Batudaka *i.* Indon. **73** C2
Bat'umi Georgia **93** C1
Batu Pahat Malaysia **72** B1
Baubau Indon. **73** C2
Bauchi Nigeria **101** C3
Baugé France **58** B2
Baume-les-Dames France **59** D2
Bauru Brazil **154** C2
Baús Brazil **154** B1
Bauska Latvia **42** B2
Bautzen Ger. **56** C2
Bavispe *r.* Mex. **142** B2
Bavly Rus. Fed. **41** E3
Bawdwin Myanmar **74** A1
Bawean *i.* Indon. **73** C2
Bawku Ghana **100** B3
Bayamo Cuba **145** C2
Bayanhongor Mongolia **80** C1
Bayan Hot China **82** A2
Bayan Obo Kuangqu China **82** A1
Bayan Ul Hot China **82** B1
Bayawan Phil. **76** B3
Bayburt Turkey **92** C1
Bay City *MI* U.S.A. **136** D2
Bay City *TX* U.S.A. **141** E3
Baydaratskaya Guba Rus. Fed. **40** F2
Baydhabo Somalia **103** C4
Bayeux France **53** C5
Bayji Iraq *see* Bayjī
Baykal, Ozero *l.* Rus. Fed. *see*
    Baikal, Lake
Baykal'skiy Khrebet *mts* Rus. Fed.
    95 J3
Baykonyr Kazakh. **88** C2
Baymak Rus. Fed. **41** E3
Bayombong Phil. **76** B2
Bayonne France **58** B3
Bayramiç Turkey **65** C3
Bayreuth Ger. **55** E3
Bayt al Faqīh Yemen **90** B3

Baza Spain 60 C2
Baza, Sierra de *mts* Spain 60 C2
Bazardyuzyu, Gora *mt.* Azer./Rus. Fed.
　93 C1
Bazas France 58 B3
Bazdar Pak. 86 A2
Bazhong China 82 A2
Bāzmān Iran 91 D2
Bazmān, Kūh-e *mt.* Iran 91 D2
Be, Nosy *i.* Madag. 107 [inset] D1
Beachy Head U.K. 51 D4
Beacon Bay S. Africa 109 C3
Beagle Gulf Austr. 114 B1
Bealanana Madag. 107 [inset] D1
Beardmore Can. 128 B2
Bear Paw Mountain U.S.A. 132 E1
Beata, Cabo *c.* Dom. Rep. 145 C3
Beata, Isla *i.* Dom. Rep. 145 C3
Beatrice U.S.A. 135 D2
Beatty U.S.A. 133 C3
Beaudesert Austr. 117 E1
Beaufort Austr. 116 C3
Beaufort Malaysia 73 C1
Beaufort U.S.A. 139 D2
Beaufort Sea Can./U.S.A. 124 D2
Beaufort West S. Africa 108 B3
Beauly *r.* U.K. 50 B2
Beaumont Belgium 54 B2
Beaumont N.Z. 118 A4
Beaumont U.S.A. 141 F2
Beaune France 59 C2
Beauraing Belgium 54 B2
Beauséjour Can. 127 F2
Beauvais France 58 C2
Beauval Can. 127 E2
Beaver *r.* Can. 127 E2
Beaver U.S.A. 133 D3
Beaver Creek Can. 126 A1
Beaver Dam U.S.A. 136 C2
Beaver Hill Lake Can. 127 F2
Beaver Island U.S.A. 136 C1
Beaverlodge Can. 126 D2
Beawar India 86 B2
Bebedouro Brazil 154 C2
Bebra Ger. 55 D2
Becerreá Spain 60 B1
Béchar Alg. 100 B1
Beckley U.S.A. 136 D3
Bedelē Eth. 103 B4
Bedford U.K. 53 C3
Bedford U.S.A. 136 C3
Bedum Neth. 54 C1
Beecroft Peninsula Austr. 117 E2
Beelitz Ger. 55 F1
Beenleigh Austr. 117 E1
Beersheba Israel 92 B2
Beeville U.S.A. 141 E3
Bega Austr. 117 D3
Begur, Cap de *c.* Spain 61 D1
Behshahr Iran 93 D2
Bei'an China 81 E1
Beihai China 83 A3
Beijing China 82 B2
Beilen Neth. 54 C1
Beilngries Ger. 55 E3
Beinn Mhòr *h.* U.K. 50 A2
Beira Moz. 107 C1
Beirut Lebanon 92 B2
Beja Port. 60 B2
Bejaïa Alg. 101 C1
Béjar Spain 60 B1
Beji *r.* Pak. 86 A2
Bekdash Turkm. 88 C2
Békés Hungary 57 E3
Békéscsaba Hungary 57 E3
Bekily Madag. 107 [inset] D2
Bela Pak. 86 A2
Bela-Bela S. Africa 109 C1
Bélabo Cameroon 104 B2
Bela Crkva Serb. and Mont. 64 B2

Belaga Malaysia 73 C1
Belarus *country* Europe 42 C3
Bela Vista Brazil 154 C2
Bela Vista Moz. 109 D2
Belawan Indon. 72 A1
Belaya *r.* Rus. Fed. 95 N2
Belaya Glina Rus. Fed. 45 E3
Belaya Kalitva Rus. Fed. 45 F2
Belchatów Pol. 57 D2
Belcher Islands Can. 125 G3
Beledweyne Somalia 103 C4
Belém Brazil 151 E3
Belen U.S.A. 140 C2
Belev Rus. Fed. 43 E3
Belfast U.K. 51 D1
Belfast U.S.A. 137 G2
Belfort France 59 D2
Belgaum India 85 B3
Belgium *country* Europe 54 B2
Belgorod Rus. Fed. 45 E1
Belgrade Serb. and Mont. 64 B2
Belgrade U.S.A. 132 D1
Beli Nigeria 101 D4
Belinyu Indon. 72 B2
Belitung *i.* Indon. 72 B2
Belize Belize 144 B3
Belize *country* Central America 144 B3
Bel'kovskiy, Ostrov *i.* Rus. Fed. 95 L1
Bella Bella Can. 126 C2
Bellac France 58 C2
Bella Coola Can. 126 C2
Bellata Austr. 117 D1
Belle Fourche U.S.A. 134 C2
Belle Fourche *r.* U.S.A. 134 C2
Belle Glade U.S.A. 139 D3
Belle-Île *i.* France 58 B2
Belle Isle *i.* Can. 129 E1
Belle Isle, Strait of Can. 129 E1
Belleville Can. 128 C2
Belleville *IL* U.S.A. 136 C3
Belleville *KS* U.S.A. 135 D3
Bellevue U.S.A. 132 B1
Bellingham U.S.A. 132 B1
Bellinzona Switz. 59 D2
Belluno Italy 62 B1
Bellville S. Africa 108 A3
Belmonte Brazil 155 E1
Belmopan Belize 144 B3
Belmullet Rep. of Ireland 51 B1
Belogorsk Rus. Fed. 81 E1
Beloha Madag. 107 [inset] D2
Belo Horizonte Brazil 155 D1
Beloit U.S.A. 136 C2
Belomorsk Rus. Fed. 40 C2
Belorechensk Rus. Fed. 45 E3
Beloretsk Rus. Fed. 41 E3
Beloyarskiy Rus. Fed. 40 F2
Beloye, Ozero *l.* Rus. Fed. 43 E1
Beloye More *sea* Rus. Fed. *see*
　White Sea
Belozersk Rus. Fed. 43 E1
Belukha, Gora *mt.* Kazakh./Rus. Fed.
　89 F2
Belush'ye Rus. Fed. 40 D2
Belyy Rus. Fed. 43 D2
Belyy, Ostrov *i.* Rus. Fed. 40 G1
Belzig Ger. 55 F1
Bemidji U.S.A. 135 E1
Bena Dibele Dem. Rep. Congo 104 C3
Benalla Austr. 117 D3
Benavente Spain 60 B1
Benbecula *i.* U.K. 50 A2
Bend U.S.A. 132 B2
Bendearg *mt.* S. Africa 109 C3
Bendigo Austr. 116 C3
Bene Moz. 107 C1
Bengal, Bay of *sea* Indian Ocean
　85 C3

Bengbu China 82 B2
Benghazi Libya 101 E1
Bengkayang Indon. 72 B1
Bengkulu Indon. 72 B2
Benguela Angola 106 A1
Beni *r.* Bol. 152 B2
Beni Dem. Rep. Congo 105 C2
Beni-Abbès Alg. 100 B1
Benidorm Spain 61 C2
Beni Mellal Morocco 100 B1
Benin *country* Africa 100 C4
Benin, Bight of *g.* Africa 100 C4
Benin City Nigeria 101 C4
Beni-Saf Alg. 61 C2
Benito Juárez Arg. 153 C4
Benjamim Constant Brazil 150 C3
Benjamín Hill Mex. 142 A1
Benjina Indon. 71 C3
Ben Lawers *mt.* U.K. 50 B2
Ben Lomond *h.* U.K. 50 B2
Ben Macdui *mt.* U.K. 50 C2
Ben More *h.* U.K. 50 A2
Benmore, Lake N.Z. 118 B3
Ben More Assynt *h.* U.K. 50 B1
Bennett Can. 126 B2
Bennetta, Ostrov *i.* Rus. Fed. 95 L1
Ben Nevis *mt.* U.K. 50 B2
Bennington U.S.A. 137 F2
Benoni S. Africa 109 C2
Benson U.S.A. 140 B2
Benteng Indon. 73 D2
Benton Harbor U.S.A. 136 C2
Bentonville U.S.A. 138 B1
Benue *r.* Nigeria 101 C4
Ben Wyvis *mt.* U.K. 50 B2
Benxi China 82 C1
Beograd Serb. and Mont. *see* Belgrade
Beohari India 87 C2
Beppu Japan 79 B4
Berane Serb. and Mont. 64 A2
Berat Albania 65 A2
Berau, Teluk *b.* Indon. 71 C3
Berber Sudan 102 B3
Berbera Somalia 103 C3
Berbérati C.A.R. 104 B2
Berck France 58 C1
Berdyans'k Ukr. 45 E2
Berdychiv Ukr. 44 C2
Berehove Ukr. 44 B2
Bereina P.N.G. 71 D3
Berens River Can. 127 F2
Berezhany Ukr. 44 B2
Berezivka Ukr. 44 D2
Berezne Ukr. 44 C1
Bereznik Rus. Fed. 40 D2
Berezniki Rus. Fed. 40 E3
Berezovo Rus. Fed. 40 F2
Berga Spain 61 D1
Bergama Turkey 65 C3
Bergamo Italy 62 A1
Bergen Mecklenburg-Vorpommern Ger.
　56 C2
Bergen Niedersachsen Ger. 55 D1
Bergen Norway 47 B3
Bergen op Zoom Neth. 54 B2
Bergerac France 58 C3
Bergheim (Erft) Ger. 54 C2
Bergisch Gladbach Ger. 54 C2
Bergland Namibia 108 A1
Bergsviken Sweden 46 E2
Bergues France 54 A2
Beringen Belgium 54 B2
Bering Sea N. Pacific Ocean 95 O2
Bering Strait Rus. Fed./U.S.A. 95 O3
Berkeley U.S.A. 133 B3
Berkhout Neth. 54 B1
Berkner Island Antarctica 119 A2

erkovitsa Bulg. 64 B2
Lillevåg Norway 46 F1
erlin Ger. 55 F1
erlin U.S.A. 137 F2
erlingerode Ger. 55 E2
ermagui Austr. 117 E3
ermejillo Mex. 142 B2
ermejo Bol. 152 B3
ermen, Lac l. Can. 129 D1
ermuda terr. N. Atlantic Ocean
  160 B3
ern Switz. 59 D2
ernau Ger. 55 F1
ernburg (Saale) Ger. 55 E2
erkastel-Kues Ger. 54 C3
eroroha Madag. 107 [inset] D2
erounka r. Czech Rep. 55 G3
erri Austr. 116 C2
errouaghia Alg. 61 D2
erry Islands Bahamas 145 C2
ersenbrück Ger. 54 C1
ershad' Ukr. 44 D2
erté, Lac l. Can. 129 D1
ertoua Cameroon 104 B2
eru atoll Kiribati 110
eruri Brazil 150 C3
erwick-upon-Tweed U.K. 52 B2
eryslav Ukr. 45 D2
esalampy Madag. 107 [inset] D2
esnard Lake Can. 127 E2
esshoky, Gora h. Kazakh. 88 C2
etaré Oya Cameroon 104 B2
ethanie Namibia 108 A2
ethlehem S. Africa 109 C2
ethlehem U.S.A. 137 E2
éthune France 54 A2
etioky Madag. 107 [inset] D2
etroka Madag. 107 [inset] D2
etpak-Dala plain Kazakh. 89 E2
etsiboka r. Madag. 107 [inset] D1
ettiah India 87 C2
etul India 87 B2
etwa r. India 87 B2
etws-y-coed U.K. 52 B3
everley U.K. 52 C3
everungen Ger. 55 D2
everwijk Neth. 54 B1
exhill U.K. 53 D4
eykoz Turkey 65 C4
eyla Guinea 100 B4
eyneu Kazakh. 88 C2
eypazari Turkey 92 B1
eyrouth Lebanon see Beirut
eysehir Turkey 92 B2
eysehir Gölü l. Turkey 92 B2
eysug r. Rus. Fed. 45 E2
ezhanitsy Rus. Fed. 42 C2
ezhetsk Rus. Fed. 43 E2
éziers France 59 C3
hadrak India 87 C2
hadravati India 85 B3
hagalpur India 87 C2
hairi Hol mt. Pak. 86 A2
hakkar Pak. 86 B2
hamo Myanmar 74 A1
hanjanagar India 87 C3
haratpur India 86 B2
haruch India 86 B2
havnagar India 86 B2
hawanipatna India 87 C3
hekuzulu S. Africa 109 D2
hilwara India 86 B2
hima r. India 85 B3
hiwani India 86 B2
hongweni S. Africa 109 C3

Bhopal India 86 B2
Bhubaneshwar India 87 C2
Bhuj India 86 A2
Bhumiphol Dam Thai. 74 A2
Bhusawal India 86 B2
Bhutan country Asia 87 D2
Bia, Phou mt. Laos 74 B2
Biak Indon. 71 D3
Biak i. Indon. 71 D3
Biała Podlaska Pol. 57 E2
Białogard Pol. 57 D2
Białystok Pol. 57 E2
Bianco Italy 60 C2
Biarritz France 58 B3
Biasca Switz. 59 D2
Bibai Japan 78 D2
Bibala Angola 106 A1
Biberach an der Riß Ger. 56 B3
Bida Nigeria 101 C4
Biddeford U.S.A. 137 F2
Bideford U.K. 53 A4
Bideford Bay U.K. 53 A4
Biedenkopf Ger. 55 D2
Biel Switz. 59 D2
Bielefeld Ger. 55 D1
Biella Italy 62 A1
Bielsko-Biała Pol. 57 D3
Biên Hoa Vietnam 75 B2
Bienville, Lac l. Can. 128 C1
Bièvre Belgium 54 B3
Bifoun Gabon 104 B3
Biga Turkey 65 C2
Big Bend Swaziland 109 D2
Biggar Can. 124 E3
Biggar U.K. 50 C3
Big Hole r. U.S.A. 132 D1
Bighorn r. U.S.A. 134 F3
Bighorn Mountains U.S.A. 134 F3
Big Lake U.S.A. 141 D2
Big Rapids U.S.A. 136 C2
Big River Can. 127 E2
Big Sand Lake Can. 127 F2
Big Sioux r. U.S.A. 135 D2
Big Spring U.S.A. 141 D2
Big Timber U.S.A. 132 E1
Big Trout Lake Can. 128 B1
Big Trout Lake l. Can. 128 A1
Bihać Bos.-Herz. 63 C2
Bihar Sharif India 87 C2
Bihor, Vârful mt. Romania 44 B2
Bijagós, Arquipélago dos is
  Guinea-Bissau 100 A3
Bijār Iran 93 C2
Bijeljina Bos.-Herz. 63 C2
Bijelo Polje Serb. and Mont. 64 A2
Bijie China 83 A3
Bikaner India 86 B2
Bikin Rus. Fed. 78 B1
Bikin r. Rus. Fed. 78 B1
Bikoro Dem. Rep. Congo 104 B3
Bilad Bani Bu 'Ali Oman 91 C2
Bilaspur India 87 C2
Bila Tserkva Ukr. 44 D2
Bilauktaung Range mts Myanmar/Thai.
  75 A2
Bilbao Spain 60 C1
Bilecik Turkey 65 C2
Bilgoraj Pol. 57 E2
Bilhorod-Dnistrovs'kyy Ukr. 44 D2
Bili Dem. Rep. Congo 105 C2
Bilibino Rus. Fed. 95 N2
Billings U.S.A. 132 E1
Bill of Portland hd U.K. 53 B4
Bilma Niger 101 D3
Biloela Austr. 115 E2
Bilohir's'k Ukr. 45 D2
Bilohir''ya Ukr. 44 C1
Bilopillya Ukr. 45 D1
Bilovods'k Ukr. 45 E2
Biloxi U.S.A. 138 C2

Bilpa Morea Claypan salt flat Austr.
  115 C2
Bilshausen Ger. 55 E2
Biltine Chad 101 E3
Bilyayivka Ukr. 44 D2
Bimini Islands Bahamas 139 E3
Bina-Etawa India 87 B2
Binaija, Gunung mt. Indon. 71 C3
Bindu Dem. Rep. Congo 104 B3
Bindura Zimbabwe 107 C1
Binefar Spain 61 D1
Bingara Austr. 117 E1
Bingen am Rhein Ger. 54 C3
Bingham U.S.A. 137 G1
Binghamton U.S.A. 137 E2
Bingöl Turkey 93 C2
Binjai Indon. 72 A1
Bintuhan Indon. 72 B2
Bintulu Malaysia 73 C1
Binzhou China 82 B2
Bioco i. Equat. Guinea 104 A2
Biograd na Moru Croatia 62 C2
Birao C.A.R. 104 C1
Biratnagar Nepal 87 C2
Birch Mountains Can. 126 D2
Birdsville Austr. 115 C2
Birecik Turkey 92 B2
Bireun Indon. 72 A1
Birganj Nepal 87 C2
Birhan mt. Eth. 103 B3
Birigüi Brazil 154 B2
Birjand Iran 88 C3
Birkenhead U.K. 52 B3
Birmingham U.K. 53 C3
Birmingham U.S.A. 138 C2
Bïr Mogreïn Maur. 100 A2
Birnin-Kebbi Nigeria 100 C3
Birnin Konni Niger 101 C3
Birobidzhan Rus. Fed. 81 E1
Birr Rep. of Ireland 51 C2
Birsay U.K. 50 C1
Bir Shalatayn Egypt 90 A2
Biržai Lith. 42 B2
Bisalpur India 87 B2
Bisbee U.S.A. 140 C2
Biscay, Bay of sea France/Spain 58 A2
Bischofshofen Austria 56 C3
Biscotasi Lake Can. 128 B2
Bishkek Kyrg. 89 E2
Bisho S. Africa 109 C3
Bishop U.S.A. 133 C3
Bishui China 81 E1
Bisinaca Col. 150 C3
Biskra Alg. 101 C1
Bismarck U.S.A. 134 C1
Bismarck Archipelago is P.N.G. 71 D3
Bismarck Sea P.N.G. 110
Bissa, Djebel mt. Alg. 61 D2
Bissamcuttak India 85 C3
Bissau Guinea-Bissau 100 A3
Bissett Can. 127 F2
Bistcho Lake Can. 126 D2
Bistrița Romania 44 B2
Bistrița r. Romania 44 C2
Bitburg Ger. 54 C3
Bitche France 59 D2
Bitkine Chad 101 D3
Bitola Macedonia 65 B2
Bitonto Italy 63 C2
Bitterfontein S. Africa 108 A3
Bitterroot r. U.S.A. 132 D1
Bitterroot Range mts U.S.A. 132 C1
Bityug r. Rus. Fed. 43 E3
Biu Nigeria 101 D3
Biwa-ko l. Japan 79 C3
Biysk Rus. Fed. 89 F1
Bizerte Tunisia 101 C1
Bjargtangar hd Iceland 46 [inset]
Bjästa Sweden 46 D3
Bjerkvik Norway 46 D2

Bjørnøya i. Arctic Ocean **94** D2
Bla Mali **100** B3
Black r. U.S.A. **138** D1
Blackall Austr. **116** D2
Blackburn U.K. **52** B3
Blackfoot U.S.A. **132** D2
Black Forest mts Ger. **56** B3
Black Hills U.S.A. **134** C2
Black Isle pen. U.K. **50** D2
Black Lake Can. **127** E2
Black Lake l. Can. **127** E2
Blackpool U.K. **52** B3
Black River r. Vietnam **74** B1
Black River Falls U.S.A. **136** B2
Blacksburg U.S.A. **137** D3
Black Sea Asia/Europe **92** D2
Blacksod Bay Rep. of Ireland **51** A1
Blackstairs Mountains Rep. of Ireland **51** C2
Black Volta r. Africa **100** B4
Blackwater r. Rep. of Ireland **51** C2
Blackwater Lake Can. **126** C1
Blackwood r. Austr. **114** A3
Blagoevgrad Bulg. **64** B2
Blagoveshchensk Rus. Fed. **81** E1
Blaine Lake Can. **127** E2
Blair U.S.A. **135** D2
Blair Atholl U.K. **50** C2
Blairgowrie U.K. **50** C2
Blakely U.S.A. **139** D2
Blanc, Mont mt. France/Italy **59** D2
Blanca, Bahía b. Arg. **153** B4
Blanche, Lake salt flat Austr. **116** B1
Blanco r. Bol. **152** B2
Blanco, Cape U.S.A. **120**
Blanc-Sablon Can. **129** E1
Blanda r. Iceland **46** [inset]
Blandford Forum U.K. **53** B4
Blanding U.S.A. **133** E3
Blanes Spain **60** D1
Blangkejeren Indon. **72** A1
Blankenheim Ger. **54** C2
Blankenrath Ger. **54** C2
Blansko Czech Rep. **57** D3
Blantyre Malawi **107** C1
Blaydon U.K. **52** C2
Blayney Austr. **117** D2
Blenheim N.Z. **118** B3
Blida Alg. **100** C1
Blind River Can. **128** B2
Bloemfontein S. Africa **109** C2
Bloemhof S. Africa **109** C2
Bloemhof Dam S. Africa **109** C2
Blönduós Iceland **46** [inset]
Bloody Foreland pt Rep. of Ireland **51** B1
Bloomfield U.S.A. **140** C1
Bloomington IL U.S.A. **136** C2
Bloomington IN U.S.A. **136** C3
Blosseville Kyst coastal area Greenland **125** K2
Bluefield U.S.A. **136** D3
Bluefields Nic. **144** B3
Blue Mountains Austr. **117** D2
Blue Mountains U.S.A. **132** C1
Blue Nile r. Eth./Sudan **103** B3
Blue Ridge mts U.S.A. **139** D1
Blue Stack Mountains Rep. of Ireland **51** B1
Bluff N.Z. **118** A4
Bluff U.S.A. **133** E3
Blumenau Brazil **154** C3
Blyth Austr. **116** B2
Blyth U.K. **52** C2
Blythe U.S.A. **133** D4
Blytheville U.S.A. **138** C1
Bo Sierra Leone **100** A4
Boac Phil. **76** B2

Boa Esperança, Açude resr Brazil **151** E3
Boa Vista Brazil **150** C2
Bobadah Austr. **117** D2
Bobai China **83** B3
Bobaomby, Tanjona c. Madag. **107** [inset] D1
Bobo-Dioulasso Burkina **100** B3
Bobrov Rus. Fed. **43** F3
Bobrovytsya Ukr. **45** D1
Bobrynets' Ukr. **45** D2
Boby mt. Madag. **107** [inset] D2
Boca do Acre Brazil **150** C3
Bocaiúva Brazil **155** D1
Bocaranga C.A.R. **104** B2
Bochnia Pol. **57** E3
Bocholt Ger. **54** C2
Bochum Ger. **54** C2
Bochum S. Africa **109** C1
Bockenem Ger. **55** E1
Boda C.A.R. **104** B2
Bodaybo Rus. Fed. **95** J3
Bodélé reg. Chad **101** D3
Boden Sweden **46** E2
Bodmin U.K. **53** A4
Bodmin Moor moorland U.K. **53** A4
Bodø Norway **46** C2
Bodrum Turkey **65** C3
Boende Dem. Rep. Congo **104** C3
Bogalusa U.S.A. **138** C2
Bogandé Burkina **100** B3
Bogda Shan mts China **89** F2
Boggabilla Austr. **117** E1
Boggeragh Mountains Rep. of Ireland **51** B2
Bogny-sur-Meuse France **54** B3
Bog of Allen reg. Rep. of Ireland **51** C2
Bogong, Mount Austr. **117** D3
Bogor Indon. **72** B2
Bogoroditsk Rus. Fed. **43** E3
Bogotá Col. **150** B2
Bogotol Rus. Fed. **94** H3
Boguchany Rus. Fed. **95** I3
Boguchar Rus. Fed. **45** F2
Bo Hai g. China **82** B2
Bohain-en-Vermandois France **54** A3
Bohai Wan b. China **82** B2
Bohlokong S. Africa **109** C2
Böhmer Wald mts Ger. **55** F3
Bohodukhiv Ukr. **45** D1
Bohol i. Phil. **76** B3
Bohol Sea Phil. **76** B3
Bohu China **89** F2
Boi, Ponta do pt Brazil **155** C2
Bois r. Brazil **154** B1
Boise U.S.A. **132** C2
Boise City U.S.A. **141** D1
Boitumelong S. Africa **109** C2
Boizenburg Ger. **55** E1
Bojnūrd Iran **93** D2
Bokatola Dem. Rep. Congo **104** B3
Boké Guinea **100** A3
Bokele Dem. Rep. Congo **104** C3
Boknafjorden sea chan. Norway **47** B4
Bokoro Chad **101** D3
Bokovskaya Rus. Fed. **45** F2
Bokpyin Myanmar **75** A2
Boksitogorsk Rus. Fed. **43** D2
Bokspits S. Africa **108** B2
Bolama Guinea-Bissau **100** A3
Bolangir India **87** C2
Bolbec France **58** C2
Bole China **89** F2
Boleko Dem. Rep. Congo **104** B3
Bolgatanga Ghana **100** B3
Bolhrad Ukr. **44** C2
Boli China **78** B1
Bolintin-Vale Romania **44** C3
Bolívar U.S.A. **135** E3
Bolívar, Pico mt. Venez. **150** B2

Bolivia country S. America **152** B2
Bolkhov Rus. Fed. **43** E3
Bollène France **59** C3
Bollnäs Sweden **47** D3
Bollon Austr. **117** D1
Bollstedt Ger. **55** E2
Bolmen l. Sweden **47** C4
Bolobo Dem. Rep. Congo **104** B3
Bologna Italy **62** B2
Bologovo Rus. Fed. **43** D2
Bologoye Rus. Fed. **43** D2
Bolomba Dem. Rep. Congo **104** B2
Bol'shaya Martinovka Rus. Fed. **45** F2
Bol'shevik, Ostrov i. Rus. Fed. **95** I1
Bol'shezemel'skaya Tundra lowland Rus. Fed. **40** E2
Bol'shoy Aluy r. Rus. Fed. **95** M2
Bol'shoy Kamen' Rus. Fed. **78** B2
Bol'shoy Kavkaz mts Asia/Europe see Caucasus
Bol'shoy Lyakhovskiy, Ostrov i. Rus. Fed. **95** M2
Bolsward Neth. **54** B1
Bolton U.K. **52** B3
Bolu Turkey **92** B1
Bolungarvík Iceland **46** [inset]
Bolzano Italy **62** B1
Boma Dem. Rep. Congo **104** B3
Bomaderry Austr. **117** E2
Bombala Austr. **117** D3
Bombay India see Mumbai
Bom Despacho Brazil **155** C1
Bomdila India **87** D2
Bom Jesus da Lapa Brazil **151** E4
Bom Jesus do Itabapoana Brazil **155** D2
Bømlo i. Norway **48** C3
Bon, Cap c. Tunisia **101** D1
Bonaire i. Neth. Antilles **145** D3
Bonaparte Archipelago is Austr. **114** B1
Bonavista Can. **129** E2
Bonavista Bay Can. **129** E2
Bondo Dem. Rep. Congo **104** C2
Bondoukou Côte d'Ivoire **100** B4
Bône, Teluk b. Indon. **73** D2
Bonerate, Kepulauan is Indon. **73** D2
Bonete, Cerro mt. Bol. **147**
Bonfinópolis de Minas Brazil **155** C1
Bonga Eth. **103** B4
Bongaigaon India **87** D2
Bongandanga Dem. Rep. Congo **104** C2
Bongor Chad **101** D3
Bonguanou Côte d'Ivoire **100** B4
Bông Son Vietnam **75** B2
Bonham U.S.A. **141** E2
Bonifacio France **59** D3
Bonifacio, Strait of France/Italy **62** A2
Bonito Brazil **154** A2
Bonn Ger. **54** C2
Bonners Ferry U.S.A. **132** C1
Bonnie Rock Austr. **114** A3
Bonnyville Can. **127** D2
Bonorva Italy **62** A2
Bontang Indon. **73** C1
Bontoc Phil. **76** B2
Bontosunggu Indon. **73** C2
Bontrug S. Africa **109** C3
Booligal Austr. **116** C2
Boomi Austr. **117** D1
Boonah Austr. **117** E1
Boone IA U.S.A. **135** E2
Boone NC U.S.A. **136** D3
Booneville U.S.A. **138** C2
Boonville U.S.A. **135** E3
Boorowa Austr. **117** D2

oothia, Gulf of Can. **125** G2
oothia Peninsula Can. **124** F2
oppard Ger. **54** C2
oquilla, Presa de la *resr* Mex.
 142 B2
or Serb. and Mont. **64** B2
or Sudan **103** B4
or Turkey **92** B2
oraha, Nosy *i.* Madag. **107** [inset] E1
orås Sweden **47** C4
oräzjän Iran **93** D3
orba Brazil **150** D3
ordeaux France **58** B3
ordertown Austr. **116** C3
ordj Bou Arréridj Alg. **61** D2
ordj Bounaama Alg. **61** D2
ordj Messaouda Alg. **101** C2
ordj Omer Driss Alg. **101** C2
orðoy *i.* Faroe Is **48** B1
organes Iceland **46** [inset]
orgosesia Italy **62** A1
orisoglebsk Rus. Fed. **45** F1
orisoglebskiy Rus. Fed. **43** E2
orisovka Rus. Fed. **45** E1
orisovo-Sudskoye Rus. Fed. **43** E2
orken Ger. **54** C2
orkenes Norway **46** D2
orkum Ger. **54** C1
orkum *i.* Ger. **54** C1
orlänge Sweden **47** D3
orna Ger. **55** F2
orneo *i.* Asia **73** C3
ornholm *i.* Denmark **47** C4
ornova Turkey **65** C3
orodyanka Ukr. **44** C1
orovichi Rus. Fed. **43** D2
orovsk Rus. Fed. **43** E2
orroloola Austr. **115** C1
orşa Romania **44** B2
orshchiv Ukr. **44** C2
orshchovochnyy Khrebet *mts*
 Rus. Fed. **81** D1
örŻum Ger. **55** E1
orüjerd Iran **93** C2
oryslav Ukr. **44** B2
oryspil' Ukr. **44** D1
orzna Ukr. **43** D1
orzya Rus. Fed. **81** D1
osanska Dubica Bos.-Herz. **63** C1
osanska Gradiška Bos.-Herz. **63** C1
osanski Krupa Bos.-Herz. **63** C2
osanski Novi Bos.-Herz. **63** C1
osanski Samac Bos.-Herz. **63** C2
ose China **83** A3
oshof S. Africa **109** C2
osnia-Herzegovina *country* Europe
 63 C2
osobolo Dem. Rep. Congo **104** B2
osporus *str.* Turkey **65** C2
ossangoa C.A.R. **104** B2
ossembélé C.A.R. **104** B2
oston Hu *i.* China **89** F2
oston U.K. **52** C3
oston U.S.A. **137** F2
oston Mountains U.S.A. **138** B1
otany Bay Austr. **117** E2
otev *mt.* Bulg. **64** B2
otevgrad Bulg. **92** A1
othnia, Gulf of Fin./Sweden **47** D3
otoşani Romania **44** C2
otshabelo S. Africa **109** C2
otswana *country* Africa **106** C2
otte Donato, Monte *mt.* Italy **63** C3
ottineau U.S.A. **134** C1
ottrop Ger. **54** C2
otucatu Brazil **154** C2
ouaké Côte d'Ivoire **100** B4
ouar C.A.R. **104** B2
ouârfa Morocco **100** B1
ouctouche Can. **129** D2

Bougaa Alg. **61** E2
Bougainville Island P.N.G. **110**
Bougaroûn, Cap *c.* Alg. **61** E2
Bougouni Mali **100** B3
Bouillon Belgium **54** B3
Bouira Alg. **61** D2
Boujdour Western Sahara **100** A2
Boulder U.S.A. **134** B2
Boulder City U.S.A. **133** D3
Boulia Austr. **115** C2
Boulogne-Billancourt France **58** C2
Boulogne-sur-Mer France **53** D4
Boumango Gabon **104** B3
Boumba *r.* Cameroon **104** B2
Boumerdes Alg. **61** D2
Bouna Côte d'Ivoire **100** B4
Boundiali Côte d'Ivoire **100** B4
Bountiful U.S.A. **132** C2
Bourem Mali **100** B3
Bourganeuf France **58** C2
Bourg-en-Bresse France **59** D2
Bourges France **58** C2
Bourke Austr. **117** D2
Bournemouth U.K. **53** C4
Bou Saâda Alg. **101** C1
Bousso Chad **101** D3
Boutilimit Maur. **100** A3
Bouy France **54** B3
Bow *r.* Can. **127** D3
Bowen Austr. **115** D3
Bow Island Can. **127** D3
Bowling Green *KY* U.S.A. **136** C3
Bowling Green *OH* U.S.A. **136** D2
Bowman U.S.A. **134** C1
Boxberg Ger. **55** D3
Boxtel Neth. **54** B2
Boyabat Turkey **92** B1
Boyang China **83** B3
Boyle Rep. of Ireland **51** B2
Boyne *r.* Rep. of Ireland **51** B2
Boysen Reservoir U.S.A. **134** B2
Boyuibe Bol. **152** B3
Bozburun Turkey **65** C3
Bozcaada *i.* Turkey **65** C3
Bozdağ *mt.* Turkey **65** C3
Boz Dağları *mts* Turkey **65** C3
Bozdoğan Turkey **65** C3
Bozeman U.S.A. **132** D1
Bozoum C.A.R. **104** B2
Bozüyük Turkey **65** D3
Brač *i.* Croatia **63** C2
Bracebridge Can. **128** C2
Brachet, Lac au *l.* Can. **129** D2
Bracknell U.K. **53** C4
Bradano *r.* Italy **63** C2
Bradenton U.S.A. **139** D3
Bradford U.K. **52** C3
Bradford U.S.A. **137** E2
Brady U.S.A. **141** E2
Braemar U.K. **50** C2
Braga Port. **60** B1
Bragança Brazil **151** E3
Bragança Port. **60** B1
Bragança Paulista Brazil **155** C2
Brahin Belarus **43** D3
Brahmanbaria Bangl. **74** A1
Brahmapur India **86** B1
Brahmaputra *r.* China/India **74** A1
Brăila Romania **44** C2
Brainerd U.S.A. **135** E1
Braintree U.K. **53** D4
Braives Belgium **54** C2
Brake (Unterweser) Ger. **55** D1
Brakwater Namibia **108** A1
Bramsche Ger. **54** D1
Branco *r.* Brazil **150** D3
Brandenburg Ger. **55** F1
Brandon Can. **127** F3
Brandon Mountain *h.* Rep. of Ireland
 51 A2

Brandvlei S. Africa **108** B3
Braniewo Pol. **57** D2
Brantford Can. **128** B2
Bras d'Or Lake Can. **129** D2
Brasil, Planalto do *plat.* Brazil **155** D1
Brasilândia Brazil **154** C1
Brasília Brazil **154** C1
Brasília de Minas Brazil **155** D1
Braslaw Belarus **42** C2
Braşov Romania **44** C2
Bratislava Slovakia **57** D3
Bratsk Rus. Fed. **95** I3
Braunau am Inn Austria **56** C3
Braunschweig Ger. **55** E1
Brautarholt Iceland **46** [inset]
Bråviken *inlet* Sweden **42** A2
Bravo del Norte, Río *r.* Mex./U.S.A. *see*
 Rio Grande
Brawley U.S.A. **133** C4
Bray Rep. of Ireland **51** C2
Brazil *country* S. America **151** D3
Brazilian Highlands *mts* Brazil **146**
Brazos *r.* U.S.A. **141** E3
Brazzaville Congo **104** B3
Brčko Bos.-Herz. **63** C2
Brechin U.K. **50** C2
Brecht Belgium **54** B2
Breckenridge U.S.A. **141** E2
Břeclav Czech Rep. **57** D3
Brecon U.K. **53** C4
Brecon Beacons *reg.* U.K. **53** B4
Breda Neth. **54** B2
Bredasdorp S. Africa **108** B3
Bregenz Austria **56** D3
Breivikbotn Norway **46** E1
Brekstad Norway **46** B3
Bremen Ger. **55** D1
Bremerhaven Ger. **55** D1
Bremerton U.S.A. **132** B1
Bremervörde Ger. **55** D1
Brenham U.S.A. **141** E2
Brennero Italy **56** D2
Brenner Pass Austria/Italy **56** C3
Brentwood U.K. **53** D4
Brescia Italy **62** D1
Bressanone Italy **62** D1
Bressay *i.* U.K. **50** [inset]
Bressuire France **58** B2
Brest Belarus **42** B1
Brest France **58** B2
Breton Sound *b.* U.S.A. **138** C3
Breves Brazil **151** D3
Brewarrina Austr. **117** D1
Brewster U.S.A. **132** C1
Brezovo Polje *plain* Croatia **63** C1
Bria C.A.R. **104** C2
Briançon France **59** D3
Briceni Moldova **44** C2
Bridgend U.K. **53** B4
Bridgeport *CT* U.S.A. **137** F2
Bridgeport *NE* U.S.A. **134** C2
Bridgetown Barbados **145** E3
Bridgewater Can. **129** D2
Bridgwater U.K. **53** B4
Bridlington U.K. **52** C2
Bridlington Bay U.K. **52** C2
Brig Switz. **59** D2
Brigham City U.S.A. **132** D2
Brighton N.Z. **118** B4
Brighton U.K. **53** C4
Brignoles France **59** D3
Brilon Ger. **55** D2
Brindisi Italy **63** C2
Brisbane Austr. **117** E1
Bristol U.K. **53** B4
Bristol U.S.A. **139** D1
Bristol Bay U.S.A. **95** F3
Bristol Channel *est.* U.K. **53** A4
British Columbia *prov.* Can. **126** C2

175

British Indian Ocean Territory *terr.*
  Indian Ocean **69**
Britstown S. Africa **108** B3
Brittany *reg.* France **58** B2
Brive-la-Gaillarde France **58** C2
Briviesca Spain **60** C1
Brno Czech Rep. **57** D3
Broad *r.* U.S.A. **139** D2
Broadback *r.* Can. **128** C1
Broad Law *h.* U.K. **50** C3
Brochet Can. **127** E2
Brochet, Lac *l.* Can. **127** E2
Bröckel Ger. **55** E1
Brockville Can. **128** C2
Brodeur Peninsula Can. **125** G2
Brodick U.K. **50** B3
Brodnica Pol. **57** D2
Brody Ukr. **44** C1
Broken Arrow U.S.A. **141** E1
Broken Bow U.S.A. **135** D2
Broken Hill Austr. **116** C2
Bromsgrove U.K. **53** B3
Brønderslev Denmark **47** B4
Brønnøysund Norway **46** C2
Brooke's Point Phil. **76** A3
Brookhaven U.S.A. **138** B2
Brookings *OR* U.S.A. **132** B3
Brookings *SD* U.S.A. **135** D2
Brooks Can. **127** D2
Brooks Range *mts* U.S.A. **124** C2
Brookville U.S.A. **139** D3
Brooms, Loch *inlet* U.K. **50** B2
Broome Austr. **114** B1
Brothers U.S.A. **132** B2
Brovary Ukr. **44** D1
Brownfield U.S.A. **141** D2
Browning U.S.A. **126** D3
Brownsville *TN* U.S.A. **138** C1
Brownsville *TX* U.S.A. **141** E3
Brownwood U.S.A. **141** D2
Brú Iceland **46** [inset]
Bruay-la-Bussière France **58** C2
Bruce Crossing U.S.A. **136** C1
Bruchsal Ger. **55** D3
Bruck an der Mur Austria **57** D3
Bruges Belgium see **Brugge**
Brugge Belgium **54** A2
Brühl Ger. **55** D3
Bruint India **74** A1
Brûlé Can. **126** D2
Brumado Brazil **151** E4
Brumunddal Norway **47** C3
Brunei *country* Asia **73** C1
Brunico Italy **56** C3
Brunswick *GA* U.S.A. **139** D2
Brunswick *ME* U.S.A. **137** G2
Brunswick Head Austr. **117** E1
Brush U.S.A. **134** C2
Brussels Belgium **54** B2
Bruxelles Belgium see **Brussels**
Bryan U.S.A. **141** E2
Bryansk Rus. Fed. **43** D3
Bryne Norway **48** E2
Bryn'kovskaya Rus. Fed. **45** E2
Bryukhovetskaya Rus. Fed. **45** E2
Brzeg Pol. **57** D2
Buba Guinea-Bissau **100** A3
Bucak Turkey **92** B2
Bucaramanga Col. **150** B2
Buchan Austr. **117** D3
Buchanan Liberia **100** A4
Bucharest Romania **44** E3
Bucholz in der Nordheide Ger. **55** D1
Buchy France **53** I5
Bucin, Pasul *pass* Romania **44** C2
Buckeburg Ger. **55** D1
Buckeye U.S.A. **140** B2
Buckhaven U.K. **50** C2
Buckie U.K. **50** C2

Buckingham Bay Austr. **115** C1
Buckland Tableland *reg.* Austr. **115** D2
Buckleboo Austr. **116** B2
Bucksport U.S.A. **137** G2
București Romania see **Bucharest**
Buda-Kashalyova Belarus **43** D3
Budapest Hungary **57** D3
Budaun India **87** B3
Buddusò Italy **62** A2
Bude U.K. **53** A4
Budennovsk Rus. Fed. **41** D4
Budogoshch' Rus. Fed. **43** D2
Budoni Italy **62** A2
Buea Cameroon **104** A2
Buenaventura Mex. **142** B2
Buendia, Embalse de *resr* Spain
  60 C1
Buenópolis Brazil **155** D1
Buenos Aires Arg. **153** C4
Buenos Aires, Lago *l.* Arg./Chile
  153 A5
Buffalo *NY* U.S.A. **137** E2
Buffalo *SD* U.S.A. **134** C1
Buffalo *WY* U.S.A. **134** B2
Buffalo Narrows Can. **124** E3
Buffels *watercourse* S. Africa **108** A2
Buftea Romania **44** C3
Bug *r.* Pol. **57** E2
Bugel, Tanjung *pt* Indon. **73** C2
Bugojno Bos.-Herz. **63** C2
Bugsuk *i.* Phil. **76** A3
Buguruslan Rus. Fed. **41** E3
Buhl U.S.A. **132** D3
Buíllth Wells U.K. **53** B3
Buir Nur *l.* Mongolia **81** D1
Buitepos Namibia **108** A1
Bujanovac Serb. and Mont. **64** B2
Bujumbura Burundi **105** C3
Bukachacha Rus. Fed. **81** D1
Bukavu Dem. Rep. Congo **105** C3
Bukhara Uzbek. see **Buxoro**
Bukittinggi Indon. **72** B2
Bukoba Tanz. **105** D3
Bulahdelal Austr. **117** E2
Bulawayo Zimbabwe **107** B2
Buldan Turkey **65** C3
Bulembu Swaziland **109** D2
Bulgan Mongolia **80** C1
Bulgaria *country* Europe **64** B2
Buller *r.* N.Z. **118** B3
Bulloo Downs Austr. **116** C1
Büllsport Namibia **108** A1
Bulukumba Indon. **73** D2
Bumba Dem. Rep. Congo **104** B3
Bumhkang Myanmar **74** A1
Buna Dem. Rep. Congo **104** B3
Bunbury Austr. **114** A3
Buncrana Rep. of Ireland **51** C1
Bunda Tanz. **105** D3
Bundaberg Austr. **115** E2
Bundarra Austr. **117** E2
Bundi India **86** B2
Bundoran Rep. of Ireland **51** B1
Bungendore Austr. **117** D3
Bungo-suidō *sea chan.* Japan **79** B4
Bunia Dem. Rep. Congo **105** D2
Bunianga Dem. Rep. Congo **104** C3
Buôn Mê Thuột Vietnam **75** B2
Bura Kenya **105** D3
Buraydah Saudi Arabia **90** B2
Burbach Ger. **54** D2
Burco Somalia **103** C4
Burdaard Neth. **54** B1
Burdur Turkey **92** B2
Bure Eth. **103** B3
Bure *r.* U.K. **53** D3
Burgas Bulg. **64** C2
Burg bei Magdeburg Ger. **55** E1
Burgdorf *Niedersachsen* Ger. **55** E1

Burgdorf *Niedersachsen* Ger. **55** E1
Burgeo Can. **129** E2
Burgersfort S. Africa **109** D1
Burgh-Haamstede Neth. **54** A2
Burglengenfeld Ger. **55** F3
Burgos Mex. **143** C2
Burgos Spain **60** C1
Burhaniye Turkey **65** C3
Burhanpur India **86** B2
Burhave (Butjadingen) Ger. **55** D1
Burin Can. **129** E2
Buriti Bravo Brazil **151** E3
Buritis Brazil **155** C1
Burketown Austr. **115** C1
Burkina *country* Africa **100** B3
Burley U.S.A. **132** D2
Burlington *CO* U.S.A. **134** C3
Burlington *IA* U.S.A. **135** E2
Burlington *NC* U.S.A. **139** E1
Burlington *VT* U.S.A. **137** F2
Burney U.S.A. **132** B2
Burnie Austr. **115** D4
Burnley U.K. **52** B3
Burns U.S.A. **132** C2
Burns Lake Can. **126** C2
Burqin China **89** F2
Burra Austr. **116** B2
Burrel Albania **64** B2
Burren *reg.* Rep. of Ireland **51** B2
Burrendong Reservoir Austr. **117** D2
Burren Junction Austr. **117** D2
Burriana Spain **61** C2
Burrinjuck Reservoir Austr. **117** D3
Burro, Serranías del *mts* Mex. **142** B3
Bursa Turkey **65** C2
Būr Safājah Egypt **102** B2
Būr Sa'īd Egypt see **Port Said**
Burton, Lac *l.* Can. **128** C1
Burtonport Rep. of Ireland **51** B1
Burton upon Trent U.K. **52** C3
Buru *i.* Indon. **71** C3
Burundi *country* Africa **105** D3
Bururi Burundi **105** C3
Burwash Landing Can. **126** B1
Buryn' Ukr. **45** D1
Burynshyk Kazakh. **88** C2
Bury St Edmunds U.K. **53** D3
Busanga Dem. Rep. Congo **104** C3
Büshehr Iran **93** D3
Bushenyi Uganda **105** D3
Businga Dem. Rep. Congo **104** C2
Busselton Austr. **114** A3
Bustamante Mex. **143** C2
Busuanga Phil. **76** A2
Buta Dem. Rep. Congo **104** C2
Butare Rwanda **105** C3
Butha-Buthe Lesotho **109** C2
Butler U.S.A. **137** E2
Buton *i.* Indon. **73** D2
Butte U.S.A. **132** D1
Butterworth Malaysia **72** B1
Butt of Lewis *hd* U.K. **50** A1
Button Bay Can. **127** F2
Butuan Phil. **76** B3
Buturlinovka Rus. Fed. **43** F3
Butwal Nepal **87** C2
Butzbach Ger. **55** D2
Buulobarde Somalia **103** C4
Buur Gaabo Somalia **103** C5
Buurhabaka Somalia **103** C4
Buxoro Uzbek. **88** D3
Buxtehude Ger. **55** D1
Buy Rus. Fed. **43** F2
Buynaksk Rus. Fed. **41** D4
Büyükmenderes *r.* Turkey **65** C3
Buzai Gumbad Afgh. **86** B1
Buzău Romania **44** C2
Búzi Moz. **107** C1
Buzuluk Rus. Fed. **41** E3
Byala Bulg. **64** C2

Byalynichy Belarus 42 C3
Byarezina r. Belarus 42 D3
Byaroza Belarus 42 B3
Bydgoszcz Pol. 57 D2
Byerazino Belarus 42 C3
Byeshankovichy Belarus 42 C2
Bykhaw Belarus 43 D3
Bylot Island Can. 125 G2
Byrkjelo Norway 48 E1
Byron Bay Austr. 117 E1
Bytantay r. Rus. Fed. 95 K2
Bytom Pol. 57 D2
Bytów Pol. 57 D2

C

Caaguazú, Cordillera de hills Para. 154 A3
Caarapó Brazil 154 A3
Caazapá Para. 154 A3
Cabanatuan Phil. 76 B2
Cabdul Qaadir Somalia 103 C3
Cabeceira Rio Manso Brazil 154 A1
Cabeza del Buey Spain 60 B2
Cabezas Bol. 152 B2
Cabimas Venez. 150 B1
Cabinda Angola 104 B3
Cabinda prov. Angola 104 B3
Cabo Frio Brazil 155 D2
Cabo Frio, Ilha do i. Brazil 155 D2
Cabonga, Réservoir resr Can. 128 C2
Caboolture Austr. 117 E1
Cabo Pantoja Peru 150 B3
Cabora Bassa, Lake resr Moz. 107 C1
Caborca Mex. 142 A1
Cabot Strait Can. 129 D2
Cabral, Serra do mts Brazil 155 D1
Cabrera i. Spain 61 D2
Cabrera, Sierra de la mts Spain 60 B1
Cabri Can. 127 E2
Cabriel r. Spain 61 C2
Caçador Brazil 154 B3
Čačak Serb. and Mont. 64 B2
Caccia, Capo c. Italy 62 A2
Cáceres Brazil 151 D4
Cáceres Spain 60 B2
Cache Creek Can. 126 C2
Cacheu Guinea-Bissau 100 A3
Cachimbo, Serra do hills Brazil 151 D3
Cachoeira Alta Brazil 154 B1
Cachoeiro de Itapemirim Brazil 155 D2
Cacine Guinea-Bissau 100 A3
Cacolo Angola 104 B4
Caçu Brazil 154 B1
Cadenberge Ger. 55 D1
Cadereyta Mex. 143 B2
Cadillac U.S.A. 136 C2
Cádiz Spain 60 B2
Cádiz, Golfo de g. Spain 60 B2
Cadotte Lake Can. 126 D2
Caen France 58 B2
Caernarfon U.K. 52 A3
Caernarfon Bay U.K. 52 A3
Cafayate Arg. 152 B3
Cagli Italy 62 C2
Cagliari Italy 62 A3
Cagliari, Golfo di b. Italy 62 A3
Caha Mountains Rep. of Ireland 51 B3
Cahersiveen Rep. of Ireland 51 A3
Cahir Rep. of Ireland 51 C2
Cahore Point pt Rep. of Ireland 51 C2

Cahors France 58 C3
Cahul Moldova 44 C2
Caia Moz. 107 C1
Caiabis, Serra dos hills Brazil 151 D4
Caianda Angola 106 B1
Caiapó, Serra de mts Brazil 154 B1
Caiapônia Brazil 154 B1
Caicos Islands Turks and Caicos Is 145 C2
Cairngorm Mountains U.K. 50 C2
Cairnryan U.K. 50 B3
Cairns Austr. 115 D1
Cairo Egypt 102 B1
Caistor U.K. 52 C3
Caiundo Angola 106 A1
Cajamarca Peru 150 B3
Cajàzeiras Brazil 151 E3
Čakovec Croatia 63 C1
Cala S. Africa 109 C3
Calabar Nigeria 104 A2
Calabozo Venez. 150 C2
Calafat Romania 44 B3
Calafate Arg. 153 A6
Calahorra Spain 61 C1
Calais France 58 C1
Calais U.S.A. 137 G1
Calama Chile 152 B3
Calamian Group is Phil. 76 A2
Calamocha Spain 61 C1
Calandula Angola 104 B3
Calang Indon. 72 A1
Calanscio Sand Sea des. Libya 101 E1
Calapan Phil. 76 B2
Călăraşi Romania 44 C3
Calatayud Spain 61 C1
Calau Ger. 55 F2
Calayan i. Phil. 76 B1
Calbayog Phil. 76 B2
Calcanhar, Ponta do pt Brazil 151 F3
Calçoene Brazil 151 D2
Calcutta India see Kolkata
Caldas da Rainha Port. 60 B2
Caldas Novas Brazil 154 C1
Caldera Chile 152 A3
Caldwell U.S.A. 132 C2
Caledon r. Lesotho/S. Africa 109 C3
Caledon S. Africa 108 A3
Caleta Olivia Arg. 153 B5
Calf of Man i. Isle of Man 52 A2
Calgary Can. 126 D2
Cali Col. 150 B2
Calicut India 85 B3
Caliente U.S.A. 133 D3
California state U.S.A. 132 C2
California, Gulf of Mex. 133 D4
California Aqueduct canal U.S.A. 133 B3
Calitzdorp S. Africa 108 B3
Calkini Mex. 143 C2
Callabonna, Lake salt flat Austr. 116 C1
Callander U.K. 50 B2
Callao Peru 150 B4
Caltagirone Italy 62 B3
Caltanissetta Italy 62 B3
Caluquembe Angola 106 A1
Caluula Somalia 103 D3
Calvi France 59 D3
Calvià Spain 61 D2
Calvillo Mex. 142 B2
Calvinia S. Africa 108 A3
Calvo, Monte mt. Italy 63 C2
Camacho Mex. 142 B2
Camacupa Angola 106 A1
Camagüey Cuba 144 C2
Camana Peru 150 B4
Camapuã Brazil 154 B1
Camargo Mex. 143 C2
Ca Mau Vietnam 75 B3
Ca Mau, Mui c. Vietnam 75 B3

Cambodia country Asia 75 B2
Camborne U.K. 53 A4
Cambrai France 59 C1
Cambrian Mountains U.K. 53 B3
Cambridge N.Z. 118 C2
Cambridge U.K. 53 D3
Cambridge MA U.S.A. 137 F2
Cambridge MD U.S.A. 137 E3
Cambridge MN U.S.A. 135 E1
Cambridge OH U.S.A. 136 D2
Cambrien, Lac l. Can. 129 D1
Camden Austr. 117 E2
Camden AR U.S.A. 138 B2
Camden ME U.S.A. 137 G2
Cameroon country Africa 104 B2
Cameroun, Mont vol. Cameroon 96
Cametá Brazil 151 E3
Camiguin i. Phil. 76 B2
Camiri Bol. 152 B3
Camocim Brazil 151 E3
Camooweal Austr. 115 C1
Camorta i. India 73 A3
Campana, Isla i. Chile 153 A5
Campbell S. Africa 108 B2
Campbell, Cape N.Z. 118 B3
Campbell Island N.Z. 110
Campbell River Can. 126 C2
Campbellsville U.S.A. 136 C3
Campbellton Can. 137 G1
Campbeltown U.K. 50 B3
Campeche Mex. 143 C3
Campeche, Bahía de g. Mex. 143 C3
Camperdown Austr. 116 C3
Câmpina Romania 44 C2
Campina Grande Brazil 151 F3
Campinas Brazil 154 C2
Campina Verde Brazil 154 C1
Campobasso Italy 62 B2
Campo Belo Brazil 155 C2
Campo Florido Brazil 154 C1
Campo Gallo Arg. 152 B3
Campo Grande Brazil 154 B2
Campo Maior Brazil 151 E3
Campo Maior Port. 60 B2
Campo Mourão Brazil 154 B2
Campos Brazil 155 D2
Campos Altos Brazil 155 C1
Campos do Jordão Brazil 155 C2
Câmpulung Romania 44 C2
Camp Verde U.S.A. 140 B2
Cam Ranh Vietnam 75 B2
Camrose Can. 127 D2
Camsell Portage Can. 127 E2
Can Turkey 65 C2
Canada country N. America 124 D2
Canadian U.S.A. 141 D1
Canadian r. U.S.A. 141 E1
Canadian Shield reg. Can. 121
Çanakkale Turkey 65 C2
Cananea Mex. 142 A1
Cananéia Brazil 154 C2
Canary Islands terr. N. Atlantic Ocean 100 A2
Canastra, Serra da mts Brazil 155 C1
Canatlán Mex. 142 B2
Canaveral, Cape U.S.A. 139 D3
Canavieiras Brazil 155 E1
Canberra Austr. 117 D3
Cancún Mex. 143 D2
Çandarlı Turkey 65 C3
Candelaria Mex. 143 C3
Candle Lake Can. 127 E2
Cangamba Angola 106 A1
Cangas del Narcea Spain 60 B1
Canguçu Brazil 152 C4
Cangzhou China 82 B2
Caniapiscau Can. 129 D1
Caniapiscau r. Can. 129 D1
Caniapiscau, Lac l. Can. 129 C1
Canicattì Italy 62 B3

Canindé Brazil **151** F3
Cañitas de Felipe Pescador Mex. **142** B2
Çankırı Turkey **92** B1
Canna i. U.K. **50** A2
Cannanore India **85** B3
Cannes France **59** D3
Cannock U.K. **53** B3
Cann River Austr. **117** D3
Canoas Brazil **152** C3
Canoe Lake Can. **127** E2
Canoinhas Brazil **154** B3
Canon City U.S.A. **134** B3
Canora Can. **124** F3
Canowindra Austr. **117** D2
Cantábrica, Cordillera mts Spain **60** C1
Cantábrico, Mar sea Spain **60** B1
Canterbury U.K. **53** D4
Canterbury Bight b. N.Z. **118** B3
Canterbury Plains N.Z. **118** B3
Cân Thơ Vietnam **75** B2
Canto do Buriti Brazil **151** E3
Canton China see Guangzhou
Canton MS U.S.A. **138** C2
Canton OH U.S.A. **136** D2
Canyon U.S.A. **141** D1
Canyon Ferry Lake U.S.A. **132** D3
Cao Bǎng Vietnam **74** B1
Capão Bonito Brazil **154** C2
Caparaó, Serra do mts Brazil **155** D2
Cape Barren Island Austr. **115** D4
Cape Borda Austr. **116** B3
Cape Breton Island Can. **129** D2
Cape Coast Ghana **100** B4
Cape Cod Bay U.S.A. **137** F2
Cape Dorset Can. **125** G2
Cape Fear r. U.S.A. **139** E2
Cape Girardeau U.S.A. **135** F3
Capelinha Brazil **155** D1
Capelle aan de IJssel Neth. **54** B2
Capenda-Camulemba Angola **104** B3
Cape Town S. Africa **108** A3
Cape Verde country
   N. Atlantic Ocean **98**
Cape York Peninsula Austr. **115** C1
Cap-Haïtien Haiti **145** C3
Capim r. Brazil **151** E3
Capitol Hill N. Mariana Is **71** D1
Čapljina Bos.-Herz. **63** C2
Capo d'Orlando Italy **62** B3
Capraia, Isola di i. Italy **62** A2
Caprara, Punta pt Italy **62** A2
Capri, Isola di i. Italy **62** B2
Caprivi Strip reg. Namibia **106** B1
Caquetá r. Col. **150** C3
Caracal Romania **44** B3
Caracas Venez. **150** C1
Caracol Brazil **151** E3
Caraguatatuba Brazil **155** C2
Carahue Chile **153** A4
Caraí Brazil **155** D1
Carangola Brazil **155** D2
Caransebeş Romania **44** B2
Caraquet Can. **129** D2
Caratasca, Laguna de lag. Hond. **144** B3
Caratinga Brazil **155** D1
Carauari Brazil **150** C3
Caravaca de la Cruz Spain **61** C2
Caravelas Brazil **155** E1
Carberry Can. **127** F3
Carbó Mex. **142** A2
Carbonara, Capo c. Italy **62** A3
Carbondale CO U.S.A. **134** B3
Carbondale IL U.S.A. **136** C3
Carbonear Can. **129** E2
Carbonita Brazil **155** D1
Carcaixent Spain **61** C2
Carcassonne France **58** C3

Carcross Can. **126** B1
Cárdenas Mex. **143** C3
Cardiff U.K. **53** B4
Cardigan U.K. **53** A3
Cardigan Bay U.K. **53** A3
Cardston Can. **132** D1
Carei Romania **44** B2
Carentan France **58** B2
Carey, Lake salt flat Austr. **114** B2
Cargados Carajos Islands
   Mauritius **97**
Caribbean Sea N. Atlantic Ocean **144** B3
Caribou U.S.A. **137** G1
Caribou Lake Can. **128** B1
Caribou Mountains Can. **126** C2
Carichic Mex. **142** B2
Carignan France **54** B3
Carinda Austr. **117** D2
Cariñena Spain **61** C1
Carleton Place Can. **128** C2
Carletonville S. Africa **109** C2
Carlingford Lough inlet
   Rep. of Ireland/U.K. **51** C1
Carlisle U.K. **52** B2
Carlisle U.S.A. **137** E2
Carlos Chagas Brazil **155** D1
Carlow Rep. of Ireland **51** C2
Carlsbad CA U.S.A. **133** C4
Carlsbad NM U.S.A. **140** D2
Carlyle Can. **124** C1
Carmacks Can. **126** B1
Carman Can. **127** F3
Carmarthen U.K. **53** A4
Carmarthen Bay U.K. **53** A4
Carmaux France **58** C3
Carmelita Guat. **143** C3
Carmen, Isla i. Mex. **142** A2
Carnac France **58** B2
Carnarvon S. Africa **108** B3
Carndonagh Rep. of Ireland **51** C1
Carnegie, Lake salt flat Austr. **114** B2
Carn Eighe mt. U.K. **50** B2
Car Nicobar i. India **75** A3
Carnot C.A.R. **104** B2
Carnot, Cape Austr. **116** B2
Carnsore Point pt Rep. of Ireland **51** C2
Carolina Brazil **151** E3
Caroline Island atoll Kiribati **111**
Caroline Islands N. Pacific Ocean **71** D2
Carpathian Mountains Europe **44** A2
Carpaţii Meridionali mts Romania see
   Transylvanian Alps
Carpentaria, Gulf of Austr. **115** C1
Carpentras France **59** D3
Carrantuohill mt. Rep. of Ireland **51** B3
Carrara Italy **62** B2
Carrickmacross Rep. of Ireland **51** C2
Carrick-on-Shannon Rep. of Ireland **51** B2
Carrick-on-Suir Rep. of Ireland **51** C2
Carrington U.S.A. **135** D1
Carrizo Springs U.S.A. **141** E3
Carrizozo U.S.A. **140** C2
Carroll U.S.A. **135** E2
Carrollton U.S.A. **139** C2
Carrot River Can. **127** E2
Carson City U.S.A. **133** C3
Cartagena Col. **150** B1
Cartagena Spain **61** C2
Cartago Costa Rica **144** B4
Carthage MO U.S.A. **135** E3
Carthage TX U.S.A. **141** E2
Cartwright Can. **129** E1
Caruarú Brazil **151** F3
Casablanca Morocco **100** B1
Casa Branca Brazil **154** C2

Casa de Janos Mex. **142** B1
Casa Grande U.S.A. **140** B2
Casale Monferrato Italy **62** A1
Casarano Italy **63** C2
Cascade U.S.A. **132** C2
Cascade Range mts Can./U.S.A. **132** B2
Cascais Port. **60** B2
Cascavel Brazil **154** B2
Caserta Italy **62** B2
Cashel Rep. of Ireland **51** C2
Casino Austr. **117** E1
Caspe Spain **61** C1
Casper U.S.A. **134** B2
Caspian Lowland Kazakh./Rus. Fed. **88** B2
Caspian Sea l. Asia/Europe **88** B2
Cassel France **54** A2
Cássia Brazil **154** C2
Cassiar Can. **126** C2
Cassiar Mountains Can. **126** B2
Cassilândia Brazil **154** B1
Cassino Italy **62** B2
Cassley r. U.K. **50** B2
Castanhal Brazil **151** E3
Castaño r. Arg. **152** B4
Castaños Mex. **142** B2
Casteljaloux France **58** C3
Castelló de la Plana Spain **61** C2
Castelo Branco Port. **60** B2
Castelvetrano Italy **62** B3
Casterton Austr. **116** C3
Castiglione della Pescaia Italy **62** B2
Castlebar Rep. of Ireland **51** B2
Castlebay U.K. **50** A2
Castleblayney Rep. of Ireland **51** C1
Castlederg U.K. **51** C1
Castle Douglas U.K. **50** C3
Castlegar Can. **126** D3
Castleisland Rep. of Ireland **51** B2
Castlemaine Austr. **116** C3
Castle Mountain Can. **126** B1
Castlerea Rep. of Ireland **51** B2
Castlereagh r. Austr. **117** D2
Castle Rock U.S.A. **134** C3
Castor Can. **127** D2
Castres France **58** C3
Castricum Neth. **54** B1
Castries St Lucia **145** D3
Castro Brazil **154** B2
Castro Chile **153** A5
Castro Verde Port. **60** B2
Castrovillari Italy **63** C3
Catacaos Peru **150** A3
Cataguases Brazil **155** D2
Catalão Brazil **154** C1
Cataluña aut. comm. Spain **61** D1
Catamarca Arg. **152** B3
Catanduanes i. Phil. **76** B2
Catanduva Brazil **154** C2
Catanduvas Brazil **154** B3
Catania Italy **62** C3
Catanzaro Italy **63** C3
Catarman Phil. **76** B2
Catbalogan Phil. **76** B2
Catemaco Mex. **143** C3
Catherine, Mount Egypt see
   Kātrīnā, Jabal
Cat Island Bahamas **145** C2
Cat Lake Can. **128** A1
Catoche, Cabo c. Mex. **143** D2
Catskill Mountains U.S.A. **137** F2
Cauayan Phil. **76** B3
Cauca, Mount Can. **129** D1
Cauca r. Col. **150** B2
Caucaia Brazil **151** F3
Caucasus mts Asia/Europe **93** C1
Caudry France **54** A2
Caulonia Italy **63** C3
Causapscal Can. **129** D2

Cavaillon France **59** D3
avalcante Brazil **151** E4
avan Rep. of Ireland **51** C2
Cavernoso, Serra do mts Brazil **154** B3
axias Brazil **151** E3
axias do Sul Brazil **152** C3
axito Angola **104** B3
ayenne Fr. Guiana **151** D2
Cayman Islands terr. West Indies **144** B3
aynabo Somalia **103** C4
azombo Angola **106** B1
Ceballos Mex. **142** B2
ebu Phil. **76** B2
ebu i. Phil. **76** B2
ecil Plains Austr. **117** E1
ecina Italy **62** B2
edar r. U.S.A. **136** D2
edar City U.S.A. **133** D3
edar Falls U.S.A. **135** E2
edar Lake Can. **127** E2
edar Rapids U.S.A. **135** E2
edros, Isla i. Mex. **142** A2
eduna Austr. **114** C3
eeldheere Somalia **103** C4
eerigaabo Somalia **103** C3
efalù Italy **62** B3
elaya Mex. **143** E2
Celebes i. Indon. **73** D2
Celebes Sea Indon./Phil. **70** C2
elestún Mex. **143** C2
elle Ger. **55** E1
Celtic Sea Rep. of Ireland/U.K. **49** B3
enderawasih, Teluk b. Indon. **71** D3
entral, Cordillera mts Col. **150** B2
entral, Cordillera mts Peru **150** B4
entral, Cordillera mts Phil. **76** B2
Central African Republic country Africa **104** C2
Central Brahui Range mts Pak. **86** A2
Central City U.S.A. **135** D2
entralia IL U.S.A. **136** C3
entralia WA U.S.A. **132** B1
Central Makran Range mts Pak. **86** A2
Central Range mts P.N.G. **71** D3
Central Russian Upland hills Rus. Fed. **43** E3
Central Siberian Plateau Rus. Fed. **95** J2
Cephalonia i. Greece **65** B3
Ceram Sea Indon. see Seram, Laut
Ceres Arg. **152** B3
Ceres S. Africa **108** A3
Céret France **58** C3
Cerezo de Abajo Spain **60** C1
Cerignola Italy **62** C2
Cernavodă Romania **44** C3
Cēsis Latvia **42** C2
Cerralvo Mex. **143** C2
Cerralvo, Isla i. Mex. **142** B2
Cerritos Mex. **143** D2
Cerro Azul Brazil **154** C2
Cerro Azul Mex. **143** C2
Cerro de Pasco Peru **150** B4
Cervione France **59** D3
Cervo Spain **60** B1
Cesena Italy **62** D2
Cesson Austr. **117** C2
České Budějovice Czech Rep. **56** C3
Český Les mts Czech Rep./Ger. **55** F3
Çeşme Turkey **65** C3
Cetraro Italy **63** C3
Cetinje Serb. and Mont. **64** A2
Ceuta N. Africa **60** B2
Cévennes mts France **59** C3
Chābahār Iran **91** D2
Chabyêr Caka salt l. China **87** C1
Chachapoyas Peru **150** B3

Chachersk Belarus **43** D3
Chachoengsao Thai. **75** B2
Chad country Africa **101** D3
Chad, Lake Africa **101** D3
Chadaasan Mongolia **80** C1
Chadan Rus. Fed. **89** G1
Chadibe Botswana **109** C1
Chadron U.S.A. **134** C2
Chaeryŏng N. Korea **77** B2
Chaghcharān Afgh. **86** A1
Chagny France **56** A3
Chagoda Rus. Fed. **43** E2
Chagos Archipelago is B.I.O.T. **66**
Chagyl Turkm. **88** C2
Chaibasa India **87** C2
Chainat Thai. **75** B2
Chaiyaphum Thai. **75** B2
Chajari Arg. **152** C4
Chakonipau, Lac l. Can. **129** D1
Chala Peru **150** B4
Chalap Dalan mts Afgh. **86** A1
Chaleur Bay inlet Can. **129** D2
Chalisgaon India **86** B2
Chalki i. Greece **65** C3
Chalkida Greece **65** B3
Challans France **58** B2
Challenger Deep sea feature N. Pacific Ocean **158** C4
Challis U.S.A. **132** D2
Châlons-en-Champagne France **59** C2
Chalon-sur-Saône France **59** C2
Cham Ger. **55** F3
Chama U.S.A. **140** C1
Chama Zambia **107** C1
Chaman Pak. **86** A1
Chamba India **86** B1
Chambal r. India **86** B2
Chamberlain U.S.A. **135** D2
Chambersburg U.S.A. **137** E3
Chambéry France **59** D2
Chambeshi Zambia **107** C1
Champaign U.S.A. **136** C2
Champlain, Lake Can./U.S.A. **128** C2
Champotón Mex. **143** C2
Chañaral Chile **152** A3
Chandalar r. U.S.A. **124** C2
Chandeleur Islands U.S.A. **138** C3
Chandigarh India **86** B1
Chandler U.S.A. **140** B2
Chandrapur India **87** B3
Chang, Ko i. Thai. **75** B2
Changane r. Moz. **107** C2
Changbai China **77** B1
Changbai Shan mts China/N. Korea **77** B1
Changchun China **77** B1
Changde China **83** B3
Ch'angdo N. Korea **77** B2
Changhua Taiwan **83** C3
Changhung S. Korea **77** B3
Changjin N. Korea **77** B1
Changjin-gang r. N. Korea **77** B1
Changsha China **83** B3
Changsŏng S. Korea **77** B3
Changting China **83** B3
Ch'angwŏn S. Korea **77** B2
Changyuan China **82** B2
Changzhi China **82** B2
Changzhou China **82** B2
Chania Greece **65** B3
Channel Islands English Chan. **53** B5
Channel Islands U.S.A. **133** C4
Channel-Port-aux-Basques Can. **129** E2
Chanthaburi Thai. **75** B2
Chantilly France **58** C2

Chanute U.S.A. **135** D3
Chany, Ozero salt l. Rus. Fed. **89** E1
Chaouèn Morocco **60** B2
Chaoyang Guangdong China **83** B3
Chaoyang Liaoning China **82** C1
Chaozhou China **83** B3
Chapala, Laguna de l. Mex. **142** B2
Chapayev Kazakh. **88** C1
Chapecó Brazil **154** B3
Chapel Hill U.S.A. **139** E1
Chapleau Can. **128** B2
Chaplygin Rus. Fed. **43** E3
Chaplynka Ukr. **45** D2
Charcas Mex. **143** C2
Chard U.K. **53** B4
Chardzhev Turkm. see Turkmenabat
Charente r. France **58** B2
Chārīkār Afgh. **86** A1
Charkayuvom Rus. Fed. **40** E2
Charleroi Belgium **54** B2
Charles, Cape U.S.A. **137** E3
Charles City U.S.A. **135** E2
Charleston IL U.S.A. **136** C3
Charleston SC U.S.A. **139** E2
Charleston WV U.S.A. **136** D3
Charleston Peak U.S.A. **133** C3
Charleville Austr. **115** D2
Charleville-Mézières France **59** C2
Charlotte U.S.A. **139** D1
Charlotte Harbor b. U.S.A. **139** D3
Charlottesville U.S.A. **137** E3
Charlottetown Can. **129** D2
Charlton Austr. **116** C3
Charlton Island Can. **128** C1
Charozero Rus. Fed. **43** E1
Charters Towers Austr. **115** D2
Chartres France **58** C2
Chase Can. **126** D2
Chashniki Belarus **42** C3
Chasŏng N. Korea **77** B1
Chassiron, Pointe de pt France **58** B2
Châteaubriant France **58** B2
Château-du-Loir France **58** C2
Châteaudun France **58** C2
Châteaulin France **58** B2
Châteauneuf-les-Martigues France **59** D3
Châteauneuf-sur-Loire France **58** C2
Château-Thierry France **59** C2
Chateh Can. **126** D2
Châtelet Belgium **54** B2
Châtellerault France **58** C2
Chatham Can. **136** D2
Chatham Islands N.Z. **111**
Châtillon-sur-Seine France **59** C2
Chattahoochee r. U.S.A. **139** D2
Chattanooga U.S.A. **139** C1
Châu Đốc Vietnam **75** B2
Chauk Myanmar **74** A1
Chaumont France **59** D2
Chauny France **59** C2
Chaves Brazil **151** E2
Chaves Port. **60** B1
Chavigny, Lac l. Can. **128** C1
Chavusy Belarus **43** D3
Chayevo Rus. Fed. **43** E2
Chaykovskiy Rus. Fed. **40** E3
Cheb Czech Rep. **56** C2
Cheboksary Rus. Fed. **41** D3
Cheboygan U.S.A. **136** D1
Chech'ŏn S. Korea **77** B2
Chegga Maur. **100** B2
Chehalis U.S.A. **132** B1
Cheju S. Korea **77** B3
Cheju-do i. S. Korea **77** B3
Cheju-haehyŏp sea chan. S. Korea **77** B3
Chekhov Rus. Fed. **43** E2
Chelan, Lake U.S.A. **132** B1
Cheleken Turkm. **93** D2

Chelghoum el Aïd Alg. 61 E2
Chélif, Oued r. Alg. 61 D2
Chełm Pol. 57 E2
Chełmno Pol. 57 D2
Chelmsford U.K. 53 B4
Cheltenham U.K. 53 B4
Chelyabinsk Rus. Fed. 41 F3
Chemnitz Ger. 55 F2
Chenachane Alg. 100 B2
Chengde China 82 B1
Chengdu China 82 A2
Chengmai China 83 B4
Chengxian China 82 A2
Chennai India 85 C3
Chenzhou China 83 B3
Chepstow U.K. 53 B4
Cherbourg France 58 B2
Cheremisinovo Rus. Fed. 43 E3
Cheremkhovo Rus. Fed. 80 C1
Cherepovets Rus. Fed. 42 C2
Cherkasy Ukr. 45 D2
Cherkessk Rus. Fed. 41 D4
Chernihiv Ukr. 45 D1
Cherninivka Ukr. 45 E2
Chernivtsi Ukr. 44 C2
Chernyakhiv Ukr. 44 C1
Chernyakhovsk Rus. Fed. 42 B3
Chernyanka Rus. Fed. 43 E3
Chernyshevskiy Rus. Fed. 95 J2
Chernyshkovskiy Rus. Fed. 45 F2
Cherokee U.S.A. 135 D2
Cherskogo, Khrebet mts Rus. Fed. 95 L2
Chertkovo Rus. Fed. 45 F2
Chervonohrad Ukr. 44 B1
Chervyen' Belarus 42 C3
Cherykaw Belarus 43 D3
Chesapeake Bay U.S.A. 137 E3
Cheshskaya Guba b. Rus. Fed. 40 D2
Chester U.K. 52 B3
Chester IL U.S.A. 136 C3
Chester SC U.S.A. 139 D2
Chesterfield U.K. 52 C3
Chesterfield, Îles is New Caledonia 115 E1
Chesterfield Inlet Can. 127 F1
Chesterfield Inlet inlet Can. 127 F1
Chesuncook Lake U.S.A. 137 G1
Chéticamp Can. 129 D2
Chetumal Mex. 143 D3
Chetwynd Can. 126 C2
Cheviot Hills U.K. 52 C2
Cheyenne U.S.A. 134 C2
Cheyenne r. U.S.A. 134 C2
Cheyenne Wells U.S.A. 134 C3
Chhapra India 87 C2
Chhatarpur India 87 B2
Chiai Taiwan 83 C3
Chiang Dao Thai. 74 A2
Chiang Mai Thai. 74 A2
Chiang Rai Thai. 74 A2
Chiavenno Italy 62 A1
Chibi China 83 B3
Chiboma Moz. 107 C2
Chibougamau Can. 128 C2
Chibuto Moz. 109 D1
Chicago U.S.A. 136 C2
Chichagof Island U.S.A. 126 B2
Chichester U.K. 53 C4
Chichester Range mts Austr. 114 A2
Chickasha U.S.A. 141 E1
Chiclayo Peru 150 B2
Chico r. Arg. 153 B5
Chico U.S.A. 133 B3
Chicoutimi Can. 129 C2
Chidley, Cape Can. 121
Chieti Italy 62 B2
Chietla Mex. 143 C3
Chifeng China 82 B1
Chifre, Serra do mts Brazil 155 D1

Chiganak Kazakh. 89 E2
Chignahuapán Mex. 143 C3
Chigubo Moz. 107 C2
Chigu Co l. China 74 A1
Chihuahua Mex. 142 B2
Chikhachevo Rus. Fed. 42 C2
Chikuma-gawa r. Japan 79 C3
Chilanko r. Can. 126 C2
Chilas Jammu and Kashmir 86 B1
Childress U.S.A. 141 D2
Chile country S. America 152 A4
Chilecito Arg. 152 B3
Chilika Lake India 87 C3
Chililabombwe Zambia 106 B1
Chilko r. Can. 126 C2
Chilko Lake Can. 126 C2
Chillán Chile 153 A4
Chillicothe MO U.S.A. 135 E3
Chillicothe OH U.S.A. 136 D3
Chilliwack Can. 126 C3
Chiloé, Isla de i. Chile 153 A5
Chilpancingo Mex. 143 C3
Chiltern Austr. 117 D3
Chilung Taiwan 83 C3
Chimala Tanz. 105 D3
Chimbas Arg. 152 B4
Chimborazo mt. Ecuador 150 B3
Chimbote Peru 150 B3
Chimboy Uzbek. 88 C2
Chimoio Moz. 107 C1
Chimtargha, Qullai mt. Tajik. 89 D3
China country Asia 80 B2
China Mex. 143 C2
Chincha Alta Peru 150 B4
Chinchaga r. Can. 126 C2
Chinchorro, Banco sea feature Mex. 143 D3
Chinde Moz. 107 C1
Chindo S. Korea 77 B3
Chin-do i. S. Korea 77 B3
Chindu China 80 C2
Chindwin r. Myanmar 74 A1
Chingwha N. Korea 77 B2
Chingola Zambia 106 B1
Chinguar Angola 106 A1
Chinhae S. Korea 77 B2
Chinhoyi Zimbabwe 107 C1
Chiniot Pak. 86 B1
Chinipas Mex. 142 B2
Chinju S. Korea 77 B2
Chinko r. C.A.R. 104 C2
Chinle U.S.A. 140 C1
Chinmen Taiwan 83 B3
Chino Japan 79 C3
Chinon France 58 C2
Chino Valley U.S.A. 140 B2
Chinsali Zambia 105 D4
Chioggia Italy 62 B1
Chios Greece 65 C3
Chios i. Greece 65 C3
Chipata Zambia 107 C1
Chipindo Angola 106 A1
Chipinge Zimbabwe 107 C2
Chiplun India 85 B3
Chippenham U.K. 53 B4
Chipping Norton U.K. 53 C4
Chir r. Rus. Fed. 45 F2
Chirchiq Uzbek. 89 D2
Chiredzi Zimbabwe 107 C2
Chiricahua Peak U.S.A. 140 C2
Chiriquí, Golfo de b. Panama 144 B4
Chiri-san mt. S. Korea 77 B2
Chirripo mt. Costa Rica 144 B4
Chirundu Zimbabwe 107 B1
Chisasibi Can. 128 C1
Chisholm U.S.A. 135 E1
Chişinău Moldova 44 C2
Chistopol' Rus. Fed. 43 E3
Chita Rus. Fed. 81 D1
Chitado Angola 106 A1

Chitambo Zambia 107 C1
Chitato Angola 104 C3
Chitipa Malawi 105 D3
Chitradurga India 85 B3
Chitral Pak. 86 B1
Chitré Panama 144 B4
Chittagong Bangl. 87 D2
Chittaurgarh India 86 B2
Chitungwiza Zimbabwe 107 C1
Chiume Angola 106 B1
Chivhu Zimbabwe 107 C1
Chizhou China 83 B2
Chkalovsk Rus. Fed. 43 F2
Choele Choel Arg. 153 B4
Choiseul i. Solomon Is 110
Choix Mex. 142 B2
Chojnice Pol. 57 D2
Ch'ok'ē Mountains Eth. 103 B3
Chokurdakh Rus. Fed. 95 L2
Chókwé Moz. 107 C2
Cholet France 58 B2
Choma Zambia 106 B1
Chomutov Czech Rep. 56 C2
Chona r. Rus. Fed. 95 J2
Ch'ōnan S. Korea 77 B2
Chone Ecuador 150 A3
Ch'ōngjin N. Korea 77 B1
Chōngju N. Korea 77 B2
Chŏngp'yŏng N. Korea 77 B2
Chongqing China 83 A3
Chongqing mun. China 82 A2
Chŏngŭp S. Korea 77 B3
Chongzuo China 83 A3
Chōnju S. Korea 77 B2
Chonos, Archipiélago de los is Chile 153 A5
Chopimzinho Brazil 154 B3
Chorley U.K. 52 B3
Chornomors'ke Ukr. 45 D2
Chortkiv Ukr. 44 C2
Ch'ōrwōn S. Korea 77 B2
Ch'osan N. Korea 77 B1
Chōshi Japan 79 D3
Choszczno Pol. 57 D2
Choûm Maur. 100 A2
Choybalsan Mongolia 81 D1
Choyr Mongolia 81 D1
Christchurch N.Z. 118 B3
Christchurch U.K. 53 C4
Christian, Cape Can. 125 H2
Christiana S. Africa 109 C2
Christina, Mount N.Z. 118 A3
Christmas Island terr. Indian Ocean 70 B3
Chrysi i. Greece 65 C4
Chubut r. Arg. 153 B5
Chudniv Ukr. 44 C1
Chudovo Rus. Fed. 43 D2
Chugach Mountains U.S.A. 124 C2
Chūgoku-sanchi mts Japan 79 B4
Chuguyevka Rus. Fed. 78 B2
Chuhuyiv Ukr. 45 E2
Chukchi Sea Rus. Fed./U.S.A. 95 O2
Chukhloma Rus. Fed. 43 F2
Chukotskiy Poluostrov pen. Rus. Fed. 95 O2
Chula Vista U.S.A. 133 C4
Chulym Rus. Fed. 94 H3
Chumbicha Arg. 152 B3
Chumikan Rus. Fed. 95 L3
Chumphon Thai. 75 A2
Ch'unch'ōn S. Korea 77 B2
Chungking China see Chongqing
Chunya r. Rus. Fed. 95 I2
Chuquibamba Peru 150 B4
Chuquicamata Chile 152 B3
Chur Switz. 60 C2
Churachandpur India 74 A1
Churchill Can. 127 F2
Churchill r. Man. Can. 127 F2
Churchill r. Nfld. and Lab. Can. 129 D1

Churchill, Cape Can. **127** F2
Churchill Falls Can. **129** D1
Churchill Lake Can. **127** E2
Churu India **86** B2
Chute-des-Passes Can. **129** C2
Chuuk *i.* Micronesia **110**
Chuxiong China **74** B1
Ciadîr-Lunga Moldova **44** C2
Ciamis Indon. **72** B2
Cianjur Indon. **72** B2
Cianorte Brazil **154** B2
Ciechanów Pol. **57** E2
Ciego de Ávila Cuba **144** C2
Cienfuegos Cuba **144** B2
Cieza Spain **61** C2
Cigüela *r.* Spain **60** C2
Cihanbeyli Turkey **92** B1
Cihuatlán Mex. **142** B3
Cijara, Embalse de *resr* Spain **60** C2
Cilacap Indon. **72** B2
Cimarron *r.* U.S.A. **141** E1
Cimişlia Moldova **44** C2
Cimone, Monte *mt.* Italy **62** B2
Cincinnati U.S.A. **136** D3
Cine Turkey **65** C3
Ciney Belgium **54** B2
Cintalapa Mex. **143** C3
Circle *AK* U.S.A. **124** C3
Circle *MT* U.S.A. **134** B1
Cirebon Indon. **72** B2
Cirencester U.K. **53** C4
Cirò Marina Italy **63** C3
Citluk Bos.-Herz. **63** C2
Citrusdal S. Africa **108** A3
Città di Castello Italy **59** E3
Ciudad Acuña Mex. **143** B2
Ciudad Altamirano Mex. **143** B3
Ciudad Bolívar Venez. **150** D2
Ciudad Camargo Mex. **142** B2
Ciudad Constitución Mex. **142** A2
Ciudad del Carmen Mex. **143** C3
Ciudad Delicias Mex. **142** B2
Ciudad de Valles Mex. **143** C2
Ciudad Guayana Venez. **150** D2
Ciudad Guerrero Mex. **140** C2
Ciudad Guzmán Mex. **142** B3
Ciudad Hidalgo Mex. **143** B3
Ciudad Ixtepec Mex. **143** C3
Ciudad Juárez Mex. **142** B1
Ciudad Mante Mex. **143** C2
Ciudad Mier Mex. **143** C2
Ciudad Obregón Mex. **142** B2
Ciudad Real Spain **60** C2
Ciudad Río Bravo Mex. **143** C2
Ciudad Rodrigo Spain **60** B1
Ciudad Victoria Mex. **143** C2
Ciutadella de Menorca Spain **61** D1
Cîvan Dağ *mt.* Turkey **65** C3
Cividale del Friuli Italy **62** B1
Civitanova Marche Italy **62** B2
Civitavecchia Italy **62** B2
Civray France **58** C2
Çivril Turkey **65** C3
Cixi China **83** C2
Clacton-on-Sea U.K. **53** D4
Claire, Lake Can. **127** D2
Clamecy France **59** C2
Clanwilliam S. Africa **108** A3
Clare Austr. **116** B2
Clare Island Rep. of Ireland **51** A2
Claremont U.S.A. **137** E2
Claremorris Rep. of Ireland **51** B2
Clarence N.Z. **118** B3
Clarenville Can. **129** E2
Claresholm Can. **126** D2
Clarinda U.S.A. **135** D2
Clarión, Isla *i.* Mex. **142** A3
Clarkebury S. Africa **109** C3
Clark Fork *r.* U.S.A. **132** C1

Clark Hill Reservoir U.S.A. **139** D2
Clarksburg U.S.A. **137** D3
Clarksdale U.S.A. **138** B2
Clarksville *AR* U.S.A. **138** B1
Clarksville *TN* U.S.A. **138** C1
Claro *r.* Brazil **154** B1
Clayton U.S.A. **141** D1
Clear, Cape Rep. of Ireland **51** B3
Cleare, Cape U.S.A. **124** C3
Clear Lake *i.* U.S.A. **133** B3
Clearwater *r.* Can. **127** D2
Clearwater U.S.A. **139** D3
Clearwater *r.* U.S.A. **132** C1
Cleburne U.S.A. **141** E2
Clermont Austr. **115** D2
Clermont-en-Argonne France **54** B3
Clermont-Ferrand France **58** C2
Cleve Austr. **116** B2
Cleveland *MS* U.S.A. **138** B2
Cleveland *OH* U.S.A. **136** D2
Cleveland *TN* U.S.A. **139** D1
Cleveland, Mount U.S.A. **132** D1
Clewiston U.S.A. **139** D3
Clifden Rep. of Ireland **51** A2
Clifton Austr. **117** E1
Clifton U.S.A. **140** C2
Clinton *IA* U.S.A. **135** E2
Clinton *MO* U.S.A. **135** E3
Clinton *OK* U.S.A. **141** E1
Clisham *h.* U.K. **50** A2
Clitheroe U.K. **52** B3
Clonakilty Rep. of Ireland **51** B3
Cloncurry Austr. **115** D2
Clones Rep. of Ireland **51** C1
Clonmel Rep. of Ireland **51** C2
Cloppenburg Ger. **54** D1
Cloud Peak U.S.A. **134** B2
Clovis U.S.A. **141** D2
Cluff Lake Mine Can. **127** E2
Cluj-Napoca Romania **44** B2
Cluny Austr. **115** C2
Cluses France **59** D2
Clutha *r.* N.Z. **118** A4
Clyde *r.* U.K. **50** B3
Clyde, Firth of *est.* U.K. **50** B3
Clydebank U.K. **50** B3
Clyde River Can. **125** H2
Coalcomán Mex. **142** B3
Coaldale U.S.A. **133** C3
Coal River Can. **126** C2
Coari Brazil **150** C2
Coari *r.* Brazil **150** C2
Coastal Plain U.S.A. **136** B2
Coast Mountains Can. **126** C2
Coast Ranges U.S.A. **132** B2
Coatbridge U.K. **50** B3
Coats Island Can. **127** G1
Coats Land *reg.* Antarctica **119** A2
Coatzacoalcos Mex. **143** C3
Cobán Guat. **144** A3
Cobar Austr. **117** D2
Cóbh Rep. of Ireland **51** B3
Cobija Bol. **152** B2
Cobourg Can. **137** E2
Cobourg Peninsula Austr. **114** C1
Cobram Austr. **117** D3
Coburg Ger. **55** E2
Cochabamba Bol. **152** B2
Cochem Ger. **54** C2
Cochin India **85** B4
Cochrane Can. **128** B2
Cochrane Chile **153** A5
Cockburn Austr. **116** C2
Cockburn Town Turks and Caicos Is
    see **Grand Turk**
Cockermouth U.K. **52** B2
Cockscomb *mt.* S. Africa **108** B3

Coco *r.* Hond./Nic. **144** B3
Cocos Islands *terr.* Indian Ocean **70** A3
Coculla Mex. **142** B2
Cocuy, Sierra Nevada del *mt.* Col.
    150 B2
Cod, Cape U.S.A. **137** F2
Codigoro Italy **62** B2
Cod Island Can. **129** D1
Codó Brazil **151** E3
Cody U.S.A. **134** B2
Coen Austr. **115** D1
Coesfeld Ger. **54** C2
Coeur d'Alene U.S.A. **132** C1
Coffee Bay S. Africa **109** C3
Coffeyville U.S.A. **135** D3
Coffs Harbour Austr. **117** E2
Cognac France **58** B2
Cogo Equat. Guinea **104** A2
Cohuna Austr. **116** C3
Coiba, Isla de *i.* Panama **144** B4
Coihaique Chile **153** A5
Coimbatore India **85** B3
Coimbra Port. **60** B1
Colac Austr. **116** C3
Colatina Brazil **155** D1
Colby U.S.A. **134** C3
Colchester U.K. **53** D4
Cold Lake Can. **127** D2
Coldstream U.K. **50** C3
Coleman U.S.A. **141** E2
Coleraine Austr. **116** C3
Coleraine U.K. **51** C1
Coles, Punta de *pt* Peru **146**
Colesberg S. Africa **109** C3
Colima Mex. **142** B3
Colima, Nevado de *vol.* Mex. **142** B3
Coll *i.* U.K. **50** A2
Collarenebri Austr. **117** D1
Collier Bay Austr. **114** B1
Collingwood N.Z. **118** B3
Collo Alg. **61** E2
Collooney Rep. of Ireland **51** B1
Colmar France **59** D2
Cologne Ger. **54** C2
Colômbia Brazil **154** C2
Colombia *country* S. America **150** B2
Colombo Sri Lanka **85** B4
Colomiers France **58** C3
Colón Arg. **152** C4
Colón Panama **144** C4
Colonna, Capo *c.* Italy **63** C3
Colonsay *i.* U.K. **50** A2
Colorado *r.* Arg. **153** B4
Colorado *r.* Mex./U.S.A. **140** A2
Colorado *r.* U.S.A **141** E3
Colorado *state* U.S.A. **134** B3
Colorado Plateau U.S.A. **134** B3
Colorado Springs U.S.A. **134** C3
Colotlán Mex. **142** B2
Cölpin Ger. **55** F1
Colstrip U.S.A. **134** B1
Columbia *MO* U.S.A. **135** E3
Columbia *SC* U.S.A. **139** D2
Columbia *TN* U.S.A. **138** C1
Columbia *r.* U.S.A. **132** B1
Columbia, Mount Can. **126** D2
Columbia Falls U.S.A. **132** D1
Columbia Mountains Can. **126** C2
Columbia Plateau U.S.A. **132** C1
Columbus *GA* U.S.A. **139** D2
Columbus *IN* U.S.A. **136** C3
Columbus *MS* U.S.A. **138** C2
Columbus *NE* U.S.A. **135** D2
Columbus *NM* U.S.A. **140** C2
Columbus *OH* U.S.A. **136** D3
Colville U.S.A. **132** C1
Colville *r.* U.S.A. **124** C2
Colville Lake Can. **124** C2
Colwyn Bay U.K. **52** B3
Comacchio Italy **62** B2

Comalcalco Mex. **143** C3
Comănești Romania **44** C2
Combles France **54** A2
Comencho, Lac l. Can. **128** C1
Comeragh Mountains Rep. of Ireland **51** C2
Comilla Bangl. **87** D2
Comines Belgium **54** A2
Comino, Capo c. Italy **62** A2
Comitán de Domínguez Mex. **143** C3
Commentry France **58** C2
Commerce U.S.A. **141** E2
Como Italy **62** A1
Como, Lake Italy **62** A1
Comodoro Rivadavia Arg. **153** B5
Comorin, Cape India **67**
Comoro Islands Africa **97**
Comoros country Africa **107** D1
Compiègne France **58** C2
Compostela Mex. **142** B2
Comrat Moldova **44** C2
Conakry Guinea **100** A4
Conceição da Barra Brazil **155** E1
Conceição do Araguaia Brazil **151** E3
Conceição do Mato Dentro Brazil **155** D1
Concepción Arg. **152** B3
Concepción Chile **153** A4
Concepción Mex. **142** B2
Conception, Point pt U.S.A. **133** B4
Conchas Brazil **154** C2
Conchas Lake U.S.A. **140** D1
Conchos r. Nuevo León/Tamaulipas Mex. **143** C2
Conchos r. Mex. **142** B2
Concord CA U.S.A. **133** B3
Concord NH U.S.A. **137** F2
Concordia Arg. **152** C4
Concordia S. Africa **108** A3
Concordia U.S.A. **135** D3
Condobolin Austr. **117** D2
Condom France **58** C3
Condon U.S.A. **132** B1
Conegliano Italy **62** D1
Conflict Group is P.N.G. **115** E1
Confolens France **58** C2
Congdü China **87** C2
Congo country Africa **104** B3
Congo r. Congo/Dem. Rep. Congo **104** C3
Congo, Democratic Republic of country Africa **104** C3
Congo Basin Dem. Rep. Congo **97**
Conklin Can. **127** D2
Conn, Lough l. Rep. of Ireland **51** B1
Connaught reg. Rep. of Ireland **51** B2
Connecticut r. U.S.A. **137** F2
Connecticut state U.S.A. **137** F2
Connemara reg. Rep. of Ireland **51** B2
Conrad U.S.A. **132** D1
Conroe U.S.A. **141** E2
Conselheiro Lafaiete Brazil **155** D2
Conselheiro Pena Brazil **155** D1
Consett U.K. **52** C2
Côn Sơn i. Vietnam **75** B3
Constanţa Romania **44** C3
Constantina Spain **60** B2
Constantine Alg. **101** C1
Contact U.S.A. **132** D2
Contamana Peru **150** B3
Contreras, Isla i. Chile **153** A6
Contwoyto Lake Can. **127** D1
Conway AR U.S.A. **138** B1
Conway NH U.S.A. **137** F2
Coober Pedy Austr. **116** A1
Cook, Mount N.Z. **118** B3
Cookeville U.S.A. **139** C1
Cook Inlet sea chan. U.S.A. **124** B2
Cook Islands S. Pacific Ocean **111**

Cook Islands terr. S. Pacific Ocean **113**
Cookstown U.K. **51** C1
Cook Strait N.Z. **118** B3
Cooktown Austr. **115** D1
Coolabah Austr. **117** D2
Coolamon Austr. **117** D2
Coolgardie Austr. **117** E1
Coolgardie Austr. **114** C3
Cooma Austr. **117** D3
Coombah Austr. **116** C2
Coonabarabran Austr. **117** D2
Coonalpyn Austr. **116** B3
Coonamble Austr. **117** D2
Cooper Creek watercourse Austr. **116** B1
Coos Bay U.S.A. **132** B2
Cootamundra Austr. **117** D2
Copainalá Mex. **143** C3
Copala Mex. **143** C3
Copiapó Chile **152** A3
Copper Harbor U.S.A. **136** C1
Coppermine r. Can. see Kugluktuk
Coppermine r. Can. **124** E2
Copperton S. Africa **108** B2
Coquimbo Chile **153** A3
Corabia Romania **44** B3
Coração de Jesus Brazil **155** D1
Coracora Peru **150** B4
Coraki Austr. **117** E1
Coral Bay Austr. **114** A2
Coral Harbour Can. **125** G2
Coral Sea S. Pacific Ocean **115** E1
Coral Sea Islands Territory terr. Austr. **112**
Corangamite, Lake Austr. **116** C3
Corby U.K. **53** C3
Corcovado, Golfo de sea chan. Chile **153** A5
Cordele U.S.A. **139** D2
Cordilleras Range mts Phil. **76** B3
Córdoba Arg. **152** B4
Córdoba Mex. **143** C3
Córdoba Spain **60** C2
Córdoba, Sierras de mts Arg. **152** B4
Cordova U.S.A. **126** A1
Corfu i. Greece **65** B3
Coria Spain **60** B2
Corinth Greece **65** B3
Corinth U.S.A. **138** C2
Corinth, Gulf of sea chan. Greece **65** B3
Corinto Brazil **155** D1
Cork Rep. of Ireland **51** B3
Corlu Turkey **65** C2
Cornélio Procópio Brazil **154** B2
Corner Brook Can. **129** E2
Corner Inlet b. Austr. **117** D3
Corning CA U.S.A. **132** B3
Corning NY U.S.A. **137** E2
Corno, Monte mt. Italy **62** B2
Cornwall Can. **128** C2
Cornwallis Island Can. **124** F1
Coro Venez. **150** C1
Coromandel Brazil **154** C1
Coromandel Peninsula N.Z. **118** C2
Coronation Can. **127** D2
Coronation Gulf Can. **124** E2
Coronel Oviedo Para. **152** C3
Coronel Suárez Arg. **153** B4
Corozal Belize **143** D2
Corpus Christi U.S.A. **141** E3
Corque Bol. **152** B2
Corrente Brazil **151** E4
Correntes Brazil **154** B1
Correntina Brazil **151** E4

Corrib, Lough l. Rep. of Ireland **51** B2
Corrientes Arg. **152** C3
Corrientes, Cabo c. Arg. **146**
Corrientes, Cabo c. Mex. **142** B2
Corryong Austr. **117** D3
Corse i. France see Corsica
Corse, Cap c. France **59** D3
Corsica i. France **59** D3
Corsicana U.S.A. **141** E2
Corte France **59** D3
Cortegana Spain **60** B2
Cortez U.S.A. **134** B3
Cortina d'Ampezzo Italy **62** B1
Cortland U.S.A. **137** E2
Cortona Italy **62** C3
Coruche Port. **60** B2
Çoruh r. Turkey **92** B1
Çoruh Turkey see Artvin
Çorum Turkey **92** B1
Corumbá Brazil **152** C1
Corumbá r. Brazil **154** C1
Corvallis U.S.A. **132** B2
Corwen U.K. **52** B3
Cosalá Mex. **142** B2
Cosamaloapan Mex. **143** C3
Cosenza Italy **63** C3
Cosne-Cours-sur-Loire France **58** C2
Costa Blanca coastal area Spain **61** C2
Costa Brava coastal area Spain **61** D1
Costa del Sol coastal area Spain **60** B2
Costa de Mosquitos coastal area Nic. **144** B3
Costa Rica Brazil **154** B1
Costa Rica country Central America **144** B3
Costa Rica Mex. **142** B2
Costeşti Romania **44** B3
Cotabato Phil. **76** B3
Côte d'Ivoire country Africa **100** B4
Cotopaxi, Volcán vol. Ecuador **150** B3
Cotswold Hills U.K. **53** B4
Cottage Grove U.S.A. **132** B2
Cottbus Ger. **56** C2
Coubre, Pointe de la pt France **58** B2
Coüedic, Cape de Austr. **116** B3
Council Bluffs U.S.A. **135** D2
Courland Lagoon b. Lith./Rus. Fed. **42** B2
Courtenay Can. **126** B3
Coutances France **58** B2
Coutras France **58** B2
Couvin Belgium **54** B2
Coventry U.K. **53** C3
Covington U.S.A. **136** D3
Cowan, Lake salt flat Austr. **114** B3
Cowdenbeath U.K. **50** C2
Cowes Austr. **117** D3
Cowlitz r. U.S.A. **132** B1
Cowra Austr. **117** D2
Coxim Brazil **154** B1
Cox's Bazar Bangl. **87** D2
Coyuca de Benítez Mex. **143** C3
Cozumel Mex. **143** D2
Cozumel, Isla de i. Mex. **143** D2
Cradock S. Africa **108** C3
Craig U.S.A. **134** B2
Crailsheim Ger. **55** E3
Craiova Romania **44** B3
Cranberry Portage Can. **127** E2
Cranbourne Austr. **117** D3
Cranbrook Can. **126** D3
Crateús Brazil **151** E3
Crato Brazil **151** F3
Crawford U.S.A. **134** C2
Crawfordsville U.S.A. **136** C2
Crawley U.K. **53** C4
Crazy Mountains U.S.A. **132** D1
Cree r. Can. **127** E2
Creel Mex. **142** B2

Cree Lake Can. **127** E2
Creil Neth. **54** B1
Crema Italy **59** D2
Cremona Italy **62** B1
Crépy-en-Valois France **54** A3
Cres i. Croatia **62** B2
Crescent City U.S.A. **132** B2
Creston Can. **126** D3
Creston U.S.A. **135** E2
Crestview U.S.A. **138** C2
Crete i. Greece **65** B3
Creus, Cap de c. Spain **61** D1
Creutzwald France **54** C3
Crewe U.K. **52** B1
Criciúma Brazil **152** D3
Crianlarich U.K. **50** B2
Crieff U.K. **50** C2
Crikvenica Croatia **62** B1
Crimea pen. Ukr. **45** D2
Crimmitschau Ger. **55** F2
Cristalina Brazil **154** C1
Crivitz Ger. **55** E1
Crna Gora aut. rep. Serb. and Mont.
  64 A2
Črnomelj Slovenia **62** C1
Croagh Patrick h. Rep. of Ireland
  51 B2
Croatia country Europe **63** C1
Crocker, Banjaran mts Malaysia **73** C1
Crockett U.S.A. **141** E2
Croker Island Austr. **71** C3
Cromer U.K. **52** D3
Cromwell N.Z. **118** A4
Crookston U.S.A. **135** D1
Crookwell Austr. **117** D3
Crosby U.S.A. **134** C1
Cross City U.S.A. **139** D3
Crossett U.S.A. **138** B2
Cross Fell h. U.K. **52** B2
Cross Lake Can. **127** F2
Crossville U.S.A. **139** C1
Crotone Italy **63** C3
Crowborough U.K. **53** D4
Crowley U.S.A. **138** B2
Crowsnest Pass Can. **126** D3
Cruz, Cabo c. Cuba **145** C3
Cruz Alta Brazil **152** C3
Cruzeiro Brazil **150** D3
Cruzeiro do Sul Brazil **150** B3
Crystal Brook Austr. **116** B2
Crystal City U.S.A. **141** D3
Crystal Falls U.S.A. **136** C1
Csongrád Hungary **57** E3
Cuando r. Angola/Zambia **106** B1
Cuangar Angola **106** A1
Cuango r. Angola/Dem. Rep. Congo
  104 B3
Cuanza r. Angola **104** A3
Cuatro Ciénegas Mex. **143** D3
Cuauhtémoc Mex. **142** B2
Cuautla Mex. **143** C3
Cuba country West Indies **144** B2
Cubal Angola **106** A1
Cubango r. Angola/Namibia **106** B1
Cúcuta Col. **150** B2
Cuddalore India **85** B3
Cuddapah India **85** B3
Cuéllar Spain **60** C1
Cuemba Angola **106** A1
Cuenca Ecuador **150** B3
Cuenca Spain **61** C1
Cuenca, Serranía de mts Spain **61** C1
Cuero U.S.A. **141** E3
Cuiabá Brazil **154** A1
Cuiabá r. Brazil **151** D4
Cuillin Sound sea chan. U.K. **50** A2
Cuilo Angola **104** B3
Cuito r. Angola **106** B1

Cuito Cuanavale Angola **106** A1
Cukai Malaysia **72** B1
Culcairn Austr. **117** D3
Culgoa r. Austr. **117** D1
Culiacán Mex. **142** B2
Culion i. Phil. **76** A2
Cullera Spain **61** C2
Cullman U.S.A. **138** C2
Cullybackey U.K. **51** C1
Culuene r. Brazil **151** D4
Cumaná Venez. **150** C1
Cumberland U.S.A. **137** E3
Cumberland r. U.S.A. **136** C3
Cumberland Lake Can. **127** E2
Cumberland Peninsula Can. **125** H2
Cumberland Plateau U.S.A. **139** C1
Cumberland Sound sea chan. Can.
  125 H2
Cumbernauld U.K. **50** C3
Cummings U.S.A. **132** B3
Cumnock U.K. **50** B3
Cumpas Mex. **142** B1
Cunduacán Mex. **143** C3
Cunene r. Angola **106** A1
Cuneo Italy **62** A1
Cunnamulla Austr. **117** D1
Cuorgnè Italy **62** A1
Cupar U.K. **50** C2
Curaçao i. Neth. Antilles **145** D3
Curaray r. Ecuador **150** B3
Curicó Chile **153** A4
Curitiba Brazil **154** C3
Curitibanos Brazil **154** B3
Curnamona Austr. **116** B2
Currie Austr. **115** D3
Curtis Island Austr. **115** E2
Curuá r. Brazil **151** D3
Curup Indon. **72** B2
Cururupu Brazil **151** E3
Curvelo Brazil **155** D1
Cusco Peru **150** B4
Cushing U.S.A. **141** E1
Cut Bank U.S.A. **132** D1
Cuttack India **87** C2
Cuxhaven Ger. **55** D1
Cuyo Islands Phil. **76** B2
Cuzco Peru see Cusco
Cyangugu Rwanda **105** C3
Cyclades is Greece **65** B3
Cypress Hills Can. **127** D3
Cyprus country Asia **102** B1
Cyprus i. Asia **92** B2
Czech Republic country Europe **56** C3
Czersk Pol. **57** D2
Częstochowa Pol. **57** D2

Daban China **82** B1
Dabola Guinea **100** A3
Dacca Bangl. see Dhaka
Dachau Ger. **56** E2
Dadu Pak. **86** A2
Daegu S. Korea see Taegu
Daet Phil. **76** B2
Dagana Senegal **100** A3
Dagupan Phil. **76** B2
Dahanu India **86** B2
Da Hinggan Ling mts China **82** B1
Dahlak Archipelago is Eritrea **102** C3
Dahlem Ger. **54** C2
Dahm, Ramlat des.
  Saudi Arabia/Yemen **90** B3
Dahme Ger. **55** F2
Dahn Ger. **54** C3
Daik Indon. **72** B2
Daimiel Spain **60** C2
Dajarra Austr. **115** C2

Dakar Senegal **100** A3
Daketa Shet' watercourse Eth. **105** E2
Dākhilah, Wāḩāt al oasis Egypt
  102 A2
Dakhla Oasis Egypt see
  Dākhilah, Wāḩāt al
Dakoank India **75** A3
Dakol'ka r. Belarus **42** C3
Đakovica Serb. and Mont. **64** B2
Đakovo Croatia **63** C1
Dala Angola **106** B1
Dalain Hob China **80** C2
Dalälven r. Sweden **47** D3
Dalaman Turkey **65** C3
Dalaman r. Turkey **65** C3
Dalandzadgad Mongolia **80** C2
Đa Lat Vietnam **75** B2
Dalbandin Pak. **86** A2
Dalbeattie U.K. **50** C3
Dalby Austr. **117** E1
Dale Hordaland Norway **48** E1
Dale Sogn og Fjordane Norway **48** E1
Dale Hollow Lake U.S.A. **139** C1
Dalgety Austr. **117** D3
Dalhart U.S.A. **141** D1
Dalhousie Can. **137** G1
Dali China **74** D1
Dalian China **82** C2
Dalkeith U.K. **50** C3
Dallas U.S.A. **141** D2
Dall Island U.S.A. **126** B2
Dalmatia reg. Bos.-Herz./Croatia **63** C2
Dal'negorsk Rus. Fed. **78** C2
Dal'nerechensk Rus. Fed. **78** B1
Daloa Côte d'Ivoire **100** B4
Dalrymple, Mount Austr. **115** C2
Dalsmynni Iceland **46** [inset]
Daltenganj India **87** C2
Dalton U.S.A. **139** C2
Daludalu Indon. **72** B1
Dalvík Iceland **46** [inset]
Daly r. Austr. **114** C1
Daly Waters Austr. **114** C1
Daman India **86** B2
Damanhûr Egypt **92** B2
Damar i. Indon. **71** C3
Damascus Syria **92** B2
Damaturu Nigeria **101** D3
Damghan Iran **93** D2
Dammam Saudi Arabia **91** C2
Damme Ger. **55** D1
Damoh India **87** B2
Damongo Ghana **100** B4
Dampir, Selat sea chan. Indon. **71** C3
Damroh India **74** A1
Damxung China **87** D1
Danané Côte d'Ivoire **100** B4
Đa Năng Vietnam **75** B2
Danbury U.S.A. **137** F2
Dandong China **82** C1
Dangriga Belize **144** B3
Dangshan China **82** B2
Danilov Rus. Fed. **43** F2
Danilovskaya Vozvyshennost' hills
  Rus. Fed. **43** E2
Danjiangkou China **82** B2
Dankov Rus. Fed. **43** E3
Danlí Hond. **144** B3
Dannenberg (Elbe) Ger. **55** E1
Dannevirke N.Z. **118** C3
Dan Sai Thai. **74** B2
Dantu China **82** B2
Danube r. Austria/Ger. **56** D3
Danube r. Bulg./Croatia/Serb. and
  Mont. **64** C2
Danube r. Hungary **57** D3
Danube r. Romania **44** C2
Danube Delta Romania/Ukr. **44** C2
Danville IL U.S.A. **136** C2
Danville KY U.S.A. **136** D3

Danville VA U.S.A. **137** E3
Danzhou China **83** A4
Daoxian China **83** B3
Dapaong Togo **100** C3
Da Qaidam Zhen China **80** C2
Daqing China **81** E1
Dar'ā Syria **92** B2
Dārāb Iran **93** D3
Daraj Libya **101** D1
Dārān Iran **93** C2
Đa Răng, Sông r. Vietnam **75** B2
Darbhanga India **87** C2
Dar es Salaam Tanz. **105** D3
Dargai Pak. **86** B1
Dargaville N.Z. **118** B2
Dargo Austr. **117** D3
Darhan Mongolia **80** D1
Darién, Golfo del g. Col. **150** B2
Darjiling India **87** C2
Darlag China **80** C2
Darling r. Austr. **116** C2
Darling Downs hills Austr. **117** D1
Darling Range hills Austr. **114** A3
Darlington U.K. **52** C3
Darlington Point Austr. **117** D3
Darłowo Pol. **57** D2
Darmstadt Ger. **55** D3
Darnah Libya **101** E1
Darnick Austr. **116** C2
Daroca Spain **61** C1
Dartford U.K. **53** D4
Dartmoor hills U.K. **53** A4
Dartmouth Can. **129** D2
Dartmouth U.K. **53** B4
Daru P.N.G. **71** D3
Darvaza Turkm. **88** C2
Darwin Austr. **114** C1
Dashoguz Turkm. **88** C2
Dasht r. Pak. **86** A2
Datadian Indon. **73** C1
Datça Turkey **65** C3
Datong China **82** B1
Datu Piang Phil. **76** B3
Daud Khel Pak. **86** B1
Daugava r. Latvia **42** B2
Daugavpils Latvia **42** C2
Daun Ger. **54** C2
Dauphin Can. **127** E2
Dauphin Lake Can. **127** F2
Davangere India **85** B3
Davao Phil. **76** B3
Davao Gulf Phil. **76** B3
Davenport U.S.A. **135** E2
Daventry U.K. **53** C3
Daveyton S. Africa **109** C2
David Panama **144** B4
Davidson Can. **127** E2
Davis U.S.A. **133** B3
Davis Inlet Can. **129** D1
Davis Sea Antarctica **119** F3
Davis Strait Can./Greenland **125** I2
Davos Switz. **59** D2
Dawqah Oman **91** C3
Dawson r. Austr. **117** D2
Dawson U.S.A. **139** D2
Dawson Can. **126** B1
Dawson Creek Can. **126** C2
Dawsons Landing Can. **126** C2
Dawu China **80** C2
Dax France **58** B3
Da Xueshan mts China **80** C2
Dayr az Zawr Syria **92** C2
Dayton U.S.A. **136** D3
Daytona Beach U.S.A. **139** D3
Da Yunhe canal China **82** B2
Dazhou China **82** A2
De Aar S. Africa **108** B3
Dead Sea salt l. Asia **92** B2
De'an China **83** B2
Deán Funes Arg. **152** B4

Death Valley depr. U.S.A. **133** C3
Deauville France **58** C2
Debak Malaysia **73** C1
Debar Macedonia **65** B2
Debrecen Hungary **57** E3
Debre Markos Eth. **103** B3
Debre Tabor Eth. **103** B3
Debre Zeyit Eth. **103** B4
Decatur AL U.S.A. **138** C2
Decatur IL U.S.A. **136** C3
Deccan plat. India **85** B3
Děčín Czech Rep. **56** C2
Decorah U.S.A. **135** E2
Dedovichi Rus. Fed. **42** C2
Dedza Malawi **107** C1
Dee r. England/Wales U.K. **52** B3
Dee r. Scotland U.K. **50** C2
Deepwater Austr. **117** E1
Deer Lake Can. **129** E2
Deer Lodge U.S.A. **132** D1
Defiance U.S.A. **136** D2
Dêgê China **80** C2
Degeh Bur Eth. **103** C4
Deggendorf Ger. **56** C3
Degtevo Rus. Fed. **45** F2
Dehra Dun India **87** B1
Dehri India **87** C2
Dehui China **81** E2
Deinze Belgium **54** A2
Dej Romania **44** B2
De Kalb U.S.A. **136** C2
Dekemhare Eritrea **90** A3
Dekese Dem. Rep. Congo **104** C3
Delano U.S.A. **133** C3
Delano Peak U.S.A. **133** D3
Delap-Uliga-Djarrit Marshall Is **112**
Delārām Afgh. **86** A1
Delareyville S. Africa **109** C2
Delaronde Lake Can. **127** E2
Delaware U.S.A. **136** D2
Delaware r. U.S.A. **137** E3
Delaware state U.S.A. **137** E3
Delaware Bay U.S.A. **137** E3
Delegate Austr. **117** D3
Delémont Switz. **59** D2
Delft Neth. **54** B1
Delfzijl Neth. **54** C1
Delgado, Cabo c. Moz. **105** E4
Delhi India **86** B2
Deli i. Indon. **72** B2
Déline Can. **126** C1
Delitzsch Ger. **55** F2
Dellys Alg. **61** D2
Delmenhorst Ger. **55** D1
Delnice Croatia **62** B1
De-Longa, Ostrova is Rus. Fed. **95** M1
Deloraine Can. **127** E3
Delphi tourist site Greece **65** B3
Del Rio U.S.A. **141** D3
Delta CO U.S.A. **134** B3
Delta UT U.S.A. **133** D3
Delta Junction U.S.A. **124** C2
Delvinë Albania **65** B3
Demanda, Sierra de la mts Spain **60** C1
Demba Dem. Rep. Congo **104** C3
Dembī Dolo Eth. **103** B4
Demidov Rus. Fed. **43** D2
Deming U.S.A. **140** C2
Demirci Turkey **65** C3
Demirköy Turkey **64** C2
Demmin Ger. **56** C2
Demopolis U.S.A. **138** C2
Dempo, Gunung vol. Indon. **72** B2
Demyansk Rus. Fed. **43** D2
De Naawte S. Africa **108** B3
Denakil reg. Eritrea/Eth. **103** C3
Den Burg Neth. **54** B1
Dendermonde Belgium **54** B2
Dengkou China **82** A1

Dengzhou China **82** B2
Den Haag Neth. see The Hague
Denham Austr. **114** A2
Den Helder Neth. **54** B1
Deniliquin Austr. **116** C3
Denio U.S.A. **132** C2
Denison IA U.S.A. **135** D2
Denison TX U.S.A. **141** E2
Denizli Turkey **65** C3
Denman Austr. **117** E2
Denmark Austr. **114** A3
Denmark country Europe **47** C4
Denmark Strait Greenland/Iceland **125** K2
Denpasar Indon. **73** C2
Denton U.S.A. **141** E2
D'Entrecasteaux, Point pt Austr. **114** A3
Denver U.S.A. **134** B3
Deogarh Orissa India **87** C2
Deogarh Rajasthan India **86** B2
Deoghar India **87** C2
Deputatskiy Rus. Fed. **95** L2
Dêqên China **74** A1
De Queen U.S.A. **138** B2
Dera Bugti Pak. **86** A2
Dera Ghazi Khan Pak. **86** B1
Dera Ismail Khan Pak. **86** B1
Derbent Rus. Fed. **41** D4
Derby Austr. **114** B1
Derby U.K. **52** C3
Dereham U.K. **53** D3
Derg, Lough l. Rep. of Ireland **51** B2
Derhachi Ukr. **45** E1
De Ridder U.S.A. **138** B2
Derkul r. Rus. Fed./Ukr. **45** E2
Dêrub China **87** B1
Derudeb Sudan **102** B3
De Rust S. Africa **108** B3
Derwent r. U.K. **52** C3
Derwent Water l. U.K. **52** B2
Derzhavinsk Kazakh. **89** D1
Desaguadero r. Bol. **152** B2
Désappointement, Îles du is Fr. Polynesia **111**
Deschambault Lake Can. **127** E2
Deschutes r. U.S.A. **132** B1
Desē Eth. **103** B3
Deseado Arg. **153** B5
Deseado r. Arg. **153** B5
Des Moines U.S.A. **135** E2
Des Moines r. U.S.A. **135** E2
Desna r. Rus. Fed./Ukr. **45** D1
Desnogorsk Rus. Fed. **43** D3
Dessau Ger. **55** F2
Destruction Bay Can. **126** B1
Desventurados, Islas de los is S. Pacific Ocean **149**
Detah Can. **126** D1
Detmold Ger. **55** D2
Detroit U.S.A. **136** D2
Detroit Lakes U.S.A. **135** D1
Deurne Neth. **54** B2
Deva Romania **44** B2
Deventer Neth. **54** C1
Deveron r. U.K. **50** C2
Devét Skal h. Czech Rep. **57** D3
Devil's Lake U.S.A. **135** D1
Devil's Paw mt. U.S.A. **126** B2
Devizes U.K. **53** C4
Devli India **86** B2
Devnya Bulg. **64** C2
Devon Can. **126** D2
Devon Island Can. **125** F1
Devonport Austr. **115** D4
Dewas India **86** B2
Dexter U.S.A. **135** F3
Deyang China **82** A2
Deyong, Tanjung pt Indon. **71** D3

Dezfūl Iran **93** C2
Dezhou China **82** B2
Dhahran Saudi Arabia **91** C2
Dhaka Bangl. **87** D2
Dhamār Yemen **90** B3
Dhamtari India **87** C2
Dhanbad India **87** C2
Dhankuta Nepal **87** C2
Dharmanagar India **74** A1
Dharmjaygarh India **87** C2
Dharwad India **88** B3
Dhasa India **86** B2
Dhubāb Yemen **90** B3
Dhule India **86** B2
Diablo, Picacho del *mt.* Mex. **142** A1
Diamantina *watercourse* Austr. **115** C2
Diamantina Brazil **155** D1
Diamantina, Chapada *plat.* Brazil **151** E4
Diamantino Brazil **151** D4
Dianbai China **83** B3
Dianópolis Brazil **151** E4
Dianra Côte d'Ivoire **100** B4
Diapaga Burkina **100** C3
Dibā al Ḥiṣn U.A.E. **91** C2
Dibaya Dem. Rep. Congo **104** C3
Dibrugarh India **84** D2
Dickinson U.S.A. **134** C1
Dickson U.S.A. **138** C1
Dicle *r.* Turkey *see* Tigris
Die France **59** D3
Diefenbaker, Lake Can. **127** E2
Diéma Mali **100** B3
Diên Châu Vietnam **74** B2
Diepholz Ger. **55** D1
Dieppe France **58** C2
Diffa Niger **101** D3
Digby Can. **129** D2
Digne-les-Bains France **59** D3
Digos Phil. **76** B2
Digul *r.* Indon. **71** D3
Dijlah, Nahr *r.* Iraq/Syria **66**
Dijon France **59** D2
Dikhil Djibouti **103** C3
Dikili Turkey **65** C3
Dikwa Nigeria **101** D3
Dila Eth. **103** B4
Dili East Timor **71** C3
Dillenburg Ger. **55** D2
Dillon U.S.A. **132** D1
Dilolo Dem. Rep. Congo **104** C4
Dimapur India **74** A1
Dimashq Syria *see* Damascus
Dimbokro Côte d'Ivoire **100** B4
Dimboola Austr. **116** C3
Dimitrovgrad Bulg. **64** C2
Dimitrovgrad Rus. Fed. **41** D3
Dinagat *i.* Phil. **76** B2
Dinan France **58** B2
Dinant Belgium **54** B2
Dinar Turkey **92** B2
Dinār, Kūh-e *mt.* Iran **93** C2
Dinaric Alps *mts* Bos.-Herz./Croatia **36**
Dindigul India **88** B3
Dindiza Moz. **109** D1
Dingelstädt Ger. **55** E2
Dingle Rep. of Ireland **51** A2
Dingle Bay Rep. of Ireland **51** A2
Dingwall U.K. **50** B2
Dingxi China **82** A2
Dinkelsbühl Ger. **55** E3
Dinngyê China **87** C2
Dionisio Cerqueira Brazil **154** B3
Diourbel Senegal **100** A3
Diplog Phil. **76** B3
Dir Pak. **86** B1

Dirē Dawa Eth. **103** C4
Dirico Angola **106** B1
Dirk Hartog Island Austr. **114** A2
Dirranbandi Austr. **117** D1
Dirs Saudi Arabia **90** B3
Disappointment, Cape S. Georgia **153** E6
Disappointment, Lake *salt flat* Austr. **114** B2
Discovery Bay Austr. **116** C3
Dismal Swamp U.S.A. **137** E3
Diss U.K. **53** D3
Dittaino *r.* Italy **62** C3
Diu India **86** B2
Divinópolis Brazil **155** D2
Divnoye Rus. Fed. **43** D3
Divo Côte d'Ivoire **100** B4
Divriği Turkey **92** C2
Dixon U.S.A. **136** C2
Dixon Entrance *sea chan.* Can./U.S.A. **126** B2
Diyarbakır Turkey **92** C2
Diz Pak. **86** A2
Djado Niger **101** D2
Djado, Plateau du Niger **101** D2
Djambala Congo **104** B3
Djanet Alg. **101** D2
Djéma Cent. Afr. Rep. **105** C2
Djenné Mali **100** B3
Djibo Burkina **100** B3
Djibouti *country* Africa **103** C3
Djibouti Djibouti **103** C3
Djougou Benin **100** C4
Djúpivogur Iceland **46** [inset]
Dmitriyevka Rus. Fed. **43** F3
Dmitriyev-L'govskiy Rus. Fed. **43** E3
Dmitrov Rus. Fed. **43** E2
Dnepr *r.* Rus. Fed. *see* Dnieper
Dnieper *r.* Rus. Fed. **43** D3
Dnieper *r.* Ukr. **45** D2
Dniester *r.* Ukr. **44** C2
Dnipro *r.* Ukr. *see* Dnieper
Dniprodzerzhyns'k Ukr. **45** D2
Dnipropetrovs'k Ukr. **45** E2
Dniprorudne Ukr. **45** D2
Dnister *r.* Ukr. *see* Dniester
Dno Rus. Fed. **42** C2
Doba Chad **101** D4
Dobele Latvia **42** B2
Döbeln Ger. **55** F2
Doberai, Jazirah *pen.* Indon. **71** C3
Dobo Indon. **71** C3
Doboj Bos.-Herz. **63** C2
Dobrich Bulg. **64** C2
Dobrinka Rus. Fed. **43** F3
Dobrush Belarus **43** D3
Doce *r.* Brazil **155** E1
Doctor Arroyo Mex. **143** B2
Doctor Belisario Domínguez Mex. **142** B2
Dodecanese *is* Greece **65** C3
Dodekanisos *is* Greece *see* Dodecanese
Dodge City U.S.A. **134** C3
Dodoma Tanz. **105** D3
Doetinchem Neth. **54** C2
Dofa Indon. **71** C3
Dogai Coring *salt l.* China **87** C1
Dog Creek Can. **126** C2
Dōgo *i.* Japan **79** B3
Dogondoutchi Niger **100** C3
Doğubeyazıt Turkey **93** C2
Doha Qatar **91** C2
Doi Saket Thai. **74** A2
Dokkum Neth. **54** B1
Dokshytsy Belarus **42** C3
Dokuchayevs'k Ukr. **45** E2
Dolak, Pulau *i.* Indon. **71** D3

Dolbeau Can. **129** C2
Dol-de-Bretagne France **58** B2
Dole France **59** D2
Dolgellau U.K. **53** B3
Dolgorukovo Rus. Fed. **43** E3
Dolgoye Rus. Fed. **43** E3
Dolinsk Rus. Fed. **81** F1
Dolisie Congo *see* Loubomo
Dolomites *mts* Italy **62** B1
Dolo Odo Eth. **103** C4
Dolyna Ukr. **44** B2
Domažlice Czech Rep. **56** C3
Dombås Norway **47** B3
Dombóvár Hungary **57** D3
Dome Creek Can. **126** C2
Dominica *country* West Indies **145** D3
Dominican Republic *country* West Indies **145** C3
Domodedovo Rus. Fed. **43** E2
Domokos Greece **65** B3
Dompu Indon. **73** C2
Don *r.* Rus. Fed. **43** E3
Don *r.* U.K. **50** C2
Donaghadee U.K. **51** D1
Donald Austr. **116** C3
Donau *r.* Austria/Ger. *see* Danube
Donauwörth Ger. **56** C3
Don Benito Spain **60** B2
Doncaster U.K. **52** C3
Dondo Angola **104** B3
Dondo Moz. **107** C3
Dondra Head Sri Lanka **85** C4
Donegal Rep. of Ireland **51** B1
Donegal Bay Rep. of Ireland **51** B1
Donets'k Ukr. **45** E2
Donets'kyy Kryazh *hills* Rus. Fed./Ukr. **45** E2
Dongara Austr. **114** A2
Dongchuan China **83** A3
Dongfang China **83** A4
Dongfanghong China **78** B1
Donggala Indon. **73** C2
Donggang China **77** A2
Dongguan China **83** B3
Đông Ha Vietnam **74** B2
Đông Hôi Vietnam **74** B2
Dongou Congo **104** B2
Dongshan China **83** B3
Dongsheng China *see* Ordos
Dongtai China **82** C2
Dongting Hu *l.* China **83** B3
Dongying China **82** B2
Donnellys Crossing N.Z. **118** B2
Donostia - San Sebastián Spain **61** C1
Dooxo Nugaaleed *val.* Somalia **103** C4
Dorchester U.K. **53** B4
Dordabis Namibia **108** A1
Dordogne *r.* France **58** B2
Dordrecht Neth. **54** B2
Dordrecht S. Africa **109** C3
Doré Lake Can. **127** E2
Dorfmark Ger. **55** D1
Dori Burkina **100** B3
Doring *r.* S. Africa **108** A3
Dormans France **54** A3
Dornoch U.K. **50** B2
Dornoch Firth *est.* U.K. **50** B2
Dorogobuzh Rus. Fed. **43** D2
Dorohoi Romania **44** C2
Dörön Nuur *salt l.* Mongolia **80** C1
Dorotea Sweden **46** D3
Dorre Island Austr. **114** A2
Dorrigo Austr. **117** E2
Dorsale Camerounaise *slope* Cameroon/Nigeria **104** B2
Dortmund Ger. **54** C2
Dortmund-Ems-Kanal *canal* Ger. **54** C2
Dos Bahías, Cabo *c.* Arg. **153** B5

Dosse r. Ger. **55** F1
Dosso Niger **100** C3
Dothan U.S.A. **139** C2
Dötlingen Ger. **55** D1
Douai France **58** C1
Douala Cameroon **104** A2
Douarnenez France **58** B2
Doubtful Sound N.Z. **118** A4
Douentza Mali **100** B3
Douglas Isle of Man **52** A2
Douglas S. Africa **108** B2
Douglas AK U.S.A. **126** B3
Douglas AZ U.S.A. **140** C2
Douglas GA U.S.A. **139** D2
Douglas WY U.S.A. **134** B2
Doullens France **58** C1
Dourada, Serra hills Brazil
  154 B1
Dourados Brazil **154** B2
Dourados, Serra dos hills Brazil
  154 B2
Douro r. Port. **60** B1
Dover U.K. **53** D4
Dover U.S.A. **137** E3
Dover, Strait of France/U.K. **49** D3
Dover-Foxcroft U.S.A. **137** G1
Dowlatābād Büshehr Iran **93** C3
Dowlatābād Kermän Iran **91** C2
Downpatrick U.K. **51** D1
Dowshi Afgh. **86** A1
Dōzen is. Japan **79** B3
Dozois, Réservoir resr Can. **128** C2
Dracena Brazil **154** B2
Drachten Neth. **54** B1
Drăgăneşti-Olt Romania **44** B3
Drăgăşani Romania **44** B3
Drahichyn Belarus **42** F2
Drakensberg mts Lesotho/S. Africa
  109 C2
Drakensberg mts S. Africa **109** C2
Drake Passage S. Atlantic Ocean
  119 L4
Drama Greece **65** B3
Drammen Norway **47** C4
Drau r. Austria **62** B1
Drava r. Europe **62** C1
Drayton Valley Can. **126** D2
Dreieich Ger. **55** D2
Drepano, Akra pt Greece **65** B3
Dresden Ger. **55** F2
Dreux France **58** C2
Driemond Neth. **54** B1
Drina r. Bos.-Herz./Serb. and Mont.
  63 C2
Drniš Croatia **62** C2
Drobeta - Turnu Severin Romania
  44 B3
Drochtersen Ger. **55** D1
Drogheda Rep. of Ireland **51** C2
Drohobych Ukr. **44** B2
Dromore U.K. **51** C1
Drosh Pak. **86** B1
Drouin Austr. **117** D3
Drumheller Can. **127** D2
Drummond Island U.S.A. **136** D1
Drummondville Can. **129** C2
Druskininkai Lith. **42** E3
Druzhkivka Ukr. **45** E2
Druzhnaya Gorka Rus. Fed. **42** D2
Dryden Can. **128** A2
Drysdale r. Austr. **114** B1
Dubā Saudi Arabia **90** A2
Dubai U.A.E. **91** C2
Dubawnt Lake Can. **127** E1
Dubayy U.A.E. see Dubai
Dubbagh, Jabal ad mt. Saudi Arabia
  90 A2
Dubbo Austr. **117** D2
Dublin Rep. of Ireland **51** C2
Dublin U.S.A. **139** D2
Dubno Ukr. **44** C1

Du Bois U.S.A. **137** E2
Dubréka Guinea **100** A4
Dubrovnik Croatia **63** C2
Dubrovytsya Ukr. **44** C1
Dubrowna Belarus **43** D3
Dubuque U.S.A. **135** E2
Ducie Island atoll Pitcairn Is **111**
Đức Trong Vietnam **75** B2
Duderstadt Ger. **55** E2
Dudinka Rus. Fed. **94** H2
Dudley U.K. **53** B3
Duero r. Spain **60** C1
Duffreboy, Lac l. Can. **129** C1
Dufftown U.K. **50** C2
Dugi Rat Croatia **63** C2
Duisburg Ger. **54** C2
Duiwelskloof S. Africa **109** D1
Dukathole S. Africa **109** C3
Dukhān Qatar **91** C2
Dukhovshchina Rus. Fed. **43** D2
Dūkštas Lith. **42** C2
Dulan China **80** C2
Dulce r. Arg. **152** B4
Dülmen Ger. **54** C2
Dulovo Bulg. **64** C2
Duluth U.S.A. **135** E1
Dumaguete Phil. **76** B3
Dumai Indon. **72** B1
Dumaran i. Phil. **76** B2
Dumas AR U.S.A. **138** B2
Dumas TX U.S.A. **141** D1
Dumbarton U.K. **50** B3
Ďumbier mt. Slovakia **57** D3
Dumfries U.K. **50** C3
Dumyāţ Egypt **102** B1
Duna r. Hungary see Danube
Dunakeszi Hungary **57** D3
Dunărea r. Romania see Danube
Dunaújváros Hungary **57** D3
Dunayivtsi Ukr. **44** C2
Dunbar U.K. **50** C3
Dunbeath U.K. **50** C1
Duncan Can. **126** C3
Duncan U.S.A. **141** E2
Duncansby Head U.K. **50** C1
Dundalk Rep. of Ireland **51** C1
Dundalk Bay Rep. of Ireland **51** C2
Dundas Greenland **125** H1
Dundee S. Africa **109** D2
Dundee U.K. **50** C2
Dundrum Bay U.K. **51** D1
Dunedin N.Z. **118** B4
Dunfermline U.K. **50** C2
Dungannon U.K. **51** C1
Dungarpur India **86** B2
Dungarvan Rep. of Ireland **51** C2
Dungeness hd U.K. **53** D4
Dungiven U.K. **51** C1
Dungog Austr. **117** E2
Dungu Dem. Rep. Congo **105** C2
Dungun Malaysia **72** B1
Dungunab Sudan **102** B2
Dunhua China **77** B1
Dunhuang China **80** C2
Dunkerque France see Dunkirk
Dunkirk France **58** C1
Dunkirk U.S.A. **137** E2
Dún Laoghaire Rep. of Ireland **51** C2
Dunmurry U.K. **51** D1
Dunnet Head U.K. **50** C1
Duns U.K. **50** C3
Dunstable U.K. **53** C4
Dupnitsa Bulg. **64** B2
Dupree U.S.A. **134** C1
Durack r. Austr. **114** B1
Durango Mex. **142** B2
Durango Spain **60** C1
Durango U.S.A. **134** B3
Durant U.S.A. **141** E2

Durazno Uru. **153** C4
Durban S. Africa **109** D2
Durban-Corbières France **58** C3
Durbanville S. Africa **108** A3
Durbuy Belgium **54** B2
Düren Ger. **54** C2
Durg India **87** C2
Durham U.K. **52** C2
Durham U.S.A. **139** E1
Duri Indon. **72** B1
Durmitor mt. Serb. and Mont. **64** A2
Durness U.K. **50** B1
Durrës Albania **65** A2
Dursey Island Rep. of Ireland **51** A3
Dursunbey Turkey **65** C3
D'Urville, Tanjung pt Indon. **71** D3
D'Urville Island N.Z. **118** B3
Dushan China **83** A3
Dushanbe Tajik. **89** D3
Düsseldorf Ger. **54** C2
Duyun China **83** A3
Dvorichna Ukr. **45** E2
Dwarka India **86** A2
Dwarsberg S. Africa **109** C1
Dworshak Reservoir U.S.A. **132** C1
Dyat'kovo Rus. Fed. **43** D3
Dyce U.K. **50** C2
Dyer, Cape Can. **125** H2
Dyersburg U.S.A. **138** C1
Dyfrdwy r. England/Wales U.K. see Dee
Dyje r. Austria/Czech Rep. **57** D3
Dylewska Góra h. Pol. **57** D2
Dymytrov Ukr. **45** E2
Dyoki S. Africa **109** C3
Dyurtyuli Rus. Fed. **41** E3
Dzamïn Üüd Mongolia **81** D2
Dzhanga Turkm. **93** D1
Dzhangala Kazakh. **88** C2
Dzhankoy Ukr. **45** D2
Dzhizak Uzbek. see Jizzax
Dzhubga Rus. Fed. **45** E3
Dzhugdzhur, Khrebet mts Rus. Fed.
  95 L3
Dzhungarskiy Alatau, Khrebet mts
  China/Kazakh. **89** E2
Dzhusaly Kazakh. **88** D2
Działdowo Pol. **57** E2
Dzuunmod Mongolia **80** D1
Dzyarzhynsk Belarus **42** C3
Dzyatlavichy Belarus **42** C3

E

Eagle r. Can. **129** E1
Eagle Cap mt. U.S.A. **132** C1
Eagle Lake Can. **128** A2
Eagle Lake U.S.A. **132** B2
Eagle Pass U.S.A. **141** D3
Eagle Plain Can. **124** C2
Ear Falls Can. **128** A1
East Antarctica reg. Antarctica **119** F2
Eastbourne U.K. **53** D4
East China Sea N. Pacific Ocean
  81 E2
East Coast Bays N.Z. **118** B2
Eastend Can. **132** E1
Eastern Cape prov. S. Africa **109** C3
Eastern Desert Egypt **102** B2
Eastern Ghats mts India **85** B3
Easterville Can. **127** F2
East Falkland i. Falkland Is **153** C6
East Frisian Islands Ger. **54** C1
East Kilbride U.K. **50** B3
Eastleigh U.K. **53** C4
East Liverpool U.S.A. **137** D2
East London S. Africa **109** C3
Eastmain Can. **128** C1

Eastmain r. Can. **128** C1
Eastman U.S.A. **139** D2
East Sea N. Pacific Ocean *see*
 Japan, Sea of
East Siberian Sea Rus. Fed. **95** L2
East St Louis U.S.A. **136** B3
East Timor *country* Asia **69**
Eau Claire U.S.A. **136** B2
Eau Claire, Lac à l' *l.* Can. **128** C1
Eauripik *atoll* Micronesia **71** D2
Ebano Mex. **143** C2
Ebbw Vale U.K. **53** B4
Eberswalde-Finow Ger. **55** F1
Eboli Italy **62** C2
Ebolowa Cameroon **104** B2
Ebro r. Spain **61** D1
Echeverria, Pico *mt.* Mex. **142** A2
Echoing r. Can. **127** F2
Echternach Lux. **54** C3
Echuca Austr. **116** C3
Écija Spain **60** B2
Eckernförde Ger. **56** B2
Ecuador *country* S. America **150** B3
Ed Eritrea **102** C3
Ed Da'ein Sudan **103** A3
Ed Damazin Sudan **103** B3
Ed Damer Sudan **102** B3
Ed Debba Sudan **102** B3
Ed Dueim Sudan **102** B3
Ede Neth. **54** B1
Edéa Cameroon **104** B2
Edéia Brazil **154** C1
Eden r. U.K. **52** B2
Eden Austr. **117** D3
Eden r. U.K. **52** B2
Edenburg S. Africa **109** C2
Edenderry Rep. of Ireland **51** C2
Edenhope Austr. **116** C3
Edessa Greece **65** B2
Edgeoya i. Svalbard **94** D1
Edinburg U.S.A. **141** E3
Edinburgh U.K. **50** C3
Edirne Turkey **64** C2
Edmonton Can. **126** D2
Edmundston Can. **137** G1
Edson Can. **126** D2
Edward, Lake
 Dem. Rep. Congo/Uganda **105** C3
Edward's Creek Austr. **116** B1
Edwards Plateau U.S.A. **141** D2
Eenrum Neth. **54** C1
Éfaté i. Vanuatu **110**
Effingham U.S.A. **136** C3
Egan Range *mts* U.S.A. **133** D3
Eger Hungary **57** E3
Egersund Norway **47** B4
Egilsstaðir Iceland **46** [inset]
Eğirdir Turkey **92** B2
Eğirdir Gölü *l.* Turkey **92** B2
Egletons France **58** C2
Egvekinot Rus. Fed. **95** O2
Egypt *country* Africa **102** A2
Ehen Hudag China **82** A2
Eibergen Neth. **54** C1
Eifel *hills* Ger. **54** C2
Eigg i. U.K. **50** A2
Eight Degree Channel India/Maldives
 85 B4
Eighty Mile Beach Austr. **114** B1
Eilat Israel **92** B3
Eilenburg Ger. **55** F2
Einbeck Ger. **55** D2
Eindhoven Neth. **54** B2
Eirunepé Brazil **150** C3
Eiseb *watercourse* Namibia **106** B1
Eisenach Ger. **55** E2
Eisenhüttenstadt Ger. **56** C2

Eisenstadt Austria **57** D3
Eisleben Lutherstadt Ger. **55** E2
Eivissa Spain **61** D2
Eivissa i. Spain *see* Ibiza
Ejea de los Caballeros Spain **61** C1
Ejeda Madag. **107** [inset]
Ekenäs Fin. **47** E4
Ekibastuz Kazakh. **89** E1
Ekostrovskaya Imandra, Ozero *l.*
 Rus. Fed. **46** G2
Eksjö Sweden **47** C4
Eksteenfontein S. Africa **108** A2
Ekwan r. Can. **128** B1
Ela Myanmar **74** A2
Elandsdoorn S. Africa **109** C2
Elassona Greece **65** B3
Elazığ Turkey **92** B2
Elba, Isola d' i. Italy **62** B2
El Banco Col. **150** B2
Elbasan Albania **65** B2
El Baúl Venez. **150** C2
El Bayadh Alg. **100** C1
Elbe r. Ger. **55** D1
Elbert, Mount U.S.A. **134** B3
Elberton U.S.A. **139** D2
Elbeuf France **58** C2
Elbistan Turkey **92** B2
Elbląg Pol. **57** D2
El'brus *mt.* Rus. Fed. **41** D4
El Callao Venez. **150** C2
El Campo U.S.A. **141** E3
El Centro U.S.A. **133** C4
El Cerro Bol. **152** B2
Elche-Elx Spain **61** C2
Elda Spain **61** C2
Eldon U.S.A. **135** E3
Eldorado Arg. **154** B3
El Dorado Mex. **142** B2
El Dorado AR U.S.A. **138** B2
El Dorado KS U.S.A. **135** D3
El Eglab *plat.* Alg. **100** B2
El Ejido Spain **60** C2
Elektrostal' Rus. Fed. **43** E2
El Encanto Col. **150** B3
El Eulma Alg. **61** D2
Eleuthera i. Bahamas **145** C2
El Fuerte Mex. **142** B2
El Geneina Sudan **103** A3
El Geteina Sudan **102** B3
Elgin U.K. **50** C2
Elgin U.S.A. **136** C2
El Golea Alg. **100** C1
El Golfo de Santa Clara Mex. **142** A1
Elgon, Mount Uganda **105** D2
El Hammâmi *reg.* Maur. **100** A2
El Hierro i. Canary Is **100** A2
El Higo Mex. **143** C2
El Homr Alg. **100** C2
Elim U.S.A. **124** B2
Elista Rus. Fed. **41** D4
Elizabeth U.S.A. **137** F2
Elizabeth City U.S.A. **139** E1
Elizabethtown U.S.A. **136** C3
El Jadida Morocco **100** B1
Ełk Pol. **57** E2
Elk City U.S.A. **141** E1
Elkford Can. **126** D2
Elkhart U.S.A. **136** C2
Elkhovo Bulg. **64** C2
Elko Can. **126** D3
Elko U.S.A. **132** C2
Elk Point Can. **127** D2
Ellef Ringnes Island Can. **124** F1
Ellendale U.S.A. **135** D1
Ellensburg U.S.A. **132** B1
Ellesmere, Lake N.Z. **118** B3
Ellesmere Island Can. **125** G1

Ellesmere Port U.K. **52** B3
Ellice r. Can. **124** F2
Elliotdale S. Africa **109** C3
Ellon U.K. **50** C2
Ellsworth U.S.A. **137** G2
Ellsworth Mountains Antarctica
 119 K2
Elmalı Turkey **65** C3
El Meghaïer Alg. **101** C1
El Milia Alg. **61** D2
Elmira U.S.A. **137** E2
El Moral Spain **61** C2
Elmshorn Ger. **55** D1
El Muglad Sudan **103** A3
El Nido Phil. **76** A2
El Obeid Sudan **103** B3
El Oro Mex. **142** B2
El Oued Alg. **101** C1
Eloy U.S.A. **140** B2
El Paso U.S.A. **140** C2
El Porvenir Mex. **142** B1
El Prat de Llobregat Spain **61** D1
El Progreso Hond. **143** D3
El Reno U.S.A. **141** E1
Elsa Can. **126** B1
El Salado Mex. **143** B2
El Salto Mex. **142** B2
El Salvador *country* Central America
 144 B3
El Salvador Mex. **143** B2
El Sauz Mex. **140** C3
El Socorro Mex. **142** A1
Elsterwerda Ger. **55** F2
El Temascal Mex. **143** C2
El Tigre Venez. **150** C2
El Tocuyo Venez. **145** D4
Elva Estonia **42** C2
Elvas Port. **60** B2
Elverum Norway **47** C3
El Wak Kenya **105** E2
Ely U.K. **53** D3
Ely MN U.S.A. **135** E1
Ely NV U.S.A. **133** D3
Emämrüd Iran **93** D2
Emån r. Sweden **47** D4
Emba Kazakh. **88** C2
Emba r. Kazakh. **88** C2
Embalenhle S. Africa **109** C2
Emborcação, Represa de *resr* Brazil
 154 C1
Embu Kenya **105** D3
Emden Ger. **54** C1
Emerald Austr. **115** D2
Emerson Can. **127** F3
Emet Turkey **65** C3
eMgwenya S. Africa **109** D2
eMijindini S. Africa **109** D2
Emi Koussi *mt.* Chad **101** D3
Emine, Nos *pt* Bulg. **64** C2
Emirdağ Turkey **92** B2
Emmaste Estonia **42** B2
Emmeloord Neth. **54** B1
Emmelshausen Ger. **54** C2
Emmen Neth. **54** C1
Emory Peak U.S.A. **141** D3
Empalme Mex. **142** A2
Empangeni S. Africa **109** D2
Empoli Italy **62** B2
Emporia KS U.S.A. **135** D3
Emporia VA U.S.A. **137** E3
Ems r. Ger. **55** C1
Emsdetten Ger. **54** C1
Enarotali S. Africa **109** C3
Enarotali Indon. **71** D3
Encarnación Mex. **142** B2
Encarnación Para. **152** C3
Encruzilhada Brazil **155** D1
Ende Indon. **73** D2
Endicott Mountains U.S.A. **124** B2
Enerhodar Ukr. **45** D2

Engel's Rus. Fed. **41** D3
Enggano *i.* Indon. **72** B2
England *admin. div.* U.K. **52** C3
English *r.* Can. **128** A1
English Channel France/U.K. **53** C5
Enid U.S.A. **141** E1
Enkhuizen Neth. **54** B1
Enköping Sweden **47** D4
Enna Italy **62** B3
Ennadai Lake Can. **127** E1
En Nahud Sudan **103** A3
Ennedi, Massif *mts* Chad **101** E3
Enngonia Austr. **117** D1
Ennis Rep. of Ireland **51** B2
Ennis U.S.A. **141** E2
Enniscorthy Rep. of Ireland **51** C2
Enniskillen U.K. **51** C1
Ennistymon Rep. of Ireland **51** B2
Enns *r.* Austria **56** E3
Enontekiö Fin. **46** E2
Ensay Austr. **117** D3
Enschede Neth. **54** C1
Ensenada Mex. **142** A1
Enshi China **83** A2
Enterprise Can. **126** G2
Enterprise *AL* U.S.A. **139** C2
Enterprise *OR* U.S.A. **132** C1
Entre Rios Bol. **152** B3
Entroncamento Port. **60** B2
Enugu Nigeria **101** C4
Envira Brazil **150** B3
Épernay France **54** A3
Ephraim U.S.A. **133** D3
Ephrata U.S.A. **132** C1
Épinal France **59** D2
Epsom U.K. **53** C4
Equatorial Guinea *country* Africa **104** A2
Erbendorf Ger. **55** F3
Erbeskopf *h.* Ger. **54** C3
Erciş Turkey **93** C2
Erdao Jiang *r.* China **77** B1
Erdek Turkey **65** C2
Erdemli Turkey **92** B2
Erechim Brazil **152** C3
Ereentsav Mongolia **81** D1
Ereğli *Konya* Turkey **92** B2
Ereğli *Zonguldak* Turkey **92** B1
Erenhot China **82** B1
Erevan Armenia *see* Yerevan
Erfurt Ger. **55** E2
Ergani Turkey **92** B2
'Erg Chech *des.* Alg./Mali **100** B2
Ergene *r.* Turkey **65** C2
Erie U.S.A. **137** D2
Erie, Lake Can./U.S.A. **136** D2
Erimo-misaki *c.* Japan **78** D2
Eritrea *country* Africa **102** B3
Erkner Ger. **55** F1
Erlangen Ger. **56** E3
Erldunda Austr. **114** C2
Ermelo S. Africa **109** C2
Ermenek Turkey **92** B2
Ermoupoli Greece **65** B3
Ernakulam India **85** B4
Erode India **85** B3
Erp Neth. **54** B2
Er Rachidia Morocco **100** B1
Er Rahad Sudan **103** B3
Errigal *h.* Rep. of Ireland **51** B1
Erris Head Rep. of Ireland **51** A2
Erromango *i.* Vanuatu **110**
Ersekë Albania **65** B2
Ertil' Rus. Fed. **43** F3
Erwitte Ger. **55** D2
Erzgebirge *mts* Czech Rep./Ger. **56** C2
Erzincan Turkey **92** B2
Erzurum Turkey **41** D5
Esbjerg Denmark **47** B4
Escalante U.S.A. **133** D3

Escalón Mex. **142** B2
Escanaba U.S.A. **136** C1
Escárcega Mex. **143** C3
Escatrón Spain **61** C1
Escaut *r.* Belgium **54** A2
Eschede Ger. **55** E1
Esch-sur-Alzette Lux. **54** B3
Eschwege Ger. **55** E2
Eschweiler Ger. **54** C2
Escondido U.S.A. **133** C4
Escuinapa Mex. **142** B2
Eşen Turkey **65** C3
Eşfahān Iran **93** D2
Esikhawini S. Africa **109** D2
Esk *r.* U.K. **52** B2
Esker Can. **129** D1
Eskifjörður Iceland **46** [inset]
Eskilstuna Sweden **47** D4
Eskişehir Turkey **92** B2
Eslāmābād-e Gharb Iran **93** C2
Esler Dağı *mt.* Turkey **65** C3
Eşme Turkey **65** C3
Esmeraldas Ecuador **150** B2
Espakeh Iran **91** D2
Espalion France **58** C3
Espanola Can. **128** B2
Espanola U.S.A. **140** C1
Esperance Austr. **114** B3
Esperanza Mex. **142** B2
Espichel, Cabo *c.* Port. **60** B2
Espinhaço, Serra do *mts* Brazil **155** D1
Espinosa Brazil **151** E4
Espíritu Santo *i.* Vanuatu **158** D6
Espíritu Santo, Isla *i.* Mex. **142** A2
Espoo Fin. **47** E3
Esquel Arg. **153** A5
Essaouira Morocco **100** B1
Es Semara Western Sahara **100** A2
Essen Ger. **54** C2
Essequibo *r.* Guyana **150** D2
Esso Rus. Fed. **95** M3
Estados, Isla de los *i.* Arg. **153** B6
Eşţahbān Iran **93** D3
Estância Brazil **151** F4
Estcourt S. Africa **109** C2
Estella Spain **61** C1
Estepona Spain **60** B2
Esteras de Medinaceli Spain **60** C1
Esterhazy Can. **127** E2
Esteros Arg. **152** B3
Estes Park U.S.A. **134** B2
Estevan Can. **134** C1
Estherville U.S.A. **135** E2
Eston Can. **127** E2
Estonia *country* Europe **42** C2
Estrela, Serra da *mts* Port. **60** B1
Estremoz Port. **60** B2
Etadunna Austr. **116** B2
Étain France **54** B3
Étampes France **58** C2
Étaples France **58** C1
Etawah India **87** B2
eThandukukhanya S. Africa **109** D2
Ethiopia *country* Africa **103** B4
Ethiopian Highlands *plat.* Eth. **96**
Etna, Monte *vol.* Italy **62** B3
Etne Norway **48** E2
Etolin Island U.S.A. **126** B2
Etosha Pan *salt pan* Namibia **106** A1
Ettelbruck Lux. **54** C3
Etten-Leur Neth. **54** B2
Etxarri-Aranatz Spain **61** C1
Eu France **53** D4
Euabalong Austr. **117** D2
Euboea *i.* Greece *see* Evvoia
Eucla Austr. **114** B3
Eufaula U.S.A. **139** C2
Eufaula Lake *resr* U.S.A. **141** E1
Eugene U.S.A. **132** B2

Eugenia, Punta *pt* Mex. **142** A2
Eulo Austr. **117** D1
Eumungerie Austr. **117** D2
Euphrates *r.* Asia **92** C2
Eureka *CA* U.S.A. **132** B2
Eureka *MT* U.S.A. **132** C1
Eureka *NV* U.S.A. **133** C3
Euriowie Austr. **116** C2
Euroa Austr. **117** D3
Europa Point *pt* Gibraltar **60** B2
Eutsuk Lake Can. **126** C2
Evans, Lac *l.* Can. **128** C1
Evans Head Austr. **117** E1
Evans Strait Can. **127** G1
Evanston U.S.A. **134** A2
Evansville U.S.A. **136** C3
Evaton S. Africa **109** C2
Evaz Iran **91** C2
Evensk Rus. Fed. **95** M2
Everard, Lake *salt flat* Austr. **116** B2
Everest, Mount China/Nepal **87** C2
Everett U.S.A. **132** B1
Evergem Belgium **54** A2
Everglades *swamp* U.S.A. **139** D3
Evinayong Equat. Guinea **104** B2
Evje Norway **47** B4
Évora Port. **60** B2
Évreux France **58** C2
Évvoia *i.* Greece **65** B3
Evrotas *r.* Greece **65** B3
Evrychou Cyprus **92** B2
Evvoia *i.* Greece **65** B3
Ewaso Ngiro *r.* Kenya **105** E2
Exaltación Bol. **152** B2
Exe *r.* U.K. **53** B4
Exeter U.K. **53** B4
Exmoor *hills* U.K. **53** B4
Exmouth U.K. **53** B4
Exmouth Gulf Austr. **114** A2
Exuma Cays *is* Bahamas **145** C2
Eya *r.* Rus. Fed. **45** E2
Eyl Somalia **103** C4
Eyre, Lake *salt flat* S.A. Austr. **116** B1
Eyre Peninsula Austr. **116** B2
Eysturoy *i.* Faroe Is **48** B1
Ezakheni S. Africa **109** D2
Ezenzeleni S. Africa **109** C2
Ezhou China **83** B2
Ezhva Rus. Fed. **40** E2
Ezine Turkey **65** C3

Fabens U.S.A. **140** C2
Fåborg Denmark **56** C1
Fabriano Italy **62** B2
Fachi Niger **101** D3
Fada-N'Gourma Burkina **100** C3
Faenza Italy **62** B2
Fafanlap Indon. **71** C3
Făgăraş Romania **44** B2
Fagatogo American Samoa **113**
Fagernes Norway **47** B3
Fagersta Sweden **47** D4
Fagnano, Lago *l.* Arg./Chile **153** B6
Faguibine, Lac *l.* Mali **100** B3
Fagurhólsmýri Iceland **46** [inset]
Fairbanks U.S.A. **124** C2
Fairbury U.S.A. **135** D2
Fairfield U.S.A. **133** B3
Fair Isle *i.* U.K. **50** [inset]
Fairmont *MN* U.S.A. **135** E2
Fairmont *WV* U.S.A. **137** D3
Fairview Can. **126** C2
Fairweather, Mount Can./U.S.A. **126** B2
Fais *i.* Micronesia **71** D2

Faisalabad Pak. **86** B1
Faith U.S.A. **134** C1
Faizabad India **87** D2
Fakarava *atoll* Fr. Polynesia **111**
Fakfak Indon. **75** C3
Faku China **77** A1
Falaba Sierra Leone **100** A4
Falcon Lake Mex./U.S.A. **141** E3
Falfurrias U.S.A. **141** E3
Falher Can. **126** D2
Falkenberg Ger. **55** F2
Falkenberg Sweden **47** C4
Falkensee Ger. **55** F1
Falkirk U.K. **50** C3
Falkland Islands *terr.* S. Atlantic Ocean
  153 C6
Falköping Sweden **47** C4
Fallon U.S.A. **133** C3
Fall River U.S.A. **137** F2
Falls City U.S.A. **135** D2
Falmouth U.K. **53** A4
False Bay S. Africa **108** A3
Falso, Cabo *c.* Mex. **120**
Falster *i.* Denmark **47** C5
Fălticeni Romania **44** C2
Falun Sweden **47** D3
Fameck France **54** C3
Fangchenggang China **83** A3
Fangshan Taiwan **83** C3
Fangzheng China **81** E1
Fano Italy **62** B2
Fan Si Pan *mt.* Vietnam **74** B1
Faradje Dem. Rep. Congo **105** C2
Farafangana Madag. **107** [inset] D2
Farafirah, Wāḥāt al *oasis* Egypt
  102 A2
Farāh Afgh. **86** A1
Farah Rūd *watercourse* Afgh. **86** A1
Faranah Guinea **100** A3
Farasān, Jazā'ir *is* Saudi Arabia **90** B3
Farewell, Cape Greenland **125** J2
Farewell, Cape N.Z. **118** B3
Fargo U.S.A. **135** D1
Farg'ona Uzbek. **89** E2
Faribault U.S.A. **135** E2
Faribault, Lac *l.* Can. **129** C3
Farmington *ME* U.S.A. **137** F2
Farmington *NM* U.S.A. **140** C1
Farnville U.S.A. **137** E3
Farnborough U.K. **53** C4
Farnham, Mount Can. **126** D2
Faro Can. **126** B1
Faro Port. **60** B2
Färö *i.* Sweden **42** A2
Faroe Islands *terr.* N. Atlantic Ocean
  48 B1
Farrāshband Iran **93** D3
Farwell U.S.A. **141** D2
Fāryāb Iran **91** C2
Fasā Iran **93** D3
Fasano Italy **63** C2
Fastiv Ukr. **44** C1
Fatehgarh India **87** D2
Fatehpur India **87** C2
Faulquemont France **54** C3
Fauske Norway **46** C2
Faxaflói *b.* Iceland **46** [inset]
Faxälven *r.* Sweden **46** D3
Faya Chad **101** D3
Fazilka India **86** B1
Fderîk Maur. **100** A2
Fear, Cape U.S.A. **139** E2
Featherston N.Z. **118** C3
Fécamp France **58** C2
Fehmarn *i.* Ger. **56** C2
Fehrbellin Ger. **55** F1
Feia, Lagoa *lag.* Brazil **155** D2

Feijó Brazil **150** B3
Feilding N.Z. **118** C3
Feira de Santana Brazil **151** F4
Felanitx Spain **61** D2
Feldberg Ger. **55** D2
Felipe C. Puerto Mex. **143** D3
Felixlândia Brazil **155** D1
Felixstowe U.K. **53** D4
Felsberg Ger. **55** D2
Feltre Italy **62** B1
Femunden *l.* Norway **47** C3
Fengcheng *Jiangxi* China **83** B3
Fengcheng *Liaoning* China **77** A1
Fengqing China **74** A1
Fengxian China **82** B3
Fengyüan Taiwan **83** C3
Fengzhen China **82** B1
Feno, Capo di *c.* France **59** D3
Fenoarivo Atsinanana Madag.
  107 [inset] D1
Feodosiya Ukr. **45** E2
Fer, Cap de *c.* Alg. **62** A3
Fergus Falls U.S.A. **135** D1
Ferkessédougou Côte d'Ivoire
  100 B4
Fermo Italy **62** B2
Fermont Can. **129** D1
Fermoselle Spain **60** B1
Fermoy Rep. of Ireland **51** B2
Fernandina Beach U.S.A. **139** D2
Fernandópolis Brazil **154** B2
Fernie Can. **126** D3
Ferrara Italy **62** B2
Ferreiros Brazil **154** B2
Ferro, Capo *c.* Italy **62** A2
Ferrol Spain **60** B1
Ferwert Neth. **54** B1
Fès Morocco **100** B1
Feshi Dem. Rep. Congo **104** B3
Festus U.S.A. **135** E3
Fethiye Turkey **65** C3
Fetlar *i.* U.K. **50** [inset]
Feucht Ger. **55** E3
Feuilles, Rivière aux *r.* Can. **128** C1
Feyzābād Afgh. **86** B1
Fichê Eth. **103** B4
Fier Albania **65** A2
Fife Ness *pt* U.K. **50** C2
Figeac France **58** C3
Figueira da Foz Port. **60** B1
Figueres Spain **61** D1
Figuig Morocco **100** B1
Fiji *country* S. Pacific Ocean **112**
Fik' Eth. **105** E2
Filadelfia Para. **152** B3
Filchner Ice Shelf Antarctica **119** A2
Filey U.K. **52** C2
Filippiada Greece **65** B3
Filipstad Sweden **47** C4
Findhorn *r.* U.K. **50** C2
Findlay U.S.A. **136** D2
Fingal Austr. **115** D4
Finger Lakes U.S.A. **137** E2
Finisterre, Cape Spain **60** B1
Finland *country* Europe **46** F3
Finland, Gulf of Europe **47** E4
Finlay *r.* Can. **126** C2
Finley Austr. **117** D3
Finne *ridge* Ger. **55** E2
Finnmarksvidda *reg.* Norway **46** E2
Finnsnes Norway **46** D2
Finspång Sweden **47** D4
Finsterwalde Ger. **55** F2
Fionnphort U.K. **50** A2
Firenze Italy *see* Florence
Firminy France **58** C2
Firozabad India **87** B2
Firozpur India **86** B1

Fīrūzābād Iran **93** D3
Fish *r.* S. Africa **108** A3
Fish *watercourse* Namibia **108** A2
Fisher Strait Can. **127** G1
Fishguard U.K. **53** A4
Fismes France **59** D2
Fisterra, Cabo *c.* Spain *see*
  Finisterre, Cape
Fitchburg U.S.A. **137** F2
Fitzgerald U.S.A. **127** D2
Fitzroy Crossing Austr. **114** B1
Fivizzano Italy **62** B2
Fizi Dem. Rep. Congo **105** C3
Fjällsjöälven *r.* Sweden **46** D3
Flagstaff S. Africa **109** C3
Flagstaff U.S.A. **140** B1
Flaherty Island Can. **128** C1
Flamborough Head U.K. **52** C2
Fläming *hills* Ger. **55** F1
Flaming Gorge Reservoir U.S.A.
  134 B2
Flathead *r.* U.S.A. **132** C1
Flathead Lake U.S.A. **132** D1
Flattery, Cape Austr. **115** D1
Flattery, Cape U.S.A. **132** B1
Fleetwood U.K. **52** B3
Flekkefjord Norway **47** B4
Flen Sweden **42** A2
Flensburg Ger. **56** C2
Flers France **58** B2
Flinders *r.* Austr. **115** D1
Flinders Bay Austr. **114** A3
Flinders Island Austr. **115** D3
Flinders Ranges *mts* Austr. **116** C2
Flin Flon Can. **127** E2
Flint U.S.A. **136** D2
Flint *i.* Kiribati **111**
Florac France **61** D1
Florence Italy **62** B2
Florence *AL* U.S.A. **138** C2
Florence *AZ* U.S.A. **140** B2
Florence *OR* U.S.A. **132** B2
Florence *SC* U.S.A. **139** E2
Florencia Col. **150** B2
Flores Guat. **144** B3
Flores *i.* Indon. **73** D2
Flores, Laut Indon. **73** D2
Flores Sea Indon. *see* Flores, Laut
Floresta Brazil **151** F3
Floresville U.S.A. **141** E3
Floriano Brazil **151** E3
Florianópolis Brazil **154** C3
Florida Uru. **153** C4
Florida *state* U.S.A. **139** D2
Florida, Straits of Bahamas/U.S.A.
  144 D2
Florida Keys *is* U.S.A. **139** D3
Florina Greece **65** B2
Florø Norway **47** B3
Foam Lake Can. **127** E2
Foča Bos.-Herz. **63** C2
Focşani Romania **44** C2
Fogang China **83** B3
Foggia Italy **62** C2
Fogo Island Can. **129** E2
Foix France **58** C3
Fokino Rus. Fed. **43** D3
Foleyet Can. **128** B2
Foligno Italy **62** B2
Folkestone U.K. **53** D4
Folkston U.S.A. **139** D2
Follonica Italy **62** B2
Fond-du-Lac Can. **124** E3
Fond du Lac *r.* Can. **127** E2
Fond du Lac U.S.A. **136** C2
Fondevila Spain **60** B1
Fondi Italy **62** B2
Fonseca, Golfo de *b.* Central America
  144 B3
Fonte Boa Brazil **150** C3
Fontenay-le-Comte France **58** B2

Fontur *pt* Iceland **46** [inset]
Forbes Austr. **117** D2
Forchheim Ger. **55** E3
Ferde Norway **47** B3
Fords Bridge Austr. **117** D1
Fordyce U.S.A. **138** B2
Forest U.S.A. **138** C2
Forest Hill Austr. **117** D3
Forestville Can. **129** D2
Forfar U.K. **50** C2
Forks U.S.A. **132** B1
Forlì Italy **62** B2
Formentera *i.* Spain **61** D2
Formentor, Cap de *c.* Spain **61** D2
Formiga Brazil **155** C2
Formosa Arg. **152** C3
Formosa Brazil **154** C1
Forres U.K. **50** C2
Forrest Austr. **114** B3
Forrest City U.S.A. **138** B1
Forsayth Austr. **115** D1
Forssa Fin. **47** E3
Forster Austr. **117** E2
Forsyth U.S.A. **132** E1
Fort Abbas Pak. **86** B2
Fort Albany Can. **128** B1
Fortaleza Brazil **151** F3
Fort Assiniboine Can. **126** D2
Fort Augustus U.K. **50** B2
Fort Benton U.S.A. **132** E1
Fort Bragg U.S.A. **133** B3
Fort Chimo Can. *see* Kuujjuaq
Fort Chipewyan Can. **127** D2
Fort Collins U.S.A. **134** B2
Fort-de-France Martinique **145** D3
Fort Dodge U.S.A. **135** E2
Fort Frances Can. **128** A2
Fort George Can. *see* Chisasibi
Fort Good Hope Can. **124** D2
Forth *r.* U.K. **50** C2
Forth, Firth of *est.* U.K. **50** C2
Fortín Madrejón Para. **152** C3
Fort Lauderdale U.S.A. **139** D3
Fort Liard Can. **126** C1
Fort Mackay Can. **127** D2
Fort McMurray Can. **127** D2
Fort McPherson Can. **124** D2
Fort Morgan U.S.A. **134** C2
Fort Myers U.S.A. **139** D3
Fort Nelson Can. **126** C2
Fort Nelson *r.* Can. **126** C2
Fort Payne U.S.A. **139** C2
Fort Peck U.S.A. **134** E1
Fort Peck Reservoir U.S.A. **134** B1
Fort Pierce U.S.A. **139** D3
Fort Providence Can. **126** D1
Fort Qu'Appelle Can. **127** C2
Fort Resolution Can. **126** D1
Fort Rupert Can. *see* Waskaganish
Fort Saskatchewan Can. **126** D2
Fort Scott U.S.A. **135** E3
Fort Severn Can. **128** B1
Fort-Shevchenko Kazakh. **88** C2
Fort Simpson Can. **126** C1
Fort Smith Can. **127** D1
Fort Smith U.S.A. **138** B1
Fort St James Can. **126** C2
Fort St John Can. **126** C2
Fort Stockton U.S.A. **141** D2
Fort Sumner U.S.A. **140** D2
Fort Vermilion Can. **126** D2
Fort Walton Beach U.S.A. **138** C2
Fort Wayne U.S.A. **136** C2
Fort William U.K. **50** B2
Fort Worth U.S.A. **141** E2
Fort Yukon U.S.A. **124** C2
Foshan China **83** B3
Fosna *pen.* Norway **46** C3
Fosnavåg Norway **47** B3
Foss Iceland **46** [inset]

Fossá Iceland **46** [inset]
Fossano Italy **62** A2
Foster Austr. **117** D3
Fougères France **58** B2
Foula *i.* U.K. **50** [inset]
Fournoi *i.* Greece **65** C3
Fouta Djallon *reg.* Guinea **100** A3
Foveaux Strait N.Z. **118** A4
Fowler U.S.A. **134** C3
Fowlers Bay Austr. **114** C3
Fox Creek Can. **126** D2
Foxe Basin *g.* Can. **125** G2
Foxe Channel Can. **125** G2
Fox Glacier N.Z. **118** B3
Fox Lake Can. **126** D2
Fox Mountain Can. **126** B1
Foxton N.Z. **118** E2
Fox Valley Can. **127** E2
Foyle, Lough *b.* Rep. of Ireland/U.K. **51** C1
Foz de Areia, Represa de *resr* Brazil **154** B3
Foz do Cunene Angola **106** A1
Foz do Iguaçu Brazil **154** B3
Fraga Spain **61** D1
Franca Brazil **154** C2
Francavilla Fontana Italy **63** C2
France *country* Europe **58** C2
Franceville Gabon **104** B3
Francis Case, Lake U.S.A. **135** D2
Francisco Sá Brazil **155** D1
Francistown Botswana **106** B2
François Lake Can. **126** C2
Frankenberg (Eder) Ger. **55** D2
Frankenhöhe *hills* Ger. **55** E3
Frankenthal (Pfalz) Ger. **55** D3
Frankenwald *mts* Ger. **55** E2
Frankfort U.S.A. **136** D3
Frankfurt am Main Ger. **55** D2
Frankfurt an der Oder Ger. **56** C2
Fränkische Alb *hills* Ger. **55** E2
Fränkische Schweiz *reg.* Ger. **55** E3
Franklin U.S.A. **137** E2
Franklin D. Roosevelt Lake *resr* U.S.A. **132** C1
Franklin Mountains Can. **126** C1
Frantsa-Iosifa, Zemlya *is* Rus. Fed. **94** F1
Franz Josef Glacier N.Z. **118** B3
Frasca, Capo della *c.* Italy **62** A3
Frascati Italy **59** E3
Fraser *r. B.C.* Can. **126** C3
Fraser *r. Nfld. and Lab.* Can. **129** D1
Fraserburg S. Africa **108** B3
Fraserburgh U.K. **50** C2
Fraserdale Can. **128** B2
Fraser Island Austr. **115** E2
Fraser Lake Can. **126** C2
Fray Bentos Uru. **153** C4
Fredericia Denmark **47** B4
Frederick U.S.A. **141** E2
Fredericksburg *TX* U.S.A. **141** E2
Fredericksburg *VA* U.S.A. **137** D3
Frederick Sound *sea chan.* U.S.A. **126** B2
Fredericton Can. **125** H3
Frederikshavn Denmark **47** C4
Fredrikstad Norway **47** C4
Freeport *IL* U.S.A. **136** C2
Freeport *TX* U.S.A. **141** E3
Freeport City Bahamas **144** C2
Freer U.S.A. **141** E3
Free State *prov.* S. Africa **109** C2
Freetown Sierra Leone **100** A4
Fregenal de la Sierra Spain **60** B2
Fréhel, Cap *c.* France **58** B2
Freiberg Ger. **55** F2
Freiburg im Breisgau Ger. **56** B3
Freising Ger. **56** C3

Freistadt Austria **56** C3
Freital Ger. **55** F2
Fréjus France **59** D3
Fremantle Austr. **114** A3
Fremont *NE* U.S.A. **135** D2
Fremont *OH* U.S.A. **136** D2
French Guiana *terr.* S. America **151** D2
Frenchman *r.* U.S.A. **132** E1
French Polynesia *terr.* S. Pacific Ocean **113**
Frenda Alg. **61** D2
Fresnillo Mex. **142** B2
Fresno U.S.A. **133** C3
Freu, Cap de *c.* Spain **61** D2
Freyming-Merlebach France **59** D2
Fria Guinea **100** A3
Frias Arg. **152** B3
Friedland Ger. **55** F1
Friedrichshafen Ger. **56** B3
Friesack Ger. **55** F1
Friesoythe Ger. **54** C1
Frobisher Bay Can. *see* Iqaluit
Frobisher Bay *b.* Can. **125** H2
Frohburg Ger. **55** F2
Frolovo Rus. Fed. **41** D4
Frome, Lake *salt flat* Austr. **116** B2
Frome Downs Austr. **116** B2
Fröndenberg Ger. **54** C2
Frontera Mex. **143** C3
Fronteras Mex. **142** B1
Frosinone Italy **62** B2
Frøya *i.* Norway **46** B3
Frutigen Switz. **59** D2
Frýdek-Místek Czech Rep. **57** D3
Fu'an China **83** B3
Fuenlabrada Spain **60** C1
Fuerte Olimpo Para. **152** C3
Fuerteventura *i.* Canary Is **100** A2
Fuga *i.* Phil. **76** B2
Fujairah U.A.E. **91** C2
Fuji Japan **79** C3
Fujian *prov.* China **83** B3
Fujinomiya Japan **79** C3
Fuji-san *vol.* Japan **79** C3
Fukui Japan **79** C3
Fukuoka Japan **79** B4
Fukushima Japan **79** D3
Fulda Ger. **55** D2
Fulda *r.* Ger. **55** D2
Fuling China **83** A3
Fulton U.S.A. **135** E3
Fumay France **59** C2
Funafuti *atoll* Tuvalu **110**
Funchal Madeira **100** A1
Fundão Port. **60** B1
Fundy, Bay of *g.* Can. **129** D2
Funhalouro Moz. **109** D1
Funing *Jiangsu* China **82** B2
Funing *Yunnan* China **83** A3
Funtua Nigeria **101** C3
Fürgun, Küh-e *mt.* Iran **91** C2
Furmanov Rus. Fed. **43** F2
Furnas, Represa *resr* Brazil **155** C2
Furneaux Group *is* Austr. **115** D4
Fürstenau Ger. **54** C1
Fürstenwalde Ger. **55** G1
Fürth Ger. **55** E3
Furth im Wald Ger. **55** F3
Furukawa Japan **78** D3
Fushun China **82** C1
Fusong China **77** B1
Fuwayriṭ Qatar **91** C2
Fuxin China **82** C1
Fuyang China **82** B2
Fuyu China **81** E1
Fuyun China **89** F2
Fuzhou *Fujian* China **83** B3
Fuzhou *Jiangxi* China **83** B3
Fyn *i.* Denmark **47** C4

Kaalkacyo Somalia **103** C4
Kabela Angola **106** A1
Kabès Tunisia **101** D1
Kabès, Golfe de *g.* Tunisia **101** D1
Kaïlçac France **58** C3
Kaïlbag, Wadi *watercourse* Sudan **90** A2
Kabon *country* Africa **104** B3
Kaborone Botswana **109** C1
Kabrovo Bulg. **64** C2
Kabú Guinea-Bissau **100** A3
Kadag India **85** B3
Kadchiroli India **87** C2
Kadebusch Ger. **55** E1
Kadsden U.S.A. **139** C2
Kaesti Romania **44** C3
Kaeta Italy **62** B2
Kaferut *i.* Micronesia **110**
Kaffney U.S.A. **139** D1
Kafsa Tunisia **101** C1
Kagarin Rus. Fed. **43** E2
Kagnon Côte d'Ivoire **100** B4
Kagnon Can. **129** D1
Kagra Georgia **93** C1
Kaia *r.* Kenya **105** E3
Kaillac France **58** C3
Kainesville *FL* U.S.A. **139** D3
Kainesville *GA* U.S.A. **139** D2
Kainesville *TX* U.S.A. **141** E2
Kainsborough U.K. **52** C3
Kairdner, Lake *salt flat* Austr. **116** B2
Kairloch U.K. **50** D1
Kalana *r.* Kenya **105** E3
Kalanta Slovakia **57** D3
Kalapagos Islands Ecuador **148**
Kalashiels U.K. **50** C3
Kalați Romania **44** F2
Kaldhopiggen *mt.* Norway **47** B3
Kaleana Mex. **143** B2
Kalena Bay Can. **126** D2
Kalera, Punta *pt* Chile **147**
Kaleshewe S. Africa **108** B2
Kalich Rus. Fed. **43** F2
Kalichskaya Vozvyshennost' *hills* Rus. Fed. **43** F2
Kalicia *aut. comm.* Spain **60** B1
Kalilee, Sea of *l.* Israel **92** B2
Kallatin U.S.A. **139** C1
Kalle Sri Lanka **85** C4
Kallinas, Punta *pt* Col. **150** B1
Kallipoli Italy **63** C2
Kallipoli Turkey **65** C2
Kallup U.S.A. **140** C1
Kaltat Zemmour Western Sahara **100** A2
Kaltymore Rep. of Ireland **51** B2
Kalveston U.S.A. **141** F3
Kalveston Bay U.S.A. **141** F3
Kalway Rep. of Ireland **51** B2
Kalway Bay Rep. of Ireland **51** B2
Kamá Brazil **154** C1
Kamalakhe S. Africa **109** D3
Kambia, The *country* Africa **100** A3
Kambier, Îles *is* Fr. Polynesia **111**
Kambier Islands Austr. **116** B2
Kambo Can. **129** C2
Kamboma Congo **104** B3
Kanado U.S.A. **140** C1
Kanäveh Iran **93** D2
Käncä Azer. **93** C1
Kandadanah, Bukit *mt.* Indon. **73** C2
Kandajika Dem. Rep. Congo **104** C2
Kander Can. **129** E2
Kander *r.* Can. **129** E2
Kanderkesee Ger. **55** D1

Gandesa Spain **61** D1
Gandhidham India **86** B2
Gandhinagar India **86** B2
Gandhi Sagar *resr* India **86** B2
Gandía Spain **61** C2
Ganga *r.* Bangl./India **87** D2
Gangán Arg. **153** B5
Ganganagar India **86** B2
Gangca China **80** C2
Gangdisê Shan *mts* China **87** C1
Ganges France **59** C3
Ganges, Mouths of the Bangl./India **87** C2
Gangtok India **87** C2
Gannat France **59** C2
Gannett Peak U.S.A. **134** B2
Gansbaai S. Africa **108** A3
Gansu *prov.* China **82** A2
Ganzhou China **83** B3
Gao Mali **100** B3
Gaoual Guinea **100** A3
Gaoyou China **82** B2
Gaoyou Hu *l.* China **82** B2
Gap France **59** D3
Gap Carbon *hd* Alg. **61** C2
Gar China **87** C1
Garah Austr. **117** D1
Garanhuns Brazil **151** F3
Garbahaarrey Somalia **105** E2
Garberville U.S.A. **132** B2
Garbsen Ger. **55** D1
Garça Brazil **154** C2
Garda, Lake Italy **62** B1
Gardelegen Ger. **55** E1
Garden City U.S.A. **134** C3
Garden Hill Can. **127** F2
Gardēz Afgh. **86** A1
Gargždai Lith. **42** B2
Gariep Dam *resr* S. Africa **109** C3
Garies S. Africa **108** A3
Garissa Kenya **105** D3
Garmisch-Partenkirchen Ger. **56** C3
Garnpung Lake *imp. l.* Austr. **116** C2
Garonne *r.* France **58** B3
Garoowe Somalia **103** C4
Garoth India **86** B2
Garoua Cameroon **104** B2
Garry *r.* U.K. **50** B2
Garry Lake Can. **127** E1
Garsen Kenya **105** E3
Garut Indon. **72** B2
Gary U.S.A. **136** C2
Garza García Mex. **143** B2
Garzê China **80** C2
Gascony, Gulf of France **58** B3
Gascoyne *r.* Austr. **114** A2
Gashua Nigeria **101** D3
Gaspé Can. **129** D2
Gaspé, Péninsule de *pen.* Can. **129** D2
Gaston, Lake U.S.A. **139** E1
Gastonia U.S.A. **139** D1
Gata, Cabo de *c.* Spain **61** C2
Gatchina Rus. Fed. **42** D2
Gateshead U.K. **52** C2
Gatesville U.S.A. **141** E2
Gatineau *r.* Can. **128** C2
Gatton Austr. **117** E1
Gauer Lake Can. **127** F2
Gausta *mt.* Norway **47** B4
Gāvbandī Iran **91** C2
Gavdos *i.* Greece **65** B4
Gävle Sweden **47** D3
Gavrilov Posad Rus. Fed. **43** F2
Gavrilov-Yam Rus. Fed. **43** F2
Gawai Myanmar **74** A1
Gawler Austr. **116** B2
Gawler Ranges *hills* Austr. **116** B2
Gaya India **87** C2

Gaya Niger **100** C3
Gaylord U.S.A. **136** D1
Gayny Rus. Fed. **40** E2
Gaza *terr.* Asia **92** B2
Gaza Gaza **92** B2
Gaz-Achak Turkm. **88** D2
Gazandzhyk Turkm. **88** C3
Gaziantep Turkey **102** B1
Gbarnga Liberia **100** B4
Gdańsk Pol. **57** D2
Gdańsk, Gulf of Pol./Rus. Fed. **57** D2
Gdov Rus. Fed. **42** C2
Gdynia Pol. **57** D2
Gedaref Sudan **102** B3
Gedern Ger. **55** D2
Gediz *r.* Turkey **65** C3
Gedser Denmark **56** C2
Geel Belgium **54** B2
Geelong Austr. **116** C3
Geesthacht Ger. **55** E1
Gê'gyai China **87** C1
Geikie *r.* Can. **124** F3
Geilo Norway **47** B3
Gejiu China **83** A3
Gela Italy **62** C3
Gelendzhik Rus. Fed. **45** E3
Gelibolu Turkey *see* Gallipoli
Gelsenkirchen Ger. **54** C2
Gemena Dem. Rep. Congo **104** B3
Gemlik Turkey **65** C2
Gemona del Friuli Italy **59** E2
Genalê Wenz *r.* Eth. **103** C4
General Acha Arg. **153** B4
General Alvear Arg. **153** B4
General Belgrano Arg. **153** C4
General Cepeda Mex. **142** B2
General Pico Arg. **153** B4
General Roca Arg. **153** B4
General Santos Phil. **76** B3
Genesee *r.* U.S.A. **137** E2
Geneseo U.S.A. **137** E2
Geneva Switz. **59** D2
Geneva U.S.A. **137** E2
Geneva, Lake France/Switz. **59** D2
Genève *see* Geneva
Genil *r.* Spain **60** B2
Genk Belgium **54** B2
Genoa Italy **62** A1
Genova Italy *see* Genoa
Gent Belgium *see* Ghent
Genthin Ger. **55** F1
Geographe Bay Austr. **114** A3
George *r.* Can. **129** D1
George S. Africa **108** B3
George, Lake *FL* U.S.A. **139** D3
George, Lake *NY* U.S.A. **137** F2
Georgetown Gambia **100** A3
Georgetown Guyana **151** D2
George Town Malaysia **72** B1
Georgetown *SC* U.S.A. **139** E2
Georgetown *TX* U.S.A. **141** E2
George V Land *reg.* Antarctica **119** H3
Georgia *country* Asia **93** C1
Georgia *state* U.S.A. **139** D2
Georgian Bay Can. **137** D1
Georgina *watercourse* Austr. **115** C2
Georgiyevka Kazakh. **89** F2
Georgiyevsk Rus. Fed. **41** D4
Gera Ger. **55** F2
Geral, Serra *mts* Brazil **154** C3
Geraldine N.Z. **118** B3
Geraldton Austr. **114** A2
Gerede Turkey **92** B1
Gereshk Afgh. **86** A1
Gerlach U.S.A. **132** C2
Gerlachovský štit *mt.* Slovakia **57** E3
Germany *country* Europe **56** B2
Gerolstein Ger. **54** C2
Gerolzhofen Ger. **55** E3
Gersfeld (Rhön) Ger. **55** D2

Gêrzê China **87** C1
Gettysburg *PA* U.S.A. **137** E3
Gettysburg *SD* U.S.A. **134** D1
Gevgelija Macedonia **65** B2
Geyikli Turkey **65** C3
Ghaap Plateau S. Africa **108** B2
Ghadāmis Libya **101** C1
Ghaghara *r.* India **87** C2
Ghana *country* Africa **100** B4
Ghanzi Botswana **106** C2
Ghardaïa Alg. **100** C1
Gharyān Libya **101** D1
Ghatal India **87** C2
Ghazaouet Alg. **61** C2
Ghaziabad India **87** B2
Ghazipur India **87** C2
Ghaznī Afgh. **86** A1
Ghent Belgium **54** A2
Gherla Romania **44** B2
Ghisonaccia France **59** D3
Ghotaru India **86** B2
Ghotki Pak. **86** A2
Giant's Causeway *lava field* U.K. **51** C1
Gianyar Indon. **73** C2
Giarre Italy **62** C3
Giaveno Italy **62** A1
Gibeon Namibia **108** A2
Gibraltar Gibraltar **60** C4
Gibraltar, Strait of Morocco/Spain **60** B2
Gibson Desert Austr. **114** B2
Gichgeniyn Nuruu *mts* Mongolia **80** C1
Gidolē Eth. **103** B4
Gien France **58** C2
Gießen Ger. **55** D2
Gifhorn Ger. **55** E1
Gift Lake Can. **126** D2
Gifu Japan **79** C3
Gigha *i.* U.K. **50** B3
Gijón-Xixón Spain **60** B1
Gila *r.* U.S.A. **140** B2
Gila Bend U.S.A. **140** B2
Gilbert *r.* Austr. **115** D1
Gilbert Islands Kiribati **110**
Gildford U.S.A. **132** D1
Gilgandra Austr. **117** D2
Gilgit Jammu and Kashmir **86** B1
Gilgit *r.* Jammu and Kashmir **86** B1
Gilgunnia Austr. **117** D2
Gillam Can. **127** F2
Gillette U.S.A. **134** B2
Gillingham U.K. **53** D4
Gilmour Island Can. **128** C1
Gimli Can. **127** F2
Ginir Eth. **103** C4
Ginosa Italy **63** C2
Gippsland *reg.* Austr. **117** D3
Girdar Dhor *r.* Pak. **86** A2
Girdi Iran **91** D1
Giresun Turkey **92** B1
Girona Spain **61** D1
Girvan U.K. **50** B3
Gisborne N.Z. **118** C2
Gislaved Sweden **47** C4
Gitarama Rwanda **105** C3
Giulianova Italy **62** B2
Giurgiu Romania **44** C3
Giuvala, Pasul *pass* Romania **44** C2
Givors France **59** C2
Giyani S. Africa **109** D1
Giza Egypt **102** B2
Gjirokastër Albania **65** B2
Gjoa Haven Can. **124** F2
Gjøvik Norway **47** C3
Glace Bay Can. **129** E2
Gladstone Austr. **115** E2

Gláma *mts* Iceland **46** [inset]
Glamoč Bos.-Herz. **63** C2
Glan *r.* Ger. **54** C3
Glanaruddery Mountains
Rep. of Ireland **51** B2
Glasgow U.K. **50** B3
Glasgow *KY* U.S.A. **136** C3
Glasgow *MT* U.S.A. **132** E1
Glastonbury U.K. **53** B4
Glauchau Ger. **55** F2
Glazov Rus. Fed. **40** E3
Glazunovka Rus. Fed. **43** E3
Glen Coe *val.* U.K. **50** B2
Glendale U.S.A. **140** B2
Glen Davis Austr. **117** E2
Glendive U.S.A. **134** C1
Glenelg *r.* Austr. **116** C3
Glen Innes Austr. **117** E1
Glenmorgan Austr. **117** D1
Glennallen U.S.A. **124** C2
Glenrothes U.K. **50** C2
Glens Falls U.S.A. **137** F2
Glen Shee *val.* U.K. **50** C2
Glenties Rep. of Ireland **51** B1
Glenwood U.S.A. **140** C2
Glenwood Springs U.S.A. **134** B3
Gliwice Pol. **57** D2
Globe U.S.A. **140** B2
Głogów Pol. **57** D2
Glomfjord Norway **46** C2
Glomma *r.* Norway **47** C4
Gloucester Austr. **117** E2
Gloucester U.K. **53** B4
Głowen Ger. **55** F1
Glubokoye Kazakh. **89** F1
Glückstadt Ger. **55** D1
Gmünd Austria **56** C2
Gmunden Austria **56** C3
Gnarrenburg Ger. **55** D1
Gniezno Pol. **57** D2
Gnjilane Serb. and Mont. **64** B2
Goalpara India **87** D2
Goat Fell *h.* U.K. **50** B3
Goba Eth. **103** C4
Gobabis Namibia **108** A1
Gobernador Gregores Arg. **153** A5
Gobi *des.* China/Mongolia **82** A1
Goch Ger. **54** C2
Gochas Namibia **108** A1
Godavari *r.* India **85** C3
Goderich Can. **128** B2
Godhra India **86** B2
Gods *r.* Can. **127** F2
Gods Lake Can. **127** F2
Godthåb Greenland *see* Nuuk
Godwin Austen *mt.*
China/Jammu and Kashmir *see* K2
Goéland, Lac au *l.* Can. **128** C2
Goélands, Lac aux *l.* Can. **129** D1
Goes Neth. **54** A2
Goiandira Brazil **154** C1
Goiânia Brazil **154** C1
Goiás Brazil **154** B1
Goio-Erê Brazil **154** B2
Gökçeada *i.* Turkey **65** C2
Gökçedağ Turkey **65** C3
Gokwe Zimbabwe **107** B1
Gol Norway **47** B3
Golaghat India **74** A1
Gol'chikha Rus. Fed. **40** H1
Gölcük Turkey **65** C2
Goldap Pol. **57** E2
Goldberg Ger. **55** F1
Gold Coast Austr. **117** E1
Gold Coast *coastal area* Ghana **100** B4
Golden Can. **126** D2
Golden Bay N.Z. **118** B3
Golden Hinde *mt.* Can. **126** C3
Golden Vale *lowland* Rep. of Ireland
51 B2

Goldfield U.S.A. **133** C3
Gold River Can. **126** C3
Goldsboro U.S.A. **139** E1
Goleta U.S.A. **133** C4
Golmud China **80** C2
Golpāyegān Iran **93** D2
Golspie U.K. **50** C2
Goma Dem. Rep. Congo **105** C3
Gomati *r.* India **87** C2
Gombe Nigeria **101** D3
Gombi Nigeria **101** D3
Gómez Palacio Mex. **142** B2
Gonaïves Haiti **145** C3
Gonâve, Île de la *i.* Haiti **145** C3
Gonbad-e Kavus Iran **93** D2
Gonder Eth. **103** B3
Gondia India **87** C2
Gönen Turkey **65** C2
Gongola *r.* Nigeria **101** D4
Gongolgon Austr. **117** D2
Gongzhuling China **77** A1
Gonzáles Mex. **143** C2
Gonzales U.S.A. **141** E3
Good Hope, Cape of S. Africa **108** A3
Gooding U.S.A. **132** D2
Goodland U.S.A. **134** C3
Goodooga Austr. **117** D1
Goole U.K. **52** C3
Goolgowi Austr. **117** D2
Goolwa Austr. **116** B3
Goondiwindi Austr. **117** E1
Goose Lake U.S.A. **132** B2
Göppingen Ger. **56** B2
Gorakhpur India **87** C2
Goražde Bos.-Herz. **63** C2
Gördes Turkey **65** C3
Gordeyevka Rus. Fed. **43** D3
Goré Chad **101** D4
Gorē Eth. **103** B4
Gore N.Z. **118** A4
Gorey Rep. of Ireland **51** C2
Gorgān Iran **93** D2
Gori Georgia **93** C1
Gorizia Italy **62** B1
Gorlice Pol. **57** E3
Görlitz Ger. **56** C2
Gornji Milanovac Serb. and Mont.
64 B2
Gornji Vakuf Bos.-Herz. **63** C2
Gorno-Altaysk Rus. Fed. **89** F1
Gornotrakiyska Nizina *lowland* Bulg.
64 C2
Gornyak Rus. Fed. **89** F1
Goroka P.N.G. **71** D3
Gorokhovets Rus. Fed. **43** F2
Gorom Gorom Burkina **100** B3
Gorontalo Indon. **73** D1
Gorshechnoye Rus. Fed. **43** E3
Gorumna Island Rep. of Ireland **51** B2
Goryachiy Klyuch Rus. Fed. **45** E3
Gorzów Wielkopolski Pol. **56** C2
Gosford Austr. **117** E2
Goshogawara Japan **78** D2
Goslar Ger. **55** E2
Gospić Croatia **62** C2
Gosport U.K. **53** C4
Gostivar Macedonia **64** B2
Göteborg Sweden *see* Gothenburg
Gotha Ger. **55** E2
Gothenburg Sweden **47** C4
Gothenburg U.S.A. **134** C2
Gotland *i.* Sweden **47** D4
Gotse Delchev Bulg. **65** B2
Gotska Sandön *i.* Sweden **47** D4
Gotsu Japan **79** B4
Göttingen Ger. **55** D2
Gott Peak Can. **126** C2
Gouda Neth. **54** B1
Goudiri Senegal **100** A3
Goudoumaria Niger **101** D3

ouin, Réservoir resr Can. **128** C2
oulburn Austr. **117** D2
oulburn r. N.S.W. Austr. **117** C3
oulburn r. Vic. Austr. **117** C3
oundam Mali **100** B3
ouraya Alg. **61** D2
ourdon France **58** C3
ouré Niger **101** D3
ourits r. S. Africa **108** B3
ourma-Rharous Mali **100** B3
ourock Range mts Austr. **117** D3
overnador Valadares Brazil **155** D1
overnor's Harbour Bahamas **139** E3
oví Altayn Nuruu mts Mongolia **80** C2
ovind Ballash Pant Sagar resr India **87** C2
ower pen. U.K. **53** A4
oya Arg. **152** C3
öyçay Azer. **93** C1
ozha Co salt l. China **87** C1
raaf-Reinet S. Africa **108** B3
rabow Ger. **55** E1
račac Croatia **63** C2
rachevka Rus. Fed. **41** E3
räfenhainichen Ger. **55** F2
rafton Austr. **117** E1
rafton U.S.A. **135** D1
raham U.S.A. **141** E2
raham Island Can. **126** B2
raham Land reg. Antarctica **119** K3
rahamstown S. Africa **109** C3
rajaú Brazil **151** E3
rammos mt. Greece **65** B2
rampian Mountains U.K. **50** B2
ranada Nic. **144** B3
ranada Spain **60** C2
ranby Can. **137** F1
rand U.S.A. **134** F2
rand Bahama i. Bahamas **144** C2
rand Bank Can. **129** E2
rand Canal China see Da Yunhe
rand Canyon U.S.A. **140** B1
rand Canyon gorge U.S.A. **140** B1
rand Cayman i. Cayman Is **144** B3
rand Centre Can. **127** D2
rand Coulee U.S.A. **132** C1
rande r. Bol. **152** B2
rande r. Brazil **155** B2
rande, Bahía arg. **153** B6
rande, Ilha i. Brazil **155** D2
rande Cache Can. **126** D2
rande Comore i. Comoros see Njazidja
rande Prairie Can. **126** D2
rand Erg de Bilma des. Niger **101** D3
rand Erg Occidental des. Alg. **100** B1
rand Erg Oriental des. Alg. **101** C2
rande-Rivière Can. **129** D2
randes, Salinas salt marsh Arg. **152** B4
rand Falls N.B. Can. **137** G1
rand Falls Nfld. and Lab. Can. **129** E2
rand Forks Can. **126** D3
rand Forks U.S.A. **135** D1
randin, Lac l. Can. **126** D1
rand Island U.S.A. **135** D2
rand Isle U.S.A. **138** B3
rand Junction U.S.A. **134** B3
rand-Lahou Côte d'Ivoire **100** B4
rand Lake N.B. Can. **129** D2
rand Lake Nfld. and Lab. Can. **129** E2
rand Marais U.S.A. **135** E1
rándola Port. **60** B2
rand Rapids Can. **127** F2
rand Rapids MI U.S.A. **136** C2
rand Rapids MN U.S.A. **135** E1

Grand Teton mt. U.S.A. **134** A2
Grand Turk Turks and Caicos Is **145** C2
Grangeville U.S.A. **132** C1
Granisle Can. **126** C2
Granite Peak U.S.A. **132** E1
Granitola, Capo c. Italy **62** B3
Gränna Sweden **47** C4
Gransee Ger. **55** F1
Grantham U.K. **52** C3
Grantown-on-Spey U.K. **50** C2
Grants U.S.A. **140** C1
Grants Pass U.S.A. **132** B2
Granville France **58** B2
Granville Lake Can. **127** E2
Grão Mogol Brazil **155** D1
Grarem Alg. **61** E2
Graskop S. Africa **109** D1
Grasse France **59** D3
Graus Spain **61** D1
Gravdal Norway **46** C2
Grave, Pointe de pt France **58** B2
Gravelbourg Can. **127** E3
Gravenhurst Can. **126** C2
Gravesend Austr. **117** E1
Gravesend U.K. **53** D4
Gray France **59** D2
Graz Austria **57** D3
Great Abaco i. Bahamas **145** C2
Great Australian Bight g. Austr. **114** B3
Great Barrier Island N.Z. **118** C2
Great Barrier Reef Austr. **115** D1
Great Basin U.S.A. **133** C3
Great Bear Lake Can. **126** D1
Great Belt sea chan. Denmark **47** C4
Great Bend U.S.A. **135** D3
Great Coco Island Cocos Is **75** A2
Great Dividing Range mts Austr. **117** C3
Greater Antilles is Caribbean Sea **144** B2
Great Falls U.S.A. **132** C1
Great Fish r. S. Africa **109** C3
Great Fish Point pt S. Africa **109** C3
Great Inagua i. Bahamas **145** C2
Great Karoo plat. S. Africa **108** B3
Great Kei r. S. Africa **109** C3
Great Malvern U.K. **53** B3
Great Namaqualand reg. Namibia **108** A2
Great Nicobar i. India **75** A3
Great Ouse r. U.K. **53** D3
Great Plains reg. U.S.A. **121**
Great Rift Valley Africa **105** D3
Great Ruaha r. Tanz. **105** D3
Great Salt Lake U.S.A. **132** D2
Great Salt Lake Desert U.S.A. **132** D2
Great Sand Sea des. Egypt/Libya **102** A2
Great Sandy Desert Austr. **114** B2
Great Slave Lake Can. **126** D1
Great Smoky Mountains U.S.A. **139** D1
Great Victoria Desert Austr. **114** B2
Great Yarmouth U.K. **53** D3
Gredos, Sierra de mts Spain **60** B1
Greece country Europe **65** B3
Greeley U.S.A. **134** F2
Greem-Bell, Ostrov i. Rus. Fed. **94** C1
Green r. Can. **136** U1
Green r. KY U.S.A. **139** C1
Green r. WY U.S.A. **134** B3
Green Bay U.S.A. **136** C2
Green Bay b. U.S.A. **136** C1
Greenbrier r. U.S.A. **137** D3
Greencastle U.S.A. **136** C3
Greeneville U.S.A. **139** D1
Greenfield U.S.A. **137** E2
Green Lake Can. **127** E2

Greenland terr. N. America **125** J2
Greenland Sea Greenland/Svalbard **94** B1
Greenock U.K. **50** B3
Green River UT U.S.A. **133** D3
Green River WY U.S.A. **134** B2
Greensburg IN U.S.A. **136** C3
Greensburg PA U.S.A. **137** E2
Green Swamp U.S.A. **139** E2
Green Valley U.S.A. **140** B2
Greenville Liberia **100** B4
Greenville AL U.S.A. **138** C2
Greenville MS U.S.A. **138** B2
Greenville NC U.S.A. **139** E1
Greenville SC U.S.A. **139** D2
Greenville TX U.S.A. **141** E2
Greenwell Point Austr. **117** D2
Greenwood U.S.A. **139** D2
Gregory, Lake salt flat Austr. **114** B2
Gregory Range hills Austr. **115** D1
Greifswald Ger. **56** C2
Greiz Ger. **55** F2
Grená Denmark **47** C4
Grenada country West Indies **145** D3
Grenade France **58** C3
Grenen spit Denmark **47** C4
Grenfell Austr. **117** D2
Grenfell Can. **127** E2
Grenoble France **59** D2
Grenville, Cape Austr. **115** D1
Gresham U.S.A. **132** B1
Greven Ger. **54** C1
Grevena Greece **65** B2
Grevenbroich Ger. **54** C2
Greybull U.S.A. **134** B2
Grey Hunter Peak Can. **126** B1
Grey Islands Can. **129** E1
Greymouth N.Z. **118** B3
Grey Range hills Austr. **116** C1
Greystones Rep. of Ireland **51** C2
Gribanovskiy Rus. Fed. **45** F1
Griffin U.S.A. **139** D2
Griffith Austr. **117** D2
Grimma Ger. **55** F2
Grimmen Ger. **56** C2
Grimsby U.K. **52** C3
Grimshaw Can. **126** D2
Grímsstaðir Iceland **46** [inset]
Grimstad Norway **47** B4
Grinnell U.S.A. **135** D2
Griqualand East reg. S. Africa **109** C3
Griqualand West reg. S. Africa **108** B2
Grise Fiord Can. **125** G1
Gritley U.K. **50** C1
Groblersdal S. Africa **109** C2
Groblershoop S. Africa **108** B2
Groix, Île de i. France **58** B2
Gronau (Westfalen) Ger. **54** C1
Grong Norway **46** C3
Groningen Neth. **54** C1
Grootdrink S. Africa **108** B2
Groote Eylandt i. Austr. **115** C1
Grootfontein Namibia **106** A1
Groot Karas Berg plat. Namibia **108** A2
Groot Swartberge mts S. Africa **108** B3
Groot Winterberg mt. S. Africa **109** C3
Großenlüder Ger. **55** D2
Großer Rachel mt. Ger. **55** F3
Grosser Speikkogel mt. Austria **56** C3
Grosseto Italy **62** B3
Groß-Gerau Ger. **55** D3
Großglockner mt. Austria **56** C3
Groß-Hesepe Ger. **54** C1
Großlohra Ger. **55** E2
Groß Schönebeck Ger. **55** F1
Gross Ums Namibia **108** A1
Groswater Bay Can. **129** E1
Groundhog r. Can. **128** B2

Grover Beach U.S.A. **133** B3
Groveton U.S.A. **137** F2
Groznyy Rus. Fed. **41** D4
Grubišno Polje Croatia **63** C1
Grudziądz Pol. **57** D2
Grünau Namibia **108** A2
Grundarfjörður Iceland **46** [inset]
Gryazi Rus. Fed. **43** E3
Gryazovets Rus. Fed. **43** F2
Gryfice Pol. **56** D2
Gryfino Pol. **56** C2
Grytviken S. Georgia **153** E6
Guacanayabo, Golfo de *b.* Cuba **144** C2
Guadalajara Mex. **142** B2
Guadalcanal *i.* Solomon Is **110**
Guadalope *r.* Spain **61** C1
Guadalquivir *r.* Spain **60** B2
Guadalupe *i.* Mex. **130** B4
Guadalupe, Sierra de *mts* Spain **60** B2
Guadalupe Peak U.S.A. **140** D2
Guadalupe Victoria Mex. **142** B2
Guadalupe y Calvo Mex. **142** B2
Guadarrama, Sierra de *mts* Spain **60** C1
Guadeloupe *terr.* West Indies **145** D3
Guadiana *r.* Port./Spain **60** B2
Guadix Spain **60** C2
Guaíra Brazil **154** B2
Guajira, Península de la *pen.* Col. **145** C3
Gualaceo Ecuador **150** B3
Guam *terr.* N. Pacific Ocean **71** D2
Guamúchil Mex. **142** B2
Guanacevi Mex. **142** B2
Guanambi Brazil **151** E4
Guanare Venez. **150** C2
Guane Cuba **144** B2
Guang'an China **83** A2
Guangchang China **83** B3
Guangdong *prov.* China **83** B3
Guangxi Zhuangzu Zizhiqu *aut. reg.* China **83** A3
Guangyuan China **82** A2
Guangzhou China **83** B3
Guanhães Brazil **155** D1
Guanipa *r.* Venez. **145** D4
Guanling China **83** A3
Guanshui China **77** B3
Guansu Brazil **154** B3
Guapo Venez. **145** D4
Guápore *r.* Bol./Brazil **152** B2
Guarapuava Brazil **154** B3
Guaraqueçaba Brazil **154** C3
Guaratinguetá Brazil **155** C3
Guarda Port. **60** B1
Guarda Mor Brazil **155** C1
Guardo Spain **60** C1
Guarujá Brazil **155** C2
Guasave Mex. **142** B2
Guatemala *country* Central America **144** A3
Guatemala City Guat. **144** A3
Guaviare *r.* Col. **150** C2
Guaxupé Brazil **155** C2
Guayaquil Ecuador **150** B3
Guayaquil, Golfo de *g.* Ecuador **146**
Guayaramerín Bol. **152** B2
Guaymas Mex. **142** A2
Guba Eth. **103** D3
Guba Dolgaya Rus. Fed. **40** E1
Gubbio Italy **59** E3
Gubkin Rus. Fed. **43** E3
Guelma Alg. **101** C1
Guelmine Morocco **100** A2
Guelph Can. **128** B2
Guémez Mex. **143** C2
Guénange France **54** C3
Guéret France **58** C2
Guernsey *i.* Channel Is **53** B5

Guerrero Negro Mex. **142** A2
Guers, Lac *l.* Can. **129** D1
Guiana Highlands *mts* Guyana/Venez. **150** C2
Guider Cameroon **104** B3
Guidonia-Montecelio Italy **62** B2
Guigang China **83** A3
Guignicourt France **54** A3
Guija Moz. **109** D1
Guildford U.K. **53** C4
Guilin China **83** B3
Guillaume-Delisle, Lac *l.* Can. **128** C1
Guimarães Port. **60** B1
Guinea *country* Africa **100** A3
Guinea, Gulf of Africa **100** C4
Guinea-Bissau *country* Africa **100** A3
Guingamp France **58** B2
Guipavas France **58** B2
Guiratinga Brazil **154** B1
Güiria Venez. **150** C1
Guise France **54** A3
Guiyang China **83** A3
Guizhou *prov.* China **83** A3
Gujranwala Pak. **86** B1
Gujrat Pak. **86** B1
Gukovo Rus. Fed. **45** E2
Gulang China **82** A2
Gulbarga India **85** B3
Gulbene Latvia **42** C2
Gulfport U.S.A. **138** C2
Gulian China **81** E1
Guliston Uzbek. **89** D2
Gul'kevichi Rus. Fed. **45** F2
Gull Lake Can. **127** E2
Güllük Turkey **65** C3
Gulu Uganda **105** D2
Gumare Botswana **106** B1
Gumdag Turkm. **88** C3
Gumla India **87** C2
Gummersbach Ger. **54** C2
Guna India **86** B2
Gundagai Austr. **117** D3
Güney Turkey **65** C3
Gungu Dem. Rep. Congo **104** B3
Gunisao *r.* Can. **127** F2
Gunnedah Austr. **117** E2
Gunnison U.S.A. **134** B3
Gunnison *UT* U.S.A. **133** D3
Gunnison *r.* U.S.A. **134** B3
Guntakal India **85** B3
Gunungsitoli Indon. **72** A1
Gunungtua Indon. **72** A1
Günzburg Ger. **56** C2
Gunzenhausen Ger. **55** E3
Guojiaba China **82** B2
Gurgaon India **86** B2
Gurgueia *r.* Brazil **151** E3
Guri, Embalse de *resr* Venez. **150** C2
Gurinhatã Brazil **154** C1
Gürpinar Turkey **92** C2
Guru Sikhar *mt.* India **86** B2
Gusau Nigeria **101** C3
Gushan China **77** B3
Gushi China **82** B2
Gusinoozersk Rus. Fed. **95** J3
Gus'-Khrustal'nyy Rus. Fed. **43** F2
Guspini Italy **62** A3
Gustavus U.S.A. **126** B2
Güstrow Ger. **55** F1
Gütersloh Ger. **55** D2
Gutu Zimbabwe **107** C1
Guwahati India **87** D2
Guyana *country* S. America **150** D2
Guymon U.S.A. **141** D1
Guyra Austr. **117** E2
Guyuan China **82** A2
Guzmán Mex. **142** B1

Guzmán, Lago de *l.* Mex. **142** B1
Gwadar Pak. **86** A2
Gwalior India **87** B2
Gwanda Zimbabwe **107** B2
Gwardafuy, Gees *c.* Somalia **103** D3
Gweebarra Bay Rep. of Ireland **51** B1
Gweedore Rep. of Ireland **51** B1
Gweru Zimbabwe **107** B1
Gwoza Nigeria **101** D3
Gwydir *r.* Austr. **117** E2
Gyangzê China **87** C2
Gyaring Co *l.* China **87** C1
Gyaring Hu *l.* China **80** C2
Gydan Peninsula Rus. Fed. **40** G1
Gydanskiy Poluostrov *pen.* Rus. Fed. *see* Gydan Peninsula
Gyigang China **74** A1
Gympie Austr. **115** E2
Gyöngyös Hungary **57** D3
Győr Hungary **57** D3
Gypsumville Can. **127** F2
Gyrfalcon Islands Can. **129** D1
Gyula Hungary **57** E3
Gyumri Armenia **93** C1
Gyzylarbat Turkm. **88** C3

Haapsalu Estonia **42** B2
Haarlem Neth. **54** B1
Haarstrang *ridge* Ger. **55** C2
Haast N.Z. **118** A3
Habbān Yemen **90** B3
Habbānīyah, Hawr al *l.* Iraq **93** C2
Hachijō-jima *i.* Japan **79** C4
Hachinohe Japan **78** D2
Hacufera Moz. **107** C2
Hadd, Ra's al *pt* Oman **91** C2
Haddington U.K. **50** C3
Hadejia Nigeria **101** D3
Haderslev Denmark **47** B4
Hadyach Ukr. **45** D1
Haeju N. Korea **77** B2
Haeju-man *b.* N. Korea **77** B2
Haenam S. Korea **77** B3
Ḥafar al Bāţin Saudi Arabia **90** B2
Haflong India **74** A1
Hafnarfjörður Iceland **46** [inset]
Hagar Nish Plateau Eritrea **90** A3
Hagåtña Guam **71** D2
Hagen Ger. **54** C2
Hagenow Ger. **55** E1
Hagensborg Can. **126** C2
Hagerstown U.S.A. **137** E3
Hagfors Sweden **47** C3
Hagi Japan **79** B4
Ha Giang Vietnam **74** B1
Hag's Head Rep. of Ireland **51** B2
Hague, Cap de la *c.* France **58** B2
Hai Tanz. **105** D3
Haicheng China **77** A1
Hai Duong Vietnam **74** B1
Haifa Israel **92** B2
Haifeng China **83** B3
Haikou China **83** B3
Ḥā'il Saudi Arabia **90** B2
Hailar China *see* Hulun Buir
Hailuoto *i.* Fin. **46** E2
Hainan *i.* China **83** D3
Hainan *prov.* China **83** A4
Haines U.S.A. **126** B2
Haines Junction Can. **126** B1
Hainich *ridge* Ger. **55** E2
Hainleite *ridge* Ger. **55** E2
Hai Phong Vietnam **74** B1
Haiti *country* West Indies **145** C3
Haiya Sudan **102** B3
Hajdúböszörmény Hungary **57** E3

ajhir *mt.* Yemen **91** C3
ajjah Yemen **90** B3
ajjiābād Iran **93** D3
ajmā' Oman **91** C3
aka Myanmar **74** A1
akkâri Turkey **93** C2
akkâri Turkey **93** C2
akodate Japan **78** D2
alab Syria *see* Aleppo
alabān Saudi Arabia **90** B2
alaib Sudan **102** B2
alāniyāt, Juzur al *is* Oman **91** C3
ālat 'Ammār Saudi Arabia **90** A2
alban Mongolia **80** C1
alberstadt Ger. **55** E2
alcon, Mount Phil. **76** B2
alden Norway **47** C4
aldensleben Ger. **55** E1
aldwani India **87** B2
āleh Iran **91** C2
alfmoon Bay N.Z. **118** A4
alifax Can. **129** D2
alifax U.K. **52** C5
alifax U.S.A. **137** E3
alla-san *mt.* S. Korea **77** B3
all Beach Can. **125** G2
alle Belgium **54** B2
allein Austria **56** C2
alle (Saale) Ger. **55** E2
allock U.S.A. **135** D1
alls Creek Austr. **114** B1
almahera *i.* Indon. **71** C2
almstad Sweden **47** C4
am France **54** A3
amada Japan **79** C4
amadān Iran **93** C2
amāh Syria **92** B2
amamatsu Japan **79** C4
amar Norway **47** C3
amāṭah, Jabal *mt.* Egypt **102** B2
ambantota Sri Lanka **85** C4
amburg Ger. **55** D1
amḍ, Wādī al *watercourse*
 Saudi Arabia **90** B3
amḍah Saudi Arabia **90** B3
ämeenlinna Fin. **47** E3
ameln Ger. **55** D1
amersley Range *mts* Austr. **114** A2
amhŭng N. Korea **77** B2
ami China **80** C2
amid Sudan **102** B2
amilton Austr. **116** C3
amilton Can. **128** C2
amilton U.K. **50** B3
amilton *AL* U.S.A. **138** C2
amilton *MT* U.S.A. **132** D1
amilton *OH* U.S.A. **136** D3
amina Fin. **47** F3
amm Ger. **54** C2
ammada du Drâa *plat.* Alg. **100** B2
ammamet Japan **78** D3
ammburg Ger. **55** D2
ammerdale Sweden **46** D3
ammerfest Norway **46** E1
ammond U.S.A. **136** C2
ammonton U.S.A. **137** F3
āmūn-e Jaz Mūriān *salt marsh* Iran
 91 C2
amun-i-Lora *dry lake* Afgh./Pak.
 86 A2
āmūn-i Mashkel *salt flat* Iran **91** C2
amun-i Mashkel *salt flat* Pak. **86** A2
anak Saudi Arabia **90** A2
anamaki Japan **78** D3
anau Ger. **55** D2
ancheng China **82** B2
ancock U.S.A. **136** C1
andan China **82** B2
anford U.S.A. **133** C3

Hangayn Nuruu *mts* Mongolia **80** C1
Hangzhou China **83** C2
Hangzhou Wan *b.* China **82** C2
Hanko Fin. **47** E4
Hanksville U.S.A. **133** D3
Hanmer Springs N.Z. **118** B3
Hanna Can. **127** D2
Hannibal U.S.A. **135** E3
Hannover Ger. **55** D1
Hannoversch Münden Ger. **55** D2
Hanöbukten *b.* Sweden **47** C4
Ha Nôi Vietnam **74** B1
Hanoi Vietnam *see* Ha Nôi
Hanover Can. **128** B2
Hanover S. Africa **108** B3
Hanstholm Denmark **47** B4
Hantsavichy Belarus **42** B3
Hanumana India **87** C2
Hanumangarh India **86** B2
Hanzhong China **82** A2
Hao *atoll* Fr. Polynesia **111**
Haparanda Sweden **46** E2
Hapert Neth. **54** B2
Happy Valley - Goose Bay Can.
 129 D1
Haql Saudi Arabia **90** A2
Haraḍh Saudi Arabia **91** B2
Haradok Belarus **42** C2
Harajā Saudi Arabia **90** B3
Harare Zimbabwe **107** C1
Harāsis, Jiddat al *des.* Oman **91** C3
Har-Ayrag Mongolia **81** D1
Harbin China **81** E1
Harbour Breton Can. **129** E2
Harda India **86** B2
Hardangerfjorden *sea chan.* Norway
 47 B4
Hardenberg Neth. **54** C1
Harderwijk Neth. **54** B1
Hardeveld *mts* S. Africa **108** A3
Hardin U.S.A. **132** E1
Hardisty Lake Can. **126** D1
Haren (Ems) Ger. **54** C1
Härer Eth. **103** C4
Hargeysa Somalia **103** C4
Harghita-Mădăraş, Vârful *mt.* Romania
 44 C2
Har Hu *l.* China **80** C2
Haripur Pak. **86** B1
Hari Rūd *r.* Afgh./Iran **86** A1
Harlingen Neth. **54** B1
Harlingen U.S.A. **141** E3
Harlow U.K. **53** D4
Harlowton U.S.A. **132** E1
Harney Basin U.S.A. **132** C2
Harney Lake U.S.A. **132** C2
Härnösand Sweden **47** D3
Har Nur China **81** C1
Har Nuur *l.* Mongolia **80** C1
Harper Liberia **100** B4
Harpstedt Ger. **55** D1
Harricanaw *r.* Can. **128** C1
Harrington U.S.A. **137** E2
Harrington Harbour Can. **129** E1
Harris *pen.* U.K. **50** A2
Harris, Lake *salt flat* Austr. **116** B2
Harris, Sound of *sea chan.* U.K. **50** A2
Harrisburg *IL* U.S.A. **136** C3
Harrisburg *PA* U.S.A. **137** E2
Harrismith S. Africa **109** C2
Harrison U.S.A. **138** B1
Harrison, Cape Can. **129** E1
Harrison Bay U.S.A. **124** C2
Harrisonburg U.S.A. **137** E3
Harrisonville U.S.A. **135** E3
Harrogate U.K. **52** C3
Hârşova Romania **44** C3
Harstad Norway **46** C3
Hartbees *watercourse* S. Africa **108** B2

Hartberg Austria **57** D3
Hartford U.S.A. **137** F2
Hartland Point *pt* U.K. **53** C4
Hartlepool U.K. **52** C2
Hartley Bay Can. **126** C2
Harts *r.* S. Africa **109** B2
Hartwell Reservoir U.S.A. **139** D2
Har Us Nuur *l.* Mongolia **80** C1
Harvey U.S.A. **134** C1
Harwich U.K. **53** D4
Harz *hills* Ger. **55** E2
Hassan India **85** B3
Hasselt Belgium **54** B2
Hassi Messaoud Alg. **101** C1
Hässleholm Sweden **47** C4
Hastière-Lavaux Belgium **54** B2
Hastings Austr. **117** D3
Hastings N.Z. **118** C2
Hastings U.K. **53** D4
Hastings *MN* U.S.A. **135** E2
Hastings *NE* U.S.A. **135** D2
Hatay Turkey *see* Antalya
Hatchet Lake Can. **127** E2
Hatfield Austr. **116** C2
Hatgal Mongolia **80** C1
Ha Tinh Vietnam **74** D2
Hatteras, Cape U.S.A. **139** E1
Hattiesburg U.S.A. **138** C2
Hattingen Ger. **54** C2
Hat Yai Thai. **75** B3
Haud *reg.* Eth. **103** C4
Haugesund Norway **47** B4
Haukeligrend Norway **47** B4
Haukipudas Fin. **46** F2
Hauraki Gulf N.Z. **118** C2
Haut Atlas *mts* Morocco **100** B1
Hauterive Can. **129** D2
Hauts Plateaux Alg. **100** B1
Havana Cuba **144** B2
Havant U.K. **53** C4
Havel *r.* Ger. **55** F1
Havelberg Ger. **55** F1
Havelock N.Z. **118** B3
Havelock North N.Z. **118** C2
Haverfordwest U.K. **53** A4
Havlíčkův Brod Czech Rep. **57** D3
Havøysund Norway **46** F1
Havran Turkey **59** C3
Havre U.S.A. **132** E1
Havre Aubert Can. **129** D2
Havre-St-Pierre Can. **129** D1
Hawaii *i.* U.S.A. **120**
Hawaiian Islands N. Pacific Ocean
 158 E3
Hawarden U.K. **52** B3
Hawea, Lake N.Z. **118** A3
Hawera N.Z. **118** B2
Hawes U.K. **52** B2
Hawick U.K. **50** C3
Hawke Bay N.Z. **118** C2
Hawker Austr. **116** B2
Hawkers Gate Austr. **116** C1
Hawthorne U.S.A. **133** C3
Hay Austr. **116** C2
Hay *r.* Can. **126** D2
Hayden U.S.A. **132** C1
Hayes *r.* Man. Can. **127** F2
Hayes *r.* Nunavut Can. **125** F2
Hayotboshi tog'i *mt.* Uzbek. **89** D2
Hayrabolu Turkey **65** C2
Hay River Can. **126** D1
Hays U.S.A. **135** D3
Hays Yemen **90** B3
Haysyn Ukr. **44** C2
Haywards Heath U.K. **53** C4
Hazarajat *reg.* Afgh. **86** A1
Hazard U.S.A. **136** D3
Hazaribagh India **87** C2
Hazaribagh Range *mts* India **87** C2
Hazebrouck France **54** A2

Hazelton Can. **126** C2
Healesville Austr. **117** D3
Hearst Can. **128** B2
Hebei prov. China **82** B2
Hebel Austr. **117** D1
Heber Springs U.S.A. **138** B1
Hebi China **82** B2
Hebron Can. **129** D1
Hecate Strait Can. **126** B2
Hechi China **83** A3
Hede Sweden **47** C3
Heerenveen Neth. **54** B2
Heerhugowaard Neth. **54** B1
Heerlen Neth. **54** B2
Hefa Israel see Haifa
Hefei China **82** B2
Hefeng China **83** B3
Hegang China **81** E1
Heide Ger. **56** B2
Heide Namibia **108** A1
Heidelberg Ger. **55** D3
Heidelberg S. Africa **108** B3
Heilbronn Ger. **55** D3
Heilongjiang prov. China **78** B1
Heilong Jiang r. China **81** E1
Heinola Fin. **47** F3
Helagsfjället mt. Sweden **46** C3
Helena AR U.S.A. **138** C2
Helena MT U.S.A. **132** D1
Helensburgh U.K. **50** B3
Helgoland i. Ger. **56** B2
Helgoländer Bucht g. Ger. **56** B2
Hella Iceland **46** [inset]
Hellevoetsluis Neth. **54** B2
Hellín Spain **61** C2
Helmand r. Afgh. **86** A1
Helmbrechts Ger. **55** F2
Helmeringhausen Namibia **108** A2
Helmond Neth. **54** B2
Helmsdale U.K. **50** C1
Helmsdale r. U.K. **50** C1
Helmstedt Ger. **55** E1
Helong China **77** B1
Helsingborg Sweden **47** C4
Helsingfors Fin. see Helsinki
Helsingør Denmark **47** C4
Helsinki Fin. **47** F3
Helvick Head Rep. of Ireland **51** C2
Hemel Hempstead U.K. **53** C4
Hemmoor Ger. **55** D1
Hemnesberget Norway **46** C2
Henan prov. China **82** B2
Henderson KY U.S.A. **136** C3
Henderson NC U.S.A. **139** E1
Henderson NV U.S.A. **133** D3
Henderson TX U.S.A. **141** F2
Hendersonville U.S.A. **139** D1
Hendon U.K. **53** C4
Hengduan Shan mts China **74** A1
Hengelo Neth. **54** C1
Hengshui China **82** B2
Hengxian China **83** A3
Hengyang China **83** B3
Henichesʹk Ukr. **45** D2
Hennef (Sieg) Ger. **54** C2
Henrietta Maria, Cape Can. **128** B1
Henryetta U.S.A. **141** E1
Henry Kater, Cape Can. **125** H2
Henstedt-Ulzburg Ger. **55** D1
Hentiesbaai Namibia **106** A2
Hepu China **83** A3
Herāt Afgh. **86** A1
Herbert Can. **127** E2
Herbstein Ger. **55** D2
Hereford U.K. **53** B3
Hereford U.S.A. **141** D2
Herford Ger. **55** D1
Herkenbosch Neth. **54** C2
Herma Ness hd U.K. **50** [inset]
Hermanus S. Africa **108** A3

Hermidale Austr. **117** D2
Hermiston U.S.A. **132** C1
Hermit Islands P.N.G. **71** D3
Hermosillo Mex. **142** A2
Hernandarias Para. **154** B3
Herne Ger. **54** C2
Herning Denmark **47** B4
Herrieden Ger. **55** E3
Hertford U.K. **53** C4
Hertzogville S. Africa **109** C2
Hervey Bay Austr. **115** E2
Herzberg Ger. **55** F2
Herzogenaurach Ger. **55** E3
Heshan China **83** A3
Hess r. Can. **126** B1
Hesselberg h. Ger. **55** E3
Hessisch Lichtenau Ger. **55** D2
Hettinger U.S.A. **134** C1
Hettstedt Ger. **55** E2
Hexham U.K. **52** B2
Heyuan China **83** B3
Heywood Austr. **116** C3
Heze China **82** B2
Hezhou China **83** B3
Hiawatha U.S.A. **135** D3
Hibbing U.S.A. **135** E1
Hicks Bay N.Z. **118** C2
Hidaka-sanmyaku mts Japan **78** D2
Hidalgo Mex. **142** C2
Hidalgo del Parral Mex. **142** B2
Hidrolândia Brazil **154** C1
High Atlas mts Morocco see Haut Atlas
Highland Desert U.S.A. **132** B2
High Level U.S.A. **126** D2
High Point U.S.A. **139** E1
High Prairie Can. **126** D2
High River Can. **126** D2
Highrock Lake Can. **127** E2
High Wycombe U.K. **53** C4
Hilton Head Island U.S.A. **139** D2
Hilversum Neth. **54** B1
Himalaya mts Asia **87** B1
Himeji Japan **79** B4
Himeville S. Africa **109** C2
Hinchinbrook Island Austr. **115** D1
Hindu Kush mts Afgh./Pak. **86** A1
Hinesville U.S.A. **139** D2
Hinganghat India **87** B2
Hinton Can. **126** D2
Hinnøya i. Norway **46** C2
Hinojosa del Duque Spain **60** B2
Hinthada Myanmar **74** A2
Hirakud Reservoir India **87** C2
Hirosaki Japan **78** D2
Hiroshima Japan **79** B4
Hirschaid Ger. **55** E3
Hirschberg Ger. **55** E2
Hirson France **59** C2
Hirtshals Denmark **47** B4
Hisar India **86** B2
Hispaniola i. Caribbean Sea **145** C2
Hīt Iraq **93** C2
Hitachi Japan **79** D3
Hitachinaka Japan **79** D3
Hitra i. Norway **46** B3
Hiva Oa i. Fr. Polynesia **111**
Hjälmaren l. Sweden **47** C4
Hjalmar Lake Can. **127** E1

Hjørring Denmark **47** C4
Hlabisa S. Africa **109** D2
Hlíð Iceland **46** [inset]
Hlobyne Ukr. **45** D2
Hlohlowane S. Africa **109** C2
Hlotse Lesotho **109** C2
Hlukhiv Ukr. **45** D1
Hlybokaye Belarus **42** C2
Ho Ghana **100** C4
Hoachanas Namibia **108** A1
Hobart Austr. **115** D4
Hobart U.S.A. **141** E1
Hobbs U.S.A. **141** D2
Hobro Denmark **47** B4
Hobyo Somalia **103** C4
Hoceima, Baie d'Al b. Morocco **60** C2
Hô Chi Minh City Vietnam **75** B2
Hôd reg. Maur. **100** B3
Hodeidah Yemen **90** B3
Hódmezővásárhely Hungary **57** E3
Hodna, Chott el salt l. Alg. **61** D2
Hoek van Holland Neth. see
Hook of Holland
Hoeyang N. Korea **77** B2
Hof Ger. **55** F2
Hofheim in Unterfranken Ger. **55** E2
Höfn Austurland Iceland **46** [inset]
Höfn Vestfirðir Iceland **46** [inset]
Hofsjökull ice cap Iceland **46** [inset]
Höfu Japan **79** B4
Hoggar plat. Alg. **101** C2
Högsby Sweden **47** D4
Høgste Breakulen mt. Norway **47** B3
Hohe Rhön mts Ger. **55** D2
Hohe Venn moorland Belgium **54** C2
Hohhot China **82** B1
Hoh Xil Shan mts China **87** C1
Hôi An Vietnam **75** B2
Hojai India **74** A1
Hokitika N.Z. **118** B3
Hokkaidō i. Japan **78** D2
Holberg Can. **126** C2
Holbrook U.S.A. **140** B2
Holdrege U.S.A. **135** D2
Holguín Cuba **145** C2
Hóll Iceland **46** [inset]
Holland U.S.A. **136** C2
Hollum Neth. **54** B1
Holly Springs U.S.A. **138** C2
Hollywood CA U.S.A. **133** C4
Hollywood FL U.S.A. **139** D3
Holm Norway **46** C2
Holman Can. **124** E2
Holmsund Sweden **46** E3
Holoog Namibia **108** A2
Holstebro Denmark **47** B4
Holston r. U.S.A. **139** D1
Holyhead U.K. **52** A3
Holy Island England U.K. **52** C2
Holy Island Wales U.K. **52** A3
Holyoke U.S.A. **134** C2
Holzminden Ger. **55** D2
Homalin Myanmar **74** A1
Homberg (Efze) Ger. **55** D2
Hombori Mali **100** B3
Homburg Ger. **54** C3
Home Bay Can. **125** H2
Homestead U.S.A. **139** D3
Hommelvik Norway **46** C3
Homs Syria **92** B2
Homyel' Belarus **43** D3
Hondeklipbaai S. Africa **108** A3
Hondo r. Belize/Mex. **143** D3
Hondo U.S.A. **141** E3
Honduras country Central America **144** B3
Hønefoss Norway **47** C3
Honey Lake salt l. U.S.A. **132** B2
Honfleur France **58** C2
Hông Gai Vietnam **74** B1

Honghu China **83** B3
Hongjiang China **83** A3
Hong Kong China **83** B3
Hong Kong *aut. reg.* China **83** B3
Hongwŏn N. Korea **77** B1
Hongze Hu *l.* China **82** B2
Honiara Solomon Is **112**
Honjō Japan **78** D3
Honshū *i.* Japan **79** B3
Honningsvåg Norway **46** F1
Hood, Mount *vol.* U.S.A. **132** B1
Hood Point *pt* Austr. **114** A3
Hood River U.S.A. **132** B1
Hoogeveen Neth. **54** C1
Hoogezand-Sappemeer Neth. **54** C1
Hoog-Keppel Neth. **54** C2
Hoonah U.S.A. **126** B2
Hoorn Neth. **54** B1
Hoorn, Îles de *is* Wallis and Futuna Is
  111
Hope Can. **126** C3
Hope U.S.A. **138** B2
Hope, Point *pt* U.S.A. **95** O2
Hopedale Can. **129** D1
Hopetoun Austr. **116** C3
Hopetown S. Africa **108** B3
Hopewell U.S.A. **137** E3
Hopewell Islands Can. **128** C1
Hopkins, Lake *salt flat* Austr. **114** B2
Hopkinsville U.S.A. **136** C3
Hoquiam U.S.A. **132** B1
Horasan Turkey **93** C1
Horažďovice Czech Rep. **55** F3
Hörby Sweden **47** C4
Horki Belarus **43** D3
Horlivka Ukr. **45** E2
Hormak Iran **91** D2
Hormuz, Strait of Iran/Oman **91** C2
Horn Austria **57** D3
Horn *c.* Iceland **46** [inset]
Horn, Cape Chile **153** B6
Hornell U.S.A. **137** E2
Hornepayne Can. **128** B2
Hornsea U.K. **52** C3
Horodenka Ukr. **44** C2
Horodnya Ukr. **45** D1
Horodok *Khmel'nyts'ka Oblast'* Ukr.
  44 C2
Horodok *L'vivs'ka Oblast'* Ukr. **44** B2
Horokhiv Ukr. **44** B1
Horse Islands Can. **129** E1
Horsham Austr. **116** C3
Horton *r.* Can. **124** D2
Hosa'ina Eth. **103** B4
Horton *r.* Can. **124** D2
Hosa'ina Eth. **103** B4
Hoshab Pak. **86** A2
Hoshiarpur India **86** B1
Hotan China **87** C1
Hotazel S. Africa **108** B2
Hot Springs *AR* U.S.A. **138** B2
Hot Springs *SD* U.S.A. **134** C2
Hottah Lake Can. **126** D1
Houffalize Belgium **54** B2
Houma China **82** B2
Houma U.S.A. **138** B3
Houston Can. **126** C2
Houston U.S.A. **141** E3
Houwater S. Africa **108** B3
Hovd Mongolia **80** C1
Hove U.K. **53** C4
Hövsgöl Nuur *l.* Mongolia **80** C1
Höviün Mongolia **80** C1
Howar, Wadi *watercourse* Sudan
  102 A3
Howe, Cape Austr. **117** D3
Howland Island *terr.* N. Pacific Ocean
  113
Howlong Austr. **117** D3
Höxter Ger. **55** D2

Hoy *i.* U.K. **50** C1
Høyanger Norway **47** B3
Hoyerswerda Ger. **56** C2
Hpapun Myanmar **74** A2
Hradec Králové Czech Rep. **57** D2
Hrasnica Bos.-Herz. **63** C3
Hrebinka Ukr. **45** D1
Hrodna Belarus **42** B3
Hsi-hseng Myanmar **74** A1
Hsinchu Taiwan **83** C3
Hsinying Taiwan **83** C3
Hsipaw Myanmar **74** A1
Huachi China **82** A2
Huacho Peru **150** B4
Huade China **82** B1
Huadian China **77** B1
Huai'an China **82** B2
Huaibei China **82** B2
Huaihua China **83** A3
Huainan China **82** B2
Huaiyang China **82** B2
Huaiyin China *see* Huai'an
Huajuapan de Leon Mex. **143** C3
Huaki Indon. **71** C3
Hualien Taiwan **83** C3
Huallaga *r.* Peru **150** B3
Huambo Angola **106** A1
Huancavelica Peru **150** B4
Huancayo Peru **150** B4
Huangchuan China **82** B2
Huang Hai *sea* N. Pacific Ocean *see*
  Yellow Sea
Huang He *r.* China *see* Yellow River
Huangliu China **83** A4
Huangnihe China **77** B1
Huangshan China **83** B3
Huangshi China **83** B2
Huangtu Gaoyuan *plat.* China **82** A2
Huangyan China **83** C3
Huanren China **77** B1
Huánuco Peru **150** B3
Huanuni Bol. **152** B2
Huaráz Peru **150** B3
Huarmey Peru **150** B4
Huascarán, Nevado de *mt.* Peru **146**
Huasco Chile **152** A3
Huasco *r.* Chile **152** A3
Huatabampo Mex. **142** B2
Huatusco Mex. **143** C3
Huayuan China **83** A3
Huayxay Laos **74** B1
Hubei *prov.* China **82** B2
Hubli India **85** B3
Hückelhoven Ger. **54** C2
Hucknall U.K. **52** C3
Huddersfield U.K. **52** C3
Hudiksvall Sweden **47** D3
Hudson *r.* U.S.A. **137** F2
Hudson Bay Can. **127** E2
Hudson Bay *sea* Can. **125** G3
Hudson's Hope Can. **126** C2
Hudson Strait Can. **125** H2
Huê̂ Vietnam **74** B2
Huehuetenango Guat. **144** A3
Huehueto, Cerro *mt.* Mex. **142** B2
Huejutla Mex. **143** C2
Huelva Spain **60** B2
Huércal-Overa Spain **61** C2
Huesca Spain **61** C1
Huéscar Spain **60** C2
Hughes Austr. **114** B3
Hugo U.S.A. **141** E3
Huhudi S. Africa **108** B2
Huib-Hoch Plateau Namibia
  108 A2
Huichang China **83** B3
Huich'ŏn N. Korea **77** B1
Huilai China **83** B3
Huíla Plateau Angola **106** A1
Huili China **74** B1

Huinan China **77** B1
Huittinen Fin. **47** E3
Huixtla Mex. **143** C3
Huize China **83** A3
Huizhou China **83** B3
Hujirt Mongolia **80** C1
Hujr Saudi Arabia **90** B2
Hukuntsi Botswana **108** B1
Hulayfah Saudi Arabia **90** B2
Hulin China **78** B1
Hull Can. **128** C2
Hulun Buir China **81** D1
Hulun Nur *l.* China **81** D1
Hulwan U.K. **45** E2
Hulyaypole Ukr. **45** E2
Huma China **81** E1
Humaitá Brazil **150** C3
Humansdorp S. Africa **108** B3
Humber *est.* U.K. **52** C3
Humboldt Can. **124** E3
Humboldt U.S.A. **138** C1
Humboldt *r.* U.S.A. **132** C2
Humenné Slovakia **57** E3
Hume Reservoir Austr. **117** D3
Humphreys Peak U.S.A. **140** B1
Húnaflói *b.* Iceland **46** [inset]
Hunan *prov.* China **83** B3
Hunchun China **77** C1
Hunedoara Romania **44** B2
Hünfeld Ger. **55** D2
Hungary *country* Europe **57** D3
Hungerford Austr. **116** C1
Hŭngnam N. Korea **77** B2
Hun He *r.* China **77** A1
Hunstanton U.K. **52** D3
Hunter *r.* Ger. **55** D1
Hunter Island
  S. Pacific Ocean **110**
Hunter Islands Austr. **115** D4
Huntingdon U.K. **53** C3
Huntington *IN* U.S.A. **136** C2
Huntington *WV* U.S.A. **136** C3
Huntly N.Z. **118** C1
Huntly U.K. **50** C2
Huntsville Can. **128** C2
Huntsville *AL* U.S.A. **138** C2
Huntsville *TX* U.S.A. **141** E2
Huon Peninsula P.N.G. **71** D3
Huozhou China **82** B2
Huron U.S.A. **135** D2
Huron, Lake Can./U.S.A. **136** D2
Hurricane U.S.A. **133** D3
Húsavík Iceland **46** [inset]
Huşi Romania **44** C2
Huslia U.S.A. **124** B2
Husn Āl 'Abr Yemen **90** B3
Husnes Norway **48** E2
Husum Ger. **56** B2
Hutag Mongolia **80** C1
Hutanopan Indon. **72** A1
Hutchinson U.S.A. **135** D3
Huzhou China **82** C2
Hvalnes Iceland **46** [inset]
Hvannadalshnúkur *vol.* Iceland
  46 [inset]
Hvar *i.* Croatia **63** C2
Hwange Zimbabwe **106** B1
Hyannis U.S.A. **134** C2
Hyargas Nuur *salt l.* Mongolia
  80 C1
Hyden Austr. **114** A3
Hyderabad India **85** B3
Hyderabad Pak. **86** A2
Hyères France **59** D3
Hyères, Îles d' *is* France **59** D3
Hyesan N. Korea **77** B1
Hyland Post Can. **126** C2
Hyllestad Norway **48** E1
Hyōno-sen *mt.* Japan **79** B3
Hythe U.K. **53** D4
Hyvinkää Fin. **47** E3

I

Iaco r. Brazil **150** C3
Ialomiţa r. Romania **44** C3
Ianca Romania **44** C3
Iaşi Romania **44** C2
Iba Phil. **76** A2
Ibadan Nigeria **100** C4
Ibagué Col. **150** B2
Ibarra Ecuador **150** B2
Ibb Yemen **90** B3
Ibbenbüren Ger. **54** C1
Ibi Nigeria **101** C4
Ibiá Brazil **155** C1
Ibiraçu Brazil **155** D1
Ibiza i. Spain **61** D2
Ibotirama Brazil **151** E4
Ibrā' Oman **91** C2
Ibrī Oman **91** C2
Ica Peru **150** B4
İçel Turkey see Mersin
Iceland country Europe **46** [inset]
Ichinoseki Japan **78** D3
Ichnya Ukr. **45** D1
Ich'ŏn N. Korea **77** B2
Idabel U.S.A. **141** F2
Idaho state U.S.A. **132** D2
Idaho Falls U.S.A. **132** D2
Idar-Oberstein Ger. **54** C3
Idfū Egypt **102** B2
Idhān Awbārī des. Libya **101** D2
Idhān Murzūq des. Libya **101** D2
Idiofa Dem. Rep. Congo **104** B3
Idlib Syria **92** B2
Iepê Brazil **154** B2
Ieper Belgium **54** A2
Ifakara Tanz. **105** D3
Ifanadiana Madag. **107** [inset] D2
Ife Nigeria **100** C4
Ifóghas, Adrar des hills Mali **100** C3
Igan Malaysia **73** C1
Igarapava Brazil **154** C2
Igarka Rus. Fed. **94** H2
Iqatpuri India **86** B3
Iğdır Turkey **93** C2
Iglesias Italy **62** A3
Igloolik Can. **125** G2
Ignace Can. **128** A2
Ignalina Lith. **42** C2
İğneada Turkey **64** C2
Igoumenitsa Greece **65** B3
Igra Rus. Fed. **40** F2
Iguaçu r. Brazil **154** B3
Iguaçu Falls Arg./Brazil **154** B3
Iguala Mex. **143** C3
Igualada Spain **61** D1
Iguape Brazil **154** C2
Iguatemi Brazil **154** B2
Iguatemi r. Brazil **154** B2
Iguatu Brazil **151** F3
Iguéla Gabon **104** A3
Iqunga Tanz. **105** D3
Ihbulag Mongolia **81** D2
Ihosy Madag. **107** [inset] D2
Iisalmi Fin. **46** F3
Ijebu-Ode Nigeria **100** C4
IJmuiden Neth. **54** B1
IJssel r. Neth. **54** B1
IJsselmeer l. Neth. **54** B1
Ikageng S. Africa **109** C2
Ikaria i. Greece **65** C3
Ikela Dem. Rep. Congo **104** C3
Ikhtiman Bulg. **64** B2
Iki i. Japan **79** A4
Ikongo Madag. **107** [inset] D2
Iksan S. Korea **77** B2
Ilagan Phil. **76** B2

Īlām Iran **93** C2
Ilam Nepal **87** C2
Iława Pol. **57** D2
Ilazārān, Kūh-e mt. Iran **91** C2
Île-à-la-Crosse Can. **127** E2
Île-à-la-Crosse, Lac l. Can. **127** E2
Ilebo Dem. Rep. Congo **104** C3
Ileret Kenya **105** D2
Ilford U.K. **53** D4
Ilfracombe U.K. **53** A4
Ilha Grande, Baía da b. Brazil **155** D2
Ilha Grande, Represa resr Brazil **154** B2
Ilha Solteira, Represa resr Brazil **154** B2
Ílhavo Port. **60** B1
Ilhéus Brazil **151** F4
Iligan Phil. **76** B3
Illapel Chile **152** A4
Illichivs'k Ukr. **44** D2
Illinois r. U.S.A. **136** B3
Illinois state U.S.A. **136** C3
Illintsi Ukr. **44** C2
Iliçi Alg. **100** C2
Il'men', Ozero l. Rus. Fed. **43** D2
Ilmenau Ger. **55** E2
Ilo Peru **150** B4
Iloilo Phil. **76** B2
Ilomantsi Fin. **46** G3
Ilorin Nigeria **100** C4
Iluka Austr. **117** E1
Ilulissat Greenland **125** I2
Imari Japan **79** A4
Imatra Fin. **46** F2
Imbituba Brazil **154** C3
Imi Eth. **103** C4
Imola Italy **62** B2
Imperatriz Brazil **151** E3
Imperial U.S.A. **134** C2
Impfondo Congo **104** B2
Imphal India **74** A1
İmroz Turkey **65** C2
Inambari r. Peru **150** C4
In Aménas Alg. **100** C2
Inanwatan Indon. **71** C3
Inari Fin. **46** F2
Inarijärvi l. Fin. **46** F2
Inawashiro-ko l. Japan **79** D3
İnce Burun pt Turkey **92** B1
Inch'ŏn S. Korea **77** B2
Incomati r. Moz. **109** D2
Indalstø Norway **48** E1
Inda Silasē Eth. **90** A3
Indé Mex. **142** B2
Independence IA U.S.A. **133** C3
Independence KS U.S.A. **135** E3
Independence MO U.S.A. **135** D3
Independence Mountains U.S.A. **132** C2
Inderborskiy Kazakh. **88** C2
India country Asia **84** B2
Indiana U.S.A. **137** E2
Indiana state U.S.A. **136** C2
Indianapolis U.S.A. **136** C3
Indian Head Can. **127** F2
Indian Ocean **161**
Indianola IA U.S.A. **135** E2
Indianola MS U.S.A. **138** B2
Indian Springs U.S.A. **133** C3
Indiga Rus. Fed. **40** E2
Indigirka r. Rus. Fed. **95** L2
Indija Serb. and Mont. **64** B1
Indio U.S.A. **133** C4
Indonesia country Asia **72** B3
Indore India **86** B2
Indramayu, Tanjung pt Indon. **72** B2
Indre r. France **58** C2
Indus r. China/Pakistan **86** B1
Indus r. China/Pakistan **84** A2
Indus, Mouths of the Pak. **86** A2
İnebolu Turkey **92** B1

İnegöl Turkey **65** C2
Infiernillo, Presa resr Mex. **142** B3
Inglewood Austr. **117** E1
Ingolstadt Ger. **56** C3
Ingomar Austr. **116** A1
Ingraj Bazar India **87** C2
Inhaca Moz. **109** D2
Inhambane Moz. **107** C2
Inishbofin i. Rep. of Ireland **51** A2
Inishmore i. Rep. of Ireland **51** B2
Inishowen pen. Rep. of Ireland **51** C1
Inland Kaikoura Range mts N.Z. **118** B3
Inn r. Europe **56** C3
Innaanganeq c. Greenland **125** H1
Inner Mongolia aut. reg. China see
  Nei Mongol Zizhiqu
Inner Sound sea chan. U.K. **50** B2
Innisfail Austr. **115** D1
Innsbruck Austria **56** C3
Inocência Brazil **154** B1
Inongo Dem. Rep. Congo **104** B3
Inowrocław Pol. **57** D2
In Salah Alg. **100** C2
Insein Myanmar **74** A2
Inta Rus. Fed. **40** F2
International Falls U.S.A. **135** E1
Inukjuak Can. **128** C1
Inuvik Can. **124** D2
Inveraray U.K. **50** B2
Invercargill N.Z. **118** A4
Inverell Austr. **117** E1
Invergordon U.K. **50** B2
Invermere Can. **126** D2
Inverness U.K. **50** B2
Inverness U.K. **50** B2
Inverurie U.K. **50** C2
Investigator Strait Austr. **116** B3
Inya Rus. Fed. **89** F1
Inyonga Tanz. **105** D3
Inza Rus. Fed. **41** D3
Ioannina Greece **65** B3
Iola U.S.A. **135** E3
Iona i. U.K. **50** A2
Ionian Islands admin. reg. Greece
  65 A3
Ionian Sea Greece/Italy **65** A3
Ionioi Nisoi admin. reg. Greece see
  Ionian Islands
Ios i. Greece **65** C3
Iowa state U.S.A. **135** E2
Iowa City U.S.A. **135** E2
Ipameri Brazil **154** C1
Ipatinga Brazil **155** D1
Ipatovo Rus. Fed. **93** C1
Ipelegeng S. Africa **109** C2
Ipiales Col. **150** B2
Ipiranga Brazil **154** B3
Ipoh Malaysia **72** B1
Iporá Brazil **154** B1
Ippy C.A.R. **104** C2
Ipsala Turkey **65** C2
Ipswich Austr. **117** E1
Ipswich U.K. **53** D3
Iqaluit Can. **125** H2
Iquique Chile **152** A3
Iquitos Peru **150** B3
Irai Brazil **154** B3
Irakleio Greece see Iraklion
Iraklion Greece **65** C3
Iran country Asia **93** D2
Iran, Pegunungan mts Indon. **73** C1
Īrānshahr Iran **91** D2
Irapuato Mex. **142** B2
Iraq country Asia **93** C2
Irati Brazil **154** B3
Irbid Jordan **92** B2
Irbit Rus. Fed. **40** F3
Irecê Brazil **151** E4

Ireland i. Rep. of Ireland/U.K. **36**
Ireland, Republic of country Europe **51** B2
Irema Dem. Rep. Congo **104** C3
Irgiz Kazakh. **88** D2
Irigui reg. Mali/Maur. **100** B3
Iringa Tanz. **105** D3
Iriri r. Brazil **151** D3
Irish Sea Rep. of Ireland/U.K. **49** B3
Irkutsk Rus. Fed. **80** C1
Iron Knob Austr. **116** B2
Iron Mountain U.S.A. **136** C1
Ironwood U.S.A. **136** B1
Irosin Phil. **76** B2
Irpin' Ukr. **44** D1
Irrawaddy r. Myanmar **74** A2
Irrawaddy, Mouths of the Myanmar **75** A2
Irtysh r. Kazakh./Rus. Fed. **89** E1
Irún Spain **61** C1
Irvine U.S.A. **54**
Isabela Phil. **76** B3
Isabela, Cordillera mts Nic. **144** B3
Ísafjörður Iceland **46** [inset]
Isahaya Japan **79** B4
Isar r. Ger. **59** E2
Isbister U.K. **50** [inset]
Ischia, Isola d' i. Italy **62** B2
Ise Japan **79** C4
Isengi Dem. Rep. Congo **104** C2
Isère, Pointe pt Fr. Guiana **146**
Iserlohn Ger. **54** C2
Isernhagen Ger. **55** D1
Ise-wan b. Japan **79** C4
Iseyin Nigeria **100** C4
Ishikari-wan b. Japan **78** D2
Ishim r. Kazakh./Rus. Fed. **89** E1
Ishinomaki Japan **78** D3
Ishioka Japan **79** D3
Ishpeming U.S.A. **136** C1
Işıklar Dağı mts Turkey **65** C5
Işıklı Turkey **65** C3
Isil'kul' Rus. Fed. **89** E1
Isipingo S. Africa **109** D2
Iskenderun Turkey **92** B2
Iskitim Rus. Fed. **94** H3
Iskür r. Bulg. **64** B2
Iskut r. Can. **126** B2
Islamabad Pak. **86** B1
Island Lagoon salt flat Austr. **116** B2
Island Lake Can. **127** F2
Islands, Bay of N.Z. **118** B2
Islay i. U.K. **50** A3
Isle of Man i. Irish Sea **52** A2
Isna Egypt **90** A2
Isoka Zambia **105** C4
Isperikh Bulg. **64** C2
Issoire France **57** C2
Istanbul Turkey **65** C3
Istanbul Boğazı str. Turkey see Bosporus
Istiaia Greece **65** B3
Istres France **57** D3
Istria pen. Croatia **62** B1
Itaberaba Brazil **151** E4
Itabira Brazil **155** D1
Itabirito Brazil **155** D2
Itabuna Brazil **151** F4
Itacoatiara Brazil **150** D3
Itaguajé Brazil **154** B2
Itaí Brazil **154** C2
Itaipu, Represa de resr Brazil **154** B3
Itaituba Brazil **151** D3
Itajaí Brazil **154** C3
Itajubá Brazil **155** C2

Itajuípe Brazil **155** E1
Itaju do Colônia Brazil
Itália country Europe **62** B2
Itamaraju Brazil **155** D1
Itamarandiba Brazil **155** D1
Itambacuri Brazil **155** D1
Itambé, Pico de mt. Brazil **155** D1
Itanagar India **74** A1
Itanhaém Brazil **154** C2
Itanhém Brazil **155** D1
Itaobím Brazil **155** D1
Itapajipe Brazil **154** C1
Itapebi Brazil **155** E1
Itapemirim Brazil **155** D2
Itaperuna Brazil **155** D2
Itapetinga Brazil **151** E4
Itapetininga Brazil **154** C2
Itapeva Brazil **154** C2
Itapicuru r. Brazil **151** F4
Itapicuru Mirim Brazil **151** E3
Itapuranga Brazil **154** C1
Itararé Brazil **154** C2
Itarsi India **87** B2
Itarumã Brazil **154** B1
Itaúna Brazil **155** C2
Itbayat i. Phil. **76** B1
Ithaca U.S.A. **137** E2
Ith Hils ridge Ger. **55** D1
Itimbiri r. Dem. Rep. Congo **104** C3
Itinga Brazil **155** D1
Itiquira Brazil **154** B1
Itiquira r. Brazil **154** A1
Itō Japan **79** C4
Ittoqqortoormiit Greenland **125** K2
Itu Brazil **154** C2
Ituí r. Brazil **150** B3
Ituiutaba Brazil **154** C1
Itula Dem. Rep. Congo **105** C3
Itumbiara Brazil **154** C1
Iturama Brazil **154** B1
Itzehoe Ger. **56** B2
Iul'tin Rus. Fed. **95** O2
Ivaí r. Brazil **154** B2
Ivalo Fin. **46** J2
Ivanava Belarus **42** C3
Ivanhoe Austr. **116** C2
Ivankiv Ukr. **44** C1
Ivano-Frankivs'k Ukr. **44** B2
Ivanovo Rus. Fed. **43** F2
Ivatsevichy Belarus **42** C3
Ivaylovgrad Bulg. **65** C2
Ivdel' Rus. Fed. **40** F2
Ivinheima Brazil **154** B2
Ivinheima r. Brazil **154** B2
Ivittuut Greenland **125** I2
Ivrea Italy **61** A1
Ivrindi Turkey **65** C2
Ivujivik Can. **125** G2
Iwaki Japan **79** D3
Iwakuni Japan **79** B4
Iwamizawa Japan **78** D2
Iwanai Japan **78** D2
Iwye Belarus **42** C3
Ixopo S. Africa **109** D3
Ixtlán Mex. **142** B2
Izabal, Lago de l. Guat. **143** D3
Izamal Mex. **143** D2
Izberbash Rus. Fed. **93** C1
Izhevsk Rus. Fed. **40** E3
Izhma Rus. Fed. **40** E2
Izmalkovo Rus. Fed. **43** E3
Izmayil Ukr. **44** C2
İzmir Turkey **65** C3
İznik Gölü l. Turkey **65** C2
Izumo Japan **79** B3
Izyaslav Ukr. **44** C1
Izyum Ukr. **45** C2

Jabalón r. Spain **60** C2

Jabalpur India **87** B2
Jabiru Austr. **114** C1
Jablanica Bos.-Herz. **63** C2
Jaboatão Brazil **151** F4
Jabotícabal Brazil **154** C2
Jaca Spain **61** C1
Jacala Mex. **143** C2
Jacareacanga Brazil **151** D3
Jacareí Brazil **155** C2
Jacinto Brazil **155** D1
Jackman U.S.A. **137** F1
Jackson AL U.S.A. **138** C2
Jackson MI U.S.A. **136** C2
Jackson MS U.S.A. **138** B2
Jackson TN U.S.A. **138** C1
Jackson WY U.S.A. **134** A2
Jackson Head N.Z. **118** A3
Jacksonville AR U.S.A. **138** B2
Jacksonville FL U.S.A. **139** D2
Jacksonville IL U.S.A. **136** B3
Jacksonville NC U.S.A. **139** E2
Jacksonville TX U.S.A. **141** D2
Jacmel Haiti **145** C3
Jacobabad Pak. **86** A2
Jacobina Brazil **151** E4
Jacques Cartier, Mont mt. Can. **129** D2
Jacunda Brazil **151** E3
Jacupiranga Brazil **154** C2
Jadovnik mt. Bos.-Herz. **63** C2
Jaén Peru **150** B3
Jaén Spain **60** C2
Jaffa, Cape Austr. **116** B3
Jaffna Sri Lanka **85** B4
Jagdalpur India **85** C3
Jagersfontein S. Africa **109** C2
Jaghín Iran **91** C2
Jagtial India **85** B2
Jaguariaíva Brazil **154** C2
Jahrom Iran **93** D3
Jaipur India **86** B2
Jaisalmer India **86** B2
Jajarkot Nepal **87** C2
Jajce Bos.-Herz. **63** C2
Jakarta Indon. **72** B2
Jakes Corner Can. **126** B1
Jäkkvik Sweden **46** J2
Jakobstad Fin. **46** E3
Jalālābād Afgh. **86** B1
Jalal-Abad Kyrg. **89** E2
Jalandhar India **86** B1
Jalapa Mex. **143** C3
Jales Brazil **154** B2
Jalgaon India **86** B2
Jalingo Nigeria **101** D4
Jalna India **86** B3
Jalpa Mex. **142** B2
Jalpaiguri India **87** C2
Jalpan Mex. **143** C2
Jālū Libya **101** E2
Jamaica country West Indies **144** C3
Jamalpur Bangl. **87** C2
Jambi Indon. **72** B2
James r. N. Dakota/S. Dakota U.S.A. **135** D2
James r. VA U.S.A. **137** E3
James Bay Can. **125** G3
Jameson Land reg. Greenland **125** K2
Jamestown Austr. **116** B2
Jamestown ND U.S.A. **135** D1
Jamestown NY U.S.A. **137** E2
Jammu India **86** B1
Jammu and Kashmir terr. Asia **86** B1
Jamnagar India **86** B2
Jämsä Fin. **47** F3
Jamshedpur India **87** C2
Jamuna r. Bangl. **87** C2
Janakpur Nepal **87** C2
Janaúba Brazil **155** D1
Jandaq Iran **93** D2
Janesville U.S.A. **136** C2

Jan Mayen *terr.* Arctic Ocean **94** B2
Jansenville S. Africa **108** B3
Januária Brazil **151** E4
Jaora India **86** B2
Japan *country* Asia **79** C3
Japan, Sea of N. Pacific Ocean
81 E2
Japurá *r.* Brazil **150** C3
Jaraguá Brazil **154** C1
Jaraguari Brazil **154** B2
Jardim Brazil **154** A2
Jargalant Mongolia **81** D1
Jarocin Pol. **57** D2
Jarosław Pol. **57** E2
Järpen Sweden **46** C3
Jartai China **82** A2
Jarú Brazil **150** C3
Jarud China *see* Lubei
Järvenpää Fin. **42** C1
Jarvis Island *terr.* S. Pacific Ocean
113
Jäsk Iran **91** C3
Jasło Pol. **57** E3
Jasper Can. **126** D2
Jasper *IN* U.S.A. **136** C3
Jasper *TX* U.S.A. **141** F2
Jastrzębie-Zdrój Pol. **57** D3
Jászberény Hungary **57** D3
Jataí Brazil **154** B1
Jati Pak. **86** A2
Jaú Brazil **154** C2
Jaú *r.* Brazil **150** C3
Jaumave Mex. **143** C2
Jaunpur India **87** C2
Jauru Brazil **154** B1
Java *i.* Indon. **72** B2
Javarthushuu Mongolia **81** D1
Java Sea Indon. *see* Jawa, Laut
Java Trench *sea feature* Indian Ocean
161 H6
Jawa *i.* Indon. *see* Java
Jawa, Laut sea Indon. **72** C2
Jawhar Somalia **103** C4
Jawor Pol. **57** D2
Jaworzno Pol. **57** D2
Jaya, Puncak *mt.* Indon. **71** D3
Jayapura Indon. **71** D3
Jean Marie River Can. **126** C1
Jeannin, Lac *l.* Can. **129** D1
Jebel, Bahr el *r.* Sudan/Uganda *see*
White Nile
Jebel Abyad Plateau Sudan **102** A3
Jedburgh U.K. **50** C3
Jeddah Saudi Arabia **90** A2
Jeetze *r.* Ger. **55** E1
Jefferson, Mount U.S.A. **133** C3
Jefferson City U.S.A. **135** E3
Jejuí Guazú *r.* Para. **154** A2
Jēkabpils Latvia **42** C2
Jelenia Góra Pol. **57** D2
Jelgava Latvia **42** B2
Jember Indon. **73** C2
Jena Ger. **55** E2
Jengish Chokusu *mt.* China/Kyrg. *see*
Pobeda Peak
Jenin West Bank **92** B3
Jennings U.S.A. **138** D2
Jequié Brazil **151** E4
Jequitaí Brazil **155** B2
Jequitinhonha Brazil **155** D1
Jequitinhonha *r.* Brazil **155** E1
Jérémie Haiti **145** C3
Jerez Mex. **142** D2
Jerez de la Frontera Spain **60** B2
Jergucat Albania **65** B3
Jerid, Chott el *salt l.* Tunisia **101** C1
Jerome U.S.A. **132** D2
Jersey *i.* Channel Is **53** B5
Jerumenha Brazil **151** E3
Jerusalem Israel/West Bank **92** B3

Jervis Bay Territory *admin. div.* Austr.
117 E3
Jesenice Slovenia **62** B1
Jesi Italy **62** B2
Jessen Ger. **55** F2
Jessore Bangl. **87** C2
Jesup U.S.A. **139** D2
Jesús Carranza Mex. **143** C3
Jhalawar India **86** B2
Jhang Pak. **86** B1
Jhansi India **87** B2
Jharsuguda India **87** C2
Jhelum Pak. **86** B1
Jiading China **82** C2
Jiamusi China **78** B1
Ji'an *Jiangxi* China **83** B3
Ji'an *Jilin* China **77** B1
Jianchuan China **74** A1
Jiangsu *prov.* China **82** B2
Jiangxi *prov.* China **83** B3
Jiangyou China **82** A2
Jianli China **83** B3
Jianqiao China **82** B2
Jianyang *Fujian* China **83** B3
Jianyang *Sichuan* China **83** A2
Jiaohe China **77** B1
Jiaozhou China **82** C2
Jiaozuo China **82** B2
Jiaxing China **82** C2
Jiayuguan China **80** C2
Jiddah Saudi Arabia *see* Jeddah
Jiehkkevárri *mt.* Norway **46** D2
Jiexiu China **82** B2
Jigzhi China **80** C2
Jihlava Czech Rep. **57** D3
Jijel Alg. **61** C2
Jijiga Eth. **103** C4
Jilib Somalia **103** C4
Jilin China **77** B1
Jilin *prov.* China **82** C1
Jilin Hada Ling *mts* China **77** A1
Jima Eth. **103** B4
Jiménez *Chihuahua* Mex. **142** B2
Jiménez *Tamaulipas* Mex. **143** C2
Jinan China **82** B2
Jinchang China **82** A2
Jincheng China **82** B2
Jindabyne Austr. **117** D3
Jindřichův Hradec Czech Rep. **56** D3
Jingdezhen China **83** B3
Jinghong China **74** B1
Jingmen China **82** B2
Jingning China **82** A2
Jingtai China **82** A2
Jingxi China **83** A3
Jingyu China **77** B1
Jingyuan China **82** A2
Jingzhou *Hubei* China **83** B3
Jingzhou *Hubei* China **83** B3
Jinhua China **83** B3
Jining *Nei Mongol* China **82** B1
Jining *Shandong* China **82** B2
Jinja Uganda **105** D2
Jinka Eth. **103** B4
Jinotepe Nic. **144** B3
Jinping China **83** A3
Jinsha Jiang *r.* China *see* Yangtze
Jinshi China **83** B3
Jinzhong China **82** B2
Jinzhou China **82** C2
Jiparaná *r.* Brazil **150** C3
Jirang China **87** C1
Jirkov Czech Rep. **55** F2
Jiroft Iran **91** C2
Jishou China **83** A3
Jiu *r.* Romania **44** B3
Jiuding Shan *mt.* China **82** A2

Jiujiang China **83** B3
Jiwani Pak. **91** D2
Jixi China **78** B1
Jīzān Saudi Arabia **90** B3
Jizzax Uzbek. **89** D2
Joaçaba Brazil **154** B3
João Pessoa Brazil **151** F3
João Pinheiro Brazil **155** C1
Jodhpur India **86** B2
Joensuu Fin. **46** F3
Jōetsu Japan **79** C3
Jofane Moz. **107** C2
Jõgeva Estonia **42** C2
Johannesburg S. Africa **109** C2
John Day U.S.A. **132** C2
John Day *r.* U.S.A. **132** B1
John d'Or Prairie Can. **126** D2
John H. Kerr Reservoir U.S.A. **137** E3
John o'Groats U.K. **50** C1
Johnson City U.S.A. **139** D1
Johnson's Crossing Can. **126** B1
Johnstone U.K. **50** D3
Johnstown U.S.A. **137** E2
Johor Bahru Malaysia **72** C1
Jõhvi Estonia **42** C2
Joinville Brazil **154** C3
Joinville France **59** D2
Jokkmokk Sweden **46** C3
Jökulsá á Fjöllum *r.* Iceland **46** [inset]
Joliet U.S.A. **136** C2
Joliette Can. **128** C2
Jolo Phil. **76** B3
Jolo *i.* Phil. **76** B3
Jombang Indon. **73** C2
Jomsom Nepal **87** C2
Jonava Lith. **42** B2
Jonesboro *AR* U.S.A. **138** B1
Jonesboro *LA* U.S.A. **138** B2
Jones Sound *sea chan.* Can. **125** G1
Jönköping Sweden **47** C4
Jonquière Can. **129** C2
Jonuta Mex. **143** C3
Joplin U.S.A. **135** E3
Jordan *country* Asia **92** B2
Jordan *r.* Asia **92** B2
Jordan U.S.A. **132** E1
Jordan Valley U.S.A. **132** C2
Jorhat India **74** D1
Jørpeland Norway **47** B4
Jos Nigeria **101** C4
José Cardel Mex. **143** C3
Joseph, Lac *l.* Can. **129** D1
Joseph Bonaparte Gulf Austr. **114** B1
Jos Plateau Nigeria **101** C4
Jotunheimen *mts* Norway **47** B3
Joubertina S. Africa **108** B3
Jouberton S. Africa **109** C2
Joutseno Fin. **47** F3
Juan de Fuca Strait Can./U.S.A.
132 B1
Juan Fernández, Archipiélago *is*
S. Pacific Ocean **149**
Juárez Mex. **143** B2
Juàzeiro Brazil **151** E3
Juàzeiro do Norte Brazil **151** F3
Juba Sudan **103** B4
Jubba *r.* Somalia **103** C5
Jubbah Saudi Arabia **90** B2
Júcar *r.* Spain **61** C2
Juchitán Mex. **143** C3
Judenburg Austria **56** C3
Jühnde Ger. **55** D2
Juigalpa Nic. **144** B3
Juist *i.* Ger. **54** C1
Juiz de Fora Brazil **155** D2
Juliaca Peru **150** B4
Jumla Nepal **87** C2
Junagadh India **86** B2
Junction U.S.A. **141** E2
Junction City U.S.A. **135** D3

Jundiaí Brazil **154** C2
Juneau U.S.A. **126** B3
Junee Austr. **117** D2
Jungfrau *mt.* Switz. **59** D2
Juniata *r.* U.S.A. **137** E2
Junsele Sweden **46** B3
Juntura U.S.A. **132** C2
Juquiá Brazil **154** C2
Jur *r.* Sudan **103** A4
Jura *i.* U.K. **50** B2
Jura *mts* France/Switz. **59** D2
Jurbarkas Lith. **42** B2
Jūrmala Latvia **42** B2
Juruá *r.* Brazil **150** C3
Juruena *r.* Brazil **150** D3
Jutaí *r.* Brazil **150** C3
Jüterbog Ger. **55** F2
Jutland *pen.* Denmark **36**
Juventud, Isla de la *i.* Cuba **144** B2
Juxian China **82** B2
Jūyom Iran **93** D3
Jwaneng Botswana **108** B1
Jyväskylä Fin. **47** F3

K2 *mt.* China/Jammu and Kashmir
86 B1
Kaarina Fin. **42** B1
Kabaena *i.* Indon. **73** D2
Kabalo Dem. Rep. Congo **105** C3
Kabare Dem. Rep. Congo **105** C3
Kabinakagami Lake Can. **128** B2
Kabo C.A.R. **104** B2
Kabompo Zambia **106** C1
Kabongo Dem. Rep. Congo **105** C3
Kābul Afgh. **86** A1
Kaburuang *i.* Indon. **76** B3
Kabwe Zambia **107** B1
Kachchh, Gulf of India **86** A2
Kachchh, Rann of *marsh* India **86** B2
Kachug Rus. Fed. **95** J3
Kaçkar Dağı *mt.* Turkey **93** C1
Kadavu *i.* Fiji **110**
Kadiéwo Rus. Fed. **40** E2
Kadiolo Mali **100** B3
Kadmat *atoll* India **85** B3
Kadom Rus. Fed. **43** F3
Kadoma Zimbabwe **107** B1
Kadonkani Myanmar **75** A2
Kadugli Sudan **103** A3
Kaduna Nigeria **100** C3
Kaduy Rus. Fed. **43** E2
Kadzherom Rus. Fed. **40** E2
Kaédi Maur. **100** A3
Kaélé Cameroon **104** B1
Kaeo N. Korea **77** B2
Kaesŏng N. Korea **77** B2
Kafireas, Akra *pt* Greece **65** B3
Kaffrine Senegal **100** A3
Kafue Zambia **107** B1
Kafue *r.* Zambia **106** B1
Kaga Bandoro C.A.R. **104** B2
Kagal'nitskaya Rus. Fed. **45** F2
Kagoshima Japan **79** B4
Kaharlyk Ukr. **44** D2
Kahayan *r.* Indon. **73** C2
Kahemba Dem. Rep. Congo **104** B3
Kahla Ger. **55** E2
Kahnūj Iran **91** C2
Kahperusvaarat Fin. **46** E2
Kahūrak Iran **91** C2
Kai, Kepulauan *is* Indon. **71** C3
Kaiama Nigeria **100** C4
Kaiapoi N.Z. **118** B3
Kai Besar *i.* Indon. **71** C3

Kaifeng China **82** B2
Kaiingveld *reg.* S. Africa **108** B2
Kai Kecil *i.* Indon. **71** C3
Kaikoura N.Z. **118** B3
Kailahun Sierra Leone **100** A4
Kaili China **83** A3
Kaimana Indon. **71** C3
Kaimanawa Mountains N.Z. **118** C2
Kainan Japan **79** C4
Kainji Reservoir Nigeria **100** C3
Kaipara Harbour N.Z. **118** B2
Kairana India **86** B2
Kairouan Tunisia **101** D1
Kaitaia N.Z. **118** B2
Kaitawa N.Z. **118** C2
Kaiwatu Indon. **71** C3
Kaiyuan *Liaoning* China **77** A1
Kaiyuan *Yunnan* China **83** A3
Kajaani Fin. **46** F3
Kajabbi Austr. **115** D2
Kakamas S. Africa **108** B2
Kakamega Kenya **105** D2
Kakhovka Ukr. **45** E2
Kakhovs'ke Vodoskhovyshche *resr*
Ukr. **45** D2
Kakinada India **85** C3
Kakisa Can. **126** D1
Kakoswa Dem. Rep. Congo **105** C3
Kaktovik U.S.A. **124** C2
Kalabahi Indon. **71** C3
Kalabo Zambia **106** B1
Kalach Rus. Fed. **45** F1
Kalacha Dida Kenya **105** D2
Kaladan *r.* India/Myanmar **74** A1
Kalahari Desert Africa **106** C3
Kalajoki Fin. **46** E3
Kalamare Botswana **109** C1
Kalamaria Greece **65** B2
Kalamata Greece **65** B3
Kalamazoo U.S.A. **136** C2
Kalampaka Greece **65** B3
Kalanchak Ukr. **45** D2
Kalao *i.* Indon. **73** C2
Kalaotoa *i.* Indon. **73** D2
Kalasin Thai. **74** B2
Kalāt Afgh. **86** A1
Kalāt Iran **91** C2
Kalat Pak. **86** A2
Kalbarri Austr. **114** A2
Kale Turkey **65** C3
Kalecik Turkey **92** B1
Kalema Dem. Rep. Congo **104** C3
Kalemie Dem. Rep. Congo **105** C3
Kalemyo Myanmar **74** A1
Kalevala Rus. Fed. **46** G2
Kalgoorlie Austr. **114** B3
Kali Croatia **62** C2
Kaliakra, Nos *pt* Bulg. **64** C2
Kalima Dem. Rep. Congo **105** C3
Kalimantan *reg.* Indon. **73** C2
Kaliningrad Rus. Fed. **42** B3
Kalininskaya Rus. Fed. **45** E2
Kalinkavichy Belarus **42** C3
Kalispell U.S.A. **132** D1
Kalisz Pol. **57** D2
Kalitva *r.* Rus. Fed. **45** F2
Kalix Sweden **46** E2
Kalixälven *r.* Sweden **46** E2
Kalkan Turkey **65** C3
Kalkfeld Namibia **106** A2
Kallavesi *l.* Fin. **46** F3
Kallsjön *l.* Sweden **46** C3
Kalmar Sweden **47** D4
Kalmarsund *sea chan.* Sweden **47** D4
Kalomo Zambia **106** B1
Kalone Peak Can. **126** C2
Kalpa India **87** B1
Kalpeni *atoll* India **85** B3
Kalpi India **87** B2
Kaltag U.S.A. **124** B2

Kaltenkirchen Ger. **55** D1
Kaluga Rus. Fed. **43** E3
Kalundborg Denmark **47** C4
Kalush Ukr. **44** B2
Kalyazin Rus. Fed. **43** E2
Kalymnos *i.* Greece **65** C3
Kama Dem. Rep. Congo **105** C3
Kama Myanmar **74** A2
Kama *r.* Rus. Fed. **40** E3
Kamaishi Japan **78** D3
Kaman Turkey **92** B2
Kamanjab Namibia **106** A1
Kamarán *i.* Yemen **90** B3
Kamarod Pak. **86** A2
Kambalda Austr. **114** B3
Kambove Dem. Rep. Congo **105** C4
Kamchatka Peninsula Rus. Fed. **67**
Kamchiya *r.* Bulg. **64** C2
Kamenitsa *mt.* Bulg. **64** B2
Kamenjak, Rt *pt* Croatia **62** B2
Kamenka Kazakh. **88** C1
Kamenka Rus. Fed. **45** E1
Kamen'-na-Obi Rus. Fed. **89** F1
Kamennomostskiy Rus. Fed. **45** F3
Kamenolomni Rus. Fed. **45** F2
Kamenskoye Rus. Fed. **95** N2
Kamensk-Shakhtinskiy Rus. Fed.
45 F2
Kamensk-Ural'skiy Rus. Fed. **40** F3
Kamiesberge *mts* S. Africa **108** A3
Kamieskroon S. Africa **108** A3
Kamilukuak Lake Can. **127** E1
Kamina Dem. Rep. Congo **105** C3
Kaminak Lake Can. **127** F1
Kamin'-Kashyrs'kyy Ukr. **44** B1
Kamloops Can. **126** C2
Kamonia Dem. Rep. Congo **104** C3
Kampala Uganda **105** D2
Kampar *r.* Indon. **72** B1
Kampar Malaysia **72** B1
Kampen Neth. **54** B1
Kampene Dem. Rep. Congo **105** C3
Kamphaeng Phet Thai. **74** A2
Kâmpóng Cham Cambodia **75** B2
Kâmpóng Chhnăng Cambodia **75** B2
Kâmpóng Spœ Cambodia **75** B2
Kâmpôt Cambodia **75** B2
Kamsack Can. **127** E2
Kamskoye Vodokhranilishche *resr*
Rus. Fed. **40** E3
Kamsuuma Somalia **103** C4
Kam"yanets'-Podil's'kyy Ukr. **44** C2
Kam"yanka-Buz'ka Ukr. **44** B1
Kamyanets Belarus **42** B3
Kamyshevatskaya Rus. Fed. **45** E2
Kamyshin Rus. Fed. **41** D3
Kanab U.S.A. **133** D3
Kananga Dem. Rep. Congo **104** C3
Kanash Rus. Fed. **41** D3
Kanawha *r.* U.S.A. **137** D3
Kanazawa Japan **79** C3
Kanbalu Myanmar **74** A1
Kanchanaburi Thai. **75** A2
Kanchipuram India **85** B3
Kandahār Afgh. **86** A1
Kandalaksha Rus. Fed. **46** G2
Kandangan Indon. **73** C2
Kandhkot Pak. **86** A2
Kandi Benin **100** C3
Kandla India **86** B2
Kandos Austr. **117** D2
Kandreho Madag. **107** [inset] D1
Kandy Sri Lanka **85** C4
Kandyagash Kazakh. **88** C2
Kanevskaya Rus. Fed. **45** E2
Kang Botswana **108** B1
Kangaatsiaq Greenland **125** I2
Kangaba Mali **100** B3
Kangal Turkey **92** B2
Kangān Iran **91** C2

Kangar Malaysia **72** B1
Kangaroo Island Austr. **116** B3
Kangchenjunga *mt.* India/Nepal **87** C2
Kangdong N. Korea **77** B2
Kangean, Kepulauan *is* Indon. **73** C2
Kangeq *c.* Greenland **125** J2
Kangersuatsiaq Greenland **125** I2
Kanggye N. Korea **77** B1
Kangiqsualujjuaq Can. **129** D1
Kangiqsujuaq Can. **125** H2
Kangirsuk Can. **125** H2
Kangnüng S. Korea **77** B2
Kangping China **77** A1
Kangto *mt.* China/India **87** D2
Kani Myanmar **74** A1
Kanin, Poluostrov *pen.* Rus. Fed.
    40 D2
Kanin Nos Rus. Fed. **40** D2
Kaniv Ukr. **45** D1
Kankaanpää Fin. **47** E3
Kankakee U.S.A. **136** C2
Kankan Guinea **100** B3
Kanker India **87** C2
Kano Nigeria **101** C3
Kanonpunt *pt* S. Africa **108** B3
Kanoya Japan **79** B4
Kanpur India **87** C2
Kansas *r.* U.S.A. **134** E3
Kansas *state* U.S.A. **135** D3
Kansas City U.S.A. **135** E3
Kansk Rus. Fed. **95** I3
Kantchari Burkina **100** C3
Kantemirovka Rus. Fed. **45** E2
Kanton *atoll* Kiribati **111**
Kanturk Rep. of Ireland **51** B2
KaNyamazane S. Africa **109** D2
Kanye Botswana **109** C1
Kaohsiung Taiwan **83** C1
Kaokoveld *plat.* Namibia **106** A1
Kaolack Senegal **100** A3
Kaoma Zambia **106** B1
Kapanga Dem. Rep. Congo **104** C3
Kapchagay Kazakh. **89** E2
Kapchagayskoye Vodokhranilishche
    resr Kazakh. **89** E2
Kapellen Belgium **54** B2
Kapiri Mposhi Zambia **107** B1
Kapisillit Greenland **125** I2
Kapiskau *r.* Can. **128** C1
Kapit Malaysia **73** C1
Kapoe Thai. **75** A3
Kapoeta Sudan **103** B4
Kaposvár Hungary **57** D3
Kapuas *r.* Indon. **73** B2
Kapunda Austr. **116** B2
Kapuskasing Can. **128** C2
Kapuvár Hungary **57** D3
Kapyl' Belarus **42** C3
Kara Togo **100** C3
Kara Ada *i.* Turkey **65** C3
Karabalyk Kazakh. **88** D1
Karabaur, Uval *hills* Kazakh./Uzbek.
    93 D1
Kara-Bogaz-Gol, Zaliv *b.* Turkm.
    88 C2
Karabogazkel' Turkm. **88** C2
Karabük Turkey **92** B1
Karabutak Kazakh. **88** D2
Karachev Rus. Fed. **43** D3
Karachi Pak. **86** A2
Karaganda Kazakh. **89** E2
Karagayly Kazakh. **89** E2
Karaginskiy Zaliv *b.* Rus. Fed. **95** M3
Karaj Iran **93** D2
Karakelong *i.* Indon. **76** B3
Kara-Köl Kyrg. **89** E2
Karakol Kyrg. **89** E2
Karakoram Range *mts* Asia **89** E3

Karakum, Peski *des.* Kazakh. *see*
    Karakum Desert
Karakum Desert Kazakh. **88** C2
Karakum Desert Turkm. *see*
    Karakumy, Peski
Karaman Turkey **102** B1
Karamay China **89** F2
Karamea N.Z. **118** B3
Karamea Bight *b.* N.Z. **118** B3
Karapınar Turkey **92** B2
Karasburg Namibia **108** A2
Kara Sea Rus. Fed. **40** G1
Kárášjohka Norway *see* Karasjok
Karasjok Norway **46** F2
Karasuk Rus. Fed. **89** E1
Karatau Kazakh. **89** D2
Karatau, Khrebet *mts* Kazakh. **89** D2
Karatayka Rus. Fed. **40** F2
Karatsu Japan **79** A4
Karawang Indon. **72** B2
Karbalā' Iraq **92** C2
Karcag Hungary **57** E3
Karditsa Greece **65** B3
Kärdla Estonia **42** B2
Kareeberge *mts* S. Africa **108** B3
Kareli India **87** B2
Kargil India **86** B1
Kariba Zimbabwe **107** B1
Kariba, Lake *resr* Zambia/Zimbabwe
    107 B1
Karimata, Pulau-pulau *is* Indon. **72** B2
Karimata, Selat *str.* Indon. **72** B2
Karimnagar India **85** B3
Karimunjawa, Pulau-pulau *is* Indon.
    73 C2
Karkinits'ka Zatoka *g.* Ukr. **45** D2
Karkinits'ka Zatoka *b.* Ukr. **37**
Karlivka Ukr. **45** E2
Karl Marx, Qullai *mt.* Tajik. **89** E3
Karlovac Croatia **62** C1
Karlovy Vary Czech Rep. **56** C2
Karlshamn Sweden **47** C4
Karlskrona Sweden **47** D4
Karlsruhe Ger. **55** D3
Karlstad Sweden **47** C4
Karlstadt Ger. **55** D3
Karma Belarus **43** D3
Karmøy *i.* Norway **47** B4
Karnafuli Reservoir Bangl. **87** D2
Karnal India **86** B2
Karnobat Bulg. **64** C2
Karodi Pak. **86** A2
Karoi Zimbabwe **107** B1
Karonga Malawi **105** D3
Karora Eritrea **102** B3
Karpathos *i.* Greece **65** C3
Karpenisi Greece **65** B3
Karpogory Rus. Fed. **40** D2
Karratha Austr. **114** A2
Kars Turkey **93** C1
Kārsava Latvia **42** C2
Karshi Turkm. **41** E4
Karshi Uzbek. *see* Qarshi
Karskiye Vorota, Proliv *str.* Rus. Fed.
    40 F2
Karskoye More *sea* Rus. Fed. *see*
    Kara Sea
Karstädt Ger. **55** E1
Kartal Turkey **65** C2
Kartaly Rus. Fed. **41** F3
Karwar India **85** B3
Karymskoye Rus. Fed. **95** J3
Karystos Greece **65** B3
Kaş Turkey **92** A2
Kasabonika Lake Can. **128** B1
Kasaji Dem. Rep. Congo **104** C4
Kasama Zambia **105** D4
Kasane Botswana **106** B1
Kasangulu Dem. Rep. Congo **104** B3

Kasaragod India **85** B3
Kasba Lake Can. **127** E1
Kasempa Zambia **106** B1
Kasenga Dem. Rep. Congo **105** C4
Kasese Dem. Rep. Congo **105** C3
Kasese Uganda **105** D2
Kâshân Iran **93** D2
Kashary Rus. Fed. **45** F2
Kashi China **89** E3
Kashima-nada *b.* Japan **79** D3
Kashin Rus. Fed. **43** E2
Kashira Rus. Fed. **43** E3
Kashirskoye Rus. Fed. **43** E3
Kashiwazaki Japan **79** C3
Kâshmar Iran **88** C3
Kashmir *terr.* Asia *see* Jammu and
    Kashmir
Kashmor Pak. **86** A2
Kashyukulu Dem. Rep. Congo **105** C3
Kasimov Rus. Fed. **43** F3
Kaskinen Fin. **47** E3
Kasongo Dem. Rep. Congo **105** C3
Kasongo-Lunda Dem. Rep. Congo
    104 B3
Kasos *i.* Greece **65** C3
Kassala Sudan **102** B3
Kassel Ger. **55** D2
Kastamonu Turkey **92** B1
Kastelli Greece **65** B3
Kastoria Greece **65** B3
Kastsyukovichy Belarus **43** D3
Kasulu Tanz. **105** D3
Kasungu Malawi **107** C1
Katahdin, Mount U.S.A. **137** G1
Katako-Kombe Dem. Rep. Congo
    104 C3
Katanning Austr. **114** A3
Katchall *i.* India **75** A3
Katerini Greece **65** B3
Kate's Needle *mt.* Can./U.S.A. **126** B2
Katete Zambia **107** C1
Katha Myanmar **74** A1
Katherine *r.* Austr. **114** C1
Katherine *r.* India **86** B2
Kathiéhong *b.* Africa **109** C2
Kathmandu Nepal **87** C2
Kathu S. Africa **108** B2
Kati Mali **100** B3
Katihar India **87** C2
Katikati N.Z. **118** C2
Kati-Kati S. Africa **109** C3
Katima Mulilo Namibia **106** B1
Kato Achaïa Greece **65** B3
Katoomba Austr. **117** E2
Katowice Pol. **57** D2
Kâtrînâ, Jabal *mt.* Egypt **92** B3
Katrineholm Sweden **47** D4
Katsina Nigeria **101** C3
Katsina-Ala Nigeria **101** C4
Kattaqo'rg'on Uzbek. **89** D2
Kattegat *str.* Denmark/Sweden **47** C4
Katwijk aan Zee Neth. **54** B1
Kauai *i.* U.S.A. **120**
Kauhajoki Fin. **47** E3
Kaunas Lith. **42** B3
Kaura-Namoda Nigeria **101** C3
Kautokeino Norway **46** E2
Kavala Greece **65** B2
Kavalerovo Rus. Fed. **78** C3
Kavali India **85** C3
Kavaratti *atoll* India **85** B3
Kavarna Bulg. **64** C2
Kaveri *r.* India **85** B3
Kavīr, Dasht-e *des.* Iran **93** D2
Kawagoe Japan **79** C3
Kawakawa N.Z. **118** B2
Kawanishi Japan **79** C3
Kawartha Lakes Can. **128** C2
Kawasaki Japan **79** C3
Kawerau N.Z. **118** C2

Kawkareik Myanmar **74** A2
Kawlin Myanmar **74** A1
Kawmapyin Myanmar **75** A2
Kawm Umbū Egypt **90** A2
Kawthaung Myanmar **75** A2
Kaxgar He r. China **89** E3
Kaya Burkina **100** B3
Kayan r. Indon. **73** C1
Kaycee U.S.A. **134** B2
Kayenta U.S.A. **140** B1
Kayes Mali **100** A3
Kaynar Kazakh. **89** E2
Kayseri Turkey **92** B1
Kazakhskiy Melkosopochnik plain Kazakh. **89** E1
Kazakhskiy Zaliv b. Kazakh. **93** D1
Kazakhstan country Asia **88** D2
Kazan' Rus. Fed. **41** D3
Kazanlŭk Bulg. **92** A1
Kazanskaya Rus. Fed. **45** F2
Kazbek mt. Georgia/Rus. Fed. **41** D4
Käzerūn Iran **93** D3
Kazincbarcika Hungary **57** E3
Kazymskiy Mys Rus. Fed. **40** F3
Kea i. Greece **65** B3
Keady U.K. **51** C1
Kearney U.S.A. **135** D2
Kearny U.S.A. **140** B1
Kebkabiya Sudan **102** A3
Kebnekaise mt. Sweden **46** D2
Kebumen Indon. **73** D2
Kechika r. Can. **126** C2
Kédainiai Lith. **42** B2
Kédougou Senegal **100** A3
Kedzierzyn-Koźle Pol. **57** D2
Keele r. Can. **126** C1
Keele Peak mt. Can. **126** B1
Keeling Taiwan see Chilung
Keene U.S.A. **137** F2
Keetmanshoop Namibia **108** A2
Keewatin Can. **127** F3
Kefallonia i. Greece see Cephalonia
Kefamenanu Indon. **71** C3
Keflavík Iceland **46** [inset]
Kegen Kazakh. **89** E2
Keg River Can. **126** D2
Kehsi Mansam Myanmar **74** A1
Keighley U.K. **52** C3
Keila Estonia **42** B2
Keimoes S. Africa **108** B2
Keitele l. Fin. **46** F3
Keith Austr. **116** C3
Keith Arm b. Can. **126** C1
Kékes mt. Hungary **57** E3
Kelheim Ger. **56** C3
Kelkit r. Turkey **92** B1
Keller Lake Can. **126** C1
Kellosełkä Fin. **46** F2
Kells Rep. of Ireland **51** C2
Kelmé Lith. **42** B2
Kelo Chad **101** D4
Kelowna Can. **126** D3
Kelso U.K. **50** C3
Kelso U.S.A. **132** C1
Keluang Malaysia **72** B1
Kelvington Can. **127** E2
Kem' Rus. Fed. **40** C2
Kemano Can. **126** C2
Kemer Turkey **65** C3
Kemerovo Rus. Fed. **94** H3
Kemi Fin. **46** E2
Kemijärvi Fin. **46** F2
Kemijoki r. Fin. **46** F2
Kemmerer U.S.A. **134** A2
Kempele Fin. **46** F3
Kempsey Austr. **117** E2

Kempt, Lac l. Can. **128** C2
Kempten (Allgäu) Ger. **56** C3
Kempton Park S. Africa **109** C2
Kemujan i. Indon. **73** C2
Kenai U.S.A. **124** B2
Kendari Indon. **73** D2
Kendawangan Indon. **73** C2
Kendal U.K. **52** B2
Kendari Indon. **73** D2
Kendégué Chad **101** D3
Kenema Sierra Leone **100** A4
Kenge Dem. Rep. Congo **104** B3
Kengtung Myanmar **74** A1
Kenhardt S. Africa **108** B2
Kenitra Morocco **100** B1
Kenmare Rep. of Ireland **51** B3
Kenmare U.S.A. **134** C1
Kenmare River inlet Rep. of Ireland **51** A3
Kenn Ger. **54** C3
Kennett U.S.A. **135** E3
Kennewick U.S.A. **132** C1
Kenora Can. **127** F3
Kenosha U.S.A. **136** C2
Kent U.S.A. **140** D2
Kentau Kazakh. **89** D2
Kentucky r. U.S.A. **136** C3
Kentucky state U.S.A. **136** D3
Kentucky Lake U.S.A. **136** C3
Kenya country Africa **105** D2
Kenya, Mount Kenya **105** D3
Keokuk U.S.A. **135** E2
Keonjhar India **87** C2
Kepsut Turkey **65** C3
Kerang Austr. **116** C3
Kerava Fin. **42** C1
Kerch Ukr. **45** D2
Kerema P.N.G. **71** D3
Keremeos Can. **126** D3
Keren Eritrea **102** B3
Kericho Kenya **105** D3
Kerikeri N.Z. **118** B2
Kerinci, Gunung vol. Indon. **72** B2
Kerkyra Greece **65** A3
Kerkyra i. Greece see Corfu
Kerma Sudan **102** B3
Kermadec Islands S. Pacific Ocean **111**
Kermān Iran **91** C1
Kermānshāh Iran **93** C2
Kermit U.S.A. **141** D2
Kern r. U.S.A. **133** C3
Kerpen Ger. **54** C2
Kerrobert Can. **127** E2
Kerrville U.S.A. **141** E2
Keryneia Cyprus see Kyrenia
Kesagami Lake Can. **128** C1
Keşan Turkey **65** C2
Kesennuma Japan **78** D3
Keshod India **86** B2
Kessel Neth. **54** C2
Keswick U.K. **52** B2
Keszthely Hungary **57** D3
Ket' r. Rus. Fed. **94** H3
Ketapang Indon. **73** C2
Ketchikan U.S.A. **126** B2
Ketchum U.S.A. **132** D2
Kettering U.K. **53** C3
Keuruu Fin. **47** F3
Kevelaer Ger. **54** C2
Kewanee U.S.A. **136** C2
Keweenaw Bay U.S.A. **136** C1
Keweenaw Peninsula U.S.A. **136** C1
Key Largo U.S.A. **139** D3
Keyser U.S.A. **137** E3
Key West U.S.A. **139** D4
Kgotsong S. Africa **109** C2
Khabarovsk Rus. Fed. **81** F1
Khadyzhensk Rus. Fed. **92** B1

Khagrachari Bangl. **74** A1
Khairpur Pak. **86** A2
Khakhea Botswana **108** B1
Khamar-Daban, Khrebet mts Rus. Fed. **80** C1
Khambhat India **86** B2
Khambhat, Gulf of India **86** B3
Khamgaon India **86** B2
Khamir Yemen **90** B3
Khamis Mushayṭ Saudi Arabia **90** B3
Khammam India **85** C3
Khānābād Afgh. **86** A1
Khandwa India **86** B2
Khandyga Rus. Fed. **95** L2
Khanewal Pak. **86** B1
Khanka, Lake China/Rus. Fed. **78** B2
Khanpur Pak. **86** B2
Khantau Kazakh. **89** E2
Khantayskoye, Ozero l. Rus. Fed. **95** I2
Khanty-Mansiysk Rus. Fed. **40** F2
Khao Chum Thong Thai. **75** A3
Khao Laem Reservoir Thai. **75** A2
Kharabali Rus. Fed. **41** D4
Kharagpur India **87** C2
Khārān r. Iran **91** C2
Khārijah, Wāḥāt al oasis Egypt **102** B2
Kharkiv Ukr. **45** D2
Khar'kov Ukr. see Kharkiv
Kharmanli Bulg. **64** C2
Kharovsk Rus. Fed. **43** F2
Khartoum Sudan **102** B3
Khasav'yurt Rus. Fed. **41** D4
Khāsh Iran **91** D2
Khashm el Girba Sudan **90** A3
Khashm el Girba Dam Sudan **90** A3
Khasi Hills India **87** D2
Khaskovo Bulg. **64** C2
Khayamnandi S. Africa **109** C3
Khaybar Saudi Arabia **90** A2
Khayelitsha S. Africa **108** A3
Khê Bo Vietnam **74** B2
Khemis Miliana Alg. **61** D2
Khemmarat Thai. **75** B2
Khenchela Alg. **101** C1
Kherämeh Iran **93** D3
Kherson Ukr. **45** D2
Kheta r. Rus. Fed. **95** I2
Khilok Rus. Fed. **81** D1
Khimki Rus. Fed. **43** E2
Khlevnoye Rus. Fed. **43** E3
Khmel'nyts'kyy Ukr. **44** C2
Khobda Kazakh. **88** C1
Khokhol'skiy Rus. Fed. **43** E3
Khokhropar Pak. **86** B2
Kholm Afgh. **86** A1
Kholm Rus. Fed. **43** D2
Kholmsk Rus. Fed. **78** D1
Kholm-Zhirkovskiy Rus. Fed. **43** D2
Khomas Highland hills Namibia **108** A1
Khonj Iran **91** C2
Khon Kaen Thai. **74** B2
Khonsa India **74** A1
Khonuu Rus. Fed. **95** L2
Khoper r. Rus. Fed. **45** F2
Khoreyver Rus. Fed. **40** E2
Khorinsk Rus. Fed. **81** D1
Khorol Ukr. **45** D2
Khorramābād Iran **93** C2
Khorramshahr Iran **93** C2
Khorugh Tajik. **89** E3
Khowst Afgh. **86** A1
Khreum Myanmar **74** A1
Khromtau Kazakh. **88** C1
Khrystynivka Ukr. **44** C2
Khūjand Tajik. **89** D2
Khu Khan Thai. **75** B2
Khulays Saudi Arabia **90** A2

203

Khulna Bangl. **87** C2
Khunsar Iran **93** D2
Khurays Saudi Arabia **91** B2
Khushab Pak. **86** B1
Khust Ukr. **44** B2
Khuzdar Pak. **86** A2
Khvormüj Iran **93** D3
Khvoy Iran **93** C2
Khvoynaya Rus. Fed. **43** D2
Khyber Pass Afgh./Pak. **86** B1
Kiama Austr. **117** E2
Kiambi Dem. Rep. Congo **105** C3
Kibiti Tanz. **105** D3
Kičevo Macedonia **65** B2
Kidal Mali **100** C2
Kidderminster U.K. **53** B3
Kidira Senegal **100** A3
Kidnappers, Cape N.Z. **118** C2
Kiel Ger. **56** C2
Kielce Pol. **57** E2
Kielder Water resr U.K. **52** B2
Kieler Bucht b. Ger. **47** C5
Kiev Ukr. **44** D1
Kiffa Maur. **100** A3
Kigali Rwanda **105** D3
Kigoma Tanz. **105** C3
Kihnu i. Estonia **42** B2
Kiiminki Fin. **46** F2
Kii-suidō sea chan. Japan **79** B4
Kikinda Serb. and Mont. **64** B1
Kikondja Dem. Rep. Congo **105** C3
Kikori r. P.N.G. **71** D3
Kikwit Dem. Rep. Congo **104** B3
Kilchu N. Korea **77** B1
Kilembe Dem. Rep. Congo **104** B3
Kilgore U.S.A. **141** E2
Kilimanjaro vol. Tanz. **105** D3
Kilis Turkey **92** D2
Kiliya Ukr. **44** C2
Kilkee Rep. of Ireland **51** B2
Kilkeel U.K. **51** D1
Kilkenny Rep. of Ireland **51** C2
Kilkis Greece **65** B2
Killala Bay Rep. of Ireland **51** B1
Killaloe Rep. of Ireland **51** B1
Killam Can. **127** D2
Killarney Rep. of Ireland **51** B2
Killeen U.S.A. **141** E2
Killin U.K. **50** B2
Killybegs Rep. of Ireland **51** B1
Kilmarnock U.K. **50** B3
Kilmore Austr. **117** C3
Kilosa Tanz. **105** D3
Kilrush Rep. of Ireland **51** B2
Kilwa Dem. Rep. Congo **105** C3
Kilwa Masoko Tanz. **105** D3
Kimambi Tanz. **105** D3
Kimba Austr. **116** B2
Kimball U.S.A. **134** C2
Kimberley Can. **126** D3
Kimberley S. Africa **108** C2
Kimberley Plateau Austr. **114** B1
Kimch'aek N. Korea **77** B1
Kimch'ŏn S. Korea **77** B2
Kimmirut Can. **125** H2
Kimovsk Rus. Fed. **43** E3
Kimpese Dem. Rep. Congo **104** B3
Kimry Rus. Fed. **43** E2
Kinabalu, Gunung mt. Malaysia **73** C1
Kinbasket Lake Can. **126** D2
Kincardine Can. **128** B2
Kinchang Myanmar **74** A1
Kinda Dem. Rep. Congo **105** C3
Kinder Scout h. U.K. **52** C3
Kindersley Can. **124** B2
Kindia Guinea **100** A3
Kindu Dem. Rep. Congo **105** C3
Kineshma Rus. Fed. **43** F2
Kingaroy Austr. **115** E2

King City U.S.A. **133** B3
King George Islands Can. **128** C1
Kingisepp Rus. Fed. **42** C2
King Island Austr. **115** D3
King Leopold Ranges hills Austr. **114** B1
Kingman U.S.A. **140** B1
Kings r. U.S.A. **133** B3
Kingscote Austr. **116** B3
King's Lynn U.K. **53** D3
Kingsmill Group is Kiribati **110**
King Sound b. Austr. **114** B1
Kings Peak U.S.A. **132** D2
Kingsport U.S.A. **139** D1
Kingston Can. **128** C2
Kingston Jamaica **145** C3
Kingston U.S.A. **137** F2
Kingston South East Austr. **116** B3
Kingston upon Hull U.K. **52** C3
Kingstown St Vincent **145** D3
Kingsville U.S.A. **141** E3
Kingswood U.K. **53** B4
Kingussie U.K. **50** B2
King William Island Can. **124** F2
King William's Town S. Africa **109** C3
Kinka-san i. Japan **78** D3
Kinna Sweden **47** C4
Kinsale Rep. of Ireland **51** B3
Kinshasa Dem. Rep. Congo **104** B3
Kinston U.S.A. **139** E1
Kintai Lith. **42** B2
Kintampo Ghana **100** B4
Kintyre pen. U.K. **50** B3
Kipawa, Lac l. Can. **128** C2
Kirensk Rus. Fed. **95** J3
Kireyevsk Rus. Fed. **43** E3
Kiribati country Pacific Ocean **113**
Kırıkkale Turkey **92** B2
Kirillov Rus. Fed. **43** E2
Kirinyaga mt. Kenya see Kenya, Mount
Kirishi Rus. Fed. **43** D2
Kiritimati atoll Kiribati **111**
Kırkağaç Turkey **65** C3
Kirkcaldy U.K. **50** C2
Kirkcudbright U.K. **50** B3
Kirkenes Norway **46** G2
Kirkkonummi Fin. **42** B1
Kirkland Lake Can. **128** B2
Kirksville U.S.A. **135** E2
Kirkūk Iraq **93** C2
Kirkwall U.K. **50** C1
Kirov Kaluzhskaya Oblast' Rus. Fed. **43** D3
Kirov Kirovskaya Oblast' Rus. Fed. **40** D3
Kirovo-Chepetsk Rus. Fed. **40** E3
Kirovohrad Ukr. **45** D2
Kirovsk Rus. Fed. **46** G2
Kirovs'ke Ukr. **45** D2
Kirriemuir U.K. **50** C2
Kirs Rus. Fed. **40** E3
Kirsanov Rus. Fed. **45** F1
Kirthar Range mts Pak. **86** A2
Kiruna Sweden **46** E2
Kiryū Japan **79** C3
Kirzhach Rus. Fed. **43** E2
Kisangani Dem. Rep. Congo **105** C2
Kisantu Dem. Rep. Congo **104** B3
Kisaran Indon. **72** A1
Kiselevsk Rus. Fed. **94** H3
Kishanganj India **87** C2
Kishi Nigeria **100** C4
Kishinev Moldova see Chişinău
Kishkenekol' Kazakh. **89** E1
Kishorganj Bangl. **74** A1
Kishtwar Jammu and Kashmir **86** B1
Kisii Kenya **105** D3
Kiskunfélegyháza Hungary **57** D3
Kiskunhalas Hungary **57** D3
Kislovodsk Rus. Fed. **41** D4

Kismaayo Somalia **103** C5
Kisoro Uganda **105** C3
Kissidougou Guinea **100** A4
Kissimmee U.S.A. **139** D3
Kissimmee, Lake U.S.A. **139** D3
Kississing Lake Can. **127** E2
Kisumu Kenya **105** D3
Kita Mali **100** B3
Kitakami Japan **78** D3
Kitakami-gawa r. Japan **78** D3
Kita-Kyūshū Japan **79** B4
Kitale Kenya **105** D2
Kitami Japan **78** D2
Kitchener Can. **128** B2
Kitee Fin. **47** G3
Kitgum Uganda **105** D2
Kitona Dem. Rep. Congo **104** B3
Kitunda Tanz. **105** D3
Kitwanga Can. **126** C2
Kitwe Zambia **107** B1
Kitzingen Ger. **55** E3
Kiuruvesi Fin. **46** F3
Kivu, Lake Dem. Rep. Congo/Rwanda **105** C3
Kıyıköy Turkey **64** C2
Kizel Rus. Fed. **40** E3
Kızılca Dağ mt. Turkey **65** C3
Kizlyar Rus. Fed. **41** D4
Kjøllefjord Norway **46** F1
Kjøpsvik Norway **46** D2
Kladno Czech Rep. **56** C2
Klagenfurt Austria **56** C3
Klaipėda Lith. **42** B2
Klaksvík Faroe Is **48** B1
Klamath r. U.S.A. **132** B2
Klamath Falls U.S.A. **132** B2
Klamath Mountains U.S.A. **132** B2
Klang Malaysia **72** B1
Klatovy Czech Rep. **56** C3
Klawer S. Africa **108** A3
Klawock U.S.A. **126** B2
Kleena Kleene Can. **126** C2
Kleinbegin S. Africa **108** B2
Kleinsee S. Africa **108** A2
Klerksdorp S. Africa **109** C2
Kletnya Rus. Fed. **43** D3
Kleve Ger. **54** C2
Klimavichy Belarus **43** D3
Klimovo Rus. Fed. **43** D3
Klimovsk Rus. Fed. **43** E2
Klin Rus. Fed. **43** E2
Klínovec mt. Czech Rep. **55** F2
Klintehamn Sweden **47** D4
Klintsy Rus. Fed. **43** D3
Ključ Bos.-Herz. **63** C2
Kłodzko Pol. **57** D2
Kloosterhaar Neth. **54** C1
Klosterneuburg Austria **57** D3
Klötze (Altmark) Ger. **55** E1
Kluane Lake Can. **126** B1
Kluczbork Pol. **57** D2
Klukwan U.S.A. **126** B2
Klupro Pak. **86** A2
Klyaz'ma r. Rus. Fed. **43** F2
Klyetsk Belarus **42** C3
Knaresborough U.K. **52** C2
Knästen h. Sweden **47** C3
Knee Lake Can. **127** F2
Knesebeck Ger. **55** E1
Knetzgau Ger. **55** E2
Knin Croatia **63** C2
Knittelfeld Austria **56** C3
Knjaževac Serb. and Mont. **64** B2
Knokke-Heist Belgium **54** A2
Knoxville U.S.A. **139** D1
Knysna S. Africa **108** B3
Kōbe Japan **79** C4
København Denmark see Copenhagen
Koblenz Ger. **54** C2

obroðr i. Indon. **71** C3
obryn Belarus **42** B3
oćani Macedonia **64** B2
ocasu r. Turkey **65** C2
och Bihar India **87** C2
ōchi Japan **79** B4
odchubey Rus. Fed. **41** D4
odiak Island U.S.A. **124** B3
odok Sudan **103** B4
odyma India **87** C2
odzhaele mt. Bulg./Greece **65** C2
oës Namibia **108** A2
offiefontein S. Africa **108** C2
oforidua Ghana **100** B4
ōfu Japan **79** C3
ogaluk r. Can. **129** D1
ohat Pak. **86** B1
ohima India **74** A1
ohtla-Järve Estonia **42** C2
okand Uzbek. see Qo'qon
okkola Fin. **46** E3
okomo U.S.A. **136** C2
okpekti Kazakh. **89** F2
okshetau Kazakh. **89** D1
oksoak r. Can. **129** D1
oktokay China see Fuyun
olaka Indon. **73** D2
ola Peninsula Rus. Fed. **40** C2
olari Fin. **46** F3
olda Senegal **100** A3
oléa Alg. **61** D2
olguyev, Ostrov i. Rus. Fed. **40** D2
olhapur India **85** B3
olkata India **87** C2
öln Ger. see Cologne
ołobrzeg Pol. **57** D2
olokani Mali **100** B3
olomna Rus. Fed. **43** E2
olomyya Ukr. **44** C2
olonedale Indon. **73** D2
olonkwaneng Botswana **108** B2
olpashevo Rus. Fed. **94** H3
olpny Rus. Fed. **43** E3
ol'skiy Poluostrov pen. Rus. Fed. see
  Kola Peninsula
oluli Eritrea **90** B3
olwezi Dem. Rep. Congo **105** C4
olyma r. Rus. Fed. **95** M2
olymskaya Nizmennost' lowland
  Rus. Fed. **95** M2
olymskiy, Khrebet mts Rus. Fed.
  95 N2
omaki Japan **79** C3
omandorskiye Ostrova is Rus. Fed.
  95 N3
omárno Slovakia **57** D3
omati r. Swaziland **109** D2
omatsu Japan **79** C3
ombe Dem. Rep. Congo **105** C3
ominternivs'ke Ukr. **44** D2
omiža Croatia **63** C2
omló Hungary **57** D3
omono Congo **104** B3
omotini Greece **65** C2
omsberg mts S. Africa **108** B3
omsomolets, Ostrov i. Rus. Fed.
  95 I1
omsomol'sk Rus. Fed. **43** F2
omsomol's'k Ukr. **45** D2
omsomol'skiy Rus. Fed. **41** D4
omsomol'sk-na-Amure Rus. Fed.
  81 F1
onakovo Rus. Fed. **43** E2
ondagaon India **87** C3
ondinskoye Rus. Fed. **40** F2

Kondoa Tanz. **105** D3
Kondopoga Rus. Fed. **40** C2
Kondūz Afgh. see Kunduz
Kong Christian IX Land reg. Greenland
  125 J2
Kong Frederik VI Kyst coastal area
  Greenland **125** J3
Kongju S. Korea **77** B2
Kongolo Dem. Rep. Congo **105** C3
Kongsberg Norway **47** B4
Kongsvinger Norway **47** C3
Kongur Shan mt. China **89** E3
Königswinter Ger. **54** C2
Königs Wusterhausen Ger. **55** F1
Konin Pol. **57** D2
Konjic Bos.-Herz. **63** C2
Konkiene watercourse Namibia **108** A2
Konotop Ukr. **45** D1
Konstantinovsk Rus. Fed. **45** F2
Konstanz Ger. **56** B3
Kontagora Nigeria **101** C3
Kon Tum Vietnam **75** B2
Kon Tum, Cao Nguyên plat. Vietnam
  75 B2
Konya Turkey **92** B3
Konz Ger. **54** C3
Konzhakovskiy Kamen', Gora mt.
  Rus. Fed. **40** E3
Kooskia U.S.A. **132** C1
Kootenay Lake i. Can. **126** D3
Kootjieskolk S. Africa **108** B3
Koper Slovenia **62** B1
Kopparberg Sweden **47** D4
Koprivnica Croatia **63** C1
Korablino Rus. Fed. **43** F3
Koraput India **85** C3
Korbach Ger. **55** D2
Korçë Albania **65** B2
Korčula i. Croatia **63** C2
Korčula i. Croatia **63** C2
Korea, North country Asia **77** B1
Korea, South country Asia **77** B2
Korea Bay g. China/N. Korea **77** A2
Korea Strait Japan/S. Korea **77** B3
Korenovsk Rus. Fed. **45** E2
Korets' Ukr. **44** C1
Körfez Turkey **65** C2
Korhogo Côte d'Ivoire **100** B4
Korinthos Greece see Corinth
Kőris-hegy h. Hungary **57** D3
Koritnik mt. Albania **64** B3
Köriyama Japan **79** D3
Korkuteli Turkey **92** B3
Koro Mali **100** B3
Koroc r. Can. **129** D1
Korocha Rus. Fed. **45** E1
Korogwe Tanz. **105** D3
Koror Palau **71** C2
Korosten' Ukr. **44** C1
Korostyshiv Ukr. **44** C1
Koro Toro Chad **101** D3
Korsakov Rus. Fed. **78** D1
Korsør Denmark **56** C1
Korsun'-Shevchenkivs'kyy Ukr. **45** D2
Korsze Pol. **57** E2
Kortrijk Belgium **54** A2
Koryakskaya, Sopka vol. Rus. Fed.
  95 M3
Koryakskiy Khrebet mts Rus. Fed.
  95 N2
Koryazhma Rus. Fed. **40** D2
Koryŏng S. Korea **77** B2
Koryukivka Ukr. **45** D1
Kos Greece **65** C3
Kos i. Greece **65** C3
Kosan N. Korea **77** B2
Kościan Pol. **57** D2

Kosciuszko, Mount Austr. **117** D3
Kosh-Agach Rus. Fed. **89** F2
Košice Slovakia **57** E3
Koskullskulle Sweden **46** E2
Košong N. Korea **77** B2
Kosovo prov. Serb. and Mont. **64** B2
Kosovska Mitrovica Serb. and Mont.
  64 B2
Kosrae atoll Micronesia **110**
Kossou, Lac de l. Côte d'Ivoire **100** B4
Kostanay Kazakh. **88** D1
Kostenets Bulg. **64** B2
Koster S. Africa **109** C2
Kosti Sudan **103** B3
Kostomuksha Rus. Fed. **46** G3
Kostopil' Ukr. **44** C1
Kostroma Rus. Fed. **43** F2
Kostroma r. Rus. Fed. **43** F2
Kostrzyn Pol. **56** C2
Koszalin Pol. **57** D2
Kőszeg Hungary **57** D3
Kota India **86** B2
Kotaagung Indon. **72** B2
Kotabaru Indon. **73** C2
Kota Belud Malaysia **73** C1
Kota Bharu Malaysia **72** B1
Kotabumi Indon. **72** B2
Kota Kinabalu Malaysia **73** C1
Kota Samarahan Malaysia **73** C1
Kotel'nich Rus. Fed. **40** D3
Kotel'nikovo Rus. Fed. **41** D4
Kotel'nyy, Ostrov i. Rus. Fed. **95** L1
Köthen (Anhalt) Ger. **55** E2
Kotka Fin. **47** F3
Kotlas Rus. Fed. **40** D2
Kotlik U.S.A. **124** B2
Kotor Varoš Bos.-Herz. **63** C2
Kotovo Rus. Fed. **41** D3
Kotovsk Rus. Fed. **43** F3
Kotovs'k Ukr. **44** C2
Kotuy r. Rus. Fed. **95** I2
Kotzebue U.S.A. **124** B2
Kotzebue Sound sea chan. U.S.A.
  124 B2
Kötzting Ger. **55** F3
Koudekerke Neth. **54** A2
Koudougou Burkina **100** B3
Kougaberge mts S. Africa **108** B3
Koulamoutou Gabon **104** B3
Koulikoro Mali **100** B3
Koundâra Guinea **100** A3
Kourou Fr. Guiana **151** D2
Kouroussa Guinea **100** B3
Koussëri Cameroon **104** B1
Koutiala Mali **100** B3
Kouvola Fin. **47** F3
Kovdor Rus. Fed. **46** G2
Kovel' Ukr. **44** B1
Kovrov Rus. Fed. **43** F2
Kowhitirangi N.Z. **118** B3
Köyceğiz Turkey **65** C3
Koyda Rus. Fed. **40** D2
Koyukuk r. U.S.A. **124** C3
Kozani Greece **65** B2
Kozelets' Ukr. **45** D1
Kozel'sk Rus. Fed. **43** E3
Kozyatyn Ukr. **44** C2
Krabi Thai. **75** A3
Kra Buri Thai. **75** A2
Krâchéh Cambodia **75** B2
Kragerø Norway **47** B4
Kraggenburg Neth. **54** B1
Kragujevac Serb. and Mont. **64** B2
Krakatau i. Indon. **72** B2
Kraków Pol. **57** D2
Kralovice Czech Rep. **55** F3
Kramators'k Ukr. **45** E2
Kramfors Sweden **46** D3
Kranidi Greece **65** B3
Krasino Rus. Fed. **40** E1

Kräslava Latvia **42** C2
Kraslice Czech Rep. **55** F2
Krasnapollye Belarus **43** D3
Krasnaya Gora Rus. Fed. **43** D3
Krasnaya Gorbatka Rus. Fed. **43** F2
Krasnoarmeysk Rus. Fed. **41** D3
Krasnoarmiys'k Ukr. **45** E2
Krasnoborsk Rus. Fed. **40** D2
Krasnodar Rus. Fed. **45** E3
Krasnodon Ukr. **45** E2
Krasnogorodskoye Rus. Fed. **42** C2
Krasnogvardeyskoye *Belgorodskaya Oblast'* Rus. Fed. **45** E1
Krasnogvardeyskoye *Stavropol'skiy Kray* Rus. Fed. **45** E2
Krasnohrad Ukr. **45** E2
Krasnohvardiys'ke Ukr. **45** D2
Krasnokamsk Rus. Fed. **40** E3
Krasnomayskiy Rus. Fed. **43** D3
Krasnoperekops'k Ukr. **45** D2
Krasnoslobodsk Rus. Fed. **41** D3
Krasnouflimsk Rus. Fed. **40** E3
Krasnoyarsk Rus. Fed. **95** I3
Krasnoye-na-Volge Rus. Fed. **43** F2
Krasnyy Rus. Fed. **43** D3
Krasnyy Kholm Rus. Fed. **43** E2
Krasnyy Luch Ukr. **41** C4
Krasnyy Sulin Rus. Fed. **45** F2
Krasyliv Ukr. **44** C2
Krefeld Ger. **54** C2
Kremenchuk Ukr. **45** D2
Kremenchuts'ka Vodoskhovyshche *resr* Ukr. **45** D2
Kremešník *h.* Czech Rep. **57** D3
Kreminna Ukr. **45** E2
Krems an der Donau Austria **57** D3
Kresttsy Rus. Fed. **43** D2
Kretinga Lith. **42** B2
Kreuzau Ger. **54** C2
Kreuztal Ger. **54** C2
Kribi Cameroon **104** A2
Krikellos Greece **65** B3
Kril'on, Mys *c.* Rus. Fed. **78** D1
Krishna *r.* India **87** C2
Krishnanagar India **87** C2
Kristiansand Norway **47** B4
Kristianstad Sweden **47** C4
Kristiansund Norway **46** B3
Kristinehamn Sweden **47** C4
Kriti *i.* Greece *see* Crete
Križevci Croatia **63** C1
Krk *i.* Croatia **62** B1
Krokom Sweden **46** C3
Krolevets' Ukr. **45** D1
Kronach Ger. **55** E2
Krŏng Kaôh Kŏng Cambodia **75** B2
Kronprins Frederik Bjerge *nunataks* Greenland **125** J2
Kroonstad S. Africa **109** C2
Kropotkin Rus. Fed. **45** F2
Krosno Pol. **57** E3
Krotoszyn Pol. **57** D2
Krui Indon. **72** B2
Krujë Albania **64** A2
Krumovgrad Bulg. **65** C2
Krupki Belarus **42** C3
Kruševac Serb. and Mont. **64** B2
Krušné Hory *mts* Czech Rep. **55** F2
Kruzof Island U.S.A. **126** B3
Krychaw Belarus **43** D3
Krymsk Rus. Fed. **45** E3
Krytiko Pelagos *sea* Greece **65** C3
Kryvyy Rih Ukr. **45** D2
Ksabi Alg. **100** B2
Ksar Chellala Alg. **61** D2
Ksar el Boukhari Alg. **61** D2
Ksar el Kebir Morocco **100** B1
Kshenskiy Rus. Fed. **43** E3
Kŭ', Jabal al *h.* Saudi Arabia **90** B2

Kuala Belait Brunei **73** C1
Kuala Kerai Malaysia **72** B1
Kuala Lipis Malaysia **72** B1
Kuala Lumpur Malaysia **72** B1
Kualapembuang Indon. **73** C2
Kuala Terengganu Malaysia **72** B1
Kualatungal Indon. **72** B2
Kuamut Malaysia **73** C1
Kuandian China **77** A1
Kuantan Malaysia **72** B1
Kuban' *r.* Rus. Fed. **45** E2
Kubenskoye, Ozero *l.* Rus. Fed. **43** E2
Kubrat Bulg. **64** C2
Kubuang Indon. **73** C1
Kuching Malaysia **73** C1
Kuçovë Albania **65** A2
Kudat Malaysia **73** C1
Kudus Indon. **73** C2
Kufstein Austria **56** C3
Kugaaruk Can. **125** G2
Kugluktuk Can. **124** E2
Kuhmo Fin. **46** F3
Kührān, Kūh-e *mt.* Iran **91** C2
Kuiseb *watercourse* Namibia **108** A1
Kuito Angola **106** A1
Kuivaniemi Fin. **46** F2
Kujang N. Korea **77** B2
Kukës Albania **64** A2
Kula Turkey **65** C3
Kula Kangri *mt.* Bhutan/China **87** D2
Kulandy Kazakh. **88** C2
Kuldīga Latvia **42** B2
Kule Botswana **108** B1
Kulebaki Rus. Fed. **43** F2
Kulmbach Ger. **55** E2
Kŭlob Tajik. **89** D3
Kul'sary Kazakh. **88** C2
Kulunda Rus. Fed. **89** E1
Kulundinskoye, Ozero *salt l.* Rus. Fed. **89** E1
Kulusuk Greenland **125** J2
Kumagaya Japan **79** C3
Kumamoto Japan **79** B4
Kumanovo Macedonia **64** B2
Kumasi Ghana **100** B4
Kumba Cameroon **104** A2
Kumdah Saudi Arabia **90** B2
Kumertau Rus. Fed. **41** E3
Kumi S. Korea **77** B2
Kumla Sweden **47** D4
Kumo Nigeria **101** D3
Kumon Range *mts* Myanmar **74** A1
Kumphawapi Thai. **74** B2
Kumylzhenskiy Rus. Fed. **45** F2
Kunashir, Ostrov *i.* Rus. Fed. **78** E2
Kunene *r.* Angola/Namibia **106** A1
Kungei *Alatau mts* Kazakh./Kyrg. **89** E2
Kungsbacka Sweden **47** C4
Kungu Dem. Rep. Congo **104** B3
Kungur Rus. Fed. **40** E3
Kunhing Myanmar **74** A1
Kunlun Shan *mts* China **87** B1
Kunming China **83** A3
Kunsan S. Korea **77** B2
Kununurra Austr. **114** B1
Künzelsau Ger. **55** D3
Kuopio Fin. **46** F3
Kupa *r.* Croatia/Slovenia **62** C1
Kupang Indon. **71** C3
Kupiškis Lith. **42** B2
Küplü Turkey **65** C2
Kupreanof Island U.S.A. **126** B3
Kup"yans'k Ukr. **45** E2
Kuqa China **89** F2
Kurashiki Japan **79** B4
Kurayoshi Japan **79** B3
Kurchatov Rus. Fed. **43** E3
Kürdzhali Bulg. **64** C2
Kure Japan **79** B4

Kuressaare Estonia **42** B2
Kurgan Rus. Fed. **41** F3
Kurganinsk Rus. Fed. **45** F3
Kurikka Fin. **47** E3
Kuril Islands Rus. Fed. **95** L3
Kuril'sk Rus. Fed. **78** E2
Kurkino Rus. Fed. **43** E3
Kurmuk Sudan **103** B3
Kurnool India **85** B3
Kuroiso Japan **79** D3
Kurri Kurri Austr. **117** E2
Kursk Rus. Fed. **43** E3
Kuruman S. Africa **108** B2
Kuruman *watercourse* S. Africa **108** B2
Kurume Japan **79** B4
Kurumkan Rus. Fed. **95** J3
Kurunegala Sri Lanka **85** C4
Kuşadası Turkey **65** C3
Kuş Gölü *l.* Turkey **65** C2
Kushchevskaya Rus. Fed. **45** E2
Kushiro Japan **78** D2
Kushmurun Kazakh. **88** D1
Kushtia Bangl. **87** C2
Kuskokwim *r.* U.S.A. **124** B2
Kuskokwim Mountains U.S.A. **124** B2
Kussharo-ko *l.* Japan **78** D2
Kütahya Turkey **65** C3
K'ut'aisi Georgia **93** C1
Kutjevo Croatia **63** C1
Kutno Pol. **57** D2
Kutu Dem. Rep. Congo **104** B3
Kuujjua *r.* Can. **124** E2
Kuujjuaq Can. **129** D1
Kuujjuarapik Can. **128** C1
Kuusamo Fin. **46** F2
Kuvango Angola **106** A1
Kuvshinovo Rus. Fed. **43** D2
Kuwait *country* Asia **91** B2
Kuwait Kuwait **91** B2
Kuybysheve Ukr. **45** E2
Kuybyshevskoye Vodokhranilishche *resr* Rus. Fed. **41** D3
Kuytun China **89** F2
Kuyucak Turkey **65** C3
Kuznetsk Rus. Fed. **41** D3
Kuznetsovs'k Ukr. **44** C1
Kvalsund Norway **46** E1
Kwajalein *atoll* Marshall Is **110**
KwaMashu S. Africa **109** D2
Kwandang Indon. **73** C1
Kwangju S. Korea **77** B2
Kwanmo-bong *mt.* N. Korea **77** B1
Kwanobuhle S. Africa **109** C3
Kwanonzame S. Africa **108** B3
Kwatinidubu S. Africa **109** C3
KwaZamokhule S. Africa **109** C2
Kwazulu-Natal *prov.* S. Africa **109** D2
Kwekwe Zimbabwe **107** B1
Kwenge *r.* Dem. Rep. Congo **104** B3
Kwidzyn Pol. **57** D2
Kwilu *r.* Angola/Dem. Rep. Congo **104** B3
Kwoka *mt.* Indon. **71** C3
Kyabram Austr. **117** D3
Kyaikto Myanmar **74** A2
Kyakhta Rus. Fed. **80** D1
Kyancutta Austr. **116** B2
Kyaukpadaung Myanmar **74** A1
Kyaukpyu Myanmar **74** A2
Kybartai Lith. **42** B3
Kyebogyi Myanmar **74** A2
Kyeintali Myanmar **74** A2
Kyelang India **86** B1
Kyiv Ukr. *see* Kiev
Kyklades *is* Greece *see* Cyclades
Kyle Can. **127** E2
Kyle of Lochalsh U.K. **50** B2
Kyll *r.* Ger. **54** C3
Kyllini *mt.* Greece **65** B3

ymi Greece **65** B3
yneton Austr. **116** C3
yoga, Lake Uganda **105** D2
yogle Austr. **117** E1
yönggi-man b. S. Korea **77** B2
yŏngju S. Korea **77** B2
yōto Japan **79** C4
yparissia Greece **65** B3
ypshak, Ozero salt l. Kazakh. **89** D1
yrenia Cyprus **92** B3
yrgyzstan country Asia **89** E2
yritz Ger. **55** F1
yrönjoki r. Fin. **46** E3
yrta Rus. Fed. **40** E2
yssa Rus. Fed. **40** D2
ythira i. Greece **65** B3
ythnos i. Greece **65** B3
yuquot Can. **126** C2
yūshū i. Japan **79** B4
yustendil Bulg. **64** D2
yyivs'ke Vodoskhovyshche resr Ukr. **44** D1
yyjärvi Fin. **46** E3
yzyl Rus. Fed. **80** C1
yzylkum Desert Kazakh./Uzbek. **88** D2
yzyl-Mazhalyk Rus. Fed. **89** G1
yzylorda Kazakh. **89** D2

L

a Angostura, Presa de resr Mex. **143** C3
aascaanood Somalia **103** C4
a Asunción Venez. **150** C1
aâyoune Western Sahara **100** A2
aba r. Rus. Fed. **45** F2
a Banda Arg. **152** B3
a Baule-Escoublac France **58** B2
abé Guinea **100** A3
aberge, Lake Can. **126** B1
a Biche, Lac l. Can. **127** C2
abinsk Rus. Fed. **45** F3
abo Phil. **76** B2
aboheyre France **58** B3
abrador reg. Can. **129** D1
abrador City Can. **129** D1
abrador Sea Can./Greenland **125** I2
ábrea Brazil **150** C3
abuan Malaysia **73** C1
abuhanbajo Indon. **73** C2
abuhanbilik Indon. **72** B1
abuna Indon. **71** C3
abutta Myanmar **74** A2
abytnangi Rus. Fed. **40** F2
aç Albania **64** A2
a Capelle France **59** C2
accadive Islands India **85** B3
ac du Bonnet Can. **127** F2
a Ceiba Hond. **144** B3
achlan r. Austr. **117** C2
achute Can. **137** F1
a Ciotat France **59** D3
ac-Mégantic Can. **129** C2
acombe Can. **126** C2
a Concepción Panama **144** B4
a Concordia Mex. **143** C3
aconi Italy **62** A3
aconia U.S.A. **137** F2
a Crete Can. **126** C2
a Crosse U.S.A. **136** B2
a Cruz Mex. **142** B2
a Cuesta Mex. **142** B2
adakh Range mts India **87** B1
adismith S. Africa **108** B3

Lādīz Iran **91** D2
Ladozhskoye Ozero l. Rus. Fed. see Lagoda, Lake
Ladysmith Can. **126** C3
Ladysmith S. Africa **109** C2
Lae P.N.G. **71** D3
La Esmeralda Bol. **152** B3
Læsø i. Denmark **47** C4
La Fayette U.S.A. **139** C2
Lafayette IN U.S.A. **136** C2
Lafayette LA U.S.A. **138** C2
La-Ferté-Milon France **54** A3
Lafia Nigeria **101** C4
La Flèche France **58** B2
La Follette U.S.A. **139** D1
Laforge Can. **129** C1
La Galite i. Tunisia **62** A3
Lagan' Rus. Fed. **41** D4
Lagdo, Lac de l. Cameroon **104** B2
Laghouat Alg. **100** C1
Lagoa Santa Brazil **155** D1
Lagoda, Lake Rus. Fed. **43** D1
La Gomera i. Canary Is **100** A2
Lagos Nigeria **100** C4
Lagos Port. **60** B2
La Grande U.S.A. **132** C1
a Grande 2, Réservoir resr Can. **128** C1
La Grande 3, Réservoir resr Can. **128** C1
LLa Grande 4, Réservoir resr Can. **129** C1
Lagrange Austr. **114** B1
La Grange U.S.A. **139** C2
La Gran Sabana plat. Venez. **150** C2
Laguna Brazil **152** D3
Laguna, Picacho de la mt. Mex. **142** A2
Lagunas Peru **150** B3
La Habana Cuba see Havana
Lahad Datu Malaysia **73** C1
Lahat Indon. **72** B2
Lahij Yemen **90** B3
Lāhījān Iran **93** C2
Lahnstein Ger. **54** C2
Lahore Pak. **86** B1
Lahri Pak. **86** A2
Lahti Fin. **47** F3
Laï Chad **101** D4
Laidley Austr. **117** E1
L'Aigle France **58** C2
Laingsburg S. Africa **108** B3
Lainioälven r. Sweden **46** E2
Lairg U.K. **50** E1
Laives Italy **62** B1
Laiwu China **82** B2
Laiyang China **82** C2
Laizhou China **82** B2
Laizhou Wan b. China **82** B2
Lajamanu Austr. **114** C1
Lajes Brazil **152** C3
La Junta Mex. **142** B2
La Junta U.S.A. **134** C3
Lake Cargellligo Austr. **117** D2
Lake Cathie Austr. **117** E2
Lake Charles U.S.A. **138** B2
Lake City FL U.S.A. **139** D2
Lake City SC U.S.A. **139** E2
Lake Cowichan Can. **126** C3
Lake Havasu City U.S.A. **140** B2
Lakeland U.S.A. **139** D3
Lake Louise Can. **126** C2
Lake Oswego U.S.A. **132** B1
Lake Paringa N.Z. **118** A3
Lake Providence U.S.A. **138** B2
Lakeview U.S.A. **132** B2
Lakewood CO U.S.A. **134** B3
Lakewood NJ U.S.A. **137** F2

Lake Worth U.S.A. **139** D3
Lakhpat India **86** A2
Lakki Pak. **86** B1
Lakonikos Kolpos b. Greece **65** B3
Lakselv Norway **46** E1
La Libertad Guat. **143** C3
Lalín Spain **60** B1
Lalitpur India **87** B2
La Loche Can. **124** E3
La Louvière Belgium **54** B2
La Maddalena Italy **62** A2
Lamag Malaysia **73** C1
La Manche str. France/U.K. see English Channel
Lamar U.S.A. **134** C3
Lamard Iran **91** C2
La Marmora, Punta mt. Italy **62** A3
La Martre, Lac l. Can. **126** D1
Lambaréné Gabon **104** B3
Lambert's Bay S. Africa **108** A3
Lambeyri Iceland **46** [inset]
Lamego Port. **60** B1
La Merced Peru **150** B4
Lameroo Austr. **116** C3
Lamesa U.S.A. **141** D2
Lamia Greece **65** B3
Lamoni U.S.A. **135** E2
Lampang Thai. **74** A2
Lampasas U.S.A. **141** E2
Lampazos Mex. **143** B2
Lampeter U.K. **53** A3
Lamphun Thai. **74** A2
Lamu Kenya **105** E3
Lanark U.K. **50** C3
Lanbi Kyun i. Myanmar **75** A2
Lancang Jiang r. China see Mekong
Lancaster U.K. **52** B2
Lancaster CA U.S.A. **133** C4
Lancaster OH U.S.A. **136** D3
Lancaster SC U.S.A. **139** D2
Lancaster Sound str. Can. **125** G2
Landau in der Pfalz Ger. **54** D3
Landeck Austria **56** C3
Lander U.S.A. **134** B2
Land's End pt U.K. **53** A4
Landshut Ger. **56** C3
Landskrona Sweden **47** C4
Landstuhl Ger. **54** C3
Lanett U.S.A. **139** C2
Langberg mts S. Africa **108** B2
Langdon U.S.A. **135** D1
Langeland i. Denmark **47** C4
Langen Ger. **55** D1
Langeoog Ger. **54** C1
Langeoog i. Ger. **54** C1
Langgöns Ger. **55** D2
Langjökull ice cap Iceland **46** [inset]
Langogne France **59** C3
Langon France **58** B3
Langres France **59** D2
Langsa Indon. **72** A1
Lang Son Vietnam **74** B1
Langwedel Ger. **55** D1
Lanigan Can. **127** E2
Lanín, Volcán vol. Arg./Chile **153** A4
Länkäran Azer. **93** C2
Lannion France **58** B2
Lansing U.S.A. **136** D2
Lanxi China **83** B3
Lanya Sudan **103** B4
Lanzarote i. Canary Is **100** A2
Lanzhou China **82** A2
Laoag Phil. **76** B2
Lao Cai Vietnam **74** B1
Laohekou China **82** B2
Laoling China **77** B1
Lao Ling mts China **77** B1
Laon France **59** C2

Laos *country* Asia **74** B2
Laotougou China **77** B1
Lapa Brazil **154** C3
La Palma *i.* Canary Is **100** A2
La Palma Panama **144** C4
La Paraguа Venez. **150** C2
La Paz Bol. **152** B2
La Paz Hond. **143** D3
La Paz Mex. **142** A2
La Pedrera Col. **150** C3
La Pérouse Strait Japan/Rus. Fed. **78** D1
La Pesca Mex. **143** C2
La Piedad Mex. **142** B2
La Plata Arg. **153** C4
La Plata, Río de *sea chan.* Arg./Uru. **153** C4
La Potherie, Lac *l.* Can. **129** C1
Lappeenranta Fin. **47** F3
Lappersdorf Ger. **55** F3
Lappland *reg.* Europe **46** D2
Lāpseki Turkey **65** C2
Laptev Sea Rus. Fed. **95** K1
Laptevykh, More *sea* Rus. Fed. *see* Laptev Sea
Lapua Fin. **46** E3
La Quiaca Arg. **152** B3
Lār Iran **91** C2
Larache Morocco **100** B1
Laramie U.S.A. **134** B2
Laramie Mountains U.S.A. **134** B2
Laranda Turkey *see* Karaman
Laranjeiras do Sul Brazil **154** B3
Larantuka Indon. **73** D2
Larat *i.* Indon. **71** C3
Larba Alg. **61** D2
Laredo Spain **60** C1
Laredo U.S.A. **141** E3
Largs U.K. **50** B3
La Rioja Arg. **152** B3
Larisa Greece **65** B3
Larkana Pak. **86** A2
Larnaca Cyprus **92** B2
Larne U.K. **51** D1
La Roche-en-Ardenne Belgium **54** B2
La Rochelle France **58** B2
La Roche-sur-Yon France **58** B2
La Roda Spain **61** C2
La Romana Dom. Rep. **145** D3
La Ronge Can. **124** E3
La Ronge, Lac *l.* Can. **124** F3
Larrimah Austr. **114** C1
Larsen Ice Shelf Antarctica **119** K3
Larvik Norway **47** C4
La Sarre Can. **128** C2
Las Cruces U.S.A. **140** C2
La Serena Chile **152** A3
Las Flores Arg. **153** C4
Las Heras Arg. **153** B4
Lashio Myanmar **74** A1
Lashkar Gāh Afgh. **86** A1
La Sila *reg.* Italy **63** C3
Las Lomitas Arg. **152** B3
Las Nieves Mex. **142** B2
Las Palmas de Gran Canaria Canary Is **100** A2
La Spezia Italy **62** A1
Las Plumas Arg. **153** B5
Last Mountain Lake Can. **127** C2
Las Tórtolas, Cerro *mt.* Chile **152** B3
Lastoursville Gabon **104** B3
Lastovo *i.* Croatia **63** C2
Las Tres Vírgenes, Volcán *vol.* Mex. **142** A2
Las Tunas Cuba **145** C2
Las Varas Chihuahua Mex. **142** B2
Las Varas Nayarit Mex. **142** B2
Las Vegas NM U.S.A. **140** C1
Las Vegas NV U.S.A. **133** C3
La Tabatière Can. **129** E1

Latakia Syria **92** B2
La Teste-de-Buch France **58** B3
Latina Italy **62** B2
La Tortuga, Isla *i.* Venez. **145** D3
La Trinidad Phil. **76** B2
Latskoye Rus. Fed. **43** E2
La Tuque Can. **129** C2
Latvia *country* Europe **42** B2
Lauchhammer Ger. **55** F2
Lauf an der Pegnitz Ger. **55** E3
Laufen Switz. **59** C2
Launceston Austr. **115** D4
Launceston U.K. **53** A4
Launggyaung Myanmar **74** A1
Laura Austr. **115** D1
Laurel MS U.S.A. **138** C2
Laurel MT U.S.A. **132** E1
Lauria Italy **63** C2
Laurinburg U.S.A. **139** E2
Lausanne Switz. **59** D2
Laut *i.* Indon. **73** C2
Lautersbach (Hessen) Ger. **55** D2
Laut Kecil, Kepulauan *is* Indon. **73** C2
Lauwersmeer *l.* Neth. **54** C1
Laval France **58** B2
Lavapié, Punta *pt* Chile **147**
Laverton Austr. **114** B2
Lavras Brazil **155** D2
Lavumisa Swaziland **109** D2
Lawas Malaysia **73** C1
Lawksawk Myanmar **74** A1
Lawra Ghana **100** B3
Lawrence U.S.A. **136** D3
Lawrenceburg U.S.A. **138** C1
Lawton U.S.A. **141** E2
Lawz, Jabal al *mt.* Saudi Arabia **90** A2
Laxá Sweden **47** C4
Lazarevac Serb. and Mont. **64** B2
Lázaro Cárdenas Baja California Mex. **142** A1
Lázaro Cárdenas Michoacán Mex. **142** B3
Lazdijai Lith. **42** B3
Lead U.S.A. **134** C2
Leader Can. **127** E2
Leadville U.S.A. **134** B3
Leaf Rapids Can. **127** F2
Leane, Lough *l.* Rep. of Ireland **51** B2
Leavenworth U.S.A. **135** E3
Lebach Ger. **54** C3
Lebanon *country* Asia **92** B2
Lebanon MO U.S.A. **135** E3
Lebanon NH U.S.A. **137** F2
Lebanon OH U.S.A. **132** D2
Lebanon PA U.S.A. **137** E2
Lebedyan' Rus. Fed. **43** E3
Lebedyn Ukr. **45** D1
Le Blanc France **58** C2
Lębork Pol. **57** D2
Lebowakgomo S. Africa **109** C1
Lebrija Spain **60** B2
Lebu Chile **153** A4
Le Bugue France **58** C3
Le Catelet France **54** A2
Lecce Italy **63** C2
Lecco Italy **62** A1
Lech *r.* Austria/Ger. **56** C3
Lechaina Greece **65** B3
Lechang China **83** B3
Leck Ger. **56** B2
Lectoure France **58** C3
Ledesma Spain **60** B1
Le Dorat France **58** C2
Leduc Can. **126** D2
Leech Lake U.S.A. **135** E1
Leeds U.K. **52** C3
Leek U.K. **52** B3
Leer (Ostfriesland) Ger. **54** C1
Leesburg U.S.A. **139** D3
Leesville U.S.A. **138** B2

Leeton Austr. **117** D2
Leeu-Gamka S. Africa **108** B3
Leeuwarden Neth. **54** B1
Leeuwin, Cape Austr. **114** A3
Leeward Islands Caribbean Sea **145** D3
Lefkada Greece **65** B3
Lefkada *i.* Greece **65** B3
Lefkosia Cyprus *see* Nicosia
Legaspi Phil. **76** B2
Legnago Italy **62** B1
Legnica Pol. **57** D2
Leh India **87** B1
Le Havre France **58** C2
Lehututu Botswana **108** B1
Leiah Pak. **86** B1
Leibnitz Austria **57** D3
Leicester U.K. **53** C3
Leichhardt *r.* Austr. **115** C1
Leiden Neth. **54** B1
Leie *r.* Belgium **54** A2
Leigh Creek Austr. **116** B2
Leikanger Norway **47** B3
Leimen Ger. **55** D3
Leine *r.* Ger. **55** D1
Leinster *reg.* Rep. of Ireland **51** C2
Leipzig Ger. **55** F2
Leiranger Norway **46** C2
Leiria Port. **60** B2
Leirvik Norway **47** B4
Leixlip Rep. of Ireland **51** C2
Leiyang China **83** B3
Leizhou China **83** B3
Leizhou Bandao *pen.* China **83** A3
Lékana Congo **104** B3
Lelystad Neth. **54** B1
Le Maire, Estrecho de *sea chan.* Arg. **153** B6
Léman, Lac *l.* France/Switz. *see* Geneva, Lake
Le Mans France **58** C2
Le Mars U.S.A. **135** D2
Leme Brazil **154** C2
Lemesos Cyprus *see* Limassol
Lemförde Ger. **55** D1
Lemieux Islands Can. **125** H2
Lemmon U.S.A. **134** C1
Lemoore U.S.A. **133** C3
Le Moyne, Lac *l.* Can. **129** D1
Lemro *r.* Myanmar **74** A1
Le Murge *hills* Italy **63** C2
Lena *r.* Rus. Fed. **95** K2
Lendery Rus. Fed. **46** G3
Lengerich Ger. **54** C1
Lengshuijiang China **83** B3
Lengshuitan China **83** B3
Lenine Ukr. **45** E2
Leningradskaya Rus. Fed. **45** E2
Lenin Peak Kyrg./Tajik. **89** E3
Leninskiy Rus. Fed. **43** E3
Lens Belgium **54** A2
Lens France **58** C1
Lensk Rus. Fed. **95** J2
Lenti Hungary **57** D3
Lentini Italy **62** A1
Léo Burkina **100** B3
Leoben Austria **56** D3
Leominster U.K. **53** B3
León Mex. **142** B2
León Nic. **144** B3
León Spain **60** B1
Leonardville Namibia **108** A1
Leonora Austr. **114** B3
Leopoldina Brazil **155** D2
Lephalale S. Africa **109** C1
Lephepe Botswana **109** C1
Lephoi S. Africa **109** C3
Leping China **83** B3
Le Puy-en-Velay France **59** C2
Lerala Botswana **109** C1

érida Col. **150** B3
erma Spain **60** C1
eros i. Greece **65** C3
e Roy, Lac l. Can. **128** C1
erum Sweden **47** C4
erwick U.K. **50** [inset]
esbos i. Greece **65** C3
es Cayes Haiti **145** C3
eshan China **80** C3
eshukonskoye Rus. Fed. **40** D2
eskovac Serb. and Mont. **64** D3
esneven France **58** B2
esnoye Rus. Fed. **43** E2
esosibirsk Rus. Fed. **95** I3
esotho country Africa **109** C2
esozavodsk Rus. Fed. **78** B1
es Sables-d'Olonne France **58** B2
esser Antilles is Caribbean Sea
  145 D3
esser Caucasus mts Asia **93** C1
esser Slave Lake can. **126** D2
es Vans France **59** C3
esvos i. Greece see Lesbos
eszno Pol. **57** D2
etchworth U.K. **53** C4
ethbridge Can. **127** D3
ethem Guyana **150** D2
eti, Kepulauan is Indon. **71** C3
eticia Col. **150** C3
ethlakeng Botswana **109** C1
e Touquet-Paris-Plage France **58** C1
e Tréport France **53** D4
etsok-aw Kyun i. Myanmar **75** A2
etspa S. Africa **108** C3
etterkenny Rep. of Ireland **51** C1
eucate, Étang de l. France **58** C3
euser, Gunung mt. Indon. **72** A1
euven Belgium **54** B2
evadeia Greece **65** B3
evanger Norway **46** C3
evelland U.S.A. **141** D2
everkusen Ger. **54** C2
evice Slovakia **57** D3
évis Can. **129** C2
ev Tolstoy Rus. Fed. **43** E3
ewes U.K. **53** D4
ewis, Isle of i. U.K. **50** A1
ewis Range mts U.S.A. **132** D1
ewisburg U.S.A. **137** D3
ewiston ID U.S.A. **132** C1
ewiston ME U.S.A. **137** F2
ewistown U.S.A. **132** E1
exington KY U.S.A. **136** D3
exington NE U.S.A. **134** D2
exington VA U.S.A. **137** E3
eyte i. Phil. **76** B2
ezhë Albania **64** A2
ezhnevo Rus. Fed. **43** F2
'gov Rus. Fed. **43** E3
ianhua China **83** B3
ianjiang China **83** B3
ianshan China **82** C1
ianyungang China **82** B2
ianzhou China **83** B2
iaodong Bandao pen. China **82** C1
iaodong Wan b. China **82** C1
iao He r. China **77** A1
iaoning prov. China **82** C1
iaoyang China **82** C1
iaoyuan China **77** B1
iard r. Can. **124** D2

Libby U.S.A. **132** C1
Libenge Dem. Rep. Congo **104** B2
Liberal U.S.A. **134** C3
Liberec Czech Rep. **56** D2
Liberia country Africa **100** B4
Liberia Costa Rica **144** B3
Libertad Venez. **145** D4
Libin Belgium **54** B3
Libourne France **58** B3
Libreville Gabon **104** A2
Libya country Africa **101** D2
Libyan Desert Egypt/Libya **101** E2
Libyan Plateau Egypt **102** A1
Licata Italy **62** B3
Lichinga Moz. **107** C1
Lichte Ger. **55** E2
Lichtenburg S. Africa **109** C2
Lichtenfels Ger. **55** E2
Lida Belarus **42** C5
Lidköping Sweden **47** C4
Liebenwalde Ger. **55** F1
Liebig, Mount Austr. **114** C2
Liechtenstein country Europe **59** D2
Liège Belgium **54** B2
Lieksa Fin. **46** G3
Lienart Dem. Rep. Congo **105** C2
Lienz Austria **56** E2
Liepāja Latvia **42** B2
Liévin France **53** D4
Liezen Austria **56** C3
Liffey r. Rep. of Ireland **51** C2
Lifford Rep. of Ireland **51** C1
Lightning Ridge Austr. **117** D1
Ligonha r. Moz. **107** C1
Ligurian Sea France/Italy **62** A2
Likasi Dem. Rep. Congo **105** C2
Likely Can. **126** C2
Likhoslavl' Rus. Fed. **43** E2
Liku Indon. **72** B1
L'Île-Rousse France **59** D3
Liling China **83** B3
Lilla Edet Sweden **47** C4
Lille Belgium **54** B2
Lille France **58** C1
Lille Bælt sea chan. Denmark see
  Little Belt
Lillehammer Norway **47** C3
Lillestrøm Norway **47** C4
Lillooet Can. **126** C2
Lilongwe Malawi **107** C1
Lima Phil. **76** B3
Lima Peru **150** B4
Lima U.S.A. **136** C2
Limassol Cyprus **92** B2
Limavady U.K. **51** C1
Limay r. Arg. **153** B4
Limbach-Oberfrohna Ger. **55** F2
Limbaži Latvia **42** B2
Limbe Cameroon **104** A2
Limburg an der Lahn Ger. **54** D2
Lime Acres S. Africa **108** B2
Limeira Brazil **154** C2
Limerick Rep. of Ireland **51** B2
Limfjorden sea chan. Denmark **47** B4
Limnos i. Greece **65** C3
Limoges France **58** C2
Limón Costa Rica **144** B4
Limon U.S.A. **134** C3
Limoux France **58** C3
Limpopo prov. S. Africa **109** C1
Limpopo r. S. Africa/Zimbabwe **109** D2
Linapacan i. Phil. **76** A3
Linares Chile **153** A4
Linares Mex. **143** C2
Linares Spain **60** C2
Lincang China **74** B1
Lincoln U.K. **52** C3
Lincoln IL U.S.A. **136** C2
Lincoln ME U.S.A. **137** G1
Lincoln NE U.S.A. **135** D2
Linden Guyana **151** D2

Linden U.S.A. **138** C1
Lindi r. Dem. Rep. Congo **105** C2
Lindi Tanz. **105** D3
Lindisfarne i. U.K. see Holy Island
Lindos Greece **92** A2
Lindsay Can. **137** E2
Line Islands Kiribati **159** E4
Linfen China **82** B2
Lingayen Phil. **76** B2
Lingbao China **82** B2
Lingelethu S. Africa **109** C3
Lingelihle S. Africa **109** C3
Lingen (Ems) Ger. **54** C1
Lingga, Kepulauan is Indon. **72** B2
Lingshan China **83** A3
Lingshui China **83** A4
Linguère Senegal **100** A3
Linhares Brazil **155** D1
Linhe China **82** A1
Linköping Sweden **47** D4
Linkou China **79** C1
Linnhe, Loch inlet U.K. **50** B2
Linqing China **82** B2
Lins Brazil **154** C2
Linton U.S.A. **134** C1
Linxi China **82** B1
Linxia China **80** C3
Linyi Shandong China **82** B2
Linyi Shandong China **82** B2
Linying China **82** B2
Linz Austria **56** C3
Lion, Golfe du g. France **59** C3
Lipari Italy **62** B3
Lipari, Isole is Italy **62** B3
Lipetsk Rus. Fed. **43** E3
Lipin Bor Rus. Fed. **43** E1
Lipova Romania **44** B2
Lippstadt Ger. **55** D2
Lipu China **83** B3
Lisakovsk Kazakh. **88** D1
Lisala Dem. Rep. Congo **104** C2
Lisboa Port. see Lisbon
Lisbon Port. **60** B2
Lisburn U.K. **51** C1
Liscannor Bay Rep. of Ireland **51** B2
Lisieux France **58** C2
Liskeard U.K. **53** A4
Liski Rus. Fed. **43** E3
Lismore Austr. **117** E1
Lisnaskea U.K. **51** C1
Listowel Rep. of Ireland **51** B2
Litang Guangxi China **83** A3
Litang Sichuan China **80** C2
Litchfield IL U.S.A. **136** C3
Litchfield MN U.S.A. **135** E1
Lithgow Austr. **117** E2
Lithino, Akra c. pt Greece **65** B4
Lithuania country Europe **42** B2
Litoměřice Czech Rep. **56** C2
Little Abaco i. Bahamas **145** C2
Little Andaman i. India **75** A2
Little Belt sea chan. Denmark **47** B4
Little Falls U.S.A. **135** E1
Littlefield U.S.A. **141** D2
Littlehampton U.K. **53** C4
Little Karas Berg plat. Namibia
  108 A2
Little Karoo plat. S. Africa **108** B3
Little Minch sea chan. U.K. **50** A2
Little Missouri r. U.S.A. **134** C1
Little Nicobar i. India **75** A3
Little Rock U.S.A. **138** B2
Littleton U.S.A. **137** F2
Liujiachang China **83** B2
Liuzhou China **83** B3
Līvāni Latvia **42** C2
Liveringa Austr. **114** B1
Livermore, Mount U.S.A. **140** D2
Liverpool Can. **129** D2
Liverpool U.K. **52** B3

Liverpool Range *mts* Austr. **117** D2
Livingston *MT* U.S.A. **132** D1
Livingston *TX* U.S.A. **141** F2
Livingston, Lake U.S.A. **141** E2
Livingstone Zambia **106** B1
Livno Bos.-Herz. **63** C2
Livny Rus. Fed. **43** E3
Livonia U.S.A. **136** D2
Livorno Italy **62** B2
Liwale Tanz. **105** D3
Lizard Point *pt* U.K. **53** A5
Lizy-sur-Ourcq France **54** A3
Ljubljana Slovenia **62** B1
Ljungan *r.* Sweden **47** D3
Ljungby Sweden **47** C4
Ljusdal Sweden **47** D3
Ljusnan *r.* Sweden **47** D3
Llandeilo U.K. **53** B4
Llandovery U.K. **53** B4
Llandrindod Wells U.K. **53** B3
Llandudno U.K. **52** B3
Llanelli U.K. **53** A4
Llangefni U.K. **52** A3
Llano Estacado *plain* U.S.A. **141** D2
Llanos *reg.* Col./Venez. **150** C2
Lleida Spain **61** D1
Lliria Spain **61** C2
Llodio Spain **60** C1
Lloyd George, Mount Can. **126** C2
Lloyd Lake Can. **127** E2
Lloydminster Can. **127** D2
Llullaillaco, Volcán *vol.* Chile **152** B3
Lobatse Botswana **109** C2
Lobito Angola **106** A1
Loburg Ger. **55** F1
Lochaber *reg.* U.K. **50** B2
Lochboisdale U.K. **50** A2
Loches France **58** C2
Lochgilphead U.K. **50** B2
Lochinver U.K. **50** B1
Lochmaddy U.K. **50** A2
Lochnagar *mt.* U.K. **50** C2
Lock Austr. **116** B2
Lockerbie U.K. **50** C3
Lockhart U.S.A. **141** E3
Lock Haven U.S.A. **137** E2
Lockport U.S.A. **137** E2
Lộc Ninh Vietnam **75** B2
Lodève France **59** C3
Lodeynoye Pole Rus. Fed. **40** C2
Loding Norway **46** C2
Lodwar Kenya **105** D2
Łódź Pol. **57** D2
Loei Thai. **74** B2
Loeriesfontein S. Africa **108** A3
Lofoten *is* Norway **46** C2
Logan U.S.A. **132** D2
Logan, Mount Can. **126** A1
Logansport U.S.A. **136** C2
Logatec Slovenia **62** B1
Logroño Spain **60** C1
Löhne Ger. **55** D1
Loikaw Myanmar **74** A2
Loi Lun *mt.* Myanmar/Thai. **74** A2
Loire *r.* France **58** B2
Loja Ecuador **150** B3
Loja Spain **60** C2
Lokan tekojärvi *l.* Fin. **46** F2
Lokeren Belgium **54** B2
Lokgwabe Botswana **108** B1
Lokichar Kenya **105** D2
Lokichokio Kenya **105** D2
Loknya Rus. Fed. **43** D2
Lokoja Nigeria **101** C4
Lokot' Rus. Fed. **43** D3
Loksa Estonia **42** C2
Loks Land *i.* Can. **125** H2
Lolland *i.* Denmark **47** C5
Lollondo Tanz. **105** D3

Lolwane S. Africa **108** B2
Lom Bulg. **64** B2
Lom Norway **47** B3
Lomami *r.* Dem. Rep. Congo **105** C2
Lomas de Zamora Arg. **153** C4
Lombok *i.* Indon. **73** C2
Lombok, Selat *sea chan.* Indon. **73** C2
Lomé Togo **100** C4
Lomela *r.* Dem. Rep. Congo **104** C3
Lomme France **54** A2
Lommel Belgium **54** B2
Lomond, Loch *l.* U.K. **50** B2
Lomonosov Rus. Fed. **42** C2
Lompobattang, Gunung *mt.* Indon. **73** C2
Lompoc U.S.A. **133** B4
Lom Sak Thai. **74** B2
Łomża Pol. **57** E2
London Can. **128** B2
London U.K. **53** C4
Londonderry U.K. **51** C1
Londonderry, Cape Austr. **114** B1
Londrina Brazil **154** B2
Longa, Proliv *sea chan.* Rus. Fed. **95** N2
Long Akah Malaysia **73** C1
Long Bay U.S.A. **139** E2
Long Beach U.S.A. **133** C4
Longford Rep. of Ireland **51** C2
Longiram Indon. **73** C2
Long Island Bahamas **145** C2
Long Island Can. **128** C1
Long Island P.N.G. **71** D3
Long Island U.S.A. **137** F2
Longlac Can. **128** B2
Long Lake Can. **128** B2
Longmont U.S.A. **134** B2
Long Point *pt* Can. **137** D2
Longquan China **83** B3
Long Range Mountains Can. **129** E2
Longreach Austr. **115** D2
Long Stratton U.K. **53** D3
Longtown U.K. **52** B2
Longuyon France **59** D2
Longview *TX* U.S.A. **141** F2
Longview *WA* U.S.A. **132** B1
Longxi China **82** A2
Longxi Shan *mt.* China **83** B3
Long Xuyên Vietnam **75** B2
Longyan China **83** B3
Longyearbyen Svalbard **94** D1
Lons-le-Saunier France **56** B3
Lookout, Cape U.S.A. **139** E2
Loop Head Rep. of Ireland **51** B2
Lop Buri Thai. **75** B2
Lopez Phil. **76** B2
Lop Nur *salt flat* China **80** C2
Lopori *r.* Dem. Rep. Congo **104** B2
Lora del Río Spain **60** B2
Lorain U.S.A. **136** D2
Loralai Pak. **86** A1
Lorca Spain **61** C2
Lord Howe Island Austr. **115** E3
Lordsburg U.S.A. **140** C2
Lorena Brazil **155** C2
Loreto Brazil **151** D2
Loreto Mex. **142** B2
Lorient France **58** B2
Lorn, Firth of *est.* U.K. **50** B2
Lorne Austr. **116** C3
Los Alamos U.S.A. **140** C1
Los Aldamas Mex. **141** E3
Los Ángeles Chile **153** A4
Los Angeles U.S.A. **133** C4
Los Banos U.S.A. **133** B3
Los Blancos Arg. **152** B3
Losevo Rus. Fed. **45** F1
Lošinj *i.* Croatia **62** B2
Los Mochis Mex. **142** B2

Losombo Dem. Rep. Congo **104** B2
Los Roques, Islas *is* Venez. **145** D3
Lossiemouth U.K. **50** C2
Los Teques Venez. **150** C1
Los Vilos Chile **152** A4
Lot *r.* France **58** C3
Loth U.K. **50** C1
Lotikipi Plain Kenya **105** D2
Loto Dem. Rep. Congo **104** C3
Lotoshino Rus. Fed. **43** E2
Louangnamtha Laos **74** B1
Louangphabang Laos **74** B2
Loubomo Congo **104** B3
Loudéac France **58** B2
Loudi China **83** B3
Louga Senegal **100** A3
Loughborough U.K. **53** C3
Loughrea Rep. of Ireland **51** B2
Louhans France **59** D2
Louisburgh Rep. of Ireland **51** B2
Louisiade Archipelago *is* P.N.G. **115** E1
Louisiana *state* U.S.A. **138** B2
Louisville *KY* U.S.A. **136** C3
Louisville *MS* U.S.A. **138** C2
Loukhi Rus. Fed. **46** G2
Louny Czech Rep. **55** F2
Loups Marins, Lacs des *lakes* Can. **128** C1
Lourdes France **58** B3
Lourenço Brazil **151** D2
Lousã Port. **60** B1
Louth Austr. **117** D2
Louth U.K. **52** C3
Lovat' *r.* Rus. Fed. **43** D2
Lovech Bulg. **64** B2
Loveland U.S.A. **134** B2
Lovelock U.S.A. **132** C2
Loviisa Fin. **42** C1
Lovington U.S.A. **141** D2
Lowa Dem. Rep. Congo **105** C3
Lowell U.S.A. **137** E2
Lower Arrow Lake Can. **126** D3
Lower Hutt N.Z. **118** B3
Lower Lough Erne *l.* U.K. **51** C1
Lower Post Can. **126** C2
Lowestoft U.K. **53** D3
Lowville U.S.A. **137** E2
Łowicz Pol. **57** D2
Loxton Austr. **116** C2
Loyauté, Îles *is* New Caledonia **110**
Loyew Belarus **43** D3
Løypskardtinden *mt.* Norway **46** C2
Loznica Serb. and Mont. **64** A2
Lozova Ukr. **45** E2
Luacano Angola **106** B1
Lu'an China **82** B2
Luanda Angola **104** B3
Luang, Thale *lag.* Thai. **75** B3
Luangwa *r.* Zambia **107** C1
Luanshya Zambia **107** B1
Luarca Spain **60** B1
Luau Angola **106** B1
Lubaczów Pol. **57** E2
Lubango Angola **106** A1
Lubao Dem. Rep. Congo **105** C3
Lubartów Pol. **57** E2
Lübbecke Ger. **55** D1
Lübben Ger. **55** F2
Lübbenau Ger. **55** F2
Lubbock U.S.A. **141** D2
Lübeck Ger. **56** C1
Lubei China **82** C1
Lubenka Kazakh. **88** C1
Lubin Pol. **57** D2
Lublin Pol. **57** E2
Lubny Ukr. **45** D1
Lubok Antu Malaysia **73** C1
Lübtheen Ger. **55** E1
Lubudi Dem. Rep. Congo **105** C3
Lubuklinggau Indon. **72** B2

Lubumbashi Dem. Rep. Congo **105** C4
Lubungu Zambia **106** B1
Lubutu Dem. Rep. Congo **105** C3
Lucala Angola **104** B3
Lucan Rep. of Ireland **51** C2
Lucapa Angola **104** C3
Luce Bay U.K. **50** B3
Lucélia Brazil **154** B2
Lucena Phil. **76** B2
Lucena Spain **60** C2
Lučenec Slovakia **57** D3
Lucera Italy **62** C2
Lucerne Switz. **59** D2
Lüchow Ger. **55** E1
Lucira Angola **106** A1
Luckau Ger. **55** F2
Luckenwalde Ger. **55** F1
Luckhoff S. Africa **108** B2
Lucknow India **87** C2
Lucusse Angola **106** B1
Lüdenscheid Ger. **54** C2
Lüder Ger. **55** E1
Lüderitz Namibia **108** A2
Ludhiana India **86** B1
Ludington U.S.A. **136** C2
Ludlow U.K. **53** B3
Ludlow U.S.A. **133** C4
Ludogorie *reg.* Bulg. **64** C2
Ludvika Sweden **47** D3
Ludwigsburg Ger. **56** B3
Ludwigsfelde Ger. **55** F1
Ludwigshafen am Rhein Ger. **55** D3
Ludwigslust Ger. **55** E1
Ludza Latvia **42** C2
Luebo Dem. Rep. Congo **104** C3
Luena Angola **106** B1
Lueyang China **82** A2
Lufeng China **83** B3
Lufkin U.S.A. **141** F2
Luga Rus. Fed. **42** C2
Luga *r.* Rus. Fed. **42** C2
Lugano Switz. **59** D2
Lugenda *r.* Moz. **107** C1
Lugenda *r.* Moz. **107** C1
Lugo Spain **60** B1
Lugoj Romania **44** B2
Luhans'k Ukr. **45** E2
Luhombero Tanz. **105** D3
Luhyny Ukr. **44** C1
Luiana Angola **106** B1
Luilaka *r.* Dem. Rep. Congo **104** C3
Luino Italy **56** B3
Luiro *r.* Fin. **46** F2
Luiza Dem. Rep. Congo **104** C3
Lujiang China **82** B2
Lukavac Bos.-Herz. **63** C2
Lukenie *r.* Dem. Rep. Congo **104** B3
Lukeville U.S.A. **140** B2
Lukh *r.* Rus. Fed. **43** F2
Lukhovitsy Rus. Fed. **43** E3
Łuków Pol. **57** E2
Lukulu Zambia **106** B1
Luleå Sweden **46** E2
Luleälven *r.* Sweden **46** E2
Lüleburgaz Turkey **64** C2
Luliang Shan *mts* China **82** B2
Lumajang Indon. **73** C2
Lumajangdong Co *salt l.* China **87** C1
Lumbala Kaquengue Angola **106** B1
Lumberton U.S.A. **139** E2
Lumbis Indon. **73** C1
Lumbrales Spain **60** B1
Lumphăt Cambodia **75** B2
Lumsden N.Z. **118** A4
Lund Sweden **47** C4
Lundazi Zambia **107** C1
Lundy *i.* U.K. **53** A4

Lüneburg Ger. **55** E1
Lüneburger Heide *reg.* Ger. **55** E1
Lünen Ger. **54** C2
Lunéville France **59** D2
Lunga *r.* Zambia **106** B1
Lungi Sierra Leone **100** A4
Lunglei India **74** A1
Lungnaquilla Mountain *h.*
  Rep. of Ireland **51** C2
Luni *r.* India **86** B2
Luninyets Belarus **42** C3
Lunsar Sierra Leone **100** A4
Luntai China **89** F2
Luodian China **83** A3
Luoding China **83** B3
Luohe China **82** B2
Luoyang China **82** B2
Lupane Zimbabwe **106** B1
Lupanshui China **83** A3
Lupeni Romania **44** B2
Lupilichi Moz. **107** C1
Luppa Ger. **55** F2
Lúrio Moz. **107** D1
Lurio *r.* Moz. **107** D1
Lusaka Zambia **107** B1
Lusambo Dem. Rep. Congo **104** C3
Lushnjë Albania **65** A2
Lusk U.S.A. **134** C2
Lut, Dasht-e *des.* Iran **88** C3
Lutherstadt Wittenberg Ger. **55** F2
Luton U.K. **53** C4
Lutong Malaysia **73** C1
Lutsel'k Can. **127** D1
Luts'k Ukr. **44** C1
Lutzputs S. Africa **108** B2
Lutzville S. Africa **108** A3
Luuq Somalia **103** C4
Luverne U.S.A. **135** D2
Luvua *r.* Dem. Rep. Congo **105** C3
Luvuvhu *r.* S. Africa **109** D1
Luwero Uganda **105** D2
Luwuk Indon. **73** D2
Luxembourg *country* Europe
  54 C3
Luxembourg Lux. **54** C3
Luxeuil-les-Bains France **59** D2
Luxolweni S. Africa **109** C3
Luxor Egypt **102** B2
Luyksgestel Neth. **54** B2
Luza Rus. Fed. **40** D2
Luzern Switz. *see* Lucerne
Luzhou China **83** A3
Luziânia Brazil **154** C1
Luzilândia Brazil **151** D2
Luzon *i.* Phil. **76** B2
Luzon Strait Phil. **76** B1
L'viv Ukr. **44** C2
L'vov Ukr. *see* L'viv
Lyakhavichy Belarus **42** C3
Lyckele Sweden **46** D3
Lydenburg S. Africa **109** D2
Lyel'chytsy Belarus **42** C3
Lyepyel' Belarus **42** C3
Lyme Bay U.K. **53** B4
Lynchburg U.S.A. **137** E3
Lynn Lake Can. **127** E2
Lynx Lake Can. **127** E1
Lyon France **59** C2
Lyozna Belarus **43** D2
Lys'va Rus. Fed. **40** E3
Lysychans'k Ukr. **45** E2
Lytham St Anne's U.K. **52** B3
Lyuban' Belarus **42** C3
Lyubertsy Rus. Fed. **43** E2
Lyubeshiv Ukr. **44** C1
Lyubim Rus. Fed. **43** F2
Lyubotyn Ukr. **45** E2
Lyubytino Rus. Fed. **43** D2
Lyudinovo Rus. Fed. **43** D3

Ma'ān Jordan **92** B2
Maardu Estonia **42** C2
Maas *r.* Neth. **54** B2
Maaseik Belgium **54** B2
Maasin Phil. **76** B2
Maastricht Neth. **54** B2
Mabalane Moz. **107** C2
Mabaruma Guyana **150** D2
Mabote Moz. **107** C2
Mabule Botswana **108** B2
Mabutsane Botswana **108** B1
Macaé Brazil **155** D2
Macaloge Moz. **107** C1
Macapá Brazil **151** D2
Macará Ecuador **150** B3
Macarani Brazil **155** D1
Macassar Strait Indon. *see*
  Makassar, Selat
Macau China **81** D3
Macau *aut. reg.* China **83** B3
Maccaretane Moz. **107** D1
Macclesfield U.K. **52** B3
Macdonald, Lake *salt flat* Austr.
  114 B2
Macdonnell Ranges *mts* Austr. **114** C2
MacDowell Lake Can. **128** A1
Macedo de Cavaleiros Port. **60** B1
Macedon *mt.* Austr. **116** C3
Macedonia *country* Europe **64** B2
Maceió Brazil **151** F3
Macerata Italy **62** B2
Macfarlane, Lake *salt flat* Austr.
  116 B2
Macgillycuddy's Reeks *mts*
  Rep. of Ireland **51** B3
Mach Pak. **86** A2
Machado Brazil **155** C2
Machaila Moz. **107** C2
Machakos Kenya **105** D3
Machala Ecuador **150** B3
Machanga Moz. **107** C2
Machault France **54** C3
Macheng China **82** B2
Machias U.S.A. **137** G2
Machiques Venez. **150** B1
Macia Moz. **109** D2
Măcin Romania **44** C2
Macintyre *r.* Austr. **117** E1
Mackay Austr. **116** D2
Mackay, Lake *salt flat* Austr. **114** B2
MacKay Lake Can. **127** D1
Mackenzie Can. **126** C2
Mackenzie *r.* Can. **126** B1
Mackenzie Bay Can. **124** E1
Mackenzie King Island Can. **124** E1
Mackenzie Mountains Can. **126** B1
Macklin Can. **127** E2
Macksville Austr. **117** E2
Maclean Austr. **117** E1
MacLeod, Lake *imp. l.* Austr. **114** A2
Macomb U.S.A. **136** B2
Macomer Italy **62** A2
Mâcon France **59** C2
Macon *GA* U.S.A. **139** D2
Macon *MO* U.S.A. **135** E3
Macquarie *r.* Austr. **117** D2
Macquarie Island
  S. Pacific Ocean **110**
Macquarie Marshes Austr. **117** D2
Macroom Rep. of Ireland **51** B3
Macumba *watercourse* Austr. **116** B1
Macuspana Mex. **143** C3
Macuzari, Presa *resr* Mex. **142** B2
Madadeni S. Africa **109** D2
Madagascar *country* Africa
  107 [inset] D2

Madama Niger **101** D2
Madan Bulg. **65** B2
Madang P.N.G. **71** D3
Madeira r. Brazil **150** D3
Madeira terr. N. Atlantic Ocean **100** A1
Madeleine, Îles de la is Can. **129** D2
Madera Mex. **142** B2
Madera U.S.A. **133** B3
Madgaon India **85** B3
Madison IN U.S.A. **136** C3
Madison SD U.S.A. **135** D2
Madison WI U.S.A. **136** C2
Madison WV U.S.A. **136** D3
Madison r. U.S.A. **132** D1
Madisonville U.S.A. **136** C3
Madiun Indon. **73** D3
Mado Gashi Kenya **105** D2
Madona Latvia **42** C2
Madrakah Saudi Arabia **90** A2
Madras India see Chennai
Madras U.S.A. **132** B2
Madre, Laguna lag. Mex. **143** C2
Madre de Dios r. Peru **150** D2
Madre del Sur, Sierra mts Mex. **143** B3
Madre Occidental, Sierra mts Mex. **142** B2
Madre Oriental, Sierra mts Mex. **143** B2
Madrid Spain **60** C1
Madridejos Spain **60** C2
Madura i. Indon. **73** C2
Madura, Selat sea chan. Indon. **73** C2
Madurai India **85** B4
Maebashi Japan **79** C3
Mae Hong Son Thai. **74** A2
Mae Sai Thai. **74** A1
Mae Sariang Thai. **74** A2
Mae Suai Thai. **74** A2
Mafeteng Lesotho **109** C2
Mafia Island Tanz. **105** D3
Mafikeng S. Africa **109** C2
Mafinga Tanz. **105** D3
Mafra Brazil **154** C3
Magadan Rus. Fed. **95** Q3
Magangue Col. **145** C4
Magdalena r. Col. **148**
Magdalena Mex. **142** A1
Magdalena U.S.A. **140** C2
Magdalena, Bahía b. Mex. **142** A2
Magdeburg Ger. **55** E1
Magellan, Strait of Chile **153** A6
Magherafelt U.K. **51** C1
Magnitogorsk Rus. Fed. **41** E3
Magnolia U.S.A. **138** B2
Magpie, Lac l. Can. **129** D1
Magta' Lahjar Maur. **100** A3
Maguarinho, Cabo c. Brazil **151** E3
Magude Moz. **109** D2
Magwe Myanmar **74** A1
Mahābād Iran **93** C2
Mahajan India **86** B2
Mahajanga Madag. **107** [inset] D1
Mahakam r. Indon. **73** C2
Mahalapye Botswana **109** C1
Mahalevona Madag. **107** [inset] D1
Mahanadi r. India **87** C2
Mahanoro Madag. **107** [inset] D1
Mahbubnagar India **85** B3
Mahd adh Dhahab Saudi Arabia **90** B2
Mahdia Alg. **61** D2
Mahdia Guyana **150** D2
Mahesana India **86** B2
Mahi r. India **86** B2
Mahia Peninsula N.Z. **118** C2
Mahilyow Belarus **43** D3

Mahón Spain **61** D2
Mahony Lake Can. **126** C1
Mahuva India **86** B2
Mahya Dağı mt. Turkey **64** C2
Maidstone Can. **127** E2
Maidstone U.K. **53** D4
Maiduguri Nigeria **101** D3
Mailani India **87** C2
Main r. Ger. **55** D2
Mai-Ndombe, Lac l. Dem. Rep. Congo **104** B3
Main-Donau-Kanal canal Ger. **55** E3
Maine state U.S.A. **137** G1
Maingkwan Myanmar **74** A1
Mainland i. Scotland U.K. **50** C1
Mainland i. Scotland U.K. **50** [inset]
Maintirano Madag. **107** [inset] D1
Mainz Ger. **55** D2
Maiquetía Venez. **145** D3
Maitland N.S.W. Austr. **117** E2
Maitland S.A. Austr. **116** B2
Maíz, Islas del is Nic. **144** B3
Maizuru Japan **79** C3
Maja Jezercë mt. Albania **64** A2
Majene Indon. **73** C2
Majorca i. Spain **61** D2
Majuro atoll Marshall Is **110**
Majwemasweu S. Africa **109** C2
Makabana Congo **104** B3
Makale Indon. **73** C2
Makanchi Kazakh. **89** F2
Makarska Croatia **63** C2
Makassar Indon. **73** C2
Makassar, Selat str. Indon. **73** C2
Makat Kazakh. **88** C2
Makatini Flats lowland S. Africa **109** D2
Makeni Sierra Leone **100** A4
Makgadikgadi salt pan Botswana **106** B2
Makhachkala Rus. Fed. **41** D4
Makhado S. Africa **109** C1
Makhambet Kazakh. **88** C2
Makhazine, Barrage El dam Morocco **60** B1
Makindu Kenya **105** D3
Makinsk Kazakh. **89** E1
Makiyivka Ukr. **45** E2
Makkah Saudi Arabia see Mecca
Makkovik Can. **129** E1
Makó Hungary **57** E3
Makokou Gabon **104** B2
Makongolosi Tanz. **105** D3
Makopong Botswana **108** B2
Makran reg. Iran/Pak. **91** D2
Makran Coast Range mts Pak. **86** A2
Maksatikha Rus. Fed. **43** E2
Mākū Iran **93** C2
Makum India **74** A1
Makurazaki Japan **79** B4
Makurdi Nigeria **101** C4
Malā Sweden **46** D2
Mala, Punta pt Panama **144** B4
Malabo Equat. Guinea **104** A2
Malacca, Strait of Indon./Malaysia **72** A1
Malad City U.S.A. **132** D2
Maladzyechna Belarus **42** C3
Málaga Spain **60** C2
Malaita i. Solomon Is **110**
Malakal Sudan **103** B4
Malakula i. Vanuatu **110**
Malamala Indon. **73** D2
Malang Indon. **73** C2
Malanje Angola **104** B3
Mälaren l. Sweden **47** D4
Malargüe Arg. **153** B4
Malatya Turkey **92** B2
Malawi country Africa **107** C1
Malawi, Lake Africa see Nyasa, Lake

Malaya Vishera Rus. Fed. **43** D2
Malaybalay Phil. **76** B3
Malāyer Iran **93** C2
Malaysia country Asia **72** B1
Malazgirt Turkey **93** C2
Malbork Pol. **57** D2
Malchin Ger. **55** F1
Maldegem Belgium **54** A2
Malden Island Kiribati **111**
Maldives country Indian Ocean **85** B4
Male Maldives **85** B4
Maleas, Akra pt Greece **65** B3
Male Atoll Maldives **85** B4
Malé Karpaty hills Slovakia **57** D3
Malheur Lake U.S.A. **132** C2
Mali country Africa **100** B3
Malili Indon. **73** D2
Malindi Kenya **105** D3
Malin Head Rep. of Ireland **51** C1
Malin More Rep. of Ireland **51** B1
Malkara Turkey **65** C2
Mal'kavichy Belarus **42** C3
Malko Tŭrnovo Bulg. **64** C2
Mallacoota Austr. **117** D3
Mallacoota Inlet b. Austr. **117** D3
Mallaig U.K. **50** B2
Mallery Lake Can. **127** F1
Mallorca i. Spain see Majorca
Mallow Rep. of Ireland **51** B2
Malmberget Sweden **46** E2
Malmédy Belgium **54** C2
Malmesbury S. Africa **108** A3
Malmö Sweden **47** C4
Malong China **83** A3
Malonga Dem. Rep. Congo **104** C4
Måløy Norway **47** B3
Maloyaroslavets Rus. Fed. **43** E2
Maloye Borisovo Rus. Fed. **43** E2
Malta country Europe **101** D1
Malta Latvia **42** C2
Malta i. Malta **36**
Malta U.S.A. **132** E1
Maltahöhe Namibia **108** A1
Malton U.K. **52** C2
Maluku is Indon. see Moluccas
Maluku, Laut sea Indon. **71** C3
Malung Sweden **47** C3
Maluti Mountains Lesotho **109** C2
Malvan India **85** B3
Malvern U.S.A. **138** B2
Malyn Ukr. **44** C1
Malyy Anyuy r. Rus. Fed. **95** M2
Malyy Lyakhovskiy, Ostrov i. Rus. Fed. **95** L2
Mamafubedu S. Africa **109** C2
Mambasa Dem. Rep. Congo **105** C2
Mambéré r. C.A.R. **104** B2
Mamelodi S. Africa **109** C2
Mamoré r. Bol./Brazil **152** B2
Mamou Guinea **100** A3
Mamuju Indon. **73** C2
Man Côte d'Ivoire **100** B4
Man, Isle of i. Irish Sea **52** A2
Manacapuru Brazil **150** C3
Manacor Spain **61** D2
Manado Indon. **71** C2
Managua Nic. **144** B3
Manakara Madag. **107** [inset] D2
Manākhah Yemen **90** B3
Manama Bahrain **91** C2
Manam Island P.N.G. **71** D3
Mananara r. Madag. **107** [inset] D2
Mananara Avaratra Madag. **107** [inset] D1
Mananjary Madag. **107** [inset] D2
Manantali, Lac de l. Mali **100** A3
Manas Hu l. China **89** F2
Manatuto East Timor **71** C2
Man-aung Kyun i. Myanmar **74** A2

anaus Brazil **150** C3
anavgat Turkey **92** B2
anchester U.K. **52** B3
anchester U.S.A. **137** F2
andabe Madag. **107** [inset] D2
andal Norway **47** B4
andala, Puncak *mt.* Indon. **71** D3
andalay Myanmar **74** A1
andalgovī Mongolia **80** D1
andan U.S.A. **134** C1
andara Mountains Cameroon/Nigeria **104** B1
andas Italy **62** A3
anderscheid Ger. **54** C2
andi India **86** B1
andiana Guinea **100** B3
andi Burewala Pak. **86** B3
andla India **87** C2
andritsara Madag. **107** [inset] D1
andsaur India **86** B2
andurah Austr. **114** A3
andya India **85** B3
anerbio Italy **62** B1
anevyči Ukr. **44** C1
anfredonia Italy **63** C2
anga Burkina **100** B3
angai Dem. Rep. Congo **104** B3
angakino N.Z. **118** C2
angalia Romania **44** C3
angalore India **85** B3
angaung S. Africa **109** C2
angnai China **80** C2
angoei Indon. **71** C3
angueirinha Brazil **154** B3
angui China **81** E1
angystau Kazakh. **88** C2
anhattan U.S.A. **135** D3
anhica Moz. **107** C2
anhuaçu Brazil **155** D2
ania *r.* Madag. **107** [inset] D1
aniago Italy **62** B1
anicoré Brazil **150** C3
anicouagan *r.* Can. **129** D2
anicouagan, Petit Lac *l.* Can. **129** D1
anicouagan, Réservoir *resr* Can. **129** D1
anifah Saudi Arabia **91** B2
anihiki *atoll* Cook Is **111**
anila Phil. **76** B2
anilla Austr. **117** E2
anisa Turkey **65** C3
anistee U.S.A. **136** C2
anitoba *prov.* Can. **127** F2
anitou Islands U.S.A. **136** C1
anitoulin Island Can. **128** B2
anitowoc U.S.A. **136** C2
aniwaki Can. **128** C2
anizales Col. **150** B2
ankato U.S.A. **135** E2
ankono Côte d'Ivoire **100** B4
ankota Can. **132** E1
ankulam Sri Lanka **85** C4
annad India **86** B2
annar, Gulf of India/Sri Lanka **85** B4
annheim Ger. **55** D3
anning Can. **126** D3
annum Austr. **116** B2
annville Can. **127** D2
anokwari Indon. **71** C3
anoron Myanmar **75** A2
anosque France **59** D3
anouane, Lac *l.* Can. **129** C1
anresa Spain **61** D1
ansa Zambia **107** B1
ansel Island Can. **125** G2

Mansel'kya *ridge* Fin./Rus. Fed. **46** F2
Mansfield Austr. **117** D3
Mansfield U.K. **52** C3
Mansfield *LA* U.S.A. **138** B2
Mansfield *OH* U.S.A. **136** D2
Mansfield *PA* U.S.A. **137** E2
Manta Ecuador **150** A3
Manteo U.S.A. **139** E1
Mantes-la-Jolie France **58** C2
Mantiqueira, Serra da *mts* Brazil **155** C2
Mantova Italy *see* Mantua
Mantua Italy **62** B1
Manuelzinho Brazil **151** D3
Manui *i.* Indon. **73** D2
Manukau N.Z. **118** B2
Manus Island P.N.G. **71** D3
Many U.S.A. **138** B2
Manych-Gudilo, Ozero *l.* Rus. Fed. **41** D4
Manyoni Tanz. **105** D3
Manzanares Spain **60** C2
Manzanillo Mex. **142** B3
Manzhouli China **81** F1
Manzini Swaziland **109** D2
Mao Chad **101** D3
Maoke, Pegunungan *mts* Indon. **71** D3
Maokeng S. Africa **109** C2
Maokui Shan *mt.* China **77** A1
Maoming China **83** B3
Mapai Moz. **107** C1
Mapam Yumco *l.* China **87** C3
Mapane Indon. **73** D2
Mapastepec Mex. **143** C3
Mapimí Mex. **142** B2
Mapimí, Bolsón de *des.* Mex. **142** B2
Mapin *i.* Phil. **76** A3
Mapinhane Moz. **107** C2
Maple Creek Can. **127** E3
Maputo Moz. **107** C2
Maputo *r.* Moz./S. Africa **109** D2
Maquela do Zombo Angola **104** B3
Maquinchao Arg. **153** B5
Maquoketa U.S.A. **135** E2
Mar, Serra do *mts* Brazil **147**
Marabá Brazil **150** C3
Maraba U.S.A. **139** C2
Maracá *i.* Brazil **151** D2
Maracaibo Venez. **150** B1
Maracaibo, Lake Venez. **150** B2
Maracaju Brazil **154** B2
Maracajú, Serra de *hills* Brazil **154** A2
Maracay Venez. **150** C1
Marādah Libya **101** D2
Maradi Niger **101** C3
Marāgheh Iran **93** C2
Marajó, Baía de *est.* Brazil **151** E3
Marajó, Ilha de *i.* Brazil **151** D2
Marāki Iran **91** C2
Maralal Kenya **105** D2
Maralinga Austr. **114** C3
Marand Iran **93** C2
Maranoa *r.* Austr. **117** D1
Marañón *r.* Peru **150** B3
Marathon Can. **128** B2
Marathon U.S.A. **139** D4
Marbella Spain **60** C2
Marble Bar Austr. **114** A2
Marble Hall S. Africa **109** C1
Marburg S. Africa **109** D3
Marburg an der Lahn Ger. **55** D2
March U.K. **53** D3
Marche-en-Famenne Belgium **54** B2
Marchena Spain **60** B2
Mar Chiquita, Lago *l.* Arg. **152** B4
Marchtrenk Austria **59** F2
Marcoing France **54** A2
Marcy, Mount U.S.A. **137** F2
Mardan Pak. **86** B1

Mar del Plata Arg. **153** C4
Mardın Turkey **93** C2
Maree, Loch *l.* U.K. **50** B2
Marettimo, Isola *i.* Italy **62** B3
Marevo Rus. Fed. **43** D2
Marfa U.S.A. **140** D2
Margaret River Austr. **114** A3
Margarita, Isla de *i.* Venez. **145** D3
Margate S. Africa **109** D3
Margate U.K. **53** D4
Margherita Peak Dem. Rep. Congo/
 Uganda **105** C2
Mārgow, Dasht-e *des.* Afgh. **86** A1
Marhanets' Ukr. **45** D2
Maria Elena Chile **152** B3
Mariana Trench *sea feature*
 N. Pacific Ocean **158** C4
Marianna *AR* U.S.A. **138** B2
Marianna *FL* U.S.A. **139** C2
Mariánské Lázně Czech Rep. **56** C3
Marias, Islas *is* Mex. **142** B2
Mariato, Punta *pt* Panama **150** A2
Ma'rib Yemen **90** B3
Maribor Slovenia **62** C1
Maridi *watercourse* Sudan **103** A4
Marie Byrd Land *reg.* Antarctica
 119 I2
Marie-Galante *i.* Guadeloupe **145** D3
Mariehamn Fin. **47** D3
Mariental Namibia **108** A1
Mariestad Sweden **47** C4
Marietta *GA* U.S.A. **139** D2
Marietta *OH* U.S.A. **136** D3
Marignane France **59** D3
Marii, Mys *pt* Rus. Fed. **95** L3
Marijampolė Lith. **42** B3
Marília Brazil **154** C2
Marín Spain **60** B1
Marina di Gioiosa Ionica Italy **63** C3
Mar"ina Horka Belarus **42** C3
Marinette U.S.A. **136** C1
Maringá Brazil **154** B2
Marinha Grande Port. **60** B2
Marion *IN* U.S.A. **136** C2
Marion *OH* U.S.A. **136** D2
Marion *SC* U.S.A. **139** E2
Marion *VA* U.S.A. **136** D3
Marion, Lake U.S.A. **139** D2
Marion Bay Austr. **116** B3
Mariscal Estigarribia Para. **152** B3
Maritsa *r.* Bulg. **64** C2
Mariupol' Ukr. **45** E2
Marka Somalia **103** C4
Marken S. Africa **109** C1
Markermeer *l.* Neth. **54** B1
Markha *r.* Rus. Fed. **95** J2
Markivka Ukr. **45** E2
Marksville U.S.A. **138** B2
Marktheidenfeld Ger. **55** D3
Marktredwitz Ger. **55** F2
Marl Ger. **54** C2
Marle France **54** A3
Marlin U.S.A. **141** E2
Marmande France **58** C3
Marmara, Sea of *g.* Turkey **65** C2
Marmara Denizi *g.* Turkey *see*
 Marmara, Sea of
Marmaris Turkey **65** C3
Marne *r.* France **54** A3
Marne-la-Vallée France **58** C2
Maroantsetra Madag. **107** [inset] D1
Maroldsweisach Ger. **55** E2
Maromokotro *mt.* Madag.
 107 [inset] D1
Marondera Zimbabwe **107** C1
Maroni *r.* Fr. Guiana **151** D2
Marotiri *i.* Fr. Polynesia **111**
Maroua Cameroon **104** B3
Marovoay Madag. **107** [inset] D1

213

Marquesas Islands Fr. Polynesia **111**
Marquette U.S.A. **136** C1
Marquion France **54** A2
Marra, Jebel *mt.* Sudan **103** A3
Marracuene Moz. **109** D2
Marrakech Morocco **100** B1
Marra Plateau Sudan **103** A3
Marree Austr. **116** B1
Marresale Rus. Fed. **40** F2
Marromeu Moz. **107** C1
Marrupa Moz. **107** C1
Marsá al'Alam Egypt **102** B2
Marsa al Burayqah Libya **101** D1
Marsabit Kenya **105** D2
Marsala Italy **62** B3
Marsá Matrúh Egypt **102** A1
Marsberg Ger. **55** D2
Marsciano Italy **62** B2
Marsden Austr. **117** D2
Marseille France **59** D3
Marshall *MN* U.S.A. **135** E2
Marshall *MO* U.S.A. **135** E3
Marshall *TX* U.S.A. **141** E5
Marshall Islands *country*
  N. Pacific Ocean **112**
Marshalltown U.S.A. **135** E2
Marshfield U.S.A. **136** B2
Marsh Harbour Bahamas **139** E3
Marsh Island U.S.A. **138** B3
Märsta Sweden **42** A2
Martapura *Kalimantan Selatan* Indon.
  73 C2
Martapura *Sumatera Selatan* Indon.
  72 B2
Martha's Vineyard *i.* U.S.A. **137** F2
Martigny Switz. **59** D2
Martin Slovakia **57** D3
Martin U.S.A. **134** C2
Martínez Mex. **143** C2
Martinique *terr.* West Indies **145** D3
Martinsburg U.S.A. **137** E3
Martinsville U.S.A. **137** E3
Marton N.Z. **118** C3
Martorell Spain **61** D1
Martos Spain **60** C2
Marvejols France **59** C3
Mary Turkm. **88** D3
Maryborough Austr. **115** E2
Marydale S. Africa **108** B2
Maryland *state* U.S.A. **137** E3
Marysville U.S.A. **135** D3
Maryville *MO* U.S.A. **135** E2
Maryville *TN* U.S.A. **139** D1
Masai Steppe *plain* Tanz. **105** D3
Masaka Uganda **105** D3
Masamba Indon. **73** D2
Masan S. Korea **77** B2
Masasi Tanz. **105** D4
Masbate Phil. **76** B2
Masbate *i.* Phil. **76** B2
Mascara Alg. **61** D2
Maseru Lesotho **109** C2
Mashhad Iran **88** C3
Masibambane S. Africa **109** C3
Masilah, Wādī al *watercourse* Yemen
  91 C3
Masilo S. Africa **109** C2
Masindi Uganda **105** D2
Maşīrah, Jazīrat *i.* Oman **91** C2
Maşīrah, Khalīj *b.* Oman **91** C3
Masjed Soleymān Iran **93** C2
Mask, Lough *l.* Rep. of Ireland **51** B2
Masoala, Tanjona *c.* Madag.
  107 [inset] E1
Mason City U.S.A. **135** E2
Masqaṭ Oman *see* Muscat
Massa Italy **62** B2
Massachusetts *state* U.S.A. **137** F2
Massachusetts Bay U.S.A. **137** F2

Massangena Moz. **107** C2
Massango Angola **104** B3
Massawa Eritrea **102** B3
Massena U.S.A. **137** F2
Masset Can. **126** B2
Massif Central *mts* France **58** C2
Massif de l'Aïr *mts* Niger **101** C3
Massillon U.S.A. **136** D2
Massina Mali **100** B3
Massinga Moz. **107** C2
Massingir Moz. **107** C2
Mastābah Saudi Arabia **90** A2
Masterton N.Z. **118** C3
Mastung Pak. **86** A2
Masturah Saudi Arabia **90** A2
Masty Belarus **42** B3
Masuda Japan **79** B4
Masvingo Zimbabwe **107** C2
Matadi Dem. Rep. Congo **104** B3
Matagalpa Nic. **144** B3
Matagami Can. **128** C2
Matagami, Lac *l.* Can. **128** C2
Matagorda Island U.S.A. **141** E5
Matala Angola **106** A1
Matam Senegal **100** A3
Matamoros *Coahuila* Mex. **142** B2
Matamoros *Tamaulipas* Mex. **143** C2
Matandu *r.* Tanz. **105** D3
Matane Can. **129** D2
Matanzas Cuba **144** B2
Matara Sri Lanka **85** C4
Mataram Indon. **73** C2
Mataranka Austr. **114** C1
Mataró Spain **61** D1
Matatiele S. Africa **109** C3
Mataura N.Z. **118** A4
Mata'utu Wallis and Futuna Is **113**
Matawai N.Z. **118** C2
Mategua Bol. **152** B2
Matehuala Mex. **143** B2
Matera Italy **63** C2
Mathis U.S.A. **141** E3
Mathura India **87** B2
Mati Phil. **76** B3
Matías Romero Mex. **144** A3
Matlock U.K. **52** C3
Mato Grosso Brazil **150** D4
Mato Grosso, Planalto do *plat.* Brazil
  154 B1
Matola Moz. **109** D2
Matsue Japan **79** B3
Matsumae Japan **78** D2
Matsusaka Japan **79** C4
Matsu Tao *i.* Taiwan **83** C3
Matsuyama Japan **79** B4
Mattagami *r.* Can. **128** B1
Matterhorn *mt.* Italy/Switz. **62** A1
Matterhorn *mt.* U.S.A. **132** C2
Mattoon U.S.A. **136** C3
Maturín Venez. **150** C2
Matwabeng S. Africa **109** C2
Maubeuge France **54** A2
Maubourguet France **58** C3
Maui *i.* U.S.A. **120**
Maumee *r.* U.S.A. **136** D2
Maumere Indon. **73** D2
Maun Botswana **106** B1
Maunatlala Botswana **109** C1
Maungdaw Myanmar **74** A1
Maurice, Lake *salt flat* Austr. **114** C2
Mauritania *country* Africa **100** A3
Mauritius *country* Indian Ocean **99**
Māwān, Khashm n. Saudi Arabia
  90 B2
Mawanga Dem. Rep. Congo **104** B3
Mawei China **83** B3
Mawkmai Myanmar **74** A1
Mawlaik Myanmar **74** A1
Mawlamyaing Myanmar **74** A2
Mawqaq Saudi Arabia **90** B2

Mawza Yemen **90** B3
Maxia, Punta *mt.* Italy **62** A3
Maya *r.* Rus. Fed. **95** K2
Mayaguana *i.* Bahamas **145** C2
Mayamey Iran **93** D2
Maybole U.K. **50** B3
Mayenne France **58** B2
Mayenne *r.* France **58** B2
Mayerthorpe Can. **126** D2
Mayfield U.S.A. **136** C3
Maykop Rus. Fed. **45** F3
Mayo Can. **126** B1
Mayoko Congo **104** B3
Mayotte *terr.* Africa **107** D1
Mayskiy Rus. Fed. **95** K3
Maysville U.S.A. **136** D3
Mayumba Gabon **104** B3
Mayville U.S.A. **135** D1
Mazagão Brazil **151** D3
Mazamet France **58** C3
Mazar China **86** B1
Mazara del Vallo Italy **62** B3
Mazār-e Sharīf Afgh. **86** A1
Mazatán Mex. **142** A2
Mazatenango Guat. **144** A3
Mazatlán Mex. **142** B2
Mažeikiai Lith. **42** B2
Mazirbe Latvia **42** B2
Mazunga Zimbabwe **107** B2
Mazyr Belarus **42** C3
Mbabane Swaziland **109** D2
Mbaïki C.A.R. **104** B2
Mbala Zambia **105** D3
Mbale Uganda **105** D2
Mbalmayo Cameroon **104** B2
Mbandaka Dem. Rep. Congo **104** B3
Mbanga Cameroon **104** A2
M'banza Congo Angola **104** B3
Mbeya Tanz. **105** D3
Mbinga Tanz. **105** D4
Mbomo Congo **104** B3
Mbouda Cameroon **104** B2
Mbour Senegal **100** A3
Mbout Maur. **100** A3
Mbuji-Mayi Dem. Rep. Congo **104** C3
Mbuyuni Tanz. **105** D3
McAlester U.S.A. **141** E2
McAllen U.S.A. **141** E3
McBride Can. **126** C2
McCall U.S.A. **132** C2
McClintock Channel Can. **124** F2
McClure Strait Can. **124** E2
McComb U.S.A. **138** B2
McConaughy, Lake U.S.A. **134** C2
McCook U.S.A. **134** C2
McDermitt U.S.A. **132** C2
McDonald Peak U.S.A. **132** D1
McGrath U.S.A. **124** B2
McGuire, Mount U.S.A. **132** D1
McKinley, Mount U.S.A. **124** B2
McLennan Can. **126** D2
McLeod Lake Can. **126** C2
McMinnville *OR* U.S.A. **132** B1
McMinnville *TN* U.S.A. **139** C1
McPherson U.S.A. **135** D3
McTavish Arm *b.* Can. **126** D1
Mdantsane S. Africa **109** C3
Mead, Lake *resr* U.S.A. **133** D3
Meadow Lake Can. **127** D2
Meadville U.S.A. **137** D2
Meaken-dake *vol.* Japan **78** D2
Mealhada Port. **60** B1
Mealy Mountains Can. **129** E1
Meander River Can. **126** D2
Meaux France **54** A3
Mecca Saudi Arabia **90** A2
Mechelen Belgium **54** B2
Mechelen Neth. **54** B2
Mecherich Ger. **54** C2

Meckenheim Ger. **54** C2
Mecklenburger Bucht *b.* Ger. **47** C5
Meda Port. **60** B1
Medan Indon. **72** A1
Medanosa, Punta *pt* Arg. **153** B5
Medawachchiya Sri Lanka **85** C4
Médéa Alg. **61** D2
Medellín Col. **150** B2
Medenine Tunisia **101** D1
Medford U.S.A. **132** B2
Medgidia Romania **44** C3
Mediaş Romania **44** B2
Medicine Bow Mountains U.S.A. **134** B2
Medicine Bow Peak U.S.A. **134** B2
Medicine Hat Can. **127** D2
Medicine Lodge U.S.A. **135** D3
Medina Saudi Arabia **90** A2
Medinaceli Spain **60** C1
Medina del Campo Spain **60** C1
Medina de Rioseco Spain **60** B1
Mediterranean Sea **61** C2
Medjedel Alg. **61** D2
Medley Can. **127** D2
Mednogorsk Rus. Fed. **41** E3
Medvezh'i, Ostrova *is* Rus. Fed. **95** M2
Medvezh'yegorsk Rus. Fed. **40** C2
Meekatharra Austr. **114** A2
Meeker U.S.A. **134** B2
Meerut India **87** B2
Meetkerke Belgium **54** A2
Megalopoli Greece **65** B3
Meghasani *mt.* India **87** C2
Megisti *i.* Greece **65** C3
Mehamn Norway **46** F1
Meharry, Mount Austr. **114** A2
Mehrān *watercourse* Iran **91** C2
Meia Ponte *r.* Brazil **154** C1
Meiganga Cameroon **104** B2
Meihekou China **77** B1
Meiktila Myanmar **74** A1
Meiningen Ger. **55** E2
Meißen Ger. **55** F2
Meizhou China **83** B3
Mejicana *mt.* Arg. **152** B3
Mejillones Chile **152** A3
Mek'elē Eth. **103** B3
Mekerrhane, Sebkha *salt pan* Alg. **100** C2
Meknès Morocco **100** B1
Mekong *r.* Asia **73** B2
Mekong *r.* China **74** B1
Mekong, Mouths of the Vietnam **75** B3
Melaka Malaysia **72** B1
Melanesia *is* Pacific Ocean **158** D5
Melbourne Austr. **117** C3
Melbourne U.S.A. **139** D3
Mele, Capo *c.* Italy **62** A2
Melenki Rus. Fed. **43** F2
Mélèzes, Rivière aux *r.* Can. **129** C1
Melfi Chad **101** D3
Melfi Italy **62** C2
Melfort Can. **127** E2
Melhus Norway **46** C3
Melide Spain **60** B1
Melilla N. Africa **60** C2
Melitopol' Ukr. **45** E2
Melle Ger. **55** D1
Mellerud Sweden **47** C4
Mellrichstadt Ger. **55** E2
Mellum *i.* Ger. **54** D1
Melo Uru. **152** C4
Melrhir, Chott *salt* l. Alg. **101** C1
Melton Mowbray U.K. **53** C3
Melun France **58** C2
Melville Can. **127** E2
Melville, Cape Austr. **115** D1
Melville, Lake Can. **129** E1

Melville Island Austr. **114** C1
Melville Island Can. **124** E1
Melville Peninsula Can. **125** G2
Memboro Indon. **73** C2
Memmingen Ger. **56** C3
Mempawah Indon. **72** B1
Memphis *tourist site* Egypt **92** B3
Memphis *TN* U.S.A. **138** B1
Memphis *TX* U.S.A. **141** D2
Mena Ukr. **45** D1
Mena U.S.A. **138** B2
Ménaka Mali **100** C3
Mènam Khong *r.* Asia *see* Mekong
Mende France **59** C3
Mendefera Eritrea **102** B3
Méndez Mex. **143** C2
Mendī Eth. **105** B4
Mendi P.N.G. **71** D3
Mendip Hills U.K. **53** B4
Mendoza Arg. **153** B4
Menemen Turkey **65** C3
Menggala Indon. **72** B2
Mengzi China **83** A3
Menihek Can. **129** D1
Menindee Austr. **116** C2
Menindee, Lake Austr. **116** C2
Meningie Austr. **116** B3
Mennecy France **58** C2
Menominee U.S.A. **136** C1
Menongue Angola **106** A1
Menorca *i.* Spain *see* Minorca
Mentawai, Kepulauan *is* Indon.
72 A2
Mentok Indon. **72** B2
Menzies Austr. **114** B3
Meppel Neth. **54** C1
Meppen Ger. **54** C1
Mepuze Moz. **109** D1
Meqheleng S. Africa **109** C2
Merano Italy **62** B1
Merauke Indon. **71** D3
Merbein Austr. **116** C2
Merced U.S.A. **133** B3
Mercedes Arg. **152** C3
Mercy, Cape Can. **125** H2
Meredith, Lake U.S.A. **141** D1
Merefa Ukr. **45** E2
Mergui Archipelago *is* Myanmar **75** A2
Meriç *r.* Greece/Turkey **65** C2
Mérida Mex. **143** D2
Mérida Spain **60** B2
Mérida Venez. **150** B2
Meridian U.S.A. **138** C2
Mérignac France **58** B3
Merimbula Austr. **117** D3
Mérouana Alg. **61** D2
Merowe Sudan **102** B3
Merredin Austr. **114** A3
Merrick *h.* U.K. **50** B3
Merrill U.S.A. **136** C1
Merrillville U.S.A. **136** C2
Merritt Can. **126** C2
Merrygoen Austr. **117** D2
Mersa Fatma Eritrea **102** C3
Mersch Lux. **54** C3
Merseburg (Saale) Ger. **55** E2
Mersey *r.* U.K. **52** B3
Mersin Turkey **90** B2
Mersing Malaysia **72** B1
Mers-les-Bains France **53** D4
Merta India **86** B2
Merthyr Tydfil U.K. **53** B4
Mértola Port. **60** B2
Mertvyg Kultuk, Sor *dry lake* Kazakh.
88 C2
Meru *vol.* Tanz. **105** D3
Merzig Ger. **54** C3
Mesa U.S.A. **140** B2
Mesagne Italy **63** C2

Meschede Ger. **55** D2
Meshchovsk Rus. Fed. **43** E3
Meshkovskaya Rus. Fed. **45** F2
Mesimeri Greece **65** B2
Mesolongi Greece **65** B3
Messalo *r.* Moz. **107** D1
Messina Italy **62** C3
Messina, Stretta di *str.* Italy **63** C3
Messiniakos Kolpos *b.* Greece **65** B3
Mesta *r.* Bulg. **64** B2
Meta *r.* Col./Venez. **150** C2
Metán Arg. **152** B3
Methoni Greece **65** B3
Metković Croatia **63** C2
Metro Indon. **72** B2
Metu Eth. **103** B4
Metz France **59** D2
Meuse *r.* Belgium/France **54** B2
Mexia U.S.A. **141** E2
Mexicali Mex. **142** A1
Mexico *country* Central America
142 B2
Mexico U.S.A. **135** E3
Mexico, Gulf of Mex./U.S.A. **144** A2
Mexico City Mex. **143** C3
Meyenburg Ger. **55** F1
Meymaneh Afgh. **86** A1
Mezen' Rus. Fed. **40** D2
Mezen' *r.* Rus. Fed. **40** D2
Mezhdusharskiy, Ostrov *i.* Rus. Fed.
40 E1
Mezőtúr Hungary **57** E3
Mezquitic Mex. **142** B2
Meždvidi Latvia **42** C2
Mfuwe Zambia **107** C1
Mhlume Swaziland **109** D2
Mhow India **86** B2
Miahuatlán Mex. **143** C3
Miajadas Spain **60** B2
Miami *FL* U.S.A. **139** D3
Miami *OK* U.S.A. **141** F1
Miami Beach U.S.A. **139** D3
Miandowāb Iran **93** C2
Miandrivazo Madag. **107** [inset] D1
Miäneh Iran **93** C2
Mianwali Pak. **86** B1
Mianyang China **82** A2
Miarinarivo Madag. **107** [inset] D1
Miass Rus. Fed. **41** F3
Mica Creek Can. **126** C2
Michalovce Slovakia **57** E3
Michigan *state* U.S.A. **136** C1
Michigan, Lake U.S.A. **136** C2
Michigan City U.S.A. **136** C2
Michipicoten Island Can. **128** B2
Michipicoten River Can. **128** B2
Michurinsk Rus. Fed. **43** F3
Micronesia *is* Pacific Ocean **158** D4
Micronesia, Federated States of
country N. Pacific Ocean **71** D2
Middelburg Neth. **54** A2
Middelburg *E. Cape* S. Africa **109** C3
Middelburg *Mpumalanga* S. Africa
109 C2
Middelharnis Neth. **54** B2
Middle Alkali Lake U.S.A. **132** B2
Middle Andaman *i.* India **75** A2
Middle Loup *r.* U.S.A. **134** D2
Middlesboro U.S.A. **138** D3
Middlesbrough U.K. **52** C2
Middletown *NY* U.S.A. **137** F2
Middletown *OH* U.S.A. **136** D3
Midi Yemen **90** B3
Midland Can. **128** C2
Midland *MI* U.S.A. **136** D2
Midland *TX* U.S.A. **141** D2
Midleton Rep. of Ireland **51** B3
Miðvágur Faroe Is **48** B1
Midzhur *mt.* Bulg./Serb. and Mont.
64 B2

Mielec Pol. **57** E2
Miercurea-Ciuc Romania **44** C2
Mieres Spain **60** B1
Mieste Ger. **55** E2
Migriggyangzham Co *l.* China **87** D1
Miguel Alemán, Presa *resr* Mex. **143** C3
Miguel Auza Mex. **142** D2
Miguel Hidalgo, Presa *resr* Mex. **142** B2
Migyaunglaung Myanmar **75** A2
Mikhaylov Rus. Fed. **43** E3
Mikhaylovka Rus. Fed. **78** B2
Mikhaylovskiy Rus. Fed. **89** E1
Mikkeli Fin. **47** F3
Mikun' Rus. Fed. **40** E2
Mikuni-sanmyaku *mts* Japan **79** C3
Mila Alg. **61** E2
Miladhunmadulu Atoll Maldives **85** B4
Milan Italy **62** A1
Milange Moz. **107** C1
Milano Italy *see* Milan
Milas Turkey **65** C3
Milbank U.S.A. **135** D2
Mildenhall U.K. **53** D3
Mildura Austr. **116** C1
Mile China **83** A3
Miles City U.S.A. **134** B1
Milford *DE* U.S.A. **137** E3
Milford *UT* U.S.A. **133** D3
Milford Haven U.K. **53** A4
Milford Sound N.Z. **118** A3
Miliana Alg. **61** D2
Milk, Wadi el *watercourse* Sudan **102** B3
Mil'kovo Rus. Fed. **95** M3
Milk River Can. **127** D3
Millau France **58** C3
Milledgeville U.S.A. **139** D2
Mille Lacs U.S.A. **135** E1
Mille Lacs, Lac des *l.* Can. **128** A2
Millennium Island *atoll* Kiribati *see* Caroline Island
Miller U.S.A. **135** D2
Millerovo Rus. Fed. **45** F2
Millers Creek Austr. **116** B2
Millicent Austr. **116** C3
Millinocket U.S.A. **137** G1
Millmerran Austr. **117** E1
Millom U.K. **52** B2
Mills Lake Can. **126** D1
Milos *i.* Greece **65** C3
Miloslavskoye Rus. Fed. **43** E3
Milowe Ukr. **45** F2
Milparinka Austr. **116** C1
Milton N.Z. **118** A4
Milton Keynes U.K. **53** C3
Milwaukee U.S.A. **136** C2
Milwaukee Deep *sea feature* Caribbean Sea **160** B4
Mimizan France **58** B3
Mimongo Gabon **104** B3
Mina Iran **91** C2
Minahasa, Semenanjung *pen.* Indon. **73** D1
Mina Jebel Ali U.A.E. **91** C2
Minas Indon. **72** B1
Minas Uru. **153** C4
Minas Novas Brazil **155** C1
Minatitlán Mex. **143** C3
Minbu Myanmar **74** A1
Mindanao *i.* Phil. **76** B3
Minden Ger. **55** D2
Minden *LA* U.S.A. **138** B2
Minden *NE* U.S.A. **135** D2
Mindoro *i.* Phil. **76** B2
Mindoro Strait Phil. **76** A2
Minehead U.K. **53** D4
Mineiros Brazil **154** B1
Mineral Wells U.S.A. **141** E2

Minfeng China **87** C1
Minga Dem. Rep. Congo **105** C4
Mingäçevir Azer. **93** C1
Mingan Can. **129** E1
Mingary Austr. **116** C2
Mingguang China **82** B2
Mingin Myanmar **74** A1
Minglanilla Spain **61** C2
Mingoyo Tanz. **105** D4
Mingxi China **83** B3
Minhe China **82** A2
Minicoy *atoll* India **85** B4
Minilya Austr. **114** A2
Minipi Lake Can. **129** D1
Miniss Lake Can. **128** C1
Minna Nigeria **101** C4
Minneapolis U.S.A. **135** E2
Minnedosa Can. **127** F2
Minnesota *r.* U.S.A. **135** E2
Minnesota *state* U.S.A. **135** E1
Miño *r.* Port./Spain **60** B1
Minorca *i.* Spain **61** D1
Minot U.S.A. **134** C1
Minsk Belarus **43** F3
Mińsk Mazowiecki Pol. **57** E2
Minto Can. **129** D2
Minto, Lac *l.* Can. **128** C1
Minutang India **74** B1
Minxian China **82** A1
Mirabela Brazil **155** C1
Miralta Brazil **155** C1
Miramichi Can. **129** D2
Mirampello, Kolpos *b.* Greece **65** C3
Miranda Brazil **154** A2
Miranda *r.* Brazil **154** A1
Miranda de Ebro Spain **60** C1
Mirandela Port. **60** B1
Mirandópolis Brazil **154** B2
Mirbāṭ Oman **91** C3
Miri Malaysia **73** C1
Mirim, Lagoa *l.* Brazil **153** C4
Mirjāveh Iran **91** D2
Mirnyy Rus. Fed. **95** J2
Mirow Ger. **55** F1
Mirpur Khas Pak. **86** A2
Mirtoö Pelagos *sea* Greece **65** B3
Miryang S. Korea **77** B2
Mirzapur India **87** C2
Mishan China **80** C2
Miskitos, Cayos *is* Nic. **144** B3
Miskolc Hungary **57** E3
Misoöl *i.* Indon. **71** C3
Miṣrātah Libya **101** D1
Missinaibi *r.* Can. **128** B1
Missinaibi Lake Can. **128** B2
Mission Can. **126** C3
Missisa Lake Can. **128** B1
Mississippi *r.* U.S.A. **138** C2
Mississippi *state* U.S.A. **138** C2
Mississippi Delta U.S.A. **138** C3
Missoula U.S.A. **132** D1
Missouri *r.* U.S.A. **135** E3
Missouri *state* U.S.A. **135** E3
Mistassibi *r.* Can. **129** C2
Mistassini, Lac *l.* Can. **128** C2
Mistastin Lake Can. **129** D1
Mistelbach Austria **57** D3
Mistinibi, Lac *l.* Can. **129** D1
Mistissini Can. **128** C2
Mitchell Austr. **115** D2
Mitchell *r.* Austr. **115** D1
Mitchell U.S.A. **134** D2
Mitchelstown Rep. of Ireland **51** B2
Mithi Pak. **86** A2
Mito Japan **79** D3
Mitole Tanz. **105** D3
Mittagong Austr. **117** E2
Mittelhausen Ger. **55** E2
Mittellandkanal *canal* Ger. **55** D1

Mitterteich Ger. **55** F3
Mitú Col. **150** B2
Mitumba, Chaîne des *mts* Dem. Rep. Congo **105** C4
Mitumba, Monts *mts* Dem. Rep. Congo **105** C3
Mitzic Gabon **104** B2
Miyah, Wādī al *watercourse* Saudi Arabia **90** B2
Miyake-jima *i.* Japan **79** C4
Miyako Japan **78** D3
Miyakonojō Japan **79** B4
Miyaly Kazakh. **88** C2
Miyazaki Japan **79** B4
Mizdah Libya **101** D1
Mizen Head Rep. of Ireland **51** B3
Mizhhir''ya Ukr. **44** B2
Mjölby Sweden **47** D4
Mjøsa *l.* Norway **47** C3
Mkomazi Tanz. **105** D3
Mladá Boleslav Czech Rep. **56** C2
Mladenovac Serb. and Mont. **64** B2
Mława Pol. **57** E2
Mlungisi S. Africa **109** C3
Mlyniv Ukr. **44** C1
Mmabatho S. Africa **109** C2
Mmathethe Botswana **109** C2
Mo Norway **48** I1
Moab U.S.A. **133** E3
Moamba Moz. **109** D2
Moba Dem. Rep. Congo **105** C3
Mobayi-Mbongo Dem. Rep. Congo **104** C2
Moberly U.S.A. **135** E3
Mobile U.S.A. **138** C2
Mobile Bay U.S.A. **138** C2
Mobridge U.S.A. **134** C1
Moçambique Moz. **107** D1
Môc Châu Vietnam **74** B1
Mocha Yemen **90** B3
Mochudi Botswana **109** C1
Mocimboa da Praia Moz. **107** D1
Möckmühl Ger. **55** D3
Mocoa Col. **150** B2
Mococa Brazil **154** C2
Mocorito Mex. **142** B2
Mocuba Moz. **107** C1
Modane France **59** D2
Modder *r.* S. Africa **108** B2
Modena Italy **62** B2
Modesto U.S.A. **133** B3
Modimolle S. Africa **109** C1
Moe Austr. **117** D3
Moers Ger. **54** C2
Moffat U.K. **50** C3
Mogadishu Somalia **103** C4
Mogalakwena *r.* S. Africa **109** C1
Mogaung Myanmar **74** A1
Mogi-Mirim Brazil **154** C2
Mogocha Rus. Fed. **95** J3
Mogok Myanmar **74** A1
Mohács Hungary **57** D3
Mohale's Hoek Lesotho **109** C3
Mohammadia Alg. **61** D2
Mohawk *r.* U.S.A. **137** F2
Mohoro Tanz. **105** D3
Mohyliv Podil's'kyy Ukr. **44** C2
Moijabana Botswana **109** C1
Moineşti Romania **44** C2
Mo i Rana Norway **46** C2
Moissac France **58** C3
Mojave U.S.A. **133** C3
Mojave Desert U.S.A. **133** C3
Mojiang China **74** B1
Moji das Cruzes Brazil **155** C2
Moji-Guaçu *r.* Brazil **154** C2

Mokau N.Z. **118** B2
Mokhotlong Lesotho **109** C2
Mokopane S. Africa **109** C1
Mokp'o S. Korea **77** B3
Molango Mex. **143** C2
Molde Norway **46** B3
Moldova country Europe **44** C2
Moldoveanu, Vârful mt. Romania
 44 B2
Moldovei Centrale, Podişul plat.
 Moldova **44** C2
Molepolole Botswana **109** C1
Molétai Lith. **42** C2
Molfetta Italy **63** C2
Molina de Aragón Spain **61** C1
Mollenbeck Ger. **55** F1
Mollendo Peru **150** B4
MollOpolo watercourse
 Botswana/S. Africa **108** B2
Moloundou Cameroon **104** B2
Moluccas is Indon. **71** C3
Molucca Sea Indon. see Maluku, Laut
Momba Austr. **116** C2
Mombasa Kenya **105** D3
Mombuca, Serra da hills Brazil **154** B1
Momchilgrad Bulg. see Momchilgrad
Mon Ra's pt Yemen **91** C3
Møn i. Denmark **47** C3
Monaco country Europe **59** D3
Monadhliath Mountains U.K. **50** B2
Monaghan Rep. of Ireland **51** C1
Monastyrshchina Rus. Fed. **43** D3
Monastyryshche Ukr. **44** C2
Monbetsu Japan **78** D2
Moncalieri Italy **62** A1
Monchegorsk Rus. Fed. **46** G2
Mönchengladbach Ger. **54** C2
Monclova Mex. **142** B2
Moncton Can. **129** D2
Mondego r. Port. **60** B1
Mondlo S. Africa **109** D2
Mondovì Italy **62** A2
Monemvasia Greece **65** B3
Moneron, Ostrov i. Rus. Fed.
 78 D1
Monett U.S.A. **135** E3
Monfalcone Italy **62** B1
Monforte Spain **60** B1
Mông Cai Vietnam **74** B1
Mong Lin Myanmar **74** B1
Mong Pawk Myanmar **74** A1
Mong Ping Myanmar **74** A1
Mongu Zambia **106** B1
Monitor Range mts U.S.A. **133** C3
Monmouth U.K. **53** C4
Mono Lake U.S.A. **133** C3
Mono r. Togo **100** C4
Monopoli Italy **63** C2
Monreal del Campo Spain **61** C1
Monroe LA U.S.A. **138** B2
Monroe WI U.S.A. **138** C2
Monroeville U.S.A. **138** C2
Monrovia Liberia **100** A4
Mons Belgium **54** A2
Montagu S. Africa **108** B3
Montalto mt. Italy **63** C3
Montana Bulg. **64** B2
Montana state U.S.A. **130** C2
Montargis France **58** C2
Montauban France **58** C3
Montauk Point pt U.S.A. **137** F2
Mont-aux-Sources mt. Lesotho
 109 C2
Montbard France **59** C2
Mont Blanc mt. France/Italy **59** D2
Montbrison France **59** C2
Montcornet France **54** B3
Mont-de-Marsan France **58** B3
Montdidier France **58** C2

Monte Alegre Brazil **151** D3
Monte-Carlo Monaco **59** D3
Monte Caseros Arg. **152** C4
Montego Bay Jamaica **144** B3
Montélimar France **59** C3
Montella Italy **62** C2
Montemorelos Mex. **143** C2
Montendre France **58** B2
Montenegro aut. rep. Serb. and Mont.
 see Crna Gora
Montepuez Moz. **107** C1
Montepulciano Italy **62** B2
Monterey U.S.A. **133** B3
Monterey Bay U.S.A. **133** B3
Montería Col. **150** B2
Montero Bol. **152** B2
Monterrey Mex. **143** C2
Montesano sulla Marcellana Italy
 63 C2
Monte Sant'Angelo Italy **63** C2
Monte Santo Brazil **151** F4
Montes Claros Brazil **155** D1
Montevideo Uru. **153** C4
Montevideo U.S.A. **135** D2
Monte Vista U.S.A. **134** B3
Montgomery U.S.A. **138** C2
Monthey Switz. **59** D2
Monticello AR U.S.A. **138** B2
Monticello UT U.S.A. **133** C3
Montignac France **58** C2
Montilla Spain **60** C2
Mont-Joli Can. **129** D2
Mont-Laurier Can. **128** C2
Montluçon France **58** C2
Montmagny Can. **129** C2
Montmorillon France **58** C2
Monto Austr. **115** E2
Montpelier ID U.S.A. **132** D2
Montpelier VT U.S.A. **137** F2
Montpellier France **59** C3
Montréal Can. **128** C2
Montreal Lake Can. **127** E2
Montreal Lake l. Can. **127** E2
Montreux Switz. **59** D2
Montrose U.K. **50** C2
Montrose U.S.A. **134** B3
Montserrat terr. West Indies **145** D3
Monywa Myanmar **74** A1
Monza Italy **62** A1
Monzón Spain **61** D1
Mookane Botswana **109** C1
Moonie Austr. **117** E1
Moonie r. Austr. **117** D1
Moonta Austr. **116** B2
Moore, Lake salt flat Austr. **114** A2
Moorhead U.S.A. **135** D1
Moorreesburg S. Africa **108** A3
Moose r. Can. **128** B1
Moose Factory Can. **128** B1
Moosehead Lake U.S.A. **137** G1
Moose Jaw Can. **124** E3
Moose Lake U.S.A. **135** E1
Moosomin Can. **124** F3
Moosonee Can. **128** B1
Mootwingee Austr. **116** C2
M'Ooukal Alg. **61** C1
Mopane S. Africa **109** C1
Mopti Mali **100** B3
Moquegua Peru **150** B4
Mora Sweden **47** C3
Mora U.S.A. **135** E1
Moradabad India **87** B2
Moramanga Madag. **107** [inset] D1
Moray Firth b. U.K. **50** B2
Morbach Ger. **54** C3
Morbi India **86** B2
Morcenx France **58** B3
Mordaga China **81** E1

Morden Can. **127** F3
Mordovo Rus. Fed. **43** F3
Morecambe U.K. **52** B2
Morecambe Bay U.K. **52** B2
Moree Austr. **117** D1
Morehead P.N.G. **71** D3
Morehead U.S.A. **136** D3
Morehead City U.S.A. **139** E2
Morelia Mex. **143** B3
Morella Spain **61** C1
Morena, Sierra mts Spain **60** B2
Moreni Romania **44** C3
Moresby, Mount Can. **126** B2
Moresby Island Can. **126** B2
Moreton Island Austr. **117** E1
Morgan City U.S.A. **138** B3
Morganton U.S.A. **139** D1
Morgantown U.S.A. **137** E3
Morges Switz. **59** D2
Mori Japan **78** D2
Morice Lake Can. **126** C2
Morioka Japan **78** D3
Morisset Austr. **117** E2
Morlaix France **58** B2
Mornington Island Austr. **115** C1
Morobe P.N.G. **71** D3
Morocco country Africa **100** B1
Morogoro Tanz. **105** D3
Moro Gulf Phil. **76** B3
Morokweng S. Africa **108** B2
Morombe Madag. **107** [inset] D2
Mörön Mongolia **80** C1
Morondava Madag. **107** [inset] D2
Moroni Comoros **107** D1
Morotai i. Indon. **71** C2
Moroto Uganda **105** D2
Morozovsk Rus. Fed. **45** F2
Morpeth U.K. **52** C2
Morrinhos Brazil **154** C1
Morris Can. **127** F3
Morris U.S.A. **135** D2
Morristown U.S.A. **139** D1
Morshanka Rus. Fed. **43** F3
Mortes, Rio das r. Brazil **151** D4
Mortlake Austr. **116** C3
Moruya Austr. **117** E3
Morvern reg. U.K. **50** B2
Morwell Austr. **117** D3
Mosbach Ger. **55** D3
Moscow Rus. Fed. **43** E2
Moscow U.S.A. **132** C1
Mosel r. Ger. **54** C2
Moselle r. France **59** D2
Moses Lake U.S.A. **132** C1
Mosfellsbær Iceland **46** [inset]
Mosgiel N.Z. **118** B4
Moshenskoye Rus. Fed. **43** D2
Moshi Tanz. **105** D3
Mosjøen Norway **46** C2
Moskva Rus. Fed. see Moscow
Mosonmagyaróvár Hungary **57** D3
Mosquitos, Golfo de los b. Panama
 144 B4
Moss Norway **47** C4
Mossel Bay S. Africa **108** B3
Mossendjo Congo **104** B3
Mossgiel Austr. **116** C2
Mossman Austr. **115** D1
Mossoró Brazil **151** F3
Moss Vale Austr. **117** E2
Most Czech Rep. **56** C2
Mostaganem Alg. **100** C1
Mostar Bos.-Herz. **63** C2
Mostardas Brazil **152** C4
Mostovskoy Rus. Fed. **45** F3
Mosul Iraq **93** C2
Motala Sweden **47** D4
Motherwell U.K. **50** C3
Motilla del Palancar Spain **61** C2
Motokwe Botswana **108** B1

Motril Spain **60** C2
Motru Romania **44** B3
Mottama, Gulf of Myanmar **74** A2
Motul Mex. **143** D2
Motu One *atoll* Fr. Polynesia **111**
Moudros Greece **65** C3
Mouila Gabon **104** B3
Moulamein Austr. **116** C3
Moulins France **59** C2
Moultrie U.S.A. **139** D2
Moultrie, Lake U.S.A. **139** E2
Moundou Chad **101** D4
Mountain Grove U.S.A. **135** E3
Mountain Home *AR* U.S.A. **138** B1
Mountain Home *ID* U.S.A. **132** C2
Mount Airy U.S.A. **139** D1
Mount Barker Austr. **116** B3
Mount Beauty Austr. **117** D3
Mount Darwin Zimbabwe **107** C1
Mount Desert Island U.S.A. **137** G2
Mount Fletcher S. Africa **109** C3
Mount Frere S. Africa **109** C3
Mount Gambier Austr. **116** C3
Mount Hagen P.N.G. **71** D3
Mount Hope Austr. **117** C2
Mount Isa Austr. **115** C2
Mount Magnet Austr. **114** A2
Mount Manara Austr. **116** C2
Mount Maunganui N.Z. **118** E2
Mount Pleasant *IA* U.S.A. **135** E2
Mount Pleasant *MI* U.S.A. **136** D2
Mount Pleasant *TX* U.S.A. **141** F2
Mount's Bay U.K. **53** A4
Mount Shasta U.S.A. **132** B2
Mount Vernon *IL* U.S.A. **136** C3
Mount Vernon *OH* U.S.A. **136** C2
Mount Vernon *WA* U.S.A. **132** B1
Moura Austr. **115** D2
Mourdi, Dépression du *depr.* Chad **101** E3
Mourne Mountains U.K. **51** C1
Mouscron Belgium **54** A2
Moussoro Chad **101** D3
Moutong Indon. **73** D1
Mouydir, Monts du *plat.* Alg. **100** C3
Mouzon France **54** B3
Moy *r.* Rep. of Ireland **51** B1
Moyale Eth. **103** D3
Moyeni Lesotho **109** C3
Mo'ynoq Uzbek. **88** C2
Moyynty Kazakh. **89** E2
Mozambique *country* Africa **107** C2
Mozambique Channel Africa **107** D2
Mozhaysk Rus. Fed. **43** E2
Mpanda Tanz. **105** D3
Mpika Zambia **107** C1
Mporokoso Zambia **105** D3
Mpumalanga *prov.* S. Africa **109** C2
Mrauk-U Myanmar **74** A1
Mrkonjić-Grad Bos.-Herz. **64** A2
Mshinskaya Rus. Fed. **42** C2
M'Sila Alg. **61** D2
Msta *r.* Rus. Fed. **43** D2
Mstinskiy Most Rus. Fed. **43** D2
Mstsislaw Belarus **43** D3
Mtsensk Rus. Fed. **43** E3
Mtwara Tanz. **105** E4
Muanda Dem. Rep. Congo **104** B3
Muang Hinboun Laos **83** A4
Muang Khôngxédôn Laos **75** B2
Muang Ngoy Laos **74** B1
Muang Pakbeng Laos **74** B2
Muang Sing Laos **74** B1
Muang Vangviang Laos **74** B2
Muar Malaysia **72** B1
Muarabungo Indon. **72** B2
Muaradua Indon. **72** B2
Muaralaung Indon. **73** C2
Muarasiberut Indon. **72** A2

Muaratembesi Indon. **72** B2
Muarateweh Indon. **73** C2
Mubende Uganda **105** D2
Mubi Nigeria **101** D3
Muchkapskiy Rus. Fed. **45** F1
Muconda Angola **104** C4
Mucuri Brazil **155** E1
Mucuri *r.* Brazil **155** E1
Mudanjiang China **78** B1
Mudan Jiang *r.* China **78** A1
Mudanya Turkey **65** C2
Mudgee Austr. **117** D2
Mudon Myanmar **74** A2
Mudurnu Turkey **92** B1
Mueda Moz. **107** C1
Mufulira Zambia **107** B1
Mufumbwe Zambia **106** B1
Muğla Turkey **65** C3
Muhammad Qol Sudan **102** B2
Mühlberg Ger. **55** F2
Mühlhausen (Thüringen) Ger. **55** E2
Muine Bheag Rep. of Ireland **51** C2
Muite Moz. **107** C1
Muju S. Korea **77** B2
Mukacheve Ukr. **44** B2
Mukah Malaysia **73** C1
Mukalla Yemen **91** B3
Mukdahan Thai. **74** B2
Mukinbudin Austr. **114** A3
Mukomuko Indon. **72** B2
Mulanje, Mount Malawi **107** C1
Mulde *r.* Ger. **55** F2
Mulegé Mex. **142** A2
Muleshoe U.S.A. **141** D2
Mulhacén *mt.* Spain **60** C2
Mülheim an der Ruhr Ger. **54** C2
Mulhouse France **59** D2
Muling China **78** B1
Muling He *r.* China **78** B1
Mull *i.* U.K. **50** B2
Mullaley Austr. **117** D2
Mullen U.S.A. **134** C2
Mullewa Austr. **114** A2
Mullingar Rep. of Ireland **51** C2
Mull of Galloway *c.* U.K. **50** B3
Mull of Kintyre *hd* U.K. **50** B3
Mull of Oa *hd* U.K. **50** A3
Mulobezi Zambia **106** B1
Multan Pak. **86** B1
Mumbai India **85** B3
Mumbwa Zambia **106** B1
Muna *i.* Indon. **73** D2
Münchberg Ger. **55** E2
München Ger. *see* Munich
Muncie U.S.A. **136** C2
Mundrabilla Austr. **114** B3
Mungbere Dem. Rep. Congo **105** C2
Munger India **87** C2
Mungeranie Austr. **116** B1
Mungindi Austr. **117** D1
Munich Ger. **56** C2
Muniz Freire Brazil **155** D2
Münster *Niedersachsen* Ger. **55** D1
Münster *Nordrhein-Westfalen* Ger. **54** C2
Munster *reg.* Rep. of Ireland **51** B2
Münsterland *reg.* Ger. **54** C2
Mương Nhe Vietnam **74** B1
Muonio Fin. **46** E2
Muonioälven *r.* Fin./Sweden **46** E2
Muqdisho Somalia *see* Mogadishu
Mur *r.* Austria **57** D2
Muramvya Burundi **105** C3
Murang'a Kenya **105** D3
Murat *r.* Turkey **93** B2
Muratlı Turkey **65** C2
Murchison *watercourse* Austr. **114** A2

Murcia Spain **61** C2
Mürefte Turkey **65** C2
Mureşul *r.* Romania **44** B2
Muret France **58** C3
Murfreesboro U.S.A. **139** C1
Murghab *r.* Afgh. **86** A1
Murghob Tajik. **89** E3
Muriaé Brazil **155** D2
Muriege Angola **104** C3
Müritz *l.* Ger. **55** F1
Murmansk Rus. Fed. **46** G2
Murom Rus. Fed. **43** F2
Muroran Japan **78** D2
Muros Spain **60** B1
Muroto Japan **79** B4
Muroto-zaki *pt* Japan **79** B4
Murphy U.S.A. **139** D1
Murra Murra Austr. **117** D1
Murray *r.* Austr. **117** B3
Murray *r.* Can. **126** C2
Murray U.S.A. **136** C3
Murray, Lake U.S.A. **139** D2
Murray Bridge Austr. **116** B3
Murraysburg S. Africa **108** B3
Murrayville Austr. **116** C3
Murrumbidgee *r.* Austr. **116** C2
Murrupula Moz. **107** C1
Murrurundi Austr. **117** E2
Murska Sobota Slovenia **63** C1
Murupara N.Z. **118** C2
Mururoa *atoll* Fr. Polynesia **111**
Murwara India **87** C2
Murwillumbah Austr. **117** E1
Murzechirla Turkm. **41** F5
Murzūq Libya **101** D2
Mürz Turkey **93** C2
Musala *mt.* Bulg. **64** B2
Musan N. Korea **77** B1
Musaymir Yemen **90** B3
Muscat Oman **91** C2
Muscatine U.S.A. **135** E2
Musgrave Ranges *mts* Austr. **114** C2
Mushie Dem. Rep. Congo **104** B3
Musi *r.* Indon. **72** B2
Musina S. Africa **109** D1
Muskegon U.S.A. **136** C2
Muskogee U.S.A. **141** E1
Muskwa *r.* Can. **126** C2
Muslimbagh Pak. **86** A1
Musmar Sudan **90** A3
Musoma Tanz. **105** D3
Musselburgh U.K. **50** C3
Mustjala Estonia **42** B2
Muswellbrook Austr. **117** E2
Mūţ Egypt **102** A2
Mutare Zimbabwe **107** C1
Mutsu Japan **78** D2
Mutuali Moz. **107** C1
Muurola Fin. **46** F2
Mu Us Shamo *des.* China **82** A2
Muxaluando Angola **104** B3
Muyezerskiy Rus. Fed. **46** C2
Muyinga Burundi **105** D3
Muzaffargarh Pak. **86** B1
Muzaffarpur India **87** C2
Muzamane Moz. **109** D1
Múzquiz Mex. **142** B2
Muztag *mt.* China **87** C1
Muz Tag *mt.* China **87** C1
Mwanza Dem. Rep. Congo **105** C3
Mwanza Tanz. **105** D3
Mweka Dem. Rep. Congo **104** C3
Mwenda Zambia **105** C3
Mwene-Ditu Dem. Rep. Congo **104** C3
Mwenezi Zimbabwe **107** C2
Mweru, Lake Dem. Rep. Congo/Zambia **105** C3
Mwimba Dem. Rep. Congo **104** C3
Mwinilunga Zambia **106** B1
Myadzyel Belarus **42** C3

Myanaung Myanmar **74** A2
Myanmar *country* Asia **74** A1
Myaungmya Myanmar **74** A2
Myeik Myanmar **75** A2
Myingyan Myanmar **74** A1
Myitkyina Myanmar **74** A1
Mykolayiv Ukr. **45** D2
Mykonos Greece **65** C3
Mykonos *i.* Greece **65** C3
Myla Rus. Fed. **40** E2
Mymensingh Bangl. **87** D2
Myŏnggan N. Korea **77** B1
Myory Belarus **42** C2
Mýrdalsjökull *ice cap* Iceland **46** [inset]
Myrhorod Ukr. **45** D2
Myronivka Ukr. **44** D2
Myrtle Beach U.S.A. **139** E2
Myrtleford Austr. **117** D3
Myrtle Point U.S.A. **132** B2
Myshkin Rus. Fed. **43** E2
Myślibórz Pol. **56** C2
Mysore India **85** B3
Mys Shmidta Rus. Fed. **95** O2
My Tho Vietnam **75** B2
Mytilini Greece **65** C3
Mytishchi Rus. Fed. **43** E2
Mzamomhle S. Africa **109** C3
Mzimba Malawi **107** C1
Mzuzu Malawi **107** C1

N

Naas Rep. of Ireland **51** C2
Nababeep S. Africa **108** A2
Naberezhnyye Chelny Rus. Fed. **41** E3
Nabire Indon. **71** D3
Nāblus West Bank **92** B2
Naboomspruit S. Africa **109** C1
Nacala Moz. **107** D1
Nachuge India **75** A2
Nacogdoches U.S.A. **141** F2
Nacozari de García Mex. **142** B1
Nadiad India **86** B2
Nador Morocco **60** C2
Nadvirna Ukr. **44** B2
Nadvoitsy Rus. Fed. **40** C2
Nadym Rus. Fed. **40** G2
Næstved Denmark **47** C4
Nafplio Greece **65** B3
Nafy Saudi Arabia **90** B2
Naga Phil. **76** B2
Nagagami *r.* Can. **128** C1
Nagano Japan **79** C3
Nagaoka Japan **79** C3
Nagaon India **87** D2
Nagar India **86** B1
Nagar Parkar Pak. **86** B2
Nagasaki Japan **79** A4
Nagato Japan **79** B4
Nagaur India **86** B2
Nagercoil India **85** B4
Nagha Kalat Pak. **86** A2
Nag' Ḩammādī Egypt **90** A2
Nagina India **87** B2
Nagoya Japan **79** C3
Nagpur India **87** B2
Nagqu China **87** D1
Nagyatád Hungary **57** D3
Nagykanizsa Hungary **57** D3
Nahanni Butte Can. **126** C1
Nahāvand Iran **93** C2
Nahrendorf Ger. **55** E1
Nahuel Huapí, Lago *l.* Arg. **153** A5
Nain Can. **129** D1
Nā'īn Iran **93** D2
Naim U.K. **50** C2
Nairobi Kenya **105** D3

Naivasha Kenya **105** D3
Najafābād Iran **93** D2
Najd *reg.* Saudi Arabia **90** B2
Nájera Spain **60** C1
Najin N. Korea **77** C1
Najrān Saudi Arabia **90** B3
Nakatsugawa Japan **79** C3
Nakfa Eritrea **90** A3
Nakhodka Rus. Fed. **78** B2
Nakhon Pathom Thai. **75** B2
Nakhon Ratchasima Thai. **75** B2
Nakhon Sawan Thai. **75** B2
Nakhon Si Thammarat Thai. **75** A3
Nakina Can. **128** B1
Nakonde Zambia **105** D3
Nakskov Denmark **47** C5
Nakuru Kenya **105** D3
Nakusp Can. **126** D2
Nalbari India **87** D2
Nal'chik Rus. Fed. **41** D4
Nālūt Libya **101** D1
Namahadi S. Africa **109** C2
Namakzar-e Shadad *salt flat* Iran **91** C1
Namangan Uzbek. **89** E2
Namaqualand S. Africa **108** A2
Nambour Austr. **115** E2
Nambucca Heads Austr. **117** E2
Nam Co *salt l.* China **87** D1
Nam Định Vietnam **74** B1
Namib Desert Namibia **106** A2
Namibe Angola **106** A1
Namibia *country* Africa **108** A1
Namjagbarwa Feng *mt.* China **84** D2
Namlea Indon. **71** C3
Namoi *r.* Austr. **117** D2
Nampa U.S.A. **132** C2
Nampala Mali **100** B3
Namp'o N. Korea **77** B2
Nampula Moz. **107** C1
Namrup India **74** A1
Namsang Myanmar **74** A1
Namsos Norway **46** C3
Nam Tok Thai. **75** A2
Namtsy Rus. Fed. **95** K2
Namtu Myanmar **74** A1
Namur Belgium **54** B2
Namwala Zambia **106** B1
Namwŏn S. Korea **77** B2
Namya Ra Myanmar **74** A1
Nan Thai. **74** B2
Nanaimo Can. **126** C3
Nan'an China **83** B3
Nananib Plateau Namibia **108** A1
Nanao Japan **79** C3
Nanchang *Jiangxi* China **83** B3
Nanchang *Jiangxi* China **83** B3
Nanchong China **82** A2
Nancowry *i.* India **75** A3
Nancy France **59** D2
Nanda Devi *mt.* India **87** C1
Nandan China **83** A3
Nanded India **85** B3
Nandurbar India **86** B2
Nandyal India **85** B3
Nanfeng China **83** B3
Nanga Eboko Cameroon **104** B2
Nangahpinoh Indon. **73** C2
Nanga Parbat *mt.* Jammu and Kashmir **86** B1
Nangatayap Indon. **73** C2
Nangong China **82** B2
Nangulangwa Tanz. **105** D3
Nanjing China **82** B2
Nanking China *see* Nanjing
Nankova Angola **106** A1
Nan Ling *mts* China **83** B3
Nanning China **83** A3
Nanortalik Greenland **125** I2
Nanpan Jiang *r.* China **83** A3

Nanpara India **87** C2
Nanping China **83** B3
Nansei-shotō *is* Japan *see*
   Ryukyu Islands
Nantes France **58** B2
Nantong China **82** C2
Nantucket Island U.S.A. **137** G2
Nanumea *atoll* Tuvalu **110**
Nanuque Brazil **155** D1
Nanusa, Kepulauan *is* Indon. **76** B3
Nanxiong China **83** B3
Nanyang China **82** B2
Nanzhang China **82** B2
Nao, Cabo de la *c.* Spain **61** D2
Naococane, Lac *l.* Can. **129** C1
Naokot Pak. **86** A2
Napa U.S.A. **133** B3
Napaktulik Lake Can. **126** E1
Napasoq Greenland **125** I2
Napier N.Z. **118** C2
Naples Italy **62** B2
Naples U.S.A. **139** D3
Napo *r.* Ecuador **150** B3
Napoli Italy *see* Naples
Nara Mali **100** B3
Narach Belarus **42** C3
Naracoorte Austr. **116** C3
Naranjos Mex. **143** C2
Narathiwat Thai. **75** B3
Narbonne France **58** C3
Narcondam Island India **75** A2
Nares Strait Can./Greenland **125** H1
Narib Namibia **108** A1
Narimanov Rus. Fed. **41** D4
Narita Japan **79** D3
Narmada *r.* India **86** B2
Narnaul India **86** B2
Narni Italy **62** B2
Narodychi Ukr. **44** C1
Naro-Fominsk Rus. Fed. **43** E2
Narooma Austr. **117** E3
Narowlya Belarus **42** C3
Narrabri Austr. **117** D2
Narrandera Austr. **117** D2
Narromine Austr. **117** D2
Narva Estonia **42** C2
Narva Bay Estonia/Rus. Fed. **42** C2
Narvik Norway **46** C2
Narvskoye Vodokhranilishche *resr*
   Estonia/Rus. Fed. **42** C2
Nar'yan-Mar Rus. Fed. **40** E2
Naryn Kyrg. **89** E2
Nashik India **86** B2
Nashua U.S.A. **137** F2
Nashville U.S.A. **138** C1
Nasir Sudan **103** B4
Nass *r.* Can. **126** C2
Nassau Bahamas **145** C2
Nasser, Lake *resr* Egypt **102** B2
Nässjö Sweden **47** C4
Nastapoca *r.* Can. **128** C1
Nastapoka Islands Can. **128** C1
Nata Botswana **106** B2
Natal Brazil **151** F3
Natal *prov.* S. Africa *see* Kwazulu-Natal
Natashquan Can. **129** D1
Natashquan *r.* Can. **129** D1
Natchez U.S.A. **138** B2
Natchitoches U.S.A. **138** B2
Nathalia Austr. **117** D3
Nati, Punta *pt* Spain **61** D1
Natitingou Benin **100** C3
Natividade Brazil **151** E4
Natori Japan **78** D3
Natuashish Can. **129** D1
Natuna, Kepulauan *is* Indon. **72** B1
Natuna Besar *i.* Indon. **72** B1
Nauchas Namibia **108** A1
Nauen Ger. **55** F1
Naujoji Akmenė Lith. **42** B2

Naumburg (Saale) Ger. **55** E2
Nauru *country* S. Pacific Ocean **112**
Naustdal Norway **48** E1
Nautla Mex. **143** C2
Navahrudak Belarus **42** C3
Navalmoral de la Mata Spain **60** B2
Navalvillar de Pela Spain **60** B2
Navan Rep. of Ireland **51** C2
Navapolatsk Belarus **42** C2
Navarin, Mys c. Rus. Fed. **95** N2
Navarino, Isla *i*. Chile **153** B6
Navashino Rus. Fed. **43** F2
Naver *r*. U.K. **50** B1
Navlya Rus. Fed. **43** D3
Nävodari Romania **44** C3
Navoiy Uzbek. **89** D2
Navojoa Mex. **142** B2
Navolato Mex. **142** B2
Nawabshah Pak. **86** A2
Nawnghkio Myanmar **74** A1
Nawngleng Myanmar **74** A1
Naxçıvan Azer. **93** C2
Naxos *i*. Greece **65** C3
Nayar Mex. **142** B2
Nayoro Japan **78** D2
Nazareth Israel **92** B3
Nazas Mex. **142** B2
Nazas *r*. Mex. **142** B2
Nazca Peru **150** B4
Nazilli Turkey **65** C3
Nazrēt Eth. **103** B4
Nazwá Oman **91** C2
Nchelenge Zambia **105** C3
Ncojane Botswana **108** B1
N'dalatando Angola **106** B1
Ndélé C.A.R. **104** C2
Ndendé Gabon **104** B3
Ndjamena Chad **101** D3
Ndola Zambia **107** B1
Neagh, Lough *l*. U.K. **51** C1
Neale, Lake *salt flat* Austr. **114** C2
Nea Roda Greece **65** B2
Neath U.K. **53** B4
Nebine Creek *r*. Austr. **117** D1
Neblina, Pico da *mt*. Brazil **150** C2
Nebolchi Rus. Fed. **43** D2
Nebraska *state* U.S.A. **134** C2
Nebraska City U.S.A. **135** D2
Nebrodi, Monti *mts* Italy **62** B3
Necochea Arg. **153** C4
Nedlouc, Lac *l*. Can. **129** C1
Nédroma Alg. **61** C2
Needles U.S.A. **133** D4
Neemuch India **86** B2
Neepawa Can. **127** F2
Neftekamsk Rus. Fed. **41** E3
Neftyugansk Rus. Fed. **40** G2
Negage Angola **104** B3
Negēlē Eth. **103** B4
Negra, Punta *pt* Peru **150** A3
Negrais, Cape Myanmar **75** A3
Negro *r*. Arg. **153** B5
Negro *r*. Brazil **154** A1
Negro *r*. S. America **150** D3
Negro *r*. Uru. **152** C4
Negro, Cabo *c*. Morocco **60** B2
Negros *i*. Phil. **76** B3
Nehbandān Iran **91** D1
Nehe China **81** D1
Neijiang China **83** A3
Neilburg Can. **127** E2
Nei Mongol Zizhiqu *aut. reg.* China
  82 A1
Neiva Col. **150** B2
Nejanilini Lake Can. **127** F2
Nek'emtē Eth. **103** B4
Nekrasovskoye Rus. Fed. **43** F2
Nelidovo Rus. Fed. **43** D2
Nellore India **85** B3
Nelson Can. **126** D3
Nelson *r*. Can. **127** F2
Nelson N.Z. **118** B3
Nelson, Cape Austr. **116** C3
Nelson Bay Austr. **117** E2
Nelson House Can. **127** F2
Nelson Reservoir U.S.A. **132** E1
Nelspruit S. Africa **109** D2
Néma Maur. **100** B3
Neman Rus. Fed. **42** B2
Nemda *r*. Rus. Fed. **43** F2
Nemours France **58** C2
Nemuro Japan **78** E2
Nemyriv Ukr. **44** C2
Nenagh Rep. of Ireland **51** B2
Nene *r*. U.K. **53** D3
Nenjiang China **81** E1
Neosho U.S.A. **135** E3
Nepal *country* Asia **87** C2
Nepalganj Nepal **87** C2
Nephi U.S.A. **133** D3
Nephin *h*. Rep. of Ireland **51** B1
Nephin Beg Range *hills* Rep. of Ireland
  51 B1
Nepisiguit *r*. Can. **129** D2
Nepoko *r*. Dem. Rep. Congo **105** C2
Nepomuk Czech Rep. **55** F3
Nérac France **58** C3
Nerang Austr. **117** E1
Nerchinsk Rus. Fed. **81** D1
Nerekhta Rus. Fed. **43** F2
Neretva *r*. Bos.-Herz./Croatia **63** C2
Neriquinha Angola **106** B1
Neris *r*. Lith. **42** B3
Nerl' *r*. Rus. Fed. **43** F2
Nerokhi Rus. Fed. **40** F2
Nerópolis Brazil **154** C1
Neryungri Rus. Fed. **95** K3
Neskaupstaður Iceland **46** [inset]
Ness, Loch *l*. U.K. **50** B2
Ness City U.S.A. **134** D3
Nestos *r*. Greece **65** C2
Netherlands *country* Europe **54** B2
Netherlands Antilles *terr.* West Indies
  145 D3
Neubrandenburg Ger. **55** F1
Neuchâtel Switz. **59** D2
Neuenhagen Berlin Ger. **55** F1
Neuerburg Ger. **54** C2
Neufchâteau Belgium **54** B3
Neufchâteau France **59** D2
Neufchâtel-en-Bray France **58** C2
Neuhof Ger. **55** D2
Neu Lübbenau Ger. **55** F1
Neumarkt in der Oberpfalz Ger. **55** E3
Neumünster Ger. **56** B2
Neunkirchen Ger. **54** C3
Neuquén Arg. **153** B4
Neuquén *r*. Arg. **153** B4
Neuruppin Ger. **55** F1
Neuss Ger. **54** C2
Neustadt am Rübenberge Ger. **55** D1
Neustadt an der Aisch Ger. **55** E3
Neustadt an der Weinstraße Ger.
  54 D3
Neustrelitz Ger. **55** F1
Neutraubling Ger. **55** F3
Neuwied Ger. **54** C2
Nevada U.S.A. **135** E3
Nevada *state* U.S.A. **133** C3
Nevada, Sierra *mts* Spain **60** C2
Nevada, Sierra *mts* U.S.A. **133** B2
Nevel' Rus. Fed. **42** C2
Nevers France **59** C2
Nevertire Austr. **117** D2
Nevesinje Bos.-Herz. **63** C2
Nevinnomyssk Rus. Fed. **41** D4
New Aiyansh Can. **126** C2
New Albany U.S.A. **136** C3
New Amsterdam Guyana **151** D2
Newark *NJ* U.S.A. **137** F2

Newark *OH* U.S.A. **136** D2
Newark-on-Trent U.K. **52** C3
New Bedford U.S.A. **137** F2
New Bern U.S.A. **139** E1
Newberry U.S.A. **139** D2
New Boston U.S.A. **141** F2
New Braunfels U.S.A. **141** E3
Newbridge Rep. of Ireland **51** C2
New Britain *i*. P.N.G. **158** D5
New Brunswick *prov.* Can. **129** D2
Newbury U.K. **53** C4
New Caledonia *terr.*
  S. Pacific Ocean **112**
Newcastle Austr. **117** E2
Newcastle S. Africa **109** C2
Newcastle U.K. **51** D1
New Castle U.S.A. **137** D2
Newcastle U.S.A. **134** C2
Newcastle-under-Lyme U.K. **52** B3
Newcastle upon Tyne U.K. **52** C2
Newcastle West Rep. of Ireland **51** B2
New Delhi India **86** B2
New Denver Can. **126** D3
New England Range *mts* Austr.
  117 E2
Newfoundland *i*. Can. **129** E2
Newfoundland and Labrador *prov.*
  Can. **129** E1
New Glasgow Can. **129** D2
New Guinea *i*. Indon./P.N.G. **71** D3
New Halfa Sudan **90** A3
New Hampshire *state* U.S.A. **137** F2
New Haven U.S.A. **137** F2
New Hazelton Can. **126** C2
New Iberia U.S.A. **138** B2
New Ireland *i*. P.N.G. **110**
New Jersey *state* U.S.A. **137** F3
New Liskeard Can. **128** C2
Newman Austr. **114** A2
New Mexico *state* U.S.A. **140** C2
New Orleans U.S.A. **138** B3
New Philadelphia U.S.A. **136** D2
New Plymouth N.Z. **118** B2
Newport England U.K. **53** C4
Newport Wales U.K. **53** B4
Newport *AR* U.S.A. **138** B1
Newport *OR* U.S.A. **132** B2
Newport *RI* U.S.A. **137** F2
Newport *VT* U.S.A. **137** F2
Newport *WA* U.S.A. **132** C1
Newport News U.S.A. **137** E3
New Providence *i*. Bahamas **139** E3
Newquay U.K. **53** A4
New Roads U.S.A. **138** B2
New Ross Rep. of Ireland **51** C2
Newry U.K. **51** C1
New Siberia Islands Rus. Fed. **95** L1
New South Wales *state* Austr. **117** D2
Newton *IA* U.S.A. **135** E2
Newton *KS* U.S.A. **135** D3
Newton Abbot U.K. **53** B4
Newton Stewart U.K. **50** B3
Newtown Rep. of Ireland **51** B2
Newtown U.K. **53** B3
New Town U.S.A. **134** C1
Newtownabbey U.K. **51** D1
Newtownards U.K. **51** D1
Newtown St Boswells U.K. **50** C3
Newtownstewart U.K. **51** C1
New Ulm U.S.A. **135** E2
New York U.S.A. **137** F2
New York *state* U.S.A. **137** E2
New Zealand *country* Oceania **118**
Neya Rus. Fed. **43** F2
Neya *r*. Rus. Fed. **43** F2
Neyrīz Iran **93** D3
Neyshābūr Iran **88** C3
Nezahualcóyotl Mex. **143** C3
Nezahualcóyotl, Presa *resr* Mex.
  143 C3

Ngabang Indon. **73** B1
Ngamring China **87** C2
Ngangla Ringco *salt l.* China **87** C1
Nganglong Kangri *mt.* China **87** C1
Nganglong Kangri *mts* China **87** C1
Ngangzê Co *salt l.* China **87** C1
Ngao Thai. **74** A2
Ngaoundéré Cameroon **104** B2
Ngaruawahia N.Z. **118** C2
Ngathainggyaung Myanmar **74** A2
Ngo Congo **104** B3
Ngoc Linh *mt.* Vietnam **75** B2
Ngol Bembo Nigeria **101** D4
Ngoring Hu *l.* China **80** C2
Ngourti Niger **101** D3
Nguigmi Niger **101** D3
Ngulu *atoll* Micronesia **71** D2
Ngwelezana S. Africa **109** D2
Nhamalabué Moz. **107** C1
Nha Trang Vietnam **75** B2
Nhill Austr. **116** C3
Nhlangano Swaziland **109** D2
Nhulunbuy Austr. **115** C1
Niagara Falls Can. **137** E2
Niangara Dem. Rep. Congo **105** C2
Niangay, Lac *l.* Mali **100** B3
Nias *i.* Indon. **72** A1
Nicaragua *country* Central America
  144 B3
Nicaragua, Lake Nic. **144** B3
Nice France **59** D3
Nicobar Islands India **85** D4
Nicosia Cyprus **92** B2
Nicoya, Golfo de *b.* Costa Rica **144** B4
Nida Lith. **42** B2
Nidzica Pol. **57** E2
Niebüll Ger. **56** B2
Niederaula Ger. **55** D2
Niefang Equat. Guinea **104** B2
Niemegk Ger. **55** F1
Nienburg (Weser) Ger. **55** D1
Nieuw-Niedorp Neth. **54** B1
Nieuw Nickerie Suriname **151** D2
Nieuwoudtville S. Africa **108** A3
Nieuwpoort Belgium **54** A2
Niğde Turkey **92** B2
Niger *country* Africa **101** C3
Niger *r.* Africa **101** C4
Niger, Mouths of the Nigeria **101** C4
Nigeria *country* Africa **101** C4
Nighthawk Lake Can. **128** C2
Nigríta Greece **65** B2
Niigata Japan **79** C3
Niihama Japan **79** B4
Nii-jima *i.* Japan **79** C4
Niitsu Japan **79** C3
Nijmegen Neth. **54** B2
Nijverdal Neth. **54** C1
Nikel' Rus. Fed. **46** G2
Nikol'skoye Rus. Fed. **95** N3
Nikopol' Ukr. **45** D2
Niksar Turkey **92** B1
Nikshahr Iran **91** D2
Nikšić Serb. and Mont. **64** A2
Nile *r.* Africa **102** B1
Niles U.S.A. **136** C2
Nîmes France **59** C3
Nimmitabel Austr. **117** D3
Nimule Sudan **103** B4
Nindigully Austr. **117** D1
Nine Degree Channel India **85** D4
Ninety Mile Beach Austr. **117** D3
Ninety Mile Beach N.Z. **118** B1
Ningbo China **83** C3
Ningde China **83** B3
Ningdu China **83** B3
Ningguo China **83** C3
Ninghai China **83** C3

Ninging India **74** A1
Ningjing Shan *mts* China **80** C2
Ningxia Huizu Zizhiqu *aut. reg.* China
  82 A2
Ningyang China **82** B2
Ninh Binh Vietnam **74** B1
Ninh Hoa Vietnam **75** B2
Ninohe Japan **78** D2
Niobrara *r.* U.S.A. **135** D2
Niono Mali **100** B3
Nioro Mali **100** B3
Niort France **58** B2
Nipawin Can. **124** F3
Nipigon Can. **128** B2
Nipigon, Lake Can. **128** B2
Nipishish Lake Can. **129** D1
Nipissing, Lake Can. **128** C2
Nipton U.S.A. **133** C3
Niquelândia Brazil **151** E4
Nirmal India **85** B3
Niš Serb. and Mont. **64** B2
Nišava *r.* Serb. and Mont. **64** B2
Niscemi Italy **62** B3
Nishino-omote Japan **79** B4
Niterói Brazil **155** D2
Nith *r.* U.K. **50** C3
Nitra Slovakia **57** D2
Niue *terr.* S. Pacific Ocean **113**
Nivala Fin. **46** E3
Nivelles Belgium **54** B2
Nizamabad India **85** B3
Nizhnekamsk Rus. Fed. **41** E3
Nizhneudinsk Rus. Fed. **95** I3
Nizhnevartovsk Rus. Fed. **94** H2
Nizhniy Kislyay Rus. Fed. **43** F3
Nizhniy Lomov Rus. Fed. **41** D3
Nizhniy Novgorod Rus. Fed. **41** D3
Nizhniy Odes Rus. Fed. **40** E2
Nizhniy Tagil Rus. Fed. **40** E3
Nizhnyaya Tunguska *r.* Rus. Fed. **95** H2
Nizhyn Ukr. **45** D1
Njazidja *i.* Comoros **107** C1
Njinjo Tanz. **105** D3
Njombe Tanz. **105** D3
Nkhotakota Malawi **107** C1
Nkongsamba Cameroon **104** A2
Nkululeko S. Africa **109** C3
Nkwenkwezi S. Africa **109** C3
Nobeoka Japan **79** B4
Noccundra Austr. **116** C1
Nogales Mex. **142** A1
Nogales U.S.A. **140** B3
Nogent-le-Rotrou France **58** C2
Noginsk Rus. Fed. **43** E2
Nohar India **86** B2
Nohfelden Ger. **54** C3
Noirmoutier, Île de *i.* France **58** B2
Noirmoutier-en-l'Île France **58** B2
Noisseville France **54** C2
Nojima-zaki *c.* Japan **79** C4
Nokha India **86** B2
Nokia Fin. **47** E3
Nok Kundi Pak. **86** A2
Nola C.A.R. **104** B2
Nolinsk Rus. Fed. **40** D3
Nomonde S. Africa **109** C3
Nondweni S. Africa **109** D2
Nong Khai Thai. **74** B2
Nonning Austr. **116** B2
Nonoava Mex. **142** B2
Nonsan S. Korea **77** B2
Nonthaburi Thai. **75** B2
Nonzwakazi S. Africa **108** B3
Norak Tajik. **89** D3
Noranda Can. **137** E1
Nordausstandet *i.* Svalbard **94** D1
Nordegg Can. **126** D2
Norden Ger. **54** C1
Nordenshel'da, Arkhipelag *is*
  Rus. Fed. **95** I1

Norderney Ger. **54** C1
Norderney *i.* Ger. **54** C1
Norderstedt Ger. **55** E1
Nordfjordeid Norway **47** B3
Nordhausen Ger. **55** E2
Nordholz Ger. **55** D1
Nordhorn Ger. **54** C1
Nordkapp *c.* Norway *see* North Cape
Nordli Norway **46** C3
Nördlingen Ger. **56** C3
Nordmaling Sweden **46** D3
Norðoyar *i.* Faroe Is **48** B1
Nore *r.* Rep. of Ireland **51** C2
Norfolk *NE* U.S.A. **135** D2
Norfolk *VA* U.S.A. **137** E3
Norfolk Island *terr.*
  S. Pacific Ocean **112**
Norheimsund Norway **47** B3
Noril'sk Rus. Fed. **94** H2
Norkyung China **87** C2
Norman U.S.A. **141** E1
Normandes, Îles *is* English Chan. *see*
  Channel Islands
Normandy *reg.* France **58** B2
Normanton Austr. **115** D1
Norman Wells Can. **126** C1
Norrköping Sweden **47** D4
Norrtälje Sweden **47** D4
Norseman Austr. **114** B3
Norsjö Sweden **46** D3
Norte, Punta *pt* Arg. **147**
Northallerton U.K. **52** C2
Northampton U.K. **53** C3
Northampton U.S.A. **137** F2
North Andaman *i.* India **75** A2
North Battleford Can. **124** E3
North Bay Can. **128** C2
North Belcher Islands Can. **128** C1
North Berwick U.K. **50** C2
North Cape Norway **46** F1
North Cape N.Z. **118** B1
North Caribou Lake Can. **128** A1
North Carolina *state* U.S.A. **139** E1
North Channel *lake channel* Can.
  128 B2
North Channel U.K. **51** C1
North Cowichan Can. **126** C3
North Dakota *state* U.S.A. **134** C1
North Downs *hills* U.K. **53** C4
Northeim Ger. **55** D2
Northern Cape *prov.* S. Africa
  108 A2
Northern Indian Lake Can. **127** F2
Northern Ireland *prov.* U.K. **51** C1
Northern Mariana Islands *terr.*
  N. Pacific Ocean **71** D1
Northern Territory *admin. div.* Austr.
  114 C1
North Esk *r.* U.K. **50** C2
Northfield U.S.A. **135** E2
North Foreland *c.* U.K. **53** D4
North Frisian Islands Ger. **56** B2
North Geomagnetic Pole **162** J2
North Island N.Z. **118** B1
North Knife Lake Can. **127** F2
North Korea *country* Asia **77** B1
North Lakhimpur India **74** A1
North Magnetic Pole Can. **162** K1
North Nahanni *r.* Can. **126** C1
North Platte U.S.A. **134** C2
North Platte *r.* U.S.A. **134** C2
North Pole Arctic Ocean **162**
North Ronaldsay *i.* U.K. **50** C1
North Sea Europe **48** D2
North Spirit Lake Can. **128** A1
North Stradbroke Island Austr.
  117 E1
North Taranaki Bight *b.* N.Z. **118** B2
North Twin Island Can. **128** C1
North Tyne *r.* U.K. **52** B2

North Uist i. U.K. 50 A2
Northumberland Strait Can. 129 D2
North West prov. S. Africa 108 C2
North West Cape Austr. 114 A2
North West River Can. 129 E1
Northwest Territories admin. div. Can. 124 E2
North York Moors moorland U.K. 52 C2
Norton U.S.A. 136 D3
Norton Zimbabwe 107 C1
Norton Sound sea chan. U.S.A. 124 B2
Norwalk U.S.A. 136 C2
Norway country Europe 47 C3
Norway House Can. 127 F2
Norwegian Sea N. Atlantic Ocean 46 B2
Norwich U.K. 53 D3
Norwich CT U.S.A. 137 F2
Norwich NY U.S.A. 137 E2
Noshiro Japan 78 D2
Nosivka Ukr. 45 D1
Nosop watercourse Africa 108 B2
Nosovaya Rus. Fed. 40 E2
Noşratābād Iran 91 C2
Nossen Ger. 55 F2
Noteć r. Pol. 57 D2
Notodden Norway 47 B4
Noto-hantō pen. Japan 79 C3
Notre Dame, Monts mts Can. 129 D2
Notre Dame Bay Can. 129 E2
Nottaway r. Can. 128 C1
Nottingham U.K. 52 C3
Nouâdhibou Maur. 100 A2
Nouakchott Maur. 100 A3
Nouâmghâr Maur. 100 A3
Nouméa New Caledonia 112
Nouna Burkina 100 B3
Nouvelle Calédonie i. S. Pacific Ocean 110
Nova Esperança Brazil 154 B2
Nova Friburgo Brazil 155 D2
Nova Gradiška Croatia 63 C1
Nova Granada Brazil 154 C2
Nova Iguaçu Brazil 155 D2
Nova Kakhovka Ukr. 45 D2
Nova Lima Brazil 155 D1
Nova Londrina Brazil 154 B2
Nova Odesa Ukr. 45 D2
Nova Paraíso Brazil 150 C2
Nova Scotia prov. Can. 129 D2
Nova Venécia Brazil 155 D1
Novaya Sibir', Ostrov i. Rus. Fed. 95 L1
Novaya Zemlya is Rus. Fed. 40 E1
Nové Zámky Slovakia 57 D3
Novhorod-Sivers'kyy Ukr. 45 D1
Novi Iskŭr Bulg. 64 B2
Novi Ligure Italy 62 A2
Novi Pazar Serb. and Mont. 64 B2
Novi Sad Serb. and Mont. 64 A1
Novoaleksandrovsk Rus. Fed. 45 F2
Novoanninskiy Rus. Fed. 45 F1
Novo Aripuanã Brazil 150 C3
Novoazovs'k Ukr. 45 E2
Novocherkassk Rus. Fed. 45 F2
Novodvinsk Rus. Fed. 40 D2
Novo Hamburgo Brazil 152 C3
Novo Horizonte Brazil 154 C2
Novohrad-Volyns'kyy Ukr. 44 C1
Novokhopersk Rus. Fed. 43 F3
Novokubansk Rus. Fed. 45 F2
Novokuznetsk Rus. Fed. 89 F1
Novo Mesto Slovenia 60 F1
Novomikhaylovskiy Rus. Fed. 45 F3
Novomoskovsk Rus. Fed. 43 E3
Novomoskovs'k Ukr. 45 D2
Novomyrhorod Ukr. 45 D2
Novonikolayevskiy Rus. Fed. 45 F1
Novooleksiyivka Ukr. 45 D2
Novopokrovskaya Rus. Fed. 45 F2
Novopskov Ukr. 45 E2
Novorossiysk Rus. Fed. 45 E3
Novorzhev Rus. Fed. 42 C2
Novosergiyevka Rus. Fed. 41 E3
Novoshakhtinsk Rus. Fed. 45 E2
Novosibirsk Rus. Fed. 94 H3
Novosibirskiye Ostrova is Rus. Fed. see New Siberia Islands
Novosil' Rus. Fed. 43 E3
Novosokol'niki Rus. Fed. 43 D2
Novotroyits'ke Ukr. 45 D2
Novoukrayinka Ukr. 45 D2
Novovolyns'k Ukr. 44 B1
Novozybkov Rus. Fed. 43 D3
Nový Jičín Czech Rep. 57 D3
Novyy Bor Rus. Fed. 40 E2
Novyy Oskol Rus. Fed. 45 E1
Novyy Port Rus. Fed. 40 G2
Novyy Urengoy Rus. Fed. 40 G2
Novyy Urgal Rus. Fed. 81 E1
Nowg ard Pol. 56 D2
Nowra Austr. 117 E2
Now Shahr Iran 93 D2
Nowshera Pak. 86 B1
Nowy Sącz Pol. 57 E3
Nowy Targ Pol. 57 E3
Noyabr'sk Rus. Fed. 41 G2
Noyon France 58 C2
Nsanje Malawi 107 C1
Ntandembele Dem. Rep. Congo 104 B3
Ntungamo Uganda 105 D3
Nu'aym reg. Oman 91 C2
Nubian Desert Sudan 102 B2
Nudo Coropuna mt. Peru 150 B4
Nueltin Lake Can. 127 F1
Nueva Lubecka Arg. 153 A5
Nueva Rosita Mex. 143 B2
Nuevo Casas Grandes Mex. 142 B1
Nuevo Ideal Mex. 142 B2
Nuevo Laredo Mex. 143 C2
Nugaal watercourse Somalia 103 C4
Nuits-St-Georges France 59 C2
Nu Jiang r. China/Myanmar see Salween
Nuku'alofa Tonga 113
Nuku Hiva i. Fr. Polynesia 111
Nukulaelae atoll Tuvalu 110
Nukunonu atoll Tokelau 111
Nukus Uzbek. 88 C2
Nullagine Austr. 114 B2
Nullarbor Plain Austr. 114 B3
Numan Nigeria 101 D4
Numazu Japan 79 C3
Numedal val. Norway 47 B3
Numfoor i. Indon. 71 C3
Numurkah Austr. 117 D3
Nunap Isua c. Greenland see Farewell, Cape
Nunavik reg. Can. 125 H3
Nunavut admin. div. Can. 124 D2
Nuneaton U.K. 53 C3
Nunivak Island U.S.A. 95 O3
Nuñomoral Spain 60 B1
Nuoro Italy 62 A2
Nuqrah Saudi Arabia 90 B2
Nuremberg Ger. 55 E3
Nuriootpa Austr. 116 B2
Nurmes Fin. 46 F3
Nürnberg Ger. see Nuremberg
Nu Shan mts China 74 A1
Nushki Pak. 86 A2
Nuuk Greenland 125 I2
Nuussuaq Greenland 125 I2
Nuussuaq pen. Greenland 125 I2
Nuwaybi' al Muzayyinah Egypt 92 B3
Nuweveldberge mts S. Africa 108 B3
Nyagan' Rus. Fed. 40 F2

Nyainqêntanglha Feng mt. China 87 D1
Nyainqêntanglha Shan mts China 87 D2
Nyala Sudan 103 A3
Nyandoma Rus. Fed. 40 D2
Nyanga r. Gabon 104 B3
Nyanga Zimbabwe 107 C1
Nyasa, Lake Africa 107 C1
Nyborg Denmark 47 C4
Nyborg Norway 46 F1
Nybro Sweden 47 D4
Nyeri Kenya 105 D3
Nyíma China 87 C1
Nyingchi China 80 D3
Nyíregyháza Hungary 57 E3
Nykøbing Denmark 47 C5
Nyköping Sweden 47 D4
Nymagee Austr. 117 D2
Nynäshamn Sweden 47 D4
Nyngan Austr. 117 D2
Nyoman r. Belarus/Lith. 42 B3
Nyons France 59 D3
Nýřany Czech Rep. 55 F3
Nyrob Rus. Fed. 40 E2
Nyssa U.S.A. 132 C2
Nyunzu Dem. Rep. Congo 105 C3
Nyzhn'ohirs'kyy Ukr. 45 D2
Nzega Tanz. 105 D3
Nzérékoré Guinea 100 B4
N'zeto Angola 104 B3

Oahe, Lake U.S.A. 134 C2
Oahu i. U.S.A. 120
Oakbank Austr. 116 C2
Oakdale U.S.A. 138 B2
Oakey Austr. 117 E1
Oak Harbor U.S.A. 132 B1
Oak Hill U.S.A. 136 D3
Oakland U.S.A. 133 B3
Oakover r. Austr. 114 B2
Oakridge U.S.A. 132 B2
Oak Ridge U.S.A. 139 D1
Oamaru N.Z. 118 B4
Oas Phil. 76 B2
Oaxaca Mex. 143 C3
Ob' r. Rus. Fed. 40 F2
Obala Cameroon 104 B2
Oban U.K. 50 B2
O Barco Spain 60 B1
Oberá Arg. 154 A3
Oberon Austr. 117 D2
Oberpfälzer Wald mts Ger. 55 F3
Oberviechtach Ger. 55 F3
Obi i. Indon. 71 C3
Óbidos Brazil 151 D3
Obihiro Japan 78 D2
Obluch'ye Rus. Fed. 81 E1
Obninsk Rus. Fed. 43 E2
Obo C.A.R. 105 C2
Obock Djibouti 103 C3
Obouya Congo 104 B3
Oboyan' Rus. Fed. 43 E3
Obregón, Presa resr Mex. 142 B2
Obrenovac Serb. and Mont. 64 B2
Obshchiy Syrt hills Rus. Fed. 41 E3
Obskaya Guba sea chan. Rus. Fed. 40 G2
Obuasi Ghana 100 B4
Obukhiv Ukr. 44 D1
Ob"yachevo Rus. Fed. 40 D2
Ocala U.S.A. 139 D3
Ocampo Mex. 142 B2
Ocaña Spain 60 C2
Occidental, Cordillera mts Col. 150 B2

ccidental, Cordillera *mts* Peru
150 B4
cean City U.S.A. 137 E3
cean Falls Can. 126 C2
ceanside U.S.A. 133 C4
chakiv Ukr. 45 D2
cher Rus. Fed. 40 E3
chsenfurt Ger. 55 E3
conee *r.* U.S.A. 139 D2
cosingo Mex. 143 C3
date Japan 78 D2
dawara Japan 79 C3
dda Norway 47 B3
demira Port. 60 B2
demiş Turkey 65 C3
dense Denmark 47 C4
denwald *reg.* Ger. 55 D3
derbucht *b.* Ger. 56 C2
desa Ukr. 44 D2
dessa U.S.A. 141 D2
dienné Côte d'Ivoire 100 B4
dra *r.* Ger./Pol. 57 D3
eiras Brazil 151 E3
elde Ger. 54 D2
elrichs U.S.A. 134 C2
elsnitz Ger. 55 F2
enkerk Neth. 54 B1
fanto *r.* Italy 63 C2
ffenbach am Main Ger. 55 D2
ffenburg Ger. 56 B3
gadën *reg.* Eth. 103 C4
gaki Japan 79 C3
ga-hantō *pen.* Japan 78 C3
gallala U.S.A. 134 C2
gbomosho Nigeria 100 C4
gden U.S.A. 132 D2
gilvie *r.* Can. 128 B1
gilvie Mountains Can. 124 C2
gilthorpe, Mount U.S.A. 139 D2
goki *r.* Can. 128 B1
goki Reservoir Can. 128 B1
gre Latvia 42 B2
gulin Croatia 62 C1
hio *r.* U.S.A. 137 C3
hio *state* U.S.A. 136 D2
hrdruf Ger. 55 E2
hringen Ger. 55 D3
hiapoque Brazil 151 D2
il City U.S.A. 137 E3
ise *r.* France 54 A3
ita Japan 79 B4
jinaga Mex. 142 B2
jos del Salado, Nevado *mt.*
Arg./Chile 152 B3
ka *r.* Rus. Fed. 43 C2
kahandja Namibia 106 A2
kakarara Namibia 106 A2
kanagan Falls Can. 126 D3
kanagan Lake Can. 126 D3
kanogan *r.* U.S.A. 132 C1
kara Pak. 86 B1
kavango *r.* Botswana/Namibia 106 B1
kavango Delta *swamp* Botswana
106 B1
kaya Japan 79 C3
kayama Japan 79 B4
kazaki Japan 79 C4
keechobee, Lake U.S.A. 139 D3
kefenokee Swamp U.S.A. 139 D2
kehampton U.K. 53 A4
kha India 86 A2
kha Rus. Fed. 95 L3
khaldhunga Nepal 87 C2
khotka *r.* Rus. Fed. 95 L3
khotsk Rus. Fed. 95 L3

Okhotsk, Sea of Japan/Rus. Fed.
95 L4
Okhtyrka Ukr. 45 D1
Okinawa *i.* Japan 81 E3
Oki-shotō *is* Japan 79 B3
Oklahoma *state* U.S.A. 141 E1
Oklahoma City U.S.A. 141 E1
Okmulgee U.S.A. 141 E1
Oko, Wadi *watercourse* Sudan 90 A2
Okondja Gabon 104 B3
Okotoks Can. 126 D2
Okovskiy Les for. Rus. Fed. 43 D3
Okoyo Congo 104 B3
Øksfjord Norway 46 E1
Oktwin Myanmar 74 A2
Oktyabr'sk *Arkhangel'skaya Oblast'*
Rus. Fed. 40 D2
Oktyabr'skiy *Kamchatskaya Oblast'*
Rus. Fed. 95 M3
Oktyabr'skiy *Respublika Bashkortostan*
Rus. Fed. 41 E3
Oktyabr'skoye Rus. Fed. 40 F2
Oktyabr'skoy Revolyutsii, Ostrov *i.*
Rus. Fed. 95 I1
Okulovka Rus. Fed. 43 D2
Okushiri-tō *i.* Japan 78 C2
Ólafsvík Iceland 46 [inset]
Öland *i.* Sweden 47 D4
Olary Austr. 116 C2
Olavarría Arg. 153 B4
Oława Pol. 57 D2
Olbernhau Ger. 55 F2
Olbia Italy 62 A2
Old Crow Can. 124 C2
Oldenburg Ger. 55 D1
Oldenburg in Holstein Ger. 56 C2
Oldenzaal Neth. 54 C1
Old Head of Kinsale *hd* Rep. of Ireland
51 B3
Olds Can. 126 D2
Old Wives Lake Can. 127 E2
Olean U.S.A. 137 E2
Olecko Pol. 57 E2
Olekminsk Rus. Fed. 95 K2
Oleksandriya Ukr. 45 D2
Ølen Norway 48 E2
Olenegorsk Rus. Fed. 46 G2
Olenek Rus. Fed. 95 J2
Olenek *r.* Rus. Fed. 95 J2
Olenino Rus. Fed. 43 D2
Olevs'k Ukr. 44 C1
Olhão Port. 60 B2
Olifants *r.* Moz./S. Africa 109 D1
Olifants *watercourse* Namibia 108 A2
Olifants S. Africa 109 D1
Olifants *r.* S. Africa 108 A3
Olifantshoek S. Africa 108 B2
Olímpia Brazil 154 C2
Olinda Brazil 151 F3
Oliphants Drift S. Africa 109 C1
Oliva Spain 61 C2
Oliveira Brazil 155 D2
Olivenza Spain 60 B2
Ollagüe Chile 152 B3
Olmos Peru 150 B3
Olney U.S.A. 136 C3
Olomouc Czech Rep. 57 D3
Olongapo Phil. 76 B2
Oloron-Ste-Marie France 58 B3
Olot Spain 61 D1
Olovyannaya Rus. Fed. 81 D1
Olpe Ger. 54 C2
Olsztyn Pol. 57 E2
Olt *r.* Romania 44 B3
Oltu Turkey 91 C1
Olympia *tourist site* Greece 65 B3
Olympia U.S.A. 132 B1
Olympus, Mount Greece 65 B2
Olympus, Mount U.S.A. 132 B1
Olyutorskiy, Mys *c.* Rus. Fed. 95 N3

Omagh U.K. 51 C1
Omaha U.S.A. 135 D2
Oman *country* Asia 91 C2
Oman, Gulf of Asia 91 C2
Omaruru Namibia 106 A2
Omatako *watercourse* Namibia 106 B1
Omdurman Sudan 102 B3
Omeo Austr. 117 D3
Ometepec Mex. 143 C3
Om Hajēr Eritrea 90 A3
Omineca Mountains Can. 126 C2
Ōmiya Japan 79 C3
Ommen Neth. 54 C1
Omolon *r.* Rus. Fed. 95 M2
Omont France 54 B3
Omsk Rus. Fed. 89 E1
Omsukchan Rus. Fed. 95 M2
Omu, Vârful *mt.* Romania 44 C2
Ōmura Japan 79 A4
Onancock U.S.A. 137 E3
Onaping Lake Can. 136 D1
Onatchiway, Lac *l.* Can. 129 C2
Oncócua Angola 106 A1
Onderstedorings S. Africa 108 B3
Ondjiva Angola 106 A1
Onega Rus. Fed. 40 C2
Onega *r.* Rus. Fed. 40 C2
Onega, Lake Rus. Fed. 40 C2
Oneida Lake U.S.A. 137 E2
O'Neill U.S.A. 135 D2
Oneonta U.S.A. 137 E2
Oneşti Romania 44 C1
Onezhskoye Ozero *l.* Rus. Fed. *see*
Onega, Lake
Ongers *watercourse* S. Africa 108 B2
Ongjin N. Korea 77 B2
Ongole India 85 C3
Onilahy *r.* Madag. 107 [inset] D2
Onitsha Nigeria 101 C4
Onotoa *atoll* Kiribati 110
Onseepkans S. Africa 108 A2
Onslow Austr. 114 A2
Onslow Bay U.S.A. 139 E2
Ontario *prov.* Can. 128 A1
Ontario U.S.A. 132 C2
Ontario, Lake Can./U.S.A. 137 E2
Oodnadatta Austr. 116 B1
Oostende Belgium *see* Ostend
Oosterhout Neth. 54 B2
Oosterschelde *est.* Neth. 54 A2
Oost-Vlieland Neth. 54 B1
Ootsa Lake Can. 126 C2
Ootsa Lake *l.* Can. 126 C2
Opala Dem. Rep. Congo 104 C3
Opataca, Lac *l.* Can. 128 C1
Opava Czech Rep. 57 D3
Opelika U.S.A. 139 C2
Opelousas U.S.A. 138 B2
Opinaca, Réservoir *resr* Can. 128 C1
Opiscotéo, Lac *l.* Can. 129 D1
Opochka Rus. Fed. 42 C2
Opodepe Mex. 142 A2
Opole Pol. 57 D2
Oporto Port. 60 B1
Opotiki N.Z. 118 C2
Oppdal Norway 47 B3
Opunake N.Z. 118 B2
Opuwo Namibia 106 A1
Oradea Romania 44 B2
Orahovac Serb. and Mont. 64 B2
Oran Alg. 100 B1
Orán Arg. 152 B3
Orang N. Korea 77 B1
Orange Austr. 117 D2
Orange France 59 C3
Orange *r.* Namibia/S. Africa 108 A2
Orange U.S.A. 141 F2
Orange, Cabo *c.* Brazil 146
Orangeburg U.S.A. 139 D2
Orangeville Can. 137 D2

Orange Walk Belize **143** D3
Oranienburg Ger. **55** F1
Oranjemund Namibia **106** A2
Orapa Botswana **106** B2
Orăştie Romania **44** B2
Orbetello Italy **62** B2
Orbost Austr. **117** D3
Ord, Mount Austr. **114** B1
Ordes Spain **60** B1
Ordos China **82** B2
Ordu Turkey **92** B1
Ordzhonikidze Ukr. **45** D2
Örebro Sweden **47** D4
Oregon *state* U.S.A. **132** B2
Oregon City U.S.A. **132** B1
Orekhovo-Zuyevo Rus. Fed. **41** C3
Orel Rus. Fed. **43** E3
Orem U.S.A. **132** D2
Ören Turkey **65** C3
Orenburg Rus. Fed. **41** E3
Orepuki N.Z. **118** A3
Öresund *str.* Denmark/Sweden **47** C4
Orford Ness *hd* U.K. **53** D3
Orhaneli Turkey **65** C3
Orhangazi Turkey **65** C2
Orhon Gol *r.* Mongolia **95** J3
Oriental, Cordillera *mts* Bol. **152** B2
Oriental, Cordillera *mts* Col. **150** C2
Oriental, Cordillera *mts* Peru **150** B4
Orihuela Spain **61** C2
Orikhiv Ukr. **45** E2
Orillia Can. **128** C2
Orinoco *r.* Col./Venez. **150** C2
Orinoco Delta Venez. **150** C2
Orissaare Estonia **42** B2
Oristano Italy **62** A3
Orivesi *l.* Fin. **46** F3
Oriximiná Brazil **151** D3
Orizaba Mex. **143** C3
Orizaba, Pico de *vol.* Mex. **143** C3
Orkanger Norway **46** B3
Örkelljunga Sweden **47** C4
Orkla *r.* Norway **46** B3
Orkney Islands *Scotland* U.K. **50** C1
Orlândia Brazil **154** C2
Orlando U.S.A. **139** D3
Orléans France **58** C2
Ormara Pak. **86** A2
Ormoc Phil. **76** B2
Ormskirk U.K. **52** B3
Örnsköldsvik Sweden **46** D3
Orodara Burkina **100** B3
Orofino U.S.A. **132** C1
Orona *atoll* Kiribati **111**
Oroquieta Phil. **76** B3
Orosei Italy **62** A2
Orosei, Golfo di *b.* Italy **62** A2
Orosháza Hungary **57** E3
Oroville U.S.A. **133** B3
Orroroo Austr. **116** B2
Orsha Belarus **43** D1
Orsk Rus. Fed. **41** E3
Ørsta Norway **47** B3
Ortegal, Cabo *c.* Spain **60** B1
Orthez France **58** B3
Ortigueira Spain **60** B1
Ortonville U.S.A. **135** D1
Orulgan, Khrebet *mts* Rus. Fed. **95** K2
Orūmīyeh, Daryācheh-ye *salt l.* Iran *see* Urmia, Lake
Oruro Bol. **152** B2
Orvieto Italy **62** B2
Osa, Península de *pen.* Costa Rica **144** B4
Osage *r.* U.S.A. **135** E3
Ōsaka Japan **79** C4
Oschersleben (Bode) Ger. **55** E1
Oschiri Italy **62** A2

Osetr *r.* Rus. Fed. **43** E3
Osh Kyrg. **89** E2
Oshakati Namibia **106** A1
Oshawa Can. **128** C2
Ō-shima *i.* Japan **78** C2
Ō-shima *i.* Japan **79** C4
Oshkosh U.S.A. **136** C2
Oshnovīyeh Iran **93** C2
Oshogbo Nigeria **100** C4
Oshwe Dem. Rep. Congo **104** B3
Osijek Croatia **63** C1
Osilinka *r.* Can. **126** C2
Ósimo Italy **62** B2
Osizweni S. Africa **109** D2
Oskaloosa U.S.A. **135** E2
Oskarshamn Sweden **47** D4
Oskol *r.* Rus. Fed. **43** E3
Oslo Norway **47** B4
Oslofjorden *sea chan.* Norway **47** C4
Osmancık Turkey **92** B1
Osmaniye Turkey **65** C2
Osmaniye Turkey **92** B2
Os'mino Rus. Fed. **42** C2
Osnabrück Ger. **54** D1
Osorno Chile **153** A5
Osorno Spain **60** C1
Osoyoos Can. **126** C3
Oseyri Norway **48** E1
Oss Neth. **54** B2
Ossa, Mount Austr. **115** D4
Ossora Rus. Fed. **95** M3
Ostashkov Rus. Fed. **43** D2
Oste *r.* Ger. **55** D1
Ostend Belgium **54** A2
Osterburg (Altmark) Ger. **55** E1
Österdalälven *l.* Sweden **47** C3
Osterholz-Scharmbeck Ger. **55** D1
Osterode am Harz Ger. **55** E2
Östersund Sweden **46** C3
Ostfriesland *reg.* Ger. **54** C1
Osthammar Sweden **47** D3
Ostrava Czech Rep. **57** D3
Ostróda Pol. **57** D2
Ostrogozhsk Rus. Fed. **43** E3
Ostrołęka Pol. **57** E2
Ostrov Czech Rep. **55** F2
Ostrov Rus. Fed. **42** C2
Ostrovskoye Rus. Fed. **43** F2
Ostrowiec Świętokrzyski Pol. **57** E2
Ostrów Mazowiecka Pol. **57** E2
Ostrów Wielkopolski Pol. **57** D2
Osüm *r.* Bulg. **64** B2
Ōsumi-kaikyō *sea chan.* Japan **79** B4
Ōsumi-shotō *is* Japan **79** B4
Osuna Spain **60** B2
Oswego U.S.A. **137** E2
Oswestry U.K. **52** B3
Ōta Japan **79** C3
Otago Peninsula N.Z. **118** B4
Otaki N.Z. **118** C3
Otaru Japan **78** C2
Otavi Namibia **106** A2
Othello U.S.A. **132** C1
Otjiwarongo Namibia **106** A2
Otoro, Jebel *mt.* Sudan **103** B3
Otra *r.* Norway **47** B4
Otranto, Strait of Albania/Italy **65** A2
Ōtsu Japan **79** C3
Otta Norway **47** B3
Ottawa Can. **128** C2
Ottawa *r.* Can. **128** C2
Ottawa *l.* U.S.A. **136** C2
Ottawa KS U.S.A. **135** D3
Ottawa Islands Can. **128** B1
Otter Rapids Can. **128** B1
Ottignies Belgium **54** B2
Ottumwa U.S.A. **135** E2

Otuzco Peru **150** B3
Otway, Cape Austr. **116** C3
Ouachita *r.* U.S.A. **138** B2
Ouachita, Lake U.S.A. **138** B2
Ouachita Mountains U.S.A. **138** B2
Ouadda C.A.R. **104** C2
Ouaddaï *reg.* Chad **101** D3
Ouagadougou Burkina **100** B3
Ouahigouya Burkina **100** B3
Oualâta Maur. **100** B3
Ouanda-Djallé C.A.R. **104** C2
Ouarâne *reg.* Maur. **100** B2
Ouargla Alg. **101** C1
Ouarzazate Morocco **100** B1
Oudenaarde Belgium **54** A2
Oudtshoorn S. Africa **108** B3
Oued Tlélat Alg. **61** C2
Ouessant, Île d' *i.* France **58** A2
Ouesso Congo **104** B2
Ouistreham France **53** C5
Oujda Morocco **100** B1
Ouled Farès Alg. **61** D2
Oulu Fin. **46** F2
Oulujärvi *l.* Fin. **46** F3
Oulx Italy **62** A1
Oum-Chalouba Chad **101** D3
Oum-Hadjer Chad **101** D3
Ounianga Kébir Chad **101** E3
Oupeye Belgium **54** B2
Our *r.* Lux. **54** C3
Ourense Spain **60** B1
Ourinhos Brazil **154** C2
Ouro Prêto Brazil **155** D2
Ourthe *r.* Belgium **54** B2
Ouse *r.* U.K. **52** C3
Outardes *r.* Can. **129** D2
Outardes Quatre, Réservoir *resr* Can. **129** D1
Outer Hebrides *is* U.K. **50** A2
Outjo Namibia **106** A2
Outlook Can. **127** E2
Outokumpu Fin. **46** F3
Ouyen Austr. **116** C3
Ovar Port. **60** B1
Överkalix Sweden **46** E2
Overton U.S.A. **133** D3
Övertorneå Sweden **46** E2
Oviedo Spain **60** B1
Øvre Årdal Norway **47** B3
Øvre Rendal Norway **47** C3
Ovruch Ukr. **44** C1
Owando Congo **104** B3
Owase Japan **79** C4
Owatonna U.S.A. **135** E2
Owensboro U.S.A. **136** C3
Owens Lake U.S.A. **133** C3
Owen Sound Can. **128** B2
Owerri Nigeria **101** C4
Owosso U.S.A. **136** C2
Owyhee U.S.A. **132** C2
Owyhee *r.* U.S.A. **132** C2
Oxelösund Sweden **42** A2
Oxford U.K. **53** C4
Oxford U.S.A. **138** C2
Oxford Lake Can. **127** F2
Oxley Austr. **116** C2
Oxnard U.S.A. **133** C4
Oyama Japan **79** C3
Oyem Gabon **104** B2
Oyen Can. **127** D2
Oyonnax France **59** D2
Ozamiz Phil. **76** B3
Ozark U.S.A. **138** C2
Ozark Plateau U.S.A. **135** E3
Ozarks, Lake of the U.S.A. **135** E3
Ozernovskiy Rus. Fed. **95** M3
Ozersk Rus. Fed. **42** B3
Ozery Rus. Fed. **43** E3
Ozinki Rus. Fed. **41** D3

P

aamiut Greenland **125** I2
aarl S. Africa **108** A3
abianice Pol. **57** D2
abna Bangl. **87** C2
ab Range *mts* Pak. **86** A2
achino Italy **62** C3
achuca Mex. **143** C2
acific Ocean 158
aczków Pol. **57** D2
adang Indon. **72** B2
adang Endau Malaysia **72** B1
adangpanjang Indon. **72** B2
adangsidimpuan Indon. **72** A1
aderborn Ger. **55** D2
adova Italy *see* **Padua**
adre Island U.S.A. **141** E3
adthaway Austr. **116** C3
adua Italy **62** B1
aducah *KY* U.S.A. **136** C3
aducah *TX* U.S.A. **141** D2
aegam N. Korea **77** B1
aengnyŏng-do *i.* S. Korea **77** A2
aeroa N.Z. **118** C2
afos Cyprus *see* **Paphos**
ag Croatia **62** C2
agadian Phil. **76** B3
agai Selatan *i.* Indon. **72** B2
agai Utara *i.* Indon. **72** B2
agan *i.* N. Mariana Is **71** D1
agatan Indon. **73** C2
age U.S.A. **140** B1
agėgiai Lith. **42** B2
agosa Springs U.S.A. **134** B3
aide Estonia **42** C2
äijänne *l.* Fin. **47** F3
aïkü Co *l.* China **87** C2
aimio Fin. **42** B1
ainted Desert U.S.A. **140** B1
aisley U.K. **50** B3
ajala Sweden **46** E2
akaraima Mountains S. America **146**
akistan *country* Asia **86** A2
akokku Myanmar **74** A1
akruojis Lith. **42** B2
aks Hungary **57** D3
akwash Lake Can. **128** A1
akxan Laos **74** B2
akxé Laos **75** B2
ala Chad **101** D4
alabuhanratu, Teluk *b.* Indon. **72** B2
alaikastro Greece **65** C3
alaiochora Greece **65** B3
alamakoloi Botswana **108** B1
alamós Spain **61** D1
alana Rus. Fed. **95** M3
alanan Phil. **76** B2
alangkaraya Indon. **73** C2
alanpur India **86** B2
alapye Botswana **109** C1
alatka Rus. Fed. **95** M2
alatka U.S.A. **139** D3
alau *country* N. Pacific Ocean **71** C2
alau Islands Palau **67**
alaw Myanmar **75** A2
alawan *i.* Phil. **76** A3
aldiski Estonia **42** B2
alekh Rus. Fed. **43** F2
alembang Indon. **72** B2
alencia Spain **60** C1
alenque Mex. **143** C3
alermo Italy **62** B3
alestine U.S.A. **141** E2
aletwa Myanmar **74** A1
ali India **86** B2
alikir Micronesia **112**
Palinuro, Capo *c.* Italy **62** C2
Paliouri, Akra *pt* Greece **65** B3
Paliseul Belgium **54** B3
Paljakka *h.* Fin. **46** F3
Palkino Rus. Fed. **42** C2
Palk Strait India/Sri Lanka **85** B4
Palliser, Îles *is* Fr. Polynesia **111**
Palma del Río Spain **60** B2
Palma de Mallorca Spain **61** D2
Palmas *Paraná* Brazil **154** B3
Palmas Brazil **151** E4
Palmas, Cape Liberia **100** B4
Palmeira Brazil **154** C3
Palmeirais Brazil **151** E3
Palmer U.S.A. **124** C2
Palmer Land *reg.* Antarctica **119** K3
Palmerston *atoll* Cook Is **111**
Palmerston North N.Z. **118** C3
Palmi Italy **63** C3
Palmillas Mex. **143** C2
Palmira Col. **150** B2
Palm Springs U.S.A. **133** C4
Palmyra Atoll *terr.* N. Pacific Ocean **113**
Paloich Sudan **103** B3
Palomares Mex. **143** C3
Palopo Indon. **73** D2
Palos, Cabo de *c.* Spain **61** C2
Paltamo Fin. **46** F3
Palu Indon. **73** C2
Palyavaam *r.* Rus. Fed. **95** N2
Pamiers France **58** C3
Pamir *mts* Asia **89** E3
Pamlico Sound *sea chan.* U.S.A. **139** E1
Pampa Grande Bol. **152** B2
Pampas *reg.* Arg. **153** B4
Pamplona Col. **150** B2
Pamplona Spain **61** C1
Pamukova Turkey **65** D2
Panaitan *i.* Indon. **72** B2
Panaji India **85** B3
Panama *country* Central America **144** B4
Panama, Gulf of Panama **144** C4
Panama Canal Panama **144** C4
Panama City Panama **144** C4
Panama City U.S.A. **139** C2
Panamint Range *mts* U.S.A. **133** C3
Panarik Indon. **72** B1
Panay *i.* Phil. **76** B2
Pančevo Serb. and Mont. **64** B2
Panda Moz. **109** D1
Pandan Phil. **76** B2
Pandaria India **87** C2
Pandharpur India **85** B3
Panevėžys Lith. **42** B2
Pangkalanbuun Indon. **73** C2
Pangkalansusu Indon. **72** A1
Pangkalpinang Indon. **72** B2
Pangnirtung Can. **125** H2
Pangody Rus. Fed. **40** G2
Panino Rus. Fed. **43** F3
Panipat India **86** B2
Panjgur Pak. **86** A2
Pan Ling *mts* China **77** C1
Panna India **87** C2
Pannawonica Austr. **114** A2
Panorama Brazil **154** B2
Panshi China **77** B1
Pantanal *reg.* Brazil **152** C2
Pánuco Mex. **143** C2
Panxian China **83** A3
Panzhihua China **74** B1
Paola Italy **63** C3
Paôy Pêt Cambodia **75** B2
Pápa Hungary **57** D3
Papakura N.Z. **118** B2
Papantla Mex. **143** C2
Papeete Fr. Polynesia **113**
Papenburg Ger. **54** C1
Paphos Cyprus **92** B2
Papua, Gulf of P.N.G. **71** D3
Papua New Guinea *country* Oceania **71** D3
Para *r.* Rus. Fed. **43** F3
Paraburdoo Austr. **114** A2
Paracatu Brazil **154** C1
Paracatu *r.* Brazil **155** C1
Parachilna Austr. **116** B2
Paraćin Serb. and Mont. **64** B2
Pará de Minas Brazil **155** D1
Paradise U.S.A. **133** B3
Paragould U.S.A. **138** B1
Paraguai *r.* Brazil **151** D4
Paraguay *r.* Arg./Para. **152** C3
Paraguay *country* S. America **152** C3
Paraíba do Sul *r.* Brazil **155** D2
Paraíso Brazil **154** B1
Paraíso Mex. **143** C3
Parakou Benin **100** C4
Paramaribo Suriname **151** D2
Paraná Arg. **152** B4
Paraná *r.* S. America **154** B2
Paranaguá Brazil **154** C3
Paranaíba Brazil **154** B1
Paranaíba *r.* Brazil **154** B2
Paranapanema *r.* Brazil **154** B2
Paranapiacaba, Serra *mts* Brazil **154** B2
Paranavaí Brazil **154** B2
Paraparaumu N.Z. **118** B3
Parati Brazil **155** D2
Paraúna Brazil **154** B1
Paray-le-Monial France **59** C2
Parbhani India **85** B3
Parchim Ger. **55** E1
Pardo *r. Bahia* Brazil **155** E1
Pardo *r. Mato Grosso do Sul* Brazil **154** B2
Pardo *r. São Paulo* Brazil **154** C2
Pardubice Czech Rep. **57** D2
Parecis, Serra dos *hills* Brazil **150** C4
Parent, Lac *l.* Can. **128** C2
Parepare Indon. **73** C2
Parfino Rus. Fed. **43** D2
Parga Greece **65** B3
Pargas Fin. **42** B1
Parghelia Italy **63** C3
Paria, Gulf of Trin. and Tob./Venez. **145** D3
Parima, Serra *mts* Brazil **150** C2
Parintins Brazil **151** D3
Paris France **58** C2
Paris *TN* U.S.A. **138** C1
Paris *TX* U.S.A. **141** E2
Parkano Fin. **47** E3
Parker U.S.A. **140** B2
Parkersburg U.S.A. **136** D3
Parkes Austr. **117** D2
Park Falls U.S.A. **136** B1
Park Rapids U.S.A. **135** D1
Parma Italy **62** B2
Parnaíba Brazil **151** E3
Parnaíba *r.* Brazil **151** E3
Parnassos *mt.* Greece **65** B3
Parnassus N.Z. **118** B3
Parnon *mts* Greece **65** B3
Pärnu Estonia **42** B2
P'aro-ho *l.* S. Korea **77** B2
Paroo *watercourse* Austr. **116** C2
Paropamisus *mts* Afgh. **86** A1
Paros *i.* Greece **65** C3
Parras Mex. **142** B2
Parry, Cape Can. **124** D2
Parry Channel Can. **120**
Parry Islands Can. **124** E1
Parry Sound Can. **128** B2
Parsons U.S.A. **135** D3

Partenstein Ger. **55** D2
Parthenay France **58** B2
Partry Mountains Rep. of Ireland
51 B2
Paru r. Brazil **151** D3
Pasadena U.S.A. **133** C4
Pasawng Myanmar **74** A2
Pascagoula U.S.A. **138** C2
Pașcani Romania **44** C2
Pasco U.S.A. **132** C1
Pasewalk Ger. **56** C2
Pasfield Lake Can. **127** E2
Pasha Rus. Fed. **43** D1
Pasir Putih Malaysia **72** B1
Pasni Pak. **86** A2
Paso Rio Mayo Arg. **153** A5
Paso Robles U.S.A. **133** B3
Passa Tempo Brazil **155** D2
Passau Ger. **56** C3
Passo Fundo Brazil **152** C3
Passos Brazil **155** C2
Pastavy Belarus **42** C2
Pastaza r. Peru **150** B3
Pasto Col. **150** B2
Pasuruan Indon. **73** C2
Pasvalys Lith. **42** B2
Patagonia reg. Arg. **153** A6
Patan Nepal **87** E2
Patea N.Z. **118** B2
Paterson U.S.A. **137** F2
Pathfinder Reservoir U.S.A. **134** B2
Pati Indon. **73** C2
Patkai Bum mts India/Myanmar **74** A1
Patmos i. Greece **65** C3
Patna India **87** F2
Patnos Turkey **93** C2
Pato Branco Brazil **154** B3
Patos, Lagoa dos l. Brazil **152** C4
Patos de Minas Brazil **155** C1
Patquía Arg. **152** B3
Patras Greece **65** B3
Patratu India **87** E2
Patrocínio Brazil **154** C1
Pattani Thai. **75** B3
Pattaya Thai. **75** B2
Patterson, Mount Can. **126** B1
Pattullo, Mount Can. **126** C2
Patuanak Can. **127** E2
Pátzcuaro Mex. **142** B3
Pau France **58** B3
Pauillac France **58** B2
Pauk Myanmar **74** A1
Paulistana Brazil **151** E3
Paulo Afonso Brazil **151** F3
Paulpietersburg S. Africa **109** D2
Pauls Valley U.S.A. **141** D2
Paungde Myanmar **74** A2
Pavão Brazil **155** D1
Pavia Italy **62** A1
Pāvilosta Latvia **42** B2
Pavlikeni Bulg. **64** C2
Pavlodar Kazakh. **89** E1
Pavlohrad Ukr. **45** E2
Pavlovo Rus. Fed. **43** F2
Pavlovsk Rus. Fed. **45** F1
Pavlovskaya Rus. Fed. **45** E2
Payakumbuh Indon. **72** B2
Payette U.S.A. **132** C2
Payette r. U.S.A. **132** C2
Pay-Khoy, Khrebet hills Rus. Fed.
40 F2
Payne, Lac l. Can. **128** C1
Paysandú Uru. **152** C4
Pazar Turkey **93** C1
Pazardzhik Bulg. **64** C2
Pazarköy Turkey **65** C3
Pazin Croatia **62** B1
Pe Myanmar **75** A2
Peace r. Can. **126** D2
Peace River Can. **126** D2

Peale, Mount U.S.A. **133** E3
Pearl r. U.S.A. **138** C2
Pearsall U.S.A. **141** E3
Pebane Moz. **107** D2
Peçanha Brazil **155** D1
Pechora Rus. Fed. **40** E2
Pechora r. Rus. Fed. **40** E2
Pechory Rus. Fed. **42** C2
Pecos U.S.A. **141** D2
Pecos r. U.S.A. **141** D3
Pécs Hungary **57** B3
Pedra Azul Brazil **155** D1
Pedregulho Brazil **154** C2
Pedreiras Brazil **151** E3
Pedro, Point pt Sri Lanka **85** C4
Pedro Afonso Brazil **151** E3
Pedro Gomes Brazil **154** B1
Pedro Juan Caballero Para. **152** C3
Peebles U.K. **50** C3
Pee Dee r. U.S.A. **139** E2
Peel r. Can. **124** D2
Peel Isle of Man **52** A2
Peerless Lake Can. **126** D2
Pegasus Bay N.Z. **118** B3
Pegnitz Ger. **55** E3
Pegu Myanmar **74** A2
Pegu Yoma mts Myanmar **74** A2
Pehuajó Arg. **153** B4
Peine Ger. **55** E1
Peipus, Lake Estonia/Rus. Fed. **42** C2
Peixe r. Brazil **154** B2
Peixoto de Azevedo Brazil **152** C2
Pekalongan Indon. **73** B2
Pekan Malaysia **72** B1
Pekanbaru Indon. **72** B1
Peking China see Beijing
Pelee Island Can. **128** B2
Peleng i. Indon. **73** C2
Pelkosenniemi Fin. **46** F2
Pella S. Africa **108** A2
Pelleluhu Islands P.N.G. **71** D3
Pello Fin. **46** E2
Pelly r. Can. **126** B1
Pelly Mountains Can. **126** B1
Pelotas Brazil **152** C4
Pelotas, Rio das r. Brazil **152** C3
Pemadumcook Lake U.S.A. **137** G1
Pemangkat Indon. **72** B1
Pematangsiantar Indon. **72** A1
Pemba Moz. **107** D1
Pemba Zambia **106** B1
Pemba Island Tanz. **105** D3
Pemberton Can. **126** C2
Pembina r. Can. **135** D1
Pembroke Can. **128** C2
Pembroke U.K. **53** A4
Peña Nevada, Cerro mt. Mex. **143** C2
Penápolis Brazil **154** B2
Peñaranda de Bracamonte Spain
60 B1
Peñarroya mt. Spain **61** C1
Peñarroya-Pueblonuevo Spain **60** B2
Peñas, Cabo de c. Spain **60** B1
Penas, Golfo de g. Chile **153** A5
Peña Ubiña mt. Spain **60** B1
Pendleton U.S.A. **132** C1
Pendleton Bay Can. **126** C2
Pend Oreille Lake U.S.A. **132** C1
Penganga r. India **86** B3
Penge S. Africa **109** C1
Penglai China **82** C2
Pengshui China **83** A3
Peniche Port. **60** B2
Penicuik U.K. **50** C3
Peninsular Malaysia Malaysia **72** B1
Penne Italy **62** B2
Pennines hills U.K. **52** B2
Pennsylvania state U.S.A. **137** D2
Penobscot r. U.S.A. **137** G2

Penola Austr. **116** C3
Penong Austr. **114** C3
Penrhyn atoll Cook Is **111**
Penrith U.K. **52** B2
Pensacola U.S.A. **138** C2
Pensacola Mountains Antarctica
119 K1
Pensiangan Malaysia **73** C1
Penticton Can. **126** D3
Pentland Firth sea chan. U.K. **50** C1
Penygadair h. U.K. **53** B3
Penza Rus. Fed. **41** D3
Penzance U.K. **53** A4
Peoria U.S.A. **136** C2
Perales del Alfambra Spain **61** C1
Percy Isles Austr. **115** E2
Peregrebnoye Rus. Fed. **40** F2
Pereira Col. **150** B2
Pereira Barreto Brazil **154** B2
Peremyshlyany Ukr. **44** B2
Pereslavl'-Zalesskiy Rus. Fed. **43** E2
Pereyaslav-Khmel'nyts'kyy Ukr. **45** D1
Pergamino Arg. **153** B4
Perhonjoki r. Fin. **46** E3
Péribonka, Lac l. Can. **129** C3
Perico Arg. **152** B3
Pericos Mex. **142** B2
Périgueux France **58** C2
Perija, Sierra de mts Venez. **145** C4
Perito Moreno Arg. **153** A5
Perleberg Ger. **55** E1
Perm' Rus. Fed. **40** E3
Pernatty Lagoon salt flat Austr. **116** B2
Pernik Bulg. **92** A1
Péronne France **58** C2
Perote Mex. **143** C3
Perpignan France **58** C3
Perranporth U.K. **53** A4
Perry r. U.S.A. **124** F2
Perry GA U.S.A. **139** D2
Perry IA U.S.A. **135** E2
Perryton U.S.A. **141** D1
Perryville U.S.A. **135** F3
Pershore U.K. **53** B3
Pershotravens'k Ukr. **45** E2
Perth Austr. **114** A3
Perth U.K. **50** C2
Pertuis France **59** D3
Pertusato, Capo c. France **62** A2
Peru country S. America **150** B3
Perugia Italy **62** B2
Peruíbe Brazil **154** C2
Péruwelz Belgium **54** A2
Pervomays'k Ukr. **44** D2
Pervomays'ke Ukr. **45** D2
Pervomayskiy Rus. Fed. **43** F3
Pervomays'kyy Ukr. **45** E2
Pesaro Italy **62** B2
Pescara Italy **62** B2
Pescara r. Italy **62** B2
Peschanokopskoye Rus. Fed. **45** F2
Peshawar Pak. **87** C1
Peshkopi Albania **64** B2
Pesnica Slovenia **62** C1
Pessac France **58** B3
Pestovo Rus. Fed. **43** E2
Pestyaki Rus. Fed. **43** F2
Petatlán Mex. **142** B3
Petenwell Lake U.S.A. **136** C2
Peterborough Austr. **116** B2
Peterborough Can. **128** C2
Peterborough U.K. **53** C3
Peterhead U.K. **50** D2
Petermann Ranges mts Austr. **114** B2
Peter Pond Lake Can. **127** E2
Petersburg AK U.S.A. **126** B2
Petersburg VA U.S.A. **137** E3
Petershagen Ger. **55** D1
Petit Mécatina r. Can. **129** E1
Peto Mex. **143** D2

etoskey U.S.A. **136** D1
etra *tourist site* Jordan **92** B2
etra Velikogo, Zaliv *b.* Rus. Fed.
78 B2
etrich Bulg. **65** B2
etrolina Brazil **151** E3
etropavlovsk Kazakh. **89** D1
etropavlovsk-Kamchatskiy Rus. Fed.
95 M3
etroşani Romania **44** B2
etrovskoye Rus. Fed. **43** F3
etrozavodsk Rus. Fed. **40** C2
etrusburg S. Africa **109** C2
etrus Steyn S. Africa **109** C2
etrusville S. Africa **108** B3
etukhovo Rus. Fed. **41** F3
etushki Rus. Fed. **43** E2
eureula Indon. **72** A1
evek Rus. Fed. **95** N2
forzheim Ger. **56** B3
fungstadt Ger. **55** D3
hahameng S. Africa **109** C2
halaborwa S. Africa **109** D1
halodi India **86** B2
hang Hoei, San Khao *mts* Thai.
75 B2
hangnga Thai. **75** A3
han Rang Vietnam **75** B2
han Thiêt Vietnam **75** B2
hatthalung Thai. **75** B3
hayao Thai. **74** A2
helps Lake Can. **127** E2
henix City U.S.A. **139** C2
het Buri Thai. **75** A2
hichit Thai. **74** B2
hiladelphia U.S.A. **137** E3
hilip U.S.A. **134** C2
hilippeville Belgium **54** B2
hilippine Neth. **54** A2
hilippines *country* Asia **76** B2
hilippine Sea N. Pacific Ocean **71** C1
hilippsburg Ger. **55** D3
hilip Smith Mountains U.S.A. **124** C2
hilipstown S. Africa **108** B3
hillipsburg U.S.A. **135** D3
hillip Island Austr. **117** D3
hiritona S. Africa **109** C2
hitsanulok Thai. **74** B2
hnom Penh Cambodia **75** B2
hoenix U.S.A. **140** B2
hoenix Islands Kiribati **111**
hon Thai. **75** A2
höngsali Laos **74** B1
hrae Thai. **74** B2
huket Thai. **75** A3
humi Sâmraông Cambodia **75** B2
huthaditjhaba S. Africa **109** C2
iacenza Italy **62** A1
ianosa, Isola *i.* Italy **59** E3
iatra Neamţ Romania **44** C2
iauí *r.* Brazil **151** E3
iave *r.* Italy **62** B1
ibor *r.* Sudan **103** B4
ibor Post Sudan **103** B4
icayune Mex. **142** C2
ichilingue Mex. **142** C2
ickle Lake Can. **128** A1
icos Brazil **151** E3
ico Truncado Arg. **153** B5
icton Austr. **117** E2
icton N.Z. **118** B3
iedras Negras Guat. **143** C3
iedras Negras Mex. **143** B3
ieksämäki Fin. **47** F3
ielinen *l.* Fin. **46** F3
ierre U.S.A. **134** C2

Pierrelatte France **59** C3
Pietermaritzburg S. Africa **109** D2
Pietersburg S. Africa *see* Polokwane
Pietrosa *mt.* Romania **44** B2
Pigeon Lake Can. **126** D2
Pigüé Arg. **153** B4
Pihtipudas Fin. **46** F3
Pijijiapan Mex. **143** C3
Pikes Peak U.S.A. **134** C3
Piketberg S. Africa **108** A3
Pikeville U.S.A. **136** D3
Piła Pol. **57** D2
Pilar Arg. **153** C4
Pilar Para. **152** C3
Pilliga Austr. **117** D2
Pilões, Serra dos *mts* Brazil
154 C1
Pimenta Bueno Brazil **150** C4
Pinamar Arg. **153** C4
Pınarbaşı Turkey **92** B2
Pinar del Río Cuba **144** B2
Pínčzów Pol. **57** E2
Pindaré *r.* Brazil **151** E3
Pindos Mountains Greece *see*
 Pindus Mountains
Pindus Mountains Greece **65** B3
Pine Bluff U.S.A. **138** B2
Pine Creek Austr. **114** C1
Pinedale U.S.A. **134** B2
Pinega Rus. Fed. **40** D2
Pinehouse Lake Can. **127** E2
Pineios *r.* Greece **65** B3
Pine Point Can. **126** D1
Pine Ridge U.S.A. **134** C2
Pinetown S. Africa **109** D2
Pingdingshan China **82** B2
Pinggu China **83** A3
Pingjiang China **83** A3
Pingliang China **82** A2
P'ingtung Taiwan **83** C3
Pingxiang *Guangxi* China **83** A3
Pingxiang *Jiangxi* China **83** B3
Pingyin China **82** B2
Pinheiro Brazil **151** E3
Pinnaberg Ger. **55** D1
Pinotepa Nacional Mex. **143** C3
Pinsk Belarus **42** C3
Pioche U.S.A. **133** D3
Piodi Dem. Rep. Congo **105** C3
Pionki Rus. Fed. **57** E2
Piotrków Trybunalski Pol. **57** D2
Pipestone U.S.A. **135** D2
Pipmuacan, Réservoir *resr* Can.
129 C2
Piquiri *r.* Brazil **154** B2
Piracanjuba Brazil **154** C1
Piracicaba Brazil **154** C2
Piracicaba *r.* Brazil **155** D1
Piraçununga Brazil **154** C2
Piraeus Greece **65** B3
Piraí do Sul Brazil **154** C2
Pirajuí Brazil **154** C2
Piranhas Brazil **154** B1
Piranhas *r.* Brazil **151** F3
Pirapora Brazil **155** D1
Pires do Rio Brazil **154** C1
Piripiri Brazil **151** E3
Pirmasens Ger. **54** C3
Pirna Ger. **55** F2
Piru Indon. **71** C3
Pisa Italy **62** B2
Pisagua Chile **152** A2
Pisco Peru **150** B4
Písek Czech Rep. **56** C3
Pishin Iran **91** D2
Pisté Mex. **143** D2
Pisticci Italy **63** C2
Pistoia Italy **62** B2
Pisuerga *r.* Spain **60** C1
Pit *r.* U.S.A. **132** B2

Pitanga Brazil **154** B2
Pitangui Brazil **155** D1
Pitcairn Island Pitcairn Is **111**
Pitcairn Islands *terr.*
 S. Pacific Ocean **113**
Piteå Sweden **46** E2
Piteälven *r.* Sweden **46** E2
Piteşti Romania **44** B3
Pithoragarh India **87** C2
Pitlochry U.K. **50** C2
Pitt Island Can. **126** C2
Pittsburg U.S.A. **135** E3
Pittsburgh U.S.A. **137** E2
Pittsfield U.S.A. **137** F2
Pittsworth Austr. **117** E1
Piumhi Brazil **155** D2
Piura Peru **150** A3
Pivdennyy Buh *r.* Ukr. **44** D2
Placentia Can. **129** E2
Placerville U.S.A. **133** B3
Placetas Cuba **144** C2
Plainview U.S.A. **141** D2
Planaltina Brazil **154** C1
Plaquemine U.S.A. **138** B2
Plasencia Spain **60** B1
Plasy Czech Rep. **55** F3
Plato Col. **145** C2
Platte *r.* U.S.A. **135** D2
Plattsburgh U.S.A. **137** F2
Plau Ger. **55** F1
Plauen Ger. **55** F2
Plauer See *l.* Ger. **55** F1
Plavsk Rus. Fed. **43** E3
Plây Cu Vietnam **75** B2
Playgreen Lake Can. **127** F2
Plaza Huincul Arg. **153** B4
Pleasanton U.S.A. **141** E3
Pleasant Point N.Z. **118** B3
Pleaux France **58** C2
Pledger Lake Can. **128** B1
Pleinfeld Ger. **55** E3
Plenty, Bay of *g.* N.Z. **118** C2
Plentywood U.S.A. **134** C1
Plesetsk Rus. Fed. **40** D2
Plétipi, Lac *l.* Can. **129** C1
Plettenberg Ger. **54** C2
Plettenberg Bay S. Africa **108** B3
Pleven Bulg. **64** B2
Pljevlja Serb. and Mont. **64** A2
Ploče Croatia **63** C2
Płock Pol. **57** D2
Pločno *mt.* Bos.-Herz. **63** C2
Ploemeur France **58** B2
Ploieşti Romania **44** C3
Ploskoye Rus. Fed. **43** F2
Plouzané France **58** B2
Plovdiv Bulg. **64** B2
Plungė Lith. **42** B2
Plyeshchanitsy Belarus **42** C3
Plymouth Montserrat **145** D3
Plymouth U.K. **53** A4
Plymouth U.S.A. **136** C2
Plyussa Rus. Fed. **42** C2
Plzeň Czech Rep. **56** C3
Pô Burkina **100** B3
Po *r.* Italy **62** B1
Pobeda Peak China/Kyrg. **89** F2
Pocahontas U.S.A. **138** B3
Pocatello U.S.A. **132** D2
Pochayiv Ukr. **44** C2
Pochep Rus. Fed. **43** D3
Pochinok Rus. Fed. **43** D3
Pochutla Mex. **143** C3
Pocomoke City U.S.A. **137** E3
Poços de Caldas Brazil **155** C2
Podbořany Czech Rep. **55** F2
Poddor'ye Rus. Fed. **43** D2
Podgorenskiy Rus. Fed. **45** E1
Podgorica Serb. and Mont. **64** A2
Podgornoye Rus. Fed. **94** H3

Podkamennaya Tunguska *r.* Rus. Fed. **95** I2
Podol'sk Rus. Fed. **43** E2
Podujevo Serb. and Mont. **64** B2
Pofadder S. Africa **108** A2
Pogar Rus. Fed. **43** D3
Pogradec Albania **65** B2
P'ohang S. Korea **77** B2
Pohnpei *atoll* Micronesia **110**
Poiana Mare Romania **44** B3
Poie Dem. Rep. Congo **104** C3
Pointe-Noire Congo **104** B3
Point Lake Can. **127** D1
Point Pleasant U.S.A. **136** D3
Poitiers France **58** C2
Pokaran India **86** B2
Pokhara Nepal **87** C2
Pokrovsk Rus. Fed. **95** K2
Pokrovskoye Rus. Fed. **45** E2
Polacca U.S.A. **140** T1
Pola de Lena Spain **60** B1
Poland *country* Europe **57** D2
Polatsk Belarus **42** C2
Pol-e Khomri Afgh. **86** A1
Polewali Indon. **73** C2
Poli Cameroon **104** B2
Police Pol. **56** C2
Policoro Italy **63** C2
Poligny France **59** D2
Polillo Islands Phil. **76** B2
Polis'ke Ukr. **44** C1
Polkowice Pol. **57** D2
Pollino, Monte *mt.* Italy **63** C3
Polohy Ukr. **45** E2
Polokwane S. Africa **109** C1
Polonne Ukr. **44** C1
Polson U.S.A. **132** D1
Poltava Ukr. **45** D2
Poltavka Rus. Fed. **78** D2
Poltavskaya Rus. Fed. **45** E2
Põlva Estonia **42** C2
Polyarnyy Rus. Fed. **46** G2
Polyarnyye Zori Rus. Fed. **46** G2
Polygyros Greece **65** B2
Polykastro Greece **92** A1
Polynesia *is* Pacific Ocean **158** E5
Pombal Port. **60** B2
Pomezia Italy **62** B2
Pomokaira *reg.* Fin. **46** F2
Pomorie Bulg. **64** C2
Pomorska, Zatoka *b.* Pol. **56** C2
Pompéu Brazil **155** D1
Ponca City U.S.A. **141** E1
Ponce Puerto Rico **145** D3
Pondicherry India **85** B3
Pond Inlet Can. **125** G2
Ponferrada Spain **60** B1
Pongo *watercourse* Sudan **103** A4
Pongola *r.* S. Africa **109** D2
Ponoka Can. **126** D2
Ponta Grossa Brazil **154** B3
Pontalina Brazil **154** C1
Pont-à-Mousson France **59** D2
Pontarlier France **59** D2
Pontcharra France **56** B3
Pontchartrain, Lake U.S.A. **138** B2
Ponte de Sor Port. **60** B2
Ponteix Can. **127** E3
Pontes-e-Lacerda Brazil **150** D4
Pontevedra Spain **60** B1
Pontiac *IL* U.S.A. **136** C3
Pontiac *MI* U.S.A. **136** D2
Pontianak Indon. **72** B2
Pontivy France **58** B2
Pontoetoe Suriname **151** C3
Pontoise France **49** D4
Ponton Can. **127** F2
Pontypool U.K. **53** B4
Ponziane, Isole *is* Italy **62** B2

Poochera Austr. **116** A2
Poole U.K. **53** C4
Poona India *see* Pune
Pooncarie Austr. **116** C2
Poopó, Lago de *l.* Bol. **152** B2
Popayán Col. **150** B2
Popigay *r.* Rus. Fed. **95** J2
Popiltah Austr. **116** C2
Poplar *r.* Can. **127** F2
Poplar Bluff U.S.A. **135** E3
Popocatépetl, Volcán *vol.* Mex. **121**
Popokabaka Dem. Rep. Congo **104** B3
Popovo Bulg. **64** C2
Poprad Slovakia **57** E3
Porangatu Brazil **151** E4
Porbandar India **86** B2
Porcupine *r.* Can./U.S.A. **124** C2
Poreč Croatia **62** B1
Pori Fin. **47** E3
Porirua N.Z. **118** B3
Porkhov Rus. Fed. **42** C2
Pornic France **58** B2
Poronaysk Rus. Fed. **81** F1
Poros Greece **65** B3
Porsgrunn Norway **47** B4
Portadown U.K. **51** C1
Portaferry U.K. **51** D1
Portage U.S.A. **136** C2
Portage la Prairie Can. **127** F3
Port Alberni Can. **126** C3
Portalegre Port. **60** B2
Portales U.S.A. **141** D2
Port Alexander U.S.A. **126** B2
Port Alice Can. **126** C2
Port Angeles U.S.A. **132** B1
Port Arthur Austr. **115** D4
Port Arthur U.S.A. **141** F3
Port Askaig U.K. **50** A3
Port Augusta Austr. **116** B2
Port-au-Prince Haiti **145** C3
Port aux Choix Can. **129** E1
Port Blair India **75** A2
Port Campbell Austr. **116** C3
Port Chalmers N.Z. **118** B4
Port Charlotte U.S.A. **139** D3
Port-de-Paix Haiti **145** C3
Port Edward Can. **126** B2
Porteirinha Brazil **155** D1
Portel Brazil **151** D3
Port Elgin Can. **128** B2
Port Elizabeth S. Africa **109** C3
Port Ellen U.K. **50** A3
Port Erin Isle of Man **52** A2
Porterville S. Africa **108** A3
Porterville U.S.A. **133** C3
Port Fairy Austr. **116** C3
Port Fitzroy N.Z. **118** C2
Port-Gentil Gabon **104** A3
Port Harcourt Nigeria **101** C4
Port Hardy Can. **126** C2
Port Hawkesbury Can. **129** D2
Port Hedland Austr. **114** A2
Porthmadog U.K. **52** A3
Port Hope Simpson Can. **129** E1
Port Huron U.S.A. **136** D2
Portimão Port. **60** B2
Portland *N.S.W.* Austr. **117** D2
Portland *Vic.* Austr. **116** C3
Portland *ME* U.S.A. **137** F2
Portland *OR* U.S.A. **132** B1
Portland Canal *inlet* Can. **126** B2
Portlaoise Rep. of Ireland **51** C2
Port Lavaca U.S.A. **141** E3
Port Lincoln Austr. **116** B2
Port Loko Sierra Leone **100** A4
Port Louis Mauritius **99**
Port Macquarie Austr. **117** E2
Port McNeill Can. **126** C2
Port-Menier Can. **129** D2

Port Moresby P.N.G. **71** D3
Port Ness U.K. **50** A1
Port Nolloth S. Africa **108** A2
Porto Port. *see* Oporto
Porto Acre Brazil **150** C3
Porto Alegre Brazil **152** C4
Porto Artur Brazil **151** D4
Porto dos Gaúchos Óbidos Brazil **151** D4
Porto Esperidião Brazil **150** D4
Portoferraio Italy **62** B2
Porto Franco Brazil **151** E3
Port of Spain Trin. and Tob. **145** D3
Portogruaro Italy **62** B1
Portomaggiore Italy **62** B2
Porto Mendes Brazil **154** B2
Porto Murtinho Brazil **152** B2
Porto Nacional Brazil **151** E4
Porto-Novo Benin **100** C4
Porto Primavera, Represa *resr* Brazil **154** B2
Porto Santana Brazil **151** D3
Porto Seguro Brazil **155** E1
Porto Tolle Italy **62** B2
Porto Torres Italy **62** A2
Porto-Vecchio France **59** D3
Porto Velho Brazil **150** C3
Portoviejo Ecuador **150** A3
Port Phillip Bay Austr. **116** C3
Port Pirie Austr. **116** B2
Portree U.K. **50** A2
Port Renfrew Can. **126** C3
Portrush U.K. **51** C1
Port Said Egypt **102** B1
Port Shepstone S. Africa **109** D3
Portsmouth U.K. **53** C4
Portsmouth *NH* U.S.A. **137** F2
Portsmouth *OH* U.S.A. **136** D3
Portsmouth *VA* U.S.A. **137** E3
Portstewart U.K. **51** C1
Port St Joe U.S.A. **139** C3
Port St Johns S. Africa **109** C3
Port Sudan Sudan **102** B3
Port Sulphur U.S.A. **138** C3
Port Talbot U.K. **53** B4
Portugal *country* Europe **60** B2
Portumna Rep. of Ireland **51** B2
Port-Vendres France **59** C3
Port Vila Vanuatu **112**
Porvoo Fin. **47** F3
Poryŏng S. Korea **77** B2
Posadas Arg. **152** C3
Poshekhon'ye Rus. Fed. **43** E2
Posio Fin. **46** F2
Poso Indon. **73** C2
Posse Brazil **151** E4
Pößneck Ger. **55** F1
Post U.S.A. **141** D2
Poste-de-la-Baleine Can. *see* Kuujjuarapik
Postmasburg S. Africa **108** B2
Posušje Bos.-Herz. **63** C2
Poteau U.S.A. **141** F1
Potenza Italy **63** C2
Poti *r.* Brazil **151** E3
P'ot'i Georgia **93** C1
Potiskum Nigeria **101** D3
Potomac, South Branch *r.* U.S.A. **137** E3
Potosí Bol. **152** B2
Pototan Phil. **76** B2
Potrero del Llano Mex. **140** C1
Potsdam Ger. **55** F1
Potsdam U.S.A. **137** F2
Pottstown U.S.A. **137** E2
Pottsville U.S.A. **137** E2
Pouch Cove Can. **129** E2
Poughkeepsie U.S.A. **137** F2
Poulton-le-Fylde U.K. **52** B3
Pouso Alegre Brazil **155** C2

pôuthĭsăt Cambodia 75 B2
ovažská Bystrica Slovakia 57 D3
ovlen *mt.* Serb. and Mont. 64 A2
óvoa de Varzim Port. 60 B1
ovorino Rus. Fed. 45 F1
owell U.S.A. 134 B2
owell, Lake *resr* U.S.A. 133 D3
oxoréu Brazil 154 B1
oyang Hu *l.* China 83 B3
ožarevac Serb. and Mont. 64 B2
oza Rica Mex. 143 C2
ožega Croatia 63 C1
ožega Serb. and Mont. 64 B2
ozm Tiăb Iran 91 D2
oznań Pol. 57 D2
ozoblanco Spain 60 C2
ozzuoli Italy 62 B2
rabumulih Indon. 72 B2
rachatice Czech Rep. 56 C3
rado Brazil 155 C1
'achuap Khiri Khan Thai. 75 A2
rague Czech Rep. 56 C2
raha Cape Verde *see* Prague
raia Cape Verde 98
rairie Dog Town Fork *r.* U.S.A.
  141 D2
rapat Indon. 72 A1
rata Brazil 154 C1
rato Italy 59 D3
ratt U.S.A. 135 D3
'aya Indon. 73 C2
reăh Vihear Cambodia 75 B2
rechistoye Rus. Fed. 43 F2
reeceville Can. 127 E2
reili Latvia 42 C2
'emer Austr. 117 D2
émery France 59 D3
remnitz Ger. 55 F1
renzlau Ger. 55 F1
reparis Island Cocos Is 75 A2
reparis North Channel Cocos Is
  75 A2
reparis South Channel Cocos Is
  75 A2
rerov Czech Rep. 57 D3
rescott U.S.A. 140 B2
reševo Serb. and Mont. 64 B2
residencia Roque Sáenz Peña Arg.
  152 B3
residente Dutra Brazil 151 E3
residente Epitácio Brazil 154 B2
residente Prudente Brazil 154 B2
residio U.S.A. 140 D3
resov Slovakia 57 E3
resque Isle U.S.A. 137 G1
ressel Ger. 55 F2
reštice Czech Rep. 55 F3
reston U.K. 52 B3
reston U.S.A. 132 D2
restwick U.K. 50 B3
'eto *r.* Brazil 155 C1
retoria S. Africa 109 C2
reveza Greece 65 B3
'rey Vêng Cambodia 75 B2
riboj Serb. and Mont. 64 A2
rice U.S.A. 133 D3
rienai Lith. 42 B3
rieska S. Africa 108 B2
rievidza Slovakia 57 D3
rijedor Bos.-Herz. 63 C2
rikaspiyskaya Nizmennost' *lowland*
  Kazakh./Rus. Fed. *see*
  Caspian Lowland
rilep Macedonia 65 B2
rimorsk Rus. Fed. 42 C1
rimorsko-Akhtarsk Rus. Fed. 45 E2
rimrose Lake Can. 127 D2
rince Albert Can. 124 E3

Prince Albert S. Africa 108 B3
Prince Albert Peninsula Can. 124 E2
Prince Albert Road S. Africa 108 B3
Prince Alfred, Cape Can. 124 D2
Prince Alfred Hamlet S. Africa 108 A3
Prince Charles Island Can. 125 G2
Prince Charles Mountains Antarctica
  119 E2
Prince Edward Island *prov.* Can.
  129 D2
Prince George Can. 126 C2
Prince of Wales Island Can. 124 F2
Prince of Wales Island U.S.A. 126 B2
Prince Patrick Island Can. 124 E1
Prince Regent Inlet *sea chan.* Can.
  125 F2
Prince Rupert Can. 126 B2
Princess Charlotte Bay Austr. 115 D1
Princess Royal Island Can. 126 C2
Princeton Can. 126 C3
Principe *i.* São Tomé and Principe
  104 A2
Prineville U.S.A. 132 B2
Priozersk Rus. Fed. 47 G3
Pripet *r.* Belarus *see* Prypyats'
Pripet Marshes Belarus/Ukr. 42 B3
Priština Serb. and Mont. 64 B2
Pritzwalk Ger. 55 F1
Privlaka Croatia 62 C2
Privolzhsk Rus. Fed. 43 F2
Prizren Serb. and Mont. 64 B2
Professor van Blommestein Meer *resr*
  Suriname 151 D2
Progreso Mex. 143 D2
Prokhladnyy Rus. Fed. 93 C1
Prokup'je Serb. and Mont. 64 B2
Proletarsk Rus. Fed. 45 F2
Prophet *r.* Can. 124 D3
Prophet River Can. 126 C2
Proserpine Austr. 115 D2
Protvino Rus. Fed. 43 E3
Provadiya Bulg. 64 C2
Provence *reg.* France 59 D3
Providence U.S.A. 137 G2
Providence River Can. 126 C2
Providencia, Isla de *i.* Caribbean Sea
  144 B3
Provideniya Rus. Fed. 95 O2
Provo U.S.A. 132 D2
Provost Can. 127 D2
Prudentópolis Brazil 154 B3
Prudhoe Bay U.S.A. 124 C2
Prüm Ger. 54 C2
Prunelli-di-Fiumorbo France 59 D3
Pruszków Pol. 57 E2
Prut *r.* Europe 44 C2
Pryluky Ukr. 45 D1
Prymors'k Ukr. 45 E1
Pryor U.S.A. 141 E1
Prypyats' *r.* Belarus 42 C3
Przemyśl Pol. 57 E3
Psara *i.* Greece 65 C3
Psebay Rus. Fed. 93 C1
Pskov Rus. Fed. 42 C2
Pskov, Lake Estonia/Rus. Fed. 42 C2
Ptolemaida Greece 65 B2
Ptuj Slovenia 62 C1
Pucallpa Peru 150 B3
Pucheng China 83 B3
Puchezh Rus. Fed. 43 F2
Puch'ŏn N. Korea 77 B2
Puck Pol. 57 D2
Pudasjärvi Fin. 46 F2
Pudong China 82 C2
Pudozh Rus. Fed. 40 C2
Puebla Mex. 143 C3
Pueblo U.S.A. 134 C3
Puelen Arg. 153 B4
Puente-Genil Spain 60 C2
Puerto Aisén Chile 153 A5

Puerto Alegre Bol. 152 B2
Puerto Ángel Mex. 143 C3
Puerto Armuelles Panama 144 B4
Puerto Ayacucho Venez. 150 C2
Puerto Barrios Guat. 143 D3
Puerto Cabezas Nic. 144 B3
Puerto Carreño Venez. 150 C2
Puerto Cisnes Chile 153 A5
Puerto Cortés Mex. 142 A2
Puerto Escondido Mex. 143 C3
Puerto Frey Bol. 152 B2
Puerto Inírida Col. 150 C2
Puerto Isabel Bol. 152 C2
Puerto Leguizamo Col. 150 B3
Puerto Libertad Mex. 142 A2
Puerto Limón Costa Rica 144 B3
Puertollano Spain 60 C2
Puerto Madryn Arg. 153 B5
Puerto Maldonado Peru 150 C4
Puerto Montt Chile 153 A5
Puerto Natales Chile 153 A6
Puerto Nuevo Col. 150 C2
Puerto Peñasco Mex. 142 A1
Puerto Pinasco Para. 152 C2
Puerto Plata Dom. Rep. 145 C3
Puerto Portillo Peru 150 B3
Puerto Princesa Phil. 76 A3
Puerto Rico Arg. 154 A3
Puerto Rico *terr.* West Indies 145 D3
Puerto Rico Trench *sea feature*
  Caribbean Sea 160 B4
Puerto San José Guat. 144 A3
Puerto Santa Cruz Arg. 153 B6
Puerto Vallarta Mex. 142 B2
Pugachev Rus. Fed. 41 D3
Pugal India 86 B2
Pukaki, Lake N.Z. 118 B3
Pukapuka *atoll* Cook Is 111
Pukatawagan Can. 127 E2
Pukchin N. Korea 77 B1
Pukch'ŏng N. Korea 77 B1
Pukekohe N.Z. 118 B2
Puksubaek-san *mt.* N. Korea 77 B1
Pula Croatia 62 B2
Pula Italy 62 A3
Pulkkila Fin. 46 F3
Pullman U.S.A. 132 C1
Pulog, Mount Phil. 76 B2
Puná, Isla *i.* Ecuador 150 A3
Punakaiki N.Z. 118 B3
Punda Maria S. Africa 109 D1
Pune India 85 B2
P'ungsan N. Korea 77 B1
Púnguè *r.* Moz. 107 C2
Punta Alta Arg. 153 B4
Punta Arenas Chile 153 A6
Punta Balestrieri *mt.* Italy 62 A2
Punta del Este Uru. 153 C4
Punta Gorda Belize 143 D3
Puntarenas Costa Rica 144 B3
Punto Fijo Venez. 150 B1
Puolanka Fin. 46 F3
Pur *r.* Rus. Fed. 40 G2
Puri India 87 C3
Purmerend Neth. 54 B1
Purnia India 87 C2
Puruliya India 87 C2
Purus *r.* Peru 150 C3
Purwakarta Indon. 72 B2
Puryŏng N. Korea 77 B1
Pusan S. Korea 77 B2
Pushkinskiye Gory Rus. Fed. 42 C2
Pustoshka Rus. Fed. 42 C2
Putao Myanmar 74 A1
Putian China 83 B3
Puting, Tanjung *pt* Indon. 73 C2
Putlitz Ger. 55 F1
Putrajaya Malaysia 72 B1
Puttgarden Ger. 56 C2
Putumayo *r.* Col. 150 B3

Putusibau Indon. **73** C1
Putyvl' Ukr. **45** D1
Puvurnituq Can. **128** C1
Puyang China **82** B2
Puylaurens France **58** C3
Pwllheli U.K. **52** A3
Pyapon Myanmar **74** A2
Pyasina r. Rus. Fed. **94** H2
Pyatigorsk Rus. Fed. **41** D4
P"yatykhatky Ukr. **45** D2
Pyè Myanmar **74** A2
Pyetrykaw Belarus **42** C3
Pyhäjärvi l. Fin. **47** E3
Pyhäjoki r. Fin. **46** E3
Pyhäsalmi Fin. **46** F3
Pyinmana Myanmar **74** A2
Pyöksŏng N. Korea **77** B2
P'yŏngang N. Korea **77** B2
P'yŏngsan N. Korea **77** B2
P'yŏngyang N. Korea **77** B2
Pyramid Lake U.S.A. **132** C2
Pyramids of Giza tourist site Egypt **92** B3
Pyrenees mts Europe **61** D1
Pyrgos Greece **65** B3
Pyryatyn Ukr. **45** D1
Pyrzyce Pol. **56** C2
Pytalovo Rus. Fed. **42** C2
Pyxaria mt. Greece **65** B3

Qaanaaq Greenland see Thule
Qacha's Nek Lesotho **109** C3
Qādub Yemen **91** C3
Qagan Nur China **82** B1
Qaidam Pendi basin China **80** C2
Qalansīyah Yemen **91** C3
Qal'at Bīshah Saudi Arabia **90** B2
Qamanirjuaq Lake Can. **127** F1
Qamar, Ghubbat al b. Yemen **91** C3
Qam Hadīl Saudi Arabia **90** B3
Qarshi Uzbek. **89** D3
Qaryat al Ulyā Saudi Arabia **91** B2
Qasigiannguit Greenland **125** I3
Qaşr-e Qand Iran **91** D2
Qaşr-e Shīrīn Iran **93** C2
Qassimiut Greenland **125** I3
Qa'ţabah Yemen **90** B3
Qatar country Asia **91** C2
Qattara Depression Egypt **102** A2
Qausuittuq Can. see Resolute
Qazax Azer. **93** C1
Qazmämmäd Azer. **93** C1
Qazvin Iran **93** C2
Qeqertarsuaq i. Greenland **125** I2
Qeqertarsuatsiaat Greenland **125** I2
Qeqertarsuup Tunua b. Greenland **125** I2
Qeshm Iran **91** D2
Qianjiang Chongqing China **83** A3
Qianjiang Hubei China **83** B2
Qian Shan mts China **77** A1
Qidong China **82** C2
Qiemo China **80** F3
Qijiang China **83** A3
Qijiaojing China **80** C2
Qikiqtarjuaq Can. **125** H2
Qila Ladgasht Pak. **86** A2
Qillak i. Greenland **125** J2
Qimen China **83** B3
Qimusseriarsuaq b. Greenland **125** H1
Qina Egypt **102** B2
Qingdao China **82** C2
Qinghai prov. China **87** D1
Qinghai Hu salt l. China **80** C2
Qinghai Nanshan mts China **80** C2

Qingyuan Guangdong China **83** B3
Qingyuan Liaoning China **77** A1
Qingzang Gaoyuan plat. China see Tibet, Plateau of
Qingzhou China **82** B2
Qinhuangdao China **82** B2
Qin Ling mts China **82** A2
Qinyang China **82** B2
Qinzhou China **83** A3
Qionghai China **83** B4
Qionglai Shan mts China **82** A2
Qiongshan China **83** B4
Qiqihar China **81** E1
Qīr Iran **93** D3
Qitaihe China **78** B1
Qixian China **82** B2
Qogir Feng mt. China/Jammu and Kashmir see **K2**
Qom Iran **93** C2
Qomolangma Feng mt. China/Nepal see Everest, Mount
Qo'ng'irot Uzbek. **88** C2
Qo'qon Uzbek. **89** C2
Qoraqalpog'iston Uzbek. **88** C2
Quakenbrück Ger. **54** C1
Quang Ngai Vietnam **75** B2
Quang Tri Vietnam **74** B2
Quanzhou Fujian China **83** B3
Quanzhou Guangxi China **83** B3
Quartu Sant'Elena Italy **62** A3
Quartzsite U.S.A. **140** B2
Quba Azer. **93** C1
Queanbeyan Austr. **117** D3
Québec Can. **129** C2
Québec prov. Can. **128** C1
Quedlinburg Ger. **55** E2
Queen Charlotte Can. **126** B2
Queen Charlotte Islands Can. **126** B2
Queen Charlotte Sound sea chan. Can. **126** C2
Queen Charlotte Strait Can. **126** C2
Queen Elizabeth Islands Can. **124** E1
Queen Maud Gulf Can. **124** F2
Queen Maud Land reg. Antarctica **119** C2
Queen Maud Mountains Antarctica **119** I1
Queensland state Austr. **115** D2
Queenstown Austr. **115** D4
Queenstown N.Z. **118** A4
Queenstown S. Africa **109** C3
Quelimane Moz. **107** C2
Quemado U.S.A. **140** B2
Querência do Norte Brazil **154** B2
Querétaro Mex. **143** B2
Querfurt Ger. **55** E2
Quesnel Can. **126** C2
Quesnel Lake Can. **126** C2
Quetta Pak. **86** A1
Quezaltenango Guat. **143** C3
Quezon Phil. **76** A3
Quezon City Phil. **76** B2
Quibala Angola **106** A1
Quibdó Col. **150** B2
Quiberon France **58** B2
Quillan France **58** C3
Quilmes Arg. **153** C4
Quilon India **85** B4
Quilpie Austr. **115** D2
Quilpué Chile **153** A4
Quimbele Angola **104** B3
Quimilí Arg. **152** B3
Quimper France **58** B2
Quimperlé France **58** B2
Quincy IL U.S.A. **136** B3
Quincy MA U.S.A. **137** F2
Qui Nhon Vietnam **75** B2
Quinto Spain **61** C1
Quionga Moz. **105** E4
Quirindi Austr. **117** E2

Quissico Moz. **107** C2
Quitapa Angola **106** B4
Quito Ecuador **150** B3
Quixadá Brazil **151** F3
Qujing China **83** A3
Qumar He r. China **87** D1
Quoich r. Can. **127** F1
Qurayat Oman **91** C2
Qŭrghonteppa Tajik. **89** D3
Quzhou China **83** B3

Raab r. Austria **57** D3
Raahe Fin. **46** E3
Raalte Neth. **54** C1
Raas i. Indon. **73** C2
Raba Indon. **73** C2
Rabat Morocco **100** B1
Rābigh Saudi Arabia **90** A2
Race, Cape Can. **129** E2
Raceland U.S.A. **138** B3
Rach Gia Vietnam **75** B3
Racine U.S.A. **136** C2
Radā' Yemen **90** B3
Rădăuţi Romania **44** C2
Radcliff U.S.A. **136** C3
Radebeul Ger. **55** F2
Radhanpur India **86** B2
Radisson Can. **128** C1
Radom Pol. **57** E2
Radomsko Pol. **57** D2
Radomyshl' Ukr. **44** C1
Radoviš Macedonia **63** D2
Radviliškis Lith. **42** B2
Raḍwá, Jabal mt. Saudi Arabia **90** A2
Radyvyliv Ukr. **44** C1
Rae Bareli India **87** C2
Rae-Edzo Can. **126** D1
Rae Lakes Can. **126** D1
Raeren Belgium **54** C2
Raetihi N.Z. **118** C2
Rafaela Arg. **152** B4
Rafaï C.A.R. **104** C2
Rafḥā' Saudi Arabia **90** B2
Rafsanjān Iran **93** D2
Ragang, Mount vol. Phil. **76** B3
Ragusa Italy **62** B3
Raha Indon. **73** C2
Rahachow Belarus **42** D3
Rahimyar Khan Pak. **86** B2
Raichur India **85** B3
Raigarh India **87** C2
Rainbow Lake Can. **126** C2
Rainier, Mount vol. U.S.A. **132** B1
Rainy Lake Can./U.S.A. **127** F3
Rainy River Can. **127** F3
Raipur India **87** C2
Raisio Fin. **47** E3
Rajahmundry India **85** C3
Rajang r. Malaysia **73** C1
Rajanpur Pak. **86** B2
Rajapalaiyam India **85** B4
Rajasthan Canal India **86** B2
Rajgarh India **86** B2
Rajkot India **86** B2
Rajpur India **86** B2
Rajshahi Bangl. **87** C2
Rakaia r. N.Z. **118** B3
Rakhiv Ukr. **44** B2
Rakitnoye Rus. Fed. **45** E1
Rakke Estonia **42** C2
Rakovník Czech Rep. **55** F2
Rakvere Estonia **42** C2
Raleigh U.S.A. **139** E1
Ralik Chain is Marshall Is **110**
Rambutyo Island P.N.G. **71** D3

Ramgarh India **86** B2
Rāmhormoz Iran **93** C2
Râmnicu Sārat Romania **44** C2
Râmnicu Vâlcea Romania **44** B2
Ramon' Rus. Fed. **43** E3
Ramotswa Botswana **109** C1
Rampur India **87** B2
Ramree Island Myanmar **74** A2
Ramsey Isle of Man **52** A2
Ramsgate U.K. **53** D4
Ramsing India **74** A1
Ranaghat India **87** D2
Ranau Malaysia **73** C1
Rancagua Chile **153** A4
Ranchi India **87** C2
Randers Denmark **47** C4
Rangiora N.Z. **118** B3
Rangitaiki r. N.Z. **118** C2
Rangpur Bangl. **87** C2
Rankin Inlet Can. **127** D2
Rankin's Springs Austr. **117** D2
Ranong Thai. **75** A3
Ransiki Indon. **71** C3
Rantaupanjang Indon. **73** C2
Rantauprapat Indon. **72** A1
Rantepao Indon. **73** C2
Ranua Fin. **46** F2
Ranyah, Wādī *watercourse*
   Saudi Arabia **90** B2
Raoul Island Kermadec Is **111**
Rapa *i.* Fr. Polynesia **111**
Rapid City U.S.A. **134** C2
Rapla Estonia **42** B2
Rapur India **86** A2
Rarotonga *i.* Cook Is **111**
Rasa, Punta *pt* Arg. **153** B5
Ra's al Khaymah U.A.E. **91** C2
Raseiniai Lith. **42** B2
Ras Dejen *mt.* Eth. **103** B3
Rasht Iran **93** C2
Ras Koh *mt.* Pak. **86** A2
Rasony Belarus **42** C2
Rasskazovo Rus. Fed. **43** F3
Ras Tannūrah Saudi Arabia **91** C2
Rastede Ger. **55** D1
Ratak Chain *is* Marshall Is **110**
Rātān Sweden **47** C3
Ratangarh India **86** B2
Rat Buri Thai. **75** A2
Rathedaung Myanmar **74** A1
Rathenow Ger. **55** F1
Rathlin Island U.K. **51** C1
Ratlam India **86** B2
Ratnagiri India **85** B3
Ratnapura Sri Lanka **85** C4
Ratne Ukr. **44** B1
Raton U.S.A. **140** C1
Rattray Head U.K. **50** D2
Ratzeburg Ger. **55** E1
Raufarhöfn Iceland **46** [inset]
Raukumara Range *mts* N.Z. **118** C2
Rauma Fin. **47** D3
Raung, Gunung *vol.* Indon. **73** C2
Raurkela India **87** C2
Ravalli U.S.A. **132** D1
Ravānsar Iran **93** C2
Ravenna Italy **62** B2
Ravensburg Ger. **56** B3
Ravi *r.* Pak. **86** B1
Rawalpindi Pak. **86** B1
Rawicz Pol. **57** D2
Rawlinna Austr. **114** B3
Rawlins U.S.A. **134** B2
Rawson Arg. **153** B5
Rayagada India **85** C2
Raychikhinsk Rus. Fed. **81** E1

Raydah Yemen **90** B3
Rayevskiy Rus. Fed. **41** E3
Raymond Can. **132** D1
Raymond U.S.A. **132** B1
Raymond Terrace Austr. **117** E2
Raymondville U.S.A. **141** E3
Rayón Mex. **143** C2
Rayong Thai. **75** B2
Rayyis Saudi Arabia **90** B2
Raz, Pointe du *pt* France **58** B2
Razāzah, Buḩayrat ar *l.* Iraq **93** C2
Razgrad Bulg. **64** C2
Razim, Lacul *lag.* Romania **44** C3
Razlog Bulg. **64** B2
Ré, Île de *i.* France **58** B2
Reading U.K. **53** C4
Reading U.S.A. **137** E2
Rebiana Sand Sea *des.* Libya **101** E2
Rebun-tō *i.* Japan **78** D1
Recherche, Archipelago of the *is*
   Austr. **114** B3
Rechytsa Belarus **43** D3
Recife Brazil **151** F3
Recife, Cape S. Africa **109** C3
Reconquista Arg. **152** C3
Red *r.* U.S.A. **141** F2
Red Bay Can. **129** E1
Red Bluff U.S.A. **132** B2
Redcar U.K. **52** C2
Redcliff Can. **127** D2
Red Cliffs Austr. **116** C3
Red Deer Can. **126** D2
Red Deer *r.* Can. **124** E3
Red Deer Lake Can. **127** E2
Redding U.S.A. **132** B2
Redditch U.K. **53** C3
Redfield U.S.A. **135** D2
Red Lake Can. **128** A1
Red Lakes U.S.A. **135** E1
Red Lodge U.S.A. **132** E1
Redmond U.S.A. **132** B2
Red Oak U.S.A. **135** D2
Redondo Port. **60** B2
Red Sea Africa/Asia **90** A2
Redstone *r.* Can. **126** C1
Reduzum Neth. **54** B1
Red Wing U.S.A. **135** E2
Redwood Falls U.S.A. **135** D2
Ree, Lough *l.* Rep. of Ireland **51** C2
Reedsport U.S.A. **132** B2
Reefton N.Z. **118** B3
Regen Ger. **55** F3
Regência Brazil **155** E1
Regensburg Ger. **55** F3
Regenstauf Ger. **55** F3
Reggane Alg. **100** C2
Reggio di Calabria Italy **63** C3
Reggio nell'Emilia Italy **62** B2
Reghin Romania **44** B2
Regina Can. **124** F3
Rehoboth Namibia **108** A1
Reichenbach Ger. **55** F2
Reichshoffen France **59** D2
Reidsville U.S.A. **139** E1
Reigate U.K. **53** C4
Reims France **59** C2
Reina Adelaida, Archipiélago de la *is*
   Chile **153** A6
Reinbek Ger. **55** E1
Reindeer *r.* Can. **127** E2
Reindeer Island Can. **127** F2
Reindeer Lake Can. **127** E2
Reine Norway **46** C2
Reinsfeld Ger. **54** C3
Reitz S. Africa **108** B2
Reivilo S. Africa **108** B2
Reliance Can. **127** E1
Relizane Alg. **61** D2
Remeshk Iran **91** C2
Remiremont France **59** D2

Remscheid Ger. **54** C2
Rendsburg Ger. **56** B2
Renfrew Can. **137** E2
Rengat Indon. **72** B2
Reni Ukr. **44** C2
Renmark Austr. **116** C2
Rennell *i.* Solomon Is **110**
Rennerod Ger. **54** D2
Rennes France **58** B2
Rennie Lake Can. **127** E1
Reno *r.* Italy **62** B2
Reno U.S.A. **133** C3
Renshou China **83** A3
Rensselaer U.S.A. **136** B2
Renukut India **87** C2
Renwick N.Z. **118** B3
Reo Indon. **73** C2
Republican *r.* U.S.A. **134** D3
Repulse Bay Can. **125** D2
Requena Peru **150** B3
Requena Spain **61** C2
Reserva Brazil **154** B2
Resistencia Arg. **152** C3
Reşiţa Romania **44** B2
Resolute Can. **124** F2
Resolution Island Can. **125** H2
Rethel France **59** C2
Rethymno Greece **65** B3
Réunion *terr.* Indian Ocean **99**
Reus Spain **61** D1
Reutlingen Ger. **56** B3
Revelstoke Can. **126** D2
Revillagigedo, Islas *is* Mex. **142** A3
Revillagigedo Island U.S.A. **126** B2
Rewa India **87** C2
Rexburg U.S.A. **132** D2
Reykjanestá *pt* Iceland **46** [inset]
Reykjavík Iceland **46** [inset]
Reynosa Mex. **143** C2
Rēzekne Latvia **42** C2
Rhein *r.* Ger. *see* Rhine
Rheine Ger. **54** C1
Rheinsberg Ger. **55** F1
Rhin *r.* France *see* Rhine
Rhine *r.* France **56** B3
Rhine *r.* Ger. **54** C2
Rhinelander U.S.A. **136** C1
Rhinluch *marsh* Ger. **55** F1
Rhinow Ger. **55** F1
Rhode Island *state* U.S.A. **137** F2
Rhodes Greece **65** C3
Rhodes *i.* Greece **65** C3
Rhodope Mountains Bulg./Greece
   64 B2
Rhône *r.* France/Switz. **59** C3
Rhoufi Alg. **61** E1
Rhyl U.K. **52** B3
Riaño Spain **60** B1
Riau, Kepulauan *is* Indon. **72** B1
Ribadeo Spain **60** B1
Ribadesella Spain **60** B1
Ribas do Rio Pardo Brazil **154** B2
Ribáuè Moz. **107** C1
Ribble *r.* U.K. **52** B3
Ribécourt-Dreslincourt France **54** A3
Ribeira *r.* Brazil **154** C2
Ribeirão Preto Brazil **154** C2
Riberac France **58** C2
Riberalta Bol. **152** B2
Rîbniţa Moldova **44** C2
Ribnitz-Damgarten Ger. **56** C2
Rice Lake U.S.A. **136** B1
Richards Bay S. Africa **109** D2
Richardson Mountains Can. **124** C2
Richfield U.S.A. **133** D3
Richland U.S.A. **132** C1
Richland Center U.S.A. **136** B2
Richmond *N.S.W.* Austr. **117** E2
Richmond *Qld* Austr. **115** D2
Richmond N.Z. **118** B3

Richmond S. Africa **108** B3
Richmond U.K. **52** C2
Richmond *IN* U.S.A. **136** D3
Richmond *KY* U.S.A. **136** D3
Richmond *VA* U.S.A. **137** E3
Rideau Lakes Can. **128** C2
Ridgecrest U.S.A. **133** C3
Riesa Ger. **55** F2
Rieste Ger. **54** D1
Riet *r.* S. Africa **109** B2
Rietberg Ger. **55** D2
Rieti Italy **62** B2
Rifle U.S.A. **134** B3
Riga Latvia **42** B2
Riga, Gulf of Estonia/Latvia **47** E4
Rīgān Iran **91** C2
Rigby U.S.A. **132** D2
Rigolet Can. **129** E1
Riihimäki Fin. **47** E3
Rijeka Croatia **62** B1
Riley U.S.A. **132** C2
Rimah, Wādī al *watercourse*
  Saudi Arabia **90** B2
Rimavská Sobota Slovakia **57** E3
Rimini Italy **62** B2
Rimouski Can. **129** D2
Ringebu Norway **47** C3
Ringkøbing Denmark **47** B4
Ringvassøya *i.* Norway **46** D2
Rinteln Ger. **55** D1
Riobamba Ecuador **150** B3
Rio Branco Brazil **150** C4
Rio Branco do Sul Brazil **154** C3
Rio Brilhante Brazil **154** B2
Rio Claro Brazil **154** C2
Rio Colorado Arg. **153** B4
Rio Cuarto Arg. **153** B4
Rio de Janeiro Brazil **155** D2
Rio do Sul Brazil **154** C3
Rio Gallegos Arg. **153** B6
Rio Grande Brazil **152** C4
Rio Grande Mex. **142** B2
Rio Grande *r.* Mex./U.S.A. **142** C2
Rio Grande City U.S.A. **141** E3
Riohacha Col. **150** B1
Rioja Peru **150** B3
Rio Lagartos Mex. **143** D2
Riom France **59** C2
Rio Mulatos Bol. **152** B2
Rio Negro Brazil **154** C3
Rio Pardo de Minas Brazil **155** D1
Rio Rancho U.S.A. **140** C1
Rio Tigre Ecuador **150** B3
Rio Verde Brazil **154** B1
Rio Verde Mex. **143** C2
Rio Verde de Mato Grosso Brazil
  154 B1
Ripky Ukr. **44** D1
Ripley U.K. **52** C3
Ripoll Spain **61** D1
Ripon U.K. **52** C2
Rishiri-tō *i.* Japan **78** D1
Risør Norway **47** B4
Ritchie S. Africa **108** B2
Ritchie's Archipelago *is* India **75** A2
Ritzville U.S.A. **132** C1
Rivadavia Arg. **152** B3
Riva del Garda Italy **62** B1
Rivas Nic. **144** B3
Rivera Uru. **152** C4
Riverhurst Can. **127** E2
Riverina *reg.* Austr. **117** D2
Riversdale S. Africa **108** B3
Riverside U.S.A. **133** C4
Riverton U.S.A. **134** B2
Riverview Can. **129** D2
Rivesaltes France **58** C3
Rivière-du-Loup Can. **129** D2
Rivne Ukr. **44** C1

Riwaka N.Z. **118** B3
Riyadh Saudi Arabia **90** B2
Rize Turkey **93** C1
Rizhao China **82** B2
Roame France **59** C2
Roanoke U.S.A. **139** E1
Roanoke *r.* U.S.A. **139** E1
Roanoke Rapids U.S.A. **139** E1
Robe Austr. **116** B3
Röbel Ger. **55** F1
Robertsfors Sweden **46** E3
Robertson S. Africa **108** A3
Robertsport Liberia **100** A4
Roberval Can. **128** C2
Robinson Range *hills* Austr. **114** A2
Robinvale Austr. **116** C2
Roblin Can. **127** E2
Robson, Mount Can. **126** D2
Rocca Busambra *mt.* Italy **62** B3
Rocha Uru. **152** C4
Rochdale U.K. **52** B3
Rochedo Brazil **154** B1
Rochefort Belgium **54** B2
Rochefort France **58** B2
Rochester *MN* U.S.A. **135** E2
Rochester *NH* U.S.A. **137** F2
Rochester *NY* U.S.A. **137** E2
Rockford U.S.A. **136** C2
Rockhampton Austr. **115** E2
Rock Hill U.S.A. **139** D2
Rockingham Austr. **114** A3
Rock Island U.S.A. **136** B2
Rock Springs *MT* U.S.A. **134** B1
Rocksprings U.S.A. **141** D3
Rock Springs *WY* U.S.A. **134** B2
Rocky Ford U.S.A. **134** C3
Rocky Mount U.S.A. **139** E1
Rocky Mountains Can./U.S.A. **130** C2
Rocourt-St-Martin France **54** A3
Rocroi France **54** A3
Rødbyhavn Denmark **56** C2
Roddickton Can. **129** E1
Rodez France **58** C3
Roding Ger. **55** F3
Rodniki Rus. Fed. **43** F2
Rodos Greece *see* Rhodes
Rodos *i.* Greece *see* Rhodes
Roebourne Austr. **114** A2
Roebuck Bay Austr. **114** B1
Roedtan S. Africa **109** C1
Roermond Neth. **54** B2
Roeselare Belgium **54** A2
Rogers U.S.A. **138** B1
Roggeveldberge *esc.* S. Africa **108** B3
Rognan Norway **46** D2
Rogue *r.* U.S.A. **132** B2
Roja Latvia **42** B2
Rokan *r.* Indon. **72** B1
Rokiškis Lith. **42** C2
Rokycany Czech Rep. **55** F3
Rokytne Ukr. **44** C1
Rolândia Brazil **154** B2
Rolla U.S.A. **135** E3
Roma Austr. **115** D2
Roma Italy *see* Rome
Roma Lesotho **109** C2
Roma U.S.A. **141** E3
Romain, Cape U.S.A. **139** E2
Roman Romania **44** C2
Roman-Kosh *mt.* Ukr. **45** D3
Romanovka *Respublika Buryatiya*
  Rus. Fed. **81** D1
Romanovka *Saratovskaya Oblast'*
  Rus. Fed. **45** F1
Rombas France **59** D2
Romblon Phil. **76** B2
Rome Italy **62** B2
Rome *GA* U.S.A. **139** C2

Rome *NY* U.S.A. **137** E2
Romford U.K. **53** D4
Romilly-sur-Seine France **59** C2
Romny Ukr. **45** D1
Romorantin-Lanthenay France **58** C2
Romsey U.K. **53** C4
Roncador, Serra do *hills* Brazil **151** D4
Ronda Spain **60** B2
Rondon Brazil **154** B2
Rondonópolis Brazil **154** B1
Rondu Jammu and Kashmir **86** B1
Rong'an China **83** A3
Rongjiang China **83** A3
Rongklang Range *mts* Myanmar **74** A1
Rønne Denmark **47** C4
Ronne Ice Shelf Antarctica **119** K2
Ronnenberg Ger. **55** D1
Ronse Belgium **54** A2
Roorkee India **87** B2
Roosendaal Neth. **54** B2
Roosevelt U.S.A. **132** E2
Roosevelt, Mount Can. **126** C2
Roosevelt Island Antarctica **119** I2
Roquefort France **58** B3
Roraima, Mount Guyana **150** C2
Røros Norway **47** C3
Rosario Arg. **153** B4
Rosario *Baja California* Mex. **142** A1
Rosario *Sinaloa* Mex. **142** B2
Rosario *Sonora* Mex. **142** B2
Rosário Brazil **151** D4
Rosarito Mex. **142** A2
Rosarno Italy **63** C3
Roscoff France **58** B2
Roscommon Rep. of Ireland **51** B2
Roscrea Rep. of Ireland **51** C2
Roseau Dominica **145** D3
Roseau U.S.A. **135** D1
Roseburg U.S.A. **132** B2
Rosenberg U.S.A. **141** E3
Rosendal Norway **48** E2
Rosengarten Ger. **55** D1
Rosenheim Ger. **56** C2
Rosetown Can. **127** E2
Roshchino Rus. Fed. **42** C1
Rosh Pinah Namibia **108** A2
Roşiori de Vede Romania **44** C3
Roskilde Denmark **47** C4
Roslavl' Rus. Fed. **43** D3
Rossano Italy **63** C3
Rossan Point *pt* Rep. of Ireland **51** B1
Ross Ice Shelf Antarctica **119** H1
Rossignol, Lake Can. **129** D2
Rossland Can. **126** D3
Rosslare Rep. of Ireland **51** C2
Rosso Maur. **100** A3
Rosso, Capo *c.* France **59** D3
Ross-on-Wye U.K. **53** B4
Rossosh' Rus. Fed. **45** E1
Ross River Can. **126** B1
Røssvatnet *l.* Norway **46** C2
Rostāq Iran **91** D3
Rosthern Can. **124** C3
Rostock Ger. **56** C2
Rostov Rus. Fed. **43** F2
Rostov-na-Donu Rus. Fed. **45** E2
Rosvik Sweden **46** D2
Roswell U.S.A. **140** D2
Rota *i.* N. Mariana Is **71** D2
Rot am See Ger. **55** E3
Rote *i.* Indon. **71** C3
Rotenburg (Wümme) Ger. **55** D1
Roth Ger. **55** E3
Rothbury U.K. **52** C2
Rothenburg ob der Tauber Ger. **55** E3
Rotherham U.K. **52** C3
Rothesay U.K. **50** B3
Roto Austr. **117** D2
Rotondo, Monte *mt.* France **59** D3
Rotorua N.Z. **118** C2

Rotorua, Lake N.Z. **118** C2
Rottenbach Ger. **55** E2
Rottenmann Austria **56** C3
Rotterdam Neth. **54** B2
Rottweil Ger. **56** B3
Rotuma *i.* Fiji **110**
Roubaix France **59** C1
Rouen France **58** C2
Round Mountain Austr. **117** E2
Round Pond *l.* Can. **129** E2
Round Rock U.S.A. **141** E2
Roundup U.S.A. **132** E1
Rousay *i.* U.K. **50** C1
Rouyn-Noranda Can. **128** C2
Rovaniemi Fin. **46** F2
Roven'ki Rus. Fed. **45** E2
Roven'ky Ukr. **45** E2
Rovereto Italy **62** B1
Rovigo Italy **62** B1
Rôviĕng Tbong Cambodia **75** B2
Rovinj Croatia **62** B1
Rowena Austr. **117** D1
Roxas Phil. **76** B2
Roxas Phil. **76** A2
Roxas Phil. **76** B3
Roxby Downs Austr. **116** B2
Roy U.S.A. **140** D1
Royale, Isle *i.* U.S.A. **136** C1
Royan France **58** B2
Roye France **54** A3
Royston U.K. **53** C3
Rozdil'na Ukr. **44** D2
Rozdol'ne Ukr. **45** D2
Rozoy-sur-Serre France **54** B3
Rtishchevo Rus. Fed. **41** D3
Ruapehu, Mount *vol.* N.Z. **118** C2
Ruapuke Island N.Z. **118** A4
Rub' al Khālī *des.* Saudi Arabia **90** B3
Rubizhne Ukr. **45** E2
Rubtsovsk Rus. Fed. **89** F1
Ruby U.S.A. **124** B2
Ruby Mountains U.S.A. **132** C2
Rudnaya Pristan' Rus. Fed. **78** C2
Rudnya Rus. Fed. **43** D3
Rudnyy Kazakh. **88** D1
Rudol'fa, Ostrov *i.* Rus. Fed. **94** F1
Rudolstadt Ger. **55** E2
Rufiji *r.* Tanz. **105** D3
Rufino Arg. **153** B4
Rufunsa Zambia **107** B1
Rugao China **82** C2
Rugby U.K. **53** C3
Rugby U.S.A. **134** C1
Rügen *i.* Ger. **56** C2
Ruhla Ger. **55** E2
Ruhnu *i.* Estonia **42** B2
Ruhr *r.* Ger. **54** C2
Rui'an China **83** C3
Ruidoso U.S.A. **140** C2
Ruiz Mex. **142** B2
Rukwa, Lake Tanz. **105** D3
Rum *i.* U.K. **50** A2
Ruma Serb. and Mont. **64** A1
Rumāh Saudi Arabia **90** B2
Rumbek Sudan **103** A4
Rumilly France **59** D2
Rum Jungle Austr. **114** C1
Runanga N.Z. **118** B3
Runcorn U.K. **52** B3
Rundu Namibia **106** A1
Ruoqiang China **89** F3
Rupert *r.* Can. **128** C1
Rupert Bay Can. **128** C1
Rusape Zimbabwe **107** C1
Ruse Bulg. **64** C2
Rushon Tajik. **89** E3
Rushville U.S.A. **134** C2
Rushworth Austr. **117** D3
Russell Can. **127** E2

Russell N.Z. **118** B2
Russellville *AL* U.S.A. **138** C2
Russellville *AR* U.S.A. **138** B1
Russellville *KY* U.S.A. **136** C3
Rüsselsheim Ger. **55** D2
Russian Federation *country*
 Asia/Europe **94** G2
Ruston U.S.A. **138** B2
Ruteng Indon. **73** D2
Ruthin U.K. **52** B3
Rutland U.S.A. **137** F2
Ruvuma *r.* Moz./Tanz. **105** E4
Ruweis U.A.E. **91** C2
Ruzayevka Kazakh. **89** D1
Ruzayevka Rus. Fed. **41** D3
Rwanda *country* Africa **105** C3
Ryazan' Rus. Fed. **43** E3
Ryazhsk Rus. Fed. **43** F3
Rybachiy, Poluostrov *pen.* Rus. Fed.
 46 G2
Rybinsk Rus. Fed. **43** E2
Rybinskoye Vodokhranilishche *resr*
 Rus. Fed. **43** E2
Rybnik Pol. **57** D2
Rybnoye Rus. Fed. **43** E3
Rye U.K. **53** D4
Ryl'sk Rus. Fed. **43** D3
Ryōtsu Japan **78** C3
Ryukyu Islands Japan **81** E3
Rzeszów Pol. **57** E2
Rzhaksa Rus. Fed. **43** F3
Rzhev Rus. Fed. **43** D2

Sa'ādatābād Iran **93** D3
Saale *r.* Ger. **55** E2
Saalfeld Ger. **55** E2
Saarbrücken Ger. **54** C3
Saaremaa *i.* Estonia **42** B2
Saarenkylä Fin. **46** F2
Saarijärvi Fin. **46** F3
Saarlouis Ger. **54** C3
Sab' Ābār Syria **92** B2
Sabadell Spain **61** D1
Sabah *state* Malaysia **73** C1
Sabalana *i.* Indon. **73** C2
Sabará Brazil **155** D1
Sabaudia Italy **62** B2
Sabhā Libya **101** D2
Sabie *r.* Moz./S. Africa **109** D2
Sabinas Mex. **143** B2
Sabinas Hidalgo Mex. **143** B2
Sable, Cape Can. **129** D2
Sable, Cape U.S.A. **139** D3
Sable Island Can. **129** E2
Sabugal Port. **60** B1
Şabyā Saudi Arabia **90** B3
Sabzevār Iran **88** C3
Sachanga Angola **106** A1
Sachigo Lake Can. **128** A1
Sach'on S. Korea **77** B3
Sachs Harbour Can. **124** D2
Sacramento U.S.A. **133** B3
Sacramento Mountains U.S.A. **140** C2
Sacramento Valley U.S.A. **132** B2
Sada S. Africa **109** C3
Sádaba Spain **61** C1
Sádiya India **74** A1
Sadoga-shima *i.* Japan **78** C3
Sa Dragonera *i.* Spain **61** D2
Säffle Sweden **47** C4
Safford U.S.A. **140** C2
Saffron Walden U.K. **53** D3
Safi Morocco **100** B1
Safonovo *Arkhangel'skaya Oblast'*
 Rus. Fed. **40** D2

Safonovo *Smolenskaya Oblast'*
 Rus. Fed. **43** D2
Safrā' as Sark *esc.* Saudi Arabia **90** B2
Saga China **87** C2
Saga Japan **79** B4
Sagaing Myanmar **74** A1
Sagamihara Japan **79** C3
Sagar India **87** B2
Saginaw U.S.A. **136** D2
Saginaw Bay U.S.A. **136** D2
Sagres Port. **60** B2
Sagua la Grande Cuba **144** B2
Saguenay *r.* Can. **137** G1
Sagunto Spain **61** C2
Sagyndyk, Mys *pt* Kazakh. **88** C2
Sahagún Spain **60** B1
Sahara *des.* Africa **100** C3
Saharan Atlas *mts* Alg. *see*
 Atlas Saharien
Saharanpur India **87** B2
Saharsa India **87** C2
Sahel *reg.* Africa **100** B3
Sahuayo Mex. **142** B2
Şāhūq *reg.* Saudi Arabia **90** B2
Saïdia Morocco **61** C2
Saidpur Bangl. **87** C2
Saigon Vietnam *see* Hồ Chí Minh City
Saiha India **74** A1
Saihan Tal China **82** B1
Saiki Japan **79** B4
Saimaa *l.* Fin. **47** F3
Sain Alto Mex. **142** B2
St Abb's Head U.K. **50** C3
St Albans U.K. **53** C4
St Alban's Head U.K. **53** B4
St Aldhelm's Head U.K.
 see St Alban's Head
St Andrews U.K. **50** C2
St Anthony Can. **129** E1
St Anthony U.S.A. **132** D2
St Arnaud Austr. **116** C3
St-Augustin Can. **129** E1
St Augustin *r.* Can. **129** E1
St Augustine U.S.A. **139** D3
St Austell U.K. **53** A4
St-Avertin France **58** C2
St-Avold France **54** C3
St Bees Head U.K. **52** B2
St-Bonnet-en-Champsaur France
 59 D3
St Bride's Bay U.K. **53** A4
St-Brieuc France **58** B2
St Catharines Can. **128** C2
St Catherine's Point *pt* U.K. **53** C4
St Charles U.S.A. **135** E3
St Clair, Lake Can./U.S.A. **128** B2
St-Claude France **59** D2
St Cloud U.S.A. **135** E1
St Croix *r.* U.S.A. **137** B2
St Croix *i.* Virgin Is (U.S.A.)
 145 D3
St David's Head U.K. **53** A4
St-Denis Réunion **99**
St-Dizier France **59** C2
Ste-Anne-des-Monts Can. **129** D2
St-Égrève France **59** D2
St Elias Mountains Can. **124** C2
Ste-Marguerite *r.* Can. **129** D1
Sainte Rose du Lac Can. **127** F2
Saintes France **58** B2
St-Étienne France **59** C2
St-Florent France **62** A2
St-Flour France **58** C2
St Francis U.S.A. **134** C3
St-Gaudens France **58** C3
St George Austr. **117** D1
St George U.S.A. **133** D3
St George Island U.S.A. **139** D3
St-Georges Can. **129** C2
St George's Grenada **145** D3

St George's Channel
Rep. of Ireland/U.K. **51** C3
St Gotthard Pass Switz. **59** D2
St Helena *i.* S. Atlantic Ocean **99**
St Helena and Dependencies *terr.*
S. Atlantic Ocean **99**
St Helena Bay S. Africa **108** A3
St Helena Bay *b.* S. Africa **108** A3
St Helens U.K. **52** B3
St Helens, Mount *vol.* U.S.A. **132** B1
St Helier Channel Is **53** B5
St-Hubert Belgium **54** B2
St-Hyacinthe Can. **137** F1
St Ignace U.S.A. **136** D1
St Ignace Island Can. **128** D2
St Ives U.K. **53** A4
St James, Cape Can. **126** D2
St-Jean, Lac *l.* Can. **129** C2
St-Jean-d'Angély France **58** B2
St-Jean-de-Monts France **58** B2
St-Jean-sur-Richelieu Can. **128** C2
St-Jérôme Can. **137** F1
St Joe *r.* U.S.A. **132** C1
Saint John Can. **125** H3
St John *r.* U.S.A. **137** G1
St John's Antigua **145** D3
St John's Can. **129** C2
St Johns U.S.A. **140** C2
St Johnsbury U.S.A. **137** F2
St Joseph U.S.A. **135** D3
St Joseph, Lake Can. **128** A1
St Joseph Island Can. **128** D2
St-Junien France **58** C2
St Kilda *is* U.K. **48** B2
St Kitts and Nevis *country* West Indies
145 D3
St-Laurent, Golfe du *g.* Can. *see*
St Lawrence, Gulf of
St-Laurent-du-Maroni Fr. Guiana
151 D2
St Lawrence *inlet* Can. **129** D2
St Lawrence, Gulf of Can. **129** D2
St Lawrence Island U.S.A. **124** A2
St-Lô France **58** B2
St Louis Senegal **100** A3
St Louis U.S.A. **135** E3
St Louis *r.* U.S.A. **135** E1
St Lucia *country* West Indies **145** D3
St Lucia Estuary S. Africa **109** D2
St-Malo France **58** B2
St-Malo, Golfe de *g.* France **58** B2
St-Martin, Cape S. Africa **108** A3
St Marys U.S.A. **137** E2
St Matthias Group *is* P.N.G. **71** D3
St-Maurice *r.* Can. **128** C2
St-Nazaire France **58** B2
St-Omer France **58** C1
St Paul Can. **127** D2
St Paul U.S.A. **135** E2
St Peter U.S.A. **135** E2
St Peter Port Channel Is **53** B5
St Petersburg Rus. Fed. **43** D7
St Petersburg U.S.A. **139** D3
St-Pierre St Pierre and Miquelon
129 C2
St Pierre and Miquelon *terr.*
N. America **129** C2
St-Pierre-d'Oléron France **58** B2
St-Pourçain-sur-Sioule France **59** C2
St Quentin Can. **137** G1
St-Quentin France **59** C2
St-Siméon Can. **129** D2
St Theresa Point Can. **127** F2
St Thomas Can. **128** B2
St-Tropez France **59** D3
St-Vaast-la-Hougue France **53** D5
St-Valery-en-Caux France **53** D5
St Vincent, Gulf Austr. **116** B3

St Vincent and the Grenadines
country West Indies **145** D3
St-Vith Belgium **54** C2
St Walburg Can. **127** C2
St-Yrieix-la-Perche France **58** C2
Saipan *i.* N. Mariana Is **71** D1
Sajama, Nevado *mt.* Bol. **152** B2
Sak *watercourse* S. Africa **108** B2
Sakai Japan **79** C4
Sakaide Japan **79** B4
Sakākah Saudi Arabia **90** B2
Sakakawea, Lake U.S.A. **134** C1
Sakarya Turkey *see* Adapazarı
Sakarya *r.* Turkey **65** D2
Sakata Japan **78** C3
Sakchu N. Korea **77** B1
Sakhalin *i.* Rus. Fed. **78** D1
Sakhile S. Africa **109** C2
Şäki Azer. **93** C1
Šakiai Lith. **42** B3
Sakishima-shotō *is* Japan **81** E3
Sakon Nakhon Thai. **74** B2
Sakrivier S. Africa **108** B3
Sakura Japan **79** D3
Saky Ukr. **45** D2
Sal *r.* Rus. Fed. **45** F2
Sala Sweden **47** D4
Salaberry-de-Valleyfield Can. **128** C2
Salacgrīva Latvia **42** B2
Sala Consilina Italy **62** C2
Salada, Laguna *l.* Mex. **140** A2
Salado *r.* Arg. **152** B4
Salado *r.* Mex. **142** C2
Salaga Ghana **100** B4
Salajwe Botswana **108** B1
Salal Chad **101** D3
Salālah Sudan **90** A2
Şalālah Oman **91** C3
Salamanca Mex. **143** B2
Salamanca Spain **60** B1
Salas Spain **60** B1
Salavan Laos **75** B2
Salawati *i.* Indon. **71** C3
Salayar *i.* Indon. **73** D2
Salbris France **58** C2
Šalčininkai Lith. **42** C3
Saldaña Spain **60** C1
Saldanha S. Africa **108** A3
Saldus Latvia **42** B2
Sale Austr. **117** D3
Salekhard Rus. Fed. **40** F2
Salem India **85** B3
Salem MO U.S.A. **135** E3
Salem OR U.S.A. **132** B2
Salen U.K. **50** B2
Salerno Italy **62** B2
Salford U.K. **52** B3
Salgado *r.* Brazil **151** F3
Salgótarján Hungary **57** D3
Salgueiro Brazil **151** F3
Salida U.S.A. **134** B3
Salihli Turkey **65** C3
Salihorsk Belarus **42** C3
Salima Malawi **107** C1
Salimo Moz. **107** C1
Salina U.S.A. **135** D3
Salina, Isola *i.* Italy **62** B3
Salina Cruz Mex. **143** C3
Salinas Brazil **155** D1
Salinas Mex. **142** B2
Salinas U.S.A. **133** B3
Salines, Cap de ses *c.* Spain **61** D2
Salinópolis Brazil **151** E3
Salisbury U.K. **53** C4
Salisbury MD U.S.A. **137** E3
Salisbury NC U.S.A. **139** D1
Salisbury Plain U.K. **53** B4
Salitre *r.* Brazil **151** E3
Salla Fin. **46** F2
Salluit Can. **125** G2

Sallyana Nepal **87** C2
Salmās Iran **93** C2
Salmon U.S.A. **132** D1
Salmon *r.* U.S.A. **132** C1
Salmon Arm Can. **126** D2
Salmon River Mountains U.S.A.
132 C2
Salmtal Ger. **54** C3
Salo Fin. **47** E3
Sal'sk Rus. Fed. **45** F2
Salt *watercourse* S. Africa **108** B3
Salt *r.* U.S.A. **140** B2
Salta Arg. **152** B3
Saltillo Mex. **143** B2
Salt Lake City U.S.A. **132** D2
Salto Brazil **154** C2
Salto Uru. **152** C4
Salto da Divisa Brazil **155** E1
Salto del Guairá Para. **154** B3
Salton Sea *salt l.* U.S.A. **133** C4
Saluda U.S.A. **139** D2
Saluzzo Italy **62** A2
Salvador Brazil **151** F4
Salwah Saudi Arabia **91** C2
Salween *r.* China/Myanmar **74** A1
Salween *r.* China/Myanmar **80** C3
Salyan Azer. **93** C2
Salzburg Austria **56** C3
Salzgitter Ger. **55** E1
Salzkotten Ger. **55** D2
Salzwedel Ger. **55** E1
Samalayuca Mex. **142** B1
Samani Japan **78** D2
Samar *i.* Phil. **76** B2
Samara Rus. Fed. **41** E3
Samarinda Indon. **73** C2
Samarqand Uzbek. **86** D3
Sämarrä' Iraq **93** C2
Şamaxı Azer. **93** C1
Samba Dem. Rep. Congo **105** C3
Sambaliung *mts* Indon. **73** C1
Sambalpur India **87** C2
Sambar, Tanjung *pt* Indon. **73** C2
Sambas Indon. **72** B1
Sambava Madag. **107** [inset] E1
Sambir Ukr. **44** D2
Samborombón, Bahía *b.* Arg. **153** C4
Samch'ŏk S. Korea **77** B2
Samdi Dag *mt.* Turkey **93** C2
Same Tanz. **105** D3
Samīrah Saudi Arabia **90** B2
Samjiyŏn N. Korea **77** B1
Samoa *country* S. Pacific Ocean **113**
Samoan Islands *is*
S. Pacific Ocean **113**
Samobor Croatia **62** C1
Samos *i.* Greece **65** C3
Samothraki Greece **65** C2
Samothraki *i.* Greece **65** C2
Sampit Indon. **73** C2
Sampwe Dem. Rep. Congo **105** C3
Sam Rayburn Reservoir U.S.A. **141** F2
Samsun Turkey **92** B1
Samtredia Georgia **93** C1
Samui, Ko *i.* Thai. **75** B3
Samut Songkhram Thai. **75** B2
San Mali **100** B3
Şan'ā' Yemen **90** B3
Sanaga *r.* Cameroon **104** A2
San Ambrosio, Isla *i.*
S. Pacific Ocean **149**
Sanandaj Iran **93** C2
San Andrés, Isla de *i.* Caribbean Sea
144 B3
San Andres Mountains U.S.A. **140** C2
San Andrés Tuxtla Mex. **143** C3
San Angelo U.S.A. **141** C2
San Antonio U.S.A. **141** E3
San Antonio, Mount U.S.A. **133** C4
San Antonio Abad Spain **61** D2**

San Antonio de los Cobres Arg. 152 B3
San Antonio Oeste Arg. 153 B5
San Benedetto del Tronto Italy 62 B2
San Benedicto, Isla i. Mex. 142 A3
San Bernardino U.S.A. 133 C4
San Bernardino Mountains U.S.A. 133 C4
San Blas, Cape U.S.A. 139 C3
San Borja Bol. 152 B2
San Buenaventura Mex. 142 B2
San Carlos Phil. 76 B2
San Carlos Venez. 145 D4
San Carlos de Bariloche Arg. 153 A5
San Carlos del Zulia Venez. 145 C4
San Clemente Island U.S.A. 133 C4
Sancoins France 57 F3
San Cristóbal i. Solomon Is 110
San Cristóbal Venez. 150 B2
San Cristóbal de las Casas Mex. 143 C3
Sancti Spíritus Cuba 144 C2
Sand r. S. Africa 109 D1
Sandakan Malaysia 73 C1
Sandane Norway 47 B3
Sandanski Bulg. 65 B2
Sanday i. U.K. 50 C1
Sanderson U.S.A. 141 D2
Sandia Peru 150 C4
San Diego U.S.A. 133 C4
Sandıklı Turkey 92 B2
Sandnes Norway 47 B4
Sandnessjøen Norway 46 C2
Sandoa Dem. Rep. Congo 104 C3
Sandomierz Pol. 57 E2
Sandovo Rus. Fed. 44 E2
Sandoy i. Faroe Is 48 B1
Sandpoint U.S.A. 132 C1
Sandu China 83 B3
Sandur Faroe Is 48 B1
Sandusky U.S.A. 136 D2
Sandveld mts S. Africa 108 A3
Sandvika Norway 47 C4
Sandviken Sweden 47 D3
Sandwich Bay Can. 129 E1
Sandy Bay Can. 127 E2
Sandy Cape Austr. 115 E2
Sandy Lake Can. 128 A1
Sandy Lake l. Can. 128 A1
San Estanislao Para. 154 A3
San Felipe Baja California Mex. 142 A1
San Felipe Guanajuato Mex. 143 B2
San Felipe Venez. 150 C1
San Félix Chile 149
San Fernando Tamaulipas Mex. 143 C2
San Fernando Phil. 76 B2
San Fernando Phil. 76 B2
San Fernando Spain 60 B2
San Fernando Trin. and Tob. 145 D3
San Fernando de Apure Venez. 150 C2
Sanford FL U.S.A. 139 D3
Sanford ME U.S.A. 137 F2
San Francisco Arg. 152 B4
San Francisco U.S.A. 133 B3
San Francisco Javier Spain 61 D2
Sangamner India 86 B3
Sangar Rus. Fed. 95 K2
San Gavino Monreale Italy 62 A3
Sangerhausen Ger. 55 E2
Sanggau Indon. 73 C1
Sangha r. Congo 104 B3
San Giovanni in Fiore Italy 63 C3
Sangir i. Indon. 76 B3
Sangir, Kepulauan is Indon. 71 C2
Sangju S. Korea 77 B2
Sangkulirang Indon. 73 C1
Sangli India 85 B3

Sangmélima Cameroon 104 B2
Sango Zimbabwe 107 C2
Sangre de Cristo Range mts U.S.A. 134 B3
Sangsang China 87 C2
San Hipólito, Punta pt Mex. 142 A2
San Ignacio Mex. 142 A2
Sanikiluaq Can. 128 C1
Sanjiang China 83 A3
San Joaquin r. U.S.A. 133 B3
San Jorge, Golfo de g. Arg. 153 B5
San Jose Phil. 76 B2
San Jose Phil. 76 B2
San Jose U.S.A. 133 B3
San José, Isla i. Mex. 142 A2
San José de Bavicora Mex. 142 B2
San José de Buenavista Phil. 76 B2
San José de Comondú Mex. 142 A2
San José del Cabo Mex. 142 B2
San José del Guaviare Col. 150 B2
San Juan Arg. 152 B4
San Juan r. Costa Rica/Nic. 144 B3
San Juan Puerto Rico 145 D3
San Juan r. U.S.A. 133 D3
San Juan Bautista Para. 152 C3
San Juan Bautista Tuxtepec Mex. 143 C3
San Juan Islands U.S.A. 132 B1
San Juanito Mex. 142 B2
San Juan Mountains U.S.A. 134 B3
San Julián Arg. 153 B5
Sankh r. India 87 C2
Sankt Gallen Switz. 59 D2
Sankt Moritz Switz. 59 D2
Sankt-Peterburg Rus. Fed. see St Petersburg
Sankt Veit an der Glan Austria 56 C3
Sankt Wendel Ger. 54 C3
Şanlıurfa Turkey 92 B2
San Lorenzo Mex. 140 C3
Sanlúcar de Barrameda Spain 60 B2
San Lucas Mex. 142 B2
San Luis Arg. 153 B4
San Luis de la Paz Mex. 142 B2
San Luisito Mex. 142 A1
San Luis Obispo U.S.A. 133 B3
San Luis Potosí Mex. 143 B2
San Luis Río Colorado Mex. 142 A1
San Marcos U.S.A. 141 E3
San Marino country Europe 62 B2
San Marino San Marino 62 B2
San Martín de Bolaños Mex. 142 B2
San Martín de los Andes Arg. 153 A5
San Matías, Golfo g. Arg. 153 B5
Sanmenxia China 82 B2
Sanming China 83 B3
San Nicolás de los Arroyos Arg. 153 B4
San Nicolas Island U.S.A. 133 C4
Sannieshof S. Africa 109 C2
Sanok Pol. 57 E3
San Pablo Phil. 76 B2
San Pablo Balleza Mex. 142 B2
San Pedro Arg. 152 B3
San Pedro Bol. 152 B2
San-Pédro Côte d'Ivoire 100 B4
San Pedro Mex. 142 B2
San Pedro watercourse U.S.A. 140 B2
San Pedro, Sierra de mts Spain 60 B2
San Pedro de las Colonias Mex. 142 B2
San Pedro Sula Hond. 144 B3
San Pietro, Isola di i. Italy 62 A3
San Quintín, Cabo c. Mex. 142 A1
San Rafael Arg. 153 B4

San Remo Italy 62 A2
San Salvador El Salvador 144 B3
San Salvador de Jujuy Arg. 152 B3
San Severo Italy 62 C2
Sanski Most Bos.-Herz. 63 C2
Santa Ana Bol. 152 B2
Santa Ana El Salvador 144 B3
Santa Ana Mex. 142 A1
Santa Ana U.S.A. 133 C4
Santa Bárbara Mex. 142 B2
Santa Barbara U.S.A. 133 C4
Santa Bárbara, Serra de hills Brazil 154 B2
Santa Catalina Chile 152 B3
Santa Clara Col. 150 C3
Santa Clara Cuba 144 C2
Santa Clarita U.S.A. 133 C4
Santa Croce, Capo c. Italy 62 C3
Santa Cruz r. Arg. 153 B6
Santa Cruz Bol. 152 B2
Santa Cruz Phil. 76 B2
Santa Cruz U.S.A. 133 B3
Santa Cruz Barillas Guat. 143 C3
Santa Cruz Cabrália Brazil 155 E1
Santa Cruz de Moya Spain 61 C2
Santa Cruz de Tenerife Canary Is 100 A2
Santa Cruz Island U.S.A. 133 C4
Santa Cruz Islands Solomon Is 110
Santa Elena, Punta pt Ecuador 146
Santa Fé Arg. 152 B4
Santa Fe U.S.A. 140 C1
Santa Helena de Goiás Brazil 154 B1
Santa Isabel Arg. 153 B4
Santa Isabel i. Solomon Is 110
Santa Luisa, Serra de hills Brazil 154 B1
Santa Maria Brazil 152 C3
Santa María r. Mex. 142 B1
Santa María U.S.A. 133 B4
Santa Maria, Cabo de c. Moz. 109 D2
Santa Maria, Cabo de c. Port. 60 B2
Santa Maria das Barreiras Brazil 151 E3
Santa Maria di Leuca, Capo c. Italy 63 C3
Santa Marta Col. 150 B1
Santa Monica U.S.A. 133 C4
Santana Brazil 151 E4
Santander Spain 60 C1
Sant'Antioco Italy 62 A3
Sant'Antioco, Isola di i. Italy 62 A3
Santarém Brazil 151 D3
Santarém Port. 60 B2
Santa Rita do Araguaia Brazil 154 B1
Santa Rosa Arg. 153 B4
Santa Rosa Brazil 152 C3
Santa Rosa CA U.S.A. 133 B3
Santa Rosa NM U.S.A. 140 D2
Santa Rosa de Copán Hond. 144 B3
Santa Rosa Island U.S.A. 133 B4
Santa Rosalía Mex. 142 A2
Santiago Brazil 152 C3
Santiago Chile 153 A4
Santiago Dom. Rep. 145 C2
Santiago Mex. 142 B2
Santiago Panama 144 B4
Santiago Phil. 76 B2
Santiago de Compostela Spain 60 B1
Santiago Ixcuintla Mex. 142 B2
Santiago Papasquiaro Mex. 142 B2
Sant Jordi, Golf de g. Spain 61 D1
Santo Amaro de Campos Brazil 155 D2
Santo André Brazil 155 C2
Santo Ângelo Brazil 152 C3
Santo Antônio, Cabo c. Brazil 146
Santo Antônio da Platina Brazil 154 B2
Santo Antônio de Jesus Brazil 151 F4

Santo Antônio do Içá Brazil **150** C3
Santo Antônio do Monte Brazil
155 C2
Santo Domingo Dom. Rep. **145** D3
Santo Domingo Pueblo U.S.A. **140** C1
Santorini *i.* Greece *see* Thira
Santos Brazil **155** C2
Santo Tomé Arg. **152** C3
San Valentín, Cerro *mt.* Chile **153** A5
San Vicente El Salvador **144** B3
San Vicente Mex. **142** A1
San Vicente de Cañete Peru **150** B4
San Vincenzo Italy **62** B2
San Vito, Capo *c.* Italy **62** B3
Sanya China **83** A4
São Bernardo do Campo Brazil
155 C2
São Borja Brazil **152** C3
São Carlos Brazil **154** C2
São Félix *Mato Grosso* Brazil **151** D4
São Félix *Pará* Brazil **151** D3
São Fidélis Brazil **155** D2
São Francisco Brazil **155** D1
São Francisco *r.* Brazil **151** E4
São Francisco, Ilha de *i.* Brazil
154 C3
São Francisco do Sul Brazil **154** C3
São Gabriel Brazil **152** C4
São Gonçalo Brazil **155** D2
São Gotardo Brazil **155** C1
São João da Barra Brazil **155** D2
São João da Boa Vista Brazil **155** C2
São João da Madeira Port. **60** B3
São João Nepomuceno Brazil **155** D2
São Joaquim da Barra Brazil **154** C2
São José do Rio Preto Brazil **154** C2
São José dos Campos Brazil **155** C2
São José dos Pinhais Brazil **154** C3
São Lourenço Brazil **155** C2
São Lourenço, Pantanal de *marsh*
Brazil **154** A1
São Luís Brazil **151** E3
São Manuel Brazil **154** C2
São Marcos *r.* Brazil **154** C1
São Mateus Brazil **155** E1
São Paulo Brazil **155** C2
São Raimundo Nonato Brazil **151** E3
São Romão Brazil **155** C1
São Roque, Cabo de *c.* Brazil **146**
São Sebastião, Ilha do *i.* Brazil
155 C2
São Sebastião do Paraíso Brazil
154 C2
São Simão Brazil **154** B1
São Simão, Barragem de *resr* Brazil
154 B1
Sao-Siu Indon. **71** C2
São Tomé São Tomé and Príncipe
104 A2
São Tomé *i.* São Tomé and Príncipe
104 A2
São Tomé, Cabo de *c.* Brazil **155** D2
São Tomé and Príncipe *country* Africa
104 A2
São Vicente Brazil **155** C2
São Vicente, Cabo de *c.* Port. **60** B2
Sapanca Indon. **71** C3
Sapozhok Rus. Fed. **43** F3
Sapporo Japan **78** D2
Sapri Italy **62** C2
Saqqez Iran **93** C2
Sarāb Iran **93** C2
Sara Buri Thai. **75** B2
Sarai Rus. Fed. **43** F3
Sarajevo Bos.-Herz. **63** C2
Saraktash Rus. Fed. **94** F3
Saranac Lake U.S.A. **137** F2
Sarandë Albania **65** B3
Sarangani Islands Phil. **76** C3
Saransk Rus. Fed. **41** D3

Sarapul Rus. Fed. **41** E3
Sarasota U.S.A. **139** D3
Sarata Ukr. **44** C2
Saratoga U.S.A. **134** B2
Saratoga Springs U.S.A. **137** F2
Saratok Malaysia **73** C1
Saratov Rus. Fed. **41** D3
Saravan Iran **91** D2
Sarawak *state* Malaysia **73** C1
Saray Turkey **64** C2
Sarayköy Turkey **65** C3
Sarbāz Iran **91** D2
Sardarshahr India **86** B2
Sardegna *i.* Italy *see* Sardinia
Sardinia *i.* Italy **62** A2
Sarektjåkkå *mt.* Sweden **46** D2
Sar-e Pol Afgh. **86** A1
Sargasso Sea N. Atlantic Ocean
160 B4
Sargodha Pak. **86** B1
Sarh Chad **101** D4
Sarhad *reg.* Iran **91** D2
Sārī Iran **93** D2
Sarıgöl Turkey **65** C3
Sarıkamış Turkey **93** C1
Sarikei Malaysia **73** C1
Sarina Austr. **115** D2
Sarīr Tibesti *des.* Libya **101** D2
Sariwŏn N. Korea **77** B2
Sarıyer Turkey **65** C2
Sarkand Kazakh. **89** E2
Şarköy Turkey **65** C2
Sarmi Indon. **71** D3
Sarnia Can. **136** D2
Sarny Ukr. **44** C1
Sarolangun Indon. **72** B2
Saronikos Kolpos *g.* Greece **65** B3
Saros Körfezi *b.* Turkey **65** C2
Sarova Rus. Fed. **41** D3
Sarrebourg France **59** D2
Sarria Spain **60** B1
Sarrión Spain **61** C1
Sartène France **59** D3
Sárvár Hungary **57** D3
Sarykamyshskoye Ozero *salt l.*
Turkm./Uzbek. **88** C2
Saryozek Kazakh. **89** E2
Saryshagan Kazakh. **89** E2
Sarysu *watercourse* Kazakh. **94** G3
Sary-Tash Kyrg. **89** E3
Sasaram India **87** C2
Sasebo Japan **79** A4
Saskatchewan *prov.* Can. **127** E2
Saskatchewan *r.* Can. **127** E2
Saskatoon Can. **124** E1
Saskylakh Rus. Fed. **95** J2
Sasolburg S. Africa **109** C2
Sasovo Rus. Fed. **43** F3
Sassandra Côte d'Ivoire **100** B4
Sassari Italy **62** A2
Sassnitz Ger. **56** C2
Satadougou Mali **100** A3
Satara S. Africa **109** D1
Satna India **87** C2
Satpura Range *mts* India **86** B2
Sattahip Thai. **75** B2
Satu Mare Romania **44** B2
Satun Thai. **75** B3
Saucillo Mex. **142** B2
Sauda Norway **47** B4
Sauðárkrókur Iceland **46** [inset]
Saudi Arabia *country* Asia **90** B2
Saugues France **59** C3
Saulieu France **59** C2
Sault Sainte Marie Can. **128** B2
Sault Sainte Marie U.S.A. **136** D1
Saumlakki *i.* Indon. **71** C3
Saumur France **58** B2
Saurimo Angola **104** C3

Sava *r.* Europe **62** D2
Savai'i *i.* Samoa **111**
Savala *r.* Rus. Fed. **43** F3
Savannah GA U.S.A. **139** D2
Savannah *TN* U.S.A. **138** C1
Savannah *r.* U.S.A. **139** D2
Savannakhét Laos **74** B2
Savant Lake Can. **128** A1
Savaştepe Turkey **65** C3
Savino Rus. Fed. **43** F2
Savinskiy Rus. Fed. **40** C2
Savona Italy **62** A2
Savonlinna Fin. **47** F3
Savu *i.* Indon. **73** D3
Savukoski Fin. **46** F2
Savu Sea Indon. *see* Sawu, Laut
Sawai Madhopur India **86** B2
Sawai Madhopur India **86** B2
Sawankhalok Thai. **74** A2
Sawatch Range *mts* U.S.A. **134** B3
Sawhāj Egypt **102** B2
Sawtell Austr. **117** E2
Sawu, Laut *sea* Indon. **73** D2
Sayhūt Yemen **91** C3
Saynshand Mongolia **81** D2
Sayre U.S.A. **137** E2
Sayula *Jalisco* Mex. **142** B3
Sayula *Veracruz* Mex. **143** C3
Sayward Can. **126** C2
Sazonovo Rus. Fed. **43** E2
Sbaa Alg. **100** B2
Scafell Pike *h.* U.K. **52** B2
Scalea Italy **63** C3
Scapa Flow *inlet* U.K. **50** C1
Scarborough Trin. and Tob. **145** D3
Scarborough U.K. **52** C2
Scarborough Shoal *sea feature*
S. China Sea **76** A2
Scarinish U.K. **50** A2
Scarpanto *i.* Greece *see* Karpathos
Schaffhausen Switz. **59** D2
Schagen Neth. **54** B1
Schärding Austria **56** C3
Scharendijke Neth. **54** A2
Scheeßel Ger. **55** D1
Schefferville Can. **129** D1
Schell Creek Range *mts* U.S.A.
133 D3
Schenectady U.S.A. **137** F2
Scheßlitz Ger. **55** E3
Schiermonnikoog *i.* Neth. **54** C1
Schio Italy **62** B1
Schkeuditz Ger. **55** F2
Schladen Ger. **55** E1
Schleiz Ger. **55** E2
Schleswig Ger. **56** B2
Schloss Holte-Stukenbrock Ger.
55 D2
Schlüchtern Ger. **55** E3
Schlüsselfeld Ger. **55** E3
Schmallenberg Ger. **55** D2
Schneverdingen Ger. **55** D1
Schönebeck (Elbe) Ger. **55** E1
Schöningen Ger. **55** E1
Schöntal Ger. **55** D3
Schoonhoven Neth. **54** B2
Schouten Islands P.N.G. **71** D3
Schwabach Ger. **55** E3
Schwäbische Alb *mts* Ger. **56** B3
Schwandorf Ger. **55** F3
Schwaner, Pegunungan *mts* Indon.
73 C2
Schwarzenbek Ger. **55** E1
Schwarzenberg Ger. **55** F2
Schwarzrand *mts* Namibia **108** A2
Schwarzwald *mts* Ger. *see*
Black Forest
Schwaz Austria **56** C3
Schwedt an der Oder Ger. **56** C2
Schweinfurt Ger. **55** E2

Schwerin Ger. **55** E1
Schweriner See *l.* Ger. **55** E1
Schwyz Switz. **59** D2
Sciacca Italy **62** B3
Scilly, Isles of U.K. **49** B4
Scioto *r.* U.S.A. **136** D3
Scobey U.S.A. **134** E1
Scone Austr. **117** C2
Scotia Sea S. Atlantic Ocean **119** A4
Scotland *admin. div.* U.K. **50** C2
Scott, Cape Can. **126** C2
Scottburgh S. Africa **109** D3
Scott City U.S.A. **134** C3
Scottsbluff U.S.A. **134** C2
Scottsboro U.S.A. **139** C2
Scourie U.K. **50** B1
Scranton U.S.A. **137** E2
Scunthorpe U.K. **52** C3
Scuol Switz. **59** E2
Seal *r.* Can. **127** F2
Seal, Cape S. Africa **108** B3
Sea Lake Austr. **116** C3
Sealy U.S.A. **141** E3
Searcy U.S.A. **138** B1
Seascale U.S.A. **52** B2
Seattle U.S.A. **132** B1
Sebago Lake U.S.A. **137** F2
Sebastián Vizcaíno, Bahía *b.* Mex. **142** A2
Sebeş Romania **44** B2
Sebesi *i.* Indon. **72** B2
Sebezh Rus. Fed. **42** C2
Şebinkarahisar Turkey **92** B1
Sebring U.S.A. **139** D3
Sechelt Can. **126** C3
Sechura Peru **150** A3
Secunderabad India **85** B3
Sedalia U.S.A. **135** C3
Sedan France **59** C2
Seddon N.Z. **118** B3
Sedona U.S.A. **140** B2
Seeburg Ger. **55** E2
Seehausen (Altmark) Ger. **55** E1
Seeheim Namibia **108** A2
Sées France **58** C2
Seesen Ger. **55** E2
Seevetal Ger. **55** E1
Sefadu Sierra Leone **100** A4
Sefare Botswana **109** C1
Segamat Malaysia **72** B1
Segezha Rus. Fed. **40** C2
Ségou Mali **100** B3
Segovia, Sierra de *mts* Spain **60** C1
Segovia Spain **60** C1
Séguédine Niger **101** D2
Séguéla Côte d'Ivoire **100** B4
Seguin U.S.A. **141** E3
Segura *r.* Spain **61** C2
Segura, Sierra de *mts* Spain **60** C2
Sehithwa Botswana **106** B2
Seinäjoki Fin. **46** E3
Seine *r.* France **59** C2
Seine, Baie de *b.* France **58** B2
Sejny Pol. **57** E2
Sekayu Indon. **72** B2
Sekondi Ghana **100** B4
Selaru *i.* Indon. **71** C3
Selatan, Tanjung *pt* Indon. **73** C2
Selawik U.S.A. **124** B2
Selby U.K. **52** C2
Selebi-Phikwe Botswana **106** B2
Selenga *r.* Rus. Fed. **67**
Sélestat France **59** D2
Selfoss Iceland **46** [inset]
Sélibabi Maur. **100** A3
Seligman U.S.A. **140** B1
Selima Oasis Sudan **102** A2
Selimiye Turkey **65** C3
Sélingué, Lac de *l.* Mali **100** B3
Selizharovo Rus. Fed. **43** D2
Seljord Norway **47** B4

Selkirk Can. **127** F2
Selkirk U.K. **50** C3
Selkirk Mountains Can. **126** D2
Selma *AL* U.S.A. **138** C2
Selma *CA* U.S.A. **133** C3
Sel'tso Rus. Fed. **43** D3
Selvas *reg.* Brazil **150** B3
Selway *r.* U.S.A. **132** C1
Selwyn Lake Can. **127** E1
Selwyn Mountains Can. **126** C1
Selwyn Range *hills* Austr. **115** C2
Semangka, Teluk *b.* Indon. **72** B2
Semarang Indon. **73** C2
Sematan Malaysia **73** B1
Sembé Congo **104** B2
Şemdinli Turkey **93** C2
Semenivka Ukr. **45** D1
Semeru, Gunung *vol.* Indon. **73** C2
Semikarakorsk Rus. Fed. **45** F2
Semiluki Rus. Fed. **43** E3
Seminoe Reservoir U.S.A. **134** B2
Seminole U.S.A. **141** D2
Seminole, Lake U.S.A. **139** D2
Semipalatinsk Kazakh. **89** F1
Semitau Indon. **73** C1
Semnan Iran **93** D2
Semporna Malaysia **73** C1
Semur-en-Auxois France **59** C2
Sena Madureira Brazil **150** C3
Senanga Zambia **106** B1
Sendai *Kagoshima* Japan **79** B4
Sendai *Miyagi* Japan **78** D3
Senegal *country* Africa **100** A3
Sénégal *r.* Maur./Senegal **100** A3
Senftenberg Ger. **55** C2
Sengerema Tanz. **105** D3
Senhor do Bonfim Brazil **151** E4
Senigallia Italy **62** B2
Senj Croatia **62** B2
Senja *i.* Norway **46** F2
Senlac S. Africa **108** B2
Senlis France **58** C2
Senmonorom Cambodia **75** B2
Sennar Sudan **103** B3
Senneterre Can. **128** C2
Senqu *r.* Lesotho **109** C3
Sens France **59** C2
Senta Serb. and Mont. **64** B1
Seoul S. Korea **77** B2
Sepetiba, Baía de *b.* Brazil **155** D2
Sepik *r.* P.N.G. **71** D3
Sepinang Indon. **73** C1
Sept-Îles Can. **129** D1
Seram *i.* Indon. **71** C3
Seram, Laut *sea* Indon. **71** C3
Serang Indon. **72** B2
Serbia *aut. rep.* Serb. and Mont. *see* Srbija
Serbia and Montenegro *country* Europe **64** B2
Serebryanyye Prudy Rus. Fed. **43** E3
Seremban Malaysia **72** B1
Serengeti Plain Tanz. **105** D3
Sergach Rus. Fed. **41** D3
Sergiyev Posad Rus. Fed. **43** E2
Seria Brunei **73** C1
Serian Malaysia **73** C1
Serifos *i.* Greece **65** B3
Serik Turkey **92** B2
Sermata, Kepulauan *is* Indon. **71** C3
Serov Rus. Fed. **40** F3
Serowe Botswana **109** C1
Serpa Port. **60** B2
Serpukhov Rus. Fed. **43** E3
Serra da Mesa, Represa *resr* Brazil **151** E4
Serranópolis Brazil **154** B1
Serre *r.* France **54** A3

Serres Greece **65** B2
Sêrro Brazil **155** D1
Sertãozinho Brazil **154** C2
Sertolovo Rus. Fed. **43** D1
Seruyan *r.* Indon. **73** C2
Sêrxü China **80** C2
Sesfontein Namibia **106** A1
Sessa Aurunca Italy **62** B2
Sestri Levante Italy **62** A2
Sestroretsk Rus. Fed. **42** C1
Sète France **59** C3
Sete Lagoas Brazil **155** D1
Setermoen Norway **46** D2
Setesdal *val.* Norway **47** B4
Sétif Alg. **101** C1
Seto-naikai *sea* Japan **79** B4
Settat Morocco **100** B1
Settle U.K. **52** B2
Setúbal Port. **60** B2
Setúbal, Baía de *b.* Port. **60** B2
Seul, Lac *l.* Can. **128** A1
Sevan Armenia **88** C2
Sevan, Lake Armenia **88** C2
Sevastopol' Ukr. **45** D3
Seven Islands Bay Can. **129** D1
Sévérac-le-Château France **58** C3
Severn *r.* Can. **128** B1
Severn S. Africa **108** B2
Severn *r.* U.K. **53** B4
Severnaya Dvina *r.* Rus. Fed. **40** D2
Severnaya Zemlya *is* Rus. Fed. **95** I1
Severnyy *Nenetskiy Avtonomnyy Okrug* Rus. Fed. **40** D2
Severnyy *Respublika Komi* Rus. Fed. **40** F2
Severodvinsk Rus. Fed. **40** C2
Severomorsk Rus. Fed. **46** C2
Severskaya Rus. Fed. **45** E3
Sevier *r.* U.S.A. **133** D3
Sevier Lake U.S.A. **133** D3
Sevilla Spain *see* Seville
Seville Spain **60** B2
Seward U.S.A. **124** C2
Seward Peninsula U.S.A. **124** B2
Sewell Inlet Can. **126** B2
Sexsmith Can. **126** D2
Sextin *r.* Mex. **142** B2
Seyakha Rus. Fed. **40** G1
Seychelles *country* Indian Ocean **99**
Seyðisfjörður Iceland **46** [inset]
Seym *r.* Rus. Fed./Ukr. **45** D1
Seymchan Rus. Fed. **95** M2
Seymour Austr. **117** D3
Seymour *IN* U.S.A. **136** C3
Seymour *TX* U.S.A. **141** E2
Sézanne France **59** C2
Sfakia Greece **65** B3
Sfântu Gheorghe Romania **44** C2
Sfax Tunisia **101** D1
's-Gravenhage Neth. *see* The Hague
Sgurr Alasdair *h.* U.K. **50** A2
Shaanxi *prov.* China **82** A2
Shabel'sk Rus. Fed. **45** E2
Shache China **89** D3
Shackleton Range *mts* Antarctica **119** A1
Shaftesbury U.K. **53** B4
Shageluk U.S.A. **124** B2
Shahdol India **87** C2
Shah Fuladi *mt.* Afgh. **86** A1
Shahjahanpur India **87** B2
Shahr-e Kord Iran **93** D2
Shahrezā Iran **93** D2
Shahrisabz Uzbek. **89** D3
Shakhovskaya Rus. Fed. **43** E2
Shakhty Rus. Fed. **45** F2
Shakhun'ya Rus. Fed. **41** D2
Shakotan-misaki *c.* Japan **78** D2
Shalkar Kazakh. **88** C2

Shaluli Shan *mts* China **80** C2
Shamattawa Can. **127** F2
Shamrock U.S.A. **141** D1
Shandan China **80** C2
Shandong *prov.* China **82** B2
Shandong Bandao *pen.* China **82** C2
Shangani *r.* Zimbabwe **107** B1
Shanghai China **82** C2
Shanghai *mun.* China **82** C2
Shanghang China **83** B3
Shangluo China **82** A2
Shangrao China **83** B3
Shangshui China **82** B2
Shangyu China **83** C2
Shangzhi China **81** E1
Shangzhou China *see* Shangluo
Shannon *r.* Rep. of Ireland **51** C2
Shannon, Mouth of the Rep. of Ireland
　51 B2
Shantou China **83** B3
Shanxi *prov.* China **82** B2
Shaoguan China **83** B3
Shaowu China **83** B3
Shaoxing China **83** C2
Shaoyang China **83** B3
Shaqrā' Saudi Arabia **102** C2
Sharhorod Ukr. **44** C2
Sharjah U.A.E. **91** C2
Sharkawshchyna Belarus **42** C2
Shark Bay Austr. **114** A2
Sharm ash Shaykh Egypt **90** A2
Sharon U.S.A. **137** D2
Shar'ya Rus. Fed. **40** D3
Shashe *r.* Botswana/Zimbabwe **107** B2
Shashemenē Eth. **103** B4
Shasta, Mount *vol.* U.S.A. **132** B2
Shasta Lake U.S.A. **132** B2
Shatsk Rus. Fed. **43** F3
Shatura Rus. Fed. **43** E2
Shaunavon Can. **127** C3
Shawano U.S.A. **136** C2
Shawinigan Can. **129** C2
Shawnee U.S.A. **141** E1
Shay Gap Austr. **114** A2
Shchekino Rus. Fed. **43** E3
Shchelkovo Rus. Fed. **43** E2
Shchigry Rus. Fed. **43** E3
Shchors Ukr. **45** D1
Shchuchyn Belarus **42** B3
Shebekino Rus. Fed. **45** E1
Sheberghān Afgh. **86** A1
Sheboygan U.S.A. **136** C2
Shebsh *r.* Rus. Fed. **45** E3
Sheelin, Lough *l.* Rep. of Ireland **51** C2
Sheffield U.K. **52** C3
Sheksna Rus. Fed. **43** E2
Sheksninskoye Vodokhranilishche
　resr Rus. Fed. **43** E2
Shelagskiy, Mys *pt* Rus. Fed. **95** N2
Shelburne Can. **129** D2
Shelby U.S.A. **132** D1
Shelbyville *IN* U.S.A. **136** C3
Shelbyville *TN* U.S.A. **139** C1
Shelikhova, Zaliv *g.* Rus. Fed. **95** M2
Shellbrook Can. **127** E2
Shelton U.S.A. **132** B1
Shenandoah U.S.A. **135** D2
Shenandoah *r.* U.S.A. **137** E3
Shendam Nigeria **104** A2
Shendi Sudan **90** A3
Shenkursk Rus. Fed. **40** D2
Shenyang China **82** C1
Shenzhen China **83** B3
Shepetivka Ukr. **44** C1
Shepparton Austr. **117** D3
Sheppey, Isle of *i.* U.K. **53** D4
Sherbrooke *N.S.* Can. **129** D2
Sherbrooke *Que.* Can. **129** C2
Shereiq Sudan **102** B3
Sheridan U.S.A. **134** B2

Sherman U.S.A. **141** E2
's-Hertogenbosch Neth. **54** B2
Shetland Islands *Scotland* U.K.
　50 [inset]
Shetpe Kazakh. **88** C2
Sheyenne *r.* U.S.A. **135** D1
Shibām Yemen **91** B3
Shicheng China **83** B3
Shiel, Loch *l.* U.K. **50** B2
Shihezi China **89** F2
Shijiazhuang China **82** B2
Shikarpur Pak. **86** A2
Shikoku *i.* Japan **79** B4
Shikotsu-ko *l.* Japan **78** D2
Shilega Rus. Fed. **40** D2
Shiliguri India **87** C2
Shillong India **87** D2
Shilovo Rus. Fed. **43** F3
Shimbiris *mt.* Somalia **103** C3
Shimizu Japan **79** C3
Shimla India **87** B1
Shimoga India **85** B3
Shimonoseki Japan **79** B4
Shin, Loch *l.* U.K. **50** B1
Shindand Afgh. **86** A1
Shingū Japan **79** C4
Shingwedzi S. Africa **109** D1
Shingwedzi *r.* S. Africa **109** D1
Shinyanga Tanz. **105** D3
Shiono-misaki *c.* Japan **79** C4
Shiprock U.S.A. **140** C1
Shiquan China **83** A3
Shirane-san *mt.* Japan **79** C3
Shīrāz Iran **93** D3
Shiretoko-misaki *c.* Japan **78** E2
Shiriya-zaki *c.* Japan **78** D2
Shiv India **86** B2
Shivpuri India **86** B2
Shiyan China **82** B2
Shizuishan China **82** A2
Shizuoka Japan **79** C4
Shklow Belarus **43** D3
Shkodër Albania **63** C2
Shmidta, Ostrov *i.* Rus. Fed. **95** I1
Shor Barsa-Kel'mes *salt marsh* Uzbek.
　93 D1
Shoshone U.S.A. **133** C3
Shoshone Mountains U.S.A. **133** C3
Shoshong Botswana **109** C1
Shostka Ukr. **45** D1
Showak Sudan **90** A3
Show Low U.S.A. **140** B2
Shpola Ukr. **45** D2
Shreveport U.S.A. **138** B2
Shrewsbury U.K. **53** B3
Shu'ab, Ra's *pt* Yemen **91** C3
Shuangjiang China **74** A1
Shuangliao China **77** A1
Shuangyang China **77** B1
Shuangyashan China **78** B1
Shubarkuduk Kazakh. **88** C1
Shubrā al Khaymah Egypt **102** B1
Shugozero Rus. Fed. **43** D2
Shumba Zimbabwe **106** B1
Shumen Bulg. **64** C2
Shumilina Belarus **42** C2
Shumyachi Rus. Fed. **43** D3
Shungnak U.S.A. **124** B2
Shuqrah Yemen **90** B3
Shushkodom Rus. Fed. **43** F2
Shushtar Iran **93** C2
Shuswap Lake Can. **126** D2
Shuya Rus. Fed. **43** F2
Shuyskoye Rus. Fed. **43** F2
Shwebo Myanmar **74** A1
Shwedwin Myanmar **74** A1
Shwegyin Myanmar **74** A2

Shymkent Kazakh. **89** D2
Shyroke Ukr. **45** D2
Sia Indon. **71** C3
Siahan Range *mts* Pak. **86** A2
Sialkot Pak. **86** B1
Siargao *i.* Phil. **76** B3
Šiauliai Lith. **42** B2
Šibenik Croatia **63** C2
Siberia *reg.* Rus. Fed. **95** J2
Siberut *i.* Indon. **72** A2
Sibi Pak. **86** A2
Sibiu Romania **44** B2
Sibolga Indon. **72** A1
Sibsagar India **74** A1
Sibu Malaysia **73** C1
Sibut C.A.R. **104** B2
Sibuyan *i.* Phil. **76** B2
Sibuyan Sea Phil. **76** B2
Sicamous Can. **126** D2
Sichon Thai. **75** A3
Sichuan *prov.* China **82** A2
Sichuan Pendi *basin* China **83** A3
Sicié, Cap *c.* France **59** D3
Sicilia *i.* Italy *see* Sicily
Sicilian Channel Italy/Tunisia **62** B3
Sicily *i.* Italy **62** B3
Sicuani Peru **150** B4
Siddhapur India **86** B2
Sideros, Akra *pt* Greece **65** C3
Sidi Aïssa Alg. **61** D2
Sidi Ali Alg. **61** D2
Sidi Bel Abbès Alg. **100** B1
Sidi Ifni Morocco **100** A2
Sidikalang Indon. **72** A1
Sidi Okba Alg. **61** E3
Sidlaw Hills U.K. **50** C2
Sidmouth U.K. **53** B4
Sidney Can. **132** B1
Sidney *MT* U.S.A. **134** C1
Sidney *NE* U.S.A. **134** C2
Sidney *OH* U.S.A. **136** C2
Sidney Lanier, Lake U.S.A. **139** D2
Sidoan Indon. **73** D1
Sidon Lebanon **92** B2
Sidrolândia Brazil **154** B2
Siedlce Pol. **57** E2
Sieg *r.* Ger. **54** C2
Siegen Ger. **54** C2
Siĕmréab Cambodia **75** B2
Siena Italy **62** B2
Sieradz Pol. **57** D2
Sierra Grande Arg. **153** B5
Sierra Leone *country* Africa **100** A4
Sierra Mojada Mex. **142** B2
Sierra Vista U.S.A. **140** B2
Sierre Switz. **59** D2
Sifnos *i.* Greece **65** B3
Sig Alg. **61** C2
Siggup Nunaa *pen.* Greenland **125** I2
Sighetu Marmaţiei Romania **44** B2
Sighişoara Romania **44** B2
Sigli Indon. **72** A1
Siglufjörður Iceland **46** [inset]
Sigmaringen Ger. **56** B3
Signy-l'Abbaye France **54** B3
Sigüenza Spain **60** C1
Siguiri Guinea **100** B3
Sigulda Latvia **42** C2
Sihanoukville Cambodia **75** B2
Siilinjärvi Fin. **46** F3
Siirt Turkey **93** C2
Sijunjung Indon. **72** B2
Sikar India **86** B2
Sikasso Mali **100** B3
Sikeston U.S.A. **135** F3
Sikhote-Alin' *mts* Rus. Fed. **78** B2
Sikinos *i.* Greece **65** C3
Silao Mex. **142** B2
Silchar India **74** A1
Siletiteniz, Ozero *salt l.* Kazakh. **89** E1

Silgarhi Nepal 87 C2
Silifke Turkey 92 B2
Siling Co salt l. China 87 C1
Silistra Bulg. 64 C2
Silivri Turkey 92 A1
Siljan l. Sweden 47 C3
Silkeborg Denmark 47 B4
Sillamäe Estonia 42 C2
Siloam Springs U.S.A. 138 B1
Silobela S. Africa 109 D2
Silutė Lith. 42 B2
Silvan Turkey 93 C2
Silver City U.S.A. 140 C2
Silverton U.S.A. 134 B3
Simao China 74 B1
Simård, Lac l. Can. 128 C2
Simav Turkey 65 C3
Simav Dağları mts Turkey 65 C3
Simba Dem. Rep. Congo 104 C2
Simcoe, Lake Can. 137 D2
Simeulue i. Indon. 72 A1
Simferopol' Ukr. 45 D3
Şimleu Silvaniei Romania 44 B2
Simmern (Hunsrück) Ger. 54 C4
Simonhouse Can. 127 E2
Simpson Desert Austr. 115 C2
Simrishamn Sweden 47 C4
Sinabang Indon. 72 A1
Sinai pen. Egypt 102 B2
Sinan China 83 B3
Sinanju N. Korea 77 B2
Sinbo Myanmar 74 A1
Sincelejo Col. 150 B2
Sındırgı Turkey 65 C3
Sindor Rus. Fed. 40 C2
Sinekçi Turkey 65 C2
Sines Port. 60 B2
Sines, Cabo de c. Port. 60 B2
Singa Sudan 90 A3
Singahi India 87 C2
Singapore Asia 72 B1
Singapore country Asia 72 B1
Singaraja Indon. 73 C2
Singida Tanz. 105 D3
Singkaling Hkamti Myanmar 74 A1
Singkang Indon. 73 D2
Singkawang Indon. 72 B1
Singkil Indon. 72 A1
Singleton Austr. 117 E2
Siniscola Italy 62 A2
Sinj Croatia 63 C2
Sinjai Indon. 73 D2
Sinkat Sudan 102 B3
Sinkiang aut. reg. China see
  Xinjiang Uygur Zizhiqu
Sinop Turkey 92 B1
Sinp'o N. Korea 77 B1
Sinsheim Ger. 55 D3
Sintang Indon. 73 C1
Saint Anthonis Neth. 54 B2
Sint-Laurens Belgium 54 A2
Sint Maarten i. Neth. Antilles 145 D3
Sint-Niklaas Belgium 54 B2
Sinton U.S.A. 141 E3
Sinüiju N. Korea 77 A1
Siófok Hungary 57 D3
Sion Switz. 59 D2
Sioux Center U.S.A. 135 D2
Sioux City U.S.A. 135 D2
Sioux Falls U.S.A. 135 D2
Sioux Lookout Can. 128 A1
Siping China 77 A1
Sipiwesk Lake Can. 127 F2
Sipura i. Indon. 72 A2
Sira r. Norway 47 B4
Sir Edward Pellew Group is Austr.
  115 C1
Sirik Iran 91 C2
Siri Kit Dam Thai. 74 B2

Sir James MacBrien, Mount Can.
  126 C1
Sirjän Iran 93 D3
Şırnak Turkey 93 C2
Sirohi India 86 B2
Sirsa India 86 B2
Sirte Libya 101 D1
Sirvintos Lith. 42 B2
Sisal Mex. 143 C2
Sishen S. Africa 108 B2
Sisian Armenia 93 C2
Sisipuk Lake Can. 127 E2
Sisöphön Cambodia 75 B2
Sisteron France 59 D3
Sitapur India 87 C2
Siteki Swaziland 109 D2
Sitka U.S.A. 126 B2
Sittard Neth. 54 B2
Sittaung r. Myanmar 74 A2
Sittwe Myanmar 74 A1
Situbondo Indon. 73 C2
Sivas Turkey 92 B2
Sivaslı Turkey 65 C3
Siverek Turkey 65 C3
Sivrihisar Turkey 92 B2
Siwah Egypt 102 A2
Siwah, Wähät oasis Egypt 92 A3
Siwalik Range mts India/Nepal 86 B1
Siwa Oasis Egypt see Siwah, Wähät
Six-Fours-les-Plages France 59 D3
Sixian China 82 B2
Siyabuswa S. Africa 109 C2
Sjenica Serb. and Mont. 64 B2
Sjøvegan Norway 46 F2
Skadovs'k Ukr. 45 D2
Skagen Denmark 47 C4
Skagerrak str. Denmark/Norway 47 B4
Skagit r. Can. 132 B3
Skagway U.S.A. 126 B2
Skardu Jammu and Kashmir 86 B1
Skarżysko-Kamienna Pol. 57 E2
Skawina Pol. 57 D3
Skeena r. Can. 126 B2
Skeena Mountains Can. 126 C2
Skegness U.K. 52 D3
Skellefteå Sweden 46 E3
Skellefteälven r. Sweden 46 E3
Skerries Rep. of Ireland 51 C2
Skiathos i. Greece 65 B3
Skibbereen Rep. of Ireland 51 B3
Skiðadals-jökull glacier Iceland
  46 [inset]
Skiddaw h. U.K. 52 B2
Skien Norway 47 B4
Skierniewice Pol. 57 E2
Skikda Alg. 101 C1
Skipton Austr. 116 C3
Skipton U.K. 52 B3
Skive Denmark 47 B4
Skjervøy Norway 46 E1
Skodje Norway 48 E1
Skopelos i. Greece 65 B3
Skopin Rus. Fed. 43 E3
Skopje Macedonia 64 B2
Skövde Sweden 47 C4
Skowhegan U.S.A. 137 G2
Skrunda Latvia 42 B2
Skukum, Mount Can. 126 B1
Skukuza S. Africa 109 D1
Skuodas Lith. 42 B2
Skye i. U.K. 50 A2
Skyros Greece 65 B3
Skyros i. Greece 65 B3
Slagelse Denmark 47 C4
Slaney r. Rep. of Ireland 51 C2
Slantsy Rus. Fed. 42 C2
Slatina Croatia 63 C1
Slatina Romania 44 B2
Slave r. Can. 127 D1

Slave Coast Africa 100 C4
Slave Lake Can. 126 D2
Slavgorod Rus. Fed. 89 E1
Slavonski Brod Croatia 63 C1
Slavuta Ukr. 44 C1
Slavutych Ukr. 44 D1
Slavyanka Rus. Fed. 78 B2
Slavyansk-na-Kubani Rus. Fed. 45 E2
Slawharad Belarus 43 D3
Sławno Pol. 57 D2
Slea Head Rep. of Ireland 51 A2
Sleeper Islands Can. 128 C1
Slieve Donard h. U.K. 51 D1
Slieve Gamph hills Rep. of Ireland
  51 B2
Sligo Rep. of Ireland 51 B1
Sligo Bay Rep. of Ireland 51 B1
Slite Sweden 47 D4
Sliven Bulg. 64 C2
Slobozia Romania 44 C3
Slocan Can. 126 D3
Slonim Belarus 42 C3
Sloten Neth. 54 B1
Slough U.K. 53 C4
Slovakia country Europe 57 D3
Slovenia country Europe 62 B1
Slov"yans'k Ukr. 45 E2
Sluch r. Ukr. 44 C1
Słupsk Pol. 57 D2
Slutsk Belarus 42 C3
Slyne Head Rep. of Ireland 51 A2
Smallwood Reservoir Can. 129 D1
Smalyavichy Belarus 42 C3
Smarhon' Belarus 42 C3
Smeaton Can. 127 E2
Smederevo Serb. and Mont. 64 B2
Smederevska Palanka Serb. and Mont.
  64 B2
Smila Ukr. 45 D2
Smiltene Latvia 42 C2
Smithers Can. 126 C2
Smithfield U.S.A. 139 E1
Smith Mountain Lake U.S.A. 137 E3
Smiths Falls Can. 128 C2
Smoky Hills U.S.A. 135 D3
Smøla i. Norway 46 E3
Smolensk Rus. Fed. 43 D3
Smolyan Bulg. 64 B2
Smooth Rock Falls Can. 128 B2
Smyrna Turkey see İzmir
Snæfell mt. Iceland 46 [inset]
Snaefell h. Isle of Man 52 A2
Snake r. U.S.A. 132 C1
Snake River Plain U.S.A. 132 D2
Sneek Neth. 54 B1
Sneem Rep. of Ireland 51 B3
Sneeuberge mts S. Africa 108 B3
Snežnik mt. Slovenia 62 B1
Snihurivka Ukr. 45 D2
Snøhetta mt. Norway 47 B3
Snowbird Lake Can. 127 E1
Snowdon mt. U.K. 52 A3
Snowdrift r. Can. 127 D1
Snowflake U.S.A. 140 B2
Snow Lake Can. 127 E2
Snowtown Austr. 116 B2
Snowy r. Austr. 117 D3
Snowy Mountains Austr. 117 D3
Snyder U.S.A. 141 D2
Soalala Madag. 107 [inset] D1
Sobat r. Sudan 103 B4
Sobernheim Ger. 54 C3
Sobinka Rus. Fed. 43 F2
Sobradinho, Barragem de resr Brazil
  151 E4
Sobral Brazil 151 E3
Sochi Rus. Fed. 45 E3
Söch'ön S. Korea 77 B2
Society Islands Fr. Polynesia 159 E6
Socorro Col. 150 B2

Socorro U.S.A. **140** C2
Socorro, Isla *i.* Mex. **142** A3
Socotra *i.* Yemen **91** C3
Soc Trăng Vietnam **75** B3
Socuéllamos Spain **60** C2
Sodankylä Fin. **46** F2
Soda Springs U.S.A. **132** D2
Söderhamn Sweden **47** D3
Söderköping Sweden **42** A2
Södertälje Sweden **47** D4
Sodiri Sudan **102** A3
Sodo Eth. **103** B4
Södra Kvarken *str.* Fin./Sweden **47** D3
Soest Ger. **54** D2
Sofia Bulg. **64** B2
Sofiya Bulg. *see* Sofia
Sofporog Rus. Fed. **46** G2
Sōfu-gan *i.* Japan **79** D5
Sog China **80** C2
Sognefjorden *inlet* Norway **47** B3
Söğüt Turkey **65** D2
Soignies Belgium **54** B2
Soissons France **59** C2
Sokal' Ukr. **44** B1
Söke Turkey **65** C3
Sokhumi Georgia **93** C1
Sokodé Togo **100** C4
Sokol Rus. Fed. **43** F2
Sokolov Czech Rep. **55** F2
Sokol'skoye Rus. Fed. **43** F2
Sokoto Nigeria **101** C3
Sokoto *r.* Nigeria **100** C3
Sokyryany Ukr. **44** C2
Solapur India **85** B3
Soledad U.S.A. **133** B3
Soligalich Rus. Fed. **43** F2
Solihull U.K. **53** C3
Solikamsk Rus. Fed. **40** E3
Sol'-Iletsk Rus. Fed. **41** E3
Solingen Ger. **54** C2
Solitaire Namibia **108** A1
Sollefteå Sweden **46** D3
Sollentuna Sweden **47** D4
Solling *hills* Ger. **55** D2
Solnechnogorsk Rus. Fed. **43** E2
Solok Indon. **72** B3
Solomon Islands *country*
  S. Pacific Ocean **112**
Solomon Sea S. Pacific Ocean **158** D5
Solothurn Switz. **59** D2
Sol'tsy Rus. Fed. **43** D2
Solway Firth *est.* U.K. **50** D3
Solwezi Zambia **106** B1
Soma Turkey **65** C3
Somalia *country* Africa **103** C4
Sombo Angola **104** C3
Sombor Serb. and Mont. **64** A1
Sombrerete Mex. **142** B2
Somerset U.S.A. **136** D3
Somerset East S. Africa **109** C3
Somerset Island Can. **124** F2
Somerset West S. Africa **108** A3
Sömmerda Ger. **55** E2
Son *r.* India **87** C2
Sønderborg Denmark **47** B5
Sondershausen Ger. **55** E2
Sông Đa, Hồ *resr* Vietnam **74** B1
Sông Da, Hô *resr* China **77** B1
Songea Tanz. **105** D4
Songhua Hu *resr* China **77** B1
Songkhla Thai. **75** B3
Sŏngnam S. Korea **77** B2
Sŏngnim N. Korea **77** B2
Songo Angola **104** B3
Songo Moz. **107** C1
Songyuan China **81** C1
Sonkovo Rus. Fed. **43** E2
Son La Vietnam **74** B1

Sonmiani Pak. **86** A2
Sonneberg Ger. **55** E2
Sonora *r.* Mex. **142** A2
Sonora *CA* U.S.A. **133** B3
Sonora *TX* U.S.A. **141** D2
Sopo *watercourse* Sudan **103** A4
Sopron Hungary **57** D3
Sora Italy **62** B2
Sorel Can. **98** C2
Sorell Austr. **115** D4
Soria Spain **60** C1
Soroca Moldova **44** D2
Sorocaba Brazil **154** C2
Sorochinsk Rus. Fed. **41** E3
Sorol *atoll* Micronesia **71** C2
Sorong Indon. **71** C3
Soroti Uganda **105** D3
Sørøya *i.* Norway **46** E1
Sorsele Sweden **46** D2
Sorsogon Phil. **76** B2
Sortavala Rus. Fed. **47** G3
Sortland Norway **46** D2
Sōsan S. Korea **77** B2
Soshanguve S. Africa **109** C2
Sosna *r.* Rus. Fed. **43** E3
Sosneado *mt.* Arg. **153** B4
Sosnogorsk Rus. Fed. **40** E2
Sosnovka *Murmanskaya Oblast'*
  Rus. Fed. **40** D2
Sosnovka *Tambovskaya Oblast'*
  Rus. Fed. **43** F3
Sosnovo Rus. Fed. **43** D1
Sosnovyy Bor Rus. Fed. **42** C1
Sosnowiec Pol. **57** D2
Sosyka *r.* Rus. Fed. **45** E2
Soto la Marina Mex. **143** C2
Souanké Congo **104** B3
Sougueur Alg. **61** D2
Souillac France **58** C3
Souilly France **54** B3
Sŏul S. Korea *see* Seoul
Soulac-sur-Mer France **58** B2
Soulom France **58** B3
Sour el Ghozlane Alg. **61** D2
Souris Man. Can. **127** E3
Souris *P.E.I.* Can. **129** C2
Souris *r.* Can. **134** D1
Sousa Brazil **151** F3
Sousse Tunisia **101** D1
Soustons France **58** B3
South Africa, Republic of *country*
  Africa **108** B3
Southampton U.K. **53** C4
Southampton, Cape Can. **127** G1
Southampton Island Can. **127** G1
South Andaman *i.* India **75** A2
South Australia *state* Austr. **116** A2
South Baymouth Can. **128** B2
South Bend U.S.A. **136** C2
South Carolina *state* U.S.A. **139** D2
South China Sea N. Pacific Ocean
  76 B2
South Dakota *state* U.S.A. **134** C2
South Downs *hills* U.K. **53** C4
Southend Can. **127** E2
Southend-on-Sea U.K. **53** D4
Southern Alps *mts* N.Z. **118** B3
Southern Cross Austr. **114** A3
Southern Indian Lake Can. **127** F2
Southern Pines U.S.A. **139** E1
Southern Uplands *hills* U.K. **50** D3
South Geomagnetic Pole Antarctica
  119 F1
South Georgia *i.* S. Atlantic Ocean
  153 E6
South Georgia and South Sandwich
  Islands *terr.* S. Atlantic Ocean **149**
South Henik Lake Can. **127** F1
South Island N.Z. **118** B3

South Korea *country* Asia **77** B2
South Lake Tahoe U.S.A. **133** B3
South Magnetic Pole Antarctica
  119 G3
South Orkney Islands
  S. Atlantic Ocean **119** A3
South Platte *r.* U.S.A. **134** C2
South Pole Antarctica **119**
Southport U.K. **52** B3
Southport U.S.A. **139** E2
South Ronaldsay *i.* U.K. **50** C1
South Sandwich Islands
  S. Atlantic Ocean **147**
South Saskatchewan *r.* Can. **127** E2
South Seal *r.* Can. **127** F2
South Shetland Islands Antarctica
  119 A3
South Shields U.K. **52** C2
South Taranaki Bight *b.* N.Z. **118** B2
South Twin Island Can. **128** C1
South Uist *i.* U.K. **50** A2
South West Rocks Austr. **117** E2
Southwold U.K. **53** D3
Soverato Italy **63** C3
Sovetsk Rus. Fed. **42** B2
Sovetskiy *Khanty-Mansiyskiy*
  Avtonomnyy Okrug Rus. Fed. **40** F2
Sovetskiy *Leningradskaya Oblast'*
  Rus. Fed. **47** G3
Sovyets'kyy Ukr. **45** D2
Soweto S. Africa **109** C2
Sōya-misaki *c.* Japan **78** D1
Sozh *r.* Europe **44** D1
Sozopol Bulg. **64** C2
Spain *country* Europe **60** C1
Spalding U.K. **52** C3
Spanish Fork U.S.A. **132** D2
Spanish Point Rep. of Ireland **51** B2
Sparagio, Monte *mt.* Italy **62** B3
Sparks U.S.A. **133** C3
Sparta U.S.A. **136** B2
Spartanburg U.S.A. **139** D2
Sparti Greece **65** B3
Spartivento, Capo *c.* Italy **63** C3
Spas-Demensk Rus. Fed. **43** D3
Spas-Klepiki Rus. Fed. **43** F2
Spassk-Dal'niy Rus. Fed. **78** B2
Spassk-Ryazanskiy Rus. Fed. **43** F3
Spatha, Akra *pt* Greece **65** B3
Spearfish U.S.A. **134** C2
Spearman U.S.A. **141** D1
Spencer U.S.A. **136** D2
Spencer Gulf *est.* Austr. **116** B2
Spennymoor U.K. **52** C2
Spenser Mountains N.Z. **118** B3
Spessart *reg.* Ger. **55** D3
Spey *r.* U.K. **50** C2
Speyer Ger. **55** D3
Spiekeroog *i.* Ger. **54** C1
Spijkenisse Neth. **54** B2
Spirit River Can. **126** D2
Spišská Nová Ves Slovakia **57** E3
Spitsbergen *i.* Svalbard **94** D1
Spittal an der Drau Austria **56** F2
Split Croatia **63** C2
Split Lake Can. **127** F2
Split Lake *l.* Can. **127** F2
Spokane U.S.A. **132** C1
Spoleto Italy **59** E3
Spooner U.S.A. **136** B1
Spree *r.* Ger. **56** C2
Springbok S. Africa **108** A2
Springdale Can. **129** E2
Springdale U.S.A. **138** B1
Springe Ger. **55** D1
Springer U.S.A. **140** D1
Springerville U.S.A. **140** C3
Springfield *CO* U.S.A. **134** C3
Springfield *IL* U.S.A. **136** C3
Springfield *MA* U.S.A. **137** F2

pringfield *MO* U.S.A. **135** E3	Stavanger Norway **47** B4	Stowbtsy Belarus **42** C3
pringfield *OH* U.S.A. **136** D3	Stavropol' Rus. Fed. **41** D4	Strabane U.K. **51** C1
pringfield *OR* U.S.A. **132** B2	Stavropol'skaya Vozvyshennost' *hills*	Strakonice Czech Rep. **56** C3
pringfontein S. Africa **109** C3	Rus. Fed. **41** D4	Stralsund Ger. **56** C2
pringhill Can. **129** D2	Stawell Austr. **116** C3	Strand S. Africa **108** A3
prings Junction N.Z. **118** B3	Steadville S. Africa **109** C2	Stranda Norway **47** B3
purn Head U.K. **52** E3	Steamboat Springs U.S.A. **134** B2	Strangford Lough *inlet* U.K. **51** D1
quamish Can. **126** C3	Stedten Ger. **55** E2	Stranraer U.K. **50** B3
quillace, Golfo di *g.* Italy **63** C3	Steen River Can. **126** D2	Strasbourg France **59** D2
bija *aut. rep.* Serb. and Mont. **64** B2	Steens Mountain U.S.A. **132** C2	Strasburg Ger. **55** F1
ebrenica Bos.-Herz. **63** C2	Steenwijk Neth. **54** C1	Stratford Can. **137** D2
edets Bulg. **64** C2	Stefansson Island Can. **124** E2	Stratford N.Z. **118** B2
edinnyy Khrebet *mts* Rus. Fed.	Steigerwald *mts* Ger. **55** E3	Stratford U.S.A. **141** D1
95 M3	Steinbach Can. **127** F3	Stratford-upon-Avon U.K. **53** C3
ednekolymsk Rus. Fed. **95** M2	Steinfurt Ger. **54** C1	Strathspey *val.* U.K. **50** C2
edne-Russkaya Vozvyshennost'	Steinhausen Namibia **106** A2	Straubing Ger. **56** C3
hills Rus. Fed. *see*	Steinkjer Norway **46** C3	Strausberg Ger. **55** F1
Central Russian Upland	Steinkopf S. Africa **108** A2	Streaky Bay Austr. **116** A2
ednogorie Bulg. **64** D2	Stella S. Africa **108** B2	Streator U.S.A. **136** C2
etensk Rus. Fed. **81** D1	Stenay France **59** D2	Strehaia Romania **44** B3
i Aman Malaysia **73** C1	Stendal Ger. **55** E1	Stroeder Arg. **153** B5
i Jayewardenepura Kotte Sri Lanka	Stephenville Can. **129** E2	Ströhen Ger. **55** D1
85 B4	Stephenville U.S.A. **141** E2	Stromboli, Isola *i.* Italy **62** C3
ikakulam India **85** C3	Sterling S. Africa **108** B3	Stromness U.K. **50** C1
inagar India **86** B1	Sterling *CO* U.S.A. **134** C2	Strömsund Sweden **46** D3
i Lanka *country* Asia **85** C4	Sterling *IL* U.S.A. **136** C2	Stronsay *i.* U.K. **50** C1
ivardhan India **85** C4	Sterlitamak Rus. Fed. **41** E3	Stroud Austr. **117** E2
i Pada *mt.* Sri Lanka **85** C4	Sternberg Ger. **55** E1	Stroud U.K. **53** B4
ade Ger. **55** D1	Stettler Can. **127** D2	Strücklingen (Saterland) Ger. **54** C1
adensen Ger. **55** E1	Steubenville U.S.A. **137** D2	Struga Macedonia **65** B2
adskanaal Neth. **54** C1	Stevenage U.K. **53** C4	Strugi-Krasnyye Rus. Fed. **42** C2
adtallendorf Ger. **55** D2	Stevenson Lake Can. **127** F2	Struis Bay S. Africa **108** B3
adthagen Ger. **55** D1	Stevens Village U.S.A. **124** C2	Strumica Macedonia **65** B2
affelstein Ger. **55** E2	Stewart Can. **126** C2	Strydenburg S. Africa **108** B2
afford U.K. **53** E2	Stewart *r.* Can. **126** B1	Stryy Ukr. **44** B2
aines U.K. **53** C4	Stewart Island N.Z. **118** A4	Stuart Lake Can. **126** C2
akhanov Ukr. **45** E2	Steyr Austria **56** C3	Stull Lake Can. **127** F2
alingrad Rus. Fed. *see* Volgograd	Steytlerville S. Africa **108** B3	Stupino Rus. Fed. **43** E3
alowa Wola Pol. **57** E2	Stikine *r.* Can. **126** B2	Sturgeon Bay U.S.A. **136** C2
amford U.K. **53** C3	Stikine Plateau Can. **126** B2	Sturgeon Falls Can. **128** C2
amford *CT* U.S.A. **137** F2	Stilbaai S. Africa **108** B3	Sturgeon Lake Can. **128** A2
amford *TX* U.S.A. **141** E2	Stillwater U.S.A. **141** E1	Sturgis *MI* U.S.A. **136** C2
amsund Norway **46** C2	Stip Macedonia **63** D2	Sturgis *SD* U.S.A. **134** C2
anderton S. Africa **109** C2	Stirling U.K. **50** C2	Sturt Creek *watercourse* Austr. **114** B1
andish U.S.A. **136** D2	Stjørdalshalsen Norway **46** C3	Sturt Stony Desert Austr. **116** C1
anger S. Africa **109** D2	Stockerau Austria **57** D3	Stutterheim S. Africa **109** C3
aňkov Czech Rep. **55** F3	Stockholm Sweden **47** D4	Stuttgart Ger. **56** B3
anley Falkland Is **153** C6	Stockport U.K. **52** B3	Stuttgart U.S.A. **138** B2
anley U.S.A. **134** C1	Stockton U.S.A. **133** B3	Stykkishólmur Iceland **46** [inset]
anovoye Nagor'ye *mts* Rus. Fed.	Stockton-on-Tees U.K. **52** C2	Styr *r.* Belarus/Ukr. **44** C1
95 J3	Stod Czech Rep. **55** F3	Suaçuí Grande *r.* Brazil **155** D1
anovoy Khrebet *mts* Rus. Fed.	Stœng Trêng Cambodia **75** B2	Suakin Sudan **102** B3
95 K3	Stoer, Point of *pt* U.K. **50** B1	Suara, Mount Eritrea **90** A3
anthorpe Austr. **117** E1	Stoke-on-Trent U.K. **52** B3	Subotica Serb. and Mont. **64** A1
arachowice Pol. **57** E2	Stol *mt.* Serb. and Mont. **64** B2	Suceava Romania **44** C2
ara Planina *mts* Bulg./Serb. and	Stolac Bos.-Herz. **63** C2	Suck *r.* Rep. of Ireland **51** B2
Mont. *see* Balkan Mountains	Stolberg (Rheinland) Ger. **54** C2	Sucre Bol. **152** B2
araya Russa Rus. Fed. **43** D2	Stolbovoy Rus. Fed. **40** E1	Sucuriú *r.* Brazil **154** B2
araya Toropa Rus. Fed. **43** D2	Stolin Belarus **42** C3	Suda Rus. Fed. **43** E2
ara Zagora Bulg. **64** C2	Stollberg Ger. **55** F2	Sudak Ukr. **45** D3
argard Szczeciński Pol. **57** D2	Stolzenau Ger. **55** D1	Sudan *country* Africa **103** A3
arkville U.S.A. **138** C2	Stonehaven U.K. **50** C2	Sudbury Can. **128** B2
arobil's'k Ukr. **45** E2	Stonewall Can. **127** F2	Sudd *swamp* Sudan **103** A4
arodub Rus. Fed. **43** D3	Stony Rapids Can. **124** E3	Sudety *mts* Czech Rep./Pol. **36**
arogard Gdański Pol. **57** D2	Storavan *l.* Sweden **46** D2	Sudislavl' Rus. Fed. **43** F2
arominskaya Rus. Fed. **45** E2	Store Bælt *sea chan.* Denmark *see*	Sudogda Rus. Fed. **43** F2
aroshcherbinovskaya Rus. Fed.	Great Belt	Suðuroy *i.* Faroe Is **48** B1
45 E2	Støren Norway **46** C3	Sueca Spain **61** C2
arotitarovskaya Rus. Fed. **45** E2	Storforshei Norway **46** C2	Suez Egypt **102** B2
aroyur'yevo Rus. Fed. **43** F3	Storkerson Peninsula Can. **124** E2	Suez, Gulf of Egypt **102** B2
art Point *pt* U.K. **53** B4	Storm Lake U.S.A. **135** D2	Suez Canal Egypt **92** B2
arya Darohi Belarus **42** C3	Stornoway U.K. **50** A1	Suffolk U.S.A. **137** E3
aryy Oskol Rus. Fed. **43** E3	Storozhevsk Rus. Fed. **40** E2	Şuhār Oman **91** C2
aßfurt Ger. **55** E2	Storozhynets' Ukr. **44** D2	Sühbaatar Mongolia **80** D1
ate College U.S.A. **137** E2	Storsjön *l.* Sweden **46** C3	Suhl Ger. **55** E2
atesboro U.S.A. **139** D2	Storslett Norway **46** E2	Suhopolje Croatia **63** C1
atesville U.S.A. **139** D1	Storuman Sweden **46** D2	Suide China **82** B2
	Stour *r. England* U.K. **53** C3	Suifenhe China **78** B2
	Stour *r. England* U.K. **53** C4	Suihua China **81** E1
	Stout Lake Can. **128** A1	Suining China **82** A2

Suiping China **82** B2
Suippes France **54** B3
Suiyang China **82** B2
Suizhou China **82** B2
Sujangarh India **86** B2
Sujanpur India **86** B1
Sujawal Pak. **86** A2
Sukabumi Indon. **72** B2
Sukadana Indon. **73** B2
Sukaraja Indon. **73** C2
Sukhinichi Rus. Fed. **43** E3
Sukhona r. Rus. Fed. **43** F2
Sukhothai Thai. **74** A2
Sukkur Pak. **86** A2
Sukromny Rus. Fed. **43** E2
Sula i. Norway **48** D1
Sula, Kepulauan is Indon. **71** C3
Sulaiman Range mts Pak. **86** A1
Sulawesi i. Indon. see Celebes
Sullana Peru **150** A3
Sullivan U.S.A. **135** E3
Sulphur Springs U.S.A. **141** E2
Sulu Archipelago is Phil. **76** B3
Sulu Sea N. Pacific Ocean **76** A3
Sulzbach-Rosenberg Ger. **55** E3
Sumāil Oman **91** C2
Sumatera i. Indon. see Sumatra
Sumatra i. Indon. **72** A1
Šumava mts Czech Rep. **55** F3
Sumba i. Indon. **73** D2
Sumba, Selat sea chan. Indon. **73** C2
Sumbawa i. Indon. **73** C2
Sumbawabesar Indon. **73** C2
Sumbawanga Tanz. **105** D3
Sumbe Angola **106** A1
Sumburgh U.K. **50** [inset]
Sumburgh Head U.K. **50** [inset]
Sumenep Indon. **73** C2
Sumisu-jima i. Japan **79** D4
Summerside Can. **129** D2
Summersville U.S.A. **136** D3
Summit Lake Can. **126** C2
Šumperk Czech Rep. **57** D3
Sumqayıt Azer. **93** C1
Sumter U.S.A. **139** D2
Sumy Ukr. **45** D1
Sunamganj Bangl. **87** D2
Sunan N. Korea **77** B2
Şunaynah Oman **91** C2
Sunbury Austr. **116** C3
Sunbury U.S.A. **137** E2
Sunch'ŏn N. Korea **77** B2
Sunch'ŏn S. Korea **77** B3
Sun City S. Africa **109** C1
Sunda, Selat str. Indon. **72** B2
Sundance U.S.A. **134** C2
Sundarbans coastal area Bangl./India **87** C2
Sunderland U.K. **52** C2
Sundre Can. **126** D2
Sundsvall Sweden **47** D3
Sundumbili S. Africa **109** D2
Sungailiat Indon. **72** B2
Sungaipenuh Indon. **72** B2
Sungai Petani Malaysia **72** B1
Sungurlu Turkey **92** B1
Sunndal Norway **48** E1
Sunndalsøra Norway **46** B3
Sunnyside U.S.A. **132** C1
Sunnyvale U.S.A. **133** B3
Suntar Rus. Fed. **95** J2
Sunyani Ghana **100** B4
Suoyarvi Rus. Fed. **94** E2
Superior AZ U.S.A. **140** D2
Superior NE U.S.A. **135** D2
Superior WI U.S.A. **136** B1
Superior, Lake Can./U.S.A. **136** C1
Suponevo Rus. Fed. **43** D3
Süq ash Shuyūkh Iraq **93** C2

Suqian China **82** B2
Sūq Suwayq Saudi Arabia **90** A2
Suqutrā i. Yemen see Socotra
Şūr Oman **91** C2
Şūr, Punta pt Arg. **147**
Surab Pak. **86** A2
Surabaya Indon. **73** C2
Surakarta Indon. **73** C2
Surat India **86** B2
Suratgarh India **86** B2
Surat Thani Thai. **75** A3
Suraxanı Rus. Fed. **43** D3
Surdulica Serb. and Mont. **64** B2
Surendranagar India **86** B2
Surgut Rus. Fed. **40** G2
Suriapo Phil. **76** B3
Surin Thai. **75** B2
Suriname country S. America **151** D2
Surulangun Indon. **72** B2
Susanino Rus. Fed. **43** F2
Susanville U.S.A. **132** B2
Suşehri Turkey **92** B1
Sušice Czech Rep. **55** F3
Sussex Can. **129** D2
Süstedt Ger. **55** D1
Sustrum Ger. **54** C1
Susuman Rus. Fed. **95** L2
Susurluk Turkey **65** C3
Sutak Jammu and Kashmir **87** B1
Sutherland S. Africa **108** B3
Sutton Coldfield U.K. **53** C3
Suttsu Japan **78** D2
Suva Fiji **112**
Suvorov Rus. Fed. **43** E3
Suwałki Pol. **57** E2
Suwannaphum Thai. **75** B2
Suwannee r. U.S.A. **139** D3
Suwarrow atoll Cook Is **111**
Suways, Qanāt as canal Egypt see
 Suez Canal
Suwŏn S. Korea **77** B2
Süzä Iran **91** C2
Suzdal' Rus. Fed. **43** F2
Suzhou Anhui China **82** B2
Suzhou Jiangsu China **82** C2
Suzu Japan **79** C3
Suzu-misaki pt Japan **79** C3
Svalbard terr. Arctic Ocean **94** C1
Svatove Ukr. **45** E2
Svay Riĕng Cambodia **75** B2
Sveg Sweden **47** C3
Svelgen Norway **48** E1
Švenčionys Lith. **42** C2
Svendborg Denmark **47** C4
Sverdlovsk Rus. Fed. see
 Yekaterinburg
Sveti Nikole Macedonia **64** B2
Svetlaya Rus. Fed. **78** C1
Svetlogorsk Rus. Fed. **42** B3
Svetlyy Rus. Fed. **42** B3
Svetogorsk Rus. Fed. **47** F3
Svilengrad Bulg. **64** C2
Svinecea Mare, Vârful mt. Romania **44** B3
Svir' r. Rus. Fed. **43** E1
Svishtov Bulg. **64** C2
Svitavy Czech Rep. **57** D3
Svitlovods'k Ukr. **45** D2
Svobodnyy Rus. Fed. **81** E1
Svolvær Norway **46** C2
Svyetlahorsk Belarus **42** C3
Swainsboro U.S.A. **139** D2
Swakop watercourse Namibia **108** A1
Swakopmund Namibia **106** A2
Swan Hill Austr. **116** C3
Swan Hills Can. **126** D2
Swan Lake Can. **127** E2
Swan River Can. **127** E2
Swansea Austr. **117** E2
Swansea U.K. **53** B4

Swartruggens S. Africa **109** C2
Swatow China see Shantou
Swaziland country Africa **109** D2
Sweden country Europe **47** D3
Sweetwater U.S.A. **141** D2
Sweetwater r. U.S.A. **134** B2
Swellendam S. Africa **108** B3
Świdnica Pol. **57** D2
Świdwin Pol. **57** D2
Świebodzin Pol. **57** D2
Świecie Pol. **57** D2
Swift Current Can. **124** E3
Swilly, Lough inlet Rep. of Ireland **51** C1
Swindon U.K. **53** C4
Świnoujście Pol. **56** C2
Switzerland country Europe **59** D2
Swords Rep. of Ireland **51** C2
Syanno Belarus **42** C3
Sychevka Rus. Fed. **43** D2
Sydney Austr. **117** E2
Sydney Can. **129** D2
Sydney Mines Can. **129** D2
Syeverodonets'k Ukr. **45** E2
Syktyvkar Rus. Fed. **40** E2
Sylacauga U.S.A. **139** C2
Sylhet Bangl. **87** D2
Sylt i. Ger. **56** B2
Symi i. Greece **65** C3
Synel'nykove Ukr. **45** E2
Syracuse Italy **62** C3
Syracuse KS U.S.A. **134** C3
Syracuse NY U.S.A. **137** E2
Syrdar'ya r. Asia **89** D2
Syria country Asia **92** B2
Syrian Desert Asia **92** B2
Syros i. Greece **65** C3
Syzran' Rus. Fed. **41** D3
Szczecin Pol. **56** C2
Szczecinek Pol. **57** D2
Szczytno Pol. **57** E2
Szeged Hungary **57** E3
Székesfehérvár Hungary **57** D3
Szekszárd Hungary **57** D3
Szentes Hungary **57** E3
Szentgotthárd Hungary **57** D3
Szigetvár Hungary **57** D3
Szolnok Hungary **57** E3
Szombathely Hungary **57** D3

T

Tābah Saudi Arabia **90** B2
Ţabas Iran **93** D2
Tābask, Kūh-e mt. Iran **93** D3
Tabatinga Brazil **150** C3
Tabelbala Alg. **100** B2
Taber Can. **127** D3
Tábor Czech Rep. **56** C3
Tabora Tanz. **105** D3
Tabou Côte d'Ivoire **100** B4
Tabrīz Iran **93** C2
Tabūk Saudi Arabia **90** A2
Täby Sweden **42** A2
Tacheng China **89** F2
Tachov Czech Rep. **56** C3
Tacloban Phil. **76** B2
Tacna Peru **150** A3
Tacoma U.S.A. **132** B1
Tacuarembó Uru. **152** C4
Tacupeto Mex. **140** C3
Tadjoura Djibouti **103** C3
Tadmur Syria **92** B2
Tadoule Lake Can. **127** F2
Taegu S. Korea **77** B2
Taejŏn S. Korea **77** B2
Taejŏng S. Korea **77** B3
T'aepaek S. Korea **77** B2

a'erqi China 81 E1
afalla Spain 61 C1
afi Viejo Arg. 152 B3
aftän, Küh-e mt. Iran 91 D2
aganrog Rus. Fed. 45 E2
aganrog, Gulf of Rus. Fed./Ukr. 45 E2
agaung Myanmar 74 A1
agaytay City Phil. 76 B2
agbilaran Phil. 76 B2
agudin Phil. 76 B2
agum Phil. 76 B3
agus r. Port. 60 B2
agus r. Spain 60 B2
ahan, Gunung mt. Malaysia 72 B1
ahat, Mont mt. Alg. 101 C2
ahe China 81 E1
ahiti i. Fr. Polynesia 111
ahlequah U.S.A. 141 F1
ahoe, Lake U.S.A. 133 B3
ahoe City U.S.A. 133 B3
ahrüd Iran 91 C2
ahsis Can. 126 C3
ai'an China 82 B2
aichung Taiwan 83 C3
ai Hu i. China 82 C2
ainan Taiwan 83 C3
aiobeiras Brazil 155 D1
aipei Taiwan 83 C3
aiping Malaysia 72 B1
aishan China 83 B3
aitao, Peninsula de pen. Chile
  153 A5
aitung Taiwan 83 C3
aivalkoski Fin. 46 F2
aivaskero h. Fin. 46 F2
aiwan country Asia 83 C3
aiwan Strait China/Taiwan 83 B3
aiyuan China 82 B2
aizhou Jiangsu China 82 B2
aizhou Zhejiang China 83 C3
aiyuan China 90 B3
a'izz Yemen 90 B3
ajamulco, Volcán de vol. Guat.
  143 C3
ajikistan country Asia 89 E3
aj Mahal tourist site India 87 B2
ajo r. Spain see Tagus
ak Thai. 74 A2
akaka N.Z. 118 B4
akamatsu Japan 79 B4
akaoka Japan 79 C3
akapuna N.Z. 118 B2
akasaki Japan 79 C3
akefu Japan 79 C3
akengon Indon. 72 A1
i Khmau Cambodia 75 B3
akikawa Japan 78 D2
akla Lake Can. 126 C2
akla Landing Can. 126 C2
aklimakan Desert China 89 F3
aklimakan Shamo des. China see
  Taklimakan Desert
aku r. Can./U.S.A. 126 B2
akum Nigeria 101 C4
akung Belarus 42 C3
alagang Pak. 86 B1
alara Peru 150 A3
alaud, Kepulauan is Indon. 71 C2
alcahuano Chile 153 A4

Taldom Rus. Fed. 43 E2
Taldykorgan Kazakh. 89 E2
Talia Austr. 116 A2
Taliabu i. Indon. 71 C2
Talisay Phil. 76 B2
Taliwang Indon. 73 C2
Tall 'Afar Iraq 93 C2
Tallahassee U.S.A. 139 D2
Tallinn Estonia 42 B2
Tallulah U.S.A. 138 B2
Talmont-St-Hilaire France 58 B2
Tal'ne Ukr. 44 D2
Talodi Sudan 103 B3
Tāloqān Afgh. 86 A1
Talovaya Rus. Fed. 43 F3
Taloyoak Can. 124 F2
Taltal Chile 152 A3
Taltson r. Can. 127 D2
Talu Indon. 72 A1
Talwood Austr. 117 D1
Tamala Rus. Fed. 45 F1
Tamale Ghana 100 B4
Tamanrasset Alg. 101 C2
Tamar r. U.K. 53 A4
Tamazunchale Mex. 143 C2
Tambacounda Senegal 100 A3
Tambelan, Kepulauan is Indon. 72 B1
Tambey Rus. Fed. 40 G1
Tambov Rus. Fed. 43 F3
Tamiahua, Laguna de lag. Mex.
  143 C2
Tampa U.S.A. 139 D3
Tampa Bay U.S.A. 139 D3
Tampere Fin. 47 E3
Tampico Mex. 143 C2
Tamsagbulag Mongolia 81 D1
Tamsweg Austria 56 C3
Tamworth Austr. 117 E2
Tamworth U.K. 53 C3
Tana r. Kenya 105 E3
Tana, Lake Eth. 103 B3
Tanabe Japan 79 C4
Tana Bru Norway 46 F1
Tanahgrogot Indon. 73 C2
Tanahjampea i. Indon. 73 C2
Tanami Desert Austr. 114 C1
Tanana U.S.A. 124 D2
Tanaro r. Italy 62 A1
Tanch'ŏn N. Korea 77 B1
Tandag Phil. 76 B3
Ţăndărei Romania 44 C3
Tandil Arg. 153 C4
Tando Adam Pak. 86 A2
Tando Muhammad Khan Pak. 86 A2
Tanezrouft reg. Alg./Mali 100 B2
Tanga Tanz. 105 D3
Tanganyika, Lake Africa 105 C3
Tanger Morocco see Tangier
Tangermünde Ger. 55 E1
Tanggula Shan mt. China 87 D1
Tanggula Shan mts China 87 D1
Tangier Morocco 100 B1
Tangra Yumco salt l. China 87 C1
Tangshan China 82 B2
Taniantaweng Shan mts China 80 C2
Tanimbar, Kepulauan is Indon. 71 C2
Tanjay Phil. 76 B3
Tanjungbalai Indon. 72 A1
Tanjungpandan Indon. 72 B2
Tanjungpinang Indon. 72 B1
Tanjungredeb Indon. 73 C1
Tanjungselor Indon. 73 C1
Tank Pak. 86 B1
Tanna i. Vanuatu 110
Tanout Niger 101 C3
Tansen Nepal 87 C2
Ţanţā Egypt 102 B1
Tanzania country Africa 105 D3
Taonan China 81 E1

Taos U.S.A. 140 E1
Taoudenni Mali 100 B2
Tapa Estonia 42 C2
Tapachula Mex. 143 C3
Tapajós r. Brazil 151 D3
Tapaktuan Indon. 72 A1
Tapanatepec Mex. 143 C3
Tapauá Brazil 150 C3
Tapeta Liberia 100 B4
Tapi r. India 86 B2
Tappahannock U.S.A. 137 E3
Tapurucuara Brazil 150 C3
Taquari r. Brazil 151 D3
Taquari, Pantanal do marsh Brazil
  154 A1
Taquari, Serra do hills Brazil 154 B1
Taquaritinga Brazil 154 C2
Taraba r. Nigeria 101 D4
Ţarābulus Libya see Tripoli
Tarakan Indon. 73 C1
Taran, Mys pt Rus. Fed. 42 A3
Taranaki, Mount vol. N.Z. 118 B2
Tarancón Spain 60 C1
Taranto Italy 63 C2
Taranto, Golfo di g. Italy 63 C2
Tarapoto Peru 150 B3
Tarasovskiy Rus. Fed. 45 F2
Tarauacá Brazil 150 B3
Tarauacá r. Brazil 150 C3
Tarawa atoll Kiribati 110
Taraz Kazakh. 89 E2
Tarazona Spain 61 C1
Tarbagatay, Khrebet mts Kazakh.
  89 F2
Tarbert Scotland U.K. 50 B3
Tarbert Scotland U.K. 50 A2
Tarbes France 58 C3
Tarbet U.K. 50 B2
Tarcoola Austr. 116 A2
Taree Austr. 117 E2
Târgovişte Romania 44 C3
Targuist Morocco 60 C3
Târgu Jiu Romania 44 B2
Târgu Mureş Romania 44 B2
Târgu Neamţ Romania 44 C2
Tarif U.A.E. 91 C2
Tarija Bol. 152 B3
Tarim Yemen 91 C3
Tarim Basin China 89 F3
Tarim He r. China 89 E3
Tarim Pendi basin China see
  Tarim Basin
Taritatu r. Indon. 71 D3
Tarko-Sale Rus. Fed. 40 G2
Tarkwa Ghana 100 B4
Tarlac Phil. 76 B2
Tärnaby Sweden 46 D2
Tarnak r. Afgh. 86 A1
Tărnăveni Romania 44 B2
Tarnobrzeg Pol. 57 E2
Tarnów Pol. 57 E2
Taroudannt Morocco 100 B1
Tarquinia Italy 62 B2
Tarragona Spain 61 D1
Tàrrega Spain 61 D1
Tarsus Turkey 92 B2
Tartagal Arg. 152 B3
Tartas France 58 B3
Tartu Estonia 42 C2
Ţarţūs Syria 92 B2
Tarumirim Brazil 155 D1
Tarusa Rus. Fed. 43 E3
Tarvisio Italy 62 B1
Tashk, Daryācheh-ye l. Iran 93 D3
Tashkent Uzbek. 89 D2
Tasialujjuaq, Lac l. Can. 129 C1
Tasiat, Lac l. Can. 128 C1
Tasiujaq Can. 129 D1
Taskesken Kazakh. 89 F2
Tasman Bay N.Z. 118 B3

Tasmania *i.* Austr. **110**
Tasmania *state* Austr. **115** D4
Tasman Islands N.Z. **118** B3
Tasman Sea S. Pacific Ocean **115** E3
Tassili du Hoggar *plat.* Alg. **101** C2
Tassili n'Ajjer *plat.* Alg. **101** C2
Tataba Indon. **73** D2
Tatabánya Hungary **57** D3
Tatarbunary Ukr. **44** C2
Tateyama Japan **79** C4
Tathlina Lake Can. **126** D1
Tathlith Saudi Arabia **90** B3
Tathlith, Wādī *watercourse*
  Saudi Arabia **90** B3
Tathra Austr. **117** D3
Tatkon Myanmar **74** A1
Tatla Lake Can. **126** C2
Tatra Mountains Pol. **57** D3
Tatsinskiy Rus. Fed. **45** F2
Tatta Pak. **86** A2
Tatui Brazil **154** C1
Tatum U.S.A. **141** D2
Tatvan Turkey **93** D2
Taua Brazil **151** E3
Taubaté Brazil **155** C2
Tauberbischofsheim Ger. **55** D3
Taumarunui N.Z. **118** C2
Taunggyi Myanmar **74** A1
Taung-ngu Myanmar **74** A2
Taungup Myanmar **74** A2
Taunton U.K. **53** B4
Taunus *hills* Ger. **54** C2
Taupo N.Z. **118** C2
Taupo, Lake N.Z. **118** C2
Tauragė Lith. **42** B2
Tauranga N.Z. **118** C2
Taurus Mountains Turkey **92** B2
Tavas Turkey **65** C3
Tavda Rus. Fed. **40** F3
Tavira Port. **60** B2
Tavistock U.K. **53** A4
Tavoy Myanmar **75** A2
Tavşanlı Turkey **65** C3
Taw *r.* U.K. **53** A4
Tawas City U.S.A. **136** D2
Tawau Malaysia **73** C1
Tawitawi *i.* Phil. **76** A3
Taxco Mex. **143** C3
Taxiatosh Uzbek. **88** C2
Taxkorgan China **89** E3
Tay *r.* U.K. **50** C2
Tay, Firth of *est.* U.K. **50** C2
Tay, Loch *l.* U.K. **50** B2
Taylor Can. **126** C2
Taylor U.S.A. **141** E2
Taylorville U.S.A. **136** C3
Taymā' Saudi Arabia **90** A2
Taymura *r.* Rus. Fed. **95** I2
Taymyr, Ozero *l.* Rus. Fed. **95** I2
Taymyr, Poluostrov *pen.* Rus. Fed. *see*
  Taymyr Peninsula
Taymyr Peninsula Rus. Fed. **95** H2
Tây Ninh Vietnam **75** B2
Taytay Phil. **76** A2
Taz *r.* Rus. Fed. **40** G2
Taza Morocco **100** B1
Tazin Lake Can. **127** D2
Tazovskaya Guba *sea chan.* Rus. Fed.
  40 G2
T'bilisi Georgia **93** C1
Tbilisskaya Rus. Fed. **45** F2
Tchibanga Gabon **104** B3
Tcholliré Cameroon **104** B2
Tczew Pol. **57** D2
Teacapán Mex. **142** B2
Te Anau N.Z. **118** A4
Te Anau, Lake N.Z. **118** A4
Teapa Mex. **143** C3

Te Awamutu N.Z. **118** C2
Tébessa Alg. **101** C1
Tebingtinggi *Sumatera Selatan* Indon.
  72 B2
Tebingtinggi *Sumatera Utara* Indon.
  72 A1
Techiman Ghana **100** B4
Tecomán Mex. **142** B3
Tecoripa Mex. **142** B2
Técpan Mex. **143** B3
Tecuala Mex. **142** B2
Tecuci Romania **44** C2
Tedzhen Turkm. **88** D3
Tedzhen *r.* Turkm. **88** D3
Teeli Rus. Fed. **89** G1
Tees *r.* U.K. **52** C3
Tefenni Turkey **65** C3
Tegal Indon. **72** B2
Tegucigalpa Hond. **144** B3
Teguidda-n-Tessoumt Niger **101** C3
Tehek Lake Can. **127** F1
Téhini Côte d'Ivoire **100** B4
Tehrān Iran **93** D2
Tehuacán Mex. **143** C3
Tehuantepec, Golfo de *g.* Mex.
  143 C3
Tehuantepec, Istmo de *isth.* Mex.
  143 C3
Teifi *r.* U.K. **53** A3
Tejo *r.* Port. *see* Tagus
Tejupilco Mex. **143** B3
Tekapo, Lake N.Z. **118** B3
Tekax Mex. **143** D2
Tekezē *Wenz r.* Eritrea/Eth. **102** B3
Tekirdağ Turkey **65** C2
Te Kuiti N.Z. **118** C2
Tel *r.* India **87** C2
T'elavi Georgia **93** C1
Tel Aviv-Yafo Israel **92** B2
Telchac Puerto Mex. **143** D2
Telegraph Creek Can. **126** B2
Telêmaco Borba Brazil **154** B2
Telford U.K. **53** B3
Telo Indon. **72** A2
Teluk Batang Indon. **73** B2
Telukbatang Indon. **73** B2
Telukdalam Indon. **72** A1
Teluk Intan Malaysia **72** B1
Temagami Lake Can. **128** C2
Temanggung Indon. **73** C2
Temba S. Africa **109** C2
Tembilahan Indon. **72** B2
Tembo Aluma Angola **104** B3
Teme *r.* U.K. **53** B3
Temerluh Malaysia **72** B1
Temirtau Kazakh. **89** E1
Temora Austr. **117** D2
Temple U.S.A. **141** E2
Templemore Rep. of Ireland **51** C2
Templin Ger. **55** F1
Tempoal Mex. **143** C2
Temryuk Rus. Fed. **45** E2
Temuco Chile **153** A4
Temuka N.Z. **118** B3
Tenabo Mex. **143** C3
Tenali India **87** C3
Tenasserim Myanmar **75** A2
Tenby U.K. **53** A4
Tendaho Eth. **103** C3
Tende France **59** D3
Tende, Col de *pass* France/Italy **59** D3
Ten Degree Channel India **75** A3
Tendô Japan **78** D3
Ténenkou Mali **100** B3
Ténéré, Erg du *des.* Niger **101** D3
Ténéré du Tafassâsset *des.* Niger
  101 D2
Tenerife *i.* Canary Is **100** A2
Ténès Alg. **61** D2

Tengah, Kepulauan *is* Indon. **73** C2
Tengchong China **74** A1
Tenggarong Indon. **73** C2
Tengger Shamo *des.* China **82** A2
Tengxian China **83** B3
Tenke Dem. Rep. Congo **105** C4
Tenkodogo Burkina **100** B3
Tennant Creek Austr. **114** C1
Tennessee *r.* U.S.A. **138** C1
Tennessee *state* U.S.A. **138** C1
Tenosique Mex. **143** C3
Tenteno Indon. **73** D2
Tenterfield Austr. **117** E1
Teodoro Sampaio Brazil **154** B2
Teófilo Otôni Brazil **155** D1
Teopisca Mex. **143** C3
Tepache Mex. **142** B2
Te Paki N.Z. **118** B1
Tepalcatepec Mex. **142** B3
Tepatitlán Mex. **142** B2
Tepehuanes Mex. **142** B2
Tepelenë Albania **65** A2
Tepic Mex. **142** B2
Teplice Czech Rep. **56** C2
Teploye Rus. Fed. **43** E3
Tequila Mex. **142** B2
Teramo Italy **62** B2
Terbuny Rus. Fed. **43** E3
Terebovlya Ukr. **44** C2
Terek *r.* Rus. Fed. **41** D4
Teresina Brazil **151** E3
Teresópolis Brazil **155** D2
Teressa Island India **75** A3
Tergnier France **54** A3
Terme Turkey **92** B1
Termini Imerese Italy **62** B3
Términos, Laguna de *lag.* Mex.
  143 C3
Termiz Uzbek. **89** D3
Termoli Italy **62** B2
Ternate Indon. **71** C2
Terneuzen Neth. **54** A2
Terni Italy **62** B2
Ternopil' Ukr. **44** C2
Terpeniya, Mys *c.* Rus. Fed. **81** F1
Terpeniya, Zaliv *g.* Rus. Fed. **81** F1
Terrace Can. **126** C2
Terrace Bay Can. **128** B2
Terra Firma S. Africa **108** B2
Terre Haute U.S.A. **136** C3
Terrenceville Can. **129** E2
Terschelling *i.* Neth. **54** B1
Tertenia Italy **62** A3
Teruel Spain **61** C1
Tervola Fin. **46** E2
Tešanj Bos.-Herz. **63** C2
Teseney Eritrea **102** B3
Teshio-gawa *r.* Japan **78** D2
Teslin Can. **126** B1
Teslin Lake Can. **126** B1
Tesouro Brazil **154** B1
Tessaoua Niger **101** C3
Tetas, Punta *pt* Chile **147**
Tete Moz. **107** C1
Teteriv *r.* Ukr. **44** D1
Teterow Ger. **55** F1
Tetiyiv Ukr. **44** C2
Tétouan Morocco **100** B1
Tetovo Macedonia **64** B2
Teuco *r.* Arg. **152** B3
Teul de González Ortega Mex. **142** B2
Teutoburger Wald *hills* Ger. **55** D1
Tevere *r.* Italy *see* Tiber
Teviot N.Z. **118** A4
Tewantin Austr. **115** E2
Te Wharau N.Z. **118** C3
Texarkana U.S.A. **141** F2
Texas *state* U.S.A. **141** E2
Texas City U.S.A. **141** F3

Texel i. Neth. **54** B1
Texoma, Lake U.S.A. **141** E2
Teyateyaneng Lesotho **109** C2
Teykovo Rus. Fed. **43** F2
Teza r. Rus. Fed. **43** F2
Tezpur India **87** D2
Tezu India **74** A1
Tha-anne r. Can. **127** F1
Thabana-Ntlenyana mt. Lesotho **109** C2
Thaba Putsoa mt. Lesotho **109** C2
Thabazimbi S. Africa **109** C1
Thabong S. Africa **109** C2
Thagyettaw Myanmar **75** A2
Thai Binh Vietnam **74** B1
Thailand country Asia **75** B2
Thailand, Gulf of Asia **75** B2
Thai Nguyên Vietnam **74** B1
Thakèk Laos **74** B2
Thalang Thai. **75** A3
Thal Desert Pak. **86** B1
Thale (Harz) Ger. **55** E2
Tha Li Thai. **74** B2
Thamaga Botswana **109** C1
Thamar, Jabal mt. Yemen **90** B3
Thamarit Oman **91** C3
Thames r. Can. **128** B2
Thames N.Z. **118** C2
Thames est. U.K. **53** D4
Thames r. U.K. **53** D4
Thanbyuzayat Myanmar **75** A2
Thandwè Myanmar **74** A2
Thanh Hoa Vietnam **74** B2
Thanjavur India **85** B3
Thanlyin Myanmar **74** A2
Thano Bula Khan Pak. **86** A2
Than Uyen Vietnam **74** B1
Thar Desert India/Pak. **86** A2
Thargomindah Austr. **116** C1
Tharthār, Buḩayrat ath l. Iraq **93** C2
Thasos i. Greece **65** B2
Thât Khê Vietnam **74** B1
Thaton Myanmar **74** A2
Thaungdut Myanmar **74** A1
Thayawadi Myanmar **74** A2
Thayetmyo Myanmar **74** A2
Thazi Myanmar **74** A1
The Bahamas country West Indies **145** C2
The Cheviot h. U.K. **52** B2
The Dalles U.S.A. **132** B1
The Fens reg. U.K. **53** C3
The Gambia country Africa **100** A3
The Great Oasis Egypt see Khārijah, Wāḩāt al
The Gulf Asia **91** C2
The Hague Neth. **54** B1
Thelon r. Can. **127** F1
Themar Ger. **55** E2
Theodore Roosevelt r. Brazil **150** C3
The Pas Can. **127** E2
Thermaïkos Kolpos g. Greece **65** B2
Thermopolis U.S.A. **134** B2
The Rock Austr. **117** D3
Thessalon Can. **128** B2
Thessaloniki Greece **65** B2
Thetford U.K. **53** D3
Thetford Mines Can. **129** C2
The Triangle mts Myanmar **74** A1
Thévenet, Lac l. Can. **129** C1
The Wash b. U.K. **53** D3
The Woodlands U.S.A. **141** E2
Thibodaux U.S.A. **138** B3
Thicket Portage Can. **127** F2
Thief River Falls U.S.A. **135** D1
Thiers France **59** C2
Thika Kenya **105** D3
Thiladhunmathi Atoll Maldives **85** B4

Thimphu Bhutan **87** C2
Thionville France **59** D2
Thira i. Greece **65** C3
Thirsk U.K. **52** C2
Thisted Denmark **47** B4
Thlewiaza r. Can. **127** F1
Thoen Thai. **74** A2
Thohoyandou S. Africa **109** D1
Thomasburg Ger. **55** E1
Thomastown Rep. of Ireland **51** C2
Thomasville U.S.A. **139** D2
Thommen Belgium **54** C2
Thompson Can. **127** F2
Thompson r. U.S.A. **126** D2
Thompson Falls U.S.A. **132** C1
Thompson Sound Can. **126** C3
Thornhill U.K. **50** C3
Thorshavnheiane reg. Antarctica **119** C2
Thouars France **58** B2
Three Hills Can. **126** D2
Three Points, Cape Ghana **100** B4
Three Pagodas Pass Myanmar/Thai. **75** A2
Thu Dâu Môt Vietnam **75** B2
Thuin Belgium **54** B2
Thule Greenland **125** H1
Thuli Zimbabwe **107** B2
Thunder Bay Can. **128** B2
Thung Song Thai. **75** A3
Thüringer Becken reg. Ger. **55** E2
Thüringer Wald mts Ger. **55** E2
Thurles Rep. of Ireland **51** C2
Thurso U.K. **50** C1
Thurso r. U.K. **50** C1
Tianguá Brazil **151** E3
Tianjin China **82** B2
Tianjin mun. China **82** B2
Tianlin China **83** A3
Tianmen China **82** B2
Tianshan China **82** C1
Tianshui China **82** A2
Tianzhu China **82** A2
Tiaret Alg. **61** D1
Tibagi r. Brazil **154** B3
Tibati Cameroon **104** B2
Tiber r. Italy **62** B2
Tiberias, Lake Israel see Galilee, Sea of
Tibesti mts Chad **101** D3
Tibet aut. reg. China see Xizang Zizhiqu
Tibet, Plateau of China **87** C2
Tibooburra Austr. **116** C1
Tiburón, Isla i. Mex. **142** A2
Tichît Maur. **100** B3
Tichla Western Sahara **100** A2
Ticul Mex. **143** D2
Tidjikja Maur. **100** A3
Tiel Neth. **54** B2
Tieling China **82** C1
Tielt Belgium **54** A2
Tienen Belgium **54** B2
Tien Shan mts China/Kyrg. **80** B2
Tientsin China see Tianjin
Tierp Sweden **47** D3
Tierra Blanca Mex. **143** C3
Tierra Colorada Mex. **143** C3
Tierra del Fuego, Isla Grande de i. Arg./Chile **153** B6
Tietê Brazil **154** C2
Tietê r. Brazil **154** B2
Tiflis Georgia see T'bilisi
Tifton U.S.A. **139** D2
Tighina Moldova **44** C2
Tignish Can. **129** D2
Tigre r. Ecuador/Peru **150** B3
Tigris r. Asia **102** C1
Tigris r. Turkey **93** C2
Tihuatlán Mex. **143** C2
Tijuana Mex. **142** A1

Tikhoretsk Rus. Fed. **45** F2
Tikhvin Rus. Fed. **43** D2
Tikhvinskaya Gryada ridge Rus. Fed. **43** D2
Tikokino N.Z. **118** C2
Tikrit Iraq **93** C2
Tiksi Rus. Fed. **95** K2
Tilburg Neth. **54** B2
Tilcara Arg. **152** B3
Tilcha Austr. **116** C1
Tillabéri Niger **100** C3
Tillamook U.S.A. **132** B1
Tillanchong Island India **75** A3
Tilos i. Greece **65** C3
Tilpa Austr. **116** C2
Til'tim Rus. Fed. **40** F2
Tim Rus. Fed. **43** E3
Timanskiy Kryazh ridge Rus. Fed. **40** D2
Timaru N.Z. **118** B3
Timashevsk Rus. Fed. **45** E2
Timbedgha Maur. **100** B3
Timber Creek Austr. **114** C1
Timbuktu Mali **100** B3
Timimoun Alg. **100** C2
Timiş r. Romania **44** B3
Timişoara Romania **44** B2
Timmins Can. **128** B2
Timokhino Rus. Fed. **43** E2
Timon Brazil **151** E2
Timor i. East Timor/Indonesia **71** C3
Timor Sea Austr./Indon. **70** C3
Timrå Sweden **47** D3
Tindouf Alg. **100** B2
Tingri China **87** C2
Tingsryd Sweden **47** C4
Tinian i. N. Mariana Is **71** D2
Tinogasta Arg. **152** B3
Tinos Greece **65** C3
Tinos i. Greece **65** C3
Tinqueux France **54** A3
Tinrhert, Plateau du Alg. **101** C2
Tinsukia India **74** A1
Tipasa Alg. **61** C1
Tipperary Rep. of Ireland **51** B2
Tirana Albania **65** A2
Tiranë Albania see Tirana
Tirano Italy **62** B1
Tiraspol Moldova **44** C2
Tire Turkey **65** C3
Tiree i. U.K. **50** A2
Tirich Mir mt. Pak. **86** B1
Tiruchchirappalli India **85** B3
Tirunelveli India **85** B4
Tirupati India **85** B3
Tiruppattur India **85** B3
Tiruppur India **85** B3
Tisa r. Serb. and Mont. **64** B1
Tisdale Can. **127** E2
Tissemsilt Alg. **61** D2
Titicaca, Lake Bol./Peru **152** B2
Titlagarh India **87** C2
Titu Romania **44** C3
Titusville U.S.A. **139** D3
Tiverton U.K. **53** B4
Tivoli Italy **62** B2
Tiwi Oman **91** C2
Tizimín Mex. **143** D2
Tizi Ouzou Alg. **61** D2
Tiznit Morocco **100** B2
Tlacotalpán Mex. **143** C3
Tlahualilo Mex. **142** B2
Tlapa Mex. **143** C3
Tlaxcala Mex. **143** C3
Tlaxiaco Mex. **143** C3
Tlemcen Alg. **100** B1
Tlokweng Botswana **109** C1
Toad River Can. **126** C2
Toamasina Madag. **107** [inset] D1
Toba, Danau l. Indon. **72** A1

Toba and Kakar Ranges *mts* Pak. **86** A1
Tobago *i.* Trin. and Tob. **145** D3
Tobelo Indon. **71** C2
Tobermory Can. **128** B2
Tobermory U.K. **50** A2
Tobin Lake Can. **127** E2
Toboali Indon. **72** B2
Tobol *r.* Kazakh./Rus. Fed. **88** D1
Tobol'sk Rus. Fed. **40** F3
Tocantinópolis Brazil **151** E3
Tocantins *r.* Brazil **151** E3
Toccoa U.S.A. **139** D2
Toce *r.* Italy **62** A1
Tocopilla Chile **152** A3
Todos Santos Mex. **142** A2
Tofino Can. **126** C3
Toft U.K. **50** [inset]
Tofua *i.* Tonga **111**
Togian *i.* Indon. **73** D2
Togian, Kepulauan *is* Indon. **73** D2
Togo *country* Africa **100** C4
Tohana India **86** B2
Tok U.S.A. **126** A1
Tokar Sudan **102** B3
Tokara-rettō *is* Japan **81** E3
Tokarevka Rus. Fed. **43** F3
Tokelau *terr.* S. Pacific Ocean **113**
Tokelau *is* Tokelau **111**
Tokmak Ukr. **45** E2
Tokmok Kyrg. **89** E2
Tokoroa N.Z. **118** C2
Toksun China **89** F2
Tokushima Japan **79** B4
Tōkyō Japan **79** C3
Tôlañaro Madag. **107** [inset] D2
Toledo Brazil **154** B2
Toledo Spain **60** C2
Toledo U.S.A. **136** D2
Toledo, Montes de *mts* Spain **60** C2
Toledo Bend Reservoir U.S.A. **138** B2
Toliara Madag. **107** [inset] D2
Tolitoli Indon. **73** D1
Tolmezzo Italy **62** B1
Tolosa Spain **58** B3
Toluca Mex. **143** C3
Tol'yatti Rus. Fed. **41** D3
Tomah U.S.A. **136** B2
Tomakomai Japan **78** D2
Tomar Port. **60** B2
Tomaszów Lubelski Pol. **57** E2
Tomaszów Mazowiecki Pol. **57** E2
Tomatlán Mex. **142** B3
Tombigbee *r.* U.S.A. **138** C2
Tombos Brazil **155** D2
Tombouctou Mali *see* Timbuktu
Tombua Angola **106** A1
Tom Burke S. Africa **109** C1
Tomingley Austr. **117** D2
Tomini, Teluk *g.* Indon. **73** D2
Tomislavgrad Bos.-Herz. **63** C3
Tomi Price Austr. **114** A2
Tomsk Rus. Fed. **94** H3
Tomtabacken *h.* Sweden **47** C4
Tonalá Mex. **143** C3
Tonantins Brazil **150** C3
Tondano Indon. **71** C2
Tønder Denmark **56** B2
Tonga *country* S. Pacific Ocean **113**
Tongatapu Group *is* Tonga **111**
Tongcheng China **83** B3
Tongchuan China **82** A2
Tongdao China **83** A3
Tongduch'ŏn S. Korea **77** B2
Tongeren Belgium **54** B2
Tonghae S. Korea **77** D2
Tonghai China **83** A3
Tonghua China **77** B1
Tongjosŏn-man *b.* N. Korea **77** B2

Tongking, Gulf of China/Vietnam **83** A3
Tongliao China **82** C1
Tongling China **82** B3
Tongo Austr. **116** C2
Tongren China **83** A3
Tongshan China *see* Wuzhishan
Tongtian He *r.* China *see* Yangtze
Tongue U.K. **50** B1
T'ongyŏng S. Korea **77** B3
Tongyu China **81** E2
Tongyuanpu China **77** A1
Tonk India **86** B2
Tonle Sap *l.* Cambodia **75** B2
Tonopah U.S.A. **133** C3
Tønsberg Norway **47** C4
Tooele U.S.A. **132** D2
Tooleybuc Austr. **116** C3
Toowoomba Austr. **117** E1
Topeka U.S.A. **135** D3
Topia Mex. **142** B2
Topolobampo Mex. **142** B2
Topozero, Ozero *l.* Rus. Fed. **46** G2
Toppenish U.S.A. **132** B1
Torbalı Turkey **65** C3
Torbat-e Heydarīyeh Iran **88** C3
Torbat-e Jām Iran **88** D3
Tordesillas Spain **60** C1
Tordesilos Spain **61** C1
Torelló Spain **61** D1
Torgau Ger. **55** F2
Torgelow Ger. **55** G1
Torhout Belgium **54** A2
Torino Italy *see* Turin
Tori-shima *i.* Japan **79** D4
Torixoréu Brazil **154** B1
Tor'kovskoye Vodokhranilishche *resr* Rus. Fed. **43** F2
Tormes *r.* Spain **60** B1
Tornälven *r.* Sweden **46** E2
Torngat Mountains Can. **129** D1
Tornio Fin. **46** E2
Toro Spain **60** B1
Toronto Can. **128** C2
Tororo Uganda **105** D2
Toros Dağları *mts* Turkey *see* Taurus Mountains
Torquay U.K. **53** B4
Torrão Port. **60** B2
Torre *mt.* Port. **60** B1
Torreblanca Spain **61** D1
Torrecerredo *mt.* Spain **60** C1
Torre de Moncorvo Port. **60** B1
Torrelavega Spain **60** C1
Torremolinos Spain **60** C2
Torrens, Lake *salt flat* Austr. **116** B2
Torrent Spain **61** C2
Torreón Mex. **142** B2
Torres Novas Port. **60** B2
Torres Strait Austr. **110**
Torres Vedras Port. **60** B2
Torrevieja Spain **61** C2
Torridon U.K. **50** B2
Tórrijos Spain **60** C2
Torrington *CT* U.S.A. **137** F2
Torrington *WY* U.S.A. **134** F2
Torroella de Montgrí Spain **61** D1
Tórshavn Faroe Is **48** B1
Tortoli Italy **62** A3
Tortosa Spain **61** D1
Toruń Pol. **57** D2
Tory Island Rep. of Ireland **51** B1
Torzhok Rus. Fed. **43** D2
Tosca S. Africa **108** B2
Tosca *r.* Africa **108** B2
Toscano, Arcipelago *is* Italy **62** A2
Tosno Rus. Fed. **43** D2
Tostado Arg. **152** C3
Tostedt Ger. **55** D1
Tosya Turkey **92** B1

Tot'ma Rus. Fed. **43** F2
Tottori Japan **79** B3
Touba Côte d'Ivoire **100** B4
Toubkal, Jbel *mt.* Morocco **100** B1
Tougan Burkina **100** B3
Touggourt Alg. **101** C1
Toul France **59** D2
Touliu Taiwan **83** C3
Toulon France **59** D3
Toulouse France **58** C3
Tourcoing France **54** A2
Tournai Belgium **54** A2
Tournus France **59** C2
Touros Brazil **151** F3
Tours France **58** C2
Tousside, Pic *mt.* Chad **101** D2
Touwsrivier S. Africa **108** B3
Towada Japan **78** D2
Townsend U.S.A. **132** D1
Townsville Austr. **115** D1
Towori, Teluk *b.* Indon. **73** D2
Toxkan He *r.* China **89** F2
Tōya-ko *l.* Japan **78** D2
Toyama Japan **79** C3
Toyota Japan **79** C3
Tozeur Tunisia **101** C1
Tqvarch'eli Georgia **93** C1
Tràblous Lebanon *see* Tripoli
Trabzon Turkey **92** B1
Trafalgar, Cabo *c.* Spain **60** B2
Trail Can. **126** D3
Trakai Lith. **42** B3
Tralee Rep. of Ireland **51** B2
Tramore Rep. of Ireland **51** C2
Trang Thai. **75** A3
Trangan *i.* Indon. **71** C3
Transantarctic Mountains Antarctica **119** H2
Transylvanian Alps *mts* Romania **44** B2
Trapani Italy **62** B3
Traralgon Austr. **117** D3
Trat Thai. **75** B2
Traunstein Ger. **56** C3
Traverse City U.S.A. **136** C2
Třebíč Czech Rep. **57** D3
Trebinje Bos.-Herz. **63** C3
Trebišov Slovakia **57** E3
Trebnje Slovenia **62** C1
Treinta y Tres Uru. **153** C4
Trelew Arg. **153** B5
Trelleborg Sweden **47** C4
Tremblant, Mont *h.* Can. **128** C2
Tremiti, Isole *is* Italy **62** C2
Tremonton U.S.A. **132** D2
Tremošná Czech Rep. **55** F3
Tremp Spain **61** D1
Trenčín Slovakia **57** D3
Trenque Lauquén Arg. **153** B4
Trent *r.* U.K. **52** C3
Trento Italy **62** B1
Trenton Can. **137** D2
Trenton *MO* U.S.A. **135** E2
Trenton *NJ* U.S.A. **137** F2
Trepassey Can. **129** E2
Tres Arroyos Arg. **153** B4
Três Corações Brazil **155** C2
Três Lagoas Brazil **154** B2
Tres Lagos Arg. **153** A5
Três Marias, Represa *resr* Brazil **155** C1
Três Pontas Brazil **155** C2
Tres Puntas, Cabo *c.* Arg. **153** B5
Três Rios Brazil **155** D2
Treuenbrietzen Ger. **55** F1
Treviglio Italy **62** A1
Treviso Italy **62** B1
Trevose Head U.K. **53** A4
Tricase Italy **63** C3
Trichur India **85** B3

rida Austr. **117** D2
rier Ger. **54** C3
rieste Italy **62** B1
riglav *mt.* Slovenia **62** B1
rikora, Puncak *mt.* Indon. **71** D3
rim Rep. of Ireland **51** C2
rincomalee Sri Lanka **85** C4
rindade Brazil **154** C1
rinidad Bol. **152** B2
rinidad *i.* Trin. and Tob. **145** D3
rinidad U.S.A. **134** C3
Trinidad and Tobago *country*
    West Indies **145** D3
rinity Bay Can. **129** E2
ripoli Greece **65** B3
ripoli Lebanon **92** B2
ripoli Libya **101** C1
ristan da Cunha *i.* S. Atlantic Ocean
    160 D8
rivandrum India **85** B4
rivento Italy **62** B2
rnava Slovakia **57** D3
rogir Croatia **62** C2
roia Italy **62** C2
roisdorf Ger. **54** C2
rois Fourches, Cap des *c.* Morocco
    60 C2
rois-Rivières Can. **129** C2
roitsko-Pechorsk Rus. Fed. **40** E2
rombetas *r.* Brazil **151** D3
rompsburg S. Africa **109** C3
rondheim Norway **46** C3
rout Lake Can. **126** D2
rout Lake *l.* N.W.T. Can. **126** C3
rout Lake *l.* Ont. Can. **128** A1
rowbridge U.K. **53** B4
roy *AL* U.S.A. **139** C2
roy *NY* U.S.A. **137** F2
royes France **59** C2
rstenik Serb. and Mont. **64** B2
rubchevsk Rus. Fed. **43** D3
ruchas Spain **60** E1
rucial Coast U.A.E. **91** C2
rujillo Hond. **144** B3
rujillo Peru **150** B3
rujillo Spain **60** B2
rujillo Venez. **145** C4
rulben Ger. **54** C3
ruro Can. **129** D2
ruro U.K. **53** A4
ruth or Consequences U.S.A.
    140 C2
rutnov Czech Rep. **57** D2
rysil Norway **47** C3
rzebiatów Pol. **56** C2
sagaannuur Mongolia **80** B1
saratanana, Massif du *mts* Madag.
    107 [inset] B1
sarevo Bulg. **64** C2
selina Rus. Fed. **45** F2
ses Namibia **108** A2
setseng Botswana **108** B1
setserleg Mongolia **80** C1
shabong Botswana **108** B2
shane Botswana **108** B2
shchikskoye Vodokhranilishche *resr*
    Rus. Fed. **45** E2
shela Dem. Rep. Congo **104** B3
shikapa Dem. Rep. Congo **104** C3
shikapa *r.* Dem. Rep. Congo **104** C3
shipise S. Africa **109** D1
shitanzu Dem. Rep. Congo
    104 C3
shuapa *r.* Dem. Rep. Congo **104** C3
shwane S. Africa *see* Pretoria
simlyanskoye Vodokhranilishche
    resr Rus. Fed. **41** D4
singtao China *see* Qingdao

Tsiroanomandidy Madag.
    107 [inset] D1
Tsna *r.* Rus. Fed. **43** F3
Tsomo S. Africa **109** C3
Tsu Japan **79** C4
Tsuchiura Japan **79** D3
Tsugarū-kaikyō *str.* Japan **78** D2
Tsumeb Namibia **106** A1
Tsumis Park Namibia **108** A1
Tsumkwe Namibia **106** B1
Tsuruga Japan **79** C4
Tsuruoka Japan **78** C2
Tsushima *is* Japan **79** A4
Tsuyama Japan **79** B3
Tswelelang S. Africa **109** C2
Tsyurupyns'k Ukr. **45** D2
Tual Indon. **71** C3
Tuam Rep. of Ireland **51** B2
Tuamotu Archipelago *is* Fr. Polynesia
    159 F6
Tuapse Rus. Fed. **45** E3
Tuatapere N.Z. **118** A4
Tuath, Loch a' *b.* U.K. **50** A1
Tuba City U.S.A. **140** B1
Tuban Indon. **73** C2
Tubarão Brazil **152** D3
Tübingen Ger. **56** B1
Tubruq Libya **101** E1
Tubuai Island Fr. Polynesia **111**
Tubutama Mex. **142** A1
Tucavaca Bol. **152** C2
Tuchitua Can. **126** C1
Tucson U.S.A. **140** B2
Tucumcari U.S.A. **141** D1
Tucupita Venez. **150** C2
Tucuruí Brazil **151** E3
Tucuruí, Represa *resr* Brazil **151** E3
Tudela Spain **61** C1
Tuela *r.* Port. **60** B1
Tuensang India **74** A1
Tugela *r.* S. Africa **109** D2
Tuguegarao Phil. **76** B2
Tui Spain **60** B1
Tukangbesi, Kepulauan *is* Indon.
    71 C3
Tuktoyaktuk Can. **124** D2
Tukums Latvia **42** B2
Tula Mex. **143** C2
Tula Rus. Fed. **43** E3
Tulancingo Mex. **143** C2
Tulare U.S.A. **133** C3
Tularosa U.S.A. **140** C2
Tulcea Romania **44** C2
Tul'chyn Ukr. **44** C2
Tulemalu Lake Can. **127** F1
Tulia U.S.A. **141** D2
Tulit'a Can. **126** C1
Tullahoma U.S.A. **139** C1
Tullamore Rep. of Ireland **51** C2
Tulle France **58** C2
Tully Austr. **115** D1
Tulsa U.S.A. **141** E1
Tuluksak U.S.A. **124** B2
Tumaco Col. **150** B2
Tumahole S. Africa **109** C2
Tumba Sweden **47** D4
Tumba, Lac *l.* Dem. Rep. Congo
    104 B3
Tumbarumba Austr. **117** D3
Tumbes Peru **150** A3
Tumbler Ridge Can. **126** C2
Tumby Bay Austr. **116** B2
Tumen China **77** B1
Tumereng Guyana **150** C2
Tumindao *i.* Phil. **76** A3
Tumkur India **85** B3
Tumnin *r.* Rus. Fed. **81** F1
Tump Pak. **86** A2
Tumucumaque, Serra *hills* Brazil
    151 D2

Tumut Austr. **117** D3
Tunbridge Wells, Royal U.K. **53** D4
Tunceli Turkey **92** B2
Tuncurry Austr. **117** E2
Tunduru Tanz. **105** D4
Tundzha *r.* Bulg. **64** C2
Tungsten Can. **126** C1
Tunis Tunisia **101** C1
Tunisia *country* Africa **101** C1
Tunja Col. **150** B2
Tunnsjøen *l.* Norway **46** C3
Tunuyán Arg. **153** B4
Tupaciguara Brazil **154** C1
Tupelo U.S.A. **138** C2
Tupiza Bol. **152** B3
Tura Rus. Fed. **95** I2
Tura *r.* Rus. Fed. **40** F3
Turabah Saudi Arabia **90** B2
Turana, Khrebet *mts* Rus. Fed. **95** K3
Turangi N.Z. **118** C2
Turan Lowland Asia **88** C3
Turayf Saudi Arabia **90** A1
Turba Estonia **42** B2
Turbat Pak. **86** A2
Turbo Col. **150** B2
Turda Romania **44** B2
Turfan China *see* Turpan
Turgay Kazakh. **88** C2
Turgutlu Turkey **65** C3
Turhal Turkey **92** B1
Turia *r.* Spain **61** C2
Turin Italy **62** A1
Turinsk Rus. Fed. **40** F3
Turiys'k Ukr. **44** B1
Turkana, Lake *salt l.* Eth./Kenya
    103 B3
Turkestan Kazakh. **89** C2
Turkey *country* Asia/Europe **92** B2
Turkmenabat Turkm. **88** D3
Turkmenbashi Turkm. **88** C2
Turkmenistan *country* Asia **88** C3
Turks and Caicos Islands *terr.*
    West Indies **145** C2
Turku Fin. **47** E3
Turlock U.S.A. **133** B3
Turnagain, Cape N.Z. **118** C3
Turneffe Islands *atoll* Belize **143** D3
Turnhout Belgium **54** B2
Turnor Lake Can. **127** E2
Turnu Măgurele Romania **64** B2
Turpan China **89** F2
Turugart Pass China/Kyrg. **89** E2
Tuscaloosa U.S.A. **138** C2
Tuskegee U.S.A. **139** C2
Tuticorin India **85** B4
Tutume Botswana **106** B2
Tuvalu *country* S. Pacific Ocean **112**
Tuwayq, Jabal *hills* Saudi Arabia **90** B2
Tuwayq, Jabal *mts* Saudi Arabia **90** B2
Tuwwal Saudi Arabia **90** A2
Tuxpan *Nayarit* Mex. **142** B2
Tuxpan *Veracruz* Mex. **143** C2
Tuxtla Gutiérrez Mex. **143** C3
Tuyên Quang Vietnam **74** B1
Tuy Hoa Vietnam **75** B2
Tuz, Lake *salt l.* Turkey **92** B2
Tuz Gölü *salt l.* Turkey *see* Tuz, Lake
Tuz Khurmātū Iraq **93** C2
Tuzla Bos.-Herz. **63** C2
Tuzlov *r.* Rus. Fed. **45** F2
Tver' Rus. Fed. **43** E2
Tweed *r.* U.K. **52** B2
Twee Rivier Namibia **108** A2
Twentynine Palms U.S.A. **133** C4
Twillingate Can. **129** E2
Twin Falls U.S.A. **132** D2
Twizel N.Z. **118** B3
Two Harbors U.S.A. **135** E1
Two Hills Can. **127** D2
Tyler U.S.A. **141** E2

Tynda Rus. Fed. **95** K3
Tynset Norway **47** C3
Tyre Lebanon **92** B2
Tyrnavos Greece **65** B3
Tyrrell, Lake *dry lake* Austr. **116** C3
Tyrrhenian Sea France/Italy **62** B2
Tyub-Karagan, Mys *pt* Kazakh. **88** C2
Tyul'gan Rus. Fed. **41** E3
Tyumen' Rus. Fed. **40** F3
Tyung *r.* Rus. Fed. **95** K2
Tywi *r.* U.K. **53** A4
Tzaneen S. Africa **109** D1

U

Uamanda Angola **106** B1
Uaupés Brazil **150** C3
Ubá Brazil **155** D2
Ubai Brazil **155** D1
Ubaitaba Brazil **151** F4
Ubangi *r.* C.A.R./Dem. Rep. Congo **104** B3
Ube Japan **79** B4
Úbeda Spain **60** C2
Uberaba Brazil **154** C1
Uberlândia Brazil **154** C1
Ubombo S. Africa **109** D2
Ubon Ratchathani Thai. **75** B2
Ubstadt-Weiher Ger. **55** D3
Ubundu Dem. Rep. Congo **105** C3
Ucayali *r.* Peru **150** B3
Uch Pak. **86** B2
Ucharal Kazakh. **89** F2
Uchiura-wan *b.* Japan **78** D2
Uchur *r.* Rus. Fed. **95** K3
Ucluelet Can. **126** C3
Udaipur India **86** B2
Uday *r.* Ukr. **45** D1
Uddevalla Sweden **47** C4
Uddjaure *l.* Sweden **46** D2
Uden Neth. **54** B2
Udhampur India **86** B1
Udine Italy **62** B1
Udomlya Rus. Fed. **43** E2
Udon Thani Thai. **74** B2
Udupi India **85** B3
Ueda Japan **79** C3
Uekuli Indon. **73** D2
Uele *r.* Dem. Rep. Congo **104** C2
Uelen Rus. Fed. **124** A2
Uelzen Ger. **55** E1
Uere *r.* Dem. Rep. Congo **105** C3
Ufa Rus. Fed. **41** E2
Ugalla *r.* Tanz. **105** D3
Uganda *country* Africa **105** D2
Uglegorsk Rus. Fed. **81** F1
Uglich Rus. Fed. **43** E2
Uglovka Rus. Fed. **43** D3
Ugra Rus. Fed. **43** D3
Uherské Hradiště Czech Rep. **57** D3
Úhlava *r.* Czech Rep. **55** F3
Uichteritz Ger. **55** E2
Uig U.K. **50** A2
Uige Angola **104** B3
Üijŏngbu S. Korea **77** B2
Uinta Mountains U.S.A. **132** D2
Uis Mine Namibia **106** A2
Uisŏng S. Korea **77** B2
Uitenhage S. Africa **109** C3
Uithuizen Neth. **54** C1
Uivak, Cape Can. **129** D1
Ujjain India **86** B2
Ukholovo Rus. Fed. **43** F3
Ukhrul India **74** A1
Ukhta Rus. Fed. **40** E2
Ukiah U.S.A. **133** B3
Ukkusissat Greenland **125** I2
Ukmergė Lith. **42** B2

Ukraine *country* Europe **44** D2
Ulaanbaatar Mongolia *see* Ulan Bator
Ulaangom Mongolia **80** C1
Ulan Bator Mongolia **80** D1
Ulanhad China *see* Chifeng
Ulanhot China **81** E1
Ulan-Khol Rus. Fed. **41** D4
Ulan-Ude Rus. Fed. **81** D1
Ulan Ul Hu *l.* China **87** D1
Ulchin S. Korea **77** D2
Ülenurme Estonia **42** C2
Ulhasnagar India **85** B3
Uliastai China **81** D1
Uliastay Mongolia **80** C1
Ulithi *atoll* Micronesia **71** D2
Ulladulla Austr. **117** E3
Ullapool U.K. **50** B2
Ullswater *l.* U.K. **52** B2
Ullŭng-do *i.* S. Korea **77** C2
Ulm Ger. **56** B2
Ulsan S. Korea **77** B2
Ulsta U.K. **50** [inset]
Ulster *reg.* Rep. of Ireland/U.K. **51** C1
Ultima Austr. **116** C3
Ulua *r.* Hond. **143** D3
Ulubey Turkey **65** C3
Uludağ *mt.* Turkey **65** C2
Ulundi S. Africa **109** D2
Ulungur Hu *l.* China **89** F2
Uluru *h.* Austr. **114** C2
Ulverston U.K. **52** B2
Ul'yanovsk Rus. Fed. **41** D3
Ulysses U.S.A. **134** C3
Uman' *r.* Ukr. **44** D2
Umba Rus. Fed. **40** C2
Umboi *i.* P.N.G. **71** D3
Umeå Sweden **46** E3
Umeälven *r.* Sweden **46** E3
Umet Rus. Fed. **45** F1
Umingmaktok Can. **124** E2
Umlazi S. Africa **109** D2
Umm Keddada Sudan **103** A3
Umm Lajj Saudi Arabia **90** A2
Umm Ruwaba Sudan **103** B3
Umm Sa'ad Libya **101** E1
Umpqua *r.* U.S.A. **132** B2
Umpulo Angola **106** A1
Umtata S. Africa **109** C3
Umuarama Brazil **154** B2
Una Brazil **151** F4
Una *r.* Bos.-Herz./Croatia **63** C1
Unalakleet U.S.A. **124** B2
'Unayzah Saudi Arabia **90** B2
Underwood U.S.A. **134** C1
Unecha Rus. Fed. **43** D3
Ungarie Austr. **117** D2
Ungarra Austr. **116** B2
Ungava, Péninsule d' *pen.* Can. **125** H2
Ungava Bay Can. **129** D1
Ŭngŏl N. Korea **77** C1
Ungheni Moldova **44** C2
Unguja *i.* Tanz. *see* Zanzibar Island
União da Vitória Brazil **154** B3
Unini *r.* Brazil **150** C3
Union City U.S.A. **138** C1
Uniondale S. Africa **108** B3
Uniontown U.S.A. **137** E3
United Arab Emirates *country* Asia **91** C2
United Kingdom *country* Europe **48** C2
United States of America *country* N. America **130** D3
Unity Can. **124** C3
Unst *i.* U.K. **50** [inset]
Unstrut *r.* Ger. **55** E2
Upa *r.* Rus. Fed. **43** E3
Upemba, Lac *l.* Dem. Rep. Congo **105** C3

Upington S. Africa **108** B2
Upolu *i.* Samoa **111**
Upper Alkali Lake U.S.A. **132** B2
Upper Arrow Lake Can. **126** D2
Upper Klamath Lake U.S.A. **132** B2
Upper Liard Can. **126** C1
Upper Lough Erne *l.* U.K. **51** C1
Uppsala Sweden **47** D4
'Uqlat aş Şuqūr Saudi Arabia **90** B2
Ural *r.* Kazakh./Rus. Fed. **88** C2
Uralla Austr. **117** E2
Ural Mountains Rus. Fed. **41** F2
Ural'sk Kazakh. **88** C1
Ural'skiy Khrebet *mts* Rus. Fed. *see* Ural Mountains
Urambo Tanz. **105** D3
Urana Austr. **117** D3
Uranium City Can. **124** E3
Uray Rus. Fed. **40** F2
Ure *r.* U.K. **52** C2
Uren' Rus. Fed. **40** D3
Urengoy Rus. Fed. **40** G2
Ures Mex. **142** A2
Urganch Uzbek. **88** D2
Urk Neth. **54** B1
Urla Turkey **65** C3
Urmia, Lake *salt l.* Iran **93** C2
Uroševac Serb. and Mont. **64** D2
Uruáchic Mex. **142** B2
Uruaçu Brazil **151** E4
Uruapan Mex. **142** B3
Urubamba *r.* Peru **150** B4
Urucara Brazil **151** D3
Uruçuí Brazil **151** E3
Urucurituba Brazil **151** D3
Uruguai *r.* Brazil **154** B3
Uruguaiana Brazil **152** C3
Uruguay *r.* Arg./Uru. **149**
Uruguay *country* S. America **153** C4
Ürümqi China **89** F2
Urunga Austr. **117** E2
Urup *r.* Rus. Fed. **45** F2
Uryupinsk Rus. Fed. **45** F1
Urziceni Romania **44** C2
Usa Japan **79** B4
Usa *r.* Rus. Fed. **94** F2
Usa *r.* Rus. Fed. **37**
Uşak Turkey **65** C3
Usakos Namibia **108** A1
Ushakova, Ostrov *i.* Rus. Fed. **94** H1
Ushtobe Kazakh. **89** E2
Ushuaia Arg. **153** B6
Usinsk Rus. Fed. **40** E2
Uskhodni Belarus **42** C3
Usman' Rus. Fed. **43** E3
Usogorsk Rus. Fed. **40** D2
Ussel France **58** C2
Ussuriysk Rus. Fed. **78** B2
Ust'-Donetskiy Rus. Fed. **45** F2
Ustica, Isola di *i.* Italy **62** B3
Ust'-Ilimsk Rus. Fed. **95** I3
Ust'-Ilych Rus. Fed. **40** E2
Ustka Pol. **57** C2
Ust'-Kamchatsk Rus. Fed. **95** M3
Ust'-Kamenogorsk Kazakh. **89** F2
Ust'-Kara Rus. Fed. **40** F2
Ust'-Kulom Rus. Fed. **40** E2
Ust'-Kut Rus. Fed. **95** J3
Ust'-Labinsk Rus. Fed. **45** E2
Ust'-Luga Rus. Fed. **42** C2
Ust'-Nem Rus. Fed. **40** E2
Ust'-Nera Rus. Fed. **95** L2
Ust'-Omchug Rus. Fed. **95** L2
Ust'-Ordynskiy Rus. Fed. **95** I3
Ust'-Port Rus. Fed. **40** H2
Ust'-Tsil'ma Rus. Fed. **40** E2
Ust'-Ura Rus. Fed. **40** D2
Ustyurt Plateau Kazakh./Uzbek. **88** C2
Ustyuzhna Rus. Fed. **43** E2

Usvyaty Rus. Fed. **43** D2
Utah state U.S.A. **133** D3
Utah Lake U.S.A. **132** D2
Utena Lith. **42** C2
Utica U.S.A. **137** E2
Utiel Spain **61** C2
Utikuma Lake Can. **126** D2
Utrecht Neth. **54** B1
Utrera Spain **60** B2
Utsjoki Fin. **46** F2
Utsunomiya Japan **79** C3
Utta Rus. Fed. **41** D4
Uttaradit Thai. **74** B2
Uummannaq Greenland see Dundas
Uummannaq Fjord inlet Greenland **125** I2
Uusikaupunki Fin. **47** E3
Uvalde U.S.A. **141** E3
Uvarovo Rus. Fed. **45** F1
Uvinza Tanz. **105** D3
Uvs Nuur salt l. Mongolia **80** C1
Uwajima Japan **79** B4
'Uwayriḍ, Ḥarrat al lava field Saudi Arabia **90** A2
Uweinat, Jebel mt. Sudan **102** A2
Uyar Rus. Fed. **95** I3
Uyo Nigeria **101** C4
Uyuni Bol. **152** B3
Uyuni, Salar de salt flat Bol. **152** B3
Uzbekistan country Asia **88** D2
Uzerche France **58** C2
Uzès France **59** C3
Uzh r. Ukr. **44** D1
Uzhhorod Ukr. **44** B2
Užice Serb. and Mont. **64** A2
Uzlovaya Rus. Fed. **43** E3
Üzümlü Turkey **65** C3
Uzunköprü Turkey **65** C2

Vaal r. S. Africa **109** B2
Vaal Dam S. Africa **109** C2
Vaalwater S. Africa **109** C1
Vaasa Fin. **46** E3
Vác Hungary **57** D3
Vacaria Brazil **152** C3
Vacaria, Serra hills Brazil **154** B2
Vacaville U.S.A. **133** B3
Vadodara India **86** B2
Vadsø Norway **46** F1
Vaduz Liechtenstein **59** D2
Vágar i. Faroe Is **48** B1
Vágur Faroe Is **48** B1
Váh r. Slovakia **57** D3
Vaiaku Tuvalu **112**
Vaida Estonia **42** B2
Vakílābād Iran **91** C3
Valday Rus. Fed. **43** D2
Valdayskaya Vozvyshennost' hills Rus. Fed. **43** D2
Valdecañas, Embalse de resr Spain **60** B2
Valdemarsvik Sweden **47** D4
Valdepeñas Spain **60** C2
Val-de-Reuil France **53** D5
Valdés, Península pen. Arg. **153** B5
Valdivia Chile **153** A4
Val-d'Or Can. **128** C2
Valdosta U.S.A. **139** D2
Valemount Can. **126** D2
Valence France **59** C3
Valencia Spain **61** C2

Valencia Venez. **150** C1
Valencia, Golfo de g. Spain **61** D2
Valenciennes France **54** A2
Valentine U.S.A. **134** C2
Valenzuela Phil. **76** B2
Valera Venez. **150** B2
Valka Latvia **42** C2
Valkeakoski Fin. **47** E3
Valkenswaard Neth. **54** B2
Valky Ukr. **45** E2
Valkyrie Dome ice feature Antarctica **119** D2
Valladolid Mex. **143** D2
Valladolid Spain **60** C1
Vall de Uxó Spain **61** C2
Valle Norway **47** B4
Vallecillos Mex. **143** B3
Valle de la Pascua Venez. **150** C2
Valledupar Col. **150** B1
Valle Hermoso Mex. **143** C2
Vallejo U.S.A. **133** B3
Vallenar Chile **152** A3
Valletta Malta **101** D1
Valley City U.S.A. **135** D1
Valley Falls U.S.A. **132** B2
Valleyview Can. **126** D2
Valls Spain **61** D1
Val Marie Can. **134** B1
Valmiera Latvia **42** C2
Valognes France **53** C5
Valozhyn Belarus **42** C3
Valparaíso Brazil **154** B2
Valparaíso Chile **153** A4
Valréas France **59** C3
Vals, Tanjung c. Indon. **71** D3
Valsad India **86** B2
Valspan S. Africa **108** B2
Valuyki Rus. Fed. **45** E1
Valverde del Camino Spain **60** B2
Van Turkey **93** C2
Van, Lake salt l. Turkey **93** C2
Vancouver Can. **126** C3
Vancouver U.S.A. **132** B1
Vancouver Island Can. **126** C3
Vandalia U.S.A. **136** C3
Vanderbijlpark S. Africa **109** C2
Vanderhoof Can. **126** C2
Van Diemen Gulf Austr. **71** C3
Vändra Estonia **42** C2
Vänern l. Sweden **47** C4
Vänersborg Sweden **47** C4
Vangaindrano Madag. **107** [inset] D2
Van Gölü salt l. Turkey see Van, Lake
Van Horn U.S.A. **140** D2
Vanimo P.N.G. **71** D3
Vanino Rus. Fed. **81** F1
Vannes France **58** C2
Van Rees, Pegunungan mts Indon. **71** D3
Vanrhynsdorp S. Africa **108** A3
Vantaa Fin. **47** E3
Vanua Levu i. Fiji **158** E6
Vanuatu country S. Pacific Ocean **112**
Van Wert U.S.A. **136** C2
Vanwyksvlei S. Africa **108** B3
Van Zylsrus S. Africa **108** B2
Varanasi India **87** C2
Varangerfjorden sea chan. Norway **46** F1
Varangerhalvøya pen. Norway **46** F1
Varaždin Croatia **63** C1
Varberg Sweden **47** C4
Vardar r. Macedonia **65** B2
Varde Denmark **47** B4
Vardø Norway **46** G1
Varel Ger. **55** D1
Vareṇa Lith. **42** B3
Varese Italy **62** A1

Varginha Brazil **155** C2
Varkaus Fin. **47** F3
Varna Bulg. **64** C2
Värnamo Sweden **47** C4
Várzea da Palma Brazil **155** D1
Varzino Rus. Fed. **40** C2
Vasknarva Estonia **42** C2
Vaslui Romania **44** C1
Västerås Sweden **47** D4
Västerdalälven r. Sweden **47** D3
Västerhaninge Sweden **42** A2
Västervik Sweden **47** D4
Vasto Italy **62** B2
Vasyl'kiv Ukr. **44** D1
Vatan France **58** C2
Vatican City Europe **62** B2
Vatnajökull ice cap Iceland **46** [inset]
Vatra Dornei Romania **44** C2
Vättern l. Sweden **47** C4
Vaughn U.S.A. **140** C2
Vauvert France **59** C3
Vava'u Group is Tonga **111**
Vawkavysk Belarus **42** B3
Växjö Sweden **47** C4
Vaygach, Ostrov i. Rus. Fed. **40** E1
Vechta Ger. **55** D1
Vedea r. Romania **44** C3
Veendam Neth. **54** C1
Veenendaal Neth. **54** B1
Vegreville Can. **127** D2
Vejer de la Frontera Spain **60** B2
Vejle Denmark **47** B4
Velbüzhchki Prokhod pass Bulg./Macedonia **64** B2
Veldhoven Neth. **54** B2
Velebit mts Croatia **62** B2
Velen Ger. **54** C2
Velenje Slovenia **62** C1
Veles Macedonia **63** D2
Vélez-Málaga Spain **60** C2
Velhas r. Brazil **155** D1
Velika Plana Serb. and Mont. **64** B2
Velikaya r. Rus. Fed. **42** C2
Velikiye Luki Rus. Fed. **43** D2
Velikiy Novgorod Rus. Fed. **43** D2
Velikiy Ustyug Rus. Fed. **40** D2
Veliko Türnovo Bulg. **64** C2
Veli Lošinj Croatia **62** B2
Velizh Rus. Fed. **43** D2
Vellberg Ger. **55** D2
Vel'sk Rus. Fed. **40** D2
Velten Ger. **55** F1
Velykyy Burluk Ukr. **45** E1
Venafro Italy **62** B2
Venceslau Bráz Brazil **154** C2
Vendôme France **58** C2
Venev Rus. Fed. **43** E3
Venezia Italy see Venice
Venezuela country S. America **150** C2
Venezuela, Golfo de g. Venez. **150** B1
Venice Italy **62** B1
Venice U.S.A. **139** D3
Venice, Gulf of Europe **62** B1
Venlo Neth. **54** C2
Venray Neth. **54** B2
Venta r. Latvia/Lith. **42** B2
Venta Lith. **42** B2
Venterstad S. Africa **109** C3
Ventnor U.K. **53** C4
Ventspils Latvia **42** B2
Ventura U.S.A. **133** C4
Venustiano Carranza, Presa resr Mex. **141** D3
Vera Spain **61** C2
Veracruz Mex. **143** C3
Veraval India **86** B2
Verbania Italy **62** A1
Vercelli Italy **62** A1
Vercors reg. France **59** D3
Verdalsøra Norway **46** C3

Verde r. Goiás Brazil **154** B1
Verde r. Mato Grosso do Sul Brazil
154 B2
Verde r. Mex. **142** B2
Verde r. U.S.A. **140** B2
Verde Grande r. Brazil **155** D1
Verden (Aller) Ger. **55** D1
Verdinho, Serra do mts Brazil **154** B1
Verdun France **59** D2
Vereeniging S. Africa **109** C2
Verín Spain **60** B1
Verkhnebakanskiy Rus. Fed. **45** E3
Verkhnetulomskiy Rus. Fed. **46** G2
Verkhniy Mamon Rus. Fed. **45** F1
Verkhov'ye Rus. Fed. **43** E3
Verkhovyna Ukr. **44** B2
Verkhoyanskiy Khrebet mts Rus. Fed.
95 K2
Vermand France **54** A3
Vermilion Can. **127** D2
Vermilion U.S.A. **135** D2
Vermilion Bay Can. **128** A2
Vermont state U.S.A. **137** F2
Vernal U.S.A. **132** E2
Vernon Can. **126** D2
Vernon U.S.A. **141** E2
Vero Beach U.S.A. **139** D3
Veroia Greece **65** D2
Verona Italy **62** B1
Versailles France **58** C2
Vert, Cape c. Senegal **96**
Vertou France **58** B2
Verulam S. Africa **109** D2
Verviers Belgium **54** B2
Vervins France **59** C2
Verzy France **54** B3
Vescovato France **59** B3
Veselaya, Gora mt. Rus. Fed. **41** E3
Vesele Ukr. **45** D2
Veselovskoye Vodokhranilishche resr
Rus. Fed. **45** F2
Veselyy Rus. Fed. **45** F2
Veshenskaya Rus. Fed. **45** F2
Vesoul France **59** D2
Vesterålen is Norway **46** C2
Vestfjorden sea chan. Norway **46** C2
Vestmanna Faroe Is **48** B1
Vestmannaeyjar is Iceland **36**
Vestnes Norway **46** B3
Vesuvius vol. Italy **62** B2
Ves'yegonsk Rus. Fed. **43** E2
Vetlanda Sweden **47** D4
Vetluga Rus. Fed. **40** D3
Veurne Belgium **54** A2
Vevey Switz. **59** D2
Veydelevka Rus. Fed. **45** E1
Vezirköprü Turkey **92** B1
Viana Brazil **151** E3
Viana do Castelo Port. **60** B1
Viangchan Laos see Vientiane
Viangphoukha Laos **74** B1
Vianópolis Brazil **154** C1
Viareggio Italy **62** B2
Viborg Denmark **47** B4
Vibo Valentia Italy **63** C3
Vic Spain **61** D1
Vicente Guerrero Mex. **142** A1
Vicenza Italy **62** B1
Vichuga Rus. Fed. **43** F2
Vichy France **59** C2
Vicksburg U.S.A. **138** B2
Viçosa Brazil **155** D2
Victor Harbor Austr. **116** B3
Victoria r. Austr. **114** C1
Victoria state Austr. **116** C3
Victoria Can. **126** C3
Victoria Chile **153** A4
Victoria Seychelles **99**
Victoria U.S.A. **141** D3
Victoria, Lake Africa **105** D3

Victoria, Lake Austr. **116** C2
Victoria, Mount Myanmar **74** A1
Victoria, Mount P.N.G. **71** B2
Victoria Falls Zambia/Zimbabwe
106 B1
Victoria Island Can. **124** E3
Victoria River Downs Austr. **114** C1
Victoria West S. Africa **108** B3
Victorville U.S.A. **133** C4
Videle Romania **44** C3
Viðidalsá Iceland **46** [inset]
Viechtach Ger. **55** F3
Viedma Arg. **153** B5
Viedma, Lago l. Arg. **153** A5
Vielsalm Belgium **54** B2
Vienenburg Ger. **55** E2
Vienna Austria **57** D3
Vienne France **59** C2
Vienne r. France **58** C2
Vientiane Laos **74** B2
Viersen Ger. **54** C2
Vierzon France **58** C2
Viesca Mex. **142** B2
Vieste Italy **63** C2
Vietnam country Asia **74** B2
Viêt Tri Vietnam **74** B1
Vigan Phil. **76** B2
Vigevano Italy **62** A1
Vigo Spain **60** B1
Vijayawada India **85** C3
Vik Iceland **46** [inset]
Viking Can. **127** D2
Vikeyri Norway **46** E1
Vila Franca de Xira Port. **60** B2
Vilagarcía de Arousa Spain **60** B1
Vilalba Spain **60** B1
Vila Nova de Gaia Port. **60** B1
Vilanova i la Geltrú Spain **61** D1
Vila Real Port. **60** B1
Vilar Formoso Port. **60** B1
Vila Velha Brazil **155** D2
Vilcabamba, Cordillera mts Peru
150 B4
Vil'cheka, Zemlya i. Rus. Fed. **94** G1
Vilhelmina Sweden **46** D3
Vilhena Brazil **150** C4
Viljandi Estonia **42** C2
Vilkaviškis Lith. **42** B3
Vil'kitskogo, Proliv str. Rus. Fed. **95** I1
Villa Ahumada Mex. **142** B1
Villablino Spain **60** B1
Villach Austria **56** C3
Villa de Cos Mex. **142** B2
Villa Dolores Arg. **152** B4
Villa Flores Mex. **143** C3
Villagrán Mex. **143** C2
Villahermosa Mex. **143** C3
Villa Insurgentes Mex. **142** A2
Villa María Arg. **152** B4
Villa Montes Bol. **152** B3
Villanueva Mex. **142** B2
Villanueva de la Serena Spain **60** B2
Villanueva de los Infantes Spain
60 C2
Villa Ocampo Arg. **152** C3
Villaputzu Italy **62** A3
Villarrica Para. **152** C3
Villarrobledo Spain **60** C2
Villa Unión Arg. **152** B3
Villa Unión Durango Mex. **142** B2
Villa Unión Sinaloa Mex. **142** B2
Villavicencio Col. **150** B2
Villazon Bol. **152** B3
Villefranche-sur-Saône France **56** A3
Villena Spain **61** C2
Villeneuve-sur-Lot France **58** C3
Ville Platte U.S.A. **138** B2
Villers-Cotterêts France **54** A3
Villeurbanne France **59** C2
Villingen Ger. **56** B3

Vilnius Lith. **42** C3
Vil'nohirs'k Ukr. **45** D2
Vil'nyans'k Ukr. **45** E2
Vilvoorde Belgium **54** B2
Vilyeyka Belarus **42** C3
Vilyuy r. Rus. Fed. **95** K2
Vimmerby Sweden **47** D4
Viña del Mar Chile **153** A4
Vinaròs Spain **61** C1
Vincennes U.S.A. **136** C3
Vineland U.S.A. **137** E3
Vinh Vietnam **74** B2
Vinh Long Vietnam **75** B3
Vinita U.S.A. **141** E1
Vinnytsya Ukr. **44** C2
Vinson Massif mt. Antarctica **119** K2
Vinstra Norway **47** B3
Vipiteno Italy **62** B1
Virac Phil. **76** B2
Virden Can. **127** E3
Vire France **58** B2
Virei Angola **106** A1
Virgem da Lapa Brazil **155** D1
Virgin r. U.S.A. **140** B1
Virginia S. Africa **109** C2
Virginia U.S.A. **135** E1
Virginia state U.S.A. **137** E3
Virginia Beach U.S.A. **137** E3
Virginia City U.S.A. **133** C3
Virgin Islands (U.K.) terr. West Indies
145 D3
Virgin Islands (U.S.A.) terr. West Indies
145 D3
Virôchey Cambodia **75** B2
Virovitica Croatia **63** C1
Virton Belgium **54** B3
Virtsu Estonia **42** B2
Vis i. Croatia **63** C2
Visaginas Lith. **42** C3
Visalia U.S.A. **133** C3
Visavadar India **86** B2
Visayan Sea Phil. **76** B2
Visby Sweden **47** D4
Viscount Melville Sound sea chan.
Can. **124** E2
Viseu Brazil **151** E3
Viseu Port. **60** B1
Vishakhapatnam India **85** C3
Viški Latvia **42** C2
Visoko Bos.-Herz. **63** C2
Vistula r. Pol. **57** D2
Viterbo Italy **62** B2
Viti Levu i. Fiji **156** E6
Vitim r. Rus. Fed. **95** J3
Vitória Brazil **155** D2
Vitória da Conquista Brazil **151** E4
Vitoria-Gasteiz Spain **60** C1
Vitré France **58** B2
Vitry-le-François France **59** C2
Vitsyebsk Belarus **43** D2
Vittel France **59** D2
Vittoria Italy **62** B3
Vittorio Veneto Italy **62** B1
Viveiro Spain **60** B1
Vizcaíno, Sierra mts Mex. **142** A2
Vize Turkey **64** C2
Vizianagaram India **85** C3
Vlaardingen Neth. **54** B2
Vladikavkaz Rus. Fed. **41** D4
Vladimir Rus. Fed. **43** F2
Vladivostok Rus. Fed. **78** B2
Vlasotince Serb. and Mont. **64** B2
Vlieland i. Neth. **54** B1
Vlissingen Neth. **54** A2
Vlorë Albania **65** A2
Vöcklabruck Austria **56** C3
Vogelsberg hills Ger. **55** D2
Vohimena, Tanjona c. Madag. **97**
Voi Kenya **105** D3
Voiron France **59** D2

Voisey Bay Can. **129** D1
Vojens Denmark **56** B1
Vojvodina *prov.* Serb. and Mont. **64** A1
Voknavolok Rus. Fed. **46** G3
Volcano Bay Japan *see* Uchiura-wan
Volda Norway **48** E1
Volga Rus. Fed. **43** E2
Volga *r.* Rus. Fed. **43** E2
Volgodonsk Rus. Fed. **41** D4
Volgograd Rus. Fed. **41** D4
Volkhov Rus. Fed. **43** D2
Volkhov *r.* Rus. Fed. **43** D1
Volkstedt Ger. **55** E2
Volnovakha Ukr. **45** E2
Volochys'k Ukr. **44** C2
Volodarsk Rus. Fed. **43** F2
Volodars'ke Ukr. **45** E2
Volodars'k-Volyns'kyy Ukr. **44** C1
Volodymyrets' Ukr. **44** C1
Volodymyr-Volyns'kyy Ukr. **44** B1
Vologda Rus. Fed. **43** E2
Volokolamsk Rus. Fed. **43** E2
Volokonovka Rus. Fed. **45** E1
Volos Greece **65** B3
Volosovo Rus. Fed. **42** C2
Volot Rus. Fed. **43** D2
Volovo Rus. Fed. **43** E3
Vol'sk Rus. Fed. **41** D4
Volta, Lake *resr* Ghana **100** C4
Volta Redonda Brazil **155** D2
Volzhskiy Rus. Fed. **41** D4
Vopnafjörður Iceland **46** [inset]
Voranava Belarus **42** C3
Voreioi Sporades *is* Greece **92** A2
Vorkuta Rus. Fed. **40** F2
Vormsi *i.* Estonia **42** B2
Vorona *r.* Rus. Fed. **45** F1
Voronezh Rus. Fed. **43** E3
Voronezh *r.* Rus. Fed. **43** E3
Vorontsovka Rus. Fed. **45** F1
Vorskla *r.* Rus. Fed. **45** D2
Võrtsjärv *l.* Estonia **42** C2
Võru Estonia **42** C2
Vosges *mts* France **59** D2
Vosoburg S. Africa **108** B3
Voss Norway **47** B4
Vostochno-Sibirskoye More *sea* Rus. Fed. *see* East Siberian Sea
Vostochnyy Sayan *mts* Rus. Fed. **95** I3
Vostok *i.* Rus. Fed. **78** C1
Votuporanga Brazil **154** C2
Voynitsa Rus. Fed. **46** G2
Voznesens'k Ukr. **45** D2
Voznesenskoye Rus. Fed. **43** F3
Vrådal Norway **47** B4
Vrangel' Rus. Fed. **78** D2
Vrangelya, Ostrov *i.* Rus. Fed. *see* Wrangel Island
Vranje Serb. and Mont. **64** B2
Vratnik *pass* Bulg. **64** C2
Vratsa Bulg. **64** B2
Vrbas *r.* Bos.-Herz. **63** C1
Vrbas Serb. and Mont. **64** A1
Vredenburg S. Africa **108** A3
Vredendal S. Africa **108** A3
Vresse Belgium **54** B3
Vršac Serb. and Mont. **64** B1
Vryburg S. Africa **108** B2
Vryheid S. Africa **109** D2
Vsevolozhsk Rus. Fed. **43** D1
Vučitrn Serb. and Mont. **64** B2
Vukovar Croatia **63** C1
Vuktyl' Rus. Fed. **40** E2
Vukuzakhe S. Africa **109** C2
Vulcano, Isola *i.* Italy **62** B3
Vung Tau Vietnam **75** D2
Vyara India **86** B2

Vyatka Rus. Fed. *see* Kirov
Vyaz'ma Rus. Fed. **43** D2
Vyazniki Rus. Fed. **43** F2
Vyborg Rus. Fed. **42** C1
Vyerkhnyadzvinsk Belarus **42** C2
Vyksa Rus. Fed. **43** F2
Vylkove Ukr. **44** D2
Vynohradiv Ukr. **44** B2
Vypolzovo Rus. Fed. **43** D2
Vyritsa Rus. Fed. **43** D2
Vyselki Rus. Fed. **45** E2
Vyshhorod Ukr. **44** D1
Vyshniy-Volochek Rus. Fed. **43** D2
Vyškov Czech Rep. **57** D3
Vytegra Rus. Fed. **40** C2

W

Wa Ghana **100** B3
Waal *r.* Neth. **54** B2
Waalwijk Neth. **54** B2
Wabasca *r.* Can. **126** D2
Wabasca-Desmarais Can. **126** D2
Wabash *r.* U.S.A. **136** C3
Wabē Gestro *r.* Eth. **103** C4
Wabē Shebelē Wenz *r.* Eth. **103** C4
Wabowden Can. **127** F2
Waccasassa Bay U.S.A. **139** D3
Wächtersbach Ger. **55** D2
Waco U.S.A. **141** D2
Wad Pak. **86** A2
Waddān Libya **101** D2
Waddenzee *sea chan.* Neth. **54** B1
Waddington, Mount Can. **126** C2
Waddinxveen Neth. **54** B1
Wadena Can. **127** E2
Wadena U.S.A. **135** D1
Wadgassen Ger. **54** C3
Wadi Halfa Sudan **102** B2
Wad Medani Sudan **102** B3
Wafangdian China **82** C2
Wageningen Neth. **54** B2
Wagga Wagga Austr. **117** D3
Wahoo U.S.A. **135** D2
Wahpeton U.S.A. **135** D1
Waiau *r.* N.Z. **118** B3
Waigeo *i.* Indon. **71** C3
Waikabubak Indon. **73** C2
Waikerie Austr. **116** B2
Waimate N.Z. **118** B3
Wainganga *r.* India **87** B3
Waingapu Indon. **73** D2
Wainwright Can. **127** D2
Wainwright U.S.A. **124** B2
Waiouru N.Z. **118** C2
Waipara N.Z. **118** B3
Waipawa N.Z. **118** C2
Wairau *r.* N.Z. **118** B3
Wairoa N.Z. **118** C2
Waitaki *r.* N.Z. **118** B3
Waitara N.Z. **118** B2
Waiuku N.Z. **118** B2
Wajir Kenya **105** E2
Wakasa-wan *b.* Japan **79** C3
Wakatipu, Lake N.Z. **118** A4
Wakaw Can. **127** E2
Wakayama Japan **79** C4
WaKeeney U.S.A. **134** D3
Wakefield N.Z. **118** B3
Wakefield U.K. **52** C3
Wake Island *terr.*
 N. Pacific Ocean **112**
Wakkanai Japan **78** D1
Wakkerstroom S. Africa **109** D2
Wałbrzych Pol. **57** D2
Walcha Austr. **117** E2
Walchum Ger. **54** C1
Wałcz Pol. **57** D2

Wales *admin. div.* U.K. **53** B3
Walgett Austr. **117** D2
Walikale Dem. Rep. Congo **105** C3
Walker Lake U.S.A. **133** C3
Wallaroo Austr. **116** B2
Walla Walla U.S.A. **132** C1
Walldürn Ger. **55** D3
Wallendbeen Austr. **117** D2
Wallis, Îles *is* Wallis and Futuna Is **111**
Wallis and Futuna Islands *terr.*
 S. Pacific Ocean **113**
Walls U.K. **50** [inset]
Walney, Isle of *i.* U.K. **52** B2
Walsall U.K. **53** C3
Walsenburg U.S.A. **134** C3
Walsrode Ger. **55** D1
Walterboro U.S.A. **139** D2
Walvis Bay Namibia **106** A2
Wamba Dem. Rep. Congo **105** C2
Wanaaring Austr. **116** C1
Wanaka N.Z. **118** A3
Wanaka, Lake N.Z. **118** A3
Wanapitei Lake Can. **128** B2
Wanda Arg. **154** B3
Wanda Shan *mts* China **78** B1
Wanding China **74** A1
Wandlitz Ger. **55** F1
Wanganui N.Z. **118** C2
Wangaratta Austr. **117** D3
Wangqing China **77** B1
Wan Hsa-la Myanmar **74** A1
Wanning China **83** B4
Wanroij Neth. **54** B2
Wantage U.K. **53** C4
Wanxian China **82** A2
Wanyuan China **82** A2
Warangal India **85** B3
Warburg Ger. **55** D2
Warburton Austr. **114** B2
Warburton *watercourse* Austr. **116** B1
Wardha India **87** B3
Ward Hill U.K. **50** C1
Ware Can. **126** C2
Waren Ger. **55** F1
Warendorf Ger. **54** C2
Warialda Austr. **117** E1
Warmbad Namibia **108** A2
Warm Springs U.S.A. **133** C3
Warner Lakes U.S.A. **132** C2
Warner Robins U.S.A. **139** D2
Warnes Bol. **152** B2
Warracknabeal Austr. **116** C3
Warrego *r.* Austr. **117** D2
Warren Austr. **117** D2
Warren *AR* U.S.A. **138** B2
Warren *OH* U.S.A. **137** D2
Warren *PA* U.S.A. **137** D2
Warrenpoint U.K. **51** C1
Warrensburg U.S.A. **135** E3
Warrenton S. Africa **108** B2
Warri Nigeria **101** C4
Warrington U.K. **52** B3
Warrnambool Austr. **116** C3
Warsaw Pol. **57** E2
Warszawa Pol. *see* Warsaw
Warta *r.* Pol. **57** C2
Warwick Austr. **117** E1
Warwick U.K. **53** C3
Wasco U.S.A. **133** C3
Washburn U.S.A. **134** C1
Washington *DC* U.S.A. **137** E3
Washington *IA* U.S.A. **135** E2
Washington *IN* U.S.A. **136** C3
Washington *MO* U.S.A. **135** E3
Washington *NC* U.S.A. **139** E1
Washington *PA* U.S.A. **137** D2
Washington *state* U.S.A. **132** B1
Washington, Mount U.S.A. **137** F2
Washington Court House U.S.A.
 136 D3

Washuk Pak. **86** A2
Waskaganish Can. **128** C1
Waskaiowaka Lake Can. **127** F2
Wasser Namibia **108** A2
Waswanipi, Lac *i.* Can. **128** C2
Watampone Indon. **73** D2
Waterbury U.S.A. **137** E2
Waterbury Lake Can. **127** E2
Waterford Rep. of Ireland **51** C2
Waterford Harbour Rep. of Ireland
  51 C2
Waterloo U.S.A. **135** E2
Waterpoort S. Africa **109** C1
Watertown *NY* U.S.A. **137** E2
Watertown *SD* U.S.A. **135** D2
Watertown *WI* U.S.A. **136** C2
Waterville U.S.A. **137** G2
Watford U.K. **53** C4
Watford City U.S.A. **134** C1
Wathaman *r.* Can. **127** E2
Watonga U.S.A. **141** E1
Watrous Can. **127** E2
Watsa Dem. Rep. Congo **105** C2
Watseka U.S.A. **136** C2
Watsi Kengo Dem. Rep. Congo **104** C3
Watsonville U.S.A. **133** B3
Watubela, Kepulauan *is* Indon. **71** C3
Wau P.N.G. **71** D3
Wau Sudan **103** A4
Wauchope Austr. **117** E2
Waukegan U.S.A. **136** C2
Waurika U.S.A. **141** E2
Wausau U.S.A. **136** C2
Waveney *r.* U.K. **53** D3
Waverly U.S.A. **135** E2
Waycross U.S.A. **139** D2
Wayne U.S.A. **136** C2
Waynesboro *GA* U.S.A. **139** D2
Waynesboro *VA* U.S.A. **137** E3
Waynesville U.S.A. **139** D1
Wazirabad Pak. **86** B1
Wear *r.* U.K. **52** C2
Weatherford U.S.A. **141** E2
Weaverville U.S.A. **132** B2
Webequie Can. **128** B1
Webi Shabeelle *r.* Somalia **103** C4
Webster U.S.A. **135** D1
Webster City U.S.A. **135** E2
Weert Neth. **54** B2
Wee Waa Austr. **117** D2
Wegberg Ger. **54** C2
Wegorzewo Pol. **57** E2
Weiden in der Oberpfalz Ger. **55** F3
Weifang China **82** B2
Weihai China **82** C2
Weilmoringle Austr. **117** D1
Weimar Ger. **55** E2
Weinan China **82** A2
Weinsberg Ger. **55** D3
Weipa Austr. **115** D1
Weir *r.* U.K. **117** D1
Weirton U.S.A. **137** D2
Weißenburg in Bayern Ger. **55** E3
Weißenfels Ger. **55** E2
Weißkugel *mt.* Austria/Italy **56** C3
Wejherowo Pol. **57** D2
Wekweti Can. **126** D1
Welch U.S.A. **136** D3
Weldiya Eth. **103** B3
Welkom S. Africa **109** C2
Welland *r.* U.K. **53** C3
Wellesley Islands Austr. **115** C1
Wellingborough U.K. **53** C3
Wellington N.Z. **118** B3
Wellington S. Africa **108** A3
Wellington U.S.A. **135** D3
Wellington, Isla *i.* Chile **153** A5
Wellington, Lake Austr. **117** D3

Wells Can. **126** C2
Wells U.K. **53** B4
Wells U.S.A. **132** D2
Wells, Lake *salt flat* Austr. **114** B2
Wellsford N.Z. **118** B2
Wells-next-the-Sea U.K. **52** D3
Wels Austria **56** C3
Welshpool U.K. **53** B3
Wembesi S. Africa **109** C2
Wemindji Can. **128** C1
Wenatchee U.S.A. **132** B1
Wenchang China **83** B4
Wenchi Ghana **100** B4
Wendelstein Ger. **55** E3
Wendeng China **82** C2
Wendisch Evern Ger. **55** E1
Wendo Eth. **103** B4
Wendover U.S.A. **132** D2
Wengyuan China **83** B3
Wenling China **83** C3
Wenshan China **83** A3
Wentworth Austr. **116** C2
Wenzhou China **83** C3
Wepener S. Africa **109** C2
Werda Botswana **108** B2
Werdau Ger. **55** F2
Werder Ger. **55** F1
Wernberg-Köblitz Ger. **55** F3
Wernigerode Ger. **55** E2
Werra *r.* Ger. **55** D2
Werris Creek Austr. **117** E2
Wertheim Ger. **55** D3
Wesel Ger. **54** C2
Wesendorf Ger. **55** E1
Weser *r.* Ger. **55** D1
Weser *sea chan.* Ger. **55** D1
Wessel, Cape Austr. **115** C1
Wessel Islands Austr. **115** C1
Wesselton S. Africa **109** C2
West Antarctica *reg.* Antarctica **119** I2
West Bank *terr.* Asia **92** B2
West Bend U.S.A. **136** C2
West Bromwich U.K. **53** C3
Westerburg Ger. **54** C2
Westerholt Ger. **54** C1
Western Australia *state* Austr. **114** B2
Western Cape *prov.* S. Africa **108** B3
Western Desert Egypt **102** A2
Western Ghats *mts* India **85** B3
Western Sahara *terr.* Africa **100** A2
Westerschelde *est.* Neth. **54** A2
Westerstede Ger. **54** C1
Westerwald *hills* Ger. **54** C2
West Falkland *i.* Falkland Is **153** B6
West Frankfort U.S.A. **136** C3
West Frisian Islands Neth. **54** B1
West Indies *is* Caribbean Sea **145**
West Loch Roag *b.* U.K. **50** A1
Westlock Can. **126** D2
Westmalle Belgium **54** B2
West Memphis U.S.A. **138** B1
Weston U.S.A. **137** D3
Weston-super-Mare U.K. **53** B4
West Palm Beach U.S.A. **139** D3
West Plains U.S.A. **135** E3
West Point U.S.A. **135** D2
Westport N.Z. **118** B3
Westport Rep. of Ireland **51** B2
Westray *i.* Austr. **54** B3
Westray *i.* U.K. **50** C1
West Siberian Plain Rus. Fed. *see*
  Zapadno Sibirskaya Ravnina
West-Terschelling Neth. **54** B1
West Town Rep. of Ireland **51** B1
West Virginia *state* U.S.A. **137** D3
West Wyalong Austr. **117** D2
West Yellowstone U.S.A. **132** D2
Wetar *i.* Indon. **71** C3
Wetaskiwin Can. **126** D2
Wetzlar Ger. **55** D2

Wewak P.N.G. **71** D3
Wexford Rep. of Ireland **51** C2
Weyakwin Can. **127** E2
Weyburn Can. **124** F3
Weyhe Ger. **55** D1
Weymouth U.K. **53** B4
Whakatane N.Z. **118** C2
Whale Cove Can. **127** F1
Whalsay *i.* U.K. **50** [inset]
Whangarei N.Z. **118** B2
Wharfe *r.* U.K. **52** C3
Wharton U.S.A. **141** E3
Wha Ti Can. **126** D1
Wheatland U.S.A. **134** B2
Wheeler Peak *NM* U.S.A. **140** C1
Wheeler Peak *NV* U.S.A. **133** D3
Wheeling U.S.A. **137** D2
Whernside *h.* U.K. **52** B2
Whistler Can. **126** C2
Whitby U.K. **52** C2
White *r.* Can./U.S.A. **126** B1
White *r.* U.S.A. **138** B2
White, Lake *salt flat* Austr. **114** B2
White Bay Can. **129** C2
White Butte *mt.* U.S.A. **134** C1
White Cliffs Austr. **116** C2
Whitecourt Can. **126** D2
Whitefish U.S.A. **132** D1
Whitehaven U.K. **52** B2
Whitehead U.K. **51** D1
Whitehorse Can. **126** B1
White Lake U.S.A. **138** B3
White Mountain Peak U.S.A. **133** C3
White Nile *r.* Sudan/Uganda **103** B3
White Sea Rus. Fed. **40** C2
White Sulphur Springs U.S.A. **132** D1
Whiteville U.S.A. **139** E2
White Volta *watercourse*
  Burkina/Ghana **100** B3
Whitewater Baldy *mt.* U.S.A. **140** C2
Whitewater Lake Can. **128** B1
Whitewood Can. **127** E2
Whithorn U.K. **50** B3
Whitianga N.Z. **118** C2
Whitney, Mount U.S.A. **133** C3
Whitsunday Island Austr. **115** D2
Whyalla Austr. **116** B2
Wichelen Belgium **54** A2
Wichita U.S.A. **135** D3
Wichita Falls U.S.A. **141** E2
Wick U.K. **50** C1
Wickenburg U.S.A. **140** B2
Wicklow Rep. of Ireland **51** C2
Wicklow Head Rep. of Ireland **51** D2
Wicklow Mountains Rep. of Ireland
  51 C2
Widnes U.K. **52** B3
Wiehengebirge *hills* Ger. **55** D1
Wiehl Ger. **54** C2
Wieluń Pol. **57** D2
Wien Austria *see* Vienna
Wiener Neustadt Austria **57** D3
Wieringerwerf Neth. **54** B1
Wiesbaden Ger. **54** D2
Wiesloch Ger. **54** C1
Wiesmoor Ger. **54** C1
Więcbórg Pol. **57** D2
Wight, Isle of *i.* U.K. **53** C4
Wigtown U.K. **50** B3
Wijchen Neth. **54** B2
Wilcannia Austr. **116** C2
Wilge *r.* S. Africa **109** C2
Wilhelm, Mount P.N.G. **110**
Wilhelmshaven Ger. **54** D1
Wilkes-Barre U.S.A. **137** E2
Wilkes Land *reg.* Antarctica **119** G2
Wilkie Can. **127** E2
Willcox U.S.A. **140** C2
Willebroek Belgium **54** B2

Villemstad Neth. Antilles **145** D3
Villiam, Mount Austr. **116** C3
Villiam Creek Austr. **116** B1
Villiams U.S.A. **140** B1
Villiamsburg U.S.A. **137** E3
Villiamson U.S.A. **136** D3
Villiamsport U.S.A. **137** E2
Villiamston U.S.A. **139** E1
Villiston S. Africa **108** B3
Villiston U.S.A. **134** C1
Villiston Lake Can. **126** C2
Villits U.S.A. **133** B3
Villmar U.S.A. **135** D1
Villowmore S. Africa **108** B3
Villowvale S. Africa **109** C3
Vills, Lake *salt flat* Austr. **114** B2
Villunga Austr. **116** B3
Vilmington Austr. **116** B2
Vilmington *DE* U.S.A. **137** E3
Vilmington *NC* U.S.A. **139** E2
Vilsdorf Ger. **54** D2
Vilson U.S.A. **139** E1
Vilson's Promontory *pen.* Austr. **117** D3
Viltz Lux. **54** B3
Viluna Austr. **114** B2
Vinchester U.K. **53** C4
Vinchester *KY* U.S.A. **136** D3
Vinchester *VA* U.S.A. **137** E3
Vind *r.* Can. **126** B2
Vindhoek Namibia **108** A1
Vindorn U.S.A. **135** D2
Vindorah Austr. **115** D2
Vind River Range *mts* U.S.A. **134** B2
Vindsor Austr. **117** E2
Vindsor Can. **128** B2
Vindward Islands Caribbean Sea **145** D3
Vindward Passage Cuba/Haiti **145** C3
Vinfield U.S.A. **135** D3
Vingene Belgium **54** A2
Vingham Austr. **117** E2
Vinisk Can. **128** B1
Vinisk *r.* Can. **128** B1
Vinisk Lake Can. **128** B1
Vinkana Myanmar **75** A2
Vinkler Can. **127** F2
Vinnebago, Lake U.S.A. **136** C2
Vinnemucca U.S.A. **132** C2
Vinner U.S.A. **134** C2
Vinnfield U.S.A. **138** B2
Vinnibigoshish, Lake U.S.A. **135** E1
Vinnipeg Can. **127** F3
Vinnipeg *r.* Can. **127** F2
Vinnipeg, Lake Can. **127** F2
Vinnipegosis, Lake Can. **127** E2
Vinnipesaukee, Lake U.S.A. **137** F2
Vinnsboro U.S.A. **138** B2
Vinona *MN* U.S.A. **135** E2
Vinona *MS* U.S.A. **138** C2
Vinschoten Neth. **54** C1
Vinsen (Aller) Ger. **55** D1
Vinsen (Luhe) Ger. **55** E1
Vinslow U.S.A. **140** B1
Vinston-Salem U.S.A. **139** D1
Vinterberg Ger. **55** D2
Vinter Haven U.S.A. **139** D3
Vinterswijk Neth. **54** C2
Vinterthur Switz. **59** D2
Vinton U.S.A. **115** D2
Vinton N.Z. **118** A4
Virrabara Austr. **116** B2
Visbech U.K. **53** D3
Visconsin *r.* U.S.A. **136** B2
Visconsin *state* U.S.A. **136** C2
Visconsin Rapids U.S.A. **136** C2
Visła *r.* Pol. *see* Vistula

Wismar Ger. **56** C2
Witbank S. Africa **109** C2
Withernsea U.K. **52** D3
Witmarsum Neth. **54** B1
Witney U.K. **53** C4
Witrivier S. Africa **109** D2
Wittenberge Ger. **55** E1
Wittenburg Ger. **55** E1
Wittingen Ger. **55** E1
Wittlich Ger. **54** C3
Wittmund Ger. **54** C1
Wittstock Ger. **55** F1
Witvlei Namibia **108** A1
Witzenhausen Ger. **55** D2
Władysławowo Pol. **57** D2
Włocławek Pol. **57** D2
Wodonga Austr. **117** D3
Woippy France **54** C3
Wokam *i.* Indon. **71** C3
Woking U.K. **53** C4
Woldegk Ger. **55** F1
Wolfen Ger. **55** F2
Wolfenbüttel Ger. **55** E1
Wolfhagen Ger. **55** D2
Wolf Point U.S.A. **134** B1
Wolfsberg Ger. **55** E1
Wolfstein Ger. **54** C3
Wolfville Can. **129** D2
Wolgast Ger. **56** C2
Wolin Pol. **56** C2
Wollaston Lake Can. **127** E2
Wollaston Lake *i.* Can. **124** F3
Wollaston Peninsula Can. **124** E2
Wollongong Austr. **117** E2
Wolmirsleben Ger. **55** E2
Wolmirstedt Ger. **55** E1
Wolvega Neth. **54** C1
Wolverhampton U.K. **53** B3
Wŏnju S. Korea **77** B3
Wonowon Can. **126** C2
Wŏnsan N. Korea **77** B2
Wonthaggi Austr. **117** D3
Woocalla Austr. **116** B2
Woodah, Isle *i.* Austr. **115** C1
Woodbridge U.K. **53** D3
Woodland Park U.S.A. **134** B3
Woodroffe, Mount Austr. **114** C2
Woods, Lake *salt flat* Austr. **114** C1
Woods, Lake of the Can./U.S.A. **135** E1
Woods Point Austr. **117** D3
Woodstock Can. **137** G1
Woodville N.Z. **118** C3
Woodward U.S.A. **141** E1
Woolgoolga Austr. **117** E2
Woomera Austr. **116** B2
Wooster U.S.A. **136** D2
Worcester S. Africa **108** A3
Worcester U.K. **53** B3
Worcester U.S.A. **137** F2
Wörgl Austria **56** F2
Workington U.K. **52** B2
Worksop U.K. **52** C3
Worland U.S.A. **134** B2
Worms Ger. **55** D3
Wörth am Rhein Ger. **55** D3
Worthing U.K. **53** C4
Worthington U.S.A. **135** D2
Wotu Indon. **73** B3
Wowoni *i.* Indon. **73** B3
Wrangel Island Rus. Fed. **95** O2
Wrangell U.S.A. **126** B2
Wrangell Mountains U.S.A. **124** B3
Wrath, Cape U.K. **50** B1
Wray U.S.A. **134** C2
Wreck Point *pt* S. Africa **108** A2
Wrexham U.K. **52** B3
Wright U.S.A. **134** B2
Wrightmyo India **75** A2
Wrigley Can. **126** C1

Wrocław Pol. **57** D2
Września Pol. **57** D2
Wu'an China **82** B2
Wudu China **82** A2
Wuhai China **82** A2
Wuhan China **83** B3
Wuhu China **82** B2
Wukari Nigeria **101** C4
Wuli China **87** D1
Wuliang Shan *mts* China **74** B1
Wuliaru *i.* Indon. **71** C3
Wumeng Shan *mts* China **83** A3
Wunnummin Lake Can. **128** B1
Wunsiedel Ger. **55** F2
Wunstorf Ger. **55** D1
Wuntho Myanmar **74** A1
Wuppertal Ger. **54** C2
Wuppertal S. Africa **108** A3
Wurzbach Ger. **55** E2
Würzburg Ger. **55** D3
Wurzen Ger. **55** F2
Wuwei China **82** A2
Wuxi *Chongqing* China **82** A2
Wuxi *Jiangsu* China **82** C2
Wuxing China *see* Huzhou
Wuxuan China **83** A3
Wuyiling China **81** E1
Wuyishan China **83** B3
Wuyi Shan *mts* China **83** B3
Wuyuan China **82** A1
Wuzhishan China **83** A4
Wuzhong China **82** A2
Wuzhou China **83** B3
Wyangala Reservoir Austr. **117** D2
Wycheproof Austr. **116** C3
Wye *r.* U.K. **53** B4
Wyndham Austr. **114** B1
Wynne U.S.A. **138** B1
Wynyard Can. **127** E2
Wyoming *state* U.S.A. **134** B2
Wyszków Pol. **57** E2
Wytheville U.S.A. **136** D3

Xaafuun Somalia **103** D3
Xaignabouli Laos **74** B2
Xai-Xai Moz. **107** C3
Xamba China **82** A1
Xam Nua Laos **74** B1
Xanagas Botswana **108** B1
Xangongo Angola **106** A1
Xankändi Azer. **93** C2
Xanthi Greece **65** B2
Xanxerê Brazil **154** B3
Xapuri Brazil **150** C4
Xàtiva Spain **61** C2
Xiamen China **83** B3
Xi'an China **82** A2
Xianfeng China **83** A3
Xiangfan China **82** B2
Xianghua Ling *mts* China **74** A1
Xianghuang Qi China *see* Xin Bulag
Xiangkhoang Laos **74** B2
Xiangtan China **83** B3
Xiantao China **83** B3
Xianyang China **82** A2
Xiaogan China **82** B2
Xiao Hinggan Ling *mts* China **81** E1
Xiaoshan China **83** B3
Xichang China **74** B1
Xicohténcatl Mex. **143** C2
Xifeng *Gansu* China **82** A2
Xifeng *Guizhou* China **83** A3
Xigazê China **87** C2
Xilinhot China **82** B1
Xin Bulag China **82** B1
Xincai China **82** B2

Xinghai China 80 C2
Xinghua China 82 B2
Xingning China 83 B3
Xingping China 82 A2
Xingtai China 82 B2
Xingu r. Brazil 151 D3
Xingyi China 83 A3
Xinhua China 83 B3
Xining China 80 C2
Xinjiang Uygur Zizhiqu aut. reg. China 87 C1
Xinmin China 77 A1
Xinning China 83 B3
Xintai China 82 B2
Xinxiang China 82 B2
Xinyang China 82 B2
Xinyu China 83 B3
Xinzhou Shanxi China 82 B2
Xinzhou Shanxi China 81 D2
Xinzo de Limia Spain 60 B1
Xiqing Shan mts China 80 C2
Xique Xique Brazil 151 E4
Xishanzui China 82 A1
Xi Ujimqin Qi China see Bayan Ul Hot
Xiushan China 83 A3
Xiuying China 83 B3
Xixia China 82 B2
Xizang Zizhiqu aut. reg. China 74 A1
Xo'jayli Uzbek. 88 C2
Xuancheng China 82 B2
Xuanwei China 83 A3
Xucheng China 82 B2
Xuddur Somalia 103 C4
Xun Jiang r. China 83 B3
Xunwu China 83 B3
Xuwen China 83 B3
Xuyong China 83 A3

Y

Ya'an China 83 A2
Yabēlo Eth. 103 B4
Yablonovyy Khrebet mts Rus. Fed. 81 D1
Yadkin r. U.S.A. 139 D1
Yadong China 87 C2
Yagnitsa Rus. Fed. 43 E2
Yagoua Cameroon 104 B1
Yahk Can. 126 D3
Yahualica Mex. 142 B2
Yaihyali Turkey 92 B2
Yaizu Japan 79 C4
Yakima U.S.A. 132 B2
Yako Burkina 100 B3
Yakumo Japan 78 D2
Yakutat U.S.A. 126 B2
Yakutat Bay U.S.A. 126 A2
Yakutsk Rus. Fed. 95 K2
Yakymivka Ukr. 45 E2
Yala Thai. 75 B3
Yalloum Austr. 117 D3
Yalova Turkey 65 C2
Yalta Ukr. 45 D3
Yalu Jiang r. China/N. Korea 77 A1
Yamagata Japan 78 D3
Yambio Sudan 103 A4
Yambol Bulg. 64 C2
Yamburg Rus. Fed. 40 G2
Yamethin Myanmar 74 A1
Yamoussoukro Côte d'Ivoire 100 B4
Yampil' Ukr. 44 C2
Yamuna r. India 87 C2
Yamzho Yumco l. China 87 D2

Yana r. Rus. Fed. 95 L2
Yan'an China 82 A2
Yanaoca Peru 150 B4
Yanbu' al Bahr Saudi Arabia 90 A2
Yancheng China 82 C2
Yanchep Austr. 114 A3
Yangcheng China 82 B2
Yangchun China 83 B3
Yangdok N. Korea 77 B2
Yangjiang China 83 B3
Yangōn Myanmar see Rangoon
Yangquan China 82 B2
Yangshuo China 83 B3
Yangtze r. Qinghai China 80 C2
Yangtze r. China 74 B1
Yangtze, Mouth of the China 82 C2
Yangzhou China 82 B2
Yanji China 77 B1
Yankton U.S.A. 135 D2
Yano-Indigirskaya Nizmennost' lowland Rus. Fed. 95 L2
Yanskiy Zaliv g. Rus. Fed. 95 L2
Yantabulla Austr. 117 D1
Yantai China 82 C2
Yaoundé Cameroon 104 B2
Yap i. Micronesia 71 D2
Yapen i. Indon. 71 D3
Yapen, Selat sea chan. Indon. 71 D3
Yaqui r. Mex. 142 A2
Yaraka Austr. 115 D2
Yaransk Rus. Fed. 40 D3
Yaren Nauru 112
Yarim Yemen 90 B3
Yarkant He r. China 89 E3
Yarlung Zangbo r. China 80 C3
Yarmouth Can. 129 D2
Yarongo Rus. Fed. 40 F2
Yaroslavl' Rus. Fed. 43 E2
Yaroslavskiy Rus. Fed. 78 B2
Yarram Austr. 117 D3
Yartsevo Rus. Fed. 43 D2
Yasnogorsk Rus. Fed. 43 E3
Yasothon Thai. 75 B2
Yass Austr. 117 D2
Yatağan Turkey 65 C3
Yathkyed Lake Can. 127 F1
Yatsushiro Japan 79 B4
Yavari r. Brazil/Peru 150 C3
Yavatmal India 87 B3
Yaví, Cerro mt. Venez. 146
Yawatahama Japan 79 B4
Yazd Iran 93 D2
Yazoo City U.S.A. 138 B2
Ydra i. Greece 65 B3
Ye Myanmar 75 A2
Yecheng China 89 E3
Yécora Mex. 142 B2
Yefremov Rus. Fed. 43 E3
Yegorlyk r. Rus. Fed. 45 F2
Yegorlykskaya Rus. Fed. 45 F2
Yegor'yevsk Rus. Fed. 43 E2
Yei Sudan 103 B4
Yekaterinburg Rus. Fed. 40 F3
Yelets Rus. Fed. 43 E3
Yélimané Mali 100 A3
Yell i. U.K. 50 [inset]
Yellowknife Can. 126 D1
Yellow River r. China 82 B2
Yellow Sea N. Pacific Ocean 81 E2
Yellowstone U.S.A. 132 E1
Yellowstone Lake U.S.A. 134 A2
Yel'sk Belarus 42 C2
Yemen country Asia 90 B3
Yemva Rus. Fed. 40 E2
Yenakiyeve Ukr. 45 E2
Yenangyaung Myanmar 74 A1
Yên Bai Vietnam 74 B1
Yendi Ghana 100 B4

Yenice Turkey 65 C3
Yenifoça Turkey 65 C3
Yenisey r. Rus. Fed. 80 C1
Yeoval Austr. 117 D2
Yeovil U.K. 53 B4
Yeppoon Austr. 115 E2
Yerbogachen Rus. Fed. 95 J2
Yerevan Armenia 93 C1
Yereymentau Kazakh. 89 E1
Yermish' Rus. Fed. 43 F3
Yershov Rus. Fed. 41 D3
Yesan S. Korea 77 B2
Yesil' Kazakh. 89 D1
Yeşilova Turkey 65 C3
Yetman Austr. 117 E1
Ye-U Myanmar 74 A1
Yeu, Île d' i. France 58 B2
Yevlax Azer. 41 D4
Yevpatoriya Ukr. 45 D2
Yeysk Rus. Fed. 45 E2
Yezyaryshcha Belarus 42 C2
Yibin China 83 A3
Yichang China 82 B2
Yichun Heilong. China 81 E1
Yichun Jiangxi China 83 B3
Yilan China 78 A1
Yıldız Dağları mts Turkey 64 C2
Yıldızeli Turkey 92 B2
Yinchuan China 82 A2
Yingchengzi China 77 B1
Yingde China 83 B3
Yingkou China 82 C1
Yingshan Hubei China 82 B2
Yingshan Sichuan China 82 A2
Yingtan China 83 B3
Yining China 89 F2
Yirga Alem Eth. 103 B4
Yishui China 82 B2
Yitong China 77 B1
Yiwu China 80 C2
Yixing China 82 B2
Yiyang China 83 B3
Yizhou China 83 A3
Yli-Kitka l. Fin. 46 F2
Ylitornio Fin. 46 E2
Ylivieska Fin. 46 E3
Yogyakarta Indon. 72 C2
Yoko Cameroon 104 B2
Yokohama Japan 79 C3
Yola Nigeria 101 D4
Yonezawa Japan 79 D3
Yong'an China 83 B3
Yongchun China 83 B3
Yongdeng China 82 A2
Yŏndŏk S. Korea 77 B2
Yongkang China 83 B3
Yongsheng China 74 B1
Yongzhou China 83 B3
Yopal Col. 150 B2
York Austr. 114 A3
York U.K. 52 C3
York NE U.S.A. 135 D2
York PA U.S.A. 137 E3
York, Cape Austr. 71 D3
Yorke Peninsula Austr. 116 B3
Yorketown Austr. 116 B3
Yorkshire Wolds hills U.K. 52 C3
Yorkton Can. 124 F3
Yoshkar-Ola Rus. Fed. 41 D3
Youghal Rep. of Ireland 51 B3
Young Austr. 117 D2
Younghusband Peninsula Austr. 116 B3
Youngstown U.S.A. 137 D2
Youvarou Mali 100 B3
Youyi Feng mt. China/Rus. Fed. 89 F2
Yozgat Turkey 92 B2
Ypé-Jhú Para. 154 A2
Yreka U.S.A. 132 B2
Yr Wyddfa mt. U.K. see Snowdon

Vssingeaux France **59** C2
Vstad Sweden **47** C4
Vsyk-Köl *salt l.* Kyrg. **89** E2
Vtri-Rangá *r.* Iceland **46** [inset]
Vuanjiang China **74** B1
Vuan Jiang *r.* China **74** B1
Vuanmou China **74** B1
Vuba City U.S.A. **133** B3
Vübari Japan **78** D2
Vucatán *pen.* Mex. **143** C3
Vucatan Channel Cuba/Mex. **144** B2
Vuendumu Austr. **114** C2
Vueyang China **83** B3
Vugorsk Rus. Fed. **40** F2
Vukagirskoye Ploskogor'ye *plat.* Rus. Fed. **95** M2
Vukon *r.* Can./U.S.A. **126** B1
Vukon Territory *admin. div.* Can. **124** C2
Vulin *Guangxi* China **83** B3
Vulin *Shaanxi* China **82** A2
Vulong Xueshan *mt.* China **74** B1
Vuma *AZ* U.S.A. **140** B2
Vuma *CO* U.S.A. **134** C2
Vumen China **80** C2
Vuncheng China **82** B2
Vunfu China **83** B3
Vungas *reg.* Bol. **146**
Vunta *prov.* China **83** A3
Vunta Austr. **116** B2
Vunyang China **82** B2
Vurimaguas Peru **150** B3
Vurungkax He *r.* China **87** C1
Vur'yevets Rus. Fed. **43** F2
Vü Shan *mt.* Taiwan **83** C3
Vushu China **80** C2
Vushkozero Rus. Fed. **46** G3
Vushu China **80** C2
Vusufeli Turkey **93** C1
Vutian China **87** C1
Vuxi China **74** B1
Vuyu Rus. Fed. **43** F2
Vuzhno-Kuril'sk Rus. Fed. **78** E2
Vuzhno-Sakhalinsk Rus. Fed. **78** D1
Vuzhnoukrayinsk Ukr. **45** D2
Vuzhou China **82** B2
Vvetot France **58** C2

Z

Zaandam Neth. **54** B1
Zabaykal'sk Rus. Fed. **81** D1
Zabīd Yemen **90** B3
Zābol Iran **91** D1
Zābolī Iran **91** D2
Zacapa Guat. **143** D3
Zacapu Mex. **142** B3
Zacatecas Mex. **142** B2
Zacatepec Mex. **143** C3
Zacatlán Mex. **143** C3
Zacharo Greece **65** B3
Zacoalco Mex. **142** B2
Zacualtipán Mex. **143** C2
Zadar Croatia **62** C2
Zadetkyi Kyun *i.* Myanmar **75** A3
Zadonsk Rus. Fed. **43** E3
Za'farānah Egypt **92** B3
Zafra Spain **60** B2
Zagreb Croatia **63** C1
Zagros Mountains Iran **93** C2
Zagros Mountains Iran see Zagros Mountains
Zāhedān Iran **91** D2
Zahlé Lebanon **92** B2
Zahrez Chergui *salt pan* Alg. **61** D2
Zahrān Saudi Arabia **90** B3
Zaječar Serb. and Mont. **64** C3
Zakharovo Rus. Fed. **43** E3

Zākhō Iraq **93** C2
Zakynthos Greece **65** B3
Zakynthos *i.* Greece **65** B3
Zalaegerszeg Hungary **57** D3
Zalău Romania **44** B2
Zalim Saudi Arabia **90** B2
Zalingei Sudan **103** A3
Zalmā, Jabal az *mt.* Saudi Arabia **90** A2
Zama City Can. **126** D2
Zambeze *r.* Angola see Zambezi
Zambezi *r.* Angola **105** B1
Zambezi Zambia **106** B1
Zambia *country* Africa **106** B1
Zamboanga Phil. **76** B3
Zamboanga Peninsula Phil. **76** B3
Zamora Spain **60** B1
Zamora de Hidalgo Mex. **142** B3
Zamość Pol. **57** E2
Zanda China **87** B2
Zandvliet Belgium **54** B2
Zanesville U.S.A. **136** D3
Zanjān Iran **93** C2
Zanskar Mountains India **87** B1
Zante *i.* Greece see Zakynthos
Zanzibar Tanz. **105** D3
Zanzibar Island Tanz. **105** D3
Zaoskiy Rus. Fed. **43** E3
Zaouatallaz Alg. **101** C2
Zaozhuang China **82** B2
Zapadnaya Dvina *r.* Europe **43** D2
Zapadnaya Dvina Rus. Fed. **43** D2
Zapadno Sibirskaya Ravnina *plain* Rus. Fed. **40** H2
Zapadnyy Sayan *reg.* Rus. Fed. **80** B1
Zapata U.S.A. **141** E3
Zapolyarnyy Rus. Fed. **46** G2
Zaporizhzhya Ukr. **45** E2
Zappendorf Ger. **55** E2
Zara Turkey **92** B2
Zaragoza Mex. **143** B2
Zaragoza Spain **61** C1
Zarand Iran **91** C1
Zaranj Afgh. **86** A1
Zarasai Lith. **42** C2
Zaraysk Rus. Fed. **43** E3
Zaraza Venez. **160** D2
Zaria Nigeria **101** C3
Zarichne Ukr. **44** C1
Zarqān Iran **93** D3
Zarubino Rus. Fed. **78** B2
Żary Pol. **56** D2
Zarzis Tunisia **101** D1
Zastron S. Africa **109** C3
Žatec Czech Rep. **55** F2
Zavitinsk Rus. Fed. **81** E1
Zavolzhsk Rus. Fed. **43** F2
Zawiercie Pol. **57** D2
Zaysan, Lake Kazakh. **89** F2
Zdolbuniv Ukr. **44** C1
Zealand *i.* Denmark **47** C4
Zeebrugge Belgium **54** A2
Zeerust S. Africa **109** C2
Zeil, Mount Austr. **114** C2
Zeitz Ger. **55** F2
Zelenogorsk Rus. Fed. **47** F3
Zelenogradsk Rus. Fed. **42** B3
Zemmora Alg. **61** D2
Zempoaltépetl, Nudo de *mt.* Mex. **143** C3
Zengfeng Shan *mt.* China **77** B1
Zenzach Alg. **61** D2
Zereh, Gowd-e *depr.* Afgh. **86** A2
Zermatt Switz. **59** D2
Zernograd Rus. Fed. **45** F2
Zeulenroda Ger. **55** E2
Zeven Ger. **55** D1
Zevenaar Neth. **54** C2
Zeya Rus. Fed. **95** K3
Zeydābād Iran **93** D3

Zeyskoye Vodokhranilishche *resr* Rus. Fed. **95** K3
Zgierz Pol. **57** D2
Zhabinka Belarus **42** B3
Zhalpaktal Kazakh. **88** B2
Zhaltyr Kazakh. **89** D1
Zhanaozen Kazakh. **88** C2
Zhangjiajie China **83** B3
Zhangjiakou China **82** B1
Zhangping China **83** B3
Zhangshu China **83** B3
Zhangwu China **77** A1
Zhangye China **80** C2
Zhangzhou China **83** B3
Zhanibek Kazakh. **88** B2
Zhanjiang China **83** B3
Zhao'an China **83** B3
Zhaoqing China **83** B3
Zhaotong China **83** A3
Zhari Namco *salt l.* China **87** C1
Zharkent Kazakh. **89** F2
Zharkovskiy Rus. Fed. **43** D2
Zharma Kazakh. **89** F2
Zhashkiv Ukr. **44** D2
Zhejiang *prov.* China **83** C3
Zhelaniya, Mys *c.* Rus. Fed. **94** G1
Zheleznogorsk Rus. Fed. **43** E3
Zhenba China **82** A2
Zheng'an China **83** A3
Zhenghe China **83** B3
Zhengzhou China **82** B2
Zhenyuan China **83** A3
Zherdevka Rus. Fed. **43** F3
Zheshart Rus. Fed. **40** D2
Zhezkazgan *Karagandinskaya Oblast'* Kazakh. **89** D2
Zhezkazgan *Karagandinskaya Oblast'* Kazakh. **89** D2
Zhicheng China see Qingzhou
Zhigansk Rus. Fed. **95** K2
Zhitikara Kazakh. **88** D1
Zhlobin Belarus **42** D3
Zhmerynka Ukr. **44** C2
Zhob Pak. **86** A1
Zhokhova, Ostrov *i.* Rus. Fed. **95** M1
Zhongba China **87** C2
Zhongning China **82** A2
Zhongshan China **83** B3
Zhongwei China **82** A2
Zhoukou China **82** B2
Zhoushan China **83** C2
Zhovti Vody Ukr. **45** D2
Zhuanghe China **77** A2
Zhucheng China **82** B2
Zhukovka Rus. Fed. **43** D3
Zhukovskiy Rus. Fed. **43** E2
Zhumadian China **82** B2
Zhuzhou *Hunan* China **83** B3
Zhuzhou *Hunan* China **83** B3
Zhydachiv Ukr. **44** B2
Zhytkavichy Belarus **42** C3
Zhytomyr Ukr. **44** C1
Žiar nad Hronom Slovakia **57** D3
Zibo China **82** B2
Zielona Góra Pol. **57** D2
Zigaing Myanmar **74** A1
Zigong China **83** A3
Ziguinchor Senegal **100** A3
Zihuatanejo Mex. **142** B3
Žilina Slovakia **57** D3
Zillah Libya **101** D2
Zima Rus. Fed. **95** I3
Zimapán Mex. **143** C2
Zimbabwe *country* Africa **107** C2
Zimmi Sierra Leone **100** A4
Zimnicea Romania **44** C3
Zinder Niger **101** C3
Zinjibār Yemen **90** B3
Zirc Hungary **57** D3
Ziro India **74** A1

Zir Rūd Iran **91** C2
Zistersdorf Austria **57** D3
Zitácuaro Mex. **143** B3
Zittau Ger. **56** C2
Zlatoust Rus. Fed. **41** E3
Zlin Czech Rep. **57** D3
Zlynka Rus. Fed. **43** D3
Zmiyevka Rus. Fed. **43** E3
Zmiyiv Ukr. **45** E2
Znamenka *Orlovskaya Oblast'* Rus. Fed. **43** E3
Znamenka *Tambovskaya Oblast'* Rus. Fed. **43** F3
Znam"yanka Ukr. **45** D2
Znojmo Czech Rep. **57** D3
Zolochiv *Kharkivs'ka Oblast'* Ukr. **45** E1
Zolochiv *L'vivs'ka Oblast'* Ukr. **44** B2
Zolotonosha Ukr. **45** D2

Zolotukhino Rus. Fed. **43** E3
Zomba Malawi **107** C1
Zonguldak Turkey **92** B1
Zonza France **59** D3
Zorzor Liberia **100** B4
Zossen Ger. **55** F1
Zouar Chad **101** D2
Zouérat Maur. **100** A2
Zrenjanin a **64** B1
Zubtsov Rus. Fed. **43** D2
Zug Switz. **59** D2
Zugdidi Georgia **93** C1
Zújar *r.* Spain **60** B2
Zülpich Ger. **54** C2
Zumbo Moz. **107** C1
Zumpango Mex. **143** C3
Zuni China **83** A3

Županja Croatia **63** C1
Zürich Switz. **59** D2
Zutphen Neth. **54** C1
Zuwārah Libya **101** D1
Zvenyhorodka Ukr. **44** D2
Zvishavane Zimbabwe **107** C2
Zvolen Slovakia **57** D3
Zvornik Bos.-Herz. **63** C2
Zwedru Liberia **100** B4
Zweibrücken Ger. **54** C3
Zwelitsha S. Africa **109** C3
Zwettl Austria **56** D3
Zwickau Ger. **55** F2
Zwolle Neth. **54** C1
Zyryanka Rus. Fed. **95** M2

All mapping in this atlas is generated from Collins Bartholomew digital databases. Collins Bartholomew, the UK's leading independent geographical information supplier, can provide a digital, custom, and premium mapping service to a variety of markets. For further information:

Tel: +44 (0) 141 306 3752
e-mail: collinsbartholomew@harpercollins.co.uk

We also offer a choice of books, atlases and maps that can be customized to suit a customer's own requirements. For further information:

Tel: +44 (0) 141 306 3209
e-mail: business.gifts@harpercollins.co.uk

or visit our website at: www.collinsbartholomew.com